The Minister's Manual

SEVENTY-FIFTH ANNUAL ISSUE

THE MINISTER'S MANUAL
2000

Edited by

JAMES W. COX

Jossey-Bass Publishers
San Francisco

Editors of THE MINISTER'S MANUAL

G. B. F. Hallock, D.D., 1926–1958
M. K. W. Heicher, Ph.D., 1943–1968
Charles L. Wallis, M.A., M.Div., 1969–1983
James W. Cox, M.Div., Ph.D.

Translations of the Bible referred to and quoted from in this book may be indicated by their standard abbreviations, such as NRSV (New Revised Standard Version) and NIV (New International Version). In addition, some contributors have made their own translations, and others have used a mixed text.

Other acknowledgments begin on page 415.

Substantial discounts on bulk quantities of Jossey-Bass books are available to corporations, professional associations, and other organizations. For details and discount information, contact the special sales department at Jossey-Bass.

 Manufactured in the United States of America on Lyons Falls Turin Book. This paper is acid-free and 100 percent totally chlorine-free.

Library of Congress Cataloging Card Number

25–21658
ISSN 0738–5323
ISBN 0–7879–4546–3

FIRST EDITION
HB Printing
10 9 8 7 6 5 4 3 2 1

CONTENTS

PREFACE

This is the seventy-fifth annual issue of *The Minister's Manual*. From my correspondence and conversations I have learned that many "can't live without it." The value of *The Minister's Manual* can best be described by first noting what it can do for the preacher, but its use extends to other ministers—musicians, directors of Christian education, teachers, youth workers, discussion group leaders, evangelists, and missionaries. As well, many others find the manual useful for private devotional reading.

For preachers it can get the creative process going and can provide a nudge toward discovering potential variety in the treatment of texts and themes. At the same time it can serve as a kind of checklist to determine if one is neglecting or overlooking important texts and themes. Also, it often provides the needed illustration to make the sermon memorable and impressive.

For musicians and sometimes for preachers it can suggest the appropriate hymn for choir or congregation—music that complements the lectionary selections for the day or that highlights the season in the Church year.

For children's workers it provides a talk for each Sunday of the year.

Three special sections in the manual deserve particular notice. Eduard Schweizer has written two Bible studies that take us verse by verse through extended passages from the Bible. Schweizer, now retired, is former professor of the New Testament and *rektor* (president) of the University of Zurich in Switzerland. Bruce E. Shields has given practical advice for preaching on hope and has written sermons on that important subject. Shields is director of the Doctor of Ministry Program for the Emmanuel School of Religion, a graduate seminary in Tennessee. The final section of the manual is "A Little Treasury of Sermon Illustrations."

Many contributors from many different denominational backgrounds have made this volume possible. They share our common faith and enrich our personal understanding and devotion. The Southern Baptist Theological Seminary, where I have taught since 1959, has provided valuable secretarial assistance in producing the manuscript. The current volume was word-processed by Linda Durkin, with the assistance of Ja-Rhonda Staples. I wish to thank all of these people and the authors and publishers from whose works I have quoted. I am again deeply grateful.

James W. Cox
The Southern Baptist Theological Seminary

SECTION I

GENERAL AIDS AND RESOURCES

CIVIL YEAR CALENDARS FOR 2000 AND 2001

2000

January	February	March	April
S M T W T F S	S M T W T F S	S M T W T F S	S M T W T F S
1	1 2 3 4 5	1 2 3 4	1
2 3 4 5 6 7 8	6 7 8 9 10 11 12	5 6 7 8 9 10 11	2 3 4 5 6 7 8
9 10 11 12 13 14 15	13 14 15 16 17 18 19	12 13 14 15 16 17 18	9 10 11 12 13 14 15
16 17 18 19 20 21 22	20 21 22 23 24 25 26	19 20 21 22 23 24 25	16 17 18 19 20 21 22
23 24 25 26 27 28 29	27 28 29	26 27 28 29 30 31	23 24 25 26 27 28 29
30 31			30

May	June	July	August
S M T W T F S	S M T W T F S	S M T W T F S	S M T W T F S
1 2 3 4 5 6	1 2 3	1	1 2 3 4 5
7 8 9 10 11 12 13	4 5 6 7 8 9 10	2 3 4 5 6 7 8	6 7 8 9 10 11 12
14 15 16 17 18 19 20	11 12 13 14 15 16 17	9 10 11 12 13 14 15	13 14 15 16 17 18 19
21 22 23 24 25 26 27	18 19 20 21 22 23 24	16 17 18 19 20 21 22	20 21 22 23 24 25 26
28 29 30 31	25 26 27 28 29 30	23 24 25 26 27 28 29	27 28 29 30 31
		30 31	

September	October	November	December
S M T W T F S	S M T W T F S	S M T W T F S	S M T W T F S
1 2	1 2 3 4 5 6 7	1 2 3 4	1 2
3 4 5 6 7 8 9	8 9 10 11 12 13 14	5 6 7 8 9 10 11	3 4 5 6 7 8 9
10 11 12 13 14 15 16	15 16 17 18 19 20 21	12 13 14 15 16 17 18	10 11 12 13 14 15 16
17 18 19 20 21 22 23	22 23 24 25 26 27 28	19 20 21 22 23 24 25	17 18 19 20 21 22 23
24 25 26 27 28 29 30	29 30 31	26 27 28 29 30	24 25 26 27 28 29 30
			31

2001

January	February	March	April
S M T W T F S	S M T W T F S	S M T W T F S	S M T W T F S
1 2 3 4 5 6	1 2 3	1 2 3	1 2 3 4 5 6 7
7 8 9 10 11 12 13	4 5 6 7 8 9 10	4 5 6 7 8 9 10	8 9 10 11 12 13 14
14 15 16 17 18 19 20	11 12 13 14 15 16 17	11 12 13 14 15 16 17	15 16 17 18 19 20 21
21 22 23 24 25 26 27	18 19 20 21 22 23 24	18 19 20 21 22 23 24	22 23 24 25 26 27 28
28 29 30 31	25 26 27 28	25 26 27 28 29 30 31	29 30

May	June	July	August
S M T W T F S	S M T W T F S	S M T W T F S	S M T W T F S
1 2 3 4 5	1 2	1 2 3 4 5 6 7	1 2 3 4
6 7 8 9 10 11 12	3 4 5 6 7 8 9	8 9 10 11 12 13 14	5 6 7 8 9 10 11
13 14 15 16 17 18 19	10 11 12 13 14 15 16	15 16 17 18 19 20 21	12 13 14 15 16 17 18
20 21 22 23 24 25 26	17 18 19 20 21 22 23	22 23 24 25 26 27 28	19 20 21 22 23 24 25
27 28 29 30 31	24 25 26 27 28 29 30	29 30 31	26 27 28 29 30 31

September	October	November	December
S M T W T F S	S M T W T F S	S M T W T F S	S M T W T F S
1	1 2 3 4 5 6	1 2 3	1
2 3 4 5 6 7 8	7 8 9 10 11 12 13	4 5 6 7 8 9 10	2 3 4 5 6 7 8
9 10 11 12 13 14 15	14 15 16 17 18 19 20	11 12 13 14 15 16 17	9 10 11 12 13 14 15
16 17 18 19 20 21 22	21 22 23 24 25 26 27	18 19 20 21 22 23 24	16 17 18 19 20 21 22
23 24 25 26 27 28 29	28 29 30 31	25 26 27 28 29 30	23 24 25 26 27 28 29
30			30 31

Church and Civic Calendar for 2000

January

1	New Year's Day
	The Name of Jesus
5	Twelfth Night
6	Epiphany
	Armenian Christmas
17	Martin Luther King Jr. Day
18	Confession of St. Peter
25	Conversion of St. Paul

February

1	National Freedom Day
2	Presentation of Jesus in the Temple
3	Four Chaplains Memorial Day
12	Lincoln's Birthday
14	St. Valentine's Day
21	President's Day
22	Washington's Birthday

March

8	Ash Wednesday
12	First Sunday in Lent
17	St. Patrick's Day
19	Second Sunday in Lent
	Joseph, Husband of Mary
21	Purim
25	The Annunciation
26	Third Sunday in Lent

April

2	Fourth Sunday in Lent
	Daylight saving time begins
9	Fifth Sunday in Lent
16	Palm/Passion Sunday
16–22	Holy Week
20	Maundy Thursday
21	Good Friday
23	Easter
25	St. Mark, Evangelist

May

1	Law Day
	Loyalty Day
	May Day
	St. Philip and St. James, Apostles
1–5	Cinco de Mayo Celebration
14	Mother's Day
20	Memorial Day

June

1	Ascension Day
9	First Day of Shavuot
11	Pentecost
	St. Barnabas, Apostle
18	Trinity Sunday
	Father's Day
24	The Nativity of St. John the Baptist
29	St. Peter and St. Paul, Apostles

July

1	Canada Day
4	Independence Day
22	St. Mary Magdalene
25	St. James, Apostle

August

1	Civic Holiday (Canada)
14	Atlantic Charter Day
15	Mary, Mother of Jesus
24	St. Bartholomew, Apostle
26	Women's Equality Day

September

3	Labor Sunday
4	Labor Day
10	National Grandparents' Day
	Rally Day
21	St. Matthew, Apostle and Evangelist

29	St. Michael and All Angels		Veterans Day
30	First Day of Rosh Hashanah		Remembrance Day (Canada)
		12	Stewardship Sunday
October		23	Thanksgiving Day
		30	St. Andrew, Apostle
1	World Communion Sunday		
9	Columbus Day	*December*	
	Thanksgiving Day (Canada)		
14	First Day of Sukkoth	3	First Sunday of Advent
15	Laity Sunday	10	Second Sunday of Advent
16	World Food Day	17	Third Sunday of Advent
18	St. Luke, Evangelist	21	Forefather's Day
23	St. James, Brother of Jesus		St. Thomas, Apostle
24	United Nations Day	22	First Day of Hanukkah
29	Daylight saving time ends	24	Fourth Sunday of Advent
31	National UNICEF Day	25	Christmas
	Reformation Day	26	Boxing Day (Canada)
	Halloween		St. Stephen, Deacon
		27	St. John, Apostle and
November			Evangelist
1	All Saints' Day	28	The Holy Innocents
2	All Souls' Day	31	New Year's Eve
11	Armistice Day		Watch Night

The Revised Common Lectionary for 2000

The following Scripture lessons are commended for use in public worship by various Protestant churches and the Roman Catholic Church and include first, second, and Gospel readings, and Psalms, according to Cycle B from January 2 to November 26 and according to Cycle C from December 3 to December 31. (Copyright 1992 Consultation on Common Texts)

Jan. 2: Jer. 31:7–14; Ps.147:12–20; Eph. 1:3–14; John 1:(1–9) 10–18

Epiphany Season

Jan. 9 (Epiphany Sunday): Isa. 60:1–6; Ps. 72:1–7, 10–14; Eph. 3:1–2; Matt. 2:1–12
Jan. 16: 1 Sam. 3:1–10 (11–20); Ps. 139:1–6, 13–18; 1 Cor. 6:12–20; John 1:43–51
Jan. 23: Jonah 3:1–5, 10; Ps. 62:5–12; 1 Cor. 7:29–31; Mark 1:14–20
Jan. 30: Deut. 18:15–20; Ps. 111; 1 Cor. 8:1–13; Mark 1:20–28
Feb. 6: Isa. 40:21–31; Ps. 147:1–11, 20c; 1 Cor. 9:16–23; Mark 1:29–39
Feb. 13: 2 Kings 5:1–14; Ps. 30; 1 Cor. 9:24–27; Mark 1:40–45
Feb. 20: Isa. 43:18–25; Ps. 41; 2 Cor. 1:18–22; Mark 2:1–12
Feb. 27: Hos. 2:14–20; Ps. 103:1–13, 22; 2 Cor. 3:1–6; Mark 2:13–22
Mar. 5 (Transfiguration Sunday): 2 Kings 2:1–12; Ps. 50:1–6; 2 Cor. 4:3–6; Mark 4:2–9

Lenten Season

Mar. 8 (Ash Wednesday): Joel 2:1–2, 12–17; Ps. 51:1–17; 2 Cor. 5:20b–6:10; Matt. 6:1–6, 16–21

Mar. 12: Gen. 9:8-17; Ps. 25:1-10; 1 Pet. 3:18-22; Mark 1:9-15

Mar. 19: Gen. 17:1-7, 15-16; Ps. 22:23-31; Rom. 4:13-25; Mark 8:31-38

Mar. 26: Exod. 20:1-17; Ps. 19; 1 Cor. 1:18-25; John 2:13-22

Apr. 2: Num. 21:4-9; Ps. 107:1-3, 17-22; Eph. 2:1-10; John 3:14-21

Apr. 9: Jer. 31:31-34; Ps. 51:1-12; Heb. 5:5-10; John 12:20-23

Holy Week

Apr. 16 (Palm/Passion Sunday): Liturgy of the Palms—Mark 11:1-11; Ps. 118:1-2, 19-29;
Liturgy of the Passion—Isa. 50:4-9a; Ps. 31:9-16; Phil. 2:5-11; Mark 14:1-15:47

Apr. 17 (Monday): Isa. 42:1-9; Ps. 36:5-11; Heb. 9:11-15; John 12:1-11

Apr. 18 (Tuesday): Isa. 49:1-7; Ps. 71:1-14; 1 Cor. 1:18-31; John 12:20-36

Apr. 19 (Wednesday): Isa. 50:4-9a; Ps. 70; Heb. 12:1-3; John 13:21-32

Apr. 20 (Holy Thursday): Exod. 12:1-4 (5-10), 11-14; Ps. 116:1-2, 12-19; 1 Cor.
11:23-26; John 13:1-7, 31b-35

Apr. 21 (Good Friday): Isa. 52-53:12; Ps. 22; Heb. 10:15-25; John 18:1-19:42

Apr. 22 (Holy Saturday): Job 14:1-14; Ps. 31:1-4, 15-16; 1 Pet. 4:1-8; Matt. 27:57-66

Apr. 23 (Easter Vigil): Gen. 1:1-2:4a; Ps. 136:1-9, 23-26; Gen. 7:1-5, 11-18; 8:6-18;
9:8-13; Ps. 46; Gen. 22:1-18; Ps. 16; Exod. 14:10-31; 15:20-21; Exod. 15:1b-13,
17-18 (resp.); Isa. 55:1-11; Isa. 12:2-6 (resp.); Bar. 3:9-15, 32; 4:4 (alt.); Prov. 8:1-8,
19-21; 9:4-6 (alt.); Ps. 19; Ezek. 36:24-28; Ps. 42-43; Ezek. 37:1-14; Ps. 143; Zeph.
3:14-20; Ps. 98; Rom. 6:3-11; Ps. 114; Luke 24:1-12

Apr. 23 (Easter): Acts 10:34-43; Ps. 118:1-2, 14-24; 1 Cor. 15:1-11; John 20:1-18

Apr. 30: Acts 4:32-35; Ps. 133; 1 John 1:1-2:2; John 20:19-31

May 7: Acts 3:12-19; Ps. 4; 1 John 3:1-7; Luke 24:36b-48

May 14: Acts 4:5-12; Ps. 23; 1 John 3:16-24; John 10:11-18

May 21: Acts 8:26-40; Ps. 22:25-31; 1 John 4:7-21; John 15:1-8

May 28: Acts 10:44-48; Ps. 98; 1 John 5:1-6; John 15:9-17

June 4: Acts 1:15-17, 21-26; Ps. 1; 1 John 5:9-13; John 17:6-19

Season of Pentecost

June 11 (Pentecost): Ezek. 37:1-14 or Acts 2:1-21; Ps. 104:24-34, 35b; Rom. 8:22-27;
John 15:26-27; 16:4b-15

June 18 (Trinity): Isa. 6:1-8; Ps. 29; Rom. 8:12-17; John 3:1-17

June 25: 1 Sam. 17:(1a, 4-11, 19-23) 32-49; Ps. 9:9-20; 2 Cor. 6:1-13; Mark 4:35-41

July 2: 2 Sam. 1:1, 17-27; Ps. 130; 2 Cor. 8:7-15; Mark 5:21-43

July 9: 2 Sam. 5:1-5, 9-10; Ps. 48; 2 Cor. 12:2-10; Mark 6:1-13

July 16: 2 Sam. 6:1-5, 12b-14; Ps. 24; Eph. 1:3-14; Mark 6:14-29

July 23: 2 Sam. 7:1-14a; Ps. 89:20-37; Eph. 2:11-22; Mark 6:30-34, 53-56

July 30: 2 Sam. 11:1-15; Ps. 14; Eph. 3:14-21; John 6:1-21

Aug. 6: 2 Sam. 11:26-12:13a; Ps. 51:1-12; Eph. 4:1-16; John 6:24-35

Aug. 13: 2 Sam. 18:5-9, 15, 31-33; Ps. 130; Eph. 4:25-5:2; John 6:35, 41-51

Aug. 20: 1 Kings 2:10-12; 3:3-14; Ps. 111; Eph. 5:15-20; John 6:51-58

Aug. 27: 1 Kings 8: (1, 6, 10-11) 22-30, 41-43; Ps. 84; Eph. 6:10-20; John 6:56-69

Sept. 3: Song of Songs 2:8-13; Ps. 45:1-2, 6-9; James 1:17-27; Mark 7:1-8, 14-15, 21-23

Sept. 10: Prov. 22:1-2, 8-9, 22-23; Ps. 125; James 2:1-10 (11-13), 14-17; Mark 7:24-37

Sept. 17: Prov. 1:20–33; Ps. 19; James 3:1–12; Mark 8:27–38
Sept. 24: Prov. 31:10–31; Ps. 1; James 3:13–4:3, 7–8a; Mark 9:30–37
Oct. 1: Esther 7:1–6, 9–10; 9:20–22; Ps. 124; James 5:13–20; Mark 9:38–50
Oct. 8: Job 1:1; 2:1–10; Ps. 26; Heb. 1:1–4; 2:5–12; Mark 10:2–16
Oct. 15: Job 23:1–9, 16–17; Ps. 22:1–15; Heb. 4:12–16; Mark 10:17–31
Oct. 22: Job 38:1–7 (34–41); Ps. 104:1–9, 24, 35; Heb. 5:1–10; Mark 10:35–45
Oct. 29: Job 42:1–6; 10:17; Ps. 34:1–8 (19–22); Heb. 7:23–28; Mark 10:46–52
Nov. 5: Ruth 1:1–18; Ps. 146; Heb. 9:11–14; Mark 12:28–34
Nov. 12: Ruth 3:1–5; Ps. 127; Heb. 9:24–28; Mark 12:38–44
Nov. 19: 1 Sam. 1:4–20; Ps. 16; Heb. 10:11–14 (15–18), 19–25; Mark 13:1–8
Nov. 26 (Christ the King): 2 Sam. 23:1–7; Ps. 132:1–12 (13–18); Rev. 1:4–8; John 18:33–37

Advent and Christmas Season

Dec. 3 (Advent): Jer. 33:14–16; Ps. 25:1–10; 1 Thess. 3:9–13; Luke 21:25–36
Dec. 10: Mal. 3:1–4; Luke 1:68–79; Phil. 1:3–11; Luke 3:1–6
Dec. 17: Zeph. 3:14–20; Isa. 12:2–6; Phil. 4:4–7; Luke 3:7–18
Dec. 24: Mic. 5:2–5a; Luke 1:47–55; Heb. 10:5–10; Luke 1:39–45 (46–55)
Dec. 25 (Christmas Day): Isa. 9:2–7; Ps. 96; Titus 2:11–14; Luke 2:1–14 (15–20) or Isa. 62:6–12; Ps. 97; Titus 3:4–7; Luke 3:(1–7) 8–20 or Isa. 52:7–10; Ps. 98; Heb. 1:1–4 (5–12); John 1:1–14
Dec. 31: 1 Sam. 2:18–20, 26; Ps. 148; Col. 3:12–17; Luke 2:41–52

Four-Year Church Calendar

	2000	2001	2002	2003
Ash Wednesday	March 8	February 28	February 13	March 5
Palm Sunday	April 16	April 8	March 24	April 13
Good Friday	April 21	April 13	March 29	April 18
Easter	April 23	April 15	March 31	April 20
Ascension Day	June 1	May 24	May 9	May 29
Pentecost	June 11	June 3	May 19	June 8
Trinity Sunday	June 18	June 10	May 26	June 15
Thanksgiving	November 23	November 22	November 28	November 27
Advent Sunday	December 3	December 2	December 1	November 30

Forty-Year Easter Calendar

2000 April 23	2010 April 4	2020 April 12	2030 April 21
2001 April 15	2011 April 24	2021 April 4	2031 April 13
2002 March 31	2012 April 8	2022 April 17	2032 March 28
2003 April 20	2013 March 31	2023 April 9	2033 April 17
2004 April 11	2014 April 20	2024 March 31	2034 April 9
2005 March 27	2015 April 5	2025 April 20	2035 March 25
2006 April 16	2016 March 27	2026 April 5	2036 April 13
2007 April 8	2017 April 16	2027 March 28	2037 April 5
2008 March 23	2018 April 1	2028 April 16	2038 April 25
2009 April 12	2019 April 21	2029 April 1	2039 April 10

Traditional Wedding Anniversary Identifications

1 Paper	7 Wool	13 Lace	35 Coral
2 Cotton	8 Bronze	14 Ivory	40 Ruby
3 Leather	9 Pottery	15 Crystal	45 Sapphire
4 Linen	10 Tin	20 China	50 Gold
5 Wood	11 Steel	25 Silver	55 Emerald
6 Iron	12 Silk	30 Pearl	60 Diamond

Colors Appropriate for Days and Seasons

White. Symbolizes purity, perfection, and joy and identifies festivals marking events in the life of Jesus, except Good Friday: Christmas, Epiphany, Easter, Eastertide, Ascension Day; also Trinity Sunday, All Saints' Day, weddings, funerals. Gold may also be used.

Red. Symbolizes the Holy Spirit, martyrdom, and the love of God: Good Friday, Pentecost, and Sundays following.

Violet. Symbolizes penitence: Advent, Lent.

Green. Symbolizes mission to the world, hope, regeneration, nurture, and growth: Epiphany season, Kingdomtide, Rural Life Sunday, Labor Sunday, Thanksgiving Sunday.

Blue. Advent, in some churches.

Flowers in Season Appropriate for Church Use

January: carnation or snowdrop	July: larkspur or water lily
February: violet or primrose	August: gladiolus poppy
March: jonquil or daffodil	September: aster or morning star
April: lily, sweet pea, or daisy	October: calendula or cosmos
May: lily of the valley or hawthorn	November: chrysanthemum
June: rose or honeysuckle	December: narcissus, holly, or poinsettia

Quotable Quotations

1. We can take a lot of physical and even mental pain when we know that it truly makes us a part of the life we live together in this world.—Henri J. M. Nouwen
2. The longest journey is the journey inward.—Dag Hammarskjöld
3. A religion that is small enough for our understanding would not be large enough for our needs.—Arthur Balfour
4. Sin is the turning towards ourselves, and making ourselves the center of our world.—Paul Tillich
5. It is very difficult to preach the gospel honestly. It means to preach the severity of God to the proud, and the mercy of God to the brokenhearted.—Reinhold Niebuhr
6. Never argue with a woman when she's tired—or rested.—H. C. Diefenbach
7. To believe only possibilities is not faith, but mere philosophy.—Sir Thomas Browne
8. The Samaritan helps without dragging in religious reasons.—Hans Küng
9. Action springs not from thought, but from a readiness for responsibility.—Dietrich Bonhoeffer
10. Each day is a little life.—Arthur Schopenhauer

11. Remorse is memory awake.—Emily Dickinson
12. Evil has no substance of its own, but is only the defect, excess, perversion, or corruption of that which has substance.—John Henry Newman
13. Punctuality is the thief of time.—Oscar Wilde
14. Many things are not believed because their current explanation is not believed.—Friedrich Nietzsche
15. A Christian man is the most free lord of all, and subject to none; a Christian man is the most dutiful servant of all, and subject to everyone.—Martin Luther, *Concerning Christian Liberty*
16. What this parish needs, what every parish needs, is a man who knows God at more than second hand.—Thomas Carlyle
17. We . . . have to say, on the basis of our present experience, that evil is really evil, really malevolent and deadly and also, on the basis of faith, that it will in the end be defeated and made to serve God's good purposes.—John Hick
18. Blessed are the young, for they shall inherit the national debt.—Herbert Hoover
19. Love is seeing butterflies inside caterpillars.—Peter Kreeft, *A Turn of the Clock*
20. Life is tons of discipline.—Robert Frost
21. The greatest use of life is to spend it for something that will outlast it.—William James
22. Life is the childhood of immortality.—Daniel A. Poling
23. Repentance may begin instantly, but reformation often requires a sphere of years.—Henry Ward Beecher
24. Experience is not what happens to a man. It is what a man does with what happens to him.—Aldous Huxley
25. The modern idol maker goes not to the forest but to the laboratory, and there with the help of scientific concepts molds the kind of god he will adore.—Fulton J. Sheen
26. Life is too short to be little.—Benjamin Disraeli
27. Community is grounded in God, who calls us together, and not in the attractiveness of people to each other.—Henri J. M. Nouwen
28. Castles in the air—they are so easy to take refuge in. And so easy to build as well.—Henrik Ibsen
29. A life spent making mistakes is not only more honorable but more useful than a life spent doing nothing.—George Bernard Shaw
30. Diligence is the mother of good luck.—Benjamin Franklin
31. If architects want to strengthen a decrepit arch, they *increase* the load upon it, for thereby the parts are joined more firmly together.—Viktor Frankl
32. Most people would succeed in small things if they were not troubled with great ambitions.—Henry Wadsworth Longfellow
33. Show me a sane man and I will cure him for you.—C. G. Jung
34. Even though God speaks to condemn me, it is the God of love who speaks. The only bad news would be that God ceases to speak to me.—Jacques Ellul
35. The sea is the universal sewer.—Jacques Cousteau
36. If my doctor told me I had only six months to live, I wouldn't brood. I'd type a little faster.—Isaac Asimov

37. When I pray, coincidences happen, and when I do not, they don't.—William Temple, Archbishop of Canterbury

38. Age is strictly a case of mind over matter. It you don't mind, it doesn't matter.—Jack Benny

39. Life is an adventure in forgiveness.—Norman Cousins

40. In connection with arson a distinction is made between setting fire to a house in the full knowledge of its being inhabited by many or being uninhabited. But candlemongering is like setting fire to a whole community and is not even regarded as a crime!—Søren Kirkegaard

41. Without soul, science is meaningless; for what need has a lump of flesh, if that is all we are, to discover electrons and classify the farthest stars?—David Seabury

42. God has promised forgiveness to your repentance, but He has not promised tomorrow to your procrastination.—St. Augustine

43. Good teaching is one-fourth preparation and three-fourths theatre.—Gail Godwin

44. One ought to pray for peace even to the last clod of earth thrown over his grave.—The Talmud

45. Love it is—not conscience—that is God's regent in the human soul, because it can govern the soul as nothing else can.—Henry Ward Beecher

46. All mankind is of one Author, and is one volume; when one Man dies, one chapter is not torn out of the book, but translated into a better language; and every chapter must be so translated.—John Donne

47. Take hold of Allah's ropes all together, and do not part in sects.—The Koran

48. The tragedy of life is not so much what men suffer, but rather what they miss.—Thomas Carlyle

49. The vanity of being known to be trusted with a secret is generally one of the chief motives to disclose it.—Samuel Johnson

50. It is easy to know God so long as you do not tax yourself with defining Him.—Joseph Joubert

51. We cannot know whether we love God, although there may be strong reasons for thinking so, but there can be no doubt about whether we love our neighbor or not.—St. Teresa

52. God can't fall in love for the same reason water can't get wet.—Peter Kreeft, *A Turn of the Clock*

Questions of Life and Religion

These questions may be useful to prime homiletic pumps, as discussion starters, or for study and youth groups.

1. Why do Christians worship?
2. Are good works an enemy of faith?
3. What do we mean by "the Word of God"?
4. In biblical history, what are some of the various roles of women in the service of God and humankind?
5. How can one achieve wholeness in personal life and in society?
6. Can wealth serve the purposes of God?

7. Does God call every Christian to a specific vocation?
8. How can we reconcile love of neighbor and the use of force in pursuit of justice?
9. Is lying ever justified?
10. Does the Trinity make sense?
11. What is the role of tradition in shaping Christian doctrine?
12. Can we reconcile evil in its various forms with the love of God?
13. Do the Ten Commandments apply today?
14. How does temptation happen to us?
15. How can we gain self-control?
16. What can we do to help individuals who are depressed and desperate?
17. Can God be glorified by human suffering?
18. How do we determine the proper stewardship of our possessions?
19. What is the meaning of the sovereignty of God?
20. Is it possible to live without sinning?
21. What is the positive place of sex in total human experience?
22. In what ways is secularism a threat to religious faith?
23. What does the inspiration of the Bible imply for its authority?
24. Is our salvation eternally secure in Christ?
25. How is the sacrifice of Christ an example for us?
26. In what ways has God revealed himself and his will to us?
27. Why is the Resurrection of Christ important to our faith?
28. How does repentance differ from remorse?
29. In what ways does the reign (kingdom) of God relate to Jesus?
30. Why is racism wrong?
31. How does the providence of God relate to the individual?
32. Which of God's promises are conditional and which are absolute?
33. What are the purposes of prayer?
34. What can we do to ease the plight of poverty?
35. Is politics essential to carrying out the responsibilities of Christian service?
36. Is peace possible?
37. Why is patience a valuable achievement?
38. Does obedience have to conflict with personal autonomy?
39. How does the New Testament use the word *mystery?*
40. Why does the Bible include miracles?
41. Who are the ministers in the Church Universal?
42. What is the importance of Mary in the Church?
43. What are the God-intended ingredients of marriage?
44. How can we define love?
45. How can we "know" God?
46. What justifies us in the eyes of God?
47. Can God's justice and mercy be reconciled?
48. How are joy and happiness different?
49. What steps can we take to normalize Jewish-Christian relations?
50. What was and is Jesus Christ?
51. In what sense is the Bible inspired?

52. What is the meaning of *incarnation?*
53. In what way or ways are we made in the image and likeness of God?

(These questions were suggested by and treated extensively in *Handbook of Themes for Preaching,* edited by James W. Cox, Westminster/John Knox Press, 1991.)

Biblical Benedictions and Blessings

The Lord watch between me and thee when we are absent from one another.—Gen. 31:49

The Lord our God be with us, as he was with our fathers; let him not leave us nor forsake us; that he may incline our hearts unto him, to walk in all his ways and to keep his commandments and his statutes and his judgments, which he commanded our fathers.—1 Kings 8:57–58

Let the words of my mouth and the meditation of my heart be acceptable in thy sight, O Lord, my strength and my redeemer.—Ps. 19:14.

Now the God of patience and consolation grant you to be like-minded one toward another according to Christ Jesus; that ye may with one mind and one mouth glorify God, even the Father of our Lord Jesus Christ. Now the God of hope fill you with all joy and peace in believing, that ye may abound in hope, through the power of the Holy Ghost. Now the God of peace be with you.—Rom. 15:5–6, 13, 33

Now to him that is of power to establish you according to my gospel and the teaching of Jesus Christ, according to the revelation of the mystery, which was kept secret since the world began but now is manifest, and by the Scriptures of the prophets, according to the commandments of the everlasting God, made known to all nations for the glory through Jesus Christ forever.—Rom. 16:25–27

Grace be unto you, and peace, from God our Father, and from the Lord Jesus Christ.—1 Cor. 1:3

The grace of the Lord Jesus Christ and the love of God and the communion of the Holy Ghost be with you all.—2 Cor. 13:14

Peace be to the brethren, and love with faith, from God the Father and the Lord Jesus Christ. Grace be with all them that love our Lord Jesus Christ in sincerity.—Eph. 6:23–24

And the peace of God, which passeth all understanding, shall keep your hearts and minds through Christ Jesus. Finally, brethren, whatsoever things are true, whatsoever things are honest, whatsoever things are just, whatsoever things are pure, whatsoever things are lovely, whatsoever things are of good report; if there be any virtue, and if there be any praise, think on these things. Those things which ye have both learned and received, and heard and seen in me, do; and the God of peace shall be with you.—Phil. 4:7–9

Wherefore also we pray always for you, that our God would count you worthy of this calling and fulfill all the good pleasure of this goodness, and the work of faith with power; that the name of our Lord Jesus Christ may be glorified in you, and ye in him, according to the grace of our God and the Lord Jesus Christ.—2 Thess. 1:11–12

Now the Lord of peace himself give you peace always by all means. The Lord be with you all. The grace of our Lord Jesus Christ be with you all.—2 Thess. 3:16–18

Grace, mercy, and peace, from God our Father and Jesus Christ our Lord.—1 Tim. 1:2

Now the God of peace, that brought again from the dead our Lord Jesus, that great shepherd of the sheep, through the blood of the everlasting covenant, make you perfect in every good work to do his will, working in you that which is well-pleasing in his sight, through Jesus Christ, to whom be glory for ever and ever.—Heb. 13:20–21

The God of all grace, who hath called us unto his eternal glory by Christ Jesus, after that ye have suffered a while, make you perfect, establish, strengthen, settle you. To him be glory and dominion for ever and ever. Greet ye one another with a kiss of charity. Peace be with you all that are in Christ Jesus.—1 Pet. 3:10–14

Grace be with you, mercy, and peace from God the Father, and from the Lord Jesus Christ, the Son of the Father, in truth and love.—2 John 3

Now unto him that is able to keep you from falling, and to present you faultless before the presence of his glory with exceeding joy, to the only wise God our Savior, be glory and majesty, dominion and power, both now and ever.—Jude 24:25

Grace be unto you, and peace, from him which was, and which is to come; and from the seven Spirits which are before his throne; and from Jesus Christ, who is the faithful witness, and the first begotten of the dead, and the prince of the kings of the earth. Unto him that loved us, and washed us from our sins in his own blood, and hath made us kings and priests unto God and his Father, to him be glory and dominion for ever and ever.—Rev. 1:4–6

SECTION II

SERMONS AND HOMILETIC AND WORSHIP AIDS FOR FIFTY-TWO SUNDAYS

SUNDAY, JANUARY 2, 2000
Lectionary Message

Topic: The Power to Become

TEXT: John 1:1–18

Other Readings: Jer. 31:7–14; Ps. 147:12–20; Eph. 1:3–14

How do we best begin a new millennium? The question is urgent on this first Sunday of the year 2000 A.D. No answer is more brilliant than the prologue to the Gospel of John, which is an overture to new life: "In the beginning was the Word, and the Word was with God, and the Word was God. Everything was made by him and without him was not anything made that was made. . . . The Word became flesh and dwelt among us. . . . As many as received him, to them gave he power to become the children of God."

Here we have a prologue to a Gospel that is a prelude to a new age. This is the new age envisioned by the biblical prophets, which is far greater than the more recent New Age movement. Here is a project worthy of our immediate and long-range plans: to become in reality what we are potentially, children of God. Here is the one with whom to begin, the Word made flesh, Jesus Christ.

And here in these sermons at the dawn of the new century and the new millennium we have a once-in-a-lifetime opportunity to announce new life for a new day.

But how do we begin? As individual persons? As a church? As a society?

With a vision. We begin with a vision.

Picture one of those rare events when a person performs a superhuman act. A woman lifts an object many times her own weight to rescue her child who is trapped beneath it. A man sets a record in a sport, going beyond what had been believed possible. When we learn of such happenings we wonder, Where did that person get the power to do such a thing? And where can I get power like that?

To make this personal, take a moment to picture yourself faced with some burden you would like to have lifted, some challenge you would like to overcome, something you would achieve if you had the power.

You may doubt that you could ever have such power. But John's Gospel assures us that you can. The generic term John uses for the vision of human potential is *children of God.* This is also for John a genetic term, that is, one that marks a new genesis in the birth of the spirit. The child of God is one who is born of the Spirit (see the story of Nicodemus in John 3). For such persons, all is possible.

The power to become is not randomly distributed but given only to those who *receive* Jesus Christ. When Jesus came to his own people, they did not receive him and they did not have the power to become.

The key word here is *receive*. It is only when we receive him that we have the power to become. But *receive* is a very difficult word for us today because it is often interpreted as passive. When we receive a report at a business meeting, for example, we do not act on it; we simply receive it, and that often means that after many meetings and much time and money, nothing comes of the report. Or we receive a letter, a fax, or an e-mail. We receive it. That does not mean that we answer it, or even read it. These contemporary usages of *receive* are not what John's Gospel has in mind.

The word John uses for receive is *lambano*. It is an active word. There is a passive verb, *dechomai*, but John does not use that here in favor of the dynamic *lambano*. But where in our world today is there an understanding of *receive* that translates *lambano*? Look at sports. The catcher in baseball is called what? The receiver. And he is perhaps the most active player in the game, involved in every play defensively and expected to produce offensively. In football also, the receiver is the acting one, without whom the pass is incomplete.

We receive Jesus Christ not as we receive a report in a meeting or a fax from the machine but as a catcher receives the baseball and the receiver catches the football: actively, with all that we have. Then and only then do we have the power to become. The power to become who we are meant to be as individuals, as Christians, as citizens: children of God.

This active receiving of Jesus Christ, which turns our vision into reality, means (in John and throughout the New Testament) that

1. We recognize and identify Jesus Christ by name and in person.
2. We welcome him into our lives and travel with him as a crew welcomes passengers aboard a cruise ship.
3. We "take in" his presence (the analogy is to eating and drinking, that is, to eat is literally to receive meat). This is the very meaning of Holy Communion.

In these ways we receive him, and are given the power to become new persons in the new millennium.—David James Randolph

ILLUSTRATIONS

TRANSFORMATION.   A great example of how this power transformed individuals and society that is of special value at the beginning of a new era is the Wesleyan revival in Great Britain. That land was saved from a bloody revolution because of those who actively received Jesus Christ. The hymns of John and Charles Wesley as well as their sermons and journals are sources of power for today and tomorrow.—David James Randolph

SOMETHING BETTER.   Where in your experience is *receiving* active rather than passive? Develop that attitude about the Gospel. For example, when I played baseball and softball in my youth, I was a catcher. I enjoyed it and my father wanted me, then my brother Jack and then my brother Harry, to be a professional catcher. Instead, all three of us became ministers, receiving in the gospel something greater than the diamond.—David James Randolph

SERMON SUGGESTIONS

Topic: When Faith Falters

TEXT: Ps. 77:1–15

(1) The price of a great faith is a great and continuous struggle to get it, to keep it, and to share it. (2) Faith falters when some tragic event contradicts or challenges the promise of faith. (3) We have no real alternative to moving ahead in search of an even greater faith than we have ever known. (4) God's steadying hand is leading us on to even greater things.—Harold A. Bosley[1]

Topic: Something to Consider

TEXT: Matt. 4:18–20

(1) Jesus is the only one who can call to life with authority to be its leader (Luke 4:18–19; 19:10; Rom. 5:6–9). (2) Jesus is the only leader who can be light (hope and assurance) when it is dark (John 8:12). (3) Jesus is the only leader who commits himself to us for the entire journey (Matt. 28:20; Heb. 13:5).—C. Neil Strait[2]

CONGREGATIONAL MUSIC

1. "Sing Praise to God Who Reigns Above," J. J. Schütz (1675)

    MIT FREUDEN ZART, Bohemian Brethren *Kirchengesänge* (1566); tr. Frances E. Cox (1864)

    Expressing the general spirit of both the Old Testament reading in the prophecy of Jeremiah and Psalm 147, this excellent hymn of praise coming from German Pietism would be appropriate as an opening hymn of praise.

2. "The Blood Will Never Lose Its Power," Andraé Crouch

    THE BLOOD, Andraé Crouch (1962)

    The apostle Paul's rehearsal of the blessings of redemption through the blood of Christ in the Ephesian passage is echoed in this popular contemporary song by an African American.

3. "Amazing Grace, How Sweet the Sound," John Newton (1779)

    NEW BRITAIN, *Virginia Harmony* (1831); adapt./harm. E. O. Excell (1900)

    This great autobiographical hymn by converted slave trader John Newton is an eighteenth-century expression of gratitude for the blessings of redemption as related by the apostle Paul in Ephesians 1:3–14.

4. "O Word of God Incarnate," William H. How (1867)

    MUNICH, *Meiningen Gesangbuch* (1693); harm. Felix Mendelssohn (1847)

    This well-known hymn is addressed to the incarnate Word—the sublime idea set forth in the prologue to John's Gospel in this day's reading.—Hugh T. McElrath

WORSHIP AIDS

CALL TO WORSHIP.   "Praise the Lord! How good it is to sing praises to our God; for he is gracious, and a song of praise is fitting" (Ps. 147:1 NRSV).

---

[1] *Sermons on the Psalms*

[2] In G. Paul Butler (ed.), *Best Sermons*, Vol. 1 (New York: Trident Press, 1968).

INVOCATION.   Eternal God, Lord of creation, everything around us points to you, telling of your wisdom and power, and we thank you for what we can know of you through nature. Yet you have given to us a savior, Jesus Christ our Lord, who alone reveals your love in all its dimensions and splendor. We praise you for your handiwork in your universe and stand in awe of your majesty. We trust you and offer ourselves to you as we bow in penitence before the cross. Help us to render true worship as our voices blend with the music of the spheres and our lives serve your perfect will.

OFFERTORY SENTENCE.   "No one can serve two masters; for either he will hate the first and love the second, or he will be devoted to the first and despise the second. You cannot serve God and money" (Matt. 6:24 NEB).

OFFERTORY PRAYER.   Today, O God, help us to set our priorities in proper order and devote ourselves to what truly matters. Help us to find our joy in doing your will and blessing the lives of others.

PRAYER.   O God, you are the First and the Last, the Beginning and the End, the Alpha and the Omega—the Eternal One; but you are our Father also. We are awed by your majesty, yet we are comforted by your love. We take refuge in the tenderness of your strength.

We bring to this beginning of a new year all the weight of sin not confessed, duties not completed, plans not fulfilled, and hopes disappointed. We bring them into your presence with the confidence that you enter into our need and do something redemptive: forgive our sins, help us to carry forward tasks unfinished, give us wisdom to reevaluate all that we have proposed, and grant us the courage to accept realities that cannot be altered. But may we not too soon give up on our duties, plans, and hopes, assured as we are that you will supply the strength to do whatever is right and needed.

We pray for patience as we experience the slow unfolding of your will for us. We pray for tolerance and charity when family, friends, or neighbors forget your commands. We pray for a spirit of sharing, so that both those who give and those who receive may know the fullness of the blessings of the gospel of Christ.

SERMON
Topic: A Crucial Faith
TEXT: 1 Cor. 1:18–25

The meaning of the word *cross* has grown out of centuries of Christian history with crosses on steeples and altars of churches, carried in processions, and worn by the pious. If something is of critical importance in our lives, it is *crucial,* "crosslike." The terminology has blended into the secular landscape so that we no longer need to be the least bit religious or even slightly concerned about Christ to speak of the cross as a central issue. We speak of the "crux"—the cross—of the matter without the slightest thought of the suffering and death of Jesus. Our words suggest that the cross lies at the center of life. X marks the spot, and the rest of history revolves around the crucial center; but I am not at all sure that Christians today really get it. In my childhood context, every soft drink was called a "Coke." As an adult, I learned why Coca-Cola battled the image. To get lost in generic language is the kiss of death in the world of commerce. The cross has gained general acceptance in our Western culture. It has become a generic symbol of anything important, healing, or nice. Removed from its historical origin, the cross has been lost in the culture and uprooted from its original meaning.

I. *The cross ought to raise our sense of indignation.* The central mark of identity of the Christian faith has always been an offensive, repugnant symbol to the non-Christian world. Jürgen Moltmann tells about graffiti on the Palatine of a crucified figure with a donkey's head and the inscription, "Alexamenos worships his god." It comes from the time before Constantine the Great when the cross became a sign of conquest for soldiers to paint on their shields. The Roman orator Cicero declared, "Let even the name of the cross be kept away not only from the bodies of the citizens of Rome, but also from their thought, sight and hearing." To speak in polite company of crucifixion was viewed as uncouth, the disgusting language of sick minds and unrefined manners. Moltmann puts the cross in perspective: "The idea of a 'crucified God' to whom veneration and worship were due was regarded in the ancient world as totally inappropriate to God." He observed that non-Christians often recognize the scandal of the cross better than folks like us who have always viewed the cross as the central symbol of our faith.

I grew up on hymns like "The Old Rugged Cross" without registering the words "so despised by the world." I can recall a few times when my sermons offended someone with a veiled political reference or a controversial moral statement, but I can never recall anyone complaining about any mention of the cross from the pulpit. I do recall early in my ministry a plea from a church member to find a place in every sermon "to tell about Jesus' death on the cross." In the Church I've never known anyone to be offended by the cross, but I've discovered a different world outside the Church. I recall a friendly discussion among clergy about an issue of war and peace. During Lent people were generally aware of the Passion of Christ, so I suggested that the cross is a model of how the strong approach the weak in this world—without the slightest concern that I would offend anyone. I rather expected accolades for my keen insight and application of faith to life. Instead I was strongly reprimanded from my friend the rabbi. He was far too big a man to be offended by the partisan symbol of the cross. His concern had nothing to do with the divide between Judaism and Christianity. In fact, he may have had a better grasp of the implication of the cross for our lives than I did. Later, in private conversation, he appealed for me to rethink the business of the cross as either the way of God or a way to deal with our enemies. The cross suggested to the rabbi an offensive, repugnant weakness unworthy of God and beneath all human dignity—Paul's sentiments exactly: "Christ crucified, a stumbling block to Jews and foolishness to Gentiles."

II. *The cross is the mystery of God's way with the world.* Jews and Gentiles included the entire population of the world for Paul. The apostle-come-lately had been to Athens and spoken to the Platonists about the identity of the "unknown god." The point of offense for the Athenians seemed to be the Resurrection rather than the cross, but Paul had been around the Hellenistic world long enough to know that the cross does not sell too well where logic reigns. Although philosophy was not so much at stake, the issue with the Jews was the same. What kind of god allows himself to get crucified? I was a graduate student in seminary during the short-lived emergence of the "death of God" theology. The suggestion "God is dead" made tremendous fodder for our pulpits. It was such an easy target to zap. We had always had atheists and agnostics question the existence of God, but we had never had Christian theologians suggest that God has expired—as if the Creator of the universe were no greater than the life forms he had created. A few books were written, but nothing really ever came of the idea. How can you start a movement with a dead God? But here is exactly the offense of the cross. To say that "God was in Christ" and to proclaim the cross as the way of God in the world is akin to declaring the death of God.

In the face of the cross, God is either powerless or dead, and we are left alone in a cruel world. That is the scandal! It is not an issue until it becomes your issue. At the crucial moment in life when everything of worth hangs in the balance, we need a God who is about the business of rescue. That helpless figure on the cross can be terrifying. Elie Wiesel tells of the horror of being a Jew in the Nazi holocaust. At Auschwitz two men and a boy were hanged and the whole camp was forced to observe the execution. Because of his weight, the child did not die immediately but struggled for half an hour against the tightening rope. Someone in the ranks asked, "Where is God now?" Wiesel said that he heard a voice within answer: "Here he is—he is hanging here on this gallows."

There is the mystery of the cross. The Almighty comes to us in humility, vulnerable to the same threats and fears as his dear children, subject to death—even death on the cross.—Larry Dipboye

ILLUSTRATIONS

IN THE CROSS OF CHRIST I GLORY.   In times of defeat, fear, disappointment, the Cross stands by with its deliverance. The poet [Sir John Bowring] does not tell us how it is able to do this, but human experience has shown that contemplation of the sufferings of Christ and the lesson of victory through self-sacrifice implicit in the Cross are a powerful inspiration.

On the other hand, when things are going well, consciousness that our lives are linked with Christ and God puts the glory of eternity under our fleeting happiness.—Albert E. Bailey[3]

SUFFERING FOR OTHERS.   The man who protests "I want no one suffering for me" is ignoring the fact that not only religion but the whole of life is built that way. What Caiaphas said in cold, calculating cynicism—"It is expedient that one man should die for the people"— may be the voice of the devil, as indeed it was on Caiaphas' unscrupulous lips. But looked at from another angle, it is the very truth of God. It *is* expedient—it always has been and always will be expedient—that one man should die for the people. David Livingstone, dying on his knees in darkest Africa; the X-ray pioneer losing limb or life for the advancement of knowledge and the relief of suffering; the Headmaster of an English school who during an air-raid marshaled his pupils into the shelters and then, going back to make sure that none had been left behind, was himself caught by a bomb and instantly killed—"one man dying for the people." This is the cosmic principle of love, the cruciform pattern on which life itself is built, the ground-plan of the universe.—James S. Stewart[4]

---

[3] *The Gospel in Hymns*
[4] *A Faith to Proclaim*

SUNDAY, JANUARY 9, 2000
Lectionary Message

Topic: Wise Guys and Wise People

TEXT: Matthew 2:1–2

Other Readings: Isa. 60:1–6; Ps. 72:1–7, 10–14; Eph. 3:1–12

Wise Guys get more attention today than Wise People. We see this on television, where far more time is devoted to Wise Guys who have smart remarks, such as Jay Leno or David Letterman, than wise people who seek the meaning of life. Yet the path the first Wise Men blazed in the gospel is still available in our Wise Guy Wasteland if we choose to follow it.

I. *We become Wise People rather than Wise Guys when we seek the ultimate rather than the convenient.* Convenience is comfortable. I enjoy the convenience stores at times. But the individual who never travels farther than the nearest 7–11 will not become much of a person.

The Wise Men were after the ultimate rather than the convenient. They were looking for destiny's end and they knew that they would have to lift their sights beyond the market as we must look beyond the mall. They knew you could never buy the ultimate, you could only discover it. There's a practical lesson for Advent and Christmas if there ever was one. What gifts would we give if we wanted the receiver to discover something new?

The Wise Men looked for a star instead of a store. A star is far away from us. It may be beautiful but it is remote. We may not even be aware of stars. Yet the stars affect us more than anything we could possibly buy or watch on television or work for or possess. The sun, after all, is a star. Without it, life could not exist on the Earth.

Truth is like that. It seems distant and often irrelevant, but we cannot live without it. We may try to live for comfort, wealth, power, but at the end of the day they fade away and we seek a real reason for living.

II. *We become Wise People rather than Wise Guys when we travel all the way to Jesus Christ.* Faith calls for a journey. We have to leave where we are to arrive at where we want to be. It is not easy.

We seldom think of the Wise Men's long journey in the dead of winter with sore-footed camels. T. S. Eliot, in "The Journey of the Magi," heard them say,

> There were times we regretted
> The summer palaces on slopes, the terraces
> And the silken girls bringing sherbet.

The poet convinces us that the power of this journey lies not just in starting out but in enduring the difficulties and making it all the way to Bethlehem. Wise Guys may live in one cheap hotel after another. But Wise People seek a building, eternal in the heavens, whose builder and maker is God.

Many people stop in the suburbs of Bethlehem and never make it to the Savior. Self-interest without social concern, power without purpose, money without meaning, lust without love, hoarding and not sharing—these are some of the suburbs of Bethlehem. We must pass through them to get to the Savior.

III. *We become Wise People rather than Wise Guys when we worship Jesus Christ and offer ourselves in service of the Kingdom of God.* We may not have much gold, and frankincense and myrrh seem strange to us, but we are wise when like the Magi we offer ourselves and the best that we have to serve the King of Kings.

In some of the cathedrals of Europe the doorway is slanted so that as one enters one is pitched forward to one's knees. Life is like that. Life is a great cathedral whose very design throws us to our knees before a great presence.

Albert Einstein wrote of a truth that is hidden behind the illusions of life. This is beautiful, but it is not Bethlehem. For here the star condensed the cloud of mystery and drew it within itself. The mystery is still there, but it is within the act of God. The ultimate truth of the universe, the truth that will be true when all other so-called truths are false, is not shrouded in a cloud. It is wrapped in swaddling clothes. It is not an "it" at all. It is a person whose name is Jesus. And in this person we find all—that God *is,* wrapped in human flesh.

We confess at last that we are not compelled by the love of a mystery. We are called by the mystery of a love. Thus we sing:

> I know not how that Bethlehem's Babe could in the godhead be.
> I only know the manger child has brought God's love to me.

We become Wise People and not Wise Guys when we seek the ultimate rather than the convenient, when we travel all the way to the Savior and when we offer our lives in service. The end of this road is the beginning of life.—David James Randolph

ILLUSTRATIONS
THE JOURNEY OF FAITH.   "The Journey of the Magi" by T. S. Eliot, along with many other examples of the journey of faith, may be found in the *New Oxford Book of Christian Verse.*[5]

WHAT BRINGS US TO GOD?   In a sermon preached in The Memorial Church, Harvard University, Charles P. Price stirred the Harvard community with a challenge to learning, religion, and the place of love. He asked, "What does bring us to God? If it is not wisdom, if it is not moral effort, what is it? The Christian Church exists to say that it is Christ, it is love. Love defined by the life of Christ puts the network of our relationships to God, and to other persons, and to ourselves, on a right basis. Love straightens them out. Love reconciles. Love justifies. When we are puffed up with pride by all we know, it takes simplicity to humble us. That innocent question from the silent student in the back row. It takes love, honesty, openness, compassion, all of those qualities which we might sum up in the name Christ, to free us from the tyranny of learning. And when we are free from the tyranny of learning, we are free to explore the excitement and glory of wisdom, which truly does come from God. But we need to be free, and it is love which frees us. Christ frees us. If wisdom keeps us from seeing the power of love, God has to make the wisdom of this world foolish."—Charles P. Price[6]

---

[5] Edited by Donald Davie (Oxford and New York: Oxford University Press, 1988).
[6] In G. Paul Butler (ed.), *Best Sermons,* Vol. 10 (New York: Trident Press, 1968), p. 368.

SERMON SUGGESTIONS

Topic: Bewildered Strangers

TEXT: Ps. 137:4

(1) Confusion explained. (2) Confusion shared. (3) Confusion dispelled.

Topic: The Shadow and the Reality

TEXT: John 1:15–18; Matt. 5:17

(1) The shadow: the eminence of Moses and the law (Heb. 10:1). (2) The reality: the preeminence of Jesus Christ (Heb. 3:1–6).

CONGREGATIONAL MUSIC

1. "As with Gladness Men of Old," William C. Dix (1860)

    DIX, Conrad Kocher (1838); adapt. William Monk (1861)

    Each stanza of this familiar hymn draws a picture of some detail from the story of the visit of the Wise Men (Matt. 2:1–12) and then makes application to the spiritual lives of the singing worshipers.

2. "Jesus Shall Reign," Isaac Watts (1719)

    DUKE STREET, John Hatton (1793)

    Watts's free paraphrase of Psalm 72 could appropriately be sung immediately following the Psalter reading.

3. "Ye Servants of God," Charles Wesley (1744)

    LYONS, W. Gardiner's *Sacred Melodies* (1815); HANOVER, attr. William Croft (1708)

    Wesley's hymn proclaiming the riches of God's grace would be a suitable response to the Epistle reading for this day in which the apostle speaks of the grace given to him to preach the blessings of Christ to the Gentiles.

4. "Arise, Shine Out, Your Light Has Come," Brian Wren (1986)

    DUNE DIN, Vernon Griffiths (1971)

    This modern hymn based on the Isaiah passage (60:1–6) and set to one of the finest long-meter tunes composed in the twentieth century would be very appropriate sung in connection with the Isaiah reading. A choir could introduce the hymn by singing the first two stanzas, after which the congregation could join the singing.—Hugh T. McElrath

WORSHIP AIDS

CALL TO WORSHIP.   "Blessed be the Lord, the God of Israel, who alone does wondrous things. Blessed be his glorious name forever; may his glory fill the whole earth. Amen and Amen" (Ps. 72:18–19 NRSV).

INVOCATION.   O God, we continue the Psalmist's prayer with our own praise, and with the desire that your glory may be known among us as we meet to worship and may be known throughout the earth.

OFFERTORY SENTENCE.   "Where someone has been given much, much will be expected of him; and the more he has had entrusted to him, the more will be demanded of him" (Luke 12:48b REB).

OFFERTORY PRAYER.   Help us, O God, to see our duties of stewardship clearly and then let the power of love drive our giving.

PRAYER.   Appearing God, Holy You who are abidingly revealing yourself to us, we pray for eyes to see clearly, ears to hear kindly, hearts to know quietly your presence, your appearance among us. Wondrous God, the deep joy of Christmas and now Epiphany is that you have also chosen to reveal yourself to us in your Son, Jesus Christ our Lord. As we celebrate the many manifestations of Jesus this season, we pray for a fresh awareness of his presence, his power, and his peace.

Understanding God, as we undecorate and pack up the things and elements of Christmas, help us, O God, not to store away the Christ. How easy it is to be consumed with the things of life, the sweep of it all, and quickly miss his presence, his appearance, the Christ's hope and word and way for our lives. Keep us open and free to your appearance in our being, Lord Jesus.

Compassionate Christ, you who came not to be served but to serve, O Suffering Servant of prophecy, O Saving Servant of the cross, whose coat of arms was a towel, today as we ponder being servants, each one of us being a servant, help us to look to you for our example and model. We give thanks that you have given each one of us a call to service and spiritual gifts for service. We give thanks for a loving, affirming community of faith in which to serve and for opportunities abounding in our journeys to care for others in your name. As with the Psalmist, may we serve the Lord with gladness. And now, "Teach us, good Lord, to serve you as you deserve; to give and not to count the costs; to fight for you and not to heed the wounds; to toil and not to seek for rest; to labor and not to ask for any reward, except the knowledge that we do your will."[7] And in Christ we worship, pray, and serve. Amen.—William M. Johnson

SERMON
Topic: The Seekers
TEXT: Matt. 2:1–23

Today is Epiphany, the day when we are by tradition supposed to think about the visit of the Wise Men. There you are: King Herod, Jesus, and the Wise Men. Each character is a type, representing a whole way of life, a whole system of choices, and by the end of the story we're supposed to have seen enough of them to be able to make choices of our own. Here we go:

I. King Herod, who comes first in the story, was "King of the Jews," appointed by the Romans to rule over Palestine. He had been in power for more than thirty years. When he'd hear of opposition anywhere in his country, even in his own house, heads would roll, people would die.

Herod was a typical thug of a third-world king, living in luxury while his people stayed poor, keeping his power by deprivation, violence, and above all, terror. When the Wise Men showed up and asked, "Where's the new king? We saw his star and have come to pay our

---

[7] Saint Ignatius of Loyola

respects," it was as if they had pushed Herod's terror button. First, find out as much information as possible: call in the analysts, find out where a new king would be born if there was one. Second, send out spies, double agents, to locate the baby so we can send in an assassination team to take the family out. Third, have a backup plan: if the information isn't specific enough for a surgical strike, then nuke the whole village just to be sure; send in the troops to kill all the infants, since you can't be sure which one is Jesus.

Herod sounds so familiar, so typical. The temptation to those in power to stay in power by the use of force and violence must be almost impossible to resist. Herod, ordering the soldiers to kill the babies of Bethlehem, was simply imitating the strategy of the Egyptian Pharaoh so many years before. When Israeli troops drove Palestinian people from their homes in a little village just outside Bethlehem, confiscated their properties to pay a tax debt, and declared that the land was now the site of a new Jewish settlement, were they not replaying their own history, in which a thousand Jewish villages in Poland and Germany were eliminated?

Terror breeds terror, does it not? Herod was afraid, and all Jerusalem with him. Terror becomes so commonplace that today there are probably a dozen armed conflicts going on that you and I don't even know about because they don't make the front page.

But Herod, for all his power to do evil, was shown up both by the Wise Men and by Jesus. Why hadn't Herod or his court advisors noticed the star hanging right outside their windows? Bethlehem, after all, was just over the hill and down the road from Jerusalem. With all his power and all his money and all his troops and all his ruthlessness, why couldn't he catch this particular peasant family? Herod, the Terror King, seemed unstoppable, but his plans were thwarted. Herod's reign must have seemed endless to those who suffered under it, but at the end of the story he died, as all tyrants do, and his network of power fell apart.

II. Enter the Wise Men. They were stereotypes, too. They were seekers: followers of new things, star watchers, dreamers. They came from the east, where the new day begins, the direction from which new ideas always filtered into Palestine. They were outsiders—Gentiles, not Jews—they didn't have access to the Bible, so they didn't know how to interpret what they were seeing, but they had seen something amazing, something compelling enough to make them pack their bags and ride their camels all the way to Jerusalem. They were determined to find this new thing, this new king. Have you ever wondered why? It really doesn't matter where the Wise Men were from, be it Persia or Arabia or Babylon. What's so great about a new king? But seekers always hope that tomorrow can be better, seekers always believe it's worth giving life one more shot. Let's go see the new king, and pay our respects, and give him gifts, and maybe—just maybe—this time will be different.

It seems to have worked out for them. When they finally found Jesus, the text says, "they were overwhelmed with joy," and just before they left God warned them about Herod's intentions and kept them safe. Don't you imagine that they went home changed by their experiences? I think so. One genuine encounter with Jesus was probably enough to make them believe that the world could be different, that the Terror King was not the world's only option.

III. And that brings us to Jesus. He's only a baby in this chapter, and so instead of doing things, he's the center of the whirl of activity: the visit, the flight to Egypt, the massacre, and the return. But even as a baby, Jesus was the embodiment of a new kingdom, a new system, just as the seekers had hoped. It's just a little thing—only a little bit of good—but it's enough to fill the hearts of the seekers with joy.

The prophets had also said that God's new kingdom would be peaceful: Herod's analysts even read the verse out loud: the new ruler would be like a shepherd, gently tending God's people. Unfortunately Herod's monstrous nature overshadows the story. Threatened by the idea of a new king, he lashed out like a wounded beast and struck down the infants in a village. But deep within that darkness there was a little light of hope, where God's angels came to protect Jesus and his family and send him away safely. It's just a little thing—one baby saved out of a whole village massacred—but maybe it's enough to show us what could be, if we turn our hearts away from the Terror King to the Prince of Peace.

When Matthew is done with us, no one would really choose Herod, right? No sane person reading this story would really want to be like the Terror King. So why are we? Why do we repeat against others the violence done to us? Why allow the hurts life inflicts on us to make us into the image of that which we hate? To be different—to live under the Prince of Peace instead of under Herod—we have to change, we have to seek, we have to ask questions, we have to look for the little goods within the great evils, we have to be willing to be confused. But the gospel says that if we seek, we will find; if we ask for directions, we will receive them; if we knock on enough doors, we will one day open the one where Jesus lives.—Richard B. Vinson

SUNDAY, JANUARY 16, 2000
Lectionary Message

Topic: Come and See
Text: John 1:43–51
Other Readings: 1 Sam. 3:1–10 (11–20); Ps. 139:1–6, 13–18; 1 Cor. 6:12–20

"You are tough to preach to!" a pastor said to a parishioner. "You sit there in your pew and the expression on your face and your posture dare me to get and hold your attention."

"Good!" the parishioner replied. "I don't want to be a pushover."

Many people to whom we preach are difficult to reach. This is good because a faith that comes easily may go easily.

I. The first hearers of the gospel were no pushovers. Jesus had a rough time with them, as did his disciples. But they loved the challenge and their ability to deal with it established the movement on a firm footing.

Consider Philip when he began to follow Jesus. In his enthusiasm he reached out to Nathaniel and declared that he had finally found the one about whom Moses and the Law and the Prophets had spoken and it was none other than Jesus, son of Joseph from Nazareth. Nathaniel's reply was the ultimate putdown: "Can anything good come out of Nazareth?"

Note that Philip did not even try to answer the question. He knew that it was not a real question. He knew that Nathaniel was from Cana, which is near Nazareth, and there was intense rivalry between the towns. Nathaniel's question was actually a statement, a claim of superiority. It must have been tempting to argue with Nathaniel, who had all but announced a debate: resolved, nothing good can come out of Nazareth. Arguing for the proposition, Nathaniel. Arguing against the proposition, Philip.

Many apologists for Christianity have taken up precisely that task across the centuries and tried to argue their opposition into faith. In some times and places that may have been appropriate. But Philip did not go the way of debate. He went the way of dialogue. He talked with Nathaniel and invited him to come and see. He chose invitation over argumentation.

Nathaniel accepted the invitation. He came, he saw Jesus, and was soon in dialogue with him. Jesus, interestingly enough, knew something about Nathaniel. He had observed him and was able to relate what he had to say to Nathaniel personally. He had done his homework, his study of those to whom he would speak. The dialogue was an ongoing one, for Nathaniel followed Jesus. It is believed by some scholars that the man called Nathaniel in John's Gospel is the disciple who in the lists in the Synoptic Gospels is called Bartholomew.

II. Anyone wishing to reach another with the gospel, like the pastor with whom we began, or any Christian who wants to share with another, can learn a lot from this encounter, which offers an approach to the unbeliever that is still effective.

(a) *Welcome skeptics.* Pay attention to them. Learn what you can about them. Listen to them. Seek the quest beneath their questions. Do not attack them or defend against them, but invite them to take part in the life of the community.

(b) *Let them come and see what Christ is doing in and through the community.* This presupposes, of course, that the community is indeed expressing this presence, however incompletely. The skeptic asks, can anything good come out of the church? We answer: Come and worship with us. Come and take part in our Bible study. Come and see our nursery school. Come and see our family life program. Come and see our community outreach program. It is our faith that Christ is at work here and that skeptical claims are best met not by counterarguments but by the appeal to what Christ is doing. This includes what Christ is doing in the world at large as well as in the Church. Contemporary parallels to the Gospel accounts should be evident, although their expression may be different. For example, the ministry of healing today may be related to hospitals and special medical procedures as well as to worship services, but Christ is present in all of it.

(c) *Follow Christ and invite others to follow him.* This is basic to Philip's appeal and must be to ours. Evangelism, presenting the good news and making disciples of hearers, is not the offer of a solid state one is in forever but an invitation to a journey.—David James Randolph

ILLUSTRATIONS

FROM DEBATE TO DIALOGUE.   Deborah Tannen, who is well known for her work in improving communication between men and women, has recently written a book that is helpful in communicating the gospel, although she does not address this subject directly. Her book is entitled *The Argument Culture: Moving from Debate to Dialogue.*[8] As her title suggests, our culture is preoccupied with arguments. These may be of a legal nature (consider the trials with which many people seem obsessed), but often they have to do with interpersonal and intergroup conflicts that take on the nature of court cases in which all parties lose. The Church sometimes gets caught in this debate mode and Tannen shows how we can break out of this into a dialogue that I find compatible with the gospel.—David James Randolph

---

[8] New York: Random House, 1998.

WHEN THE MIRACLE HAPPENS.   A nurse told me about a young man who was struck down by severe infantile paralysis and could sleep only with the aid of an artificial lung. After four years, he was completely embittered and defeated. The miracle of God happened to him when he was able to say *yes* to what he had to live with. Inwardly, he was totally free from that moment.—Edward Schweizer[9]

SERMON SUGGESTIONS

Topic: Praising Helpless Gods
TEXT: Exod. 3:1–6; Rom. 1:18–32; Isa. 46; Matt. 6:33; John 10:10
(1) The folly of idolatry. (2) Contemporary forms of idolatry. (3) The rewarding alternative to idolatry.

Topic: What Makes a Church Grow
TEXT: Acts 2:37–47
(1) Worthy objectives. (2) A vital fellowship. (3) Serious commitment.

CONGREGATIONAL MUSIC

1. "God Moves in a Mysterious Way," William Cowper (1774)
    DUNDEE, Scottish Psalter (1615)
    The Psalmist (139:6) expresses awe and wonder when contemplating the omniscience and omnipresence of God. This finely wrought hymn similarly speaks of the mystery of God's purposes and actions in the language of trust and faith.
2. "Speak to My Heart, Lord Jesus," B. B. McKinney (1927)
    HOLCOMB, B. B. McKinney (1927)
    This simple prayer song appropriately echoes the response of the boy Samuel to the Lord's prophetic calling set forth in this day's Old Testament reading.
3. "We Praise You with Our Minds, O Lord," Hugh T. McElrath (1962)
    CLONMEL, ancient Gaelic tune
    The second stanza of this hymn of consecration focuses on the idea of glorifying God in our bodies, which are to be temples of the Holy Spirit—the central theme of the Epistle reading (1 Cor. 6:12–20).
4. "I Have Decided to Follow Jesus," Garo Christian Folk Song (nineteenth century)
    ASSAM, arr. William J. Reynolds
    This folk hymn of the Garo Christians in Northern India could suitably follow the Gospel reading in which Philip and Nathaniel decided to answer Jesus' call to "Follow me."—Hugh T. McElrath

WORSHIP AIDS

CALL TO WORSHIP.   "Search me, O God, and know my heart: try me, and know my thoughts: and see if there be any wicked way in me, and lead me in the way everlasting" (Ps. 139:23).

[9] *God's Inescapable Nearness*

INVOCATION.   Our Father, we need leadership for all the worthy objectives of life. So lead us through the experience of worship in such ways that our hearts may be cleansed and the things we do may be worthy and acceptable in your sight.

OFFERTORY SENTENCE.   "Each one should give . . . as he has decided, not with regret or out of a sense of duty; for God loves the one who gives gladly" (2 Cor. 9:7 TEV).

OFFERTORY PRAYER.   We thank you, gracious God, for all that you have given us. In the gift of your Son Jesus Christ you have set the example of love, by which all our giving is to be measured.

PRAYER.   We do not think of it often, Father, this truth that we are creatures made in your image. Sometimes that image is hard to discern. Thank you for your grace which enables us to become more of what we were made to be.

We come to confess to you that it is our sins which mar your image in us. We are not worthy of your love and grace and forgiveness and restoration. But we are thankful that you do not deal with us as we deserve. Forgive us, Father, we pray. Forgive our pride and self-righteousness. Forgive our waste of time and energy. Forgive us for neglecting those who need us and those for whom we have a special and family responsibility. Forgive us, we pray, for Jesus' sake.

Today speak clearly to us. Reveal to us some truth that will enable us to be fortified in the doing of your will. Pray, show us your will just for today. We do not ask for some future vision of what we are to do, nor for the strength for tomorrow. Just give us strength for today, and in all that we do, help us to serve you better.

Here in this sacred place we pray for one another. For the anxious and troubled we ask your peace of mind. For the physically and mentally ill we ask your gift of wholeness and health. For the lonely and neglected we ask your encouraging presence. We give ourselves to being the channels through which you move, that others may be lifted and guided in your ways.

Now, in these moments, we worship, listen, and wait, that we may encounter the Holy Spirit and through him experience your presence and truth.—Henry Fields

SERMON
Topic: Running with the Truth
TEXT: Matt. 16:13–19

The challenges of the new year are outdone only by the demands of the new millennium. But even before we can determine solutions, we need mind expansion, and faith deepening, in order to envision the ways that we can get to real answers for troubling questions. We require hearts opened to the means by which the right settlements can be secured. That's a journey of discovery all its own.

In the midst of a world equally confused, surrounded by examples of pagan worship and Roman idolatry, as well as legalistic Jewish practices, Peter made a startling confession. He said of Jesus, "You are the Messiah, the Son of the living God." It was for him a claim on the future—not only for the year before them and the millennium in which they lived, but for the ages beyond. It was on a journey that this great discovery had brightened his life. He was running with the truth, and so must we.

Caesarea Philippi is in the northeastern section of Israel, butted up against both Syria to the east and Lebanon to the north and west. It is on the fringe of the notorious Golan Heights, a once-tranquil community near one of the outlets of the streams that form the Jordan River. In Old Testament times it was a Syrian worship place of the nefarious god Baal. At a cavern in the cliff, Greeks and Romans built a place of worship for their god Pan, because this was said to be his birthplace. They named it Paneas, after the god of nature and fertility. The rock cliff is filled with niches where images of Pan once stood, and the surrounding countryside is strewn with broken pieces of marble from both the statues and the temples of the Greeks and Romans, who also built lavish marble palaces nearby.

Later, in the same spot, the Jewish king Herod the Great built a temple dedicated to the worship of Caesar. Herod's son, Philip, continued to enrich and beautify this white marble edifice honoring the Roman emperor. He added his own name to the town, Caesarea Philippi, to indicate who built it and in whose honor. Herod Agrippa, a little later, renamed the town again—but this time in honor of Nero! Jewish kings paid homage to Roman emperors as gods in this strange place! Yet it was here, surrounded by all the trappings of paganism and idolatry, that Jesus asked his disciples, "Who do people say that the Son of Man is?" Here was the most significant question of the ages spoken amid the clutter and bric-a-brac of a world that was anything but righteous.

A variety of answers spilled out of the disciples' mouths. They had heard what the people said and they reported it to Jesus: "John the Baptist!" "Elijah!" "Jeremiah!" They named other prophets, too.

"But who do *you* say that I am?" queried our Lord more directly.

It was the blustery fisherman, the bold, boisterous, and ever-lovable Peter, who exclaimed, "You are the Messiah, the Son of the living God."

On this spur of the Plains of Sharon, where foreign deities had long been worshiped and where Jews had betrayed their own faith by building shrines to deified pagan Roman emperors, the disciples swept aside all the idolatrous myths and nonsense surrounding them and saw Peter run with the truth: Jesus is God. Jesus is the long-awaited Messiah, the Christ promised to the prophets by God himself, exclaimed Peter. And the eleven did not disagree. Here was the very confession needed to carry them through the rest of that century and into the next and even further into eternity. It was the journey of sublime discovery.

Jesus was quick to respond to Peter's observation. He offered him a commendation the likes of which few others received. "Blessed are you, Simon son of Jonah! For flesh and blood has not revealed this to you but my Father in heaven. And I tell you, you are Peter, and on this rock I will build my Church, and the gates of Hades will not prevail against it."

Although some believe that Jesus was choosing Peter for the top position among the apostles, it seems to me that it is Peter's confession rather than Peter himself that is to be the building block upon which the Church is to be built. Jesus, and no one else!

It was the bold Peter, resolute in faith and determined in mission, who later stood before the Jewish authorities and declared to those who crucified the Lord, "This Jesus is 'the stone that was rejected by you, the builders; it has become the cornerstone'" (Acts 4:11). It is this "rock" upon which the burly fisherman was building the Church, this truth that Jesus is the Messiah, the one who atoned for our sins, the Savior of the world—a truth worth running to the four corners of the world to announce.

Friend, before we go any further into 2000 or proceed onward toward the third millennium, we need to run with this truth ourselves. It is the joyous journey of spiritual discovery. It is only when all of us and others beyond this culture, this society and these nations from which we come, begin to know Jesus as Lord that we ourselves will joyously discover answers to the troubling questions of today.

We who look at the future (whether this year or the next millennium) can both see the boundlessness of the universe and its problems, its challenges and opportunities, as well as recognize that there are limits and barriers that need confrontation. The greatest barrier of all is to deny that Jesus is Lord. The greater opportunity of all is to proclaim the Messiah vigorously to a world needing to know we're not stuck in neutral but enabled by him to run with the truth through generations untold. The joy of the future is that it is a journey of discovery and one that can be filled with grandeur instead of grandiloquence—with human achievement due to divine encouragement.—Richard Andersen

SUNDAY, JANUARY 23, 2000
Lectionary Message

Topic: Hooked on Jesus Christ

TEXT: Mark 1:14–20

Other Readings: Jonah 3:1–5, 10; Ps. 62:5–12; 1 Cor. 7:29–31

It all could have ended with the arrest of John. Many a revolution has been halted by the imprisonment of a charismatic leader. Yet Jesus chose that moment to begin his proclamation of the good news!

I. There is a great lesson in this: the worst of times for society may become the best of times for the gospel. Many people today tell us that our time on the edge of the new millennium is not a good time for the Christian gospel. It is a confused and chaotic time dominated by commerce and consumerism, if indeed it is dominated by anything. No doubt the signs of decay are evident around us in violent crime, drug use, breakdown of families, environmental waste, and other ways.

In a situation much like this at the end of another era, Jesus said, "Now is the time." The beginning of the third millennium is a great time to be alive for those who sense what Jesus was getting at in the beginning of the first millennium.

II. There is good news today: the Kingdom of God is near and we may participate in it by repenting and believing. Our message today is fundamentally that which Jesus proclaimed, except that now we know that Jesus Christ himself is the good news. People get hooked on Jesus Christ!

(a) Simon and Andrew are examples of this. Jesus is walking the beach on the Sea of Galilee and sees two fishermen casting their nets into the water. You can still see men doing this today, as I have in Mexico. It is primitive compared to the high-tech fishing industry, but far healthier—and more interesting to watch. To see the men arranging their nets, shaping them for maximum effect, watching the waves for just the right place and moment to hurl them out, waiting to retrieve them—coming upon such a scene one is riveted and wants to stand and wait and see what will be caught, if anything. Jesus may have been doing just that when the brothers turned and Jesus caught their attention. "Follow me," he said, "and I will make you fishers of people." Immediately they turned their backs on their nets, not even taking time to examine their catch, and followed him.

(b) They followed him. That is perfectly clear. Why? That is mysterious. It seems so impulsive at first, so unreasonable. They surely must have been looking for the Messiah and felt that without a doubt this was the one who was to come. But what of those who are not looking for a messiah, like most people. Is what happened to Simon and Andrew a kind of accident of a strange time and place long ago, or is it an opportunity still open to us today?

What we do know is that they got hooked on Jesus Christ and were called to fish for others. Now there were three of them walking the beach. Just a little way down they saw James and John, the sons of Zebedee. They might have been more prosperous than Simon and Andrew, for they had a boat big enough for a crew. Jesus called out to them, to James and John. Did Jesus know their names earlier or did Simon and Andrew, who must have known them? I imagine that Simon and Andrew identified them for Jesus. In any case, James and John left the boat with the crew and their father Zebedee still in it: "So long, Dad!"

How strange. But they were hooked on Jesus Christ. Now there were five walking down the beach.

(c) Well, the rest is history, as they say. They kept on walking and eventually there were thirteen of them and then—well, you know the story. But how well do you know it? Do you know it as a *USA TODAY* factoid, that this Jesus Christ is the very individual who gave the date to our calendar and whose advent marks the first millennium?

Or are you hooked on Jesus Christ? In which case he gets you. Notice that the gospel is not defined by Jesus in an abstract way. Jesus does not point to the gospel. Jesus Christ *is* the gospel. We do not first grasp the gospel then follow Jesus Christ. We follow Jesus Christ and are grasped by the gospel. Only in following Jesus Christ do we come to understand the gospel, because Jesus Christ is the gospel.

(d) We do not know with certainty a great deal about Jesus and the first Christians. The story varies even from Gospel to Gospel. But we know the theme that is repeated again and again in all of them: they followed him, they followed him, they followed him.

We know nothing with certainty of the third millennium and the twenty-first century. With all our projections and conferences and programs on the subject of the Church in the new millennium, we are still on the verge of a great unknown. What is the one thing we must do as Christians in the twenty-first century? Follow Him, follow Him, follow Him.—David James Randolph

ILLUSTRATIONS

A SIGNIFICANT START.   A student in a class of mine at Drew in the 1960s went on to become a seminal teacher of how faith is formed and developed in stages. His name is James Fowler. He wrote *Stages of Faith*[10] and other influential books. I remember a student sermon in which Jim told about how his faith journey began. The image he used is still with me. He said, "I got hooked on Jesus Christ." There is something about Jesus Christ that hooked

---

[10] New York: HarperCollins, 1981.

Simon and Andrew and James, the sons of Zebedee, and James, the son of Mr. Fowler, and anyone else who will follow him.—David James Randolph

SAY YES!   My dear friends, we come to something that I am unable to do. I cannot tell each of you what all of this will mean for you individually in actual practice. It may be that God awaits us on a completely new way of life which opens up before us. It may be that God awaits us in the midst of our long-standing need. It may be that on this very day we will say *No* to everything that until now we have built our lives upon and will set out on an entirely new road. It may be that today, at long last, we will say *Yes* to what has been beyond us for years and see it in an altogether different light because we can say *Yes*, not *No*, to it.—Edward Schweizer[11]

SERMON SUGGESTIONS

Topic: Going the Second Mile

TEXT: Matt. 5:38–42

(1) The principle needed: (a) In our churchmanship. (b) In our stewardship. (c) In the challenge of evangelism. (d) In our various social relations. (2) The principle achieved: (a) Through enthusiasm. (b) With the help of creative tension. (c) At the urging of a deepening spirituality.

Topic: You Shall Be My People

TEXT: Lev. 26:12

The Word of God fulfilled in Jesus Christ. Read and heard, understood and believed in this light, this Word radiates infinite power. (1) It then says not only, "I will walk among you," but also, "I *walk* among you!" (2) Not only, "I will be your God," but also, "I *am* your God!" (3) Not only, "You shall be my people," but also, "You *are* my people!"—Karl Barth[12]

CONGREGATIONAL MUSIC

1. "Be Still, My Soul," Katharina von Schlegel (1752); tr. Jane Borthwick (1855)

FINLANDIA, Jean Sibelius (1899)

This fine German hymn set to the noble tune FINLANDIA by the prominent Finnish composer Jean Sibelius breathes the very spirit of the Psalter reading (particularly Ps. 62:5). It can be used as a meaningful prayer response to that reading.

2. "In the Fish for Three Days Buried," Calvin Seerveld (1982)

EIFIONYDD, John A. Lloyd (1843)

This is a modern Bible song telling the story of Jonah. It would be appropriate as an introduction to the Old Testament reading. If the fine Welsh tune is unfamiliar, the first two stanzas could be rehearsed and sung by a choir. The congregational stanzas (3 and 4) could then move from the minor key to the parallel major in keeping with their joyful content.

3. "Jesus Calls Us," Cecil Frances Alexander (1852)

GALILEE, William H. Jude (1874)

---

[11] *God's Inescapable Nearness*
[12] *Deliverance to the Captives*

This familiar hymn of commitment was written for St. Andrew's Day and is particularly suitable to use with the passage from Mark that tells of the calling of Peter and Andrew, James and John, to discipleship.

4. "I Will Trust in the Lord," African American Spiritual

I WILL TRUST, trad. African American tune; arr. Marie Gray (1991)

A spiritual expressing trust such as this one could appropriately be sung in connection with both the reading from the prophecy of Jonah and the Psalter (Ps. 62:8).—Hugh T. McElrath

WORSHIP AIDS

CALL TO WORSHIP.   "Behold, I stand at the door and knock: if any man hear my voice, and open the door, I will come in to him, and will sup with him, and he with me" (Rev. 3:20).

INVOCATION.   Lord Christ, we need your presence among us. Just now we are trying to open the door of our hearts and worship to you and to enjoy heavenly fellowship with you. Come in, Lord Jesus. Be our welcome guest.

OFFERTORY SENTENCE.   "God chose what is weak in the world to shame the strong" (1 Cor. 1:27b NRSV).

OFFERTORY PRAYER.   We offer ourselves and our gifts to you, gracious Father. Let none among us despise the day of small things, but dedicate to you what we have and what we can give, trusting that you can do with our meager talents and means exceedingly abundantly above all that we can ask or think.

PRAYER.   Sometimes, Father, we can't seem to make contact with you, and then we remember how you revealed yourself to us in the obscurity of Bethlehem. Then we begin to look for you in places and ways that are numbered among the unexpected. Such a search does not leave us unrewarded. We confess that a large part of our inability to see you is due to our desire to be the absolute masters of our fate. Thus we have bowed our knee before a host of tyrants exercising lordship over us—before the fear of failure and the greed of gain; before the opinions of our friends and the ridicule of our foes; before hatred and envy, lust and doubt.

Thinking that we are the captains of our souls, we have served as galley hands below the decks of life, never lifting our eyes to the hills of your help or seeing the far horizons of your more abundant way. Stir us until we see the need to know how you would have us live and do life in your name on the Earth.

Teach us the lessons of duty and honor, commitment and service to those commitments, we pray. Deliver us from trying to get our way by bringing pain and heartache to others. Show us the poverty in ourselves that bearing false witness against others generates. Grant us the courage to see ourselves as others see us and then strive to become what you have called us to be.

We came from you, Father, and to you we will one day return. Therefore, we commit today and ourselves to you, praying that you will lift us when we fall, bring us back to righteousness when we stray, and save us from our sins and ourselves.—Henry Fields

SERMON
Topic: The Nature of the Job
TEXT: Luke 4:14–21

I. The vision thing is so important. Human beings, groups, and corporations need to have some idea of what we are trying to accomplish. In almost every political campaign in the last twenty years there has been this cry from the people, Where is a leader who can bring us together by giving us a common vision of the future? We need to have a common dream for the nation. No wonder war has the ability to bring us together in a way no peacetime cause can. War has a very definable object.

This vision thing is so important. No wonder sports have a way of becoming so important to so many people. Look how easy it is for a group of people to focus together on the common goal of winning.

The Dream. I don't know of another speech that so set the agenda for a nation as Martin Luther King's speech about his dream. Churchill in World War II in England. FDR and his fireside chats during the Depression. "I have a dream, that someday all of God's children, white or black, red or brown or yellow, will sit down at table together. I have a dream." That has been the social vision of this nation since it was spoken. We still have seminars and discussions on what progress we have made toward the dream. Because, unfortunately, it is not as easy to measure our progress toward that dream as it is to know who won the game.

But we all need dreams. We need to have a vision of what we are supposed to be doing as a human being; that's why we accept Jesus Christ as our Lord. We want to become, in the grace of God, like Jesus. We need to have a vision of what we ought to be as a city or a county, or a company at work, a club or a church. It is the vision, the dream, as it gets into us, that directs us, changes us, pulls us up, pushes us on. It is the dream that keeps us striving.

The Dream. The vision thing. We are made by what we seek. We are changed by what we desire. The vision gives us our direction. The dream gives us the criteria to make decisions. The mission statement provides the blueprint to determine the value of what we have already done and to point us in the direction of where we should be going.

II. So it is absolutely essential that Christian people return regularly to this passage in Luke where Jesus begins his ministry, gives his first public sermon, and declares before his hometown church what his mission, what his dream, what his vision is for his work.

John the Baptist had announced that there was one coming who was to bring in the Kingdom of God. He had been preparing the people of Israel for that coming by preaching repentance and baptism. Jesus came forward and received the baptism, and the Scriptures say that the Holy Spirit took him from that place out into the wilderness for a time of testing. The Holy Spirit drove Jesus out into the desert so that he might confront all of the lesser versions of the Kingdom of God that are always being offered to us and prepare himself to respond to them. What was going to be his vision of the Kingdom of God? The tempter came and said, "If you are the Son of God, why not offer them a kingdom where all material comforts are available. Turn the stones to bread, make the streets lined with gold, turn all the water to wine, satisfy their every material want and wish." The tempter said, "If you are the Son of God, just jump off this roof and give them a kingdom of God where God takes care of and protects those who believe. Promise them a kingdom where everybody is protected from all hurts and pains." Finally the tester said, "You can become Lord of everything you see by being willing to worship what you see. Offer them a Kingdom of God where what you see is really what you get. Where the one with the most toys wins. Where power and fame matter, and character and integrity, virtues and honesty are just words to throw around."

Jesus comes from that testing and is prepared by that testing to declare as the Son of God what the Kingdom of God he is to bring will look like, and he goes to his home church and he tells them his vision. "The Spirit of the Lord is upon me, because he has chosen me to preach the good news to the poor. He has sent me to proclaim liberty to the captive, and recovery of sight to the blind; to set free the oppressed and to announce the year when the Lord will save his people." He rolled up the scroll and said, "That is what I have come to do."

III. The vision thing. That is Jesus' vision for his life. That is Jesus' vision for his Kingdom. That is Jesus' vision for his people. We who are his Church are still called by the Spirit of the Lord to shape and direct our work by that mission statement. That was his dream, and we who have publicly declared that we want to follow him as Lord and Savior need to evaluate constantly what we do as individuals and as a congregation by that vision.

Jesus' mission statement for the coming of his Kingdom put his understanding of the Kingdom of God at odds with the Kingdom of God expected by political leaders who wanted another King Solomon. It put his understanding of the Kingdom at odds with all those who think the Kingdom of God is pie in the sky when you die. This is the vision thing and we as the people of God who want to work to fulfill his vision need to measure what we are doing individually and as a people by his dream.—Rick Brand

SUNDAY, JANUARY 30, 2000
Lectionary Message

Topic: Faith and Healing
Text: Mark 1:21–28
Other Readings: Deut. 18:15–20; Ps. 111; 1 Cor. 8:1–13

Faith and healing is a hot topic of discussion and a major item on the agenda for the new century. It is on the cover of magazines from *New York* to *Life.* Not that it is novel for the Church nor reserved for the future. It is urgent because advanced means of communication and higher standards of living do not mean much if we are too ill to enjoy them. The new millennium will hold no charm for those who are sick and tired of being sick and tired. How can we be well and renew our energy? Through faith, we are now being told by physicians as well as theologians.

The relationship between faith and healing goes right back to the New Testament, as we see in this lesson and elsewhere. The Church across the ages has been involved with healing in many ways, including the establishment of many hospitals and health centers. Many people in our churches today are seeking healing.

Ironically, the Christian Church, which has a powerful legacy in this area, seems largely out of the loop in this discussion. Becoming aware of this legacy, practicing it, and sharing it will be a major task in the twenty-first century.

I. We can enter the arena of healing through study of the Bible, especially in passages such as our Gospel lesson today. Notice that Jesus' visit to Capernaum comes immediately after the calling of the first disciples. Simon and Andrew and James and John are being taught Discipleship 101. This involves using available means of worship and teaching. This Jesus does by going to the synagogue on the Sabbath. But Jesus does not lecture like the scribes. He proclaims; he preaches with authority.

Jesus' teaching draws admiration—and attack. A man suddenly cries out, "What have you to do with, Jesus of Nazareth? Have you come to destroy us? I know who you are, the Holy One of God." Mark tells the story in such a way that that man is already identified as having an unclean spirit. But Mark is writing after the fact. Imagine the scene without knowing this, as the first disciples surely would not have. It could have been any opponent confronting the speaker. But Jesus diagnosed the man. He knew that he was possessed. He commanded the spirit to come out of the man, and with a convulsion it did. The people in the synagogue were amazed. They could not stop talking about the event, and because of it, Jesus became famous. This was the breakthrough of Jesus' ministry. What was it? The event of Jesus' preaching and healing.

II. This combination of preaching and healing demonstrates what Jesus is talking about when he commissions his disciples. Mark records this in chapter 3 when he appoints twelve men to be his disciples, including the four fisherman, and sends them out to preach and to cast out demons. Luke's version in 9.2 is the *locus classicus* for Jesus' commissioning of his disciples: "He sent them out to preach the Kingdom of God and to heal." That commission extends to all who would be disciples of Jesus Christ.

III. We accept this commission when we connect preaching and healing. Across the centuries we have allowed these two practices that Jesus intended to be joined to become separated, assigning preaching to the minister and the Church and healing to the doctor and the hospital. It is time to reconnect the two as Jesus Christ intended.

Jesus began by combining preaching and healing in the context of worship, and so can we. There are services of healing, often with the Eucharist, available in the new hymnals of major denominations, including, for example, the United Methodist Church. But the problem cannot be solved ritualistically, that is, by simply going through the motions. A real commitment to preaching and healing together calls for study, action, alliances with those in the medical professions, joint projects, research, training, and above all, much prayer and spiritual preparation. Jesus said of a particularly difficult case that this kind doesn't come out without much prayer and fasting.—David James Randolph

ILLUSTRATIONS

THE POWER THAT HEALS.   I show why the Church must become more involved in healing and offer many examples of how to do so. Christian faith reveals that love is the power that heals through creating, redeeming, and supporting us, that is, through the Trinity. We make this love our own through awareness, acceptance, action, and affirmation, as I show through the experiences of individuals and groups. (See also Leonard Sweet, *The Jesus Prescription for a Healthy Life;* Larry Dossey, M.D., *Healing Words: The Power of Prayer and the Practice of Medicine;* Dean Ornish, M.D., *Love and Survival;* Herbert Benson, M.D., *Timeless*

Healing: The Power and Biology of Belief; and the groundbreaking book by Alexander Lowen, M.D., *Spirituality and the Body.*[13])—David James Randolph

THE PROMISE.   I am not promising you perfect health if you trust in God. What I, as a minister of religion, am promising you is this: that with that confidence in the eternal Source of Life, that openness toward Him which eliminates fear and frenzy, breaks through the barriers of distrust and doubt, and sets life in motion, you will have at your disposal His energy and His weapons and all the purity that comes from life to meet the enemy and to triumph over it.—Theodore Parker Ferris[14]

SERMON SUGGESTIONS

Topic: Mocking at Sin
TEXT: Prov. 14:9
Members of our generation are guilty of mocking at sin in the following ways: (1) In their idea of sin. (2) In their practice of sin. (3) In their denial that they are sinners.—R. Furman Kenney[15]

Topic: Be Angry and Sin Not
TEXT: Eph. 4:26–27
(1) Here is a command—"Be angry": (a) Let us be angry at materialism, the idolatry of our generation. (b) Let us be angry at false discipleship, the hypocrisy of our generation. (c) Let us be angry at silence in the presence of injustice, the cowardice of our generation. (2) Here is a corrective—"and sin not": Anger must be the servant of compassion if we are to sin not.—H. Gordon Clinard[16]

CONGREGATIONAL MUSIC
1. "O God, Almighty Father," anon. German; tr. Irvin Udulutsch (1955)
   GOTT VATER SEI GEPRIESEN, *Limberg Collection* (1838)
   This hymn of adoration is Trinitarian in organization and theme but in its refrain it addresses God also as "undivided unity"—the burden of the first part of the Epistle reading (1 Cor. 8:1–13). It could be used as the opening hymn for worship on this day.
2. "O Give the Lord Wholehearted Praise," *Psalter* (1912)
   GERMANY, William Gardiner's *Sacred Melodies* (1815)
   Being a paraphrase of Psalm 111, this hymn could be sung and spoken alternately stanza by stanza in place of the assigned Psalter reading.
3. "Silence, Frenzied, Unclean Spirit," Thomas H. Troeger
   AUTHORITY, Carol Doran (1984)
   This contemporary hymn recreates in searing poetry the incident described in the passage

---

[13] Leonard Sweet, *The Jesus Prescription for a Healthy Life* (Nashville: Abingdon, 1996); Larry Dossey, *Healing Words: The Power of Prayer and the Practice of Medicine* (San Francisco: HarperCollins, 1995); Dean Ornish, *Love and Survival* (New York: HarperCollins, 1998); Herbert Benson, *Timeless Healing: The Power and Biology of Belief* (New York: Simon & Schuster, 1996); Alexander Lowen, *Spirituality and the Body* (New York: Macmillan, 1990).
[14] *Selected Sermons*
[15] *More Southern Baptist Preaching*
[16] ibid.

from Mark(1:21–28) and then makes prayerful application to the lives of the ones singing. It is the ideal hymnic response to the Gospel reading. Possibly a soloist or choral group could perform the first stanza, which dramatically describes the man with the unclean spirit; then the congregation could sing the prayerful response of stanzas 2 and 3.

4. "The God of Abraham Praise," Daniel ben Judah Dayyans (c. 1400); tr. Newton Mann/Max Landberg (c. 1885)

In its second stanza, this venerable hymn sings, "In prophet's word, He spoke of old; He speaketh still," thus reinforcing the reading in Deuteronomy (18:15–20) concerning prophets being raised up to speak for God.—Hugh T. McElrath

WORSHIP AIDS

CALL TO WORSHIP.   "Praise ye the Lord. I will praise the Lord with my whole heart" (Ps. 111:1a).

INVOCATION.   Our Creator and our Father, when we think of your marvelous works and your love for us, especially in the gift of your Son, our Lord, our hearts leap up with joy and thanksgiving. Let all that we do here today express what we pray for others to know, feel, say, and do.

OFFERTORY SENTENCE.   "Every good gift and every perfect boon is from above, and comes down from the Father of lights, in whom there is no variation or changing shadow. In accordance with His will He made us His children by the message of truth, that we might be a kind of first fruits among His creatures" (James 1:17–18, *Williams New Testament*).

OFFERTORY PRAYER.   Lord, we acknowledge that all we have comes from you. We believe that these good gifts are intended to be a blessing to us and to others. Now we pray that we may enjoy the added blessing of giving to your causes in the spirit of love that you have modeled for us.

PRAYER.   O Lord of our life, whose will is to create a family of believers whose care reaches out to one another and whose common aim is to become ministers of your grace, we regret and are ashamed of our failure to turn our blessings into saving actions and our spiritual gains into contagious influences. Everywhere we turn we see opportunities slighted, privileges exploited, and the most promising day marked by a record of nothing ventured, nothing done. Too many of us are loners and we are hesitant to serve hand in hand with others of Christian strength or to come to the aid of those who are trampled underfoot. Too often we have bungled a budding friendship by our indifference or severed a wholesome bond by being in it for what we could get out of it. Lead us, O Lord, to understand that it is sinful to belittle others, to traffic in gossip, to tattle what is merely a rumor, or to place obstacles in a brother or sister's way. Forgive us, we pray, and make us into new persons through the risen and redeeming life of Jesus Christ. Let us through him be done with petty notions and selfish schemes. Catch us up into a glorious vision of the bigness of the family of your Kingdom and enlarge our arms to embrace and hold them all. In Jesus' name we offer our confession and our claim.—Donald Macleod[17]

SERMON
Topic: The Rest of the Story
TEXT: Luke 4:14–30

I. Jesus comes home and the elders are so impressed with him. "Small town boy makes good" and "Dove seen landing on young Nazarene," the headlines read. He comes to the synagogue to worship and the elder in charge of the Scriptures gives them to Jesus to read. High honor, high test. Let's hear him read the story and see if he has it correct. So Jesus reads the passage from Isaiah, but he stops before he gets to the good part. The people of Nazareth read this passage, have claimed this passage, have held on to this passage because it goes on to say to the children of Israel, "and the day of vengeance of our God to grant to those who mourn in Zion a garland of praise instead of ashes. They shall build up the ancient ruins, they shall repair the ruined cities, the devastations of many generations." That was the good part. Those who mourn now in Zion will get to celebrate in the future. Those Jews who live in ruins will see those ruins restored. And Isaiah goes on to say that the work will not even have to be done by the children of Israel. When the Spirit of the Lord is poured out onto the Servant of God and the Kingdom comes, "Aliens shall stand and feed your flocks. Foreigners shall be your plowmen and vine dressers. You shall be called priests of the Lord."

II. The story that kept the people of Nazareth going was that when the Kingdom of God came it would bring this good news to the captives (that is, the Jews under the Romans), liberate the prisoners, give sight to the blind, rebuild the cities of Israel, put them on top so that they would have slaves and captives to do the hard work. They would be people of leisure who could gather to study the Torah at the synagogue. That is the part that really got to them. It is kind of like when you listen to the president's speech about the state of the union. It ain't over till it's over and it ain't over until the president says, "God bless you and God bless the USA." It is the way you know that every fairy tale you read will end with "and they lived happily ever after."

Jesus reads the part about the Spirit being upon him and that "he has come to preach good news to the poor. He has come to proclaim release to the captives, to bring sight to the blind, to set at liberty those who are oppressed, and to proclaim the acceptable year of the Lord." And he stops. He stops before he gets to the part they always love to hear. And they are polite for a moment, but then somebody says in a kind of wounded voice, a voice from the back of the room, "Isn't he from around here? Isn't he Joseph's boy? Shouldn't he know the whole story? Why did he stop there where it makes it sound like he will preach good news just to anybody?" He didn't read the whole story. He didn't read the part that makes us special. He didn't read the "happily ever after" part.

Jesus has met this temptation in the wilderness already. This is the desire in me for the Kingdom of God to give me special blessings, to fill up my basket with biscuits, to protect

[17] *Princeton Pulpit Prayers*

me, my wife, and my son, John, and his wife—us four and no more. To bring us all the blessings of the world and to provide for us and to hell with all the rest.

I remember, maybe you can as well, how outraged people were when Billy Graham came back from Russia, the godless empire, that evil nation, and reported that the Christian Church was very much alive and well. The Russian Orthodox people were remaining steadfast and faithful even under a ban on religion under the Marxist government. The Baptist community in Russia was vigorous and evangelical, Dr. Graham reported. Large portions of the American Christian community were outraged that Dr. Graham would say such a thing. Dr. Graham was changing the story. The story was supposed to be that God was on America's side and the Russians were atheists, and Dr. Graham was changing the story. "Isn't that Joseph's boy? Shouldn't he know the story?"

We don't want anybody changing the story. We don't want anybody changing our story when it takes us out of being special. The journal of the Phi Beta Kappa society, the *American Scholar,* has been engaged in a five-year debate over the *National Standards for History.* The new *National Standards for History* call for inclusion of the story of immigrants, for the telling of the horrors of the White men's treatment of the Indians, for the telling of contributions and inventions and discoveries made by minorities, and it demands that the heretics get as much credit as those who eventually won, because there is no progress without conflict. And there are those who oppose these new standards because they do not praise the successes, do not paint the glorious American manifest destiny and build patriotism. The new standards change the story and we don't look so good, and there are many who are angry with the new telling of the story of our history.

III. Jesus, by where he stops in the story, suggests that his message is to bring the Kingdom of God to all who are captives, to all who are blind, to all who are oppressed. That the grace of God is to be shared with all people.

Don't you remember how in the days of Elijah there was that great famine and everybody was starving, and Elijah found one widow, the foreigner, the alien, who was obedient to his voice, who responded in faith to his request for bread, and Elijah kept her bowl and her family supplied with grain till the end of the famine?

Don't you remember in the time of Elisha that there were many lepers in the community, but Naaman, the Syrian, the general of the Syrian army, a foreigner with leprosy, because of the faith of his slave girl, came to see Elisha, and Elisha wouldn't even see him but told him to go bathe in that muddy creek of a Jordan and be healed. Finally he obeyed and was healed. Don't you get it? The Kingdom of God is present wherever faith in the power and mercy of God leads to obedience to the will and purpose of God. The good news is not limited just to the children of Israel. The Kingdom of God is to be proclaimed to all people who will enter it.

Jesus' telling of the story, the changes he makes, the claims he makes, gets this nice religious community, which came to worship on the Sabbath all nice and happy, so angry that they start pushing Jesus out of the temple and out to the hill to push him off to kill him. Jesus walks away.

We are called by Jesus to come and be his disciples. To take up his mission. To tell his story. To translate that good news of the Kingdom of God being for all and for any into flesh and blood. That is not going to be easy or simple or something we can do in our spare time. The story of Jesus, Jesus' reading of the story, was not different from the story expected in the village of Nazareth, but the preaching of the Kingdom of God as Jesus revealed that Kingdom are at odds with the values of Wall Street, Madison Avenue, the Pentagon, and the State Department. The story of the Kingdom of God is not interested in blessing a vision of patriotic consumerism in which America is number one in the world. The proclamation of the good news of the Kingdom of God is to enable us to see our lives not in terms of comparisons between how wealthy we were then and how well off we are now but against the backdrop of God's enduring desire to create a new heaven and a new earth for all creation. History, our lives, your life, is not about the right to be number one over others. It is not about the manifest right of any economic theory to be enthroned universally. It is not about one culture setting up its values as normative for all. Jesus reads the story in a way that says the good news is for all, and the Kingdom is God working for creation to be healed for all.

Jesus calls us to tell his old, old story and to understand clearly that his story is not the same as all those other stories.—Rick Brand

SUNDAY, FEBRUARY 6, 2000
Lectionary Message

Topic: The Triumphant God
Text: Isa. 40:21–31
Other Readings: Ps. 147:1–11, 20c; 1 Cor. 9:16–23; Mark 1:29–39

His young wife had died of cancer. I asked this young husband if I could pray with him. He glared at me and said, "No! After this, I'm through with God. God did nothing for me."

Sadly there are many who agree with him. As they look at the hard experiences of life it seems to them as if God has abandoned them. To be honest, as we look at the situations in the world, it does cause us to wonder about God. We see wars that never end, crime on our streets, brokenness and abuse in our homes, sickness that takes the lives of far too many too soon. Many experiences could be added to the list. Where is God in them? What is God doing among them? These are honest questions.

During Isaiah's time, the people of God were wondering. They had been captured by the Babylonians and thrown into exile. They didn't understand how God could let that happen. Their conclusion was that God was not strong enough to do anything about it. Even though the exile was coming to an end, they still wondered about the sufficiency of God. To that situation and mood the words of Isaiah 40 were directed. The affirmation is made—God is a triumphant God! God cannot be defeated. Trust in God was not in vain.

I. *The reminder: God is sovereign* (vv. 21–26). The writer reminded them who God was. "Do you not know? Have you not heard?" (v. 21). The reminders of the greatness of God were plenty. God sits above the earth and the people are "like grasshoppers." Princes and rulers are brought to nothing. The stars—they line up before God, a God who knows the name of each star. The Babylonians were astrologers who felt that the stars controlled their destiny. But that is not so; God controls the stars. Hear the truth about God! "The Lord is the everlasting God, the creator of the ends of the earth" (v. 28). Didn't they understand? The gods of the Babylonians were nothing. God is the Holy One, the one who can bring them into exile and take them out of it. There was and is not one like the triumphant God!

When life hits us hard and we don't understand what is going on, it is time to remember who God is. God is still the Creator, the Everlasting God. No matter what the difficulties, God has not abandoned the throne. God is able to get us through the difficult exiles. God will not let us down. God is triumphant!

II. *The instruction: Wait for God to act* (vv. 29–31). The people of God needed to wait on the Lord. *Wait* is another word for hope, a confidence that God will act in due time. This was a waiting with anticipation, wondering not *whether* God would act but *when* God would act. Many had been waiting through the years of exile for God to act and now it had happened. They were free to go home. God did act. They were to trust that truth, depend on it, live their lives in the light of it. God would always do what was needed.

In all of our experiences we are to hope in the Lord. We don't always know when God will act. We don't always know what God will do. But we live with the certain faith that God *will* act. When that happens, it will be for our good. So we must hold on, but hold on in hope. The triumphant God will not leave us but will one day do what is needed to deliver us from our unwanted exiles.

III. *The promise: Our strength is renewed* (v. 31). That was the promise they were given. Renewal was a powerful picture. They would get God's power, they would find the strength to do whatever they needed. If they were full of joy, they would find the power to soar like eagles. If they were willing to plod along, they would find the strength to run and not get tired. If all they could do was crawl, they would find the power to walk and not grow faint. Whatever strength they needed for the journey from exile to the promised land, they would find it. God would renew their strength.

To the husband struggling with the loss of his wife I said, "Don't give up on God yet. Hold on and see what God might do with you. God will get you through this, and to be truthful, God is the only one who can." This is the Word we have to say: God is able when we are not able. God can and will renew us and we will find the strength we need to keep on going. We can go on in the face of war and crime and abuse and sickness. God is triumphant and if we trust that truth, God will help us to be triumphant. There is no God like our God!—Hugh Litchfield

ILLUSTRATIONS

GOD'S SOVEREIGNTY.   Perry Biddle Jr., an Episcopalian priest, told of the time when he spoke in a church in England. The point of Biddle's message was "the Lord God Omnipotent Reigneth." In fact, he used the phrase several times in his sermon. Each time he used it, he spoke a little louder so that the last couple of times, he almost shouted out that phrase, "The Lord God Omnipotent Reigneth." As people were going out after the service, two ladies came to speak to him. The officer of the church said, "Now these two ladies are mostly deaf, they probably didn't hear much of what you said." One lady came and said, "I didn't hear much of what you said today, preacher. The only thing I heard was that "the Lord God Omnipotent Reigneth." As she went out of the door she turned and said, "but I guess that's all that really matters, isn't it?"—Perry Biddle[1]

GREATNESS OF GOD.   Adam Burnet, one-time minister of St. Cuthbert's, Edinburgh, told of an experience he had during the First World War. He was standing one evening not far

---

[1] "The Important Point," *Christian Ministry,* Sept. 1982, p. 19.

from the tall spire of a village church in France. For some unknown reason the firing on both sides of the line had died down, and in the stillness he watched the setting sun like a great ball of fire upon the horizon. Suddenly, a single shell came screaming through the twilight and the top half of the church steeple blew apart with a shocking roar. Almost simultaneously a flock of swallows, which had been nesting there, rose slowly above the smoke and flying debris. They circled in the air for a moment and then settled back quietly upon the wreckage of where they had been. Burnet said that this reminded him of the greatness of God. After the world and life are shaken, and people have done their worst, God's greatness remains unshaken, unlimited, unimpaired.—Donald Macleod[2]

SERMON SUGGESTIONS

Topic: God Carrying His People
TEXT: Isa. 46:3–4
Two kinds of religion are always with us, even in Christian circles, after all these centuries of the gospel. (1) The kind of religion that does nothing for us but has to be carried as a burden. (2) The other kind of religion, which can do something for us, carry our burdens, and carry us.—D. M. Baillie[3]

Topic: Your Search
TEXT: Luke 15:11–24
(1) A search for freedom. (2) A search for meaning. (3) A search for acceptance.—James E. Carter[4]

CONGREGATIONAL MUSIC

1. "At Evening, When the Sun Was Set," Henry Twells (1868)
   ANGELUS *Heilige Seelenlust,* Georg Joseph (1657)
   This evening hymn, based on the incident of Jesus' healing of all manner of disease after sunset, which is recorded in Mark 1:32–34, could be effectively sung at the beginning of (evening) worship or in connection with the Gospel reading.
2. "God, Who Stretched the Spangled Heavens," Catherine Cameron (1967)
   HOLY MANNA, attr. William Moore (1825)
   The vivid imagery of the Old Testament reading magnifying God's creative power (particularly Isaiah 40:22) is the inspiration for this popular contemporary hymn that would be appropriate for the beginning of worship.
3. "O Praise the Lord, for It Is Good," *Psalter* (1912)
   MINERVA (Stockton), John H. Stockton (1874)
   Set to the familiar tune for the gospel hymn "Only Trust Him," this free paraphrase of the first part of Psalm 147 could be sung at the time for the Psalter reading for the day.
4. "The Church of Christ in Every Age," Fred Pratt Green (1969)
   WAREHAM, William Knapp (1738)
   This important contemporary hymn on commitment and mission could be sung in re-

---

[2] *More Sermons I Should Like to Have Preached* (Westwood, N.J.: Fleming H. Revell, 1967), p. 43.
[3] *Out of Nazareth*
[4] *Help for the Evangelistic Preacher*

sponse to the Epistle reading in which the apostle enunciates the principle of becoming all things to all persons in order to win some to Christ.—Hugh T. McElrath

WORSHIP AIDS

CALL TO WORSHIP.   "The Lord takes pleasure in those who fear him, in those who hope in his steadfast love" (Ps. 147:11 NRSV).

INVOCATION.   Victorious God, you triumph over all your foes, winning victory after victory through your love. Help us this day to put our complete confidence in you, knowing that you can do exceeding abundantly above all that we ask or think.

OFFERTORY SENTENCE.   "But God is my helper, the Lord, the sustainer of my life" (Ps. 54:4 REB).

OFFERTORY PRAYER.   Where would we be, O God, without you? What would we have without you? You have given us good things to enjoy and share. Grant us the grace to put back into your hands a fitting portion of your bounty for your service here and anywhere and everywhere.

PRAYER.   O God, who has sent us to school in this strange life of ours and has set us tasks that test all our courage, trust, and fidelity, may we not spend our days complaining at circumstance or fretting at discipline, but give ourselves to learn of life and to profit by every experience. Make us strong to endure.

We pray that when trials come upon us we may not shirk the issue or lose our faith in Thy goodness, but committing our souls unto Thee who knowest the way that we take, come forth as gold tried in the fire.

Grant by Thy grace that we may not be found wanting in the hour of crisis. When the battle is set, may we know on which side we ought to be, and when the day goes hard, cowards steal from the field, and heroes fall around the standard, may our place be found where the fight is fiercest. If we faint, may we not be faithless; if we fall, may it be while facing the foe. Amen.—W. E. Orchard[5]

SERMON

Topic: Plain Talk

TEXT: 1 Cor. 15:12–20; Luke 6:17–26

I. Let me create the setting for Luke's version of the Beatitudes. It is here in the sixth chapter that Jesus begins to teach. He outlines what it means to be a Christian, what it means to live as a Christian in this kind of a world. Up to this point, through the first five chapters, he really hasn't taught anything. In fact, up to now he has hardly said anything. It has all been action, very little dialogue. He has healed the sick and he has sparred verbally with the Pharisees. He has called the disciples and has attracted crowds that are getting larger every time

---

[5] *The Temple*

he performs a miracle. They are now following him around from place to place. Crowds always gravitate toward the sensational.

Now we are at the sixth chapter. Jesus goes up onto a mountain with his newly recruited disciples. Then he comes down from the mountain. That's the difference between Matthew and Luke. In Matthew he goes up the mountain and takes the disciples with him. He instructs them on the mountain. In Luke he brings them down to the plain, to the crowds, to where the people are.

The text says, "There were people there who had diseases" and "he healed them all." Jesus has been doing that from the very beginning of his ministry. That is why the crowds are there. That is why they follow him around. He comes down to where the people are and he heals the crowd.

I have mentioned this before. In the New Testament there are two kinds of people: there is the crowd and there are the disciples. The crowd he heals. He doesn't ask anything of them. Out of compassion he sees their sickness and he heals them. Then they go away. We never hear of those people again. They have no names. They are the suffering in this world. He touches them and heals them.

But disciples he doesn't heal. Nor does he particularly express any compassion toward them. Nor are comfortable words uttered to them. There is nothing in the Gospels about the disciples becoming a support group. Jesus heals the crowds and he challenges the disciples into service.

The text says that when he finished healing the crowds he turned to his disciples and said, "Blessed are you who are poor, for yours is the Kingdom of God." He is talking to his disciples. "Blessed are you who are hungry now, for you will be filled. Blessed are you who weep now, for you will laugh. Blessed are you when people hate you, and exclude you, and defame you, on account of the Son of man [on account of me]." He is addressing his disciples. He is not talking to the crowd now.

II. Do you see what he is doing? He comes down to the plain, where the people are, and demonstrates what God's will for the whole world is. What he is doing is giving us a foretaste of the Kingdom of God. In the Kingdom of God there will be no more disease, no more pain, no more sorrow. Life will be whole. Life will be the way God created it to be. Later he will raise Jairus's daughter from the dead and the centurion's slave from the dead, to show that it is even God's will that we should not experience death, that we will overcome death. That is the point that Paul is making in the Epistle lesson to the Corinthians—that death is not supposed to be a part of life, and that in the future we will participate in Christ's Resurrection.

Someday life will be the way it is supposed to be. What you have just seen, he tells the disciples, is the way it will be when the Kingdom comes. So pray, "Thy kingdom come, thy will be done, on earth as it is in heaven." Pray that one day it will come to pass. Pray that it will come in the right time, in God's time.

But in the meantime, it is not that way. In the meantime, I have come to identify with the poor, the hungry, and with those who weep, to be with them, and to stand with them, and to let them know that they are God's children.

You know what the most significant part of this text is? It says he came down from the mountain to be with the people, and took his disciples with him. He is instructing his disciples now. He says, this is where Christianity is to work. This is where you are supposed to be, where people are. Not on a mountaintop.

We are not a mountaintop religion. It is always tempting to make Christianity that way, to picture Jesus as a "guru," a wise man, his teachings as inspirational thoughts, and Christianity as just another one of the philosophies about life, giving us inspiring ideals.

Jesus did not say that. Jesus would go off by himself to pray, but according to Luke, when he instructed the disciples he came down from the mountain to be in the real world. That is where he said, "Blessed are you who are poor, and who are hungry, and whose lives are filled with pain and with sorrow." He is saying, someday those things are going to change. But there are some things he can't change now. Someday they will change. Someday the world is going to be the way it is supposed to be. Someday.

In the meantime, Christians are to identify with the poor. You can't be a Christian and store up wealth for the future and ignore those people who have nothing in the present. You can't dine sumptuously every day and not be concerned about those who are hungry. You can't laugh and have a good time and not care that there are people in this world, especially children, who have never smiled. Someday that is going to be different.—Mark Trotter

SUNDAY, FEBRUARY 13, 2000
Lectionary Message

Topic: God in the Ordinary
TEXT: 2 Kings 5:1–14
Other Readings: Ps. 30; 1 Cor. 4:24–27; Mark 1:40–45

Often when we consider God acting in our lives, we think of it in extraordinary ways. We picture miraculous events, such as the parting of a sea or a fire in a bush that won't burn up or the sending of fire to wipe out a bunch of false prophets on Mount Carmel. We especially think of the Resurrection, when God did the impossible and raised Jesus from the dead. These were amazing and extraordinary events. That's the way God works.

The story in Second Kings presents us with another view. It's a story of how God works in the ordinary experiences of life. While God can and does work in extraordinary ways, we must not forget that God also often works through simple, ordinary kinds of events.

The text talks about Naaman, a Syrian general, who was a great man, honored and respected for his military exploits. He was a hero to the people. However, there was one problem: he was a leper. He suffered from that dread disease that made him a social outcast. People avoided him. His future was not hopeful. The disease would probably get worse and worse. It is at this point that we can see God begin to act in ordinary ways.

I. *God works through ordinary people* (vv. 2–5). A young slave girl enters the story. She had been captured in Israel and brought back to Syria, where she served Naaman's wife. She was a nobody in that time, a less-than-ordinary person in their thinking. However, she had a word of hope. She knew about a prophet in Israel—if only Naaman could see him, he might be healed. She dropped that suggestion to Naaman's wife, who then told her husband. Off Naaman went to find this prophet. It was no king that gave him this word of hope. It was no significant religious leader who told him what to do. It was just an ordinary slave girl. Through her God worked.

Later on, when Naaman had been told to wash in the river Jordan seven times, he was angry, was not going to do it. Again ordinary servants went to him and persuaded him to try it. Not the military leaders. Not his trusted advisors. Servants, the nobody people of his day—God used them to speak to Naaman.

Sometimes as we seek to know the word of God we go to great religious leaders to get it. We listen to seminary professors and read famous religious writers. We expect God to work through pastors and denominational leaders. Yet often God works through those we perceive as ordinary people—mothers, fathers, children, friends, the mechanic at the garage, or the salesclerk in the department store. We need to realize that God can work through anyone at any time. Maybe God will choose to work through us. To Naaman's credit, he did not dismiss the advice of the slave girl and the servants. He listened and gave them the benefit of the doubt that it just might be God speaking. Will we listen as carefully? Will we be open to what ordinary people do and say to us? They could be the means through which God speaks.

II. *God works through ordinary events* (vv. 13–14). Naaman came to the prophet Elisha's house with a great display of pomp and circumstance—horses and chariots and great gifts. Maybe he felt he could buy his healing. Elisha did not even come out to meet Naaman but sent his servant Gehazi to tell him what to do. It was a simple ordinary task: go take a bath seven times in the Jordan. Naaman was upset. He had expected some elaborate ritual and special task. He did not expect this. He wouldn't do it. He left in a rage, mumbling something about better rivers in Syria. The servants challenged him. "If the prophet had told you to do some great thing, would you have done it? How much more, then, when he tells you, 'Wash and be cleansed'" (v. 13). So Naaman did, and he was healed. It was not an extraordinary act, just a simple one. God worked through it.

Sometimes God is not in the earthquake, or wind, or thunder, but in an ordinary still, small voice. We look for God to act in extraordinary events—a miraculous healing, ending war, tearing a Berlin wall down. God does work in these, but also in not-so-spectacular ways. God might deal with us through ordinary events like reading the Bible, or prayer, or worship, or through conversation with friends. Maybe in giving water to the thirsty or food to the hungry God will speak to us. Maybe as preachers preach and as teachers teach, God might come alive. In ordinary everyday events God can act among us. Will we be open to that?

III. *God works through ordinary acts of obedience* (v. 14). Here was the heart of the matter: Would rich, powerful, respected Naaman do what Elisha commanded? Would he trust that word? Would he simply obey and do it? To his credit, he humbled himself and went and washed in the Jordan. Through that ordinary act of obedience, he was healed.

Will God work in our lives? Maybe that question needs to be turned around. Will we do what God has commanded us? Will we love one another, worship, pray, witness, be peacemakers, turn the other cheek? Will we trust God enough to follow the way set out before us in Scripture? Will we obey? It is hard to do that. We often rebel. In spite of that, will we trust God enough to obey? Here is what can happen. In the simple acts of obedience, God can speak to us, renew us, change us, heal us. Will we have faith enough to trust that truth?

Sometimes God will act in extraordinary ways in our lives. Most often, God will act through the ordinary—ordinary people, ordinary events, in the ordinary act of obedience. Look for that. God is in the ordinary.—Hugh Litchfield

ILLUSTRATIONS

GOD IN THE ORDINARY.   The town was in an uproar! The Clown was coming back! No one knew him by any other name—only "The Clown," a circus dropout whom no one had ever seen without his face paint, orange yarn hair, polka-dotted jumpsuit, and big floppy shoes. He had shown up one day to talk and forever changed all their lives. For despite his rather ridiculous appearance, his words were filled with wisdom.

That was several years ago, shortly after the flood that literally swept away half their homes, pushed the disaster relief agencies beyond their limits, and as time went on, began to separate the citizens of the community into "haves" and "have-nots." Then, seemingly out of nowhere, The Clown had come, making suggestions about how to rebuild, helping the have-nots to see the haves as persons in need of an unusual degree of understanding and love if they were to be released from the prison of their selfishness.

But after he'd been with them only a short time, The Clown had vanished as suddenly as he had appeared. Now he was coming back!

As he approached and saw the crowd gathered in welcome, The Clown knew it was time to face them without his facade. He stepped up into the bandstand, waved a silent greeting, and began to smear his face with cold cream. "What's he doing?" people asked one another in hushed, anxious whispers. The Clown, still silent, reached into his bag for a towel and began to wipe away the paint, to wipe away the face they recognized as The Clown.

Suddenly the whispering and murmuring stopped! The crowd gasped in collective surprise. John? John Jones from Elm Street? John Jones was The Clown? How could this be?

With the paint removed, John lifted off his orange wig and stepped to the microphone. "It's really very simple," he said. "Three years ago, would you have listened to John Jones from Elm Street?"[6]

FINDING GOD.   Once there was a young man who wanted to find God, so he went into a large, beautiful cathedral. He thought that under the spacious domes, in the light of the stained glass windows, and in the presence of the glittering mosaics he might experience God. Filled with feelings of God's closeness, he put his head down on the back of the pew in front of him.

A few minutes later he felt a tapping on his shoulder. Looking up, he saw an old woman. "Are you hungry?" she asked. "I could give you a few dollars to get something to eat." Realizing the risk the woman had taken and the simple love that prompted it, the man thanked her but said that he was all right. A few minutes later he left the church, knowing that he had found God in more than one way.—Paul Wharton[7]

SERMON SUGGESTIONS

Topic: Burden Bearing
TEXT: Various
(1) "Everyone has his own burden to bear" (Gal. 6:5 REB). (2) "Carry one another's burdens" (Gal. 6:2 REB). (3) "Cast your burden on the Lord, and he will sustain you" (Ps. 55:22 NRSV).

Topic: The Cross in the Marketplace
TEXT: Mark 8:34–38
When Bildad, Eliphaz, and Zophar were giving their inadequate answers, Job was asking

---

[6] *Emphasis*, July/Aug. 1994, p. 16
[7] *Stories and Parables for Teachers* (New York: Paulist Press, 1986), pp. 21–22.

the important questions. (1) Where is God? (2) Who am I? (3) What shall we do?—Foy Valentine[8]

CONGREGATIONAL MUSIC

1. "Awake, My Soul, Stretch Every Nerve," Philip Doddridge (1755)

    SIROE, George Frideric Handel (1728)

    This excellent hymn setting forth the truths of 1 Corinthians 9:24–27 would be a good beginning to worship.

2. "Come, Sing to God," Fred R. Anderson (1986)

    ELLACOMBE, *Gesangbuch der Herzogl. Wirtembergischen Katolischen Hofkapelle* (1784)

    This modern paraphrase of Psalm 30 is so well arranged that antiphonal singing line by line between choir and congregation would be quite effective.

3. "O Christ, the Healer," Fred Pratt Green (1969)

    MELCOMBE, Samuel Webbe (1791)

    Both the Old Testament reading and the Gospel for this day have to do with healing. Therefore this hymn, written by the man often considered the finest hymnist in Methodism since Charles Wesley, would be suitable for use.

4. "Fight the Good Fight," John S. B. Monsell (1863)

    PENTECOST, William Boyd (1864)

    Based on 1 Corinthians 9:24–26, this vibrant hymn could be sung either before or after the Epistle reading.—Hugh T. McElrath

WORSHIP AIDS

CALL TO WORSHIP.   "Sing praises to the Lord, O you his godly ones, and praise his holy name. For though there be a moment in his wrath, there is a lifetime in his favor. Weeping may lodge with us at evening, but in the morning there is a shout of joy" (Ps. 30:4–5 Goodspeed).

INVOCATION.   We believe that you are for us, O Lord; therefore, we come to you, recognizing your gracious presence among us and praying for your special blessing to help us to glorify you in supplication, song, and sermon.

OFFERTORY SENTENCE.   "Ye ought to support the weak, and to remember the words of the Lord Jesus, how he said, it is more blessed to give then to receive" (Acts 20:35b).

OFFERTORY PRAYER.   Again and again, O God, our cup of joy has run over when we have joined you in giving, in the spirit of him who loved us and gave himself for us. Now we thank you that again we have this wonderful privilege.

PRAYER.   Here we are, Father, part of the huddled masses yearning for that something more that completes life. In our brokenness we come, having tried in our own strength to make life work our way only to see it fall apart. In our sorrow we come, having been

---

[8] In *The Struggle for Meaning*

wounded by the events of life that tear at the heart, that bring pain to our days and tears to our nights. In our lostness we come, having chosen pathways of lesser value to follow and missing your highway of life. In our guilt we come, drowning in those feelings that haunt us with their condemnation because we know our actions, words, and thoughts were evil. In our loneliness we come, lonely many times even when we stand in the midst of people, lonely for that home where things are right and that always seems just out of sight over the horizon. In hope we come believing that you and only you have the words of life, know the way in which we should go, care for us with an unending concern, save us to the uttermost, and prepare a place for us where neither moth nor rust can corrupt and where thieves cannot break through and steal. In expectation we come, believing that you will not leave us nor forsake us, that you will not leave us comfortless, that you will not forever hide your face from us, that you will love each of us as if there were only one of us to love.

So here we are, Father, each of us here for his or her particular reason. We need to experience in this hour what we cannot find anywhere else except in the presence, power, and worship of you, the God and Father of our Lord Jesus Christ. O God of our fathers, God of all revelation, God of every person's salvation, God of unending grace and love, come to us even now, we pray, as we wait reverently and expectantly together in Jesus' name.—Henry Fields

SERMON
Topic: Being Fully You
TEXT: Luke 5:1–11; 1 Cor. 15:1–11

I. Paul was an obscure rabbi, a tent maker, a hater of Christianity, and a persecutor of its followers. But Jesus Christ transformed him from the tarnished tartar of Tarsus to the energetic, indefatigable champion of the gospel. "I worked harder than any of them," writes Paul to the Corinthians—"though it was *not* I but the grace of God that is with me." Jesus Christ made Saul the menace into Paul the apostle. It is Jesus Christ who makes us more than lumps of flesh, who makes us able leaders in the marketplace as well as his discriminating followers in the community. He adds the plus to life, and makes us fully the ones God designed.

Peter and his weary crew labored all night trying to catch fish, but they were without success. They put into port and were washing their nets when Jesus instructed them to go out into the deep water of the Sea of Galilee again and let down their nets for a catch.

Simon Peter grumbled softly. "Master," respectfully responded the fisherman to the Carpenter's command, "we have worked all night long but have caught nothing. Yet if *you say so*, we will let down the nets." Peter knew that Jesus makes a difference. He did *then;* he does *still.* Is he making a difference in your life? Are you making a difference in our world? Is your world any different because you're in it?

Jesus Christ enables us to be fully the one God intends. Peter's fishing crew caught "so many fish that their nets were beginning to break," says Luke. They did more than take Jesus on board their little boat. They took him into their hearts!

When Peter saw the amazing catch of fish, so many that they had to summon a second boat to haul them in, he was astonished. "He fell down at Jesus' knees, saying, 'Go away from me, Lord, for I am a sinful man!'" When we see Jesus fulfilling within us opportunities and capabilities far beyond our fondest dreams, are we not similarly amazed? Yet rather than driving Jesus away, we need to embrace him all the more, for Jesus is not finished empowering us to be fully the one God intends simply by achieving one success.

Certainly Jesus made a difference for that team of fishermen. He promised them even greater accomplishments. They, too, would make a difference. "Do not be afraid," consoled our Lord, "from now on you will be catching people." It was then that they left behind their fishing nets, beached their boots on the sand by the Sea of Galilee, and went fishing for Galileans—and for others as well.

Jesus enables us to be fully what we cannot be without him. I know that personally. Every time I have faced a new era in my life, I have renewed my commitment to Christ. I have asked him to enter my life anew and enable me to be the one he intended, not just the one I am alone.

II. Without him I would be like Saul of Tarsus before the Damascus Road experience, I'm afraid: bitter, hateful, out to get all I could for the sheer satisfaction of power. I would be like Peter and James and John and Andrew: fishing for fish, unsatisfied, grasping after something more, trying everything but not knowing what I'm reaching for—until Jesus enters the scene.

Peter was emboldened to fish not only for the creatures that swim the lakes and streams but also for the people who are drowning in their own sin and sorrow. He became a fisher of men, one who caught people for the Lord Christ, so they too could be more fully the ones God intends.

You and I may never be famous. Does it matter as long as we are fulfilled? You and I may never have much power or amass great fortunes. Is that essential to life now or forever? No, not at all! But Jesus *is*! If you and I let Jesus take command of our lives, we will discover that he enables us to be so much more than we ever thought possible without him. It may be on a small scale as far as the world is concerned, but gigantic for *your* world.

(a) Being fully you means living vigorously in the minutes between dangers, crises, and catastrophes, as well as when you put your foot down in the middle of a mess. That requires happily housing a resident Christ within. It is the Lord who loves you, who motivates you, and who stirs you through one perplexing crisis to another and then on to the ultimate goal ahead. It means being a Saul who turns into a Paul, a Simon Peter who is more than a big fisher of fish, who is a great fisher of souls.

It means being fully you. Without Jesus you cannot take the next step with any certainty of fulfillment; but with him, every step completes another chapter for him.

In this still fresh, new year, take the words of this covenant service seriously. Pray the prayers daily. Let Jesus board the boat of your life. Let him be seated within your soul and teach you the lessons of the kingdom as he did in Peter's little fishing boat—the lessons of life and the ways to win in a lost world. Let him be your friend.

(b) To be fully the ones God intends means being willing to accept every opportunity to share the good news with others by our words and witness. It may be the one time that we are fully what Christ promised: fishers of people! It may enable us to fish more energetically in the sea of human life.

To be fully you means letting the Christ of Calvary suffer with you when you are in pain. To be fully you means inviting the Lord of Easter to bring victory to your life when you seem defeated. To be fully you means trusting Jesus to lead you along life's journey through all its confusion to all its accomplishments. To be fully you means Jesus is on board your little boat teaching you and telling you to "let down the nets."

To be fully you, welcome Jesus to set sail with you now.—Richard Andersen

SUNDAY, FEBRUARY 20, 2000
Lectionary Message

Topic: Facing Up to Jesus
TEXT: Mark 2:1–12
Other Readings: Isa. 43:18–25; Ps. 41; 2 Cor. 1:18–22

Who do we think Jesus is? That's a question we all have to face—and answer—at some time in our life. The answer to it will determine what our lives will become. Who is this Jesus?

In our Scripture lesson, Jesus was trying to answer that question. He was running into opposition from the religious leaders of his day. They were upset and confused by his actions. Who did he think he was? They wanted to know. Through the event of the healing of the paralytic, Jesus sought to show them. That in itself is unique, for in the Gospel of Mark, often after Jesus performed a healing he admonished the person to tell no one about it. It was not the right time for his Messiahship to be revealed. However, in this story Jesus was willing to pull back the curtain of mystery and let them see in. If they really saw him, who would they see?

I. *The situation: A healing* (vv. 1–5). The situation of this story is simple. Jesus had come to Capernaum, which seemed to be his headquarters for ministry. The people flocked to hear him. He was preaching to them in a home—probably Peter's—and it was wall-to-wall crowded. No one else could get into the house. Four men showed up carrying a paralyzed man on a stretcher. They sized up the situation, climbed the outside stairway to the roof, pulled up some of the sticks and reeds and dirt, and made a hole big enough to lower down the stretcher to where Jesus was.

What ingenuity these men had! What perseverance they showed! What faith they had in Jesus' ability to heal this paralytic! Jesus was impressed with their faith (which may also include the paralytic's faith). So Jesus said to him, "Son, your sins are forgiven."

When we read about this event we are impressed by these four men. Who did they think Jesus was? They must have thought he was the answer to their prayers, their hopes. Jesus had the power to heal their friend. He was a healer. They believed that so strongly that nothing stopped them from acting on that belief. Jesus had the power!

For many today, this is who Jesus is. He is a healer, the one who has the power to take away their paralysis, whatever it is. Jesus can heal them of their cancer, put back together their broken marriage, deliver their child from drugs. That is true—Jesus does have that power. However, that is not what Jesus wants us to see. There is more to him than that.

II. *The complication: Blasphemy* (vv. 6–7). It is surprising that the first thing Jesus did was forgive the man of his sins. He didn't heal him of his physical infirmity. Instead, he declared him forgiven. That got him into trouble. The teachers of the Law accused him of blasphemy. This was slanderous language. He was assuming for himself authority that belonged only to God. That was the understanding of that day. Only God had the power to forgive sins, and then only after the sinner offered evidence of repentance. That was not the case here. Who did Jesus think he was? God?

Throughout the history of the faith, this has been a central affirmation: God was in Christ. Somehow, in what Jesus said and did, God was acting. Always there have been those who have not believed that. They have admired Jesus as a great teacher who has given us great wisdom. Others have seen him as a great moral example of how one must live courageously in the face of evil. Some have even called him a prophet of God, reminding us of what God wants us to do and be. But to think of Jesus as God come down to earth—no way! Who does he think he is—God? That is the question we have to face.

III. *The resolution: Wholeness* (vv. 8–12). Jesus knew what they were thinking and went right after them. "Which is easier? To forgive sins or to heal physical ailments? Well, I'll do both." So he told the man to get up and go home. The man got up, picked up his mat, and went on home. They couldn't miss that. Jesus even used the phrase "Son of Man" about himself. That phrase (found in Daniel 7:13–28) was identified with a messianic figure who would come with the power to execute judgment and forgive sins. Jesus said that he was that someone. The people also believed that no one could be healed of physical sickness until all of their sins had been forgiven. So because this man was healed, his sins must have been forgiven. Because only God can forgive, and because Jesus forgave his sin, the only logical conclusion was that Jesus was—? Draw the conclusion. That's what Jesus wanted them to do.

They were amazed, praised God, and said that they had never seen anything like this. Even so, the religious leaders did not get it. They would not believe that Jesus was God. Jesus had shown them clearly, but they would not change their thinking.

Who do we think Jesus is? Do we think he is God? That is what this Scripture teaches. When we see Jesus, we see God. Jesus forgives sins because God forgives sin. Jesus loves us because God loves us. Jesus brings eternal life because God does. What we need to know of God is revealed in Jesus. He is our photograph of God. When we urge others to put their trust in Jesus, we bring them to the saving arms of God. Although Jesus may or may not heal our physical sicknesses, Jesus can always heal us of our spiritual sickness. Our sins can be forgiven, our lives made whole. In Christ, we can become part of the Kingdom of God forever.

Who does Jesus think he is—God? Yes, he does! He is! Will we trust that truth?—Hugh Litchfield

ILLUSTRATIONS

POWER OF CHRIST.   Two outspoken infidels were riding in the same train and discussing Jesus. Neither believed in him. One of them said, "I think an interesting book could be written about Christ." The other replied, "Yes, and you are just the man to write it. Set forth the correct view of His life and character. Tear down the prevailing sentiment as to his divineness, and paint him as he was—a man among men."

The suggestion was followed and the book was written. The man who made the suggestion was Colonel Robert Ingersoll, notorious for his unbelief. The man who wrote the book was General Lew Wallace, and the book was *Ben-Hur*.

As a scholar, Wallace first read the Bible, books of history, fiction, religions of the East, books of geography—books of every kind. He even took a trip to the Holy Land in order to see and appreciate some of the things he would use in his book.

According to David James Burrell, in the process of writing that book, Wallace "found himself facing the unaccountable Man; until at length, like the centurion under the cross, he was constrained to cry, 'Verily, this was the Son of God.'"

Wallace's interest in Jesus was, at first, academic, but he discovered the grace of God operating in his life. He discovered who Jesus really was.[9]

CHRIST AS SAVIOR.   A girl about eight years old enjoyed chatting with a grandfatherly professor in Berkeley, California. Let Dr. Robert Rodenmayer tell this story. "Walking home one day I came to Emily's house where she was sitting on the front step. I stopped to say hello and was about to leave when she said, 'What do people preach about in your church?' I replied that they preach about the best things they know. 'What,' she asked, 'is the best thing you know?' I turned the question back, 'What is the best thing *you* know?' She considered it gravely and finally answered, 'I think the best thing is to have a friend.' I agreed."—David MacLennan[10]

SERMON SUGGESTIONS

Topic: Elijah

TEXT: 1 Kings 19:4

It has been observed of the holy men of Scripture that their most signal failures took place in those points of character for which they were remarkable in excellence. (1) The causes of Elijah's despondency: (a) relaxation of physical strength; (b) want of sympathy; (c) want of occupation; (d) disappointment in the expectation of success. (2) God's treatment of it: (a) He recruited his servant's exhausted strength. (b) He calmed his stormy mind by the healing influences of nature. (c) God made him feel the earnestness of life: "What *doest* thou here, Elijah?" (4) He completed the cure by the assurance of victory.—F. W. Robertson[11]

Topic: Doubts and Faith

TEXT: Mark 9:24

(1) Everybody doubts, skeptic and believer, pulpit and pew. (2) Everybody believes. There is the saucy story of an atheist who, when asked if he were a Christian, replied angrily, "No, I'm an atheist, thank God!" (3) The faith and the doubt come to a crux in Jesus Christ. Most people would say of him that he is "the best." In the cross of Christ we see earth's "best" at the mercy of earth's "worst." Through it men have known that the bleakest tragedy may be the most piercing and healing light. (4) Can the tension be resolved? Not fully in this life but yet with a great measure of certitude. What we need is a strategy rather than a proof, a strategy and a certain valor of the spirit. (5) Doubts are the odds that faith must meet. Otherwise faith would be a *dead* certainty, not faith.—George A. Buttrick[12]

---

[9] *Pulpit Resource*, July/Aug./Sept. 1986, pp. 39–40.
[10] *Let's Take Another Look* (Waco, Tex.: Word Books, 1970), p. 58.
[11] *Sermons*
[12] *Sermons Preached in a University Church*

CONGREGATIONAL MUSIC

1. "Praise, My Soul, the King of Heaven," Henry F. Lyte (1834)

    LAUDA ANIMA, John Goss (1869)

    Appropriate for the beginning of worship, this venerable hymn gives praise to the God who forgives and heals. Thus it is in keeping with the Gospel account of Jesus' forgiving and healing of the paralytic man.

2. "Great Is Thy Faithfulness," Thomas O. Chisholm (1923)

    FAITHFULNESS, William M. Runyan (1923)

    This song proclaiming God's faithfulness can be sung in response to either the Old Testament reading from prophecy or the reading from the Psalter. It reflects the spirit of the Psalmist, who affirms God's support against enemies and false friends, and of Isaiah, who declares God's doing of a new thing and forgiving Israel's transgressions.

3. "Come, Thou Fount," Robert Robinson (1758)

    NETTLETON, *Wyeth's Repository of Sacred Music: Part Second* (1813)

    Calling upon God to come seal the singer's wandering heart (stanza 3), this hymn suitably reflects the thought of the apostle Paul, who affirms the God who establishes, anoints, and seals all hearts, giving them his Spirit as a pledge (2 Cor. 1:21–22).

4. "How Blest Are Those Who Thoughtfully," Bert Polman (1985)

    FOREST GREEN, English tune; harm. R. V. Williams (1906)

    This contemporary paraphrase of Psalm 41 is sufficiently close to the sense of the original psalm that it could well be sung in place of the Psalm reading.—Hugh T. McElrath

WORSHIP AIDS

CALL TO WORSHIP.   "Happy is anyone who has a concern for the helpless! The Lord will save him in time of trouble" (Ps. 41:1 REB).

INVOCATION.   Lord, help us to realize that all of us are bound up together in the bundle of life and that when we do something for others we are doing something for you and for ourselves. Help us to learn to love one another, especially to love those who need it most. To that end, open our eyes more and more as we worship together.

OFFERTORY SENTENCE.   "Set your affection on things above, not on things on the earth" (Col. 3:2).

OFFERTORY PRAYER.   Lord, we know that if we love you enough, no earthly love will be able to dim our view of heavenly things or keep us from our obligations here and now.

PRAYER.   May our souls find a resting place, Father, not in creeds and designed statements of faith, but in you and you alone.

Some come here this morning worn and weary with the burdens of life. There is no seeking to turn aside from the common burdens of life. We do not seek rest from mental and manual toil. The rest we long for is deeper than struggle and toil. It is a longing for satisfying rest that settles our souls, an inner rest that is the reward of those who bring their desires into harmony with your purpose and commit themselves to doing your will. Let that inner rest and peace come as we wait together in your presence today.

Some come here restless because they have wandered far from you. Deceived by the glamour of cheap joys, many have tried to satisfy themselves with the husks of life, but there is still a deeper hunger for the very bread that you alone can give. Ashamed and homesick, they feel a longing for your presence too deep to be uttered. Give folks courage to arise and go to the Father and say, "Make me content to abide within the shelter of your grace and love and to live within your law."

Give your blessing to the Church, we pray. As it seeks to bring restless people back to their moorings, from which they have drifted, give it guidance, compassion, forgiveness, and love to accomplish your purpose. Create through the Church a fellowship that cannot be broken, a longing that will never give up on anyone, and a winsomeness that will exemplify Christ.

Whether our pathways through the coming week lead us beside still waters or through dark valleys and mountainous disappointments and difficulties, give us the ability to keep our hearts and minds on you.—Henry Fields

SERMON
Topic: Jesus Said, "Learn from Me"
TEXT: Matt. 11:25–30

It was Jesus who said, "Learn from me." The context of those words in the Gospel of Matthew tell us that Jesus possesses the power to reveal God. "All things have been handed over to me by my Father," he said. "No one knows the Son except the Father, and no one knows the Father except the Son and anyone to whom the Son chooses to reveal him." Jesus was referring to himself as the Son and to God as the Father.

God becomes known to each of us by our following, learning from, and abiding in Jesus, for Jesus, remember, possesses the power to reveal God. When he says, "Take my yoke upon you," calling us to discipleship, and when he says, "Learn from me," signifying that he will be our mentor, and when he concludes by saying, "You will find rest for your souls"—fulfillment, in other words—he is giving us more than information. He is confronting us with the very claims and purposes and blessings of God.

I. *Christlikeness.* Repeatedly Jesus called people to discipleship. "Follow me," he would command. "Come to me," he would say. "Take my yoke upon you," he would add. Jesus was pleading that life is meant to be given in homage to God. Such homage means embracing justice, mercy, service, selflessness, love—all of these things in imitation of Jesus Christ. Discipleship and Christlikeness thus are the same. Jesus explained such linkage by saying, "A disciple is not above the teacher, but everyone who is fully qualified will be like the teacher." A disciple shows or puts forth what the teacher has taught. Another way of saying it is that a disciple witnesses to the truth that has come.

All of our decisions and actions are meant to be subject to the reality of belonging to Christ—following him, assuming his yoke, sharing his life. Our faith becomes validated as it connects with the world about us, presenting to that world a testimony to the way, the truth, and the life of Jesus Christ. By this, our discipleship, we are answering God's claim on us, the claim that we become God's people, faithful to God in all things. Moreover, by our discipleship we begin to know God; we are drawn closer to him.

II. *Growth.* Besides issuing a call to discipleship, Jesus issued a call to learning. "Learn from me," he said to his followers. The things we learn from Jesus give substance to our discipleship, content to our witness. The more we learn, the more confident we become. Our Christian lives prove stronger, and the testimony we bear proves clearer and of greater influence. Learning from him never ceases.

Preeminently we learn from Jesus that God is with us. Not only is God with us but, as St. Augustine said, "God loves us every one as if there were but one of us to love." It is evident that Jesus, in his dealings with men, women, and children, consistently focused on each individual in turn.

Our learning from the master teacher could not be plainer; God is with us—knowing even the count of the hairs on our heads, loving us each one as if there were but one of us to love.

"Learn from me," said Jesus, and privileged we are to have him as our leader, counselor, helper, and guide. Our part is that of remaining humbly teachable, saying with the biblical psalmist, "Make me to know your ways, O Lord; teach me your paths. Lead me in your truth, and teach me, for you are the God of my salvation; for you I wait all day long."

III. *Fulfillment.* The yoke or mantle of discipleship we assume as Jesus' followers and the learning we gain from him have as their by-product a great blessing. Jesus called it "rest for your souls." Elsewhere he spoke of the gift of inner peace that signifies personal calm and composure. Said Jesus, "Peace I leave with you; my peace I give to you. I do not give to you as the world gives. Do not let your hearts be troubled, and do not let them be afraid." I like this way of saying it: the blessing of God's peace is nothing that the world can give; when once it is given, the world cannot take it away. Here is a promise of enormous meaning for our lives; here is a permanent and unshakable resource for the living of our days.

As hard as it may seem to perceive these blessings, the promise is that they are there. In Jesus' words, "I will not leave you comfortless." The word *comfortless* literally means "orphaned": "I will not leave you orphaned," Jesus was saying. He will instead impart peace, rest, and fulfillment for our souls. As we abide in him, there treasured blessings are bestowed.—John H. Townsend

SUNDAY, FEBRUARY 27, 2000
Lectionary Message

Topic: A New Way Coming
TEXT: Mark 2:18–22
Other Readings: Hos. 2:14–20; Ps. 103:1–13; 2 Cor. 3:1–6

In Mark's Gospel, it seems as if Jesus is always moving from one controversy to another. He heals someone and they don't understand it. He forgives a man of his sins and he is accused of blasphemy. In this Scripture lesson, he's at it again. It's over the question of fasting. As usual, Jesus will take this event and turn it into an opportunity to reveal the meaning of what he had come to do. It concerns an age-old issue—the conflict between the new and the old.

I. *The problem: Not keeping the tradition* (v. 18). Fasting was a religious practice that indicated one's sorrow over sin. It was a sign of a desire to serve God. As a matter of the Law, fasting was practiced once a year on the Day of Atonement, that sacred day when sacrifice was made in the Temple for the sins of the people. However, strict Jews fasted more than that, usually on Monday and Thursday of each week. On those days, they would not eat food from sunrise to sundown. People admired them for their devotion to God.

Now, Jesus was seen as a religious teacher, one who was supposed to be devoted to God. But he was not fasting nor did he require his disciples to fast. The fasters wanted to know why not. After all, serious disciples of God would do that. They had always done that before. So what was the matter with Jesus? Didn't he care about the Law? Wasn't he respectful of their traditions? Because Jesus and his disciples didn't fast, they didn't seem religious enough.

That is a controversy we find ourselves trapped in even today. There are those who have developed certain religious practices that they feel any dedicated Christian should do. It might be fasting, or reading the Bible daily, or praying for hours, or worshiping so many times a week, or marching in protest against some evil. Everybody does these rituals—if you are a "good" Christian. It's always been the case. Why doesn't everybody do them? There are rules you keep—that's the way it is!

In churches you hear this idea in the old phrase, "We've always done it this way." New ideas and different approaches to ministry are opposed. Because "we've never done it that way before," it can never be done that way. For example, music in worship is a controversial issue today. Shall we sing the old hymns or the new choruses? Unfortunately, churches have split because they have not found a way to resolve that issue. It's that conflict again between the old and the new. Is there a way to solve it?

II. *The solution: Be open to the new* (vv. 19–22). Jesus answered their question with the use of several images. He talked about a wedding. The bridegroom was there, so it was a time for celebration. A wedding was not a time to mourn. When the bridegroom was gone, then they could mourn and fast. Not now—it was a time to party. Scholars remind us that Jesus was referring to himself. The Kingdom of God had broken into life with his coming. New life had come to them. Jesus was there with them. Enjoy him, listen to him, learn from him, be open to the new way of life he was bringing. God was doing a new thing. Be glad about it.

Jesus talked about patches. You wouldn't use an old piece of cloth to patch up a hole in a pair of pants. If you did, it would only tear away. It would not be sufficient, it would not hold. You put a new patch on it. It's the only way to fix it. In other words, Jesus and his message were too vibrant and different to be fitted into old patterns or institutions. It was a time to reinterpret the Law, because a new way was coming.

Likewise, you don't put new wine into old wineskins. Old wineskins were little more than fragile goat hairs. Under the pressure of fermentation they would burst open when new wine was poured into them. In other words, old traditions had become so rigid, they were like brittle wineskins. They could not contain the new wine of the Kingdom of God. The new way that Jesus was bringing would "fill full" the old wineskins and bring some new ones.

Jesus came to turn their world upside down, to show them the world of God's Kingdom. That was a new world, a new way of living. To enter it, they had to be willing to be open to the new values of that Kingdom. These ideas were radical. You can't earn God's favor by keeping rules or doing good works—you have God's favor already through grace. You don't hate your enemies, you love them. You don't divide people on the basis of race or gender or social status—all are one in Christ. You don't pass by on the other side of human need, you stoop down to meet it. Peace is valued over war. Forgiveness is available to all who would seek it. Death is not the final word on life, resurrection to eternal life is. It was a new way of life!

If there is anything we can learn from this story it is to watch out. We never can know what God might do with us today through the Spirit. This is not to say that we must throw out everything that is old or traditional. There is still much good in some of the time-honored ideas and practices. It does say that we must be open to new ways of thinking and doing the gospel. We can't tie God up into a neat set of beliefs and practices and feel that's all there is. More can happen. While God can speak through old hymns, God can also speak through new choruses. Will we be open to that possibility? In the Kingdom of God there's always a new way coming.—Hugh Litchfield

ILLUSTRATIONS

WILLINGNESS TO CHANGE.   Someone told me the story of a boy who heard that the community band was looking for a trombone player. He went down and told the director that he would like to be the trombone player. The director was excited to hear that, since they were marching in a parade the next day. He gave the boy a uniform and told him to show up the next day. He did and they began to march in the parade. When they started to play the music, awful sounds were heard from the trombone section. The boy could not play the trombone! The director asked him, "Why didn't you tell me you couldn't play the trombone?" The boy answered, "Well, I didn't know. I had never tried to before." I like the willing spirit of the young boy.—Hugh Litchfield[13]

CHANGE.   An early Baptist pastor, Benjamin Keach, is credited with introducing hymn singing to English Baptist churches. Keach began with the children, for they enjoyed singing. But their parents did not, for they were convinced that singing was "foreign to evangelical worship." A controversy arose when Keach sought to introduce congregational singing to his church. With biblical evidence, he first got them to agree in 1673 to a hymn after the Lord's Supper. However, he allowed those who objected to leave before the hymn. Six years later the church agreed to sing a hymn on "public thanksgiving days." Another 14 years passed before the church could agree that singing was appropriate in worship. A full 20 years passed before one church could agree that singing was good, appropriate, and worshipful. This incident was costly, however, for 22 members of Keach's church withdrew to join a non-singing church. However, singing had caught on, and this non-singing church soon called a pastor who made hymn singing a condition of his coming. So goes the way of change.[14]

SERMON SUGGESTIONS

Topic: Temple and Town
TEXT: Gen. 12:8
We have to live between Bethel and Ai, between the House of God and the Canaanite city. And if we take our religion seriously, we must know something of the tension of such a position. (1) We must realize that that is how God intended it to be. The background against which the teachings of Christ are to be practiced is that of a sinful and difficult world. (2) Having Bethel on the west should make a difference to Ai on the east. Church should make a difference to city.—J. Ithel Jones[15]

---

[13] *Visualizing the Sermon* (Sioux Falls, S.D.: Hugh Litchfield, 1996), p. 136.
[14] *Proclaim,* Apr./May/June 1998, p. 30.
[15] *Temple and Town*

Topic: Search the Scriptures!

TEXT: John 5:39–47

(1) They testify of Christ. (2) They impart the life in Christ. (3) They glorify God through Christ.—R.C.H. Lenski[16]

CONGREGATIONAL MUSIC

1. "Praise to the Lord, the Almighty," Joachim Neander (1680)

    LOBE DEN HERREN, *Erneuerten Gesangbuch* (1665)

    Inspired by both Psalm 103 and Psalm 150, this rousing hymn of praise is ideal for the opening of worship.

2. "O My People, Turn to Me," Hosea 14:1, 4–7, vers. Marie Post (1981)

    HOSEA, Norm Jockman (1984)

    This contemporary scriptural song, based on the basic theme of Hosea—reconciliation—would make a good response to the Hosea 2:14–20 reading.

3. "I Stand Amazed in the Presence," Charles H. Gabriel (1905)

    MY SAVIOR'S LOVE, Charles H. Gabriel (1905)

    The mood and feeling of amazement of the people around Jesus upon his healing of the paralytic (Mark 2:12) is echoed in the words of this gospel song. It could be used to introduce the Gospel reading, which following this incident goes on to relate other events in Jesus' ministry.

4. "Bless His Holy Name," Andráe Crouch (1973)

    BLESS THE LORD, Andráe Crouch (1973)

    This African American interpretation of Psalm 103:1 could be used as an antiphon interspersed during the reading of the Psalter lesson for this day.—Hugh T. McElrath

WORSHIP AIDS

CALL TO WORSHIP.   "Bless the Lord, O my soul, and all that is within me, bless his holy name. Bless the Lord, O my soul, and forget not all his benefits" (Ps. 103:1–2).

INVOCATION.   To abide in your greatness is privilege beyond imagination, Father. Here in this sacred place we stand in awe of your majesty. We sing of the wonder of your greatness. We listen to the story of your love. We come to make genuine and lasting commitments to your service. Pray accept us through your grace and keep us by your power as we wait before you in anticipation.—Henry Fields

OFFERTORY SENTENCE.   "But just as you excel in everything—in faith, in speech, in knowledge, in complete earnestness and in your love for us—see that you also excel in this grace of giving" (2 Cor. 8:7 NIV).

OFFERTORY PRAYER.   Here are our bills and coins, Father. They tell as clearly as anything we can do the depth of our dedication to Christ and our concern for the world as he would

---

[16] *Eisenach Gospel Selections*

have it be. Lead us to search our hearts and motives and give liberally because we love the Lord, whose we claim to be.—Henry Fields

PRAYER.   How thankful we are, Father, that you give us the day to work and the night to rest. In the night hours may we experience renewal of our bodies that we may have the strength to do the work that is ours to perform during the day. May we be granted clear minds with which to think, joyful experiences to encourage us, and a willingness to turn our hands to whatever task arises to be done.

Deliver us from any bitterness that poisons, any frustration that maddens, all futility that deadens. We work to make our dreams become reality; show us how to dream that our work may be worthwhile. May we come to the end of the day with contentment in our hearts, goodwill toward others in our spirits, and satisfaction of a job well done in our souls.

Help us to so live each day of life that we will be better fitted to abide in your eternal presence when life's day is done and we come to the eternal shores of our true home.—Henry Fields

SERMON
Topic: Is Religion a Private Affair?
TEXT: 1 Cor. 12:12–27

I. *Lone Rangers*. Americans pride themselves on self-fulfillment and rugged individualism. In certain respects our society has a lot of men and women quite content to go it alone and live as much as possible unto themselves. Heaven forbid that there should be feelings of dependency or relationship! In modern cities people on the same block or in the same building often are strangers to one another; families frequently exist in name only, each person going his or her separate way. We like to feel self-sufficient and independent, sometimes to the extreme. Forgotten is a deeper need, the need for human community. Those who like being Lone Rangers cannot ignore the fact (as someone has said) that even the Lone Ranger had Tonto. Ultimately, life atop a pillar can be fiercely lonesome, and potentially hazardous—the hazard, of course, being falling off.

When it comes to considering Christianity, the reality is that we cannot be Christian alone. We are part of each other in the household of faith. An analogy given to us by the apostle Paul makes this point clearly, should there be any doubt. Christians, said Paul, are the body of Christ. Individually we are all members of that body, just as a foot or a hand, an ear or an eye, is integral to the whole. There always are many separate members, said Paul, yet one body. No part of that organism can exclude another by saying, "I have no need of you." On the contrary, insisted the apostle, even supposedly weaker members are indispensable. Caring for all of the parts of the body is essential, the realization being that if one part suffers, all suffer together. So also if one portion is honored, the entire body rejoices.

We may admire the devotion of any person who withdraws to seek God in prayer and meditation, but for both that person and the rest of us we need to be in fellowship as well; prayer with each other, for example, is as important as prayer in private. We could go so far as to say that vital faith begins to be fully formed only when we work at it together; God, for us, is not sought in isolation.

II. *People of koinonia.* Considerable discussion was evoked by the publication of Hillary

Rodham Clinton's book *It Takes a Village.* This book's title comes from an African proverb representing the wisdom and experience of a whole culture. The proverb says, "It takes a village to raise a child." Initial negative reactions to this idea may have related in part to the spirit of family independence and individualism we cherish in this land. Second thoughts, however, generally led to the conclusion that many, many influences go into the development of a person from infancy to maturity. It takes families and friends and teachers and peers and countless others to shape each human personality. Personal growth is limited if these influences are in short supply.

So it is with Christian formation. It takes a village to raise a Christian. It takes a community, in other words. For us, that community is the Church. For all of its weakness and faults, the local congregation of God's people is the place of Christian nurture for each of us. Beliefs are tested here, strengthened, and shared. Support is imparted in good times and bad. Appreciation for one another is encouraged; we discover ways to serve and work together.

As Catherine Marshall has done in her book *Beyond Ourselves,* we can say that "Christianity was never meant to be a lone-sheep experience."

Mrs. Marshall went on to use the Greek word *koinonia* to describe the corporate fellowship of the early Church. It was said of that company of believers that they were "of one heart and soul." In such a grouping, illumination, inspiration, and guidance flourished. "Everyone of us needs as much of the *koinonia* as he [or she] can find," said Catherine Marshall. All of us need to remain linked together, both for spiritual advancement and to be an effective witness to our world.

Interestingly, other world religions do not express themselves through communities of faith and caring. Their characteristic experience is that of an individual worshiping alone at an altar or shrine; there is no continuing social group knowing a distinctive fellowship.

What we have as a church people is precious; that fact cannot be emphasized strongly enough. How appropriate it is when we sing, "Blest be the tie that binds our hearts in Christian love; the fellowship of kindred minds is like to that above."—John H. Townsend

SUNDAY, MARCH 5, 2000
Lectionary Message

Topic: Transfiguration

TEXT: Mark 9:2–9

Other Readings: 2 Kings 2:1–12; Ps. 50:1–6; 2 Cor. 4:3–6

This Gospel reading leaves no doubt about where we are to fix our attention.

Jesus' garments are whiter than the most skilled launderer could make them; what is happening here is the work of the one who not only dazzles the eye but also says to us, "This is my beloved Son; listen to him." The cloud is the sign of the divine glory and of God's immanent presence, and just as at the Ascension, Jesus, belonging to God, appears to belong to another realm.

Here, on the verge of his Passion and death—when lifted up he will be revealed in his true glory—we see Jesus for who he is. This image is especially important to Mark, whose "messianic secret" tells the story of the one who is much more than meets the eye, who comes into the world that does not know him but in whose Passion and death the world will be saved. Here is a glimpse of that, as Jesus on the mountain is transfigured before the eyes of his disciples.

What every disciple prays for is that we may be given the eyes of faith, to keep our vision fixed on Jesus, our eyes clear to see the Savior. It was the dawning realization among those early Christians that it was the crucified who is the glorified, the one who has died who is risen and exalted, that kept them going. As we see Jesus transfigured, we pray for that steady vision.

I. *No one on earth.* An earlier translation says that Jesus' clothing is "glistening" white, utterly dazzling. Who he is and what he will accomplish by his Passion and death is beyond what we are able to fathom. Here is the one who will be lifted up, but not in the way that we would expect exaltation to occur.

The Transfiguration, then, recapitulates the gospel, that the lowly one is King, the suffering one is the Savior, the servant is the Redeemer. Jesus represents the presence of God in his down-to-earth parables, and he tells us that the way of humility and service is the way to true life and freedom. In that moment, when we see Jesus of Nazareth standing on the mountain, dazzling in his radiant majesty, we see in a flash the whole gospel, that God has chosen this man to transform the world. The one who is transfigured transfigures all, by means that no one on Earth would imagine or devise.

II. *A voice from heaven.* The voice from the cloud speaks clearly, as at Jesus' baptism: this is the one; listen to him. We are not surprised to hear the voice. We are not left with visions; there is always a voice. God speaks to us, and in this case, succinctly and clearly. The one you see, he is the one. Listen to him. Listening to him means following him, keeping focused on him, trusting that he is the one who brings to fulfillment all that is the fulfillment of the law of Moses, and all that Elijah and the prophets envisioned.

The Transfiguration gets our attention, and the voice from heaven makes our way clear. To those who are given the eyes and ears of faith, the way is clear. Keep your eyes on Jesus and listen to him, follow him. We will not be able to stay on the mountain, but wherever we must go and whatever we must do, we can keep him in view and listen to his words, knowing that he leads us toward the one from whom he comes.

III. *Jesus only.* In our pluralistic situation, texts like this are often turned toward arguing about whether there is any validity to other religions, and so on. That would have been beyond Mark's purview. He wants those who have come within sight of Jesus to know that they have found the way, the truth, and the light, that they need look no further. Look at him, keep your eyes on him, listen to him. Here before them stands the one for whom Israel and her preachers and prophets longed. This dazzling light and this clear voice make that unmistakable.—Charles Rice

ILLUSTRATIONS

CLARITY.   On a side street in our town the street lights are dim and there is not much traffic going that way. One dark night I found myself driving that way, past the mission that reaches out to addicted and homeless men. Hanging outside the mission, over the sidewalk, is a neon sign, the cross, in blue-white light: JESUS SAVES. Somehow that night, words that I had heard and spoken many times before seemed to me dazzling in their simple clarity. That is exactly what Mark, in this Gospel story, wants us to see and hear.

In the Greek Orthodox cathedral in Athens, I became aware of a large icon of Christ near the entrance. Every person coming into the church, before taking a seat, would go to the icon and kiss the glass that protected it. Being an American, I was, of course, concerned for germs. Soon, however, a sexton in black appeared, with paper towels and a bottle of window cleaner. For the rest of the service, she came back repeatedly, keeping the face of Christ clear.—Charles Rice

GLORY.   The prayer that is said at the conclusion of the eucharistic rite for the ordination of a bishop, priest, or deacon includes this petition: "We pray that [he/she] may be to us an effective example in word and action, in love and patience, and in holiness of life. Grant that we, with [him/her], may serve you now, and always rejoice in your glory." It is that phrase, "always rejoice in your glory," that evokes the scene in today's Gospel. They will soon enough come down from the mountain, and what it means to follow Jesus will become clear soon enough. But if they can keep before their eyes the vision they have seen even on the darkest, hardest day, they will be able to continue, rejoicing always in the glory revealed in Christ. [See the *Book of Common Prayer*, p. 534.]—Charles Rice

SERMON SUGGESTIONS

Topic: How to Enjoy God

TEXT: Ps. 139:7–12; Eph.3:14–21

(1) To enjoy God, we need a new perspective; that is, we need to see God as revealed in the person of Jesus Christ. (2) Also, we need a new approach; that is, we must come to God on the basis of grace, which means that God loves us first, freely, and always. (3) Furthermore, we need a new relationship. The way to get rid of that nagging feeling, that God is always on your back, is to get God into your heart.—Neil Babcox[1]

TEXT: The four verses of the hymn "O Jesus I Have Promised." (1) Verse 1: a declaration of that which lies at the heart of our Christian behavior, and our Christian commitment. (2) Verse 2: confrontation of us with our need. (3) Verse 3: the explicit help that Jesus can give you on your journey. (4) Verse 4: a double responsibility—Jesus' promise and ours.—Donald Soper[2]

CONGREGATIONAL MUSIC

1. "God, the Prophets," Dennis Wortman (1884)

   TOULON, *Genevan Psalter,* (1551)

   The first two stanzas of this hymn refer specifically to Elijah's passing his mantle to Elisha as described in today's Old Testament reading. They could be sung effectively in response to that reading.

2. "Come, Ye thankful People, Come," Henry Alford (1844)

   ST. GEORGE'S WINDSOR, George J. Elvey (1558)

---

[1] In G. Paul Butler (ed.), *Best Sermons,* Vol. 1 (New York: Trident Press, 1968).

[2] *Aflame with Faith*

Though we may be misled by the content of the first stanza to consider this hymn appropriate only for Thanksgiving worship, we should realize that the major part of the hymn has to do with Jesus' parable of the sower and the soils in the Gospel lesson for this day. Its singing could logically follow the reading of the Mark 4 passage.

3. "The Mighty God and Sovereign Lord," vers. *Psalter* (1912); rev. Marie Post (1985)

ST. PETERSBURG, Demitri S. Bortnianski (1825)

This metrical paraphrase of Psalm 50 is so faithful to the original psalm that its first two stanzas could well replace the reading of Psalm 50:1–6.

4. "Sunshine in My Soul," Eliza E. Hewitt, (1887)

SUNSHINE, John R. Sweney (1887)

The apostle's assertion that God's "light of knowledge of the glory of God in the face of Christ" shines forth in our hearts (2 Cor. 4:6) is reflected in the theme of this gospel song. Its testimonial character makes it useful as a response to the Epistle reading.—Hugh T. McElrath

WORSHIP AIDS

CALL TO WORSHIP.   "Let the giving of thanks be your sacrifice to God, and give the Almighty all that you promised. Call to me when trouble comes; I will save you, and you will praise me" (Ps. 50:14–15 TEV).

INVOCATION.   O God, we reach out for the joy that is to be found not in the chances and changes of the world but in thee. Open our eyes that we may see every sign of thy life and love moving and working among us. And raise us up that we may help others to rise, for only as we become the instruments of thy love will our gladness be unconquerable.—Theodore Parker Ferris[3]

OFFERTORY SENTENCE.   "For ye know the grace of our Lord Jesus Christ, that, though he was rich, yet for our sakes he became poor, that ye through his poverty might be rich" (2 Cor. 8:9).

OFFERTORY PRAYER.   In Jesus Christ you have enriched us, our Father, far beyond all that we could imagine. We have received many gifts, and we have much to give. In that faith and in that spirit we bring our offerings.

PRAYER.   Father of our Lord Jesus Christ, we come into this service today from a world that beckons us to be elsewhere. The enticements to abandon the practice of faithful worship in the congregation are plentiful and strong. The allurements of entertainment are everywhere, the glitter of man-created enjoyments contrasts strongly with the steady ways of the Church. We see the exciting creations of human hands and think that we are gods unto ourselves. Help us to realize that we are but temporary sojourners on this earth and that life is much more than what we see and feel and taste and experience as human pilgrims.

Remind us of what the world cannot give us, Father. Remind us that our lives and spirits

---

[3] *Prayers*

gain eternal joy by the indwelling of your Holy Spirit in us. So we bring our lives to you, polluted as they are by sins of greed, anger, mistrust; darkened by fear, anxiety, and indifference; hurt by sickness, disease, and death; defeated by doubt, misgivings, and frustrations. We bring our lives because we have been promised forgiveness of sins, light in the place of darkness, strength to bear our hurts, and victory over all defeat. Here in this sacred place, we ask for the fulfillment of these promises. As we today submit our lives to the working of the Spirit, may we go from the service fortified to manage daily life after your fashion and will.—Henry Fields

SERMON

Topic: Dancing in the Dark

TEXT: Ps. 18:28; Acts 16:16–34

What would do if you found yourself stranded in the mountains, at night, in deep snow, in subfreezing temperatures? Such is the predicament that Karen Hartley found herself in. Ms. Hartley, a thirty-three-year-old computer software developer, was skiing at Powder Mountain, a Utah ski resort, on Christmas Eve. After skiing down an ungroomed powder area at about 3:30 P.M. she became stranded. The snowcat that she had hoped would give her a ride back to the top of the mountain wasn't running that day.

Ms. Hartley yelled for help for a couple of hours before deciding that no one was going to hear her. She was too tired to hike back up the steep mountain in the deep snow. About 7:00 P.M. she ate a candy bar, the only semblance of food she had with her. The young woman realized that she was not going to be rescued, at least not before the next morning. Temperatures had dropped into the single digits. So what did Hartley do? She began to dance in the dark to tunes she kept playing in her head.

All night long Hartley sang and danced alone in the dark. "The best think I could think of was to keep my brain occupied by playing music in my head and dancing to it to keep warm," Mrs. Hartley said. "I went through all the old disco songs, show tunes, popular and current stuff, Christmas tunes, and even camp songs I'd ever known. I sang and danced all night long, from about 6:30 P.M. to dawn. It was the only way I could think of to keep warm." Dancing and singing in the dark. What imagination, creativity, and innovation! Thanks to her ingenuity and unwillingness to sit down and give up, Ms. Hartley kept herself from freezing to death. She was rescued the next morning, somewhat cold but otherwise unhurt.

Given the same situation, many folks would be tempted to curl up in the snow and give up. *But the ones who come out on top in life and faith, in the face of the challenges that rise up before us, are those who are willing to be a bit unconventional and, as it were, dance in the dark!*

I. For example, in the Bible, in the book of Acts, we have read the story of how the apostle Paul and Silas his companion were one day dragged into the marketplace, falsely accused, stripped of their clothing, and publicly flogged (beaten with rods). Then they were thrown into jail and had their feet securely fastened in stocks. Now, you would think that by this time the two missionaries of the Christian faith would be ready to pack up, call it quits, and start heading for home. But not so.

About midnight, Paul and Silas were praying and singing hymns of joy at the top of their lungs. In other words, they were singing in the dark. Their singing was so loud that the other prisoners and guards could not help but hear them. Suddenly, as the story goes, there was a violent earthquake. The foundations of the prison were shaken. Immediately all the doors flew open. The jailer ran in expecting to find his prisoners gone. But to his amazement, Paul and Silas were still in their places. The whole affair so moved the jailer that he set Paul and Silas free. Furthermore, he took them to his own house, where he fed them and cared for their wounds. He even asked the missionaries to baptize him and his family into the Christian faith!

The results of Paul and Silas's singing in the dark were that they were delivered, they were able to witness to their faith, and they saw the conversion and baptism of the jailer and his family. In short, they saw several lives changed forever!

II. We certainly cannot expect a ground-shaking earthquake every time we sing in the dark. However, experience has taught us—as in the case of Black southern slaves, for example, who gave us the great Negro spirituals—that singing through the dark nights of life can help make the burdens a little lighter and the days a little brighter. Martin Luther King Jr. wrote in this regard, "Our eternal message of hope is that dawn will come. Our slave foreparents realized this. They were never unmindful of the fact of midnight, for always there was the rawhide whip of the overseer and the auction block where families were torn asunder to remind them of its reality. When they thought of the agonizing darkness of midnight, they sang. . . . Encompassed by a staggering midnight but believing that morning would come, they sang."

When darkness falls on our lives—financial disaster, loss of a loved one, breakup of a relationship, or other troubles and trials—we can take one of two courses of action. One, we can give up in despair. We can sit down in the cold snows of life, pull ourselves up into the fetal position and give up, call it quits, wallow in our misery. But Paul and Silas didn't do this. And neither did Karen Hartley, the stranded skier.

Or two, when darkness falls on our lives we can follow the example of the apostles and Hartley and dance and sing in the dark. That is, we can keep faith, we can pray, and we can put forth our best efforts. During those dark, difficult times in our lives, let us not forget the words of the psalmist in Psalm 18:28. We might mark them in our Bibles for future reference:

It is you [O Lord] who light my lamp;
  the Lord, my God, lights up my darkness.

For those who have faith in God, the dark is not as dark.

You have often heard it said, "When life hands you lemons, make lemonade." In other words, when confronted with an obstacle, problem, or disappointment, don't give up. Work with your problem, roll with the punches, believe that all things can work for good for those who love God and seek out his purpose in their lives. Be innovative, imaginative, creative, perhaps a little unconventional if you have to. But don't give up.

In preaching this message to you today I am not mouthing armchair philosophy. I, like you perhaps, have seen times when I was so discouraged that I could hardly hold up my head. Many were the times when it would have been easy to give up and forget about my goals, dreams, and hope for the future. But somehow I was always able to be reinspired; I found the strength to begin again; I was able to hold onto a glimmer of hope.

Martin Luther King Jr. continues in that selection I quoted from earlier by saying, "Faith in the dawn arises from the faith that God is good and just. . . . Even the most starless midnight may herald the dawn of some great fulfillment." You have also heard it said that "the darkest hour is just before the dawn."

"About midnight Paul and Silas . . . were singing hymns," the Scripture says (Acts 16:25). What a concept! Singing in the dark. At midnight. In a prison cell. With feet bound securely in stocks. With backs wounded from flogging.

"I sang and danced [in the dark] all night long, from about 6:30 P.M. to dawn," Karen Hartley said. What imagination, creativity, and ingenuity! When life throws you into the dark, don't give up. Keep faith in God, pray, put forth your best effort, make your own light! In other words, be creative: be willing to sing and dance in the dark.—Randy Hammer

SUNDAY, MARCH 12, 2000
Lectionary Message

Topic: Once for All, for Us
TEXT: 1 Pet. 3:18–22
Other Readings: Gen. 9:8–17; Ps. 25:1–10; Mark 1:9–15

Today is the first Sunday of Lent, the season of forty days leading up to Palm Sunday, also known as Passion Sunday. The forty days refer to the forty days Jesus spent in the wilderness after his baptism and the forty years the Israelites spent wandering in the desert. Lent is to be the time in which Christians remember and reflect on Jesus' journey to the cross. Traditionally, it is also a time to reflect on our own lives and faith, to practice spiritual disciplines such as fasting, and to renew our baptismal covenant as disciples.

Lent is a time to consider what we need to release, which is another image of repentance. In the phrase from a *Godspell* song, it is, "Turn back, O man, forswear thy foolish ways." And we all have them—foolish ways that need a good looking over. The questions about release are, What do we need to let go? What has a hold on us to the degree that it keeps us from a daily awareness of the love and grace of God?

I. Peter tells us that Jesus was put to death in the body but made alive in the Spirit; thus it is through the Risen Christ that we are brought to God. We are brought with all our shortcomings, all our greed, all our envy, every negative thing we ever thought or did. Peter asserts that our act of baptism is our first appeal to God for a good conscience.

The word *conscience* is an interesting one in its original meaning. It means what we know in our bones. Our conscience is what we really know about ourselves, regardless of what we hope other people think of us. It is possible to hide from our conscience. We can hide in addictions, we can hide in busyness, we can hide in good works. Preachers are particularly good at this part!

One of the traditional themes of Lent is confession and there is one place where what the church has called confession is practiced religiously. That place is in twelve-step recovery programs, which have been growing by leaps and bounds over the last fifteen years. The fourth step in the recovery process that began with Alcoholics Anonymous but is now used for any number of problems is, "Make a fearless and searching moral inventory." Now there is a scary phrase. But the recovery programs are teaching responsibility—moral responsibility. And I have to ask whether that is one reason they are growing. That making an inventory of our behavior is something we know we should do and the recovery program gives a structure and support for doing so.

II. Even if we are not familiar with the practice of confession in our private prayer, even if we fear the idea of making an inventory of our Christian life, the text in First Peter reminds us of the basic assurance that every Christian has. That is that Jesus suffered for sins, once for all. Jesus paid the price for all of us. In the words of the gospel hymn, Jesus paid it all. He really did. This is why we should not fear reflection on our relationship with God or reflection on our Christian witness in the world. No matter what our favorite sins are, we will not be condemned by God. For the suffering of Jesus was to bring us to God. The crucifixion is the price that has been paid for each one of us.

One of the most common motivations for us as humans is self-interest. If we are not familiar with the practice of confession to God or examination of conscience, our first question is, What's the advantage of such reflection? How does it help our faith and our witness?

III. The reason we examine our conscience is so that whenever non-Christians question our motives, or when we are criticized, we are not threatened. We are not threatened because we know what is true about ourselves in our bones. We have reflected on our motivations for our words and actions. The phrase is, "a clear conscience." We are clear with ourselves.

With a clear conscience we are able to be confidently public about our Christian witness. We are able to follow verse 15 and make a defense of Christianity to anyone who demands the reason for our Christian hope. Peter instructs us to do this with gentleness and reverence. And when our conscience is clear, we are at peace with ourselves, so we can respond to confrontation and criticism with gentleness and reverence. This Christian way of being and relating is described in other familiar verses: "A soft answer turneth away wrath." "Turn the other cheek." In the *Peanuts* version, Snoopy says, "A kiss on the nose does much to dispel anger."

To follow this path during the season of Lent means that we spend some time in prayer reflecting on our lives as Christians. It means that if that reflection reveals some shortcoming to us, then we confess that to God. We need not fear the examination of conscience nor confession, because Jesus has already paid it all. Jesus has done that once for all, for each one of us. So reflection and confession are not supposed to be beating ourselves over the head with guilt or shame. They are our ways of recommitting our lives to Christ each year during Lent. It means that "in our hearts we sanctify Christ as Lord," in Peter's words. We renew our Christian pledge that Jesus Christ is the most sacred and holy person in our lives.—Mary Zimmer

ILLUSTRATIONS

INVITATION.   From childhood you have heard the gospel preached, are confirmed, and go to church. Very well. But are you also quite so sure that you have accepted it? Christian baptism proves nothing other than that you were once bidden to the feast. It does not prove that you are following up the invitation. Your churchgoing, your Bible reading, your prayers—all that is very well; but even that does not show that you have really accepted the invitation. The Jews, too, read their Bible, went to the synagogue, and prayed. And yet most of them did not belong to the small number of those who accepted the invitation. The inviting is God's concern: it is the word of God's unfathomable and infinite grace going out to all and

promising to all eternal life—the greatest thing that a man can hope for. But the appropria-
tion of that message is our concern, the opening of the door, for God does not deny us the
freedom of coming to Him.—Emil Brunner[4]

FULFILLMENT.   In John Marquand's novel *Point of No Return,* for instance, after years of
apple-polishing and bucking for promotion and dedicating all his energies to a single goal,
Charlie Gray finally gets to be vice-president of the fancy little New York bank where he works;
and then the terrible moment comes when he realizes that it is really not what he wanted after
all, when the prize that he has spent his life trying to win suddenly turns to ashes in his hands.
His promotion assures him and his family all of the security and standing that he has always
sought, but Marquand leaves you with the feeling that maybe the best way Charlie Gray could
have supported his family would have been by giving his life to the kind of work where he
could have expressed himself and fulfilled himself in such a way as to become in himself, as
a person, the kind of support they really needed.—Frederick Buechner[5]

SERMON SUGGESTIONS

Topic: New Life for You
TEXT: John 3:7
You must be born again. (1) To see the Kingdom of God (John 3:3). (2) To enter the King-
dom of God (John 3:5). (3) To understand spiritual things (John 3:6).—Lloyd M. Perry and
Faris D. Whitesell[6]

Topic: All Things New
TEXT: Rev. 21:1, 5
(1) The life to come is a life of vision: "We shall see him." (2) The life to come is a life of service: "His servants shall serve him" (Rev. 22:3). (3) The life hereafter is a life lived in love.—
Elam Davies[7]

CONGREGATIONAL MUSIC

1. "Lord, to You My Soul Is Lifted," vers. Stanley Wiersma (1980)
    GENEVAN 25, Louis Bourgeosis (1551)
    The Psalter reading (Psalm 25) for this Sunday could well be sung in the stanzas of this
modern paraphrase. Antiphonal singing line by line between choir and congregation would
be feasible and effective.
2. "My Song Is Love Unknown," Samuel Crossman (1664)
    LOVE UNKNOWN, John Ireland (1918)
    This lovely hymn captures the thought of 1 Peter 3:18 and makes a moving personal
response in the hearts of singers who sincerely appropriate its message to themselves.

---

[4] *The Great Invitation*
[5] *The Hungering Dark* (New York: Seabury Press, 1981).
[6] *Variety in Your Preaching*
[7] *This Side of Eden*

3. "You Are Our Lord, We Are Your People," David A. Hoekema (1978)

JANNA, David Hoekema (1978)

This contemporary hymn tells the biblical story of the flood (Genesis 9) and ends each stanza with the powerful covenant theme "I am your God; you are my people." It would be suitable for singing following the Old Testament reading.

4. "O Love, How Deep, How Broad, How High," attr. Thomas à Kempis; tr. Benjamin Webb (1851)

DEO GRACIAS, English ballad (c. 1415)

Particularly the first three stanzas of this excellent hymn form an appropriate devotional response to the Gospel account of Jesus' baptism, temptation, and ministry in Galilee.—Hugh T. McElrath

WORSHIP AIDS

CALL TO WORSHIP.   "For we do not have a high priest who is unable to sympathize with our weaknesses, but we have one who has been tempted in every way, just as we are—yet was without sin. Let us then approach the throne of grace with confidence, so that we may receive mercy and find grace to help us in our time of need" (Heb. 4:15–16 NIV).

INVOCATION.   You have given us confidence, O God, to come to you with our deep need, especially our need for forgiveness. We thank you for a Savior who sympathizes with us, who makes our forgiveness possible, and who has set us an example of obedience. As we receive your forgiveness, strengthen us against the time of temptation, and let our worship open our hearts to your mercy and grace.

OFFERTORY SENTENCE.   "But just as you excel in everything—in faith, in speech, in knowledge, in complete earnestness and in your love for us—see that you also excel in this grace of giving" (2 Cor. 8:7 NIV).

OFFERTORY PRAYER.   We confess, our Father, that sometimes our giving is the last important problem to solve in our life of faith. Help us to grow in the grace of giving as we grow in all other graces.

PRAYER.   God for the seasons, we come to you, acknowledging that you are a God known to us in change, even as you remain constant in your continuous presence. As the world moves from winter to spring, so also do you move in your continuous recreation of the universe. Life moves from its dormancy and new growth springs from the earth.

We are aware in this holy season that the miracle of new life is revealed in the person of Your Son, Jesus Christ. Easter is for us the continual hope that the old may become new, the tired refreshed, and the dead resurrected. Indeed, all of creation rejoices as you call the dead to life.

Thank you, O Lord, for a world that is about to flower and bring forth bright colors, fresh perfumes, and the sound of spring birds. All creation is in harmony with your plan of resurrection. We rejoice that your Son is the forerunner of this new experience and that he has invited each of us to follow him.

May the dawn of this new season fill our eyes with visions of what may blossom forth for all of life. Give us expectant hearts, discerning minds, listening ears, and loving hearts, as we wait to greet the Risen Christ, the very Savior who has made us new. In his name we pray.—Robert F. Langwig

SERMON
Topic: Honoring the Earth and Its Maker
Text: Ps. 104:24–34

Never far from biblical thought is praise for God and for the works of God's hands. We learn of it in the opening pages of Genesis; we hear repeated refrains of praise in the Psalms; we listen as Jesus speaks about the lilies of the field in all their glory and the birds of the air cared for by God. "O Lord, how manifold are your works! In wisdom you have made them all." Our biblical heritage and personal experience confirm for us the preciousness of nature linked with the majesty of God.

We are not alone in this understanding. If anything, others have surpassed us in honoring the earth and its maker. Others have perceived better than we the interrelationships of life, Earth, and spiritual reality. I refer to the convictions of Native Americans, convictions sadly ignored or overrun as this nation began to be settled by English and European immigrants.

We could say that Indians have possessed an ethical regard for nature and then expressed a stewardship of resources that subsequent citizens are yet challenged to match. We who stand in the Judeo-Christian tradition have our biblical basis for appreciating and acting on these very things. Blessed are we if we do them!

I. *The delights of Earth.* Never to be forgotten in all of this is faith's affirmation that God is Creator of all. The end results of the divine creative process were called "good." According to Genesis, "God saw everything that he had made, and indeed, it was very good." Being indifferent to the whole of God's creation represents a misreading of our biblical heritage and leads, sadly, to the abuse of our environment. Only in recent years have people awakened to the fact that the resources for sustaining life and the world are in shrinking supply. Doing nothing to safeguard Earth's gifts in the face of such knowledge amounts to irresponsible behavior before God—for God loves this creation and intends for it to be treated with respect.

We consume for gratification, hardly in the context of God's presence and reality. It was Gandhi who observed, "The Earth will always have enough for man's need but not for his greed." Unless our ongoing overreach of earth's resources is controlled, the human race will expel itself from a new Eden and we shall be lost, indeed.

II. *The self-expression of God.* Nature, for the indigenous peoples of this continent, testified to the handiwork of God. For us today, the same is true. Also real for us is the human face of God. Nature shows us God's handiwork; Jesus Christ reveals God's self-expression. Our relationship to the world becomes personal because we know the person behind it—the one who not only stands as Creator but also is Lord and Savior. It is in conscious alignment of our lives with the life of Christ that we most fully honor the Earth and its maker. It is in reverencing Christ that harmony is known, harmony with our environment as well as with the social order. Yes, it is right to see how nature points us to the handiwork of God; our experience then becomes complete as we look upon the human face of God, that face seen in Jesus Christ: all things come together in him. So it is that we declare with the psalmist, "I will sing to the Lord as long as I live; I will sing praise to my God while I have being."—John H. Townsend

SUNDAY, MARCH 19, 2000
Lectionary Message

Topic: Taking Up a Cross
TEXT: Mark 8: 31–38
Other Readings: Gen. 22:1–14; Ps. 16; Rom. 8:31–39

This text is not one most of us want to read or hear. We tend to hear the phrases "deny your-self" and "take up your cross" with resistance. The most common response must be, "Oh, mercy, Lord, isn't my daily life enough self-denial. I work so hard taking care of my family. I am devoted to my spouse and parents and children. I try to be the best person I know how to be. What more can I do?"

The writer of this Gospel emphasizes that Jesus has come to Earth to bring the good news of the Kingdom of God to all of us. But this good news is not a simple celebration. It is not like a bundle of bright helium balloons celebrating some occasion. How can anything called good news include the suffering Jesus indicates?

Imagine that you are in the circle of disciples around Jesus who hear him say, "I must undergo great suffering." Would your first reaction be confusion? "What can he possibly mean?" Some of us might feel irritated that the teacher who has been so close is now saying such harsh words.

I. This great suffering is not a choice for him or them, according to Mark. And Jesus will be rejected by the elders, chief priests, and scribes. Jesus then tells the disciples he will be killed and after three days rise again. "He said all this quite openly" is an interesting editor-ial comment. Jesus is not soft-pedaling this lesson. He is blunt, perhaps as a way of getting our attention.

Peter, bless his honest heart, is always the disciple who reacts. He always jumps in, open-ing his mouth before his brain is in gear. The word *rebuke* is a hard one; it sounds harsh and it means "to beat back." This news is too terrible. Peter only wants Jesus to "say it isn't so"— just what any of us wants when we hear news of the suffering of one we care about.

And Jesus' response is very hard to bear. Who is this teacher who speaks so meanly to his friend, even to the point of calling him Satan. I don't know about you but I think it took a lot of courage on Peter's part to stay put. Surely he must have wanted just to stalk off. This is a fierce exchange; their voices must have been raised and tense, the air around them full of the electricity of anger.

The problem is not that Peter disagrees with Jesus. The problem is that Peter is still stuck in the Old Testament theology of Messiah, one who was to come in glory. He does not under-stand God's true plan for redemption of the world. He wants it to be too easy.

Jesus' response to Peter seems almost cruel. Perhaps he himself is scared or terribly irri-tated with his disciples' refusal to face his truth: the truth that suffering is a part of the life of a Christian, that being the very best person we know to be and doing everything right that we know to do will not get us an insurance policy against suffering.

II. In the next few verses Jesus describes what true Christian discipleship is about. There is a cost; it is not supposed to be easy. The caution for us today on the phrase "deny themselves" is that it does not mean martyrdom, as early Christians believed. There is a legend abut one young man named Origen. In his religious fervor he intended to follow his father out into the street where Roman soldiers were murdering Christians. He wanted to be martyred. According to the legend, his mother hid all his clothes and he was too embarrassed to go out in public without them so he did not martyr himself. That's a mom for you. And Origen went on to write classics of Christian devotional prayer.

Denying self means the basic attitude of unselfishness. Denying self means that we are not on the throne of our lives. It means that the way of Christ is the way of our lives. It does not mean we give up our own life to the suffering that happens to us. We are not to abandon ourselves so that our whole life becomes suffering.

The issue for martyrs is where does the cross that is taken up come from? Is it truly a cross or burden that, through much prayer, we believe God in Christ has given us to bear? Or is it a cross of our own making? Or even worse, a cross that someone else has built for us? There are lots of folks walking around today who are carrying crosses that belong to someone else. That is not what this passage means.

III. In verse 35, Jesus describes the difference between a true disciple and one who is not. If we are focused on self-preservation and all our waking efforts are geared toward ensuring that our lives go on just as they are, then we are attempting to save our own lives, and we will lose out on the life of a disciple.

What can we give in return for the gift of our life from God? There is not anything, except living our lives as disciples of Christ. That is how we lose our life for Christ's sake and the sake of the gospel. We spend our life following the commandments of Jesus.

For a Roman execution, the prisoner was to carry part of his cross. Jesus is saying that we do have to carry for a while the suffering that comes to us. We do have to bear it up and shoulder the burden of our suffering. When we do that, we are on the road to Golgotha with Jesus. And Jesus bears the cross with us. Jesus knows the worst—death on a cross, condemnation as a common criminal after a ministry of healing. Thus the presence of the Risen Christ is with us in our suffering.

By his suffering, the presence of the Risen Christ through the Holy Spirit is with us each day, each hour of our own suffering. In the middle of the most terrible suffering we know, Jesus stands with us, holding out his love to us, telling us, "I will bear this with you. Let me help you carry this cross."—Mary Zimmer

ILLUSTRATIONS

BEYOND CAMELOT.   The ministry of the historical Jesus is over; now begins the ministry of the glorified and ascended Christ. Mary Magdalene cannot resume the old relationship with her Lord, for Christ now relates to his followers by giving them the Paraclete, the Spirit. Therefore Jesus says to her, "Do not hold me" (v. 17). She and the disciples and the Church today are not to long for the way it was, as though that time were a brief Camelot. Rather they, and we, are to believe His Word: it is best for you that I go away; if I do not go away, the Spirit will not come; the Spirit will remain with you forever; greater works than I have done, you will do because I go to my Father—Fred B. Craddock[8]

---

[8] John

A COLONY OF HEAVEN.   You do not need to wait "until the day break and the shadows flee away" before beginning to live eternally. In union with Christ, that glorious privilege is yours here and now. Risen with Him, you have passed out of relation to sin, out of the hampering limitations of this present order, out of the domain of the world and the flesh, into the realm of the Spirit, and into life that is life indeed. In short, even here on the earth you are "a colony of heaven." Never forget where your citizenship lies! "Reckon yourselves alive unto God through Jesus Christ our Lord."—James S. Stewart[9]

THE RISK OF LOVE.   Christians are called to a life of service. They are called to take up their cross and follow Jesus. Christian discipleship is always costly. It is a life of self-giving love. The risk of love for the sake of God's new community breaks the spell of narcissism that holds many people captive in our time. Narcissism is inordinate self-love. According to Greek legend, Narcissus fell in love with himself when he saw his reflection in a pool of water. Captivated by his own image, he refused to move for fear of losing his beloved. The myth of Narcissus describes one form of the human condition called sin. As sinners we are inclined to excessive self-love. We become preoccupied with ourselves or with those very much like ourselves.—Daniel L. Migliore[10]

GIVING AND KEEPING.   It is wonderful to believe enough in God and in the possibility of man so that one gladly gives all to help others. A man who lost heavily in the depression had been a generous giver to his church. A friend one day said to him, "Aren't you sorry you gave so much to that church?" After a pause, the churchman said, "All I've got is what I gave there."—Ralph E. Knudsen[11]

SERMON SUGGESTIONS

Topic: The Lord's Controversy
TEXT: Micah 6:1–8
Micah begins this remarkable speech in language that would have immediately conjured up in the minds of his audience a courtroom setting. The court is concluded by the word's of God's counsel. It has nothing to do with sacrifice and offering. (1) Do justice. (2) Love kindness. (3) Walk humbly with your God. At first it does not sound like much, but it is more than enough for one lifetime.—Peter C. Craigie[12]

Topic: Builders and Building
TEXT: Matt. 5:24–27
(1) All of us are building. (2) All builders have a choice of foundations. (3) All foundations will be tried. (4) Only one foundation will stand.—Joseph Parker

CONGREGATIONAL MUSIC
1. "Faith of Our Fathers," Frederick W. Faber (1849)
    ST. CATHERINE, Henry F. Hemy (1874)

---

[9] *A Man in Christ*
[10] *The Power of God*
[11] In G. Paul Butler (ed.), *Best Sermons* (New York: Trident Press, 1968).
[12] *Twelve Prophets*, Vol. 2

The faith of Abraham, the father of the faithful (Rom. 4:13–25), along with that of others among our forebears, can be celebrated in the singing of this familiar hymn.

2. "The Lord Our God in Mercy Spoke," Issac Watts (1707)

DUNDEE, Scottish Psalter (1615)

This little-known hymn by Watts, the great liberator of English hymnody, is based on God's promise to make Abraham the father of many nations (Gen. 17). It is a baptismal hymn but could be suitable for general worship with the omission of stanza 2.

3. "The Ends of All the Earth Shall Hear," vers. Psalter (1912)

VISION, William H. Doane (1875)

This paraphrase of the final verses of Psalm 22 is set to a gospel tune with its refrain, "All earth to him her homage brings, the Lord of Lord, the King of Kings" (Ps. 22:27). This refrain would be effective sung as an antiphon interspersed among the verses of the Psalter reading.

4. "Take Up Thy Cross," Charles W. Everest (1833)

GERMANY, William Gardiner's *Sacred Melodies* (1815)

Based on Jesus' summons (Mark 8:34) to deny self, take up the cross, and follow him, this rousing hymn would be a natural response to the Gospel lesson.—Hugh T. McElrath

WORSHIP AIDS

CALL TO WORSHIP.   "All the ends of the world shall remember and turn unto the Lord: and all the kindreds of the nations shall worship before thee. For the Kingdom is the Lord's: and he is the governor among the nations" (Ps. 22:27–28).

INVOCATION.   O God of the universe, we take heart knowing that all things and persons are in your hands. Deepen that faith as we worship together today.

OFFERTORY SENTENCE.   "None of us lives for himself only, none of us dies for himself only. If we live, it is for the Lord that we live, and if we die, it is for the Lord that we die. So whether we live or die, we belong to the Lord" (Rom. 14:7–8 TEV).

OFFERTORY PRAYER.   We thank you, Lord, that we can say that we belong to you. Make our lives and what we have useful in your service and for your glory.

PRAYER.   God of the unfolding universe, we see new revelations of you each new day. As the meaning of your word in Jesus Christ unfolds upon our journey to Easter, so also does the meaning of creation begin to come together. You are now revealing to us that the world is yours and that our journey, our pilgrimage through life, involves our returning creation to you as stewards of your gifts to us. Indeed, "the earth is the Lord's and the fullness thereof." "We give you but your own."

We thank You, O God, for the mysteries of life. In our Lenten pilgrimage we have learned that there is blessing to suffering, that joy may be found in dying, when life is placed in your hands, and that kingships often mean becoming the servant of all. Life is filled with juxtapositions and as we commend ourselves to you in servant love, all things work together for good.

Help us throughout this Holy Season to continue to hear your still, small voice speaking words of eternal life. Lead us onto the faithful pathways on which your Son walked, so that we, too, might know the joy of your nearness and reflect the brilliance of the eternal light of your presence. Let us, dear Lord, be a part of your faithful family, as your Kingdom continues to come on earth as it is in heaven.

We offer our prayer in Jesus' Name.—Robert F. Lanwig

SERMON
Topic: How Strong Is Our Faith?
TEXT: Gen. 12:1–3

Abraham was called of the Lord to an unknown land. He picked up his belongings, livestock, and servants and was joined by Lot, his nephew, who also brought his belongings to go to Canaan. When they viewed this newfound land and arrived at Shechem "by the oak of Moreh," Abraham built an altar to the Lord. What did he pray at this worship center? We are not told, but being obedient to the Lord he expressed gratitude for the promise "to your offspring I will give this land." The faith of Abraham experienced renewed hope. He was doing what he understood by "the Lord said."

When the caravan was eventually led to Egypt, away from the drought in the Negeb, the journey westward seemed to have resolved the dread of a dry and barren land where livestock and people would surely suffer and even die. Egypt seemed to be the answer, until Pharoah was afflicted with plagues because of Sarai, whom Abraham had presented as his sister and not as his wife. When Pharoah discovered this he was outraged. "And Pharoah gave his men orders concerning him and they set him on the way, with his wife and all that he had." This experience no doubt jolted the plans of Abraham, but he put himself on course by going back to where he had established an altar to the Lord at Bethel. Here Abraham did what we so often must do to find our directions from God. Abraham could easily have been detoured from following "the leading of the Lord." His unwavering faith kept him on track because he returned to the altars that he had erected for worship.

We treasure reading about the faith journey of believers in the Bible. The accounts of their ability to overcome obstacles are models for us today. Faith in God has been defined very clearly in Hebrews 11:1: "Now faith is the assurance of things hoped for, the conviction of things not seen" (RSV). The TEV translation states, "To have faith is to be sure of the things we hope for, to be certain of the things we cannot see." As we follow the journey of Abraham through the rest of his life, he seemed to live as though he was "certain of the things we cannot see." He returned to the altar repeatedly, just as we do to find clarity about what we believe is God's leading. Just as we can view the total experiences of Abraham, so it is possible later in our journey on Earth to see God's unique guidance through trying and sorrowful experiences. We cannot live without faith. We reflect on the past, which we may know, and on the present, which we can see, but when we come to the future and its possibilities, we must exercise our total capacity of faith to journey on with confidence.

The early Christians moved through great adversities. But God spoke to them through those who were unwavering in their faith. Paul the apostle wrote to the Christians, "Christ opens all the hidden treasures of God's wisdom and knowledge." "Since you have accepted Christ Jesus as Lord, live in union with him. Keep your roots deep in him. Build your lives on him and become ever stronger in your faith" (Col. 2:3, 6, 7 TEV). There are times when God seems far away. It is then that our trip back to the altar can rekindle the faith we need to journey on.

A very cherished older pastor and former seminary professor once told about his terrible struggle with depression. He described the inability to pray with meaning. What helped him return to a meaningful faith was praying many of the Psalms. He told how Psalm 77, verses 1 to 10, described his own agony, especially the words, "Then I said, 'What hurts me most is this—that God is no longer powerful'" (TEV). He said that at this point he could easily have become suicidal had he not read on in that same Psalm, verses 11 to 20. Thank God, he was restored to being able to preach until well into his eighties and departed from this life in his nineties, leaving a testimony of a triumphant faith.

Experiences in life present many meaningful illustrations of how our keeping in touch with God is so essential. My brother was a master at making large kites. In the 1930s, the drought in the Dakotas was accompanied by steady winds. We flew this kite high in the sky. We added more and more sturdy cord, helping it go higher and higher. The neighbors on the twelve-party phone line called to find out what was in the sky. It was not a plane as some thought. It was just a kite. Why did that kite stay up there day and night? It was anchored by the rock to which it was fastened and the power of the wind kept it flying. Faith is like that. As long as our faith is anchored in God and as long as the Spirit of God flows through our life, our faith will remain strong, dynamic, secure, and sure.—Gideon K. Zimmerman

SUNDAY, MARCH 26, 2000
Lectionary Message
Topic: Spring Cleaning at the Temple
TEXT: John 2:13–22
Other Readings: Exod. 20:1–17; Ps. 19; Rom. 7:13–25

Have you ever been around when someone got the cleaning bug and went on a spring cleaning spree? Jesus went on a cleaning spree that day in the Temple. It was Passover time, the Jewish holiday that recognized the passing over of the angel of death in Egypt. Jewish pilgrims came from all over to go to the great Temple in Jerusalem and thank God for their people's deliverance from slavery.

But something has happened at the Temple. In a time of Roman oppression, the religious leadership has been corrupted by commerce. The Jewish peasants who came to make their religious observance found that money changers had moved right into the court of the Temple. Not only that, they were disobeying the spirit of the Law, which forbade price-gouging. To buy animals for their Passover sacrifice, the people had to convert their own currency into the local coin and they were cheated by the money changers' high rates.

Churches would have real budget problems if we charged service fees to handle your budget pledges and offerings. We'd be functioning like any bank. But that is the equivalent of what was going on in the Temple. It was a desecration; the sacredness of the Temple's purpose for the people was violated.

I. Instead of a place where Jewish pilgrims from several nations could gather together to praise and thank Yahweh, the courtyard smelled like a barnyard. Underneath the bleating of sheep and cattle noises you could hear the doves cooing in their cages. At low tables sat the money changers. The clink, clink of heavy coins was constant. And irritated, impatient voices were raised in arguments over the rates of exchange. The Temple courtyard was full of intense, busy people trying to get the best deal on an animal for the year's Passover offering. Even the most righteous Jews would have trouble praying in this place.

And onto the scene came Jesus, brandishing a whip made from rope. Snapping it over his head he drove the animals and their keepers out of the courtyard. Almost in a frenzy, he dumped out the moneychangers' sacks. All their profits rolled into a heap on the floor. They would never get sorted out from that mess exactly what belonged to them. Jesus overturned their tables and got to the back corner where the cages of doves were. He ordered their keepers out of the Temple and yelled in an angry tone, "Stop making my Father's house a marketplace!"

II. If this stranger was going to act like a prophet, the people wanted proof of his worthiness as prophet. "Give us a sign," they said. And the response they got seemed completely preposterous. Their leaders had been collecting money and working on this building program for forty-six years. What kind of arrogant braggart was this who claimed to be able to raise up the Jerusalem Temple in only three days?

But Jesus did not mean the actual building. He referred to the Temple as the place of the worship of the one true God, and they had just about destroyed their covenant with Yahweh one more time. The situation was this: the Temple priests needed money and they found a way to get it. But their way was a horrible compromise of the principles of their own faith. Everyone who came for Passover quickly learned what the unwritten rules were. Even the poorest peasant would be cheated by the money changers; there was no justice in this Temple for the downtrodden. It was a desecration that everyone gave into, because that's just the way things were. They were all going along to get along, until Jesus showed up that day.

III. Who or what are the moneychangers in your life? What cheats you out of the time you need to spend in personal devotion to God or in reflection on just where your life in Christ is going these days? What needs to be cleaned out of your life because it is taking up too much time and space? It may be as simple as a couple of sitcoms or one evening on the Internet. What has set up tables in your life and is making so much noise that you cannot hear the still, small voice of God?

There may be some anger, you know. Sometimes it does take a little anger to make important changes and sometimes our changes make other people angry. If everyone in your family assumes you will say yes to any request, a no may bring a flare of anger. The attempt to carve time out of our day for spiritual sustenance and renewal may reveal how angry we are about what robs us of personal time and energy.

Sometimes it is a matter of learning to do our reflection and prayer while we are doing something else. A daily walk is a good time to consider what we need to release and to share time with God, to be cleaned out so that we feel connected to God each day, so that the marketplace doesn't take over our lives and separate us from the source of life and love, grace and mercy and peace.

Each day's time and energy are precious—as precious as a Temple that took more than forty-six years to build. Cleaning out the money changers that rob us of time with God is one of the tasks of the season of Lent. This week I invite you to consider how you spend your time. What needs to be cleaned out so that you feel connected to God each day? How do you leave the marketplace behind so it doesn't take over your life and separate you from the source of life and love, grace and mercy and peace?—Mary Zimmer.

ILLUSTRATIONS

LIMITATIONS.   One of the lessons of middle age for me was learning about limits. There were all kinds of limits, but the hardest to accept were the limits of time and energy. My reflections were the revelation that God wasn't going to give me more hours in the day to accomplish the long list of things I thought had to be done. There was definitely a new limit on my energy in middle age. I really can't concentrate on anything abstract after about 9 P.M. It's as if my brain has notified me it is on vacation and waved farewell.—Mary Zimmer

THE SEEKING STRANGER.   Is there anything in our church life—a snobbishness, an exclusiveness, a coldness, a lack of welcome, a tendency to make the congregation into a closed club, an arrogance, a fastidiousness—which keeps the seeking stranger out? Let us remember the wrath of Jesus against those who made it difficult and even impossible for the seeking stranger to make contact with God.—William Barclay[13]

SERMON SUGGESTIONS

Topic: When You Meet God
TEXT: Exod. 3:1–7
Have you ever stopped to consider what you might do if suddenly you met God? (1) Up to this time in the text, Jehovah God had made little difference in the life of Moses. (a) Moses learned about many gods in the pagan atmosphere in which he was reared. (b) Moses had also heard about the Lord God from his own mother. (c) Yet Moses' knowledge about God had made no real difference in his life. (2) The Lord God came to make a tremendous difference in Moses' life. (a) God spoke personally to Moses. (b) God cleansed Moses of his sins. (c) God laid claim to Moses' life. (3) How the Lord God became Moses' own personal God: (a) We must face it—some people meet God in a manner quite different from the way God met Moses; in fact, most of us do. (b) Moses came to know the living God with an abruptness that shocks us. (c) In any case, God in his grace and love is infinitely resourceful.

Topic: The Ministry of Tears
TEXT: Rev. 7:17
(1) It is the ministry of tears to keep this world from being too attractive. (2) It is the ministry of trouble to make us feel our complete dependence on God. (3) It is the ministry of tears to capacitate us for the office of sympathy.—T. DeWitt Talmage[14]

CONGREGATIONAL MUSIC
1. "The Spacious Firmament on High," Joseph Addison (1789)
   CREATION, Franz Joseph Haydn (1798)
   This classic hymn is the most familiar of several based on Psalm 19. None could be better for the opening of worship on this day.
2. "My Soul, Recall with Reverent Wonder," vers. Dewey Westra, Psalter Hymnal (1987)
   LES COMMANDEMENS, Genevan Psalter (1547)

---

[13] *The Gospel of John*, Vol. 1
[14] *The Brooklyn Tabernacle*

Since the sixteenth century this has been the tune traditionally sung to metrical versions of the Ten Commandments. The choir and congregation could sing together the first and final stanzas, then alternate in singing the internal stanzas.

3. "We Sing the Praise of Him Who Died," Thomas Kelly (1815)

BRESLAU, Lochamer Gesangbuch (fifteenth century)

The apostle Paul's eloquent statement contrasting the wisdom of God in the Word of the cross with the foolishness of the world is echoed by this passion hymn. Its singing could either introduce or follow the reading of the Epistle lesson.

4. "Strong, Righteous Man of Galilee," Harry Webb Farrington (1921)

MELITA, John Bacchus Dykes (1861)

Here is a hymn that celebrates, among other qualities, the righteous strength of the Jesus who cleansed the Temple at the Passover season. It would be appropriate for use in connection with the Gospel lesson or at any other point in a Lenten worship service.—Hugh T. McElrath

WORSHIP AIDS

CALL TO WORSHIP. "The judgments of the Lord are true and righteous altogether. More to be desired are they than gold: sweeter also than honey and the honeycomb" (Ps. 19:10b–11).

INVOCATION. Knowing that you are fair and just in all your dealings with us, even when clouds overtake us and darkness falls, we come to you again for your reassuring word and your guiding light for our daily needs. So hear us, O God, as we lift our voices in song and prayer, and open our hearts and minds in expectation.

OFFERTORY SENTENCE. "He that findeth his life shall lose it," said Jesus, "and he that loseth his life for my sake shall find it" (Matt. 10:39).

OFFERTORY PRAYER. Help us increasingly, O God, to discover what really counts toward meaning and happiness in life as we consider your will for us and the needs of all those you love and as we bring our tithes and offerings.

PRAYER. In coming now to this opportunity to pray together, we come in faith, believing that you are already turned toward us in the eternity of your love: "O love that will not let us go." You sought us out in the far country of our own willfulness, and as we turned our steps homeward we discovered you running down the road to meet us with arms outstretched in welcome and kisses for our shame. With what love you love us, that we should be your children. All that this will mean we cannot know now.

In this season, when your purpose for us and for all humankind comes into focus with burning heat and light in the Passion of Christ, we find ourselves repelled yet drawn by the compulsion of the mystery of your coming in Jesus of Nazareth. We praise you for the "Cross of Christ towering o'er the wrecks of time." May its light illuminate our every day. May we live in the hope that whatever the evils of men—no matter how twisted their ways—there is a power at work that brings order out of chaos, peace out of war, light of community out of the midnight of hatred.

We pray for our families. Where there is any brokenness of body, of mind, of spirit, we pray for the healing of your grace that alone makes whole. Let us walk as children of the light through all the valleys of the shadow that we encounter.—John Thompson

SERMON
Topic: Speaking of Jesus
TEXT: John 4:5–42

I. She's come down to us through the ages as a puzzling figure, the Samaritan woman at the well. Hers is the longest conversation with Jesus recorded in the New Testament. Yet we don't even know her name. After Jesus leaves her town, we never hear of her again.

She didn't come to Jesus seeking him out. She wasn't blind or lame or looking to be healed. She wasn't in the pits of despair. She met Jesus in the course of her daily chores, not looking to be changed, not really aware of how much better her life could be.

Hers is not the only way that people have encountered the Master. Some have been blinded by a flash of light. Some have been miraculously healed. But for all who have wondered "How do I meet Jesus?" she offers hope and inspiration, because her encounter with Jesus was similar to many of ours. It's at those places where her story and our story meet that Jesus may be waiting patiently for us, as he waited for her by a well in Samaria.

The first thing we learn about Jesus' encounter with the woman is that he came to her outside of the expected places. Jesus was coming from a place where people expected to encounter God. He had been in Jerusalem, the center of religious learning, the site of the Temple. In Jerusalem, Jesus spent time with people who knew their religion, who had the education and the time to study the Scriptures and their promises that God was going to send a savior into the world. But people in Jerusalem didn't understand Jesus. What he had to say to them went right over their heads. Jesus had talked with people like Nicodemus about being born again, and they thought he was telling them to reenter their mothers' wombs.

So Jesus went back to his home in Galilee, but to get there he passed through Samaria. Samaria was a place that good religious people tried to avoid. Even though it was the most direct route from Judah to Galilee, many people made a big detour so they wouldn't have to go through it, the way many of us will take a longer route through the city to avoid going through what is considered a bad neighborhood. Samaritans were a mixed race, which offended those who put a lot of stock in racial purity. They practiced a perverse form of Judaism. Respectable people wouldn't have anything to do with them.

That's why the woman of Samaria was shocked when Jesus spoke to her. Yet it was she, a Samaritan woman and not the learned professor Nicodemus, who understood Jesus for who he was. It was she, not those of rank and standing, whose life was changed by the Lord. She was not the one you would expect to be changed by Jesus, and it happened in a place you wouldn't expect it to happen.

II. We also encounter Jesus at the unexpected places in our lives, those places that are vulnerable and that we try to protect. Look at Jesus' conversation with the woman at the well. At first it's as if they're talking on two different planes. Jesus is talking about living water that gives eternal life, and the woman thinks he's talking about putting a spigot in her house so she would never have to walk to the well to draw water. How many times have we heard Jesus' words and completely misunderstood what he was talking about?

But then something happened that made Jesus' words connect with the woman. He asked her to go get her husband. She replied that she had no husband. "You are right," said Jesus, "for you have had five husbands and the one you have now is not your husband."

We want to know more. This sounds like the kind of story that *The National Enquirer* would pay good money for. But Jesus didn't say any more than that. He didn't lecture her on her morals. He had made his point to her—he knew her, inside and out, better than she knew herself. And that was the catalyst to her faith—when she realized that Jesus knew her.

All of us long to be known. There's something about being known by another person that validates us. It makes us feel significant and important when someone else takes an interest in what we think and how we feel and what we do. Yet, at the same time we're terrified of being known, afraid that if someone does know us they will reject us, think us foolish or weak, or somehow see through us and expose us for someone we'd rather not be. There are only a few people throughout the course of a lifetime that we allow to know us really deeply—a spouse, a trusted friend, a spiritual advisor. But even those special people know us for what we reveal to them.

Jesus knows us, the good and righteous parts of us that we haven't yet recognized and the shameful parts of us that we try to hide from ourselves. And knowing us, he accepts us and loves us and calls us his own.

III. The woman at the well offers hope to those who believe but who still have questions. When she left Jesus to go back to her town, she knew she had been changed, but she wasn't sure how or even by whom. But instead of trying to figure it all out, instead of trying to make sure all her questions were answered before she said anything to anyone, she invited her friends to share her explorations. "Come and see a man who told me everything I have ever done!" she said to the people of her town. "He cannot be the Messiah, can he?" And they all went with her to find out more. She didn't offer her friends a finished product, faith nicely wrapped up and topped with a pretty bow. She invited them to come find out more with her, to explore their questions, to encounter the man and see if their lives would be changed in ways they might not completely understand.

You don't have to have all the answers before you take up your cross. You just have to trust the man who calls to you. You'll find the answers as you go along. And you'll find that the answer is Jesus.—Stephens G. Lytch

SUNDAY, APRIL 2, 2000
Lectionary Message

Topic: From Death to Life in Grace

TEXT: Eph. 2:1–10

Other Readings: Num. 21:4–9; Ps. 107:1–3; John 3:14–21

We usually understand the gospel to mean "good news." But some New Testament passages give us pause as to just how the text can be good news. Often what we consider good news seems to be juxtaposed with a teaching that doesn't seem like good news at all. Perhaps the issue is our meaning of the phrase "good news." When someone says they have good news, our connotation usually is that *good* means something like a wish or dream fulfilled or an unexpected blessing. We don't usually expect "good news" to have the words *dead, sin,* or *children of wrath* in it, as this passage in Ephesians does.

I. For the writer of Ephesians, "following the course of the world" is a kind of living death. The language in this passage seems esoteric, but the different images all point to a life that is not lived in communion with God in Christ. The conclusion is general—regardless of cultural or religious background, as "children of wrath," to put life before knowledge and faith in Christ is to be dead because it is without a sense of the presence of Christ.

Often our casual interpretation of words like *passions of our flesh* and *desires of our senses* has come to mean only physical hungers. But for the Gospel writer, these phrases are about how, as sinful human creatures, we limit our lives to what is only human; we seek nothing more than the fulfillment of our immediate impulses and put little or no effort into a life based in Christ's gospel. In that state we are at the mercy of the power of the world around us.

II. What changes this reality of our lives lived in bondage to sin are the mercy and love of God. And that mercy and love are eternal. God's mercy and love existed for us before we heard the gospel or made any response to it. That mercy and love brought the grace of salvation and new life, not just for us as individuals, but it also "made us alive together with Christ." The power of salvation is that we are no longer held in thrall by the things and power of the world; instead, we know, experience, and live a life in which the Christ of the Resurrection is alive to us every day, and we are truly alive with Christ.

This mercy and love of God are "immeasurable riches" in our lives. We cannot measure them. We cannot even imagine their limits. This is the true gospel, the real good news. The ministry, death, and Resurrection of Jesus are the witness to us of the great good gifts of the immeasurable riches of God's love and mercy toward us.

III. The first clause of verse 8 is familiar to most Christians this side of the Reformation. That even faith itself is a matter of the grace of God, that we have both salvation and faith only because of God's grace, is something that we often don't dwell on. Most "can do" Americans would rather have just a little bit to do with their own faith. We might gladly assume the responsibility if only we could get a little of the credit.

But the New Testament is adamant. Works are not ever the cause or means of salvation or faith. Both are gifts given to us out of the mercy and love of God. The Gospel writer's insistence that faith is not the result of our effort cuts through the temptation to spiritual pride and the comparison of the strength of our faith with that of another.

We have all heard the phrase "I just don't know how he keeps his faith" or "My faith got me through it" or "She has such a strong faith." The implication behind all these statements is that faith is a human achievement and some people are better at it than others.

Such an idea is exactly the opposite of the teaching. Instead, it is the gift of faith that leads us to good works. Faith is not *by* good works; it is *for* good works. Good works are the result of our wholehearted acceptance of the gifts of salvation and faith through Christ.

IV. God prepared and intended a way of life for us. We have and we can turn away from it. The lure of the world's glitter and amusement and power can be overwhelming at times. But it is not God leaving us when we feel caught up in the alienation. What we have done is refuse grace and mercy and love. Accepting such gifts of faith means that we do live as the persons God made us to be and we do live in the way of life that God has prepared. Then good works are the expression of our faith. We don't have to make ourselves be Christ's people on Earth. Filled with God's grace, mercy, and love, we can't help but be Christ's people on Earth.

That is the great news.—Mary Zimmer

ILLUSTRATIONS

QUESTIONS AND ANSWERS.   Once I heard a man say, "I spent twenty years trying to come to terms with my doubts. Then one day it dawned on me that I had better come to terms with my faith. Now I have passed from the agony of questions I cannot answer into the agony of answers I cannot escape. And it's a great relief."—David E. Roberts[1]

VERIFICATION.   Faith is an act of self-consecration in which the will, the intellect, and the affections all have their place. It is the resolve to live as if certain things are true and we shall one day find out for ourselves that they are true. The process of verification begins as soon as we have honestly set out to climb. We ourselves change, and the world changes to our sight. The landscape opens out more and more as we get farther up the hill.—W. R. Inge

SERMON SUGGESTIONS

Topic: The Bondage of Our Feelings

TEXT: Isa. 6:1-8

Is there anything we can think and do so that the prison walls of feeling won't shut us in so desolatingly? (1) There are some things we can think: (a) Feeling must not be regarded as a clue to reality. (b) If our sentiments are right, we can dismiss transient emotion as of little account—sentiment is the deep well; emotion is the surface water. (c) Religious depression is a religious experience, a "divine discontent." (d) However we feel, God is and God is love. (2) Some things we can do to escape the bondage of bad feeling: (a) Just go doggedly on. (b) If possible, do something for somebody else. (c) Give God your will, even if you can't give him any joyous feelings. The fact of God matters, not our feeling about God.—Leslie Weatherhead[2]

Topic: What God Gives in Love

TEXT: James 4:4-10

(1) It is better than our "best-laid schemes." (2) It is offered to us in spite of our unworthiness. (3) It is to be received in humility.

CONGREGATIONAL MUSIC

1. "Come, Thou Fount of Every Blessing," Robert Robinson (1758)
   NETTLETON, *Wyeth's Repository of Sacred Music Part Second* (1813)
   A familiar hymn of praise for God's grace toward us (Eph. 2:7-8), this could be an ideal congregational invocation and gathering song for corporate worship. The folk nature of its tune would make unaccompanied singing of at least one stanza meaningful and appropriate.
2. "Lift High the Cross," George W. Kitchin and Michael R. Newholt (1916)
   CRUCIFER, Sydney H. Nicholson (1916)
   Relating both to the Old Testament passage (Num. 21:49) and the Gospel lesson (John 3:14-16), this twentieth-century hymn would be suitable as an opening hymn, particularly for a processional.

---

[1] *The Grandeur and Misery of Man*
[2] *The Eternal Voice*

3. "Redeemed, How I Love to Proclaim It," Fanny J. Crosby (1882)

REDEEMED, W. J. Kirkpatrick (1882); ADA, A. L. Butler (1966)

This gospel song that picks up the theme of Psalm 107:1–2, would be effective with either of its tunes as a response to the Psalter reading. Indeed, the chorus (refrain) could be fashioned as an antiphon to be sung before, during, and after the psalm lesson.

4. "O What a Wonder It Is," Rae E. Whitney (1978)

LeDOUX, Joanne Brown-LeDoux (1986)

Inspired in its first stanza by John 3:16, this contemporary gospel song could be appropriately sung in connection with the Gospel lesson.—Hugh T. McElrath

WORSHIP AIDS

CALL TO WORSHIP.   "O give thanks unto the Lord, for he is good: for his mercy endureth forever" (Ps. 107:1).

INVOCATION.   God of grace, help us to listen so intently on all levels that we see our failures, recognize the possibilities of reform, and rededicate ourselves to Christ our Savior, who never stops caring for us.—E. Lee Phillips

OFFERTORY SENTENCE.   "My God shall supply all your needs according to his riches in glory by Christ Jesus" (Phil. 4:19).

OFFERTORY PRAYER.   Our Father, we need our daily bread, but we need the bread of heaven more. As you continue to offer us the heavenly manna, may our willingness to share the bread of Earth deepen and increase.

PRAYER.   Thou great Father of us all, we rejoice that at last we know thee. All our soul within us is glad because we need no longer cringe before thee as slaves of holy fear, seeking to appease thine anger by sacrifice and self-inflicted pain, but may come like little children, trustful and happy, to the God of love. Thou art the only true Father, and all the tender beauty of our human love is the reflected radiance of thy loving kindness, like the moonlight from the sunlight, and testifies to the eternal passion that kindled it.

Grant us growth of spiritual vision, that with the passing years we may enter into the fullness of this our faith. Since thou art our Father, may we not hide our sins from thee, but overcome them by the stern comfort of thy presence. By this knowledge uphold us in our sorrows and make us patient even amid the unsolved mysteries of the years. Reveal to us the larger goodness and love that speak through the unbending laws of thy world. Through this faith make us the willing equals of all thy other children.—Walter Rauschenbusch[3]

SERMON

Topic: The Toughest Assignment of All

TEXT: Rom. 12:18

In one of the famous Charlie Brown cartoons by Charles Schulz, Charlie amuses Linus by saying he wants to be a doctor. "That's a big laugh," Linus responds. "You could never be a

---

[3] *Prayers of the Social Awakening*

doctor. You know why? Because you don't love mankind, that's why!" And Charlie protests, "I do love mankind; it's people I can't stand!" It is relatively easy to love mankind in general. It is quite another matter to love people in particular.

It is a plain Christian duty to learn the art of personal relationships and to ensure that, as far as we are concerned, harmony is achieved with all sorts and conditions of men. Consider some practical means to this end.

I. To begin with, *we must learn to respect the essential dignity and absolute equality of every person.* "What is hell?" asks a character in a play by Jean-Paul Sartre. The answer is "Hell? This is other people." We by nature are egocentric. Consciously or unconsciously, we put ourselves in the center of the picture and glare at other people as potential rivals waiting to usurp our position and steal our thunder. They must be exploited or eliminated.

Put God in the centre of the picture and we get things in true perspective. Our fellows are not rivals but equals. All are manifestly not equal in ability, or personality, but all are equally important in the sight of God. If we want to live in serenity and unity, we must first learn to express our respect for the equality and dignity of every man by tolerance and courtesy.

II. In the second place, *we must learn to laugh with others and at ourselves.* "There is a time to laugh," says the author of Ecclesiastes. It is the time when we are making a serious attempt to get on with other people. Do not dismiss this as mere trifling with a big theme. We err greatly if we overlook the fact that laughter is one of God's richest and sunniest gifts for maintaining the harmony of society.

III. Again, *we must learn to be appreciative.* Appreciation is a grace to be cultivated.

The difficulties of other people need to be appreciated. The Old Testament records the striking testimony of Ezekiel, the prophet. Called to serve his exiled countrymen in Babylon, he tells how he gained a genuine appreciation of their plight and a real understanding of his mission and message. He put himself in the exile's place: "I sat where they sat."

The qualities in other people need also to be appreciated. The critical spirit, necessary as it is, can easily run riot and become a destructive, disintegrating force. Unlimited faultfinding provokes dislike and hostility. On the other hand, sincere appreciation generously expressed is a tonic and a unifying force.

IV. Above and beyond all else, *we must learn to love.* "Love one another with brotherly affection," says Paul in this chapter. But that raises a question: Can we learn to love? Not if you think of love in a natural sense: the love of husband for wife, parent for child, friend for friend. Such love cannot be commanded. The thing to grasp is the supernatural nature of Christian love. When it broke upon the world it was so new, so completely new, that a Greek noun had to be coined to describe it: *agape.* Perhaps *caring* is our best English equivalent. And we can learn to care, we can will to serve one another, we can set out deliberately to seek one another's highest interests. Faults, annoying traits, accents, and distasteful habits do not vanish in our eyes, or in the eyes of others. But we can learn to love and to forgive where we cannot expect to like. Temple Gairdner of Cairo summed it up when he wrote in his diary, "From this day on, I have determined to try to see Jesus in all I meet, and to try to be Jesus to them."—John N. Gladstone[4]

---

[4] *A Magnificent Faith*

SUNDAY, APRIL 9, 2000
Lectionary Message

Topic: A Renewed Spirit to Serve and Follow

TEXT: John 12:20–23

Other Readings: Jer. 31:31–34; Ps. 51; Heb. 5:5–10

Have you ever had a terrible thing happen in your life and then looked back on it and realized that somehow good came from it? That is not always true for us. There are some tragedies that remain painful throughout our lives. However, a common theme of Christian spiritual journeys is that when something crucial is lost, very often something new and precious that is very much needed is found or given to us. When that happens, sometimes we find that we truly grow and become a new person because of the changes and crises, even because of the losses.

These life changes are the kind of experiences that fit Jesus' image of the grain of wheat falling into the ground and dying so that there can be fruit. I had to lose the old kind of ministry so that the right one could have time to grow.

I. This short text in the Gospel of John is somewhat confusing. Apparently there were Greek citizens in Jerusalem who were Jewish. They had heard of Jesus since coming to Passover that year and they hoped to meet him, this rabbi everyone was talking about who healed the sick on the Sabbath and argued with the Pharisees, who had caused such a stir by driving money changers from the temple. This teacher who people said had turned water into wine, walked on water, and fed five thousand people with just five loaves and two fishes.

So they went to Philip, one of the miracle worker's disciples. Philip seems to have had a need to get consultation from Andrew. Then they both went to Jesus to see if he would meet with these Greeks. But Jesus didn't really answer the question. Instead he made a pronouncement that "the hour has come." Somehow you can see the puzzled looks on Philip's and Andrew's faces. What *is* Jesus talking about? Then they get a parable about a grain of wheat, which seems purely obvious—*everybody* knows that the seed that is planted dies itself before the sprout and root form. What is this about losing and keeping your life? All they wanted was a simple yes or no about whether Jesus would meet the Greeks who were seeking him.

II. This passage contains in a nutshell one of the most difficult things for us to understand—that is, that Jesus considers the cross and his Crucifixion to be part of his glory as the Son of God and the Savior of the world. Compared to a grain of wheat, the Crucifixion is a much more horrible symbol of dying into eternal life.

I think Jesus is sharing with Philip and Andrew and with us one of his own revelations about his role as Savior. In the Gospel of John, for Jesus the Crucifixion is not just the result of angry religious and political leaders. It is part of God's plan for all of creation, for the redemption of all persons—not just for the Jewish people but also for the Gentiles. As hard as it is for us to contemplate the realities of Jesus' last week on Earth—his fear in the Garden of Gethsemane, a humiliating trial, and death on a cross—all those losses are part of what he brings as new life in Christ to each one of us.

III. The image of the seed coat that has to die before the plant can grow brings important questions to us today. What is wrapped around us too tightly that we can't let go? What needs to soften and fall away so that we are released and new roots of faith can grow and new sprouts of service can be offered? What are we stuck in that we cannot leave behind and make fruit for the cause of Christ in the world?

Jesus tells Philip and Andrew, "Those who love their life will lose it and those who hate their life in this world will keep it for eternal life." We don't want to hear that. What's wrong with loving our life? Aren't we supposed to try to be happy? This teaching is all about what or who comes first in our life. When we love all the things in our own life more than we seek to serve Jesus, we lose out on the life we could have with Jesus. When we are able to look inside our hearts and consider what separates us from God, then we will find repentance and cleansing. Then we will know the rejoicing and wisdom of new life that Psalm 51 describes.

Have you ever gone out to do something for another person and then discovered that you really received a blessing from your service that you never expected? That is another way in which our seed coat of self-absorption softens and we grow in new directions in our spiritual life.

Following Jesus means going all the way to the foot of the cross. It means standing there and considering whether we are always working harder at saving our own life than at serving the cause of Jesus in the world. Following Jesus means servanthood. It means following Jesus into those places listed in Matthew 25—the places where the poor and hungry are, where people are imprisoned for whatever reason, where people are lonely and sick. And as strange as it sounds, in the paradox of the gospel of Jesus Christ, it is there we will also find joy and gladness, wisdom, and a new and willing spirit. May it be so for each one of us.— Mary Zimmer

ILLUSTRATIONS

SURPRISE.   Do you remember as a small child planting a bean in a clear plastic cup? Teachers helped you do that so you could see the tiny miracle of growth as the seed coat dissolved and a white root curved downward. At the same time another white tendril curled upward to become the first leaf that would grow above ground and start the photosynthesis to make more leaves, and then many more beans. That one seed can be expected to keep producing beans throughout the summer as long as the soil is fed, tilled, and watered. If you have never grown vegetables, you haven't seen this miracle in nature—that from a single, solitary bean can come a plant that makes enough beans to fill a pot.—Mary Zimmer

BEARING CHRIST'S REPROACH.   In the late seventies of the [nineteenth century] there was a girl named Priscilla Livingstone Stewart. She was lovely to look upon: blue eyes, bright-colored golden hair, Irish gaiety. All the boys in the neighborhood thought she was grand. Her admirers lined up for a smile!

Then she met Christ. Having been heartily opposed to religion before, she became as ardent a disciple, and, soon after, the Salvation Army came to those parts. It was altogether characteristic of her that she could throw in her lot for a while with that despised people, and she chose to walk in their procession in days when they were pelted with old boots, stones, bad oranges, and worse eggs. Now, notice this! I give you the exact words of her reminiscences. She said, "None of my friends recognized me in the street, and all the young men who were fond of me walked on the other side."

I have no doubt that, being a normal girl, there was something of pain for her in that, but she felt that she had gained infinitely more than she had lost, and, truth to tell, God had other things in store for her. She went as a missionary to China and became the wife of that extraordinary missionary, C. T. Studd.—W. E. Sangster[5]

SERMON SUGGESTIONS

Topic: Missing the Remedy
TEXT: Jer. 8:22
(1) By turning to the wrong solution. (2) By refusing to acknowledge sin. (3) By not trusting God. (4) By giving up in discouragement or despair.

Topic: Superlative Life
TEXT: Phil. 1:20–30
(1) A life of fruitful service (v. 22). (2) A life of anticipation of being with Christ (v. 23). (3) A life that may include suffering (vv. 29–30).

CONGREGATIONAL MUSIC

1. "Glorify Thy Name," Donna Adkins (1975)
   GLORIFY THY NAME, Donna Adkins (1975)
   The Epistle lesson asserts that Christ did not glorify himself, and in the Gospel lesson Jesus is recorded as saying that the hour had come for him to be glorified. In response to these readings, this Trinitarian contemporary song allows the singing congregation to join in glorifying Christ's name.
2. "Though Your Sins Be As Scarlet," Fanny J. Crosby (1876)
   CRIMSON, William H. Doane (1876)
   The singing of this gospel song affords an apt response to the Old Testament reading in Jeremiah where God assures a new covenant with his people, forgiving their sin and remembering it no more.
3. "We Would See Jesus," Anna B. Warner (1852)
   CONSOLATION, arr. Felix Mendelssohn (1835); CUSHMAN, Herbert B. Turner (1907)
   Based on the Gospel reading (John 12:20–23), this hymn magnifies the request of the Greeks, "Sirs, we would see Jesus." It could thus logically be sung following the Gospel lesson.
4. "O for a Heart to Praise My God," Charles Wesley (1742)
   RICHMOND, Thomas Haweis (1792)
   This devotional song by the great hymnic poet Charles Wesley breathes the very spirit of David's prayer for pardon and cleansing (Ps. 51:10). Its singing could be varied stanza by stanza as follows: stanza 1, all singing; stanza 2, women alone; stanza 3, all; stanza 4, men alone; and stanza 5, all.—Hugh T. McElrath

WORSHIP AIDS

CALL TO WORSHIP.   "O Lord, open thou my lips; and my mouth shall show forth thy praise" (Ps. 51:15).

---

[5] *Can I Know God?*

INVOCATION.   Look on our souls, Father, as we seek to glorify thy name. Let the darkness in us vanish before the beams of your brightness. In this hour fill us with your love and open the depths of your wisdom, that we may worship you in spirit and in truth. Indeed, let mighty things be done among us today, even as they were among those first followers who learned from the Lord to pray, "Our Father. . . ."—Henry Fields

OFFERTORY SENTENCE.   "Each one should use whatever gift he has received to serve others, faithfully administering God's grace in its various forms" (1 Pet. 4:10 NIV).

OFFERTORY PRAYER.   Fill us with the compassionate spirit of the Master, Father, that we may be moved to give what we have in order that others' needs may be met through the power of his love.—Henry Fields

PRAYER.   In grateful praise we come to you this morning, Father. We have experienced you as the strong deliverer. In moments of darkness you have been light for the way and support in the journey. In times of joy you have been for us the stability we need and the companion in appreciation. From your hand we have received good gifts beyond numbering. In these moments we pause to give thanks for each one, especially family, friends, beauty, laughter, work, and prayer. Above all, we give thanks for Jesus, our Redeemer and Lord.

Forgive us, Father, when we return so little in comparison to the abundance with which you daily shower us. Our selfishness, our pride, our anxiety, our envy, our desire for praise, our chosen narrowness of vision, and our complacency before the agony of the world cause us to turn inward and fail to reach out with heart, hand, and wealth to do the work of Christ among fellow citizens of the world. By your grace heal us and remove our selfishness and unite us as the people of the Lord to follow him in making his Kingdom a reality in our world in our times. .

To that end create in us clean hearts and a right spirit. Give strength for the daily task and help each of us to see our responsibility, no matter how small, as a service done for you. Let us feel you near, Father, whatever may be our lot in life and whatever we have to manage. You know our cares, you see our tears; grant us your peace. You hear our sorrows, you understand our fears; grant us your healing. You feel our loves and listen to our laughter; grant that each may increase for your glory. In every circumstance where you find us, weave us together that we may be strong to do your will and courageous in bringing others to the Lord, in whose name we pray.—Henry Fields

SERMON
Topic: The Courage to Cry
TEXT: John 11:1–45

The most terrified I've ever been in my life was one evening in the summer of 1977. I was in Oklahoma City, doing a basic quarter of clinical pastoral education, an intensive chaplaincy experience that not only trains you to minister in a hospital but also forces you to grapple with basic issues of life and death. I saw lots of sobering things that summer, from mothers who had just lost babies to victims of motorcycle accidents lying mangled on the emergency room table. But I had never been as frightened as I was the night I was chaplain on call and the head nurse on the third floor paged me to come to the room of a patient under her care.

There was nothing dramatic about the scene I encountered when I got to the patient's room. There was no medical team responding to a code blue, trying desperately to save his life. There was no distraught family, crying and wailing in grief. The only person there was an elderly man, unconscious and breathing fitfully on his bed. He was expected to die at any time, and the nurse asked whether, if I wasn't doing anything else, I would sit at his bedside. She thought he deserved to have someone beside him in his final moments.

Had there been family there it would have been different for me. I would have focused my attention on them and their needs, offering them comfort in their distress. Had there been doctors and nurses trying frantically to save his life, I would have known what to do. I would have stayed out of the way but been nearby, available for them to debrief emotionally and unload some of their feelings when it was all over. If there had been other people there, something for me to do, I would have been in control, giving stability in the midst of emotional turmoil.

But there was no one else in the room, nothing for me to do that could distract me from the man grasping for what could be his last breath. Even if he had already been dead, it would have been different. I would have felt sadness, not terror. I had been in the same room with a recently deceased body. I had experienced the still peace that enshrouds a room when a valiant person has ended a long struggle. But I had never been in a room alone with a person who might die any minute with nothing to do but wait. Not knowing the gentleman, I didn't even have memories or emotions or grief to work through, some feelings that might shield me from the starkness of what was to come.

So I sat in the chair by his bed, listening carefully in the darkness to every breath, praying that another one would follow it. I did not want to be in that room when death stalked in and claimed that man. I wouldn't mind at all coming in right after, but I did not want to be there when he went.

After I had sat with him for about twenty minutes, the hospital operator paged me and I was summoned to the emergency room to be with the family of an accident victim. I breathed a sigh of relief and a prayer of thanks. By the time I made it back to the third floor about an hour later, the man had died. I had been spared.

There's something in us that tries valiantly to avoid confronting our limits. But that's not the world I live in, no matter how hard I wish for it. The world where I live has death, injustice, pain, and grief, forces beyond our control that put limits on our dreams. It's enough to make you angry—not just at the murderers and the cancer cells, but at God. It makes you want to cry out, with Martha and Mary and the company of mourners standing before the grave of Lazarus, "If only you had been here, Jesus."

If only, if only. If only things were the way we thought they ought to be.

They believed that there was hope for everlasting life in the future, when the Messiah would come at the end of time and put an end to all suffering and pain. But what about now? How could they explain the untimely death of their brother Lazarus when Jesus, the Son of God, was in their midst?

But Jesus didn't remove the limitations under which we all must live. He didn't miraculously change the nature of the human race into a species, like the cow or the dog, that's spared from wrestling with ultimate questions about mortality and eternity and meaning in life. He didn't eliminate pain and grief. Instead he brought the eternal power and love of God into the midst of it and transformed the nature of human suffering forever.

When Jesus called Lazarus from the tomb, he gave a sign of God's answer to our painful limitations: he resuscitated the body of a dead man. Now, what Lazarus experienced wasn't the same as Jesus' Resurrection. When Lazarus walked out of the tomb, he still had to die again. But Lazarus' resuscitation was a sign that pointed to something more significant than the resuscitation of a dead man. It pointed to Jesus' Resurrection, which occurred a little more than a week later. It was a sign to prepare Mary and Martha and others who believed in him that the one who could raise a body from death to life again would also resurrect our souls, and not only in the life to come but now. "I am the resurrection and the life," Jesus told Martha, not "I will be" but "I am."

God's power has to come to us on our own terms, in a way that's accessible to us. When Jesus speaks of his glory, he's not talking about his triumphal entry into Jerusalem, when he was adored by the crowds and welcomed as their king. When Jesus talks about his glory in the Gospel of John, he's referring to his Crucifixion. The glorious Resurrection on Easter morning took place in the graveyard where he was buried. We see his glory not by running away from our weakness, by ignoring our limitations, by pretending we're towers of unlimited power. We only know Jesus' glory by letting him break into our limits and share our pain.

Before Jesus showed Mary and Martha his power by raising their brother from the grave, he showed them something else about himself, something you have to know about him or you can't understand any of his miracles. Jesus listened to their grief and their anguish. He heard their questions, colored with disappointment and despair, and then he wept with them. Jesus wept. He knew that in a few minutes Lazarus would walk out of the grave, but he didn't come swaggering into Bethany, smiling, telling them to cheer up, minimizing their pain. Jesus wept. Even though he knew that his work was to conquer the power of death, Jesus wept.

It matters to Jesus. Our losses, our grief, the suffering we live through, they all matter to him. It matters enough that he would leave his heavenly throne to share this life with us, to bear on a cross the brunt of its death-dealing force. Jesus gives us the courage to cry as he breaks into our lives and holds us and cries with us. And standing with us before the tomb of all our sorrows, his Resurrection power breaks through our limitations and sweeps us up, not in the future, not even on the last day, but at this very moment, when he gives us the first fruits of his Resurrection to eternal life.—Stephens G. Lytch

SUNDAY, APRIL 16, 2000
Lectionary Message

Topic: Palm Sunday, 2000
Text: Mark 11:1–11
Other Readings: Ps. 118:1–2, 19–29

A useful rule of thumb in preaching is, the larger the occasion, the smaller the sermon. That would certainly be the case on this Sunday. If a congregation is ever going to have a procession it is likely to be on Palm Sunday, and the exuberance of the children waving palms and singing "All Glory, Laud, and Honor" can be counted on to carry much of the message of this day: we welcome the coming of our Savior and we walk with him in the way of the cross. That is what the day at the beginning of Holy Week is for, as it recapitulates much of the practice of the early Church in Jerusalem. A particular text connects with a place and a time to make for a powerful liturgical occasion. The preacher will do best to take his or her place on that occasion, to let the dramatic occasion both set the tone of the sermon and reinforce its message.

In many congregations there will be two readings of the Gospel on this Sunday: the narrative of the entry into Jerusalem and the Passion narrative. The preacher can actually preach in the procession, on the entry Gospel. The children process into the church and halfway through the hymn they stop for the reading of Mark 11:1–11. After the reading, the children sit down in the aisle and the congregation is seated. The preacher can then give a homily on the entry narrative. Then all stand and the procession continues. This has the advantage of giving the preacher the opportunity, at the very beginning of the service—and of Holy Week—to start the congregation on its journey toward the reading of the Passion story this morning and toward the unfolding days of Holy Week. This allows the Passion narrative to stand on its own; when it is well read—usually by a number of readers, with the congregation serving as the crowd—it speaks the message without additional homiletical comment.

The homily-in-procession also goes to the heart of today's Gospel: Jesus enters the city, our city; we welcome him but are not sure who he is or what he requires; we fail him, but in him God overcomes sin and death. The preacher could direct these three points [as developed later] of the homily-in-procession to the children, giving the adults the opportunity to listen in. (As Fred Craddock has shown in *Overhearing the Gospel,* we hear things more clearly when we are eavesdropping.) The children's homily could ask, Do you like a parade? When do we have parades (July 4, Thanksgiving, and so on)? Why do we have parades? Today we have a parade in church. Why would we do that? This gives the preacher the opportunity to communicate to both children and adults that we are welcoming Jesus as our Savior and that we want to follow him just as we are walking together today. In those churches where the procession is led by a cross, the preacher can use that visible symbol to make the point that to welcome Jesus and to follow him is to walk in the way of the cross, the theme of Holy Week.

I. *Jesus enters the city, our city.* Holy Week got started in Jerusalem as the early Christians became aware of the very places where Jesus walked, taught, suffered, and died. They wanted not so much to reenact as to connect—to enter into—those saving events by standing in the very places and reading the accounts of what happened there. The liturgical word for this is *anamnesis.* It is more than remembering, more than reenactment. It is lively participation in the saving presence of Christ. One way to achieve this, Christians have thought, is to keep Holy Week, to walk through the story of Jesus' Passion and death.

But what makes us truly rejoice is the knowledge that Jesus enters *our* city, comes to us in Montclair or Chandler or Newport; wherever people with the open hearts of children will receive him, he comes. It is a matter not of wishing that we could have "been with him then" but of welcoming him with sincerity and abandon: "Hosanna, blessed is he who comes in the name of the Lord."

II. *We still forget what he requires of us.* It is all too easy to turn this whole day into nothing more than a showy parade, to forget what it means to follow Jesus on this way. The humble beast of burden that carried Jesus into the city can remind us of the lowly service to which we are called. Though we sometimes speak of this as the "triumphal entry," the unfolding events of the week, like the whole of Jesus' life, deliver us from notions of triumphalism.

III. *Though Jesus is betrayed, through him God overcomes sin and death.* There lies the importance of keeping Holy Week. Among the early Christians, Easter was celebrated as the "Great Three Days." Those early followers of Jesus did not separate the events of this week; they were all of a piece, beginning on this day filled with expectation and uncertainty. Jesus came to a city we recognize and to people we know all too well. But among them, and in spite of them, he walks toward the salvation that comes at Easter.—Charles Rice

Collect for Monday in Holy Week: "Almighty God, whose most dear Son went not up to joy but first he suffered pain, and entered not into glory before he was crucified: Mercifully grant that we, walking in the way of the cross, may find it none other than the way of life and peace; through Jesus Christ your Son our Lord, who lives and reigns with you and the Holy Spirit, one God, for ever and ever."[6]

ILLUSTRATIONS

CONFUSED.   I remember a beautiful Palm Sunday (it is often a beautiful spring day). The church was filled with well-dressed, happy people. Sitting in front of me was a couple who I somehow knew were going out for a nice lunch after the service. This particular congregation had only started to read, in addition to the entry Gospel, the long narrative of the Passion. As that reading went on and on, the couple—whose whispered comments I could hear—became increasingly puzzled. What was going on? Had we jumped to Good Friday already? When the reading was finally done, one of my neighbors whispered to the other, "Well, that wasn't very pleasant."

No, indeed. But this is what we mark on Palm Sunday: he comes to our city; we are still confused as to who he is and what he asks of us; but even confusion and betrayal cannot thwart what God's love will do through him.—Charles Rice

THE MAGNITUDE OF ONE.   One temporary triumph offsets a hundred defeats. One man who does something because it is right and not because it will win an election will roll back the clouds of darkness for days to come. One person who is honest without any thought of what will happen to himself will make a crack in the clouds of night; one person, no matter how obscure he may be, who is willing to let the spirit of Christ live in him, that is, the spirit of good will and love and honesty, will offset a thousand defeats that scoundrels and rascals and sinners have made.—Theodore Parker Ferris[7]

---

[6] *Book of Common Prayer*, p. 220.
[7] In G. Paul Butler (ed.), *Best Sermons*, Vol. 9 (New York: Trident Press, 1968), p. 141.

SERMON SUGGESTIONS

Topic: From Here to Joy
TEXT: Ps. 50:15
(1) Prayer. (2) Promise. (3) Praise.

Topic: Running to Win
TEXT: Heb. 12:1–2
(1) The witnesses—our faithful predecessors (ch. 11). (2) The weights—our various hindrances. (3) The winners—those who make Jesus their inspiration, sustainer, and destiny.

CONGREGATIONAL MUSIC

1. "This Is the Day the Lord Has Made," Isaac Watts (1719)
    ARLINGTON, Thomas A. Arne (1762)
    Inspired by Psalm 118:24, Isaac Watts, the great eighteenth-century hymnist, had in mind, among other things, the triumphal entry of Jesus into the Holy City. Stanzas 1, 3, and 4 are most appropriate for Palm Sunday worship.
2. "At the Name of Jesus," Caroline M. Noel (1870)
    KING'S WESTON, Ralph Vaughan Williams (1925)
    Written as a processional hymn for Ascension Day, this fine hymn is on this day's Epistle lesson (Phil. 2:5–11) and thus is appropriate for Passion Sunday.
3. "He Is Lord," Linda Lee Johnson (1986)
    HE IS LORD, Linda Lee Johnson (1986)
    This contemporary song also gathers up the truths of the Philippian passage (Phil. 2:5–11). Its anonymous refrain is often sung separately and could well be used in antiphonal fashion with the reading of the Epistle.
4. "Lift Up Your Heads," George Weissel (1642); tr. Catherine Winkworth (1855)
    TRURO, Thomas Williams' *Psalmodia Evangelica* (1789)
    Although written for use at Advent, this triumphal hymn is quite suitable for the opening of worship on Palm Sunday. It relates particularly to the Psalter reading (Ps. 118:19–20).
5. "An Upper Room Did Our Lord Prepare," Fred Pratt Green (1973)
    O WALY WALY, English folk song; harm., John Weaver (1988)
    This contemporary hymn, though unfamiliar, will go well with its familiar folk song tune. It relates well to the Gospel lesson for Passion Sunday (Mark 14:1–15).
6. "O Thou, in Whose Presence," Joseph Swain (1781)
    DAVIS, *Wyeth's Repository of Sacred Music, Part Second* (1813)
    This fine old hymn affirms the truth of the Isaiah passage (Isa. 50:4–9a) that God helps us and gives strength in times of tribulation.—Hugh T. McElrath

WORSHIP AIDS

CALL TO WORSHIP.   "This is the day that the Lord has made; let us rejoice and be glad in it" (Ps. 118:24 NRSV).

INVOCATION.   Our Father God, we are in Thy presence in an especial way this morning, touching one another's lives, looking to the same God, but from such different points of view. Thou knowest all of us and everything about us and in us, and we are thankful that this is so, for Thou art all-merciful and all-kind. So this morning we come to Thee with the united song which we have offered as our praise to Thee, but we bring to Thee in this hour of prayer our open lives, the things we do not suspect, the things that Thou alone knowest about. Make this hour an hour of great, tender searching, of healing, of helping, in the Name of our Lord and Saviour, Jesus Christ.—Frank W. Gunsaulus[8]

OFFERTORY SENTENCE.   "God has chosen the weak things of the world to confound the things which are mighty" (1 Cor. 1:27b).

OFFERTORY PRAYER.   Because of your amazing resourcefulness, O Lord, we believe that even the smallest of our gifts can do astonishing things. So we give boldly, trusting in your providence and power.

PRAYER.   Forever God, Lord of this Holy Week, you are Lord of all seasons and all time; we praise you. Lord of Passion/Palm Sunday, you are Lord of all hosannas and adoration, and still ever acquainted with suffering. O Man of Sorrows!! Ever moving God, Lord of the journey, how far is it from Bethlehem to Jerusalem? For it seems as if we were just traveling with the shepherds to the manger to celebrate Jesus' birth. Yet now we enter Jerusalem, glancing timidly but knowingly toward Calvary. How far is it, O God, from the cradle to the cross, from birth to death, from wondrous joy and heavenly light to sweat like blood agony and earthquake darkness? Is it three plus months, or thirty plus years, or is it an eternity? This Holy Week we wonder, O Wondrous Love, how far shall we go with Jesus? How far will it be for us?

Holy Lord of Bethlehem, Jerusalem, Louisville, in our heart of hearts we are both drawn to and haunted by the simple words of the hymn. But we pray today and each day this week that this hymn will be our call and our commitment. So, most willingly, "Jesus keep us near the cross"—not a place of kindness or safety, but a hard place to see and to suffer, yet a place to stand and a place to be saved. With the call and demand of each day, may we be tuned to your Passion, your suffering, and your rejection, and as we see and acknowledge them, may we begin to make some better sense of our own.

Jesus keep us near the cross, for as we sing and say our hosannas today, we know they will fade into quiet indifference and even silent betrayal this week, if not today. Jesus keep us near the cross, for all the events and persons of your holy week seem so very familiar: praise turned to jeers, arguing about greatness, jockeying for a better place, sleeping instead of praying, the comfortable feel of thirty pieces of silver betrayal, the choosing of the other Jesus—the Barabbases of our days, the words of denial that fit into our mouths and hearts, too.

So, as you cleanse the Temple this week, cleanse us, too. Throw out the thieves and perpetrators that reside in our holy spaces also. As you take the towel, wash our feet and hands, hearts and wills to be anointed and made pure for your Kingdom's will and work. As you set the table, prepare a place for each one of us, if you will. By faith we know it is your will for everyone to have a place at the table.

---

[8] *Prayers*

Jesus, keep us near the cross. And as the angry, relentless crowd comes, may we stand beside you, not with a sword raised but with a heart bowed with deep sorrow. Save us, loving, suffering Lord, from the abiding temptations of this week by indeed keeping us near the cross. For there we shall wait, hoping, trusting, believing, knowing that amid the chaos we are being redeemed; and next Sunday we shall lay down the cross of death and, with you, put on the crown of life: Resurrection, Resurrection!!—William M. Johnson

SERMON

Topic: The Kind of Person the Lord Can Use
TEXT: Isa. 6:8

God does choose persons of many sorts to serve him. Some self-appointed persons have considered themselves "sons of destiny" and have inflicted their megalomania on the nation they ruled or on the little group they gathered about themselves. But bypassing those persons, let us get down to individuals such as you and I and see if it is possible that God can use us.

Isaiah was brought up in the court. He was of royal blood. He had distinct advantages above his fellows. God used Isaiah mightily in proclaiming the burning truth to the people of his day. Some of the most beautiful prophecies of the coming of Christ and his meaning are to be found in the prophecy of Isaiah. Again and again in the New Testament, Isaiah is quoted as having made the prophecy that is fulfilled in Christ. Isaiah was outstanding.

But at the same time, Micah proclaimed practically the same message, although in rough-hewn language. Micah, the man of the country, Micah, the man who had no royal blood in his veins, was one whom God had laid his hand upon, had chosen, had anointed and used as he had done with Isaiah.

The message came to Isaiah after Isaiah's conversion experience. "Whom shall I send, and who will go for us?" Isaiah responded, "Here am I; send me." He realized that God had spoken to him, that God needed someone. Isaiah was available and offered himself to God as his missionary.

Who can God use today? God today can use and does use in his service converted people. God has, to be sure, used people who have not been converted to accomplish his purpose. Cyrus of Persia was an instrument in the hands of God to bring the people of God out of their exile in Babylon and to restore them to their own land, to their happiness, and to the pursuit of their own religious heritage and insights.

Also, God has overruled such individuals as Judas Iscariot, Pontius Pilate, Caiaphas the high priest, and the Roman soldiers who nailed Christ to the cross. In his own way and providence, God has used these persons to further his purpose in the world.

Now we must make this distinction. Some people are *partners* of God in what God is doing in this world. They consciously and in fellowship with him carry out what has been revealed to them and what they believe to be his purposes. On the other hand, some individuals are *tools* of God—instruments of God, not conscious of fellowship with God and even with hearts of rebellion against God, who are nonetheless used by God in furthering his purpose. But in the action of these persons reacting against God, revolting against Jesus Christ, Satan overreaches himself to his own undoing. So in this world we are either the instruments of God or the partners of God. If we choose to be his partners, then we benefit by carrying out his purposes consciously and directly, and we are rewarded for it both here and hereafter. If we rebel against him, if we reject him, God in his infinite power will overrule our evil eventually, and God's will at last will triumph.

Nevertheless, the sort of person that God will use and can use most effectively is a converted person. The biographies of people who have been great in the service of God include persons who have been drunkards and found sobriety; adulterers and discovered purity; thieves and become honest; liars and learned to speak the truth; lustful, jealous, and envious and learned to respect the rights, property, and yearnings of others. God in his infinite mercy, grace, and compassion has been able to take some of the vilest specimens of humanity and cleaned up those lives; and he has made those persons free, forgiven, and pure and used them in his service. I'm sure that somehow in God's wisdom and providence and power he overruled what Saul of Tarsus did in helping persecute Stephen—breathing out threats against those who were of the Christian way and persecuting all of those who he recognized as Christians. I am sure that God overruled what Saul did and eventually will use it to God's glory and triumph. But God most effectively used Paul after Paul's conversion. God sent him out into the Roman empire, the length and breadth of it, to proclaim that Jesus Christ is the Son of God.

And then again God uses people to do his work who are prepared. Now the preparation of people is of different sorts. One person is prepared by poverty to do the work of God, another by being born into wealth. One person can make himself available to God for work among some people by the very fact that he has not seen much of the schools; another is able to serve God most effectively among other people because he has had superior training. God uses people of different backgrounds to reach people of varied backgrounds. The important thing is what God will make of what is made available to him. The Bible tells us that God has taken the common and despised things of this earth and made them into vessels of honor for his service. I think that one is certainly missing the point of the Christian vocation who assumes that there is nothing that can be done for God by one who has not had the training that another person has had. If we make ourselves available to God, God can use us with the preparation that we have had, which for the purposes of God may be far and away superior to that of another person that we are so envious of.

The Lord uses prepared persons, but they are the ones who have humility before God to say, "Lord, here am I. Send me. Use me as you wish. Show me what I can do and enable me to do it. What I may do in my own strength, I do not well; but what I do in your strength can be pleasing to you."

Also, the Lord uses people who are prepared through activity. The busy people are the ones God calls—the people who are doing the task closest to them instead of waiting for the big chance—the great opportunity. There are some people who have hoped to be sent out as foreign missionaries who wouldn't do anything for the Church in missionary service at home. Is it any wonder, then, that God does not use these persons?

And then, finally, the kind of person that God can use is a person who has devotion—a person who prays and who seeks God's will. The advice of our friends is often, and what we may discover concerning God's will in a general way in the Bible points in the right direction. But after all of the advice we receive from friends and after all of the profound and extensive study of the Bible we may do, we have to come to God in prayer and confess to him our dependence on him, our lack of wisdom, and look to him for wisdom, for insight, for guidance. We are told in the Bible, in the words of our Lord Jesus himself, "Go into all of the world and preach the gospel." That's the general command; but specifically and individually we do not know where, in what circumstances, and in what way we are to proclaim that gospel. Where in the world am I to go? Where in the world am I to serve? In what capacity am I to serve? Shall I be a layman? Shall I be a businessman? Shall I be a secretary? Shall I be a teacher in the schools? Shall I be an instructor in the Sunday school or in the church? Shall I serve on the committees and boards of the church? In what way can I fulfill in my own life this great commission, "Go into all of the world"? That is to be discovered through the exercise of prayer after all of the other resources have been exploited. When all of these questions have been brought to God, we may expect guidance and an answer.

But as a final word, if God uses us, we are going to have to keep ourselves clean before him. We are going to have to relinquish some things that might in themselves be legitimate but that are able to impede our progress as Christians and as the Lord's willing servants. Are you able to say, since God has converted you and turned your heart to him in faith, trust, and repentance, are you able to say to him, "Now that you have forgiven me and saved me, now use me in your service. Here am I Lord; send me." There are many tasks, there are many responsibilities—some small, some great—but they are here with their burning challenge. They are out in the community with their great needs. They are abroad in the world with their pressing urgency. Will you hear God's call and respond to him today?—James W. Cox

SUNDAY, APRIL 23, 2000
Lectionary Message

Topic: Easter Day, 2000
TEXT: John 20:1–18
Other Readings: Acts 10:34–43; Ps. 118:1–2, 14–24; 1 Cor. 15:1–11

This text makes clear once more that the empty tomb was not the basis—at least was not sufficient ground on which to stand—of the early Church's witness to the Resurrection. The vacated tomb, to which the orderly grave clothes point, is no doubt a powerful symbol of the Resurrection, as are the stone rolled away and the heavenly messengers. But what finally counts here is that Jesus speaks to Mary. Indeed, it is when he calls her name—she has to this point mistaken him for the gardener, just as she has surmised that the empty tomb means the grave has been robbed—that Mary recognizes him as her teacher and Christ. And even in this moment he makes it clear to Mary that the appropriate response is not to cling to the earthly Jesus but to go and bear witness to the one who is ascending to the Father. Based on her experience, Mary's witness is crystal clear: "I have seen the Lord."

I. *The report: The tomb is empty and the stone is rolled back.* It is a puzzling, even frightening report, and it could have a rational explanation. Mary comes to her conclusion immediately: someone has stolen the body of Jesus. Here lies the problem in viewing Scripture as historical account, and the inadequacy of established fact as the ultimate basis of faith. This report, in the form of John's narrative, has served as a powerful and formative factor in the history of faith. But as the fourth Gospel itself makes clear, we must go beyond the mere fact.

There was a time when some people seemed to put quite a lot of faith's stock in the shroud of Turin, which has been shown to come from the Middle Ages. As long as this relic is understood to be a historical corroboration, then faith stands on shaky ground.

II. John begins and ends his story with Mary coming to the tomb in the dark, finding the stone rolled back and the grave empty. She is confused and sorrowful. The heavenly messengers speak to her, and then Jesus himself appears to her. It is this that leads to her confession, "I have seen the Lord," and makes her a witness.

The evangelist is clear about his reason for giving us this story, as he tells us why he has written this Gospel: "These [things] are written that you may believe that Jesus is the Christ, the Son of God, and that believing you may live in his name." Mary meets the Risen Christ for herself, and it is that, finally, that makes all the difference.

III. *The tomb is empty: Jesus has overcome death.* The stone is rolled back; we are free. Sin cannot conquer God's Son. Death cannot hold the Lord's Christ. The empty tomb and the big stone rolled back tell us of the victory of God's love and of our freedom from sin, fear, and death. This means that the preacher will want to tell this story once more on this Easter Day—the story of a woman who has lost the one who is, no doubt, her best friend, a woman who may as well be inside a dark hole herself with a boulder blocking out the air and light. Then the heavenly messengers speak to her and Jesus himself comes to her in the midst of her confusion, speaking her name. In that moment, all is changed.

In a 1998 film there is a fine image for Easter. Melvin Udall (played by Jack Nicholson) is a prolific author. He spends every day locked in his apartment, creating the characters that have made him rich. At the same time, he is unable to relate to the people who live nearby and he is desperately afraid of the world. His bathroom is stocked with dozens of wrapped bars of soap; he uses a fresh one each time he washes his hands or bathes. When he goes out to the only restaurant he ever goes to, he takes his own sterile cutlery. Each time he returns to his apartment he bolts the door with five locks.

The movie opens with Melvin chasing the neighbor's dog, which has made a mess in the hallway. Melvin dumps the animal down the laundry chute! As things turn out, his neighbor—a young man he does not like at all—goes to the hospital and Melvin is forced to take care of the dog. The result of this is something we would never predict: as Melvin cares for the dog, he finds himself somehow changing. When his neighbor comes home from the hospital, he takes care of him, too.

Then a quite amazing thing happens. One day as Melvin is leaving the apartment, he is completely taken aback to find that he has forgotten to lock the door! By some miracle, the fearful world outside has been overcome and Melvin finds himself in a new, open place in which he can receive and give love.

This story does not, of course, exhaust the meaning of what we celebrate on this Easter Day, but it does point us to what comes through so clearly in John's story. It is where the Risen Christ comes out to meet us and speaks our names that we know the truth of the Resurrection and tell our own stories of the stone rolled away and the empty tomb. Alleluia.—Charles Rice

Collect for Easter Day: Almighty God, who through your only-begotten Son Jesus Christ overcame death and opened to us the gate of everlasting life: grant that we who celebrate with joy the day of the Lord's Resurrection may be raised from the death of sin by your life-giving Spirit; through Jesus Christ, our Lord, who lives and reigns with you and the Holy Spirit, one God, now and forever. Amen.

ILLUSTRATIONS

BEYOND CAMELOT.   The ministry of the historical Jesus is over; now begins the ministry of the glorified and ascended Christ. Mary Magdalene cannot resume the old relationship with her Lord, for Christ now relates to his followers by giving them the Paraclete, the Spirit. Therefore Jesus says to her, "Do not hold me" (v. 17). She and the disciples and the Church today are not to long for the way it was, as though the time were a brief Camelot. Rather, they and we are to believe his word: "It is best for you that I go away; if I do not go away, the Spirit will not come; the Spirit will remain with you forever; greater works than I have done, you will do because I go to my Father."—Fred B. Craddock[9]

A COLONY OF HEAVEN.   You do not need to wait "until the day break and the shadows flee away" before beginning to live eternally. In union with Christ, that glorious privilege is yours here and now. Risen with Him, you have passed out of relation to sin, out of the hampering limitations of this present order, out of the domain of the world and the flesh, into the realm of the Spirit, and into life that is life indeed. In short, even here on the earth you are "a colony of heaven." Never forget where your citizenship lies! "Reckon yourselves alive unto God through Jesus Christ our Lord."—James S. Stewart[10]

SERMON SUGGESTIONS

Topic: God's Countenance
TEXT: Isa. 54:7–8

(1) We sometimes experience what seems to be God's anger, because of what we have done, what someone else has done, or for no apparent reason. (2) But God soon shows his compassion—in his willingness to forgive us, to deal with justice toward evildoers, or to give us reassurance even before all wrongs are righted.

Topic: Take Heart!
TEXT: John 16:33b REB

"In the world you will have suffering. But take heart! I have conquered the world." (1) The scope of our suffering. (2) The signal for a right attitude in the worst of times. (3) The source of our courage.

CONGREGATIONAL MUSIC

1. "Christ Is Risen," Brian Wren (1984)

   W ZLOBIE LKEZY, Polish carol; harm. Austin Lovelace (1964)

   This joyous hymn by a living author is set to a sprightly carol tune. It reflects the hope and exhilaration of the Easter message.
2. "He Lives," Alfred H. Ackley (1933)

   ACKLEY, Alfred H. Ackley (1933)

   This twentieth-century Easter song possesses a testimonial spirit not unlike that of the apostle Paul in his Epistle to the Corinthian church (1 Cor. 15:1–11).

---

[9] *John*
[10] *A Man in Christ*

3. "Give Thanks for All His Goodness," vers. Stanley Wiersma (1982)

RENDEZ A DIEU, Louis Bourgeois (1551)

A contemporary paraphrase of Psalm 118, this hymn should accompany the Psalter reading.

4. "Easter People, Raise Your Voices," William M. James (1979)

REGENT SQUARE, Henry T. Smart (1867)

Here is a bright new hymn of the Resurrection that in a fresh way celebrates our victory over sin and death. The alleluias of each stanza could be sung alternately (antiphonally) by choir and congregation or by divisions of the singing congregation.

5. "Thine Be the Glory," Edmond L. Budry (1904)

JUDAS MACCABEUS, George F. Handel (1747)

This majestic hymn is recommended for Easter processional use. Accompanied by a group of brass instruments, it can reinforce the joy and excitement of the season.—Hugh T. McElrath

WORSHIP AIDS

CALL TO WORSHIP.   "The stone that the builders rejected has become the chief cornerstone. This is the Lord's doing; it is marvelous in our eyes" (Ps. 118:22–23 NRV).

INVOCATION.   We give thanks, O Lord, for the hope we have in Jesus, who died but is risen and rules over all. Because he lives, we look for eternal life, knowing that nothing past, present, or yet to come can separate us from your great love made known in Jesus Christ our Lord.—Robert F. Langwig

OFFERTORY SENTENCE.   "And [Jesus] went on to say to them all, 'Watch out and guard yourselves from every kind of greed; because a person's true life is not made up of the things he owns, no matter how rich he may be'" (Luke 12:15 TEV).

OFFERTORY PRAYER.   It is with a sense of joy and celebration that we come to you today, our Father. We thank you for the victory you have won for us and for all people. Our hearts swell with the love we feel from your visit with us in the midst of our darkest moments. We have been resurrected by your power, released in the Resurrection of your Son, Jesus the Christ. Thank you, Father, for new birth, new life, and new goals, through Jesus Christ our Lord.—Robert F. Langwig

PRAYER.   God of glory and Lord of love, we come to you on this Easter morning full of hope and certain of life eternal. The splash you have made in history has caused a rippling effect that has carried throughout the course of human events as the divine happening of Resurrection.

You have called Jesus from the grave and he has responded splendidly with a burst of new life that draws us all into the arms of the eternal.

We know that where the ripples of Easter have found us this morning, we have been centered on the Resurrection of Jesus, the Christ. We know that we are now focused on victory, a gift you have given to each of us as we have placed our lives in the mainstream of faith. You have called Jesus forth, and your call has been heard throughout the centuries, enabling each of us who would be followers of him to rise also with him to life eternal. We thank You, O God, for this eternal gift to us.

As we touch other lives this week, let the power you have given us bring to them a new awareness of love, a new sense of peace, a strong surge of joy. Make us instruments of your saving power as we minister to one another in reconciling ways, enabling healing to take place among the peoples of this world and in our broken relationships with one another. We would be yours, O God, as we seek to serve one another in Jesus' name, bringing a new sense of faith and trust to our relationships and allowing the kingdom of heaven to come once again on Earth.

Our prayer we offer in the name of the Risen Christ.—Robert F. Langwig

SERMON
Topic: Irrepressible Easter
TEXT: Matt. 28:1–20

I. They had come to pay homage to a dead man. Two women, both named Mary, were returning to the place where he had been buried.

But it wasn't only for Jesus that they had come to grieve. They had come to mourn for themselves and the whole human race. They had come to grieve the death of a dream they'd had, the end of a brief shining moment.

As the women approached the tomb where they had laid Jesus on Friday evening, they saw in the predawn shadows the soldiers who were assigned to guard it. The soldiers were evidence of who was in control.

You can imagine how it would have looked: two women, shattered, humiliated, and weak, cowering while the guards, secure in their armor and their brawn, hardly noticed.

But in an instant the tables were turned. As the women approached the tomb, the earth shook and an angel of the Lord appeared. His appearance was as dazzlingly bright as lightning when it flashes through a dark, overcast sky. His clothes sparkled like snow in the morning sunshine. The angel rolled back the stone that had been sealed extra tight for security, sat calmly on it, and spoke to the women. The guards, the ones with the spears and the armor, the ones who had the authority of the priests and the Pharisees, of Pontius Pilate and of Caesar, to back them up, trembled with fear and fell to the ground paralyzed by terror, while the women, the ones who were weak and helpless and lost, stood upright and heard the angel say, "He is not here, for he has been raised, as he said. Come, see the place where he lay."

For all their power, the guards couldn't keep Jesus in the tomb. They couldn't control him and make him conform to their designs. People have tried to control him ever since, to keep him confined to dark places where he can be well guarded. For two thousand years people have tried to make him conform to their idea of power. Masters called on him to bless slavery; men have invoked his name to subjugate women; nations have tried to take him to the front lines of battle in their wars of conquest.

II. And we still try to restrict him, to keep Jesus securely in those places in our lives where we can control him.

But Jesus keeps breaking through the seals and the guards we post to contain him. He lives, unrestrained, in power and glory. He won't be confined to the tomb or to any human ideology or to the cubbyholes of our lives where we try to keep him. He won't be confined even by our doubts.

After the women saw Jesus, he sent them to tell his disciples to meet him in Galilee. There he spoke to them on a mountain. Matthew says something strange about that encounter. He says that his disciples worshiped Jesus but some doubted. They were in the presence of the Risen Lord, falling at his feet in homage, but they doubted. What did they doubt? Did they doubt their own judgment for being there, their eyes for seeing him before them?

Some of us, even as we worship him on this glorious Easter morning, have doubts. Is all of this true? Is it really better to follow him and give of ourselves to others, or wouldn't we be better off not bothering with any of this religion?

But Jesus wasn't held back by the doubts of his disciples, just as he wasn't held back by the power of the guards at the tomb. Our doubts don't constrain him. Despite our doubts and our denials, our complacency and our craving for comfort, he is alive.

Do you need evidence? Just look wherever his followers are doing what he commanded them to do. Look at this congregation, which gathers every Sunday expecting to encounter him week after week. Look wherever you see someone who calls Jesus Lord performing an act of mercy and love for another person in need. Look inside your own heart to see if there's not a longing there to be close to God, to love God, and to walk beside him. Even when we keep trying to get Jesus out of the way, to make him more manageable, the way the Roman army did when they sealed his tomb and posted armed guards in front of it, Jesus keeps going ahead of us to meet us as he met his disciples on the mountain in Galilee.

But regardless of what we do, he won't be held back. Christ is risen, and he comes to us as he came to those women named Mary, as he came to his disciples who met him on a mountain. And breaking down the walls we have erected to protect ourselves from his power, he sends us into a world of need, promising us none of the things we spend most of our time striving for: money, power, popularity, health. What he promises is that he will be with us, in our certainty and in our doubts, in our defeat and in our triumph, in our obedience and in our sinfulness. The one who cannot be contained by a tomb is with us today, and will be with us until the close of the age. Christ is risen! He is risen indeed!—Stephens G. Lytch

SUNDAY, APRIL 30, 2000
Lectionary Message

Topic: We Also Believe
TEXT: John 20:19–31
Other Readings: Acts 4:32–35; Ps. 133; 1 John 1:1–2:2

Today's Gospel follows very close on the heels of the story read last Sunday of Mary, who does not come to Easter faith until Jesus speaks her name. Thomas makes it a matter of seeing evidence in the flesh—the wounds—and touching him, a hand in his pierced side. Some have taken his protesting words "Unless I see, touch, I will not believe" as a determined doubt. More likely these strong words point to a passion to believe, to a man struggling with the brute facts of Jesus' ignominious death and trying, somehow, to believe that what had been so vital and promising in him had not all been crushed forever. This, Thomas seems to say, would be too much to bear, if an apparition got our hopes up only to dash them once more. "I want to be sure," Thomas says.

I. We do rely on the word of others. There can be no doubt that it is in the company of the faithful that we come to faith, just as we rely on the words of Scripture and tradition coming down to us from those who have gone before to tell us that Jesus crucified is raised from the dead and that all who believe this will enter into life eternal. We get this news from others, just as Thomas got it from the eleven. We should keep in mind that he would not have had this trouble, probably, if he had been with them that first evening. (And we would have lost an important story for the life of faith!)

John Westerhof (*Will Our Children Have Faith?*) has shown us that people get the faith from others, in the community that listens to the Word of God, celebrates the sacraments, lives out together God's grace, forgiveness, and peace. Long before they are able to understand or articulate articles of faith, children take them in by being with and observing significant adults speaking, singing, listening, bowing, and communing. And this is true not only of children. We continue in the faith and are strengthened in our times of doubt in the fellowship of the saints. Anyone who forgets this may well find himself or herself standing on the outside, confused and full of doubt.

This is a good point at which to be reminded that a red-hot coal taken out of the fire and isolated quickly dies away. "Thomas was not with them."

II. Jesus comes to Thomas, as he has to the eleven, speaking the essential words: "Peace be with you." Before Thomas can make his demand to touch Jesus, Jesus speaks the words that matter: "Peace, Thomas. I am with you. The one who was crucified, dead, and buried, I have overcome and am with you." It is enough for Thomas to hear Jesus' voice and to hear the greeting that is a promise. He does not touch Jesus. Instead, like Mary in the garden, he speaks the words that are both confession and commitment: "My Lord and my God."

At the end of the celebration of almost every Holy Communion, as we prepare to go forth once more into the world that can lead us into doubt and betrayal, the blessing is given: "The peace of God which passes all understanding keep your hearts and minds in the knowledge and love of God and of his Son, Jesus Christ, our Lord." The peace of God which passes all understanding, Paul says, *will* keep our hearts and minds. This is the word that Thomas receives: the Crucified lives and reigns, and he will be with us to keep us, even through the times of darkness and doubt, to the end.

III. "Blessed are those who have not seen and yet believe." That would be us. That would, almost certainly, be the one who gave us these words. The community out of which the fourth Gospel comes was at least two or three generations after Jesus. They had not seen him, let alone touched him. But they—John's Gospel makes this so evident—lived in the blessedness and peace of which Jesus speaks to Thomas.

What Thomas asks for, today's reading from First John declares. We are not talking about a phantom. At the heart of our faith is the one Thomas seeks, who lived in the flesh and was pierced with nails and spear. It is this one who has conquered and is alive and present, speaking peace to all who seek him. "That which we have heard, which we have seen with our eyes, which we have looked upon and touched with our hands, we proclaim to you, so that you may have fellowship with us."

This is where we live and where we celebrate the great fifty days of Easter. We have heard the story of the one who was from the beginning and has come into the world to live and die among us and who is present speaking peace to all those who in faith and with the means of grace follow him.—Charles Rice

ILLUSTRATIONS

JESUS' REAL OPPONENTS.   It is important to remember that the continuous mention of the "Jews" here has nothing to do with the Jewish people who live in our time. The opponents of Jesus were his own people who were resistant to his message. Jesus is a Jew. People within and without the Christian community have irresponsibly used the fourth Gospel to justify racism and hatred. The Jews did not attack and kill Jesus. Each person who turns from him and sins—in every age—is the opponent of Christ.—Dennis C. Benson[11]

HONEST THOMAS.   Thomas would never say that he understood what he did not understand, or that he believed what he did not believe. There is an uncompromising honesty about Thomas. Thomas would never still his doubts by pretending that they did not exist. Thomas was not the kind of man who would rattle off a creed without understanding what it was all about. Thomas had to be sure—and Thomas was quite right. Tennyson wrote:

> There lives more faith in honest doubt,
> Believe me than in half the creeds.

There is more ultimate faith in the man who insists on being sure than in the man who glibly repeats things which he has never thought out and which he does not really believe. It is a doubt like that which in the end arrives at certainty.—William Barclay[12]

SERMON SUGGESTIONS

Topic: The Hiddenness of God

TEXT: Isa. 45:15

God is so hidden that much of the world's life goes on as if he were not there. Even his providential working and his gifts have a curious anonymity about them. (1) God is hidden because of our sin and the world's evil. Our world is not as God created it. Our humanity is a fallen humanity. (2) God is hidden because he is a holy person. Man in his pride sets himself against God, seeking to possess and control him. (3) God is hidden because this is a part of his loving purpose. Otherwise, our freedom of decision would be overwhelmed.—Eric C. Rust[13]

Topic: The Redeemer of the Cross

TEXT: Rom. 3:23–26

Righteousness means redemption. The righteousness of God is his love acting through his Son, Jesus Christ, to redeem from the bondage of sin those who believe in him. The cross reveals: (1) the meaning of the righteousness of God; (2) the awful blackness of sin; (3) the height, depth, length, and breadth of God's love; (4) the demands that the Lord makes upon his disciples.—Richard B. Sims[14]

---

[11] *The Bible Creative*
[12] *The Gospel of John*, Vol. 2
[13] *Professor in the Pulpit*
[14] *The Righteousness of God*

CONGREGATIONAL MUSIC

1. "O Sons and Daughters," sixteenth-century Latin; tr. John Mason Neale (1851)

    O FILII ET FILIAE, French tune (fifteenth century)

    One of the finest Easter carols, which relates the entire story of the Resurrection and post-Resurrection events (John 20), this could be used antiphonally between congregation (the alleluias) and a children's choir (the narrative stanzas).

2. "O Word of God Incarnate," William W. How (1867)

    MUNICH, *Meningisches Gesangbuch* (1693)

    This classic hymn takes up the theme of the Epistle lesson in 1 John dealing with the idea of the Incarnate Word.

3. "Filled with the Spirit's Power," John R. Peacey (1967)

    FARLEY CASTLE, Henry Lawes (1638)

    This contemporary hymn magnifies the spirit of unity in the early Church recorded in Acts 4. In its latter stanzas it becomes a prayer to be offered by today's worshipers in response to the Scripture lesson.

4. "Behold the Goodness of Our Lord," Fred R. Anderson (1986)

    CRIMOND, Jessie Seymour Irvine (1972)

    Alternating each verse of Psalm 133 with (before) the singing of each stanza of this modern paraphrase could bring fresh meaning to the use of this psalm in worship.—Hugh T. McElrath

WORSHIP AIDS

CALL TO WORSHIP.   "How very good and pleasant it is when kindred live together in unity!" (Ps. 133:1 NRSV).

INVOCATION.   O God, let this be a day of rejoicing and profound gladness for all of us—a day when we fully understand that, although with men the saving of man is impossible, with you all things are possible, that there is a mighty grace at work in this world for our salvation and the salvation of humankind, and that even a cross and nails cannot stop it.

Let this be a day when you surprise us with the insight that in our weakness you make perfect your strength and through the foolishness of the cross you reveal your wisdom and power.—John Thompson

OFFERTORY SENTENCE.   "Every man according as he purposeth in his heart, so let him give; not grudgingly, or of necessity; for God loveth a cheerful giver" (2 Cor. 9:7).

OFFERTORY PRAYER.   Thank you for the privilege of giving, Father. May what we bring to the altar be given willingly and generously so that others may discover the wonder of following Jesus in whose name we pray. Amen.

PRAYER.   Gracious God, Creator of the universe and of each of us, we come to you with hearts that are filled with love, hope, and affirmation.

We love, dear God, because we know that in your great mercy you have come first to love us at Christmastide and you have confirmed it through your creation come alive at Easter. In the birth, life, death, and Resurrection of Jesus, your Son, we have witnessed the fullness of your saving grace and know that all of creation is now returning to you to find new life.

In the Resurrection you have offered to each of us, we find hope. We realize that we, too, are offered the gift of becoming new creations in Christ. Through the sacrificial love you have offered to us, we are able now to share with each other in the feeding of the poor, in the clothing of the naked, in the healing of the infirm, and in bringing peace to the conflicted. In so doing, we find ourselves working with you to bring your Kingdom on Earth. In so doing, we find hope.

We are affirmed by all that you have given us. We know that you have looked upon us and seen us worthy of salvation—of being a part of your goodly and Godly creation. Thank you, Creator God, for your gracious gifts made known to us in Jesus Christ, your Son and our Lord, in whose name we pray.—Robert F. Langwig

SERMON
Topic: The Resurrection of the Body
TEXT: 1 Cor. 15:35–50

What are we to make of these bodies of ours?

How little progress we've made since the first century. It was that same confusion about the human body that was tearing apart the church in Corinth.[15]

Word of that confusion over their bodies got back to Paul, who wrote them this letter we read from. At the end of his letter, he gave the Corinthians the best reason he could think of for them to enjoy their bodies on the one hand and treat them with the utmost respect on the other.

We know that our bodies matter because of something basic that we believe as Christians. We believe in the resurrection of the dead. By the resurrection of the dead we mean that one day, at the end of time, Jesus will return to the Earth to bring in the Kingdom of God and restore the whole creation to the perfection it had when God first made it. And when he does all that, he will raise all those who have died. They—we—will have a resurrection like the one Jesus had on Easter, and we will be given brand new bodies, just like Jesus was given a new body when he was raised. We know for a fact that our bodies decay and disappear, so the thought of their being reconstituted just the way they are now is absurd. Yet to think of ourselves without bodies is also impossible, at least from the perspective of the Bible.

And even the perishability of these bodies of ours enhances rather than detracts from the beauty of life. The very sting of death, the grief it causes us, is evidence of how good this created order is. Instead of trying to escape this world that God has made, God wants us to embrace it and enjoy it, and when part of it is lost, to mourn it.[16]

So the Christian faith doesn't deny the importance of our bodies. Ours is a very worldly religion. Yet in Jesus' death and in the Resurrection of his body, we see how different our new bodies will be from the ones we have now. When Jesus rose from the dead, he had a body that looked to his disciples like the one he had before he died.

---

[15] Darrell Jodock, "Confused About the Body," *Christian Century*, Feb. 1–8, 1995, p. 107.
[16] Jack Stotts, *Austin Seminary Bulletin*, Fall 1994, pp. 5–6; Alan Lewis, ibid., p. 10.

And that's the kind of body we will be given at the resurrection of the dead—spiritual bodies that are in many ways like the ones we have now, but different.

Now that's a very hard concept to grasp. Paul struggled with it in the Scripture passage we read this morning. There's really nothing with which to compare when trying to explain what our spiritual bodies will be like. So he gropes for a comparison, trying four ways. None of those images is exactly it.

So we're left with lots of mystery about just what those spiritual bodies will be like. Maybe we're not meant to know any more details because if we did, we'd be even more discontented with these earthly bodies we have.

When we die we will still be who we are. Everything about us that makes us who we are will be the same. That's what Scripture means when it says that by death Christ has destroyed death. By dying and rising again, Christ has taken away the power of death to dismantle us. Christ has robbed death of its power so completely that even that part of us that is our body will not be destroyed, but transformed into something more glorious than we can imagine.

And those spiritual bodies will be able to have relationships with others, as we have relationships with others now. But I believe that we will be able to love others in a way we can't conceive of in this life.

I think that when we enter into God's perfect love, we'll be able to love more like God loves, in a way that's not limited to the members of our immediate family but which in no way diminishes the love we have for them.

That is why we can rejoice in the midst of our grief for those we love who have died. We know that death has not diminished their identity, that they are still who they were in this life, only now they wait for new bodies that are fit for the glory their spirits enjoy. They haven't received the full extent of their glory yet. They still await its fulfillment at the final resurrection, a hope they share with us.

Our bodies are gifts from God, gifts we use to glorify God and praise him. It does matter what we do with them.

Churches have always gone out of their way to provide food and medicine and shelter for people in addition to giving spiritual guidance. God loves us as whole persons, not as disembodied spirits.

When the Corinthians were confused about what to make of their bodies, Paul reminded them of the resurrection of the dead. He reminded them that each of us is a whole person, made up of body, mind, and spirit. You can't separate one from the others. What we do with our bodies matters—because we matter to God.—Stephens G. Lytch

SUNDAY, MAY 7, 2000
Lectionary Message

Topic: How He Became Whole
TEXT: Acts 3:12–19
Other Readings: Ps. 4; 1 John 3:1–7; Luke 24: 36b–48

We all worry about what to say in front of the crowd. We want to be articulate or we want to be quiet. In Acts 3, a spontaneous crowd gathered around the apostles Peter and John under Solomon's magnificent column-shaded porch bordering the Temple court. The crowd had gathered in response to the joy-filled jumping and rejoicing of a just-healed beggar. They wanted explanations. The apostles wanted to witness. The resulting sermonette of fourteen sentences is among the best and boldest in Scripture. Peter therein preached five truths to explain how that happy man had become whole.

I. *Truth 1: The healing of the lame is what the name of Jesus can do.* Peter first corrected the amazement of the crowd. They concluded that the healing focused on the personal power and piety of Peter and John. As flattering as this assumption might have been to the apostles, it was false. We must never allow anyone to deflect any of the glory due to the name of the Lord to ourselves. The power is in the name of Jesus so the glory must be given to that name. Preaching is only as articulate as it is able to attract people to the saving power of faith in Jesus. Having clarified for the crowd what God had done *in the name of* Jesus, Peter then reminded them what had recently been done *to* Jesus.

II. *Truth 2: The crime of the cross is what the deceitfulness of sin can do.* As Peter was apt to do in these early days of the Church in Jerusalem, he indicted the crowd for the crime of the cross. His indictment contained three charges: first, handing Jesus over to be killed; second, disowning Jesus in order to choose a real criminal to be released by Pilate; and third, by association, killing Jesus, the author of life (vv. 13–15). The crowd had allowed, if not encouraged, the crucifixion of the God of Abraham's servant, the holy and righteous one. The proof of these charges for Peter was in the Resurrection of Jesus from the dead.

III. *Truth 3: The raising of the dead is what the power of God can do.* Peter had not only piled up charges against the crowd, but he had also compiled messianic titles for Jesus. No matter, says Peter; the proof of Jesus' identity was in his Resurrection from the dead. "We are witnesses of this," stated Peter (v. 15). Furthermore, the full healing of the beggar points to and promises our healing and wholeness in Christ's name. "It is Jesus' name and the faith that comes through him that has given this man complete healing" (v. 16).

IV. *Truth 4: The provision for human ignorance is what the providence of God can do.* Peter muted the charges against the Temple crowd. "Now, brothers, I know you acted in ignorance as did your leaders" (v. 17). Those charges were further muted when Peter asserted that their crime, causing Christ's suffering, was all according to God's providential plan. This plan was fully fulfilled in the Crucifixion and Resurrection of Christ as foretold by the Hebrew prophets (v. 18; see also Psalm 22:1–18 and Isaiah 53). God always remains sovereign over his creation and his creatures. He makes history his story of redemption.

V. *Truth 5: The blotting out of sin is what repentance unto faith can do.* By this point in Peter's first sermon at Pentecost, his audience had interrupted him with the question, "Is there any way we can be saved?" (Acts 2:37). Now, in his second sermon, Peter anticipated the same question in the hearts of his hearers. Without their asking, Peter answered, "Repent, then, and turn to God, that your sins may be wiped out, that times of refreshing may come from the Lord" (v. 19). Repentance leads to refreshing. Conversion leads to cleansing from sin and guilt. If our sins are wiped out of the books, our names will not be wiped out of the book of life (Ex. 32:32–33).

VI. *Conclusion.* Peter's second sermon is here recorded by Luke. In it, Peter blends fearful warning and wonderful assurance in the name of Jesus. There still is power to heal and to save in the name of Jesus. This refreshing is, however, reserved for the repentant. This cleansing is appropriated through conversion. Will you not repent and be converted by calling on the name of Jesus? All you need to know is your need of him.—Rodrick K. Durst

ILLUSTRATIONS

FORGIVENESS.   Ink in our day usually contains acid. It bites into the paper on which it is applied so it cannot be wiped or blotted off. Ancient ink contained no acid, so scribes could alter written records by using a damp sponge to carefully blot out what was written. Forgiveness meant that God had blotted out his record of the sin confessed and forgiven.—Roderick K. Durst

REPENTANCE.   Repentance means to rethink or think after. It suggests a change in thinking and implies a resulting change in the life. Repentance involves a new world view and new values. Conversion means to change back and retool for a new life and task. Used together, they imply a renouncing of the sin-directed life and a commitment to the Christ-directed life.—Rodrick K. Durst

SERMON SUGGESTIONS

Topic: Daniel, a Man of Excellent Spirit
TEXT: Dan. 6:3
The key to Daniel's splendid fidelity may be found in the words "an excellent spirit was in him." (1) A man of purpose. (2) A man of prayer. (3) A man of perception. (4) A man of power.—G. Campbell Morgan[1]

Topic: Your True Vocation
TEXT: Col. 3:1–4
(1) A new status—"raised with Christ." (2) Worthy objectives—"things that are above." (3) An outcome to die for—"revealed with him in glory."

CONGREGATIONAL MUSIC

1. "He Is Risen! He Is Risen!" Cecil Frances Alexander (1846)
    UNSER HERRSCHER, Joachim Neander (1680)
    The appearance of Jesus to the startled disciples was to convince them of his Resurrection. Singing hymns like this one aids a congregation in their joyous affirmation of that glorious reality.
2. "Lead Me, Lord" Psalm 4:8
    LEAD ME LORD, Samuel S. Wesley (1861)
    This simple response based on the last verse of Psalm 4 would be effective sung by a congregation as an antiphon during the Psalter reading. The procedure could be as follows: Ps. 4:1–2, antiphon, Ps. 4:3–4, antiphon, Ps. 4:5–6, antiphon, Ps. 4:7–8, antiphon.
3. "Children of the Heavenly Father," Caroline V. Sandbell-Berg (1855)
    TRYGGARE KAN INGEN VARA, trad. Swedish melody (c. 1850)
    Reflecting the calm assurance of our relationship to God as children (1 John 3:1–7) is this lovely song by the "Fanny Crosby of Sweden." It offers a natural response to the reading of the Epistle lesson.

---

[1] *The Westminster Pulpit*, Vol. 8

4. "There Shall Be Showers of Blessing," Daniel W. Whittle (1883)

   SHOWERS OF BLESSING, James McGranahan (1883)

   The apostle Peter's sermon (Acts 3:12–19) called on his hearers to repent and believe in order that they might be forgiven and that spiritual refreshing might come from the presence of God. This gospel song expresses the hope and prayer that such "seasons of refreshing" may indeed come in the present as in biblical times.—Hugh T. McElrath

WORSHIP AIDS

CALL TO WORSHIP.   "Offer the right sacrifices to the Lord, and put your trust in him" (Ps. 4:5 TEV).

INVOCATION.   Help us to raise to you our sacrifice of praise, O God. And let our worship of you be matched by deeds of love for one another, even for those beyond our shores.

OFFERTORY SENTENCE.   "God hath chosen the weak things of the world to confound the things which are mighty" (1 Cor. 1:27b).

OFFERTORY PRAYER.   In faith, we pray, O God, that the offerings we bring today will make a difference in us and in our world, far beyond anything that we can imagine. May your great love be shed abroad in our hearts for your glory.

PRAYER.   Ours is a strange faith, Father. We see that, unlike other faiths, it demands that we practice life differently from the common ways of the world. This morning, help us to be more diligent in following Christ, that some of the hard strangeness may become welcome practice.

It is strange to be called on to be persecuted for the faith we hold. Yet we know that when we stand strong in the face of evil and do what is right, we will have to manage persecution in some manner. Give us the courage to stand firm in doing the will of Jesus even when persecution is inevitable.

It is strange to be called on to pray for enemies. Our desire is to destroy enemies in fits of wrath. Teach us the truth that we destroy enemies when we pray them into friendship, and lead us to be diligent in conquering in such a manner.

Forgiveness is a strange position to take toward one who has wronged us, Father. We rather like the holding of grudges and the building of walls between us and the wrongdoer. Help us to be good practitioners of forgiveness and toward another, that we may make the world a better place in which to live and eternity a reality in life.

It seems strange to follow a crucified felon, to allow such a one to have dominion over all of life, to commit all that we are to his service and will. Yet we know that until we become staunch followers of Jesus, experience his forgiveness and salvation, and allow him to be the reigning Lord of life, we cannot really live or know the certainty of eternal life. This morning, open the hearts and minds and wills of all of us that in these sacred moments we might let him be master of all that we are and ever hope to be.—Henry Fields

SERMON

Topic: What Is Man That You Think of Him?

TEXT: Ps. 8

When the Scriptures speak of "man" in Psalm 8, we know it refers to both female and male. We have searched for answers to people's being, people's purpose, and people's destiny since the beginning of time. Today we face dangers of much greater magnitude than ever before in history. We want to know why God created us and we want him to continue to reveal his will to us.

I. Our human qualities and characteristics separate us from other living beings in the following areas:

(a) *We are self-conscious beings.* We are inquisitive about ourselves in relation to others and to the world and the universe.

(b) We have specific concepts about ourselves. We develop ideas and implement them.

(c) We use language and symbols to communicate. Communicating the Scriptures to people around the world has involved studying many languages and dialects in order to translate the Bible for people to read and understand.

(d) We give varied expressions to understanding the Creator, Spirit, or God. When early immigrants encountered Native Americans, they discovered that each tribe had religious practices that identified a response to some spiritual power. When visiting mission installations in the heart of Africa, I was taken by the missionary to areas off the main road. There in the bush were piles of stones and designs made with sticks that were worship centers. They were primitive attempts to understand deity.

(e) We have been creative by designing ideas into objects useful for our livelihood. We have made tools and machines to serve ourselves. Through our language we have created books by the millions, so that libraries have to cull out those that may be obsolete.

We have been created different from other creatures. "The Lord God formed man of dust from the ground, and breathed into his nostrils the breath of life; the man became a living being" (Gen. 2:7 RSV). We are self-conscious and self-determining beings made in the image of our Creator with the unique ability to make free moral decisions between good and evil. These and other concepts of humans are the result of our basic conviction of being religious persons.

The firm belief and repeated emphasis that God created us with a divine plan and purpose has brought about contrary replies by skeptics and atheists. The attempts to delete God as an outdated concept or to delete God as our Creator are mere repetitions of what happened in the days of the psalmist when he answered the critics: "The fool says in his heart, 'There is no God.' They are corrupt, they do abominable deeds. There is none that does good. The Lord looks down from heaven upon the children of men, to see if there are any that act wisely, that seek after God" (Ps. 14:1, 2).

II. The human struggle to fulfill the purpose for which we have been created is threefold.

(a) *We must satisfy our relationship with our Creator.* The Christian view of what we are maintains that we are separated from God, in whose image we have been created. The separation from God was the result of the Fall. Our reasoning may attribute to various human acts the cause of this separation. However, the fact remains that we are sinful beings and stand in need of a right relationship with God. The teachings of the New Testament highlight the good news that God restores our faith in Jesus Christ. Faith in Christ also restores in us the image of God.

(b) *We feverishly endeavor to discover our identity.* Living in the world as we do has led us to identify with our world so much that we become swallowed up by it. We are subdued by our world and the things in it, including our problems, our frustrations, our feelings, and our occupations.

A Christian view recognizes that God created us with the privilege to make choices, to select our way of life, and to decide what we want or do not want in life. We are free to determine the identity we wish to establish for ourselves. As Christians we believe that when we identify with Christ we become a new creation and find the highest meaning in life for this world and for the life to come.

(c) *We struggle to relate ourselves to God and to our fellow human beings.* What we have received from God cannot be contained within ourselves. We must share our abundant life with others through deeds and acts generated by love and compassion. We continue throughout life to search for answers to the question, "When I consider thy heavens, the work of thy fingers, the moon and stars which thou hast ordained: what is man, that thou art mindful of him? and the son of man that thou visitest him?" (Ps. 8:3, 4).

Thousands of men, women, and children were assembled in Convention Hall, Miami Beach, Florida, in the summer of 1965 to gather new insight into the question, "What is man?" The oratorio entitled, "What Is Man?" was half-finished when a man rushed to the platform, stopped the conductor, and announced that the authorities were requesting that the hall be evacuated immediately. The reason? A man told the authorities that a bomb had been placed in the hall. Once again we witnessed how people were interrupted when trying to find an answer to the question, "What is man?" These interruptions have been in the form of hate movements, dictators, invasions, atrocities, and mob violence. In spite of these and other interruptions down through the centuries, we must continue to find answers to the question, "What is man?"

In Christ we see unveiled the true value of humankind. Jesus is never confined to boundaries we create. He crossed over boundaries to meet the needs of people, be they Samaritans, lepers, sinners, or outcasts. He considered people to be of eternal value, so valuable that he gave his life on a cross "that you may have life and have life abundantly."—Gideon K. Zimmerman

SUNDAY, MAY 14, 2000
Lectionary Message

Topic: The Politics of Jesus
Text: Acts 4:5–12
Other Readings: Ps. 23; 1 John 3:16–24; John 10:11–18

Luke records the first persecution of believers in Acts 4. After only their second public presentation of the gospel, Peter and John were arrested and held overnight in the Temple detainment center.

Arraignment the next morning was held before the high priest, his family, and the ranking seventy-one Sadducee and Pharisee members of Jewish temple court, the Sanhedrin

(v. 6). Jesus had faced this audience less than two months prior. The concern of this audience was far more serious than mere curiosity as to the healing of a lame man. Luke recorded, "They [the authorities] were greatly disturbed because the apostles were teaching the people and proclaiming in Jesus the resurrection of the dead" (v. 2).

The opening question in the arraignment was focused on the apostles' lack of authorization to teach the resurrection doctrine in the Temple courts. The Sadducee party had, in the name of Hebrew conservatism, denied the doctrine of the resurrection from the dead (Matt. 22:23ff). Despite the intimidating tactics of these keepers of the status quo, Peter's response was so effective that the charges were dropped (v. 21). Peter's effectiveness is also meant to be ours. His pattern puts three requirements on us as witnesses in the public square.

I. *Be Spirit-filled.* Peter's demeanor and response reveal that these intimidating officials were not Peter's real audience. Peter was aiming to please God (2 Cor. 5:9). Witness becomes articulate when we make God the audience. When we make God our real audience, he fills us with his Spirit. Spirit-filled people aim and are enabled to please God. You may answer to others, but the manner and content of that answer are formed out of a consciousness that God is your audience.

(a) *Peter's filling was meant to be democratic, not apostolic.* More than one biblical scholar has asserted that Peter's filling by the Spirit was special and unique. However, if the quality of Peter's filling was uniquely for the apostles, then why does Paul command the Ephesian believers to "be filled with the Spirit" (Eph. 5:18)? If this filling was only for the few, then why did Peter proclaim that the prophecy of Joel was fulfilled by the Pentecostal distribution of the Spirit to all 120 believers, male and female, youth and seniors? The presence and power of the Spirit is the norm and privilege for the believer's witness in the public square.

(b) *Peter's filling was according to Jesus' promise.* Jesus promised his followers problems, persecution, and suffering. He also promised spiritual enablement to witness for the gospel under such circumstances (Matt. 10:19–20). We need not worry. The words will come from heaven when we need to witness.

II. *Be Savior-focused.* Being Spirit-filled means that our witness will be focused on the Savior. The work of the Spirit is to bear witness to Jesus. The teaching ministry of the Spirit clarifies the meaning and measure of the life of the Son of God (John 14:25; 15:26–27). Peter's response to the Temple prosecutor transcended temple politics to embrace the politics of Jesus. "It is by the name of Jesus, the Messiah from Nazareth, whom you crucified but whom God raised from the dead, that this man stands before you completely healed" (v. 10). In the place of theoretical arguments against the resurrection from the dead, Peter presented two resurrections as his authority to follow and preach Jesus. The first resurrection was God's Easter reversal of Jesus' death and the second was the "resurrection" of the beggar to full health. Living proof is always better than the theoretical.

III. *Be Scripture-fueled.* The Hebrews were a people shaped around a book. Faithfulness meant responsiveness to the revelation of God through Moses and the prophets. As a Jew, Peter had the same need for scriptural fuel. Under the inspiration of the Spirit, Peter both quoted and concluded from classic Hebrew Scriptures.

(a) *Quoting Scripture clarifies and convinces the conscience* (2 Cor. 4:2). Peter quoted from the Septuagint translation of Psalm 118:22, "The stone you builders rejected has become the capstone [or cornerstone]" (v. 11). There is authority in the name of Jesus because God has raised the rejected rock to become the capstone of the messianic mission.

(b) *Scriptural conclusions call for personal commitment.* Peter followed the quotation from the Psalms with the following declaration: "Salvation is found in no one else, for there is no other name under heaven given to men by which we can be saved" (v. 12). Scholars have tried to mute this so-called scandalous claim that Jesus is the only way. Some scholars have suggested that Peter's assertion was a ministerial exaggeration to be excused by the pressure of the moment. Others see it as a rhetorical exaggeration acceptable in public debate. However, careful review of the great "Servant Songs" in Isaiah chapters 40 to 45 shows that Peter's assertion was a conclusion from the monotheism and monosaviorism preached by Isaiah. "I, even I, am the Lord, and apart from me there is no savior" (Isa. 43:11; see also 43:10; 45:5, 14–15, 22). Monotheism always implies monosaviorism. If we would be monotheists who worship the one God, then we must receive the salvation offered in the one name that the one God has given to us, Jesus.

IV. *Conclusion.* Peter's defense may have been interrupted by the prosecutor that day. I wonder if he wanted to conclude with Isaiah's own monotheistic invitation, "Turn to me and be saved, all you ends of the earth; for I am God and there is no other" (Isa. 45:22).—Rodrick K. Durst

ILLUSTRATIONS

WORDS.   The difference between the right word and the wrong word is the difference between a lightning bolt and a lightning bug.—Rodrick K. Durst

SPIRIT-FILLED.   The Pauline mandate to "be filled with the Spirit" is contrasted with being drunk with wine. So being filled by the Spirit means to be surrendered sufficiently to God and His will that you are effectively under his influence in your attitudes, responses, and decisions. Some alcoholics are such effective practitioners of self-chemistry that they can imbibe just enough alcohol to feel better without allowing the alcohol to take control. May it be that we believers seek the Spirit not for his "feel good" effect but rather to worship and glorify him through spiritual service to others.—Rodrick K. Durst

DELIVERANCE.   Psalm 118 was the favorite of Martin Luther, the great sixteenth-century Church reformer. In Luther's commentary on the Psalms, he gave the reason for this preference. "He has delivered me from many a sore affliction when neither the emperor nor kings nor the wise nor the saints were able or willing to help me." Every Hebrew knew this Psalm because it was sung as part of the Passover celebration every year. It is the last of the Hallel psalms (113–118) and was sung by the disciples with Jesus at the conclusion of the last supper. (See Matt. 26:30.) Even as he faced death, Jesus sang of victory.—Rodrick K. Durst

SERMON SUGGESTIONS

Topic: Escape Mechanism

TEXT: "The Eternal is my . . . retreat" (Ps. 18:2 Moffatt).

Three observations about religion as an escape from life: (1) We ought to have a sympathetic understanding of some of the exhilarations behind it. (2) We ought to do some humble heart searching—"Lord, is it I?" (3) We have only cleared the ground for some positive declarations: (a) A vital faith gives a way of escape from things that make life intolerable if one cannot escape from them. (b) A faith in the God of Jesus brings an escape from the blankness of a meaningless world. (c) Faith is an escape from the prison house of self and from the chaos and suffering of a deranged world.—Halford E. Luccock[2]

Topic: The Discipline of Disillusionment
TEXT: Heb. 12:26–29
(1) Facing the reality of disillusionment. (2) Accepting the discipline of disillusionment.—Wayne E. Oates[3]

CONGREGATIONAL MUSIC

1. "Savior, Like a Shepherd Lead Us," Dorothy A. Thrupp (1836)
   BRADBURY, William B. Bradbury (1859)
   This appealing hymn originally written for children can appropriately be sung as a response either to the reading of the Shepherd Psalm (23), to the Gospel lesson having to do with the theme of the Good Shepherd, or to both.
2. "What Wondrous Love Is This," American folk hymn (c. 1835)
   WONDROUS LOVE, from *The Southern Harmony* (1835)
   A folk hymn that is best sung with simple instrumental (dulcimer or autoharp) accompaniment, it relates beautifully to the Scripture lesson in 1 John (3:16–24) concerning the love that led Christ to lay down his life for us all.
3. "The Lord's My Shepherd," vers. Scottish Psalter (1650)
   BROTHER JAMES' AIR, J. L. Macbeth Bain (1915)
   Of the dozens of hymnic versions of Psalm 23, this Scottish Psalter rendering is probably the most well known. This musical setting is often found in choral arrangements, but there is no reason for a congregation not to sing it, possibly in alteration with a choir, stanza by stanza: choir, congregation, choir, congregation, and all together.
4. "The King of Love My Shepherd Is," Henry W. Baker (1868)
   St. COLUMBA, trad. Irish melody (c. 1855)
   This familiar paraphrase of Psalm 23 furnishes a preferable substitute for stricter metrical settings with its evangelical references to the cross (stanza 4) and the Good Shepherd (stanzas 3 and 5).
5. "The Way of the Cross Leads Home," Jessie B. Pounds
   WAY OF THE CROSS, Charles H. Gabriel (1906)
   Gospel songs are called such because in many instances they present the gospel story of Jesus' death and offer of salvation. This one, like many, refers to the truth in the apostle Peter's preaching (Acts 4:12): "There is no other name under heaven by which we must be saved."—Hugh T. McElrath

WORSHIP AIDS

CALL TO WORSHIP.   "He guides me by true paths, as he himself is true" (Ps. 23:3b Moffatt).

---

[2] *Preaching Values in the Old Testament*
[3] *Professor in the Pulpit*

INVOCATION.   Assured of your presence and your willing leadership, we walk with courage, our Father. Strengthen us for the long journey by the companionship of our fellow believers, with whom we worship, and by the joy of lifting our hearts to you in prayer and praise.

OFFERTORY SENTENCE.   "The King will reply, 'I tell you, whenever you did this for one of the least important of these brothers of mine, you did it for me'" (Matt. 25:40 TEV).

OFFERTORY PRAYER.   Help us, gracious Lord, to open our hearts wide to the needs of all your people. As we do this more and more, grant us the joy and fulfillment of service to you, realizing that you condescended to the depth of our unworthiness to save us and give us work to do.

PRAYER.   It is a day of remembrance, Father. Thinking about mothers and family, we scan the past and focus on moments that have molded our lives. Tender moments, frightening moments, secure moments, and challenging moments rise to meet us, reminding us of the forever impressions that each burned into our minds and characters. Across the stage we have played on pass the people who were significant in fixing certain character traits in us, who spoke words of guidance, who called us to high accomplishment, who entered our lives as strangers and remained to become the larger family we cherish, people of faith who believed in us because they believed in you and who gave us the sure foundation of life on which to build for time and eternity.

How grateful we are for all who shaped us and loved us and believed in us. How thankful we are for the ones who disciplined us, taught us the hard lessons of life, and challenged us as they opened our minds to worlds hidden to us before they invaded our space for living. Most of all we are grateful for our human mother and father, those two special people through whom you worked to give us human life. Today as we honor our mothers, may we cherish the sacred thoughts given by remembering. May we recall her sacrifices, her chastisements, her direction, her love, and her faith, which touched us in so many areas of our journey from childhood's beginnings. Help us to understand that we clearly reflect our parentage not only in how we look, but also in large measure in what we have become.

As mothers who still live among us continue the journey with us, may they be blessed with a sense of your presence and the power of your love. May they remain courageous in doing what is right and constant in their commitment to family and faith. And may our honor not cease when this hour is done, but remain constant as we continue our journey of life across the highway of the years.—Henry Fields

SERMON
Topic: Families Reaching Families from Strength
Text: Luke 14:28–31a

Jesus indicated that the wise person assembles the necessary resources before tackling a task. He taught that responsibilities are better carried out from strength rather than from weakness and that opportunities are better seized when we are prepared than when we are not.

So with families reaching families—a family can better reach its own members and other persons when it is stable and strong than when unstable and weak. The Bible provides guidance about what makes a family strong and how to achieve such strength.

What makes families strong? Families can be strong when the persons who make up the family are stable and strong, mature and responsible. The best gift a person can give his or her family is a mature, responsible self. Regardless of how much a person babbles on and on about love for family, that person's expression of love is a sham unless that person is developing the very best self possible. How can a person love a family and yet not do all possible to make it healthy and strong? In turn, strong families contribute to developing the individuals who make up the family.

Families can be strong when the persons who make up the family understand the nature of marriage and family according to the Word of God. The Bible teaches that a marriage is a very special union, one established by God. In Matthew 19:4–6, Jesus states the nature of this union. He indicates that it is from God, who joins the couple together; thus marriage is a divine union and family is a divine institution. The union is to last a lifetime; "let not man put asunder," Jesus declared. Lifetime commitment gives a family stability and strength. The union is to be exclusive: forsake father and mother and cleave only to each other, Jesus stated. Fidelity and loyalty give a family stability; infidelity and divided loyalty undermine a family's strength.

Families can be strong when the persons who make up the family understand the purpose of marriage and family. Anything not used according to its purpose—from a pencil to a jet airplane—is damaged, weakened, or destroyed. This is certainly true of families. God's Word clearly sets forth why he gave to us the gift of family. The Genesis account of the establishment of family (Gen. 2:18–24) indicates that the primary purpose is companionship—a very special, intimate type of sharing one with another. Human beings need the intimate relationships afforded by family. Related to this is sexual fulfillment (1 Cor. 7:3–5), because God created humans as sexual beings. The nurture of children is clearly another primary purpose (Gen. 1:27–28). No one can replace the family in nurturing children in the Lord (Eph. 6:1–4). And of course the family is to bear witness to the wonderful love and saving power of Jesus Christ (Acts 2:6–8). Mature people carrying out these purposes within God's framework will develop a strong family.

How can families develop strength? Such a challenge seems beyond human ability, doesn't it? The terrifying number of family failures seems to indicate that we are not capable of doing what needs to be done to develop strong, stable families. Indeed, we are not—at least on our own. We need help—God's help. That help comes from being in Christ, growing in Christ, and living for Christ.

Being in Christ is essential for a family to be strong. Christ is to be Lord of life, including family life. Because individuals make up a family, those individuals need to be in Christ if the family is to be in Christ. This means that each member of the family ought to be saved, born again, redeemed. When a person repents of sin and puts faith in the Lord Jesus Christ for forgiveness of sin, he or she becomes a new creation; old things pass away and all things become new (2 Cor. 5:17). This new life in Christ provides the basis for a person being the kind of family member who makes family strong.

Growing in Christ is also essential if we are to be what we ought to be for our family. Baby Christians, immature in their relationship with Jesus, are usually immature in their relationships with family members. Christian growth comes from a deep love of Jesus and a desire to be the very best person possible to serve him. Christian growth is enhanced by prayer, Bible study, Christian fellowship, worship, witness, and ministry. Christian growth is a lifelong process, something we never fully accomplish but are always in the process of achieving.

Living for Christ also contributes to our strength and thus to that of our family. Day by day we are to depend on the Holy Spirit to guide and empower us as we endeavor to follow God's will and share the good news about Jesus. Living for Christ means we live to glorify God in all that we do, especially our family life.

For its own sake and for the sake of others, a family needs to be stable and strong. Such strength doesn't just happen, anymore than successful businesses, growing churches, or winning football teams just happen. A desire to work to make it happen must be present. But work alone is not enough; we must know what we are doing. Thus family strength comes out of understanding what God's Word teaches about family strength and about how a family can gain that strength. Apart from a close relationship with Christ, we have no hope of achieving what God has for us in family life.

If you are not a believer, become one today; trust in the Lord Jesus Christ for your salvation. Apart from a church, your family cannot be all God desires; as we worship, discipleship, and serve as part of a church, our family grows stronger. If you are not growing in Christ as part of his church, become an involved member. Finally, commit your family to grow in his strength.—William M. Pinson Jr.[4]

SUNDAY, MAY 21, 2000
Lectionary Message

Topic: Hindrances to Baptism
TEXT: Acts 8:26–40
Other Readings: Ps. 22:25–31; 1 John 5:1–6; John 15:1–8

Acts records the spontaneous expansion of the Church under the compulsion of the Holy Spirit. It narrates the influence of the gospel from Jerusalem to the uttermost parts of the Earth. In Acts 8, we meet a man from Ethiopia. The Romans considered Ethiopia to be the ends of the Earth. In the climax of this story, the Ethiopian official asks the question, "What hinders me from being baptized" (v. 36)? The answer is "nothing," because five hindrances to his baptism have been removed. Listen closely to see if the removal of similar hindrances today might open millions more to immerse themselves in faith commitment to Christ.

I. *Hindrance 1: We as believers must be willing to run to catch up to what God is doing.* God is on a redemptive mission. He mobilizes us. In this text, an angel scheduled Phillip, the Hellenist evangelist, to keep a gospel rendezvous along the old road running southwest from Jerusalem through Gaza. Along this route, Phillip encountered a vehicle returning the court treasurer to his queen and home in Numidia, south of the second cataract of the Nile River. The Spirit commanded Phillip, "Go to that chariot and stay near it" (v. 29). Phillip must run

---

to catch up with what God is doing. To remove this first hindrance to the baptism of those whom God is calling, we must

- Recognize that the mission of redemption is initiated by God.
- Look for and run to where God is at work.
- Count on divine coincidence and recognize divine appointments.

Hearing and recognizing the Greek translation of Isaiah 53, Phillip asked if the Ethiopian understood what he was reading. The man's answer to Phillip identifies the hindrance most common to all seekers, the lack of a scriptural guide.

II. *Hindrance 2: We must be Spirit-directed, bold guides to the unbaptized.* "How can I understand unless someone explains it to me" (v. 31)? To Phillip's question came an invitation to come up, sit, and explain. Most unbelievers are open to the right guide into the Scriptures. To imitate Phillip here and overcome the second hindrance to baptism, we must:

- Run humbly alongside seekers until invited into their lives.
- Show respect by asking and listening to questions.

III. *Hindrance 3: As scriptural guides, we must enable the seeker to acquire enough biblical understanding to make a genuine commitment.* Phillip was asked to explain Isaiah 53:7. The Ethiopian was "ignostic," not agnostic. "Then Phillip began with that very passage of Scripture and told him the good news about Jesus" (v. 35).

(a) *Biblical ignorance does hinder baptism.* Phillip models the Reformation principle that Christ is the key to interpreting the Old Testament. He may have used the same Scriptures and insights that Jesus used on the road to Emmaus to explain why it was necessary for Christ to die and be raised from the dead (Luke 24:26–27). This classic messianic prophecy anticipated the atoning death of the Lamb of God (Isa. 53:7; John 1:29). This Lamb takes away sins and removes hindrances to relationship with God (Eph. 2:12–14; Gal. 3:28).

(b) *Through Jesus, culture is no hindrance to baptism.* Perhaps Phillip's witness included explanation of the great commission of Jesus that baptized disciples were to be made of the nations, of which Numidia-Ethiopia was certainly one. Whatever the case, the eunuch recognized the baptismal opportunity presented by a roadside pond. Seeing the water, the eunuch asked, "What hinders me from being baptized?" Lack of physical opportunity no longer presented a hindrance to baptism. However, the best understanding of the Ethiopian's question about baptismal hindrances was one of legality.

(c) *The law of Moses is no hindrance to believer's baptism.* The eunuch was returning from worship in Jerusalem. There he would have experienced two legal hindrances barring him from entering the inner courts of Temple worship. The Mosaic law prevented non-Hebrews from entering beyond the outermost court. Furthermore, the Mosaic law expressly forbade the physically emasculated from entering that assembly (Deut. 23:1). Whether from birth, accident, or intentional surgery, the eunuch's physical condition hindered him from full entrance into the assembly and prevented him from receiving circumcision as the entrance right of full conversion into the Hebrew community. In addition, as with all people except the high priest, the Ethiopian was perpetually hindered from entering into the very presence of God in the Holy of Holies area beyond the veil in the Temple.

(d) *The physically and socially challenged are not hindered from baptism.* Through Jesus, the messianic promise of including and honoring the emasculated in the assembly had been fulfilled (Isa. 56:3-6; see also Gal. 3:28). Phillip could have described to the Ethiopian that at the moment of Jesus' death the walls of hostility had come down and even the curtain had been torn from top to bottom. Therefore, by taking Jesus as high priest, all who believe may enter boldly to the throne of grace (Heb. 4:10). All hindrances to life with the holy one have been removed. With joy, the eunuch asked, "What can hinder me from baptism now?"

IV. *Hindrance 4: We must be willing to commit to Christ without reservation.* If God places no hindrance to our knowing and serving him amid his people, then we must never hinder a prompt response to his invitation. Most modern translations omit the baptismal inquiry and confession contained in verse 37 because the verse is not found in the oldest manuscripts. Verse 37 does record for us what were most likely the words exchanged in the baptismal waters of the early Church between the administrator and the candidate: "If you believe with all your heart, you may [be baptized]. I believe that Jesus Christ is the Son of God." For this reason, verse 37, although added later, is very helpful as a model for adult believers' baptism.

V. *Conclusion.* All hindrances to admission to the body of Christ have been removed for the believer. We must never put up new hindrances. What hindrances are you removing that others may be baptized? We must constantly act to remove hindrances to the reception of the repentant. We must receive new believers and encourage and equip them to live worthy of the high calling of their priesthood in Christ. Our invitation must be, "See, here is water. What hinders you from being baptized in Christ's name?"—Rodrick K. Durst

ILLUSTRATIONS

GROWTH.   The last word in the book of Acts is *unhinderedly.* The whole book is about the gospel's incredible ability to overcome hindrances. Natural church growth occurs whenever arbitrary hindrances to growth are removed or overcome.

ESTRANGEMENT.   Archaeologists have recovered a warning stone from the head of the gate entering into the Temple worship area. The inscription declares in multiple languages that the blood of any uncircumcised who entered there would be upon their own heads. Remember the riot that surrounded Paul's visit to Jerusalem when it was rumored that he had brought the Greek Timothy into the Temple area. In his autobiography, *On the Outside Looking In,*[5] Michael Reagan describes the incredible estrangement he felt growing up as a stepchild in the Reagan household. As an adopted child born out of wedlock, Michael Reagan was told by his parochial schoolmates that he could never go to heaven because he was an "illegitimate." Discovery of the injunction in Deuteronomy 23:2 against children of forbidden marriages ever entering the assembly of the Lord, even to the tenth generation, served to deepen his pain and alienation from God. It took him twenty years to open his Bible again. If only a kindly person had opened the Scriptures and gospel to him sooner, years of despair could have been avoided.

COMMITMENT.   William Borden was the heir to a great dairy empire, yet he surrendered to a call to missions to the Muslims of Egypt during the days of the student missions movement at Yale University. Soon after arriving at Cairo, Borden contracted encephalitis and

---

[5] New York: Zebra Books, 1988

died. Shortly before his death he cabled to his friends at Yale, "No reserves. No retreats. No regrets."—Rodrick K. Durst

SERMON SUGGESTIONS

Topic: Dwelling Place of Wonder

TEXT: Ps. 8:1–2

A church can become deadly, dull, boring, and stuffy. But think about the Church as the dwelling place of wonder. (1) We should observe *the wonder of its history.* (2) The Church deals with *the wonder of life.* (3) Consider *the wonder of man.* (4) The Church is the dwelling place of *the wonder of God.*—Gerald Kennedy[6]

Topic: Christ and Love

TEXT: John 13:34

(1) A new commandment in its comprehensiveness. (2) A new commandment in its emphasis on brotherhood. (3) A new commandment in its dominant note of love. (4) A new commandment in its model—"as I have loved you."—John A. Hayes[7]

CONGREGATIONAL MUSIC

1. "We've a Story to Tell to the Nations," H. Ernest Nichol (1896)

   MESSAGE, H. Ernest Nichol (1896)

   The missionary thrust as well as the vision of the future success of Christ's Kingdom portrayed by this vibrant hymn gathers up the theme both of the story of Phillip's winning of the Ethiopian eunuch in Acts and the latter part of Psalm 22. Thus its singing could function as a "bridge" between the two Scripture readings.

2. "Like the Murmur of the Dove's Song," Carl P. Daw Jr. (1982)

   BRIDEGROOM, Peter Cutts (1969)

   This contemporary hymn, especially in its second stanza, recalls the teaching of Jesus in John 15 concerning the vine and the branches. Its singing, invoking the Holy Spirit, could be effectively used as an "invocation" leading to the Gospel lesson.

3. "Oh, How I Love Jesus," Frederick Whitfield (1855)

   OH HOW I LOVE JESUS, anon. (1869)

   The apostle John's assertion in 1 John 4:19 that we love God because God first loved us is echoed in the chorus of this familiar gospel song.

4. "My Jesus, I Love Thee," William R. Featherstone (1864)

   GORDON, Adoniram J. Gordon, (1876)

   This devotional hymn would also be suitable as a response to the Epistle reading (1 John 4:7–21).

5. "I Need Thee Every Hour," Annie S. Hawks (1872)

   NEED, Robert Lowry (1873)

   The Scripture heading for the first appearance of this song was John 15:5b: "Without me you can do nothing." Given this fact, its singing in connection with the Gospel reading could be especially meaningful.—Hugh T. McElrath

---

[6] *Fresh Every Morning*

[7] *The Ten Commandments*

WORSHIP AIDS

CALL TO WORSHIP. "I will tell of your name [O Lord], to my brothers and sisters; in the midst of the congregation I will praise you: You who fear the Lord, praise him" (Ps. 22:22–23a NRSV).

INVOCATION.   O Lord, we await the wonder of your presence among us. We long for a word of guidance from you. We desire to catch a vision of what you would have us do and be when we return to the everyday world. That such might happen we commit ourselves to this high hour of holy worship.—Henry Fields

OFFERTORY SENTENCE.   "As ye have therefore received Christ Jesus the Lord, so walk ye in him: rooted and built up in him, and established in the faith, as ye have been taught, abounding therein with thanksgiving" (Col. 2:6–7).

OFFERTORY PRAYER.   We cannot contemplate your great love for us and turn aside from the opportunity to have a part in the many services of the Church to spread the good word abroad. Bless now what we bring before you, and use these offerings for the furtherance of the gospel by word and deed.

PRAYER.   Our Father and our God, as we acknowledge our own waywardness, we rejoice all the more in the abundance of your mercy, which follows us constantly all our days. From the rising of the sun to its setting at eventide, your goodness never fails to surprise and surround us. We bless you for the seasons of joy and success in life, for the quiet comfort of your Spirit when we are in pain or trouble, for your patience with us when things are in disarray and we shift the blame to you and rebel, and especially for the infusion and optimism of genuine faith that steadies our feet in our pilgrimage whenever we feel uncertain and the headwinds of adversity are overly strong. May we so appropriate your grace and favor that every time of worship will mean entering your gates with thanksgiving and treading your courts with praise. Remake us into obedient servants of your will so we shall be known as those whose confidence rests in you and who find nowhere else the secret of daily victory and strength.—Donald Macleod[8]

SERMON
Topic: The Tie That Binds
TEXT: John 15:1–17

Raymond Brown sees a connection to the Kingdom parables of the other Gospels. In the figure of the vine, Jesus is leaving final words with his closest friends, but words that seem to be intended for the whole Church of all times. He used familiar pictures. Isaiah and Ezekiel had envisioned Israel as the vineyard of God. We know well the part about pruning vines and bearing fruit. Jesus extends the image beyond judgment to the connection of our lives to God: "I am the vine, you are the branches. Apart from me you can do nothing." Jesus would not

---

[8] *Princeton Pulpit Prayers*

leave his friends without comfort, without the same kind of powerful spiritual presence that had been the dynamic of his own life. Two essential words about the Church leap out at us: (1) Life flows from the vine to the branches; Christ is the source of life. (2) The branches are connected at the vine; Christ is our link to one another.

I. As Church, we celebrate a mystical bond in Christ that exceeds all other notions of human relationship. Paul was moved toward the figure of marriage to explain the unexplainable relationship between Christ and his Church. This bond extends to our fellowship with one another. The earliest notions of the "communion of saints" in the New Testament was not so much an idea of community with the dead as of the family tie between friends in the Church. The word *communion,* or *koinonia,* addresses the shared life we have with God and with one another in Christ. The Old Testament is built on covenant relationship with God. Moses was distinct from the Prophets, for he was one whom God knew "face to face." Thus, Philo speaks of the *koinonia* between God and Moses.

We are joined at the Christ. We are more than individuals in need of only the nurture of a devotional relationship with God. We are Church. We are bound together as we pray and as we work in the name of our Lord. We are more than a huddled mass of humanity closed up to ourselves. Our forebears in Christian history, the Anabaptists, attempted to shut out the evil world by living only to themselves. We cannot minister only to ourselves and fulfill our calling in Christ. Scattered to the four winds, the people of God are never alone in the world. The only way the missionary can leave family and friends to go into a strange place to preach in a different language and culture is to know the bond that holds us together.

II. As Church, we reach across the bounds of time and place to become one body in Christ. The lifeblood of the Church flows through the cooperative labor of the people. As we share our lives with one another, we are bound together in Christ. Jesus said, "I am the vine, you are the branches" and "This is my commandment, that you love one another as I have loved you." This is the farewell discourse. Jesus was preparing his disciples for his death and for their new birth through the communion of the Church.

If death cannot break this bond, certainly distance cannot. "Out of sight, out of mind" is the whimpering sob of one who cannot face separation. Early Christians struggled initially with the reality of separation from the person of Christ and finally with the death of Christian friends. Out of the crush of life came the promise of *koinonia.* Jesus would not leave his disciples without the strengthening, comforting presence of the Spirit of God, and he would not leave them without the support of one another. The tie that binds us in Christ is a communion that crosses the lines of death and distance.—Larry Dipboye

SUNDAY, MAY 28, 2000
Lectionary Message
Topic: The Day the Church Grew Up (or The Gentile Pentecost)
TEXT: Acts 10: 44–48
Other Readings: Ps. 98; 1 John 5:1–6; John 15:9–17

Maturity is the mission of the Spirit. Learning is the way the mature express their faithfulness to the mission of the Spirit of Christ. Such faithfulness is found in Acts 10:44–48. The passage is called "the Gentile Pentecost" for good reason. On the day the Spirit fell upon the

Jewish believers at Pentecost, the Church of Christ sprang up. On the day the Spirit fell upon the Gentile believers at Caesarea, the Church of Christ grew up. On that day, the Church outgrew captivity to a single culture to become a church for the nations. At least five dimensions of Christian maturity are identifiable in this incredible passage.

I. *The mature acknowledge and accept unexpected realities.* Peter and his company had not anticipated that the Holy Spirit would fall upon the uncircumcised in the same measure and manner as he had fallen upon the circumcised. Despite his own astonishment, Peter acted responsibly by acknowledging the reality of what the Spirit of Christ had done. "Can anyone keep these people from being baptized with water? They have received the Holy Spirit just as we have" (v. 47). Leaders have a responsibility to articulate spiritual events to the congregation. Maturity depends on moving to new insights and greater values concerning redemption in Christ.

II. *The mature are able to overlook surface appearances to see deeper truths.* God had been preparing Peter and the early Church to leap to the ends of the Earth and overcome cultural comfort zones. Peter had already realized "how true it is that God does not show favoritism but accepts men from every nation who fear him and do what is right" (vv. 34–35). Peter called his Christian brothers from Joppa to a new level of insight that overlooked skin, accents, and customs to let Christ and the Church be for the nations.

III. *The mature move out of comfortable patterns and habits and into new adventures.* Peter's logic must have been something like, "If God has seen fit to baptize these Gentiles with his Spirit, then who are we not to baptize them with water in Christ's name?" Our logic then must follow: never deny the water of baptism to any whose confession of faith in Christ is accompanied by newness of spirit. New spiritual life from above is God's green light to go ahead with a person's baptism. Absence of a new spirituality or attitude in a person is a red light concerning baptism in Christ's name.

IV. *The mature discern what is authentically of God and what is not.* The mature test the spirits to see whether they are of God (1 John 4:1–3). Just as traditionalism and racism hinder the gospel, so can innovation. Only the immature think that everything new is from God. Two innovations to early Church custom are found in these four verses. First, the Spirit baptized these Gentiles before they were water baptized. That order was new. But remember, holy fire is never wildfire. Second, excluding the baptism of the Ethiopian by Phillip in Acts 8, the uncircumcised were first baptized by apostolic instruction. The culture of the baptized was new. Luke's record in Acts is very clear that "he [Peter] ordered that they [the Gentile believers] be baptized in the name of Jesus Christ" (v. 48). Appropriately enough, Peter later went up to Jerusalem to explain these actions and to articulate that they were faithful to God the Father of Jesus Christ and to the gospel (Acts 11). All our innovations and actions should meet these doctrinal tests before our brothers and sisters in Christ. The Anabaptist leader John Hubmaier once said, "I may err, but since I can always be corrected by the word of God, I can never be a heretic."

V. *The mature are willing to accept new people into the Church in Christ's spirit and in Christ's name.* New life comes to old churches through new believers, yet so many refuse to accept new people into the fellowship. We may baptize them, but must we accept them? Yes! After the baptism, Peter stayed "for a few days" for fellowship and teaching (v. 48). What does not prevent baptism must not prevent fellowship. If Christ accepts outsiders as insiders, so must we or we are not Christ's. People are to be accepted on the basis of similarity of confession and not culture. We must assimilate any whose confession is accompanied by a worshipful attitude and spirit. To do otherwise is to backslide from the call to Christian maturity and mission.

VI. *Conclusion.* In Christ, maturity is not to become old. Christian maturity is to become new. He makes all things new. If we are in Christ, then old things will be passing away and new things will be coming. Are you in Christ? Then what's new and who's new?—Rodrick K. Durst

ILLUSTRATIONS

HOSPITALITY.   The Greek word for hospitality (*zenophilia*) means love of strangers. Some people have the capacity to make even strangers feel at home. Others have the capacity to make even friends feel like strangers! Practice hospitality to make it perfect and to make it permanent. Practicing hospitality turns strangers into friends and family (Heb. 13:1–2; Rom. 12:13; 1 Pet. 4:9).—Rodrick K. Durst

RISK TAKING.   Church consultants have often concluded that churches have a very specific pattern of development. Churches tend to move from risk taking to caretaking and finally to undertaking. When a church is just starting, the members take many risks to grow. In middle age, the church just takes care of what and who it has. Finally, in old age, the church calls for an undertaker-pastor to preach until the church dies for lack of new members. The book of Acts and the Spirit call the Church to take risks ever and always.—Rodrick K. Durst

NEWNESS IN CHRIST.   Perhaps we should ask the family members of a baptismal candidate if they have detected anything new about a candidate before we baptize. The early twentieth-century Baptist missionary to China Bertha Smith claimed that many Chinese had been "buried alive" by baptism before they had genuinely died to their old selfish life. We are burying people alive whenever we baptize anyone who has not died to their old way of self and sin in order to take up the new life of the spirit in Christ (Rom. 6:1–4).—Rodrick Durst

SERMON SUGGESTIONS

Topic: God's Way of Working

TEXT: Deut. 6:23

(1) God is concerned about us, as he was concerned about the children of Israel, to deliver us from our troubles. (2) His deliverance is *from* something *to* something wonderful.

Topic: Inner Reward

TEXT: 2 Cor. 4:16–18

(1) We cannot escape the problems of aging. (2) Notwithstanding, our difficulties and challenges may be the occasions of special inner enrichment. (3) The glorious goal of our life in Christ should give us courage to face every circumstance with faith, hope, and love.

CONGREGATIONAL MUSIC

1. "What a Friend We Have in Jesus," Joseph Scriven (c. 1855)
    CONVERSE, Charles C. Converse (1868)

Friendship with God through obedience to his commandment of love is one theme of both the Gospel lesson and this familiar hymn. Its singing would logically follow the reading of John 15:9–17.

2. "My Lord, I Did Not Choose You," Josiah Conder (1843)

WHITFIELD, Anonymous (1869)

This hymn is based on Jesus' statement in John 15:16 and thus appropriately could be used in connection with the Gospel lesson.

3. "Joy to the World," Issac Watts (1719)

ANTIOCH, George F. Handel (1741)

Because this well-known hymn is usually sung only at Christmas time, it is little known that it is really based on Psalm 98:4–9. Therefore it does not have to be confined to the Christmas season but can be used to follow the Psalter reading for this day.

4. "Spirit of the Living God," Daniel Iverson (1926)

IVERSON, Daniel Iverson (1726)

As a response to the reading of Acts 10:44–48, in which the story of God's Spirit falling on the people hearing Peter's preaching is related, this appealing song is quite appropriate if sung prayerfully.—Hugh T. McElrath

WORSHIP AIDS

CALL TO WORSHIP.   "O sing to the Lord a new song, for he has done marvelous things" (Ps. 98:1a NRSV).

INVOCATION.   Lord, come to us in the music, the words, the silences of this hour of corporate worship as we bow down before you and open ourselves to your life-changing power.—E. Lee Phillips

OFFERTORY SENTENCE.   "He will always make you rich enough to be generous at all times, so that many will thank God for your gifts which they receive from us" (2 Cor. 9:11 TEV).

OFFERTORY SENTENCE.   Inspire us this morning to be generous with our giving, Father. Remind us of the needs of the world, which can be met only through the ongoing ministry of Christ's Church, which depends on our faithful and generous giving, we pray in Christ's name.—Henry Fields

PRAYER.   Risen Christ, Ascended Lord, we gather to worship surrounded by the fulfillment of your promises to us. From the beginning of creation through the birth of the Lord's day, your promises grant us assurance and hope, direction and purpose. We give you thanks.

On this special day, O living God, we peer through many windows, most in the room of gratitude. Through one window we are indeed redeemed by your Resurrection and now Ascension. May we find ourselves "lost in wonder, love, and praise" for your grandness and goodness.

Then we peer through the window for our graduating high school seniors. We pray that you continue to bless and guide them. As their church home and ship, we launch them now into a deeper and wider ocean. As they go and grow, may they learn more about how "fierce and gleaming is thy mystery drawing them to shores unknown," to new horizons, fresh challenges, wondrous discoveries. Bless them, O God.

Through a window fogged with tears and sadness, we offer thanks for these sixteen saints who have loved and served among us. The calling of each name stirs our hearts and memories with gladness and shapes a smile upon our spirit.

We rejoice that this day becomes a family reunion, for we are made kin by Christ's blood. We look forward to a grand reunion. As these join that cloud and chorus of witnesses that encourage and cheer us on, that enrich and give voice to the silence of this sanctuary, we lean into that "mystic sweet communion with those whose rest is won."

Thanks be to God, who gives them and us the victory through Jesus Christ our Lord. And we miss not the connection this day between your Ascension and the promise of ours.

On this national memorial weekend, we also glance through the window of gratitude for those who have served our country, and for the many who have given life and limb that we might enjoy freedom—life, liberty, and the pursuit of happiness. Especially we give thanks for those from this community of faith who have served our country and given much.

Understanding God, Creator of us all, looking through a dark and cloudy window, we pray for our country and particularly for our youth, our schools, our society. We are stunned by the seeds and now heavy harvest of so much violence. Make us all instruments of your peace.

Gracious God, for all the good gifts of this day, for seniors and saints and soldiers and servants, we give thanks in the name of our Risen and Ascended Lord.—William M. Johnson

SERMON
Topic: New Beginnings
TEXT: Heb. 10:20; 2 Cor. 5:17–21

The Bible is filled with stories of people, churches, and nations who have experienced new beginnings in God's revelation of his purpose in their lives. Adam and Eve were given a new beginning outside the garden. God put a mark on Cain and sent him to the land of Nod for a new beginning. Noah built an ark and God gave him and his family a new beginning. God told Abraham to go from his country, kindred, and family and said, "I will make you a great nation" (Genesis 12:2). With Isaac on the altar and knife in hand, Abraham responded to the voice of the angel of the Lord, and so began the miracle of new beginnings for people of faith like you and myself.

The history of Israel is filled with events for new beginnings for people who often went astray. Nothing is fixed in human and divine-human relationships that cannot be enriched with new beginnings. God's greatest miracle—the death, burial and Resurrection of Jesus—stands out as the eternal testimony of God's will and ability in providing new beginnings. Repentance opens the door to new beginnings. Faith brings the resources of God's grace to our needs in new beginnings.

We all need new beginnings. We need something to release us so we can walk away from the sin of our past life to a life of new beginnings. You and I are released from our past as we go to the experiences of newness in Jesus Christ—God the giver of new beginnings. Lazarus became ill, died, and was buried, and Jesus wasn't there. God sometimes is away from us, it seems, in our empty experiences. But Jesus came a few days later and Mary and Martha,

Lazarus' sisters, talked with him about his absence. Jesus went to the grave and called Lazarus from the dead. God has the power to call you and me from the deadness of our past, the emptiness of our present, and the futility of our future if we are willing to trust in and rely on him. Jesus came so our lives might be new and full again. He is wanting to bring a living resurrection into your and my life.

My favorite story of all stories of new beginnings is the story of the big fisherman—Peter, who was quick to speak and strong to act at the Lord's Last Supper. The Church was going so very well but a problem arose—what are we going to do with the Gentiles who have never been Jews who come to church? Peter said, "We better not try to put them together." Then God gave Peter a new beginning on the rooftop when a tent came down like a sheet in front of him and he was told to eat things he had never dared to eat. He came out of the experience declaring that God is no respecter of persons.

We have been called to live the resurrected life, which has the potential of new beginnings regardless of the circumstances of our present situation. Revelation 21:5 declares, "He who sat upon the throne said, 'Behold, I make all things new.'" Ours is the call to live and the hope of the resurrected life. Paul addresses this issue very clearly in his letter to the Corinthian church (2 Cor. 5:17–21).

God asked Jesus to taste sin, to become sin, to enter into the human predicament, which gives to desperate people such as you and I a new beginning. If God would invest this much in you and me for new beginnings, how grateful and thankful we ought to be.

These great truths are evident in Paul's letter to the Corinthian church. Working together with God makes everything I do sacred. There is no greater need in our country and world than for us to bring the sacred and secular together under the will and power of God, to his glory and the betterment of every living person on this Earth.

Our new beginnings come with a price—with a potential for all Christ can bring us. Revelation 3:14–22 pictures Jesus best for me. John wrote to the church at Laodicea, a church with problems that was seemingly going places, maybe even to the wrong place. He concluded his letter by saying (v. 20), "Behold, I stand at the door and knock; if anyone hears my voice and opens the door, I will come in to him and eat with him, and he with me." We are a Church that prays, searches, and hopes for a new beginning. John says, "Jesus is at the door knocking so he might bring to us our new beginning."

If Jesus were to come to church, how would he get here? Would he come through the roof, window, or door? Would he come the night before? Would he come in the middle of the service? Jesus comes to church in your experiences and mine. He comes to church with insights and teachings of Scripture, comes to church in the person of the Holy Spirit. Listen and see if he is knocking at the door of our church? Did you bring him today or did you come looking for him? So often we think we go to church to find Jesus. We really ought to bring him to church so others can find him. We need to share ourselves in an open, loving way and find among our differences the Jesus way of doing things.

Someone recently wrote an article that identified the Church as "God's New Thing." Under the Lordship of Christ we become new people whose life is from above and with a new nature and new values. We are the people of God whose life is from above. The church as God's New Thing is the agent, power, force, and instrument of the Holy Spirit. We call it the Kingdom of God.—Joe Priest Williams

SUNDAY, JUNE 4, 2000

Lectionary Message

Topic: Utmost Certainty

TEXT: 1 John 5:9–13

Other Readings: Ps. 1; Acts 1:15–17, 21–26; John 17:6–19

We live in an uncertain world. People all over the world are wondering, What is going to happen in the world in the future? Will we continue to have occasional riots? Will war break out again in the Middle East? What is really going on in Russia? Will Japan take over the economic life of the United States? Will the stock market crash? Will we have jobs tomorrow? Will the drug problem in our nation get worse?

We are living in a day in which it seems that everything we once thought was nailed down is coming loose. It is an uncertain world! Is there any certainty for such an uncertain world? I believe that there is utmost certainty, and it is found in verse 13 of 1 John 5: "that ye may know. . . ." Jesus was saying that if you believe in the name of the Son of God, you may not only know but you may be certain that you have eternal life. Here is God's great certainty, utmost certainty, and offer for certainty in an uncertain world.

One of the basic longings of the human heart is the longing for assurance and certainty, the longing for security. This is especially true in the area of spiritual life, because we know that spiritual life is eternal. When it comes to the question of where we are going when we die, we want some certainty in the answer to that question. So very simply let's draw some conclusions from the text in 1 John 5:13.

I. *It is certain that we can know that we have eternal life.* Some believe that this is sheer presumption. But the apostle says in our text, "I have written to you who believe on the name of my son that you may know that you have eternal life." God did not inspire the apostle to write that verse to say instead, "I have written that you may *hope* or *think* or *assume* that you have eternal life." He wrote, *"that you may know."*

It is possible to know that you have eternal life. It is possible for you to know that if you were to die this very day, heaven would be your home. God wants you to know this not just in the "sweet by and by" but in today's "here and now." As you confront the problems of this life, you have a heavenly home with him, if you belong to him. That is utmost certainty.

II. *We must realize that this promise of certainty that you have eternal life is limited.* This is not a blanket coverage kind of promise. It is not for everyone on Earth, although the possibility is there for them to claim it. This promise includes only a select group, a particular category of people. The promise is that only those who believe in Jesus Christ can know that they have eternal life. To believe means to trust. God's Son is the Lord Jesus, so what God promises is this: "I am writing to all of you who have trusted in the name of my Son, the Lord Jesus Christ, that you may know that you have eternal life." If you are a believer in Jesus Christ, the good news to you is that you can know that you have eternal life.

III. *You can personally know that you have eternal life.* The way you can know that you have eternal life is not on the basis of feelings. The problem with feelings is that they change. Human beings are so emotionally constituted that feelings alter, they vacillate, they fluctuate, they are not steady. For real assurance you have to have something that never changes or alters, something that is fixed. The thing that never changes is the promise of God. How do you know that you have eternal life? You know because when you became a believer God said that you do. He tells us in his Word that if we meet the condition of faith we will have eternal life. We know that God never lies to us. He always keeps his promises. He is absolutely trustworthy.

Then why do so many doubt? Sometimes it is because they have unforgiven, unconfessed sin in their lives. They let it come between them and God. Most people doubt because they are not willing to take the promises of God at face value. We must be willing to accept what God says in his Word. As long as we refuse to accept what God says in his Word, we will never have the assurance that we need.

The presence of the Holy Spirit, when we are responsive to him, gives witness to us of our salvation and gives witness to us of the promise of God for eternal life. Also look back to that time when you trusted Christ for your salvation, not at the events that have happened since, and see if that experience was real and if it was what God had promised.

That is the utmost certainty that God has given so that you may know that you have eternal life. If there has been a time in your life when you have trusted Christ for your salvation, then you can know and lay claim to the promise of God.—W. Matt Tomlin

ILLUSTRATION

One of the children in our church, a little boy ten years of age, was killed while riding a small motorcycle. He hit a bump in the road and lost control, his helmet came off, and his head hit the pavement. Three days later he died from the head injury. Just two weeks before the accident little Joey had declared his faith in Christ, accepting him as savior.

When I was preparing to conduct the funeral, the father of little Joey requested that I read the words from 2 Samuel 12, the account of King David's son dying. The father laid claim to the words of verses 22 and 23, which are, "And he said, While the child was yet alive, I fasted and wept for I said, Who can tell whether God will be gracious to me, that the child may live? But now he is dead, wherefore shall I fast? Can I bring him back again? I shall go to him, but he shall not return to me" (2 Sam. 12:22–23 KJV). The father's words to his wife and family, were these: "We cannot bring him back, but thank God we know where he is. He placed his faith in Christ, and so have we. That means that one of these days we will go where he is and we will see our precious son again."

Even though his heart was broken, through his tears he could express his utmost certainty in God's promise of eternal life.—W. Matt Tomlin

SERMON SUGGESTIONS

Topic: From Doubt to Faith
TEXT: Isa. 40:27–31
(1) Circumstances often make it easy to doubt God's goodness and justice. (2) Yet God does not give up on his weak and complaining people. (3) Two movements complete the success story: (a) our persistent expectation of God's action, and (b) God's abundant fulfillment of his gracious purpose.

Topic: The Way Through
TEXT: Matt. 11:28–30
(1) An encouraging invitation (v. 28). (2) A gentle command (v. 29). (3) A compelling secret—a yoke that fits (v. 30).

CONGREGATIONAL MUSIC

1. "Jesus Lives, and So Shall I," Christian Gellert (1757)

ZUVERSICHT, Johann Crüger (1653)

The apostle John's teaching (1 John 5:11–13) that to those who believe God has given eternal life finds a vibrant response in this great hymn of the Resurrection. Since the tune, like many from the German, is in bar form (AAB), choir and congregation could alternate on the first two sections of each stanza and come together on the triumphant affirmation: "Jesus, my hope and trust" (A, choir; A, congregation; B, all together).

2. "How Blest Are They Who, Fearing God," Psalm 1, vers. *Psalter* (1912)

ST. ANNE, William Croft (1708)

The five stanzas of this metrical version of Psalm 1 could profitably be alternated with the reading of the original verses, as follows: read Ps. 1:1, sing stanza 1; read Ps. 1:2, sing stanza 2; read Ps. 1:3, sing stanza 3; read Ps. 1:4–5, sing stanza 4; read Ps. 1:6, sing stanza 5.

3. "So Send I You," E. Margaret Clarkson (1938)

TORONTO, John W. Peterson

This contemporary missionary hymn is based on John 20:21. However, Jesus' priestly prayer in this day's Gospel lesson also contains the same idea. "So Send I You" would therefore be eminently appropriate if used with the Gospel reading (John 17:6–19).

4. "By All Your Saints in Warfare," Horatio B. Nelson (1864)

KING'S LYNN, English folk tune; arr. R. V. Williams (1906)

Matthias, who replaced Judas among the disciples, is a very minor saint, little celebrated in Christian worship. However, this hymn, composed with a general initial stanza and a concluding doxological one can have as a central stanza,

> Lord, your abiding presence
> Mysterious made the choice;
> For one in place of Judas
> The faithful now rejoice.
> From all such false apostles
> Your holy church defend
> And by your parting promise
> Be with us to the end.

This hymn could be sung or quoted following the reading from Acts (1:15–17, 21–26).—Hugh T. McElrath

WORSHIP AIDS

CALL TO WORSHIP.   "Happy are those who do not follow the advice of the wicked or take the path that sinners tread or sit in the seat of scoffers; but their delight is in the law of the Lord, and on his law they meditate day and night" (Ps. 1:1–2 NRSV).

INVOCATION.   Lord, we have eyes: open them to what you want us to see. We have hearts: turn them toward those who are lonely, discouraged, and erring. We have hands: move them to help when there are things we can do.

OFFERTORY SENTENCE.   "Let your light shine before others so that they may see your good works and give glory to your Father in heaven" (Matt. 5:16 NRSV).

OFFERTORY PRAYER.   Awaken a sense of need within us to be caretakers of your Kingdom, Father. As we give this offering, may we give because we care for the causes of Christ and the welfare of our fellow pilgrims.—Henry Fields

PRAYER.   Merciful Father, awaken us to the ways of your amazing grace as we worship here today. Open our eyes that we may behold the many times when you invaded life with presence, strength, wisdom, hope, love, and support. How many times have you come into our lives through the extended hands and hearts of people about us. Forgive us when we fail to acknowledge your presence manifested in the kind and good deeds that people constantly do for us all.

How we thank you that already in our lives and in the lives of others we have experienced the breakthrough that sets us free. Looking about us and gazing momentarily into the yesterdays of life, we marvel at the certainty of your working in lives and conditions all around us. We have seen how in moments of despair your grace has come bearing the gift of hope. We have found how in lonely hours of sorrow the comfort of your presence has seen us through. We know firsthand how when the remorse of sin had torn our souls, the way to conviction and forgiveness and the way out came to us through your grace and salvation.—Henry Fields

SERMON
Topic: On Whose Shoulders Now?
Text: 2 Kings 2:6–14; Ps. 47; Luke 24:44–53

We think of the Ascension as a cosmological event, a space flight, a transfer of a body from Earth up into heaven. But that is not what it meant to the Church. What it meant to the Church was a transfer of responsibility from Jesus to his disciples. It was not so much a cosmological event as it was a commissioning event. The mission that Jesus had, including the power with which he did it, is now transferred to his disciples. Not only does Jesus give us so much, but the Ascension means that now Jesus asks of us much.

Let's begin by looking at another ascension, the ascension of Elijah. Elijah lived 880 years before Jesus, when Ahab was king. Ahab had a Phoenician wife; her name was Jezebel. Jezebel was not a nice lady. She brought from her home country of Phoenicia the priests of Baal, who sought to make the worship of the idol Baal the official religion of Israel. So Yahweh, the God of Israel, said to Elijah, his prophet, "Go speak against the queen and her political agenda for this country," which he did. Then he called the priests of Baal to a contest on Mt. Carmel to demonstrate who was more powerful: Baal or Yahweh, the God of Israel. Elijah won.

Jezebel got angry and told Elijah she was going to get him. So Elijah went out into the desert and into a depression, asking why bad things happen to good people. He hid in a cave. There God found him and told him in a still, small voice to come out because "I have three things for you to do." The third thing that God had for Elijah to do was to pick Elijah's successor.

Which brings us to our text for this morning from the Old Testament. Elisha has been chosen as Elijah's successor. Elijah was taking Elisha around the country to all the shrines, showing him "the works." It was sort of a farewell tour for Elijah. He was showing off his powers, which were evidently related to his mantle. A mantle is a cape that goes over your shoulders. Elijah rolled it up like a wand. He waved it over things and did fantastic miracles.

They come at last to the River Jordan, at the end of the tour. Elijah waved his mantle over the waters. The waters parted. That has to be the favorite Jewish miracle. You save that one for the finale. Parting the waters of Jordan, they went across. Elisha said to Elijah, "Let me inherit your spirit so that I can do what you have done." Then a chariot of fire pulled up. Elijah got into it and closed the door. Up he went into heaven! As he climbed, the mantle fell off his shoulder and to the ground in front of Elisha. Elisha picked up the mantle, rolled it into a wand, parted the waters of the Jordan, and walked back across, to demonstrate that Elisha not only has the mission of Elijah but he also has Elijah's power.

That is called "taking up a mantle." It means that the responsibility for making society better passes from generation to generation. Those who went before us give us the task they had. We take up their mantle. That is what it means. The amazing thing about taking up a mantle is that when you do it you discover you have power inside of you that you never knew you had. You did not have that power until you took up the mantle.

I imagine that each of you can recall instances when some unlikely person was given a title, power, or responsibility and you thought they would never make it; they would never measure up, especially when you compared them with the person who was leaving that job. The person coming in would never do as well as the person they succeeded; the distance between the two was so great. But they did well. Sometimes they exceeded the accomplishments of the person that was before them. All because a mantle had fallen on their shoulders, a power had been conferred upon them.

Now go to the New Testament lesson. It is the story of the Ascension of Jesus. You notice it sounds just like Elijah being lifted up into heaven. It is supposed to. Luke wants you to see that being a Christian means that you are to take up a mantle.

In the last scene of Elijah's life he ascends into heaven. In the last scene of Jesus' life he ascends into heaven. Elijah's mantle falls to the ground. Elisha picks it up. Jesus says, "I send the promise of my Father upon you. Stay in the city until you are clothed [like with a mantle] with power from on high."

The real conclusion of the ascension of Jesus occurs in the book of Acts, which was also written by Luke, in the second chapter. Ten days after the Ascension, at the feast day called Pentecost, the Spirit of Jesus came upon the disciples, like a mantle, and empowered them now to be apostles.

Jesus is Elijah. We are to be Elisha, and take up where Jesus left off. When you read the story of the apostles in Acts you will see that is exactly what they did. They did exactly the same things that Jesus did. They preached the Kingdom, they healed the sick, they cast out demons, they converted the nations, they formed a new community of humanity called the Church. They even got into the same trouble that Jesus got into, with the same people. They even had the same trials that Jesus had. They even died the same death that Jesus died.

Luke was trying to make this point. When you take up a mantle, you do extraordinary things, things that you never thought you would ever do, things you never thought you could do. Jesus is gone. As the creed puts it, he is now "sitting at the right hand of God the Father Almighty." But his Spirit is here, like a mantle, waiting for you to take it up.—Mark Trotter

SUNDAY, JUNE 11, 2000
Lectionary Message

Topic: Powerful Restoration
TEXT: Acts 2:1–21
Other Readings: Ezek. 37:1–14; Ps.104:24–34, 35b; John 15:26–27; 16:4b–15; Rom. 8:22–27

From outcast to hero, from failure to victory. There is something in all of us that longs to know such restoration is possible. We read of characters, both real and fictional, who have made that glorious comeback, after life has seemingly defeated them. Through some chain of circumstances, they make a comeback, and their lives are restored to even greater heights than they had enjoyed before calamity struck. Perhaps we need to know that because we know what it means to fail at something and to wonder if it will ever be the same again.

Peter knew that feeling. He was one of the inner circle of disciples with whom Jesus surrounded himself. But this man whom Jesus had named "the Rock" turned to mush on the night of the arrest and trials of Jesus, denying his Lord three times. What abysmal failure! Peter knew what it was like to hit rock bottom. That is why the story of restoration is so meaningful to us, because we can see it in the life of Peter. Despite the tragedy of his denial and sin, the Lord reached out to him and drew him back into discipleship and eventual leadership in the early Church. In our text we see the culmination of the powerful restoration, as Peter preached the great sermon at Pentecost, as the Spirit came down and did its mighty work.

Jesus can take our lives, even at our deepest point of failure, and he can restore us to wholeness. Peter is a marvelous example of that truth, and Acts 2 shows us what results from such a restoration.

I. *Being restored means that we are given a new power.* When the thousands of pilgrims came to Jerusalem for the Feast of the Passover, the followers of Jesus were gathered together, and in the morning they were startled by the sound of a mighty wind as the Holy Spirit filled the space and then filled the believers.

The coming of the Spirit brought new power to Peter and his fellow believers: power to offer new life in Christ in a startling, effective way. If you have given your heart to Christ, you have the same access to the same power that Peter experienced at Pentecost. It is not power given for its own sake; rather, it is power for service and for witness. Jesus had promised them earlier, "But you will receive power when the Holy Spirit comes on you, and you will be my witnesses" (Acts 1:8a NIV). The power that had been absent in Peter's life when he denied his Lord was now clearly evident through the filling of the Holy Spirit.

God wants to bring that same power into your life. Like Peter you may feel that you are inadequate, unworthy. Yet the message is clear. No matter who you are, no matter what you have done or failed to do, God is ready to bring new life and new power to you right now. Your life can be restored to new power that you never dreamed possible.

II. *When that powerful restoration takes place, we proclaim a new message.* Peter who had sworn that he did not know Jesus now stepped before the half-inquiring, half-mocking crowd and proclaimed mightily the gospel of Jesus Christ and his allegiance to it. What was the difference? Peter had a new message, because he had been open to the coming of the Spirit and had experienced a powerful restoration. His message was that Christ is risen! The Resurrection was at the heart of the early Church's message, and it ought to be at the center of ours as well. We do not serve a Savior who died two thousand years ago; we serve one who was raised from the dead and is alive today. Peter's message was also that Jesus is Lord. He was not only the Christ; he was also the Lord of life and of history. His message was also that people must respond in faith and surrender to this Lord of life and accept him as Savior. That response must also involve service to the Lord.

III. *Powerful restoration means that we are empowered to make a new impact on the world around us.* On that great occasion of Pentecost, three thousand people responded in faith and trust to the Christ who was preached. What an amazing restoration! A weak, discouraged disciple had become a powerful deliverer of a message that had a tremendous impact on the crowd. But to accomplish this and have such an impact, Peter had to experience God's forgiving, restoring love. He had to receive the Spirit's presence and power. Then he was capable of being used in such a remarkable way.

God wants to use you and me to accomplish some powerful things in the life of the Church and in the lives of others. Like Peter we may be weak and ineffectual, but like Peter we can be transformed into powerful proclaimers of the gospel.—W. Matt Tomlin

ILLUSTRATIONS

PENTECOST TODAY.   Charles Gabriel wrote a prayer, many years ago that has become one of our greatest hymns, "Pentecostal Power." Not only did he write the words but he set it to music. The first verse and the chorus of that hymn express the powerful restoration that people need. Here are those words:

> Lord, as of old at Pentecost
> Thou didst thy pow'r display,
> With cleansing, purifying flame,
> Descend on us today.

> Lord, send the old time power, the Pentecostal power!
> Thy flood-gates of blessing on us throw open wide!
> Lord, send the old-time power, the Pentecostal power,
> That sinners be converted, and Thy name glorified.[1]

If we could pray that prayer sincerely, then perhaps we could receive that powerful restoration that we so desperately desire.—W. Matt Tomlin

SPIRITUAL PRESENCE.   One can compare the Spiritual Presence with the air we breathe, which surrounds us, is nearest to us, and works life within us. This comparison has a deep justification: In most languages, the word *spirit* means breath or wind. Sometimes the wind

---

[1] Charles Gabriel, "Pentecostal Power," *The Baptist Hymnal* (Nashville, Tenn.: Convention Press, 1991), p. 242.

becomes storm, grand and devastating; but mostly it is moving air, always present, not always noticed. In the same way the Spirit is always present, a moving power, sometimes in stormy ecstasies of individuals and groups, mostly quietly entering our human spirit and keeping it alive; sometimes manifest in great moments of history or of a personal life, mostly working hiddenly through the media of our daily encounters with men and world; sometimes using its creation, the religious communities and their Spiritual means, often making itself felt in spheres far removed from what is usually called religious. Like the wind the Spirit blows where it wills!—Paul Tillich[2]

SERMON SUGGESTIONS

Topic: Glad Worship
TEXT: Ps. 100
(1) Joyful worship is our privilege (vv. 1–2). (2) Such acknowledgment is our fitting duty because the Lord is our creator and we belong to him (v. 3). (3) Corporate worship in a dedicated place evokes thanksgiving and praise (v. 4). (4) The basis of our worship is the Lord's unfailing love (v. 5).

Topic: The Urgent Truth
TEXT: Heb. 2:1–4
(1) It is the truth of Jesus Christ, God's Son, our Savior (Heb. 1:3). (2) It is possible to drift away from this truth (v. 1). (3) There are temporal and eternal consequences to indifference to the great salvation offered to us (vv. 3–4). (4) The evidence for this truth is available to those who have hearts open to receive it (v. 4).

CONGREGATIONAL MUSIC

1. "O Worship the King" (1833)
   HANOVER, attr. William Croft (1708)
   This majestic hymn is a highly romantic metrical version of Psalm 104. Although very free in expression, it breathes the basic spirit of the original psalm and makes an excellent opening hymn for corporate worship.

2. "Hail Thee, Festival Day!" Venantius Fortunatus (fourteenth century); tr. *English Hymnal* (1906)
   SALVE FESTA DIES, Ralph Vaughan Williams (1906)
   This ancient hymn appropriate for Pentecost, paired with a fine tune, forms a magnificent setting for a processional. It lends itself naturally to having the stanzas sung by choir alone, with the congregation joining in singing the vibrant refrain.

3. "Come, Gracious Spirit, Heavenly Dove," Simon Browne (1720)
   MENDON, from *Methodist Harmonist* (1821); adapt. Lowell Mason (1831)
   Jesus' promise to send the Spirit of truth (John 16:13–15) is reflected in this prayer hymn, which would be effective sung immediately after the Gospel lesson.

4. "Eternal Spirit of the Living Christ," Frank von Christierson (1975)
   FLENTGE, Carl Flentge Schalk (1979)

---

[2] In G. Paul Butler (ed.), *Best Sermons*, Vol. 9 (New York: Trident Press, 1968).

In both words and music, this hymn is a fine example of hymnic creation by two contemporary Americans. Based on the truth that the Spirit of God intercedes for us and helps us pray as we should (Rom. 8:26–27), the hymn could be sung prayerfully in this manner: stanza 1, soloist; stanza 2, choir; stanza 3, choir and congregation.—Hugh T. McElrath

WORSHIP AIDS

CALL TO WORSHIP.   "I will sing unto the Lord as long as I live: I will sing praise to my God while I have my being" (Ps. 104:33).

INVOCATION.   Today, O God, let us taste again the joy of the Holy Spirit and bring our gladness to expression in song, prayer, fellowship, and rededication.

OFFERTORY SENTENCE.   "And though I bestow all my goods to feed the poor, and though I give my body to be burned, but have not love, it profits me nothing" (1 Cor. 13:3 NKJV).

OFFERTORY PRAYER.   With music in our souls and love in our hearts, we bring these gifts to you. Grant that our receiving and giving may draw us close to you.

PRAYER.   O God, who art the Father of our spirits, the lover of our souls, and the Lord of our lives: we offer thee our worship and our praise. With thy whole Church in heaven and on Earth, we adore thee for thy wondrous mercy in the work of our redemption through Jesus Christ, thy Son. We thank thee for the grace of thy Holy Spirit, who did brood upon the waters when darkness was upon the face of the deep, speak in the prophets to foretell the coming of thy Christ, and descend as in tongues of living fire upon thy Church at Pentecost. We bless thee that thou has never taken or withheld thy Holy Spirit from us, but that he abides with us for ever to rebuke us for our sin, to comfort us in our tribulations, to help our infirmities and teach us how to pray, and to witness with our spirits that we are thy children and joint-heirs with Christ. To thee, O God, Father, Son, and Holy Spirit, we give all praise and glory, for ever and ever.—James Todd[3]

SERMON

Topic: That's the Spirit

TEXT: Rom. 8:14–17; John 14:8–17

Paul was a genius in interpreting the gospel so that it could be heard. He essentially had two audiences for his letters: the Jews and the Greeks. To the Jews he preached one way, to the Greeks he preached another. He told us he was doing that in his letter to the Corinthians. He said he was "all things to all people."

---

[3] *Prayers and Services for Christian Festivals*

The Jews believed that God was righteous and stern, like a judge sitting on a throne, demanding righteousness from us. So the question the Jews asked was, "What is my status before this righteous judge?" Paul's answer was, "Because of Christ, we know that by God's grace we are forgiven." If you want to read about that, turn to the fifth chapter of his letter to the Romans, where he talks about being made righteous by God's grace given to us through Jesus Christ. Our righteousness is a gift given to us through forgiveness of sins. That is the way he spoke to the Jews.

In the eighth chapter, our text for this morning, Paul is talking to Gentiles, to Greeks, to people who believed, if they believed in God at all, that God was a distant, uncaring, unfeeling power that had no concern for them at all and probably had no awareness of their existence. The Gentile question was not, "Am I forgiven?" but "Am I alone? Is there a God who cares for me? Is there a God who knows me?"

If I were to pick which one of Paul's audiences comes closest to our situation today, I think I would have to say it's the Gentile audience. There are still people who feel guilt in our time, and they need to know the gospel, "You are forgiven." But increasingly in my experience I come across people who feel not that they are guilty but that they are abandoned, that they are lonely, and that they have been forgotten.

Increasingly our society is more secular, which means it is a world in which God is considered to be absent. And spiritually, in a world where God is considered to be absent, you will feel abandoned, betrayed, or alone. In a time in which it seems as if my life counts for nothing, as if this world is like a small piece of sand on an infinite beach, and that God, if there is a God, is remote and unaffected by my existence, then, I suggest, the good news is that you are not alone, and that God loves you and cares for you as if you were a child of his.

That was the way the Church translated what Jesus meant to a Gentile world. It changed that world, and it changed it most radically by asserting that our life is not controlled by fate or by chance. It is controlled by providence. You are not alone. You have received the spirit of adoption, to confirm that you are now a child of God.

I want to suggest that the way Spirit comes to us most often is quietly and gently. We have before us, in our time, the image of the Spirit coming into peoples lives dramatically and effectively. We see that and say, "That hasn't happened to me." We probably say, "I don't want that to happen to me." It happens that way, but most often I believe that the Spirit will come to us gently and quietly. That's the way I believe it was with John Wesley, who said of his experience, "My heart was strangely warmed."

What matters is not the experience itself but what results from it. The result of Wesley's experience he described as a feeling of "assurance," which is similar to the "peace which passes understanding," as described in the Gospel lesson, which was also addressed to Greeks. Or similar to what Paul was talking about, a sense that I am a child of God and an heir now to all that Christ has won for me.

When you are aware of your insignificance and feel that you are nothing, the gift of the Spirit will be a sense that you are a child of God, and you are important.

When you are sure that you have come to the end of your strength and there is nothing more that you can do, and when the world seems coldly indifferent to your plight, then you will receive strength to do what you thought you could not do.—Mark Trotter

SUNDAY, JUNE 18, 2000

Lectionary Message

Topic: Three Things God Will Do for You

TEXT: John 3:1–17

Other Readings: Ps. 29; Isa. 6:1–8; Rom. 8:12–17

Although life usually rides on an even keel, it sometimes fluctuates between extremes: from extreme sadness to extreme joy; from great confidence to great insecurity; from high experience to tedious drudgery of time and labor; from health to pain; from mountaintops of spiritual experience, where God seems so near, to the valleys, where he seems so far away; from flying like the eagle to the dull plodding footsteps of the depths; from triumph to disappointment; from success to failure; from skimming along on the surface joy to the times when "deep calleth unto deep." Life is sometimes confusing, sometimes enlightening. We have great knowledge about some things, nothing about others. There are times when we are confident in our relationships and other times when are deeply hurt by those we love. Friends and family support us and friends and family let us down. We love, we hate; we are contented and we are discontented.

We have problems in life and there is that fluctuation between all of these extremes. The number one problem affecting the lives of so many is stress, and it contributes to a host of other illnesses. We live in a stressful age, and we are confronted by the strange contrasts in life until we wonder who we are and if anyone cares about us. Is there anyone with power who can do something for us? What about God? Does he have anything to offer us, and if he does, what can he do for us? I believe that there are things he can do, and I want you to know about three of them.

I. *God will love you.* This has been true since the time referred to in the words, "In the beginning God" in the first chapter of the book of Genesis, the first words in the Bible and the story of creation. God created all of his creation and capped it off with the creation of human beings, the only part of his creation that he created to return his love and to have fellowship with him. We are the only creature with the ability to love God and respond to him.

Throughout the centuries God has demonstrated his love for us. The Old Testament is the story of the deliverance of his people. He delivered them from the flood, out of Egypt, from the Babylonian exile, and in the New Testament, through Christ from sin. He sent the patriarchs, the judges, the prophets, to tell us of his love until the fullness of time when Jesus came, the very embodiment of God's love.

The same God that has loved us throughout history loves you today. When life fluctuates to the low extreme, God loves you. When moments of hurt and insecurity come, remember that God loves you. When no one seems to care about you, remember that God loves you. When friends and family let you down, God loves you. When you are disappointed, frustrated, facing tragedy, death, and defeat, when you have cried until your tears have dried up, remember that God loves you and you are not alone. But above all, when you need a savior, remember that God loves you so much that he sent his son to save you.

II. *The second thing that God will do for you is seek you out.* When Adam and Eve sinned in the Garden of Eden, they went and hid themselves, guilt ridden with the shame of their sin, and God sought them out. Who could forget the picture of God calling, "Adam, where art thou?" (Gen. 3:9). God took the initiative in declaring to Adam his presence and in giving an invitation to come into his presence. He does the same thing for us. God took the initiative in sending his son Jesus Christ to seek and to save that which was lost.

Today God seeks you out. In the depths of your sin God finds you and sends the Holy Spirit to convict you of your sin and draw you to himself, and to invite you to salvation. He also seeks you out in the depths of the problems of life. When life is confusing, depressing, disappointing, insecure, when you are down in the valley, far from the mountaintop, God comes to you, seeking you out. But God also comes to you in the good times and reminds you of your responsibility to share, to serve him, to support his Kingdom. God's presence is always here, seeking us out. We simply have to open up and receive what he has to offer.

III. *The third thing God will do for you is take care of you.* God will take care of you in salvation; we respond and God takes care of the rest of it. God will take care of you in eternity. For the Christian there is no worry about eternity. We belong to God and he takes care of us. But God also takes care of you in the here and now, in the midst of life. If you will let him, he will take care of you in time of trouble, when tragedy comes, when you lose a loved one through death; when life gets difficult, God will take care of you.

He may not change the circumstances you are in, but he will keep them from defeating you and destroying you. He will give you the power to live within them and he will be with you every step of the way. God will take care of you! He will enter into your mind and into your life. He will give you knowledge and power to live your life successfully.

That's what God has to offer you in the midst of the fluctuations of life, in the midst of a crazy, strange, confusing world. He will love you, he will seek you out, and he will take care of you!—W. Matt Tomlin

ILLUSTRATIONS

GOD'S CARE.   In 1989 our grown daughter was critically injured in a car accident. The injuries were so severe that she had to be airlifted by helicopter to a trauma center, in a city seventy-five miles from where we live. When we arrived at the hospital, we were met by her husband, who told us that she was in a coma and it was doubtful that she would live. Thirty minutes after we arrived at the hospital, five of the deacons from our church walked into the waiting room and joined hands in a circle around my wife and me. The chairman, a public school administrator, led a prayer: "Lord, we know that you love these folks, even as we do. We simply pray that you take care of their daughter and take care of them as they wait on the outcome of this calamity. Amen!" As that prayer ended and those godly men surrounded us with their love and concern, we knew that this was a reflection of God's love for us. During the next three days, when our daughter hovered between life and death, during those long days and nights in the waiting room, we felt God's presence as never before. The truth of it is, we can tell you that no matter what life brings, God will take care of you; he took care of us. Our daughter eventually recovered and is a wonderful mother to two of the most special grandchildren in the world. We knew through those Godly men who prayed with us that God loved us and would take care of us, and he did! He will do the same for you.—W. Matt Tomlin

THE BEST.   Augustine has said, "I have looked through many of the heathen writers and have found many jewels in Cicero and in Herodotus." Yet, says he, "I never found anything like 'Come unto me all ye that labor and are heavy laden and I will give you rest.'"—F. B. Meyer

SERMON SUGGESTIONS

Topic: Getting There
TEXT: Josh. 1:1–9
(1) By seeking God's will. (2) By considering how God has helped others (v. 5). (3) By trusting God's promise (v. 9). (4) By playing by the rules (vv. 7–8).

Topic: Our Real Handicaps
TEXT: Heb. 12:1
(1) Nothing in our circumstances, such as poverty, disease, or physical handicaps. They can be a stimulus. (2) Our real handicaps: (a) the sense of grievance, (b) oversensitivity, (c) a critical spirit, (d) prejudices.—James Reid[4]

CONGREGATIONAL MUSIC

1. "O Day of Rest and Gladness," Christopher Wordsworth (1862)
   ELLACOMBE, *Gesangbuch der H. W. K. Hofkapelle* (1784)
   The trice-holy of Isaiah (6:3) in stanza 1, the threefold light of the days of creation, of Resurrection, and Pentecost in stanza 2, and the Trinitarian doxology of stanza 4 all qualify this to be the pristine hymn for Trinity Sunday.
2. "Lift Up Your Heads, O Gates," Psalm 24:7–10, vers. Bert Polman (1987)
   VINEYARD HAVEN, Richard Dirksen (1974)
   This contemporary setting of parts of Psalm 24 has as its tune one of the finest to be composed in the twentieth century. If unfamiliar, the stanzas could be sung by a choir, with the congregation coming in on the joyous refrain.
3. "As Moses Raised the Serpent Up," John 3:14–17, vers. Marie Post (1985)
   O WALY WALY, English tune; arr. Hal Hopson (1972)
   Set to a familiar folk tune, this free paraphrase of John 3:14–17 can be sung in two-part canon, with the second voice following the leading voice by one measure. Because stanza 4 is identical to stanza 2, it could be sung in full unison to reinforce its central message (John 3:16).
4. "Take My Life, Lead Me Lord," R. Maines Rawls (1968)
   LANGLEY, R. Maines Rawls (1968)
   The prophet Isaiah's response to God's call to service (Isa. 6:8b) is reflected in the words of this modern minihymn of commitment. As a climax, the third stanza voices the very word of Scripture, "Here am I; send me." Its singing could well follow the Old Testament reading for this day.
5. "Holy Is the Lord," Isaiah 6:3
   HOLY IS THE LORD, Franz Schubert (c. 1826)
   Those desiring to emphasize the Sanctus portion of the Isaiah reading could use this lovely response. It is simple enough for congregational singing. For Trinity focus, it would make either a good call to worship or a sung invocation.—Hugh T. McElrath

---

[4] *The Temple in the Heart*

WORSHIP AIDS

CALL TO WORSHIP.   "The Lord will give strength unto his people; the Lord will bless his people with peace" (Ps. 29:11).

INVOCATION.   Almighty God, whom by searching we cannot find out unto perfection, but who in Jesus Christ has revealed Thyself as Father, and who by Thy Spirit hast borne witness that we are joint-heirs with Christ; help us to confess our faith in Thee our Father by living as Thy children, our faith in Thy Son by following in His steps, and our faith in Thy Holy Spirit by our obedience to His light within our souls; through Jesus Christ our Lord.[5]

OFFERTORY SENTENCE.   "And Jesus went on to say: 'And so I tell you: make friends for yourselves with worldly wealth, so that when it gives out you will be welcomed in the eternal home'" (Luke 16:9 TEV).

OFFERTORY PRAYER.   O God, some of us have little, others of us have much, but all of us have something to give. You know our hearts; so may our offerings be acceptable in your sight.

PRAYER.   Holy, Holy, Holy, Lord God Almighty, early in this morning may our song and praise rise to thee. On this absolutely glorious morning we are clearly reminded that, indeed, "all thy works shall praise thy name in earth and sky and sea."

Holy God, high above us yet deep within us, wondrous creator of all things bright and beautiful, we pray that our presence and our worship will honor your name and renew us for the right and abundant living of these days.

Holy, Holy, Holy, Lord Christ victorious, we continue to celebrate your Resurrection and Ascension.

Holy, Holy, Holy, O Holy Spirit of Pentecost, stir within and among us. Cleanse our lips, enflame our hearts, and empower our wills to worship and sense thee in spirit and in truth.

Wondrous God, whose first creation and first word was that of light, wondrous Christ, Love's pure light, the Light of the world, wondrous Spirit, light divine, we know well and live amid the hymn line, "though the darkness hide thee." Often we are the people who walk and wander in darkness. We become children of darkness rather than your children of light. We pray for you to call forth your light again in our lives, that we may receive Christ as the light of the world and of our world, and that your Holy Spirit of comfort and light divine may accompany our daily walk. Liberate us to long for and love light. By your spirit may it be so for us as in the prayer of Mother Teresa:

> The fruit of silence is prayer,
> the fruit of prayer is faith,
> the fruit of faith is love,
> the fruit of love is service,
> the fruit of service is peace.

---

[5] *The Book of Common Order of the Church of Scotland*

And may the grace of the Lord Jesus Christ, and the love of God, and the fellowship of the Holy Spirit be with us all.—William M. Johnson

SERMON
Topic: On the Doctrine of the Trinity
TEXT: 2 Cor. 13:14

"The grace of our Lord Jesus Christ, and the love of God, and the communion of the Holy Ghost, be with you all." That is the last line of one of the finest letters of antiquity, the second letter that Paul wrote to the people in Corinth, and it comes as close as the New Testament ever comes to a doctrine of the Trinity. As a matter of fact, it isn't a doctrine at all; it is a reference to three facts of experience.

The grace of our Lord Jesus Christ. Jesus gave freely and gladly to those who wished to receive it a new lease on life which they neither expected nor, in many cases, deserved. This was the graciousness which melted many a hard heart and changed many a life. Everyone who knew Jesus knew what it was. It was a fact of experience.

The love of God. This, too, was a fact of experience, though not quite so tangible or concrete a fact as the grace of Jesus. People knew that when they made a piece of pottery or worked on a piece of land they loved, people knew what they were doing and that they put something of themselves into it. And they knew that when their children went wrong, their heart ached because they loved them so much, loved them too much to tie them down so that they couldn't go wrong. Must there not be something like that in the heart of the Eternal? Had they not felt that very thing when they had been drawn back from a disastrous course, almost against their will? Had they not felt it in the vitality and energy of grown things, and had they not seen it in the glory of the Earth when it shone in springtime splendor?

The communion of the Holy Ghost. Ghost is an Elizabethan word that means spirit, breath, wind. When we say that someone came into a room like a breath of life, we come close to what the word *spirit* or *ghost* means. You may not have stopped to think what the word *communion* means; I had to think a while about it before I could put into a few words what I thought it meant. It means being a part of the something or someone. You can listen to music, for example, and the music may be out there and you are over here, quite apart from it; but when you say you are in communion with the music, the music is in you, all through you, and you are in it. In other words, you are part of the music and the music is part of you. People knew then and they know now that in one sense God is out there—above, beyond—quite apart from them. They also knew that in another sense God is in them and they are in him. They knew that there came a time when God was not only an Object over against them, but also a Power inside them.

These, then, were three facts of experience; and they knew instinctively that they belonged together, went together. I doubt very much if they stopped to think how they went together, or why; but they instinctively put them together, grouped them together in an unforgettable cluster, the grace of our Lord Jesus Christ, the love of God, and the communion of the Holy Spirit. But that is as far as they went. There is no doctrine of the Trinity in the New Testament, no carefully worded, theoretical statement about the threefold nature of God.

Our question is—perhaps I should say your question is—why in the world didn't they stop there? Why didn't they leave well enough alone? Why in the fourth century did they feel that they had to press this precious experience into a theological formula and begin to talk about a God in three persons? Why in the fifth century did they hammer out those frigid, bloodless phrases of the Athanasian Creed, which until recent years every child of the Anglican Church had to learn by heart? "We worship one God in Trinity, and Trinity in Unity; Neither confounding the Persons: nor dividing the substance. For there is one Person of the Father, another of the Son: and another of the Holy Ghost. But the Godhead of the Father, and of the Son, and of the Holy Ghost is all one: the glory equal, the majesty co-eternal . . ." and on and on for almost three pages.

And why in the sixteenth century, when the Church of England found itself, did it put the doctrine of the Trinity in the very first Article of Religion? "There is but one living and true God, everlasting, without body, parts, or passions; of infinite power, wisdom, and goodness; the Maker and Preserver of all things both visible and invisible. And in the unity of this Godhead there be three Persons, of one substance, power, and eternity; the Father, the Son, and the Holy Ghost."

Why did these good Christian people burden the Church with a doctrine that every member is required to believe, and that every minister feels duty-bound to explain, and no one pretends to understand? They did it for good reasons, and I shall give you two. There are more, but I shall give you two good reasons.

They did it first because they had to, and they had to because they were human. As human beings, they had minds, and they were so constituted, as you are, that they could not simply let things happen to them and think no more about them.

Christians received the grace of Jesus, given so freely and so wonderfully. It was a new life, so beautiful, so pure, and so good that they thought they had never seen the likes of it before. This they received. They encountered the love of God, a power invisible that was constantly drawing them to the heart of things. They found themselves in communion with the Spirit of God, participating in the life of God, and eventually they had to explain it.

In other words, they had to make explanation; for what man experiences, he must sooner or later try to explain, and the doctrine of the Trinity was an explanation in general terms of what was originally a personal experience. That is one reason why they did it.

The other is this: they did it because they wanted to; not only because they had to, but because they wanted to. They had something they wanted to say, something which they believed to be of supreme importance. They wanted to say that these three things—the grace, the love, and the spirit—had something in common; that though outwardly they appeared to be different, actually they were all the same.

The doctrine of the Trinity is the explanation that Christians had to make, and wanted to make, of an experience that meant everything to them. One or two suggestions I should like to make in reference to it. First, don't be surprised if you find it difficult to understand the doctrine of the Trinity. It is a theoretical statement in technical language. We do not all need to be theologians and understand every word of the theoretical material, but we need theologians who do understand it and who will tell us what it means.

The second suggestion is, don't be upset when churchmen suggest that the doctrine of the Trinity may not be the final explanation. There is nothing final about any formula.

Finally, remember this: formulas come and go, doctrines rise and fall, but the experience remains. The grace of our Lord Jesus Christ, the love of God, and the communion of the Holy Spirit—these three, and these three always together—will always remain.—Theodore Parker Ferris

SUNDAY, JUNE 25, 2000
Lectionary Message

Topic: God's Faithfulness

TEXT: Mark 4:35–41

Other Readings: 1 Sam. 17:1a, 4–11, 19–23, 32–49; Ps. 9:9–20; 2 Cor. 6:1–13

Life is sometimes as it is described in Judith Viorst's children's book, *Alexander and the Terrible, Horrible, No Good, Very Bad Day.*[6] Alexander has a day in which everything goes wrong. In part it goes like this: He woke up with gum in his hair, and had problems at the dentist. He got his foot caught in the elevator door, and was not able to get the sneakers he wanted. He called Australia on his dad's office phone, and had to eat hated lima beans for dinner. His Mickey Mouse night light burned out, his bath was too hot, and he bit his tongue. The cat chose to sleep with his brother instead of with him, and he said, "Tomorrow I'm going to Australia." The story closes with Alexander saying, "It has been a terrible, horrible, no good, very bad day. My mom says some days are like that. Even in Australia!"

Have you ever had a day like that? If you haven't, you will!

The disciples of Jesus had one. Fresh from Jesus' great teachings through the parables, they were on a spiritual high. At the suggestion of Jesus, they boarded a boat to go to the other side of the Sea of Galilee. A storm struck and they feared for their lives. They were having a terrible, horrible, no good, very bad day.

I. First of all, you are going to have days like that. That's just the way life is. There are times when it seems as if life all of a sudden begins to buffet you around. You start off the day, when you didn't sleep well the night before, and on the way to work you are almost hit by an obnoxious driver. At work your supervisor chews you out, and when you get home in the evening you have problems with the children or your spouse is grouchy. Or maybe you go to the doctor and discover you have a serious illness. Or you find out you have to replace the roof on your house or your car breaks down, and a financial emergency is the result. Maybe suddenly someone you love is taken by death. Life gets difficult for all of us, and when that happens, what do you do? Do you just give up? Do you become a fatalist?

We have to be prepared to realize that God does not promise us a life free of difficulty. We are human beings and we are just going to have problems. That is the reality of life. So when life is like that, what do we do?

II. We must believe that the promises of God are true. The key promise of God to us is found in the closing phrase of the Great Commission, "and lo I am with you always, even unto the end of the age" (Matt. 28:20b). Have you ever thought seriously about what that

---

[6] New York: Macmillan, 1972.

means? Have you ever claimed it for your own? I suspect that if we read the Bible more we would discover many promises of God that would help us in life.

What are some of those promises of God? He promises to save those who respond to him. He promises to save us from our sins, from ourselves, and from an eternity in hell. We are saved to a new quality of life and service, to membership in the Kingdom of God, to relationship and fellowship with him for eternity. Then God promises to reveal himself to us. God, through his Word, has shown himself to humankind throughout the centuries and has given the zenith of his revelation to us in Jesus Christ. God guides us, inspires us, and cares for us. He is with us as Comforter. He is with us as Guide. He is with us to give us the strength to live life.

III. This means that no matter what life brings, you never lose. If you belong to God and claim his promises, those terrible, horrible, no good, very bad days will not defeat you. If you are a Christian, you can constantly pick yourself up and start over again. Regardless of how many of those days you might have, God is always with you. You may have defeats in life, it may not always be the way you would like it to be, but you never really lose, because God has already settled your eternal destiny.

It is true, God is good. But that does not mean that bad things will not happen. Floods come, the earth quakes, tornadoes and hurricanes destroy, people die, marriages break up. We cry, but so does God. Remember the powerful words of Isaiah 53:4 as he foretold the coming of the Messiah when he said, "Surely he has borne our griefs and carried our sorrows" (Isa. 53:4a, NKJV). When we hurt, God cares. When we are in pain, God is present to comfort. When we are alone, God is a strengthening companion.—W. Matt Tomlin

ILLUSTRATIONS

GOD CARES.   A Frenchman incurred the displeasure of Napoleon and was put into a dungeon. He seemed to be forsaken by his friends and forgotten by everyone in the outside world. In loneliness and despair he took a stone and scratched on the wall of his cell, "Nobody cares."

One day a green shoot came through the cracks in the stones on the floor of the dungeon and began to reach up toward the light in the tiny window at the top of the cell. The prisoner kept part of the water brought to him each day by the jailer and poured it on the blade of green. It grew until at last it became a plant with a beautiful blue flower. As the petals opened in full blossom, the solitary captive crossed out the words previously written on the wall and above them scratched, "God cares!"[7]

GOD KNOWS HIS BUSINESS.   There were three children in the home, one of whom was much younger than the others. A terrific storm came up and the two older ones were greatly frightened and cried very hard. The little fellow paid no attention to the storm and finally said to them: "Oh, stop your bawlin'! Don't you s'pose God knows His business?"

The small boy realized that God can take care of you just as well in a storm as when the sun shines.[8]

---

[7] *The Chaplain*, quoted in *Knight's Master Book of New Illustrations*
[8] *The Gospel Herald*, quoted in *ibid*.

SERMON SUGGESTIONS

Topic: What Job Learned the Hard Way

TEXT: Job 42:1–6

(1) God's purposes cannot be thwarted. (2) Yet we question both what God wills and what God permits. (3) At long last, insight comes and repentance follows.

Topic: Turn Your Scars into Stars!

TEXT: Heb. 11:34

Four things to keep in mind to handle life's hurts: (1) Don't curse them. (2) Don't rehearse and nurse them. (3) Disperse them. Through the power of God and through the power of prayer you can handle any hurt. (4) Reverse them.—Robert H. Schuller[9]

CONGREGATIONAL MUSIC

1. "Eternal Father, Strong to Save," William Whiting (1861)

    MELITA, John B. Dykes (1861)

    This "navy hymn" is a good opening hymn for a service that concentrates attention on the story of Jesus' stilling the storm at sea (Mark 4:35–41). Its first two stanzas are especially apropos, but because the entire hymn is patterned on the Trinity, no stanza should be left unsung.

2. "We Trust in You, Our Shield," Edith G. Cherry (nineteenth century)

    STRENGTH AND STAY, John B. Dykes (1875)

    As a response to the Old Testament story of David's defeat of Goliath in the strength of the Lord, this hymn would be meaningful.

3. "Let Jesus Come into Your Heart," Leila Naylor Morris (1898)

    McCONNELSVILLE, Leila Naylor Morris (1898)

    This gospel song is based on 2 Corinthians 6:2: "Now is the day of salvation." Thus it is appropriate to sing it in connection with the Epistle reading appointed for this day.

4. "Wholehearted Thanksgiving to You I Will Bring," *The Book of Psalms for Singing* (1975)

    WALTER, C. Ferdinand Walther (1860)

    The last five stanzas of this metrical paraphrase of Psalm 9 parallel the assigned Psalter reading (Ps. 9:9–20). The stanzas of the hymn follow closely the sense of the original. Therefore their singing (alternating stanzas between choir and congregation) could replace the Psalter reading.—Hugh T. McElrath

WORSHIP AIDS

CALL TO WORSHIP.   "The Lord . . . will be a refuge for the oppressed, a refuge in times of trouble. And they that know thy name will put their trust in thee: for thou, Lord, hast not forsaken them that seek thee" (Ps. 9:9–10).

---

[9] In James W. Cox (ed.), *The Twentieth Century Pulpit,* Vol. 2

INVOCATION.   Grant, O Lord, that we may live lives of faith and trust in all circumstances, and to that end let the hymns we sing, the prayers we pray, and the words and truths of Holy Scripture enrich our understanding and captivate our hearts.

OFFERTORY SENTENCE.   "And it is in God's power to provide you with all good gifts in abundance, so that, with every need always met to the full, you may have something to spare for every good cause" (2 Cor. 9:8 REB).

OFFERTORY PRAYER.   Lord God, our Heavenly Father, we thank thee for thy gracious deeds and thy wonderful evidences of compassionate mercy toward us. Wilt thou now accept these offerings as we give them in the spirit of devotion and gratitude and worship, to the glory of Jesus Christ and the strengthening of his holy Kingdom?—Lowell M. Atkinson

PRAYER.   Lord God, our Heavenly Father, we know that thou art even now looking upon us with eyes of understanding and compassion, more eager to bless our lives than we are to ask thy blessing. We turn to thee with earnest prayer that a channel be opened into thy grace through which we may receive thy love. Wilt thou bless this time of worship and the prayers of every heart and grant that we may feel thy holy presence here as our living God and savior and friend.

We come into thy presence with happy and glad remembrance of times past when thou has dealt with us according to thine infinite wisdom and mercy for our own good. Especially we thank thee for the glorious life of deliverance thou hast given us through Jesus Christ, for the light that has come into our lives through the opening of the Holy Scriptures, for the glory that has been given to our daily existence through our life of prayer when each day we speak with thee. We thank thee for the way our lives today are strengthened by these glad experiences of yesterday, for the hope thou dost give the morrow because thou art steadfast and dependable in thy compassionate character. Thy righteousness is unchanging from day to day, from generation unto generation, and thy presence as our living God is the mighty foundation on which we can surely rest our hopes. We ask that thou wilt lift us above the vicissitudes of the current events of our earthly life. Grant that we may find a higher hope and a deeper foundation for our assurance in the unchanging wonder of thy character of goodness and love and wisdom and strength. As we rest our lives in thy care and in thy keeping, may we know in our heart of hearts that all is well.

We ask this day that thou wilt bless not only our worship but the worship of all who lift their prayers to thee from earnest hearts in this land and in every land. We pray not only for this church but for every church. We pray for those outside every church whose best life is so undefined that their very poignancy of need is an unspoken prayer that they may be led into thy truth. Grant to this nation thy guidance and thy leading. May all things be done according to thy spirit working in human hearts. Bless this troubled world, and beneath the turbulence may there yet be an ongoing tide of goodwill that makes for justice and harmony. Grant that in our own prayers and devotions we may each one make a contribution toward a better world according to the pattern of thy holy will.

These mercies we ask with the forgiveness of our sins in the name of Jesus Christ, our Savior and Redeemer.—Lowell M. Atkinson

SERMON
Topic: Be Prepared
TEXT: Luke 14:25–33

There's the Scout image of "be prepared": full backpacks, utility belts hung with all sorts of handy things, Swiss army knife with twenty-five separate functions in your pocket, survival tool in a leather pouch strapped around your leg. Then there's the Pastor Bruce Wilson image of "be prepared," illustrated from his letter to the youth about the ski trip: "Do not overpack! There is not room for you to bring your whole wardrobe. All you need is your ski stuff and some casual clothes for the evenings. Don't show up with gigantic suitcases full of needless stuff." For Bruce, "be prepared" means "pack light."

I. The road stories we look at today are twins, two matched parables told on the same occasion to make the same point. The first one begins "Which of you" and is clearly aimed at us ordinary folks. "Which of you, intending to build a tower"—we're talking home improvement project here! Here's a farmer who has decided to build a raised platform next to his grain field, let's say, so that he or his boy or his servant can stand on it and get a better shot at the animals or people who might try to steal a snack. Or maybe this is a farmer who has a vineyard enclosed by a stone fence who has decided to beef up security by building a stone tower from which armed servants could defend the property.

There are two inflexible rules for home improvement projects. Number one, no job takes fewer than three trips to the hardware store; number two, no job takes less than three times the number of hours that you've allotted to spend on it. So if I'm going to tackle something like that, Jesus says, I ought to sit down and figure carefully and overbudget both my time and the money to spend on materials. Otherwise I may get it only half done and have to leave it alone for a while, and have to put up with my neighbor walking by making smart-aleck comments about how clever it was to design my garage doors slanting toward the middle, compensating for the fact that they stuck out so far into the weather, and allowing the rain to run off them into a convenient spot.

Jesus' second parable gives a situation about which most of us can only speculate: "What king," he says, "would decide to attack another kingdom and not sit down and figure out how many men he had in his army." Well, I've never done that, and don't expect I ever will, but the principle is sound. If you are going to attack someone, then you need an army of a proper size. And if you don't have the army of the proper size, you'd be better off negotiating than fighting. The stakes are so much greater here than in the first parable; if I miscalculate on my garage doors, I may be ridiculed, but if the king miscalculates, he may lose his army and his kingdom. So the principle is even more important on a large scale—the higher the stakes, the more you should be prepared. Don't rush in without counting the cost. Overbudget, overplan, have contingencies, scrutinize the risks, take it very seriously; pack extra if you think there's a chance you may run out before you're done.

II. These parables clearly lead us to the Scout image of "be prepared," but there's a problem there. That whole train of thought runs contrary to what Jesus says to the crowds who are following him on the road. He gives them three specific instructions on what they must do to follow him. First, he says, "If you want to be my disciples and follow me, you must hate your parents, your spouse, your children, your siblings." He doesn't mean "hate" in the sense of despise them, act mean to them, call them names, mark them off your Christmas list. He means that his disciples will have to act as if they hated their families. The illustration is the call of the disciples, who left families, jobs, and communities to follow Jesus. If you are Jesus' disciple, that's what you may have to do.

Next, he says, "If you want to be my disciple, you must give up all your possessions." Jesus says that we must get prepared by unloading a lot of stuff. Don't pack more, pack light, and we see the reason for that when we hear Jesus' third specific instruction. He says, "If you want to be my disciple, you must carry your cross, give up your life, and follow me." The image is of a daily sacrifice of life. We get a partial picture of this when we think of professionals who put their lives on the line for others: firefighters, the search-and-rescue teams in the armed forces, combat medics, and so on. They go into life-threatening situations to try to get someone out, and sometimes the rescuers are killed. But even that is not quite what Jesus is asking. There are rules for lifesaving crews that prevent them from taking risks where there is not chance for success, a sort of a grim calculus that says that if the odds of losing both the patient and the rescuer are very high, you have to let it go. Jesus makes no caveat like that—he just says, "Carry your cross—be ready to give up your life; and if you aren't, you shouldn't come at all."

Be prepared: in normal life it often means that we make sure we have enough nails and boards to complete our projects. But because none of us has an endless supply of money, being prepared means that we choose one project over another; extra medical bills may mean that the garage doors wait for a while. And because none of us has an endless supply of time, being prepared means that we choose what seems to us most critical; the garage doors can sag for a while if I need to help a son with a science project. And that business of priorities and choosing what's most important, I guess, is where the Scout version and the Bruce version of "be prepared" intersect. Life always comes down to what we can sacrifice in order to do what we want: Can we set aside the time? Can we manage to come up with the money? Can we marshal the energy from somewhere? And that gets us to the two inflexible rules of following Jesus on the road.

III. First, if you follow Jesus, there will come a day, somewhere, sometime, when Jesus will call you to do something that will require setting aside something really meaningful and very dear. You always have to remember where Jesus is heading: he is walking toward the Kingdom of God. In that Kingdom there won't be poor people and rich people, so no one would even think of building a tower to protect his field or his vineyard, or a stronger set of garage doors to protect his yard tools. In that Kingdom there will be peace, not violence, so kings there won't need to consider the size of their armies, because there won't be any armies. But we like our vineyards and our yard tools and our whole way of life, so we budget lots of time and money on building towers and stronger garage doors and on training armies to protect them. We've spent so much time and money on these things, it's hard to give them up. But one day Jesus will smack you right between the eyes with something—some ministry to perform, some job to do—and it will become crystal clear to you that you cannot both obey him and keep your fists closed tightly around that thing that is so dear to you.

That's the first rule of the road with Jesus. The other is that unless you give that thing away, you will never know what it is really to live. Again, you have to remember where Jesus is heading: he is walking toward the Kingdom of God, but his path goes through Jerusalem, up to the cross, then to the tomb, and only then to the Resurrection. Jesus' rule is absolute: unless you lay your life down, you lose it; but if you lay it down, then you get it back again, renewed and resurrected.

Are you prepared to lighten your load? When Jesus calls you and says, "Follow me here," are you prepared to lay down all the stuff you're trying to carry, all the stuff you've crammed into your suitcases and closets and garages, all the stuff you've tucked away inside your soul, all the things about your life that you think define you—are you prepared to lay them down to follow Jesus?

Jesus first sounds like a wise veteran of the home improvement struggles: be certain that you have enough before you start. But as we listen to him closer, he really sounds more like Bruce: Don't show up with gigantic suitcases full of useless stuff. They hold you back, and they'll keep you from finding your life. Come and follow Jesus to the Kingdom, but pack lightly. Keep a light touch on your things, even on your life. That's the gospel, brothers and sisters.—Richard B. Vinson

SUNDAY, JULY 2, 2000
Lectionary Message
Topic: The Sound of the Mighty Falling
TEXT: 2 Sam. 1:16–27
Other Readings: Ps. 130; 2 Cor. 8:7–15; Mark 5:21–43

No one notices the fall of a sparrow, but when a jumbo jet comes down, the world takes notice. Chop down a cherry tree and it falls with a whisper; cut down a sequoia and it shakes the forest for a mile in every direction. So it is with mighty people and nations: they go down with a crash that can change the course of history.

Our text rings with the words, "how the mighty have fallen." Both King Saul and the crown prince were exterminated in one senseless war. Saul, a physical giant of a man, and the first king of Israel, God's own choice for the throne, was no more. Prince Jonathan joined his father in disaster. Now David speaks of it in a lament.

Read this text with me. What a sad ending to a royal reign that began so well. Why was it so? We need to go back several chapters to discover the reason for Saul's failure. In fact, he made so many mistakes as king, we're surprised his reign didn't collapse much earlier. He had poor judgment. He didn't know how to take no for an answer. He was arrogant and proud. He couldn't control his temper. He dabbled in the occult. He was a bit insane. Even today in Israel, the site of Saul's palace is referred to as the "hill of the fool." But worst of all, he was disobedient to God, and God has a way of removing protection from such people and they cannot stand alone.

I. *The mighty fall; it happened to Saul.* It was so sad that David didn't want to tell it among the Philistines and cause them to rejoice. He called for a national mourning and remembrance of the prosperity and good things that Saul had brought to his people. David reminded them that the former king and prince had been swifter than eagles, stronger than lions, beloved and handsome. This funeral speech ignored the royal mistakes. If there is a moral to all this it is don't believe everything carved on a tombstone.

David must have been remembering his first encounter with Saul. The shepherd boy accepted the challenge of the giant Goliath to do personal battle. Saul offered David his own armor, which fit him like Emmett Smith's football gear would fit a jockey. However, David defeated and beheaded the monster Philistine. He became the king's favorite, married his daughter, and fought for him in many battles.

But something happened to Saul. He suffered from depression and rage. He was psychopathic and paranoid. David became, in his mind, his worst enemy. The prophet Samuel observed all this and anointed David king while Saul was still alive. Still, David defeated and beheaded the monster Philistine. David became the king's favorite, married his daughter, and fought for him in many battles.

The king's son, Jonathan, was David's best friend, closer than a brother. Saul's youngest daughter, Michal, was David's wife. So David had much to lose by Saul's death. We understand his sad son, "how the mighty have fallen."

II. *The mighty fall; it happens all around in politics, sports, business, entertainment, and the church.* Richard Nixon was elected president by such a majority it was considered a mandate from the people. At the same time he carried many from his party into the Senate and Congress, giving them a majority for the first time in decades. Then came Watergate. We all heard the sound of the mighty falling.

The world tuned in to watch the 1998 Winter Olympics, especially the hockey competition. The Russian team could not be beaten until they met a determined team from the Czech Republic who took the gold medal from them. What a night. What a victory. Everyone watched the fall of the mighty.

Charles Keating was the image of the successful businessman. He made millions for himself and billions for others. Then, in 1987 came the Lincoln Savings and Loan scandal, prison, and humiliation. That cost American taxpayers two billion dollars. We all felt the mighty falling on our backs!

I was in Europe in the summer of 1989 with a colleague who dared to enter Rumania and teach a Bible course. He was arrested and escorted to the border. The charge against him was that he had perverted the minds of the Rumanian people. He told us of the abuses of the people and the church under that cruel dictatorship. "Everyone in Rumania knows that communism is finished, everyone but the leadership." Within six months the dictator was overthrown and executed. Even the Berlin Wall came down. How the mighty had fallen.

The church is not immune, either. The decline and fall of the television ministry of the PTL club is a painful reminder that all human beings are susceptible and vulnerable to the weaknesses that lead to a fall.

So it is not unusual or unexpected when that sort of event occurs. In fact, we expect it and nod our heads in compliance with the truth of the saying, "the bigger they are, the harder they fall," and "pride goes before a fall."

III. *The mighty fall; it can happen to you and me.* We have been discussing such causes as misuse of authority, self-righteousness, dishonesty, pride, and evil. These are only a few of the problems that can bring you down.

There is a mystery here in that everyone else can predict it but you. There are many "little Titanics" cruising through life impervious to the danger ahead, to the warning signs, and to the cautioning of loved ones. It was boasted of the Titanic that "even God cannot sink the Titanic!" You think you can get away with it and nothing can bring you down. It is important to assess our attitudes and practices with cool objectivity and common sense.

We even come to think we are immune to such failure—spiritually, physically, morally, materially, or socially. But I do not know of any talisman or charm that prevents the fall of the arrogant, the dishonest, or the proud.

Jesus warned his disciples in advance of their fall. He told his disciples that they would all forsake him. He warned Peter that Satan desired him so he could sift him like wheat. When Peter was at his best, Jesus warned him that Peter would deny Jesus three times. He warned Judas that he was the betrayer.

So what can you and I do? Model your life on Jesus. Avoid pride and self-righteousness. Reject dishonesty and the abuse of power. Never let it be said of you, "We knew it would happen. The mighty has fallen."—David Beavers

ILLUSTRATIONS

THE VOICE OF AUTHORITY.   Police officers are taught to speak with authority. A case in point occurred when an out-of-town policeman was shopping in our city. He observed a thug snatch a woman's purse and run away down the street. The officer cut through an alley and came out just behind the thief and shouted, "Stop right there, put your hands on the wall, now!" The purse snatcher did not see him at all but immediately responded. A local police officer ran up, never did see the other officer in the alley and was completely surprised to see the crook waiting for him with the stolen purse at his feet.—David Beavers

NEVER SAY NEVER.   Kathy was married for several years and had no children. She had a habit of observing mothers with babies and saying, "I'll never do that with my baby." Then she had her first child. What a change. She said, "I always said that I would never spit-wash my baby's face; now I do it all the time. If she drops her pacifier on the pavement, I clean it in my own mouth for her. Never say never."—David Beavers

SERMON SUGGESTIONS

Topic: What Our Shepherd Does for Us
TEXT: Ps. 23
(1) He provides for us: (a) daily bread, (b) sustaining refreshment, (c) needed guidance. (2) He protects us: (a) with a rod of defense against our adversaries, (b) with a staff of discipline to keep us in line. (3) He pursues us: (a) with unfailing goodness and mercy, (b) with the result that we are more and more aware of the unending nearness of God.

Topic: Reasons to Rejoice
TEXT: 1 Pet. 1:3–9
(1) We have experienced a new birth (v. 3). (2) A sure inheritance awaits us (v. 4). (3) We are protected by the power of God (v. 5). (4) Our faith is being refined in the fire of trials (vv. 6–7). (5) Even now we are experiencing the outcome of our faith (vv. 8–9).

CONGREGATIONAL MUSIC

1. "Immortal Love, Forever Full," John G. Whittier (1866)
   SERENITY, William V. Wallace (1856)
   This deeply poetic expression of spiritual encouragement and consecration would be effec-

tive for the opening of worship that has as its central theme the healing ministry of Christ (Mark 5:21–43). The stanza that begins "The healing of his seamless dress" makes particular reference to the woman who touched Christ's garment in the "throng and press" and was instantly healed.

2. "Thine Arm, O Lord, in Days of Old," Edward H. Plumptre (1864)

ST. MATTHEW, *Supplement to the New Version of Psalms,* Tate and Brady (1708)

This hymn written for a hospital also has for its theme the compassionate touch of Christ to heal all manner of sickness. It could be sung immediately before the reading of the Markan passage.

3. "O Jesus Christ, May Grateful Hymns Be Rising," Bradford G. Webster (1954)

CHARTERHOUSE, David Evans (1927)

Here is a new hymn on the city that refers in its final phrase to Christ's healing of those who touch his garment's hem. For adventuresome congregational worship, this hymn could be substituted for either of the two mentioned previously.

4. "From Deepest Woe I Cry to Thee," Martin Luther (1523)

AUS TIEFER NOT, Martin Luther (1524)

This metrical version of Psalm 130 by Martin Luther is one of the earliest extant metrical psalms of the Reformation era. Skillfully set to its sturdy Phrygian melody, also by Luther, "From Deepest Woe" should definitely be sung in connection with the Psalter reading.—Hugh T. McElrath

WORSHIP AIDS

CALL TO WORSHIP. "Out of the depths I cry to you, O Lord. Lord, hear my voice! Let your ears be attentive to the voice of my supplications" (Ps. 130:1–2 NRSV).

INVOCATION. Never is there a time when we do not need you, O God. Whether we are at the moment in the throes of spiritual distress, we reach out for your special mercies, for the future will present us with new challenges that only your grace will enable us to meet triumphantly.

OFFERTORY SENTENCE. "May the Lord lead you into a greater understanding of God's love and the endurance that is given by Christ" (2 Thess. 3:5 TEV).

OFFERTORY PRAYER. We acknowledge our partnership with you, O God, in strengthening the weak, challenging the strong, and supporting the many causes that make life more meaningful and useful for all. So we give thanks for all your blessings and for the channels of sharing that are open to us even now.

PRAYER. Merciful Lord, enlighten us with a clear shining inward light, and remove all darkness from the habitation of our hearts. Repress our many wandering thoughts and break in pieces those temptations that violently assault us. Vanquish the evil that seeks to destroy us so that peace may be obtained by your power and abundant praise may resound in your holy court. Send out your light and your truth that they may shine upon the earth and enlighten each of us, for until we are individually enlightened we are like the earth in its infancy, without form and void. Lift up our minds, which are pressed down by a load of sin and desire. There is no human power available to give release, grant forgiveness, and provide full comfort and rest for our desires. Join us this morning to yourself with an inseparable band of love; for you alone can satisfy those who love you and seek to do your will in life.

In your power, send us forth to do your work in the world. Give us the power to care for the needy; the strength to wait on the suffering; the words to speak to the sorrowing; the witness to bear to the lost; the skills to heal the sick; the knowledge to bind up the mental, psychological, and emotional wounds of the struggling; and love for all people—the mentally limited, the languishing lonely, the least, the last, and the lost.

Come this morning and abide in us, Lord Jesus. Fill us with your spirit that we may become and be your disciples, doing your redeeming and healing work as we venture forth to meet the waiting world.—Henry Fields (based on a prayer by Thomas A. Kempis)

SERMON
Topic: The Seal of the Spirit
TEXT: Eph. 4:30

Our task is twofold: we must address the answer of the gospel to the restless insecurity of modern man, yet we must do so in a way that offers at the same time the authentic challenge of responsible discipleship. No finer guidance may be found than in the truth of our text, "Do not bring sorrow to the Holy Spirit of God, in whom you were sealed unto the Day of Redemption" (Eph. 4:30). Here the tension between comfort and courage is beautifully balanced so that apathy can no longer "wrap itself under the cloak of piety."

I. *The Spirit.* The controlling affirmation about the security of the Christian is that it is rooted in nothing less than "the Holy Spirit of God." Negatively, this assertion underscores the truth that ultimate security is not found in anything human or external. Let us be done with misplaced dependence on public profession, water baptism, or church membership as the anchor against anxiety.

Instead, let us grasp the positive truth that our confidence is in God! The deities of Greece and Rome were fickle and capricious, leaving their devotees to fret and tremble in uncertainty. By contrast, the chief characteristic of the Christian's God is his dependability. He always keeps his promise, even though we prove false (Rom. 3:3–4).

The Holy Spirit, in whom the Christian lives, is a faithful defender who never departs, who is never deceived or overcome by evil, who is never in doubt about the will of God, who is never dismayed by earthly difficulties. God would not lavish such perfect protection on his children unless he intended for them finally to enter the blessedness of heaven.

II. *The Seal.* Yet it is painfully obvious that Christians are still a long way from the Celestial City, for "the Day of Redemption" has not arrived.

How is the Christian protected during the interim while he journeys as a pilgrim in an alien land? Our text has the answer: by the "seal" of the Spirit.

The use of seals in the ancient world furnishes the clue to the threefold significance of this metaphor:

(a) Seals were used to designate *possession* by an owner. Animals were branded and slaves were tattooed with the mark of their master. Just so, Christians are not their own, for they have been bought with a price (1 Cor. 6:19–20). They discover stability in the certainty that

"God's firm foundation stands, bearing this seal: 'The Lord knows those who are his'" (2 Tim. 2:19).

(b) Seals were used to guarantee *protection* from an enemy. Valuable merchandise and documents were fastened in this way to prevent tampering or falsification. The Holy Spirit is the seal that guarantees that Christians will one day receive their full inheritance (Eph. 1:13–14).

(c) Seals were used to furnish *proof* of authenticity. They certified the outstanding service of a soldier, attested to the validity of a document, ratified the terms of a covenant, or accredited the credentials of an envoy (John 6:27). In the same way, the presence of the Holy Spirit in the lives of Christians confirms beyond any doubt that they are children of God (Rom. 8:16).

III. *The Sorrow.* Our text focuses on the fact that the Holy Spirit is the only source of ultimate security.

The admonition to "grieve not the Holy Spirit of God" throngs with important implications for an understanding of Christian security. This phrase bears witness to the personality of the Spirit and to the intense interest he takes in the Christian's life. It is impossible to speak of grief without speaking of a person, for whatever else may be true of an impersonal force, it cannot be thrown into sorrow. Sin does not merely stifle an influence—it injures a person!

Just as Jesus grieved at the hardness of men's hearts (Mark 3:5) and wept over unrepentant Jerusalem (Luke 19:41), so his Spirit is seared by sin in the Christian's life.

The present imperative used in this passage does not picture one monstrous act by which a person would presume to overthrow the work of God. Rather, it suggests a steady process of spiritual deterioration.

The entire New Testament bears witness to the possibility of a progressive erosion of one's relationship to the Spirit. It warns not only against "grieving" the Spirit (Eph. 4:30) but also against "resisting" the Spirit (Acts 7:51), "outraging" or "despising" the Spirit (Heb. 10:29), and even "quenching" the Spirit (1 Thess. 5:19).

In the light of these warnings, we cannot proclaim with conviction that Christians are "sealed unto the Day of Redemption" unless we proclaim with equal conviction that they must "not bring sorrow to the Holy Spirit of God"!

Christians are not helpless marionettes dangling by divine strings; they are responsible children set down in the disturbing intimacy of a divine-human relationship that they must cultivate at any cost.

In this day of moral indifference among Christians, it is imperative to remember that the seal of the Lord has *two sides:* "God's firm foundation stands, bearing this seal: 'The Lord knows who are his,' and 'Let every one who names the name of the Lord depart from iniquity'" (2 Tim. 2:19)!—William E. Hull

SUNDAY, JULY 9, 2000
Lectionary Message

Topic: The Prophet Comes Home

TEXT: Mark 6:1–13

Other Readings: 2 Sam. 5:1–5, 9–10; Ps. 48; 2 Cor. 12: 2–10

The Steinbeck Memorial Library in Salinas, California, displays a treasure in its museum section. It is John Steinbeck's handwritten copy, on a yellow pad, of *The Pearl*. It seems that he offered it and other items to the city of Salinas during his lifetime but no one was interested. Decades later a society purchased the handwritten copy for $70,000.00. Many famous people were never popular at home in spite of tributes and honors everywhere else.

Jesus was like that. Our text tells how the people of his hometown were embarrassed by him while other towns around them were praising him. The text contrasts the people of Nazareth with the people of the neighboring villages.

I. *The response of Nazareth* (vv. 1–6). Jesus probably lived in Nazareth more than twenty years before beginning his ministry. It was nothing new for him to go to synagogue on the Sabbath, but this day was very different.

He began to teach and they mocked his teaching. Mark doesn't tell us what Luke explains, that Jesus read from Isaiah and stated that he was the fulfillment of the messianic prophecy. For Mark it was bad enough that the people who had always known Jesus should respond with such bitterness, "Where did he get this? He didn't learn that here!"

It reminds us of the political rhetoric of a campaign year. He wasn't the favorite son so his words were wasted. They asked, "Isn't this the son of Mary?" They didn't mention Joseph, so they hadn't forgotten Mary's premarital pregnancy and they questioned the reputation of Jesus.

They complained that he hadn't done any powerful deeds at Nazareth, so the ones they'd heard about must be false and hearsay. Then Mark says something cryptic, "He could do no deed of power there." Of all the synoptic writers, Mark alone says this. Did their mockery deprive Jesus of power? Was he humiliated to helplessness? Bible students wish that Mark had said, "He would do no deed of power there."

Think about it this way. During a recent election a candidate made statements that were blatantly untrue. I could not vote for this person. Oh, I could physically go into the polling place and mark the ballot, but I could not, in good conscience vote for such a prevaricator. Almost anything Jesus did or said at Nazareth was wasted. So he couldn't because he wouldn't give them the signs and wonders they demanded.

The text says they took offense at him. The Greek reading is that they were scandalized because of him. This same Jesus who was a compliment to any home, synagogue, or organization was a disgrace to them. He was like a skunk at a picnic. He was a hillbilly at the opera. Jesus was amazed at their unbelief. Here were townspeople he had known for a lifetime; he had worshiped with them, worked with them, known their children, been in their homes, and all that goes with small-town life. They were ashamed of Jesus. How did he respond?

He laid his hands on a few sick people and cured them. This is an important statement because there was much spiritual sickness at Nazareth and only a few were cured. Then he went from Nazareth to the towns nearby.

II. *The results in the neighboring villages* (vv. 7–13). Jesus didn't make a personal appearance but only sent his representatives, who enjoyed acceptance and success. Mark explained that "they drove out many demons, anointed with oil many who were sick and cured them." Mark wants us to know that Jesus could cure the sick and overcome the evil spirits, even by remote control through his disciples. The people in the villages weren't scandalized by his disciples.

The faith of the disciples was admirable. They saw the rebuke at Nazareth and might have felt shame for Jesus on themselves. Jesus sent them out to test their mettle. He had confidence in them and, to their credit, they proclaimed, taught, and healed by his power.

III. *The response and the results in us.* Jesus' disciples continue to carry the message of his Kingdom to a skeptical community. Jesus is as wonderful as he ever was and as compelling as only he can be. It is amazing, after nineteen hundred years, that people are stirred by the gospel and change their way of thinking, acting, and speaking. The power of Jesus to convert human beings is as potent as it ever was.

We were told, as school children, of the three-thousand-year-old wheat found in a pharaoh's tomb. An archaeologist nourished the wheat and planted it. It came to life and sprouted after three millennia, vigorous as ever. The gospel is not the problem, but the people who receive it are. It is a contemporary parable.

The Nazarenes abound in American society. They grew up in Christian homes, many of them preachers' kids, elders' kids, bishops' kids, and so on. They cannot remember not being in church and in a rich atmosphere of Christian influence. Somehow that familiarity bred a noxious contempt. They now live their lives without Christ. Confronting them with their need for Christ will produce negativism, denial, even derision. They've heard it all before and walked away from it. Jesus cannot do much for them. Oh, there are some responses, but not many.

So the disciples roam out into the areas of the unchurched, never-having-heard people. Church growth specialists tell of a generation that did not grow up in church, having parents and grandparents who were not religious at all.

America is a marvelous magnet, pulling the nations as immigrants. They come from places where the gospel was suppressed or unknown. They come as worshipers of Buddha, spirits, and other gods. The mission field has come to the church. Now they are first-generation Christians.

We like to think that if we were in Nazareth that day we wouldn't have taunted Jesus and driven him away. We like to believe that we would be like the outside villages, receptive and responsive to the Kingdom.

I began this sermon taking about John Steinbeck and his rejection at home. I visited the cemetery where he is interred with a local funeral director who pointed out his gravesite. Steinbeck was cremated and placed near his parents. He said, "The only way I'll ever be welcome in Salinas is in a pine box." But he wanted to be home.

As Jesus' disciples, we continue to meet rejection or reception from those who hear us. We're tempted to go where it's easiest, but Nazarenes still need Jesus. Like Jesus, we must do what we can. He wants to be at home with us.—David Beavers

ILLUSTRATIONS

FOLLOWING THE LEADER.   I was trying to find a church in Castro Valley, California, one Sunday morning in a heavy fog. I was to preach there and was almost late. I could hardly see the street signs but knew I was within a few blocks of the church. I decided to watch for cars with people who looked like they were going to church. A van approached, a man and woman in front with several children in back, everyone dressed up, so it looked good. I pulled in behind them and noticed their bumper sticker. It said, "Don't follow me—I'm lost too!"—David Beavers

WHO IS IN CHARGE?   My brother was at boot camp in Great Lake, Illinois, the morning after the assassination of John F. Kennedy. News of the outside world is usually ignored there but when he reported for guard duty that morning he was asked, "Sailor, who is the supreme commander of the United States Navy?" Without hesitation he replied, "Lyndon Baines Johnson, sir." The officer said, softly, "Very well, sailor. Carry on."—David Beavers

SERMON SUGGESTIONS

Topic: Prepared for the Worst and Finding the Best

TEXT: Hab. 3:17–19

(1) Looking at life as it really is leads us to expect problems, trouble, even tragedy. (2) A stubborn faith will cause us to see God's faithfulness in the worst of times. (3) God will help us to make right choices when the way before us is risky.

Topic: Getting Along with Fellow Christians

TEXT: Phil. 2:1–11

(1) By honestly recognizing the worth of other believers (vv. 3–4). (2) By measuring our attitude by the example of Jesus Christ (vv. 6–8). (3) By considering how God rewarded Jesus Christ, and why (vv. 9–11).

CONGREGATIONAL MUSIC

1. "Guide Me, O Thou Great Jehovah," William Williams (1745)
   CWM RHONDDA, John Hughes (1907)
   Relating to the idea of God's companionship and guidance (Ps. 48:14), which enabled David to become a great king (2 Sam. 5:10), this grand hymn would be ideal for the opening of worship on this day.
2. "Jesus, Thou Divine Companion," Henry Van Dyke (1909)
   PLEADING SAVIOR, Joshua Leavitt, *The Christian Lyre* (1830)
   This hymn addressed to the "Carpenter of Nazareth" relates naturally to the Gospel lesson (Mark 6:1–13), in which the people of Nazareth, in their amazement at Jesus' teaching and miracle working, refer to him as "the carpenter, the son of Mary."
3. "Make Me a Captive, Lord," George Mattheson (1890)
   ST. BRIDE, Samuel Howard (1762), DIADEMATA, George J. Elvey (1868)
   The paradoxes of the Christian faith expressed in this hymn reflect the paradox in the apostle Paul's assertion (2 Cor. 12:10) that "when I am weak, then I am strong." Its singing would naturally follow the reading of the Epistle lesson.
4. "Great is the Lord, Our God," Psalm 48:1–2, *Psalter Hymnal* (1987), 3–5, vers. *Psalter* (1887)
   The stanzas of this free-composite paraphrase of Psalm 48 could alternately be sung and read at the time of the Psalter reading, as follows: stanza 1, sung; stanza 2, read; stanza 3, sung; stanza 4, read; stanza 5, sung.—Hugh T. McElrath

WORSHIP AIDS

CALL TO WORSHIP.   "God, within your temple we meditate on your steadfast love. God, the praise your name deserves is heard at Earth's farthest bounds. Your right hand is full of victory" (Ps. 48:9–10 REB).

INVOCATION.   Wherever we are, gracious God, we can know your love for us and for all humankind. Now, in this service of worship, we are especially privileged to plumb new depths of understanding and catch vaster visions of your glory. So help us now to worship you in spirit and in truth.

OFFERTORY SENTENCE.   "God is always fair. He will remember how you helped his people in the past and how you are still helping them. You belong to God, and he won't forget the love you have shown his people" (Heb. 6:10 CEV).

OFFERTORY PRAYER.   Sometimes we think we have nothing to give, Father. Our coffers are empty and our treasures seem to have vanished. Remind us again that your first desire is the gift of ourselves. When that is given, we will discover treasures for the collection we did not know we possessed. So, today inspire us to give ourselves in offering to you in Jesus' name and for his Kingdom on earth.—Henry Fields

PRAYER.   Wondrous Creator, abiding God, Lord of all, we gather in your sanctuary and around your table of glad welcome to worship and praise you. Safely through the night you have kept us and awakened us to this Lord's Day. As we worship and remember, gracious God, our hearts turn to gratitude: what a large room of gratitude you have provided us, showered with blessings, grand providence beyond measure!

Reflecting on our nation's birthday, we give thanks for our homeland. May we in all expressions become better and gentler and kinder citizens, laboring with integrity and civility and goodwill, for all to have the inalienable rights we cherish and that others have died to preserve.

O generous Provider, we thank you for your teachings, like the Sermon on the Mount; and for your table, salvation in symbol and substance; for Jesus Christ our Savior and Lord, the Alpha and Omega of all our gratitude. As we have sung, so may it be: "Take our hearts and form them, take our minds and transform them, take our wills and confirm them to yours, O Lord."—William M. Johnson

SERMON
Topic: Prophets With and Without Honor
TEXT: Ezek. 2:1–5; Mark 6:1–2; Cor. 12:1–10

I. (a) It was a bad day to be a prophet. Ezekiel the priest, who was accustomed to doing his work in the beautiful Temple of Solomon in Jerusalem, was now a prisoner in Babylon, just like several thousand other Judeans. He and they were standing by a river, by the waters of Babylon, where the people who used to run Judah—the rich, the noble, the powerful—had hung their harps and their hopes on the willow branches. Ezekiel was a priest without an altar, a pastor without a sanctuary, a preacher without a pulpit, facing a congregation of bruised, grieving, angry, disconsolate exiles.

God said, "Zeke, go tell all those sad, miserable folks that their own sins put them here and that they need to repent. They're not going to want to hear that, but you tell them anyway." Ezekiel thought, "Great, if there's anything less useful than a priest without a temple, it's a prophet with a message no one wants to hear." God said, "Yes, they won't want to hear it, but you preach it anyway. It doesn't matter if no one listens; you preach it anyway."

(b) Skip forward several hundred years to another prophet having a bad day. Paul, the peripatetic tentmaker, bivocational missionary, probably stiff and sore from his latest whipping or beating at the hands of the Ephesian city authorities, was writing another letter to the Corinthians. He had started that church a few years back and they had been nothing but trouble. They were a mixed group: some fundamentalists, some feminists, some legalists, some libertarians, and all of them caught up in the booming get-rich economy of Corinth. They thought they deserved better than Paul; they wanted a flashier preacher. Paul himself admitted that he wasn't so hot, and even his admiring biographer, Luke, told the story of how one of Paul's sermons was fatally dull to a young man in the Ephesian church. The Corinthians thought that Paul was too bossy in his letters; weren't they able to figure out God's will for themselves? They even thought that Paul was ugly—physically repulsive—not attractive enough to be the leader of a church as great as theirs.

Paul had prayed about all this, asking God for help. God said, "Paul, I like you dull, bossy, ugly, and weak. That way, when the gospel changes folks, everyone will know it wasn't because of you." God said, "I know they don't like you very much, but you keep preaching to them anyway."

(c) So far we have Ezekiel—they won't like the message but preach it anyway—and Paul—they won't like the messenger but preach anyway. Surely God can do better than that. So we find our third example, Jesus, in this story in Mark, preaching in the synagogue. Great guy, right? Always healing somebody's daughter or mother-in-law, occasionally providing an unexpected lunch, telling great stories—what's not to like? And the message was good, too. He was preaching to the people of Nazareth—mostly poor, mostly farmers, some landowners, some tenant farmers—and he was telling them that the Kingdom of God had started. The poor, folks like you, will be blessed, he said; evil will be driven out and the world will run by God's rules, not by the whims of the wealthy and powerful. But these good folks, who had known him and his family all his life, still didn't like it. They said, "Who is this guy? Who does he think he is?" But Jesus tried anyway, with only small effect.

II. The moral to these three stories?

(a) It's often a bad day to be a prophet. Being a prophet is not an easy road. For everyone who listens, there are a hundred who don't, and it seems to matter little who is doing the preaching or what the content is—people mostly don't listen to prophets. It isn't an easy job. Whew, you say, then I'm glad I'm in another line of work. I'd hate to be hated or ignored. I couldn't take it if I spent most of my time being rejected. The flip side to the stories, though, is that for every hundred who won't listen there's one who will, despite the difficulty of the message, despite the incompetence of the messenger. Somehow, through the Spirit of God, the message gets through.

(b) A prophet is someone who can see something the rest of us can't. A prophet will catch a glimpse of the way something could be, and then become convinced that it will be that way someday, through God's power. A prophet can look at a street corner and know that someday a church will grow there. A prophet can look at a dying neighborhood full of houses with holes in the roofs and picture it full of safe, quality housing, full of home owners with pride and confidence, and picture it all done by volunteer labor, and picture it happening not just once but a million times, all around the country. A prophet can look at a church parking lot and see a corral and cacti and live horses and a crowd of Baptists dancing the macarena.

(c) And because the vision is so clear, and so clearly from God, the prophets preach it. They talk, they nudge, they twist some arms, they whisper, they shout, and they talk to a hundred people to get one, but after a while they have ten, then a hundred, and then the mustard seed sprouts and grows into the bush, home for all the birds lucky enough to be in the neighborhood.

Prophets change parking lots into dance floors. Prophets transform hopeless exiles into vibrant worshiping communities. Prophets metamorphose self-focused, haughty, prejudiced yuppies into teams of caregivers, into cells of the body of Christ. It doesn't happen because of the prophet's native abilities; God often prefers that prophets be weak, dull, and ugly. The transformation comes because the prophet hears the word, sees the vision, and becomes a conduit for God's life-giving breath. God, who pursues every human heart with shameless abandon, whose nature is to give without restraint, who never knows when to quit, and who apparently is not put off by the daily rejection of millions of people—God shows the prophet something of this divine nature and the prophet is changed, and then begins to be an agent of change. And when that happens, the exiles sing, the homeless are housed, and the Baptists dance.

Prophets are so necessary to our life as a congregation that Paul directs each of us to pray for that gift to fall on us and on all those around us. Pray that you will hear the message that will give life to all the rest of us. Pray that you will hear the message that will give you life, even if it comes from an unexpected source, even if it comes from one of us. Pray that the living Word that inspires the prophets will always be alive in this place, giving us new life. "And in the last days it will be, says God, that I will pour out my spirit on all of you, and all your sons and daughters will prophesy." That's the gospel, brothers and sisters.—Richard B. Vinson

SUNDAY, JULY 16, 2000
Lectionary Message

Topic: The King of the Dance
TEXT: 2 Sam. 6:1–14
Other Readings: Ps. 24; Eph. 1:3–14; Mark 6:14–29

Picture this: King David prepared for the future construction of the Temple of God and escorted the Mosaic box to the royal capital. It contained the relics of Israel in the wilderness. It was an unusual box, or ark, in that it benefited anyone entrusted with it. It was a sinister ark, which brought instant death to anyone who touched it. Read the text with me.

This is an astonishing picture. The king of Israel worships God to the limit. There came a point when praying, singing, lyres and harps, and liturgy were not enough. David led Israel in a dance of worship. Twice the text reads that David danced with all his might. This dancing wasn't common to worship in the tabernacle, or later in the Temple and synagogue. But on this day David danced his way into the heart of God. He was the king of the dance, joined by thousands of his subjects.

What are we to make of this worship event? Is there anything there that resonates in the contemporary situation?

I. *Worship is in stormy transition in America.* The worship and music department have always been the war department of the local church, but radical change is sweeping through the American church and worship is at the center of the storm.

Especially here in California, the older and younger generations oppose each other, saying that this is worship and that is worship. When I was young it was high church and low church, or liturgical versus free worship. At this time the most controversy is between those who want traditional music and those who want contemporary music.

Worship should bring us together but it can also have the opposite effect. Why is it that our best efforts to find unity often miscarry into controversy and argument? At home we have family meals to bring parents and children together at least one time each day, and arguments fracture the peace. In business, we have company picnics for fun and fellowship, and fights break out. Our minister married a couple who telephoned him during the honeymoon and begged him to tear up their marriage license! Human nature and subjectivity work against the purposes of unity.

Each of us has a subjective view of worship that comes from our understanding of the Scriptures, our idea of what pleases God, the example of Jesus, and our personal experiences. Today's contemporary worship is tomorrow's traditional worship. We are building a tradition that may or may not be the ideal.

David broke with tradition that day when he danced before the Lord. I believe the Holy Spirit caused this. A thousand years later, on almost the same spot, the Spirit again came with power on a day of Pentecost. On that day three thousand were baptized and the Church was born. Any time the Church becomes mired in tired traditions, going through the motions of worship without any spiritual emphasis, the Spirit may intervene in surprising and dynamic ways.

II. *We are rediscovering worship.* It seems that the left wing learns from the right wing and vice versa in terms of worship. The changes in Roman Catholic liturgy are astonishing. The charismatics learn from the high-church people and the Episcopalians learn from the Pentecostals. The most dramatic changes occur on the left and the right rather than in the middle. Everyone seems to be trying to explain worship in the midst of change. What is worship?

Worship is in the substance and not the style. Jesus taught the woman at the well that a time was coming when the place would be unimportant, and that God seeks those who worship in spirit and in truth.

Worship is to please God and not self. David embarrassed his family with his worship dance. His own wife denounced him. But God seemed to be pleased. So, if I worship in a way that "zings me" but doesn't please God, what good is it?

Worship is both planned and spontaneous. David planned everything about that day—the music, the sacrifices, the installation service. What he didn't plan made it unique. We know that planning is essential for proper worship. Lack of planning is a serious problem. But rigid planning that stifles spontaneity is also a problem.

III. *Worship will continue to test our mettle.* The past is only an indication of this. New sects and denominations will emerge to please the peculiar tastes in worship. In the words of that famous Saint, Anonymous, "If we cannot worship together, we cannot worship apart."

Some want hymns while others want choruses. Some want sound systems with electronic accompaniment while others want a Hammond organ. Some want a cappella music while others want instrumental music. Some want a choir while others want a worship team.

There's a story going around about a shop that advertised, "We fix anything." A preacher asked them to fix a cracked egg, the last egg laid by the last living California Condor who had died the day before. The clerk in the store said, "I'm sorry, we can't fix this egg. Do you have anything else we might fix for you?" The preacher thought a moment and said, "Can you fix the conflict between the traditional worship people and the contemporary worship people in my church?" The clerk conferred with his supervisor and said, "Can we look at that egg again?"

Where will it end? Though I am not a prophet, I believe that we are not where we are going but the worst is past. I predict that people will get used to the changes and settle down for a while.

The church has divided more often because of worship than it has because of doctrine. It may not be all that bad. Jesus described the parameters of worship very broadly, with much room for difference in the middle and on the right and the left.

Jesus said that God seeks those who will worship him in spirit and truth. Can we practice tolerance, patience, and appreciation for those who worship God differently? If you worship God in a way that is scriptural and appropriate, you will receive criticism for that.

A young woman spoke of her relationship to Christ. Others preceded her telling of their "walk with the Lord." She said that her relationship with Christ was more than a walk, it was a dance, because in a dance someone leads and someone follows. "The Lord leads me in my dance with him." In her eyes, Jesus is King of the dance.

Remember that King David was criticized for his worship. He went home to the hurtful speech of his wife, who tongue-lashed him for being undignified, for dancing in his underwear before the servant. David replied, "I will celebrate before the Lord and I will become even more dignified than this" (2 Sam. 6:21). Thanks, David. To us, you will always be the king of the dance.—David Beavers

ILLUSTRATIONS

RETHINK DANCING.   Dancing was a religious exercise in the Old Testament and the early church. But I grew up in a church that had five don'ts; we were warned not to smoke, drink, cuss, go to movies, or dance. I came from a dancing family that square-danced, round-danced, and everything else. My grandfather won a polka contest when he was in his sixties. My mother taught me to dance, in private, of course, but we didn't mention it at church.—David Beavers

QUESTIONS AND ANSWERS.   Professor Ruben Ratzlaff taught Bible at San Jose Christian College for thirty-nine years. In his later years he wore two hearing aids. One day, when a student raised his hand with a question, the professor asked him to wait while he turned on his hearing aids. "Sir," asked the student, "why do you lecture without your hearing aids?" "Because I've already heard all the questions," said the teacher.—David Beavers

SERMON SUGGESTIONS

Topic: A Banquet of Blessing

TEXT: Isa. 55:1–5

What God offered ancient Israel he offers to individuals today. (1) He offers abundant life (vv. 1–2). (2) He offers an everlasting relationship with himself (v. 3). (3) He offers opportunity for special service in his name (vv. 4–5).

Topic: A Word to the Wealthy

TEXT: 1 Tim. 6:17–19

(1) Trust God, rather than riches (v. 17). (2) Be rich in good works (v. 18). (3) Keep moving in the right direction until you "take hold of the life that is really life" (v. 19 NRSV).

CONGREGATIONAL MUSIC

1. "Lift Up Your Heads, Ye Mighty Gates," George Weissel (seventeenth century); tr. C. Winkworth (1855)

   TRURO, *Psalmodia Evangelica* (1789)

   Based on Psalm 24, this venerable hymn is appropriate for the beginning of public worship. It makes an excellent processional hymn.

2. "Amazing Grace, How Sweet the Sound," John Newton (1779)

   NEW BRITAIN, *Virginia Harmony* (1831); harm. A. C. Lovelace (1969)

   This popular hymn from the eighteenth century has as its prevailing theme those blessings of redemptive grace delineated by the apostle Paul in the Ephesian passage (1:3–14) appointed for this day. Because NEW BRITAIN is a folk tune, it would be true to its nature that it be sung unaccompanied or with simple (autoharp) accompaniment.

3. "Give Thanks to God the Father," vers. James Quinn (1980)

   DU MEINE SEELE SINGE, Johann G. Ebeling (1666)

   In the place of the Epistle reading, this modern paraphrase of Ephesians 1:3–14 could be alternately sung and read.

4. "There's a Wideness in God's Mercy," Frederick W. Faber (1854)

   WELLESLEY, Lizzie S. Tourjee (1878)

   The truth that the apostle Paul asserts concerning the redemption that Christians have through Christ's shed blood (Eph. 1:7–8) is reflected in the mood and especially in the second stanza of this excellent hymn.—Hugh T. McElrath

WORSHIP AIDS

CALL TO WORSHIP.   "The earth is the Lord's, and the fullness thereof; the world, and they that dwell therein" (Ps. 24:1).

INVOCATION.   O God, who didst make all things, and who hast given to us the gift and wonder of life, help us to walk softly through the world, obeying its laws, respecting its wonders, and give us also that confidence that comes from knowing that all things can be remade by thy power and love.—Theodore Parker Ferris[1]

---

[1] *Prayers*

OFFERTORY SENTENCE.   "This is the Christ we proclaim; we train everyone and teach everyone the full scope of this knowledge, in order to set everyone before God mature in Christ" (Col. 1:28 Moffatt).

OFFERTORY PRAYER.   Teach us more, O God, that we may learn from the self-giving of Christ that there is more that we can be and do to fulfill your plan for the life of each of us.

PRAYER.   We are a mixed group, Father. Yet we try to blend into a sameness so that our differences, some of them painful, will not stand out. With a magician's skill we hide from one another and try to hide from you. This morning, lead us into honesty with ourselves so that we might be honest with each other and honest with you.

Some of us come today with hope destroyed. Bad news has come concerning folks we love. Securities we took for granted have been lost as jobs have been downsized and curtailed or circumstances have diminished our ability to manage as we once could, or people we once depended on have left us or disappointed us. In a hundred ways hopes get dashed, Father, and we have a hard time coping when hope is all but gone. Pray restore our hope today and enable us to face the future with courage born of hope. Then we will be more able disciples of the Lord and will be able to share hope with other strugglers beside us.—Henry Fields

SERMON
Topic: I Am a Christian—So Why Am I Tempted?
TEXT: Ps. 91 *selected;* Luke 4:1–15

A character in one of Oscar Wilde's plays says, "I can resist everything except temptation" (*Lady Windermere's Fan*), and Mae West, who immortalized the words "Why don't you come up and see me sometime?" also said, "I was pure as the driven snow—until I drifted."

Temptation. If I am a Christian, then why am I tempted? I have had a conversion experience, I am supposed to be a changed person, I am trying to follow the teachings of Jesus the best I know how—so why am I sometimes tempted? Have you ever felt this way? Some of you, at least, no doubt have. Trying to come to grips with the reality of temptation can be especially disturbing to those young in the faith. For the immature in the faith, temptation is often equated with sin, and this in turn leads to feelings of failure, guilt, and anxiety. Contemporary author Peter Gomes contends in his book *The Good Book* that "temptation is the single greatest source of human anxiety. In the thousands of people with whom I have counseled over the years of my ministry, I have found the problem of temptation to be at the heart of their personal anxiety" (p. 267).

But you know what? No one who has ever walked the earth has been exempt from temptation. It's a part of being human. Where there is life and consciousness, there is temptation in one form or another. The great fifteenth-century mystic and devotional writer Thomas à Kempis wrote, "So long as we live in this world we cannot be without . . . temptation. No one is so perfect and holy, but he has sometimes temptations. . . ." Even the most dedicated Christians have to struggle against temptations of a physical and spiritual nature. But temptation does not equal sin or failure. " 'Tis one thing to be tempted, another thing to fall" (Shakespeare, *Measure for Measure*).

I. The truth is, *temptation comes to those who are trying—trying to do what is right, that is.* The temptation of Jesus in the wilderness certainly did not constitute sin or failure. In fact, it was just the opposite. The Scripture says, "Jesus [was] full of the Holy Spirit" (Luke 4:1). He was led by the Spirit into the wilderness where he would spend several days in prayer and fasting. Yet it was at this very time when Jesus was full of the Holy Spirit and immersed in prayer and fasting that he was tempted the most. F. B. Meyer, a nineteenth-century English pastor and devotional writer, said, "You will be tempted to the end of your life, and the nearer you live to Christ the more you will be tempted. . . . But the virulence of the temptation means not that you are declining into sin, but that you are advancing in holiness." And Peter Gomes continues in his book, "The nearer one lives in proximity to God, contrary to our expectations, the greater is the influence of temptation" (p. 272). The more you try to live like Christ, and the more dedicated you strive to become in your Christian living, most likely the more you will have to struggle against the forces of temptation—at least in the early years of your Christian life. But that's OK. Temptation is not all bad. Why?

II. Because *temptation can build character.* F. B. Meyer observes, "Temptation does for us what the storms do for the oaks—it roots us—and what the fire does for the painting on porcelain—it makes us permanent." Or in the words of Thomas à Kempis, "Temptations are often very profitable to us, though they be troublesome and grievous; for in them one is humbled, purified, and instructed." The wilderness of temptation is God's training ground for us. Temptations serve to strengthen us, build up our endurance, make better persons out of us.

Again, consider the example of Jesus. Jesus was a much, much stronger man after he left the wilderness, having endured the temptations. Jesus endured temptations of a physical nature, having to do with the body. He endured temptations of an emotional nature, having to do with the ego. And he endured temptations of a spiritual nature that had to do with his relationship with God. And when he came down out of the wilderness having endured all those temptations, he was a better man for it. And so will we be.

Temptation endured is holiness gained. Temptation resisted is character strengthened. Temptation overcome is personality perfected!

III. And there is one more thing: *temptation helps us define our goals.* It was during his time of temptation in the wilderness that Jesus was able really to find himself, to come to the realization of his mission in the world, and to clarify his goals for the future. The Scripture says that having emerged from the wilderness temptations victorious, "then Jesus, filled with the power of the Spirit, returned to Galilee, and . . . began to teach in their synagogues" (Luke 4:14,15). After his wilderness experience, Jesus knew who he was, why he was born into this world, the goals he needed to set, and what he needed to accomplish in the time allotted to him. And so it can be with us. Our times of temptation can become opportunities for self-realization and self-improvement—if we are willing to see them that way.

Another great English preacher, Charles Spurgeon, noted that "we are never out of the reach of temptation. . . . Those who think themselves secure are more exposed to danger than any others." Perhaps the downfall of television evangelists a few years ago, and the trouble that other contemporary high-profile figures have gotten themselves into, resulted from the fact that those guys felt they were above temptation, so they got careless. But the truth is, those at the top have more stones or darts thrown at them than those at the bottom, and they also have further to fall when hit.

The key is never to think that we are above temptation. Nor should we think that because we have been tempted we have sinned. Our task is to be prepared to deal with temptation when it does come. Four simple steps might be of help to us:

(a) *Know and name your temptation.* Identify what is tempting you—money, lust, adultery, illegal drugs, anger, violence, covetousness, dishonesty, cheating on an exam, gluttony or overeating, what have you. It's easier to deal with your enemy when he is out in the open.

(b) *Design a plan of resistance.* Take precautions to stay away from whatever is tempting you or situations that could prove to be unhealthy.

(c) *Look to the example of Jesus.* The writer of the book of Hebrews says, "Because he himself was tested by what he suffered, he is able to help those who are being tested" (2:18). Jesus relied on prayer, Scripture, and the power of the Spirit to help him be victorious over his temptations. So can we.

d) *Call for help from God and others.* Spend time in prayer with God in which you name the temptation before God and ask for spiritual help. We can count on God's help to strengthen us. "God is faithful," the Scripture says, and he will provide us a way out of our temptation and testing (1 Cor. 10:13). And talk to a friend, pastor, or counselor so that you will have some emotional and spiritual support.

If we are Christians, then why are we tempted? It is because we are human. Even Jesus himself was not exempt from the onslaught of temptation. But temptation need not lead to our downfall. If handled properly, temptations withstood can in the end be good for us. They can help build character, they can help us clarify our goals, and they can help us become the persons God created us to be.—Randy Hammer

SUNDAY, JULY 23, 2000
Lectionary Message

Topic: God's Idea of a House

TEXT: 2 Sam. 7:1–14a

Other Readings: Ps. 89; Eph 2:11–22; Mark 6:30–34, 53–56

The situation in our text came about because King David wanted to build a house for God. A conversation developed between God and the king through the prophet Nathan. To give David credit, his heart was in the right place. Even Nathan thought it was a good idea, until God spoke. The response was, Have I asked you to do this? I don't live in a house. The tent and tabernacle—this is fine with me. In short, God told David, This is your idea not mine.

Then the prophet delivered a cryptic message, an exciting prophecy. Rather than have David build a house for God, God would build a house for David. *House* is a metaphor for family to the Hebrews, but this house would exceed any family, nation, or kingdom in human experience.

The prophecy had several aspects—five dynamics facets. And like some other prophecies, this had both a near and a far fulfillment. God would build the house of David through Solomon; this was the near realization. And God would build the house of David through Jesus, the far realization.

Some Jewish scholars and other critics complain that Christians read Jesus into the Old Testament. We may sometimes be guilty of such spiritualizing. But in this messianic text we are reading Christ out of the Old Testament. In fact, Christ springs out at us from this prophecy. Notice the near and far fulfillments for each facet of the prophecy.

I. *Facet One: "I will raise up your offspring after you, who shall come forth from your body. . . ."* This is the same kind of language used with Abraham, promising a genetic descendant. At that time David was well into his forties, already the father of several children. Which one would it be? The prophecy seemed to speak of one yet unborn. And "raise up" carries the idea of greatness.

The near fulfillment was realized only four chapters later in the same book. David took another man's wife, Bathsheba. We all know that story. Her first child died but her second son lived. They named him Solomon and he was prominent over all his brothers and expanded his father's kingdom. Astute Solomon often quoted the wisdom of his father and mother.

The ultimate fulfillment was a thousand years later in David's own Bethlehem when one of his descendants gave birth to Jesus—a genetic descendant of David who was raised up to prominence.

II. *Facet Two: "I will establish his kingdom, . . . and I will establish his kingdom forever."* This is every king's dream: an unending dynasty. This appeals to me as well. I'm interested in genealogy and now that I have the Internet I have traced my family name, with some interesting results. Last summer I located the gravestone of my great-great grandfather, who was buried only a few steps away from Thomas Lincoln, father of the president. I wondered if they did business, went to church together, or socialized. I too want to leave a legacy so that my great-great grandchildren might know about me and remember me.

The near fulfillment was realized in Solomon. He succeeded his father to bring Israel to a glory they had never known nor would ever know again. Everything he attempted succeeded. He had the golden touch. He had so much gold that silver was a common metal. The people flourished and so did their crops, and their flocks, and on and on.

But the prophecy says that the Kingdom will be established forever. We know that "forever" can mean a lifetime, or a long time. The Davidic dynasty endured only a few hundred years, until Zedekiah and Jehoichin died in Babylonian captivity. Never again did a descendant of David rule over the Hebrew people in Israel.

The far fulfillment was realized in Jesus. People approached him in the streets pleading for healing and help, addressing him as Son of David. He made his triumphal entry into Jerusalem on the day we remember as Palm Sunday to the cries of "Hosanna to the Son of David" (Matt. 21:15). Jesus asked the Pharisees who the Messiah was and they believed it was the Son of David.

The people rightly assumed he had come to renew the Davidic line. They clamored to make him king more than once. But Jesus' kingship was superior to that of his ancestor David. It was this royal claim that brought Jesus to trial before Pilate. Jesus answered, "My kingdom is not from this world. If my kingdom were from this world, my followers would be fighting to keep me from being handed over to the Jews. But as it is, my kingdom is not from here." Pilate asked him, "So you are a king?" Jesus answered, "You say that I am a king. For this I was born, and for this I came into the world, to testify to the truth. Everyone who belongs to the truth listens to my voice" (John 18:36–37 NRSV).

III. *Facet Three: "He will build a house for my name."* This issue caused the prophecy. David wanted to build a temple for God, but that would be accomplished by his offspring.

The near fulfillment was in Solomon. 1 Kings 5:5ff describes Solomon's commitment to David's dream of a temple. David dreamed of a cedar temple that was humble compared to the golden structure produced by his son. (Your homework this week is to read this passage in 1 Kings.)

The far fulfillment was in Jesus. Jesus was the temple of God among human beings. His enemies charged, "We heard him say, 'I will destroy this temple that is made with hands, and in three days I will build another, not made with hands'" (Mark 14:58).

He drew people to him and added them to the structure, with himself as the cornerstone. Matthew, Mark, Luke, Peter, and Paul describe a temple in which we are living stones. This is a temple that cannot be invaded by Babylonians or Romans. This is a temple that will never be reduced to rubble without one stone remaining on another.

IV. *Facet Four: "I will be a father to him."* This facet has the idea of discipline. Solomon believed in the discipline of children, probably because David did not and the result was a brood of self-seeking and rowdy sons. Several of the Solomonic proverbs laud the wisdom of parental discipline.

The near fulfillment of this was Solomon. "When he commits iniquity, I will punish him." And Solomon did just that. It astounds us that Solomon became a drunken womanizer who built pagan worship sites in his kingdom. God disciplined him by dividing his kingdom and reducing his holdings to a fraction of their former glory. Solomon did not believe in personal discipline but he experienced it at the hand of God.

The ultimate fulfillment of this was Jesus. "I will punish him with a rod such as mortals use, with blows inflicted by human beings." This produces vivid images of Christ being flogged by the Roman soldiers and being led to crucifixion. It stirs memories of another prophecy, "But he was wounded for our transgressions, crushed for our iniquities; upon him was the punishment that made us whole, and by his bruises we are healed" (Isa. 53:5).

I'm grateful that this text appears in the lectionary every three years. For the first time I was impressed with the power of the prophecy. It reminds me that God's ways are not our ways and that God is able to surpass our dreams and imaginations. David wanted to build a house for God but God built a house for David.—David Beavers

ILLUSTRATIONS

A HOUSE TO LIVE IN.   The story is told of a contractor who worked for a large company. When it came time to retire he was completing a new development in a plush neighborhood. He said, "This is the last house I'm ever going to build and it's going to be the best." He annoyed the architects with his demands for perfection. He called in only the best subcontractors and spared no expense on materials, with more insulation, better wiring, superior paint, and copper plumbing. He finished it off with the best bonded roof and first-class landscaping.

At his retirement dinner his coworkers honored him with stories and praise for his achievements. The president of the company was last to speak and he too spoke of the quality of the contractor's work and his loyalty to the company. "As a parting gift," he said, "for thirty years of service to the company, we award you the keys to the last house you built for us. Enjoy your final home."—David Beavers

ALL THAT GOLD.   Solomon seemed determined to collect all the gold in the world. Suppose all the gold ever found was in one place—every watch, ring, tooth and inlay, coin, brick, decoration, and so on. It would make only a fifty-four-feet-square block. That's about one-tenth the size of the Washington monument. That is the sum total of all the digging, scratching, panning, and mining on the planet since the creation. Then we take it to Ft. Knox and bury it again.—David Beavers

PARABLE OF THE TREE HOUSE.   There once was a little boy who wanted to build a tree house. His father was a contractor and offered to help him, but the boy insisted he could do it alone. He began his project with scraps of wood from a building site and put it together with old nails he straightened and lots of wire. He worked on the project every day after school. Every morning during school hours his dad came and leveled the tree house, plumbed it, strengthened it, and improved it. The boy never noticed and the weeks went by with the son cobbling the house together and his father making it secure. The day finally came when the boy announced that the tree house was finished. He and his dad climbed the rope ladder. Dad complimented how strong it was, how nice the view, and how comfortable. "Yes," said the little boy, "and I built it all myself."—David Beavers

SERMON SUGGESTIONS

Topic: Turn Away from Your Idols

TEXT: Ezek. 14:6

(1) Idolatry was a recurring problem among God's people. (2) Idolatry is a current problem for those who "take their idols into their hearts" (v. 4): (a) for people in general, (b) for church people in particular. (3) The solution is drastic: "Repent and turn away from your idols."

Topic: A Voice in the World's Wilderness

TEXT: Mark 1:4

(1) The role of John the Baptist—to prepare the way for Jesus the Christ. (2) The message of John: (a) a challenge to repent, (b) the prospect of forgiveness, (c) the appropriateness of baptism.

CONGREGATIONAL MUSIC

1. "Christ Is Made the Sure Foundation," Latin (seventh-century); tr. John Mason Neale (1851)
   WESTMINSTER ABBEY, Henry Purcell (c. 1680)
   This makes a fine processional hymn for formal worship. It relates in text to Ephesians 2:20 in this day's Epistle lesson.
2. "O Christ, the Healer," Fred Pratt Green (1967)
   ERHALT UNS HERR, Klug, *Geistliche Lieder* (1543); harm. J. S. Bach (1725)
   As a response to the Gospel reading concerning Christ's healing all manner of diseases, this contemporary hymn is relevant and appropriate. If unfamiliar, it could be introduced by a choir, with the congregation joining in the last stanza.
3. "I Will Sing of the Mercies of the Lord," Psalm 89:1, vers. James H. Fillmore (c. 1900)
   FILLMORE, James H. Fillmore (c. 1900)

The first eight measures of this Bible song based on the first verse of Psalm 89 could serve as an antiphon to be sung before, during, and after the reading of the Psalter lesson (Ps. 89:20–37).

4. "The Church's One Foundation," Samuel J. Stone (1866)

AURELIA, Samuel S. Wesley (1864)

This beloved hymn may be preferable for use in connection with the reading of the Epistle lesson (Eph. 2:11–22). It also can relate to King David's plans to establish the Temple in Jerusalem (2 Sam. 7:1–14a).—Hugh T. McElrath

WORSHIP AIDS

CALL TO WORSHIP.   "I will sing of the mercies of the Lord for ever; with my mouth will I make known thy faithfulness to all generations" (Ps. 89:1).

INVOCATION.   Almighty Lord, our everlasting God, turn us from that which blocks our vision of holy things. Bring us humbly before that throne of grace from which no one returns the same, through Christ our Savior.—E. Lee Phillips

OFFERTORY SENTENCE.   "And Moses spake unto all the congregation of the children of Israel, saying, this is the thing which the Lord commanded, saying, Take ye from among you an offering unto the Lord" (Exod. 35:4–5a).

OFFERTORY PRAYER.   Lord, we are thankful for all we have been given and now we share a portion of it, so that others may hear of the Christ who never stops giving to us.—E. Lee Phillips

PRAYER.   As the psalmist said long ago, "O magnify the Lord with me, let us call upon his name together," so we come together in this sacred hour to be met by you, Father. We gather here today to give thanks for the good earth and its bountiful provision for all our needs. Yet we know that the bounty which we enjoy in life would never be ours were it not for the work that others do to take the provisions of the earth and mold them into usable items for our consumption. Thank you for those who labor on our behalf in the fields to provide food for our tables; those who work at the machines to create all of the many things we daily use that lighten our burdens; those who search for truth to enlighten our minds; those who delve into the mysteries of the universe to bring back not only understanding but also help for living more worthily in our time. We thank you for the enlightened minds and skilled hands of those whose energies are given to help us manage our health, of those who teach that we may have knowledge and understanding, of those who stand on the frontiers of danger and protect us from invasions that would destroy us. Thank you, Father, for every task that is done to make us an interdependent family and for those who give their lives to the doing of these tasks.

Deliver us from exploiting our fellow human family members by negating their worth, underpaying them for the tasks they do, making them virtual slaves to provide for our needs and wants. Deliver us from ravaging the weak to possess their wealth, from destroying the earth to satisfy our personal and collective whims. Make us aware that when one human family member suffers because of our greed, all suffer. Remind us that we are our brother's keeper, no matter what his nationality, creed, color, or station in life. Keep ever before us the truth that Christ labored with his hands and heart to make the world what God intended it to be: a home for his children, where they could live together in harmony and love. Lead us to commit ourselves to that high calling as we follow him who has called us and claimed us. We ask this morning that we be inspired to become laborers together in love, that we might be saved from warrings and hatreds that destroy the human family and crucify again Christ and all the principles of justice, love, and caring that he embodies.

This morning we come to dedicate to you our lives and our labors as an offering before your throne, asking that these gifts of ourselves be used to the benefit of all people everywhere and the glory of Christ, in whose name we pray.—Henry Fields

SERMON
Topic: What Is Truth?
TEXT: John 14:6b

"What is truth?" (John 18:38), cried an exasperated Pilate, trying perhaps to stifle the growing suspicion that it was staring him in the face. Of all the answers ever given to that haunting question, none rivals the central claim of Jesus, "I am the truth" (John 14:6b). Never were four words more focal for an understanding of ultimate reality.

I. *Truth is personal.* At the very outset we encounter a provocative pronoun, "I am the truth," which discloses our initial insight: truth is personal.

The insight that facts do not become truth until they are related to life was the great educational discovery of the twentieth century. But John Dewey and his devotees failed to realize that not just any life will do. Only when facts are "life-centered" in Jesus' life do they find fulfillment as personal truth.

It is here that we discern the unity of mind and heart in relation to the Christian faith. If truth is personal, it cannot be coerced by self-will. If truth is a subject rather than an object, then truth will be grasped, not through "I-it" speculation but through "I-Thou" dialogue. Prayer and worship cultivate an openness that places the learner at the disposal of the one he seeks to know.

A prime reason why the church finds it so difficult to commend its faith to thoughtful persons may be found in the words of Father Victor White: "Zeal for truth has too often been a cloak for the most evil and revolting of human passions."

Jesus met this danger by describing truth in terms of a personal relationship. The disciples could not love him and share his compassion while at the same time arrogantly supposing that they had a corner on truth. The Spirit who would "lead them into all truth" (John 16:13) was the same Spirit who would bind them together in blessed fellowship. No wonder Paul insisted that the church grow up by "speaking the *truth* in *love*" (Eph. 4:15). How may truth be both dialogical and dependable at the same time? For an answer we turn to the second word of our text: "I am the truth."

II. *Truth is permanent.* Undergirding the Johannine approach to truth lies the Old Testament understanding of ultimate reality. There the characteristic emphasis was not on substance versus shadow, as with the Greeks, but on stability versus transiency, on the changeless constancy of truth. To the Hebrews, God was "true" because he was reliable. His truthfulness was seen in his dependability. Because God was faithful, his word was "true" and steadfast; it "endured forever" (see, for example, Ps. 117:2).

There is no contingency in Jesus' words, such as "I will *become* truth" in certain situations. No, "I *am* the truth!" That is, the consistency of his life provides truth with its inner integrity. With Christ as guide we may commit ourselves in confidence to any honest quest for truth. There is no need to fear new discoveries, as if they will somehow "disprove" Christ.

In the struggle to move beyond our broken vision of only a part of the truth and discover its enduring wholeness, we are not left to fight in our own strength. For truth itself fights on our side against those forces that would rend its seamless robe.

III. *Truth is powerful.* Our third insight is the sum of the first two: truth is powerful because it combines personal dynamic with permanent unity. Springing from the authority of Jesus, such truth "talks back" to thoughtful inquirers, laying claim to their total being, battering down their most stubborn defenses. The disciples did become not passive depositories of golden thoughts but active recipients of a lively word that liberated them from bondage and led them to unsuspected depths of commitment and insight (John 8:31–32).

Jesus did not simply disclose certain important teachings about God; rather, he manifested the saving activity of God. Truth included not only the words he spoke but also the deeds he did (John 3:21).

The events that unfolded with savage swiftness seemed to confirm the melancholy verdict, "Truth forever on the scaffold, Wrong forever on the throne."

But Jesus had already contemplated his grim fate. He knew only too well that everything for which he stood would be brutally destroyed. Yet, beyond disaster, he set the audacious but unshakable conviction that "truth, crushed to earth [would] rise again" and that the vindication would come in only "a little while" (John 16:16–24). The power of his cause was paradoxical: he would win by losing, rise by dying, reign by suffering.

As his followers, we are called to live in that creative tension between the "now" and the "not yet," to sacrifice the securities of the present for the certainties of the future. This is because the controlling clue to the nature of truth is disclosed in a crucified failure who became a resurrected victor. Tragedy is but the prelude to triumph.

Near the end of his conflict with the forces of darkness, Jesus summed up the central thrust of his entire life: "For this I was born, and for this I have come into the world, to bear witness to the truth" (John 18:37). To us, his followers, therefore, faith has no higher priority than a passionate commitment to truth. This does not mean that we are called to defend truth, for in the nature of the case something can be defended only by that which is stronger or higher, whereas nothing human is more ultimate than truth. No, truth seeks not a defense but a witness.—William E. Hull

SUNDAY, JULY 30, 2000
Lectionary Message

Topic: Bathsheba's Dilemma
Text: 2 Sam. 11:1–15
Other Readings: Ps. 14; Eph. 3:14–21; John 6:1–21

I. *The story.* Everything was fine with Bathsheba. She had a home in the best neighborhood, adjacent to the palace. Her husband was one of the fifty, the royal elite, renowned in all the land. There is nothing in the text to indicate that she was evil or acted inappropriately. I told my wife I wanted to tell this story from Bathsheba's viewpoint and she asked me, "Do you think you're qualified to do that?" Rethinking it, she's probably right; but I'm going to try to treat her with respect.

David was the serpent in Bathsheba's Eden. Haddon Robinson described the aging king as probably having a paunch and out of shape. Unable to sleep because of the stresses of life, David took a walk on the roof of the palace. This was the highest building in the City of David, so he could see down into the courtyards, streets, and gardens and onto the rooftops of his neighbors. There he was, leering at this young woman like an old fool with a pornographic magazine.

He sent for her and she came because she had no choice. Then he raped her and sent her home like a woman of the streets. He didn't care that she was the wife of one of his friends. He was the one with the power.

Her pregnancy was a problem for both of them. But the king had a plan, even a plan B and a plan C. Plan A was to recall Uriah from combat and give him leave with his wife. But Uriah, innocent and loyal, foils that. If he had only cooperated, how much better it would have been for them. Plan B was for the king to get Uriah drunk and send him home, so drunk he wouldn't be able to remember what happened. When the baby was born he would believe it was his. But Uriah insisted on being close to the king and slept in the barracks that night.

David never did the right thing, which was to confide in Uriah and ask forgiveness. If Uriah was true to form, he wouldn't blame Bathsheba and he would forgive David and rear the child as his own. Adultery was a capital crime for anyone, including the king. But Uriah was loyal beyond measure when it came to David. But there was no loyalty in David.

Plan C was murder. David sent Uriah to his death in combat. We can imagine the national mourning and memorial service in his name. Then David took Bathsheba as one of his wives so he could save his reputation.

II. *The implications.* What a chilling tale. Legend has it that David had killed his ten thousands in combat. He could not build a temple for God because of the blood on his hands. It was the blood of a single victim that ruined him. Like Abel before him, the blood of his victim was testimony to his arrogance, deceit, adultery, and murder.

This is a dark story about human nature that unnerves us with its foulness. We don't like David much after this. He didn't know the meaning of the word *no.* Temptation came to him at his weakest moment.

Henri Nouwen spoke of the temptation of Jesus. He asserted that the three temptations of Christ come to all of us as well, again and again. They are the temptations to be relevant (change these stones into bread), spectacular (leap from the parapet of the temple), and powerful (worship Satan and rule the world). Jesus was not like David during temptation; he resisted and said no!

Like David, we are tempted to exercise our power over others, sometimes even those we love the most. Let's not gloat over David. On the other hand, you may be the victim of someone else's conduct and you are hurt, confused, blaming others, even God.

After this event David's life became a morass of trickery and intrigue as never before. His family was a mess and became even worse as his children followed his example. One son fell in love with his sister and treated her the way David had treated Bathsheba, then sent her home in shame. Another son treated his brother the way David had treated Uriah. Evil has a way of getting into a family and bankrupting it morally.

I have always wondered what Bathsheba thought of David. She came to live in the palace, but did she miss her home with Uriah? She was one of many wives to David but the only wife of Uriah. The scriptures describe how her child was born, then sickened and died, and how David mourned him. How did this lovely woman mourn both husband and son?

As far as we know, Bathsheba was never at fault. My Sunday school teacher used to tell me that she probably took a bath in public to gain the king's attention. The Bible story has none of that.

She may have had the last laugh, if there was one. Her second son, Solomon, became king and far surpassed David as an administrator and architect. He extended the boundaries of his nation and was known for his wisdom. Best of all, she is mentioned in Jesus' genealogy, not by name but as Solomon's mother who had been Uriah's wife. She was part of Jesus, as much as Sarah, Ruth, Rebecca, and Mary.

David himself repented and was restored to favor with God. It was a long and difficult process but he found the peace he needed. He wrote a poignant psalm that blesses us all. The best news is that there is good news when we sin. Jesus Christ can forgive and change the worst of us. The repentant prayer of David has a Christian character to it: "Purge me with hyssop, and I shall be clean; wash me, and I shall be whiter than snow. Let me hear joy and gladness; let the bones that you have crushed rejoice.

"Hide your face from my sins, and blot out all my iniquities. Create in me a clean heart, O God, and put a new and right spirit within me. Do not cast me away from your presence, and do not take your holy spirit from me. Restore to me the joy of your salvation, and sustain in me a willing spirit" (Ps. 51:7–12 NRSV).—David Beavers

ILLUSTRATIONS

SPIRITUAL SURGERY.   Mildred and Claude were driving under the speed limit in a careful manner when a little boy dashed in front of their car. He was crushed to death. The couple remembered that terrible accident every day for the rest of their lives. If doctors could surgically remove a memory, it would be the most popular procedure in medicine. We each have ten or twenty minutes of mistakes that we would give anything to flush from our memory.—David Beavers

PRESIDENT CARTER ON ADULTERY.   President Jimmy Carter once consented to an interview that appeared in *Playboy* magazine. He was asked if he had ever committed adultery. He said he had never actually committed adultery but he sometimes had lustful thoughts, which were just as bad as adultery. The media ridiculed him for such nonsense—the very idea! But Mr. Carter was an old Sunday school teacher who remembered the teaching of Jesus: to stop adultery, nip it in the bud, do not lust.—David Beavers

SERMON SUGGESTIONS

Topic: A Matter of Choice
TEXT: Deut. 30:19
(1) It is God's will that we experience life at its best and fullest. (2) Immediate or ultimate success is a matter of choice: (a) in momentous matters, (b) in small things, (c) even when all seems lost and futile.

Topic: Two Sides of Salvation

TEXT: 2 Cor. 6:1

(1) Our salvation has come by God's initiative. (2) The fruition of this experience requires our action.

CONGREGATIONAL MUSIC

1. "Jesus, Thy Boundless Love to Me," Paul Gerhardt (1612); tr. John Wesley (1735)

   ST. CATHERINE, Henri Hemy (1864)

   The apostle Paul's declaration (Eph. 3:17–19) concerning the breadth, length, height, and depth of Christ's love finds response in this classic hymn translated by John Wesley. The singing might be varied by having one half of the congregation sing the first two phrases of each stanza, having the other half of the congregation sing the next two phrases, and then having them sing together the last two phrases, which musically constitute a refrain.

2. "Break Thou the Bread of Life," Mary A. Lathbury (1877)

   BREAD OF LIFE, William F. Sherwin (1877)

   This hymn on the Word of God and its reference to Jesus' breaking the bread by the sea for the thousands seeking to be fed is ideal for singing in connection with the Gospel lesson from John 6.

3. "The Foolish in Their Hearts," Psalm 14, vers. Marie J. Post (1983)

   MAPLE AVENUE, Richard L. Van Oss (1984)

   This contemporary paraphrase of Psalm 14 could be alternated with the reading of the Psalm, as follows: Ps. 14:1–2, read; stanza 1, sung; Ps. 14:3–4, read; stanza 2, sung; Ps. 14:5–7, read; stanza 3, sung.

4. "O Love, How Deep, How Broad, How High," Latin (fifteenth century); tr. Benjamin Webb (1854)

   PUER NOBIS, Latin (fifteenth century), DEO GRACIAS, English ballad (fifteenth century)

   Sung to either ancient tune, this hymn on the comprehensive nature of God's love would be appropriate sung after the Epistle reading (Eph. 3:14–21).—Hugh T. McElrath

WORSHIP AIDS

CALL TO WORSHIP.   "The Lord looks out from heaven on all the human race to see if any act wisely, if any seek God" (Ps. 14:2 REB).

INVOCATION.   We confess, O Lord, that we have not always acted wisely, but if we know our hearts we truly are seeking you. We are emboldened to seek you, for indeed your holy Word assures us that you are seeking us. Help us to meet you in spirit and in truth as we gather together in this service of worship.

OFFERTORY SENTENCE.   "And whatever you do, whether in word or deed, do it all in the name of the Lord Jesus, giving thanks to God the Father through him" (Col. 3:17 NIV).

OFFERTORY PRAYER.   Father, you have given us something special to do, even now, as we bring tithes and offerings to you. Let our giving be in the Spirit and after the example of our Lord Jesus Christ, who loved us and gave himself for us.

PRAYER.   We enter the stillness of these sacred moments, Father, that in your presence we might find renewal and direction. Through the past week we have spent energies on manifold matters and need the power for living that abiding with you in all consciousness brings. We have been pulled in so many directions by the cries and demands of life that we feel fragmented and need to be put together again in wholeness. Our emotions have run the gamut from elation to despair, from joy to sorrow, from hope to hopelessness. We come this morning that we might be reminded of the steadfastness of Christ and his eternal promise of hope and joy and peace and purpose in this daily walk we make through life.

Today, Father, make us into new creations determined and empowered to turn from our sins and failures to a life of devotion and usefulness to you. By your Spirit make this an hour of true conviction for each of us, that seeing ourselves as you see us we may initiate life change as we confess our sins, experience your forgiveness of our sins, turn from our sins, and rise to true newness of life through Christ our Lord, in whose name we pray.—Henry Fields

SERMON
Topic: Believe and Confess
TEXT: Rom. 10:5–13

The good news of the Christian faith is that our success, our salvation, our wholeness, our redemption, our citizenship in the Kingdom of God's people, our goal in life, is not based on what we do. Our salvation, our wholeness, our welcome into the people of God is grounded in what God has done in Jesus Christ already. God was in Christ reconciling the world to himself. It is done. Our success is rooted in what God has done and is still doing in history.

I. The good news of the Christian faith is that we find our joy, our delight, our peace, our contentment in the recognition that Jesus is Lord. All of our anxieties and fears, our needs to make something of ourselves, all of our questions, "What's it all about, Alfie?" are resolved when we affirm that Jesus is Lord. When we confess that Jesus is Lord, we declare that what Jesus says is what goes. What Jesus says about God is for real. Jesus is Lord. What Jesus reveals to us about the way we ought to live is true. Jesus is the voice of God speaking to our lives. When Jesus tells us that God is a kind and gracious God, he is sharing with us a true witness to the personality and heart of God. When Jesus tells us that God is like the father of the prodigal son running down Main Street to welcome home the lost, you can, as the saying goes, take it to the bank. Jesus is Lord. Jesus is the window into the heart of the Eternal.

II. Jesus is Lord is good news because it is a word of hope, joy, and possibility to all those who have worked hard and never had it work out, like all those parents who have loved their children as well as they could, done what they thought was just and good, and yet had to watch their children make mistakes and spoil their lives. Jesus is Lord is a word of great relief to those who have worked hard and have nothing to show for it, like the ninety-one-year-old writer in *Newsweek* who has always enjoyed writing, has written six books but never gotten any of them published. He loves to write, he gets up every morning and writes, but nobody is interested in publishing his works. He works hard, but few good things come. Jesus says, "Well done, good and faithful servant." The Master only asked that you use the talents given you and share and enjoy life. "Jesus is Lord" means that Jesus is the revelation to us of God.

We confess that Jesus is Lord because we believe in our hearts that God raised him from the dead. We do not believe in Jesus as Lord because he was such a clever teacher. There is no pretending that Jesus is the only one to say wonderful religious sayings. We do not claim that Jesus is Lord because he was so original. We affirm that Jesus is the picture of God for us because God has validated his life and words by the Resurrection. We accept the good news that our lives are not measured by our hard work and what we accomplish, but are valued by what God has done for us in Jesus Christ; we accept that because Jesus told us that and God has affirmed, validated, authenticated, and verified what Jesus demonstrated by raising him from the dead.

III. God keeps trying to tell us that throughout the whole New Testament. The New Testament keeps reporting that this Jesus is the one who tells us what we must know and understand about God. Jesus received his baptism from John and the story says that God tried to prepare us to listen to him with the voice from heaven saying, "This is my beloved Son, listen to him." There at Caesarea Philipi, Jesus began to tell his disciples that faithful obedience to God would take him to the cross. Jesus tried to tell them that greatness in the Kingdom of God comes by the humble heart that enjoys life and delights in being of service to others, and the disciples responded by claiming that the servants of God never have to stoop that low. Then, there on the Mount of Transfiguration, the voice came again to affirm that Jesus was telling it like it is: "Listen to him!" God continued to validate the credentials of Jesus while Jesus was alive, but old expectations die hard.

The good tidings of the Christian story is that judgment on our lives will not be made on the basis of how many good things have come into our lives. Salvation, redemption, and wholeness are built on what God has done in Jesus, and the quality and joy of our lives is whether or not we are willing to accept, to celebrate, and to live in that great gift.

If you work hard, good things happen. Nobody wants to tell you not to work hard. Gary Player chipped in from forty yards off the green. Some Arnold Palmer fan yelled, "God, how lucky can you get." Player turned and yelled back, "The more I practice, the luckier I get." Not much success comes without hard work.

The gospel message of the Christian faith is different from the gospel of hard work. The good news of the Christian faith is that Jesus is Lord, Jesus is the straight stick by which all our ideas about God are to be measured, Jesus is the authority on the grace and love of God. Jesus is Lord because God has confirmed all that Jesus said by raising him from the dead. "This is my Son, listen to him," and Jesus said that we are not forgiven and redeemed by what we do but by whether or not we, like the publican in the Temple, are willing to accept the forgiveness already offered, to allow it into the very center of our being, our heart, and to live as one who knows just how lucky we all are. Our redemption is in what God has done, and our salvation is in living in the joy of that gift.—Rick Brand

SUNDAY, AUGUST 6, 2000
Lectionary Message

Topic: Unhappily Ever After?
TEXT: 2 Sam. 11:26–12:13a (NRSV)
Other Readings: Ps. 51; Prov. 13

Many of the world's great stories conclude with the observation that the characters of the tale lived "happily ever after." But life in the real world isn't always like that. People don't always break free from their problems and go on living a merry life on a kind of mental and emotional "cruise control" for the remainder of their life. And when it comes to a life of rebellion against God, life *never* ends like that. It just isn't possible for us to sin against God and then sit down to a life of ecstasy and peace. God loves us far too much to let us simply relax and enjoy our sin or even simply move on—trying to blot out and forget our sinful past—without facing up to it. He will not let us have true peace and happiness until and unless we acknowledge the error of our ways. Unless we repair our connection with God, we are bound to live "unhappily ever after!"

I. *King David attempts to put his sin behind him* (2 Sam. 11:26–27). After Uriah's murder and Bathsheba's period of mourning, David sent for her, married her, and after the birth of their illegitimate son, tried to move on with his life (2 Sam. 11: 27). At this point, David apparently anticipated a life of happiness ever after with his beautiful, newly won bride. But she had come at a heavy cost. She cost him a loyal subject and soldier—Uriah—peace of heart, a clean conscience, and most important, a close connection with the God of heaven. David had tasted the forbidden fruit of ungodly passion and now he would never be happy again—at least in the truest sense of that word—until and unless he would acknowledge and turn from his sin.

David may not have sensed his loss immediately. He may have felt that he had sufficiently "covered his tracks" and that he was entering a new and wonderful phase of his life. He may have initially felt a rush of joy and excitement as he looked ahead. Sin sometimes creates that kind of emotion and distorted perspective. The truth is that "misfortune pursues sinners" (Prov. 13:21) and "sin overthrows the wicked" (Prov. 13:6).

II. *God is displeased and confronts David* (2 Sam. 11:27–12:12). After describing how David tried to move on after his sin—attempting to enjoy its fruit without admitting it—the text simply says, "But the thing that David had done displeased the Lord" (2 Sam. 11:27). As already suggested, God did not allow David to "live happily ever after." He didn't allow him to settle down and get comfortable with what he had done. God knew that David's sin had not occurred in a vacuum, and that its results were not just short-term and private; so, in love, he acted! He acted by pursuing and confronting David with his sin. So he does with us! He does this in different ways for different people—always keeping in mind what will be most effective in first convicting and then cleansing and restoring us to him.

In David's case, God used the prophet Nathan. Nathan, David's friend and advisor, had to become his friend and accuser! Notice that God guided Nathan to approach David indirectly, through a story (2 Sam. 12:1–4). The direct approach might have caused David to be resistant and even to threaten Nathan's life, but the well-told story of a powerful and wealthy man who abused his power and carried out an obvious injustice against a poor and powerless man helped David see with vivid clarity what he may not have seen otherwise. In righteous indignation, David rose up to demand the harshest penalty for the man in the story, saying, "The man who has done this deserves to die" (2 Sam. 12:5), not knowing that he was passing sentence on himself! It is interesting to note that David saw the moral issues and the terrible injustice in the story told by Nathan, with all of its ramifications, yet was not able to make the application to himself. That God had to do for him through the direct words of Nathan, "You are the man!" (2 Sam. 12:7).

The fact that David was able to spot sin and injustice quickly in the life of another person, analyze it clearly, and even pass judgment on it, all the while missing its application to himself, should be a warning to us. We too may be able to see sin in others readily, but not in ourselves! We may be, even now, smirkingly reading and thinking of David's awful deed and laughing at his blindness as to his role as the central character in Nathan's story when, in fact, the story of David may be *our* story and God may be saying to us, "You are the man! You are the woman!"

III. *David acknowledges his sin and finds forgiveness* (2 Sam. 12:13). The good news in this account of David, of course, is that God did not give up on David, and David ultimately chose not to give up on God. God confronted David with his sin and made it clear that he could not and would not let David go on living "happily ever after." Through Nathan, God pronounced a firm but fair judgment on David (2 Sam. 12:10–12,14), and to his credit, David acknowledged his wrong and sincerely repented. In fact, David wrote Psalm 51 as an expression of his heartfelt confession. It presents a wonderful model as to how we should think, feel, and talk to God when we have sinned. David said, "Create in me a clean heart, O God, and put a new and right spirit within me. . . . Restore to me the joy of your salvation" (Ps. 51:1–3, 10–12).

And the clear word is that God responded to David by offering him genuine forgiveness (2 Sam. 12:13). While there were some tragic future consequences for this terrible incident in David's life, as Nathan indicated (vv. 10–12, 14), God restored the joy of salvation to David and sustained him in the days ahead. He was freed from the curse of living "unhappily ever after."—Kenneth B. Stout

ILLUSTRATIONS

THE DEADLINESS OF A SIN NOT LET GO!   I remember a story of a beautiful, wild eagle that swooped down and sunk its talons into a huge snake. With its powerful wings it picked up the snake from the ground and began to rise, higher and higher, intending to carry the snake back to its nest as a feast. But before the eagle could reach its nest, it began slowly and steadily to descend, and finally crashed dead on the ground. The snake slithered away. The snake had bitten the eagle with its poisonous fangs, turning the tasty meal into a deadly encounter. In committing adultery, David embraced a sin that, if not let go, would have, like the snake's venom, destroyed him eternally (the venom of the incident contributed to rebellion and literal death within his family).—Kenneth B. Stout

THE JUDGE WHO NEEDED A MIRROR!   Imagine a judge who daily makes decisions about murder cases and passes out harsh sentences—including the death penalty—and feels that she or he is doing a great service to society yet cannot see the evil and inconsistency in personally taking bribes and kickbacks from corporations involved in product-safety lawsuits. David didn't see himself as worthy of death—like the wealthy man in the story told by

Nathan—until Nathan turned the mirror of God's word back at him and said: "You are the man."—Kenneth B. Stout

SERMON SUGGESTIONS

Topic: The Medicine Not Taken
TEXT: Jer. 8:22
(1) Common maladies: (a) arrogance (v. 6), (b) twisting the Scripture (vv. 8–9), (c) false optimism (v. 11). (2) The virus remedy: (a) the judgments of God (v. 13), (b) the mercies of God (ch. 17, v. 14).

Topic: Thanks Be to God!
TEXT: 1 Thess. 5:16–18.
(1) When it's easy to give thanks. (2) When it's difficult, even impossible to give thanks. (3) What makes giving of thanks possible: (a) faith: rejoicing always; (b) persistent prayer: assured that this is the will of God and that it enables us to work through our difficulties.

CONGREGATIONAL MUSIC
1. "Guide Me, O Thou Great Jehovah," William Williams (1745)
   CWM RHONDDA, John Hughes (1907)
   This great Welsh hymn, particularly in its first stanza, makes reference to the Bread of Heaven that Jesus speaks about as he talks to the multitudes, as recorded in the Gospel lesson for this day.
2. "Grace Greater Than Our Sin," Julia H. Johnson (c. 1911)
   MOODY, Daniel B. Tower (1910)
   Here is a gospel song that makes a gracious answer to the contrite prayer for pardon from sin of Psalm 51. It could be sung as a response to the Psalter reading.
   3. "A Charge to Keep I Have," Charles Wesley (1762)
   BOYLSTON, Lowell Mason
   Relating particularly to the Epistle reading (Eph. 4:1, 4), this Wesleyan hymn on Christian responsibility could be used to respond to the reading of that lesson.
4. "There's a Quiet Understanding," Tedd Smith (1973)
   QUIET UNDERSTANDING, Tedd Smith (1973)
   This contemporary minihymn refers to the ways Christ loves, cares for, and feeds us. Therefore it would make a suitable response to the reading of the Gospel lesson.
5. "Whiter Than Snow," James Nicholson (1872)
   FISCHER, William G. Fisher (1872)
   Based on Psalm 51:7, this gospel song could be sung as a response to the Psalter reading.—Hugh T. McElrath

WORSHIP AIDS

CALL TO WORSHIP.   "The sacrifices of God are a broken spirit: a broken and contrite heart, O God, thou wilt not despise" (Ps. 51:17).

INVOCATION.   Today, O God, as we come to you from many different experiences, some of them painful and even tragic, help us to know that you care for us and that your love can break through to us like sunlight after the storm. To that end, we lift our hearts to you with longing and faith.

OFFERTORY SENTENCE.   "The Lord is good to all: and his tender mercies are over all his works" (Ps. 145:9).

OFFERTORY PRAYER.   Lord, cause us to see the difference this fellowship of faith makes, this time of worship and prayer, then let us give with abandon that others may know the salvation we know through Christ our Lord.—E. Lee Philips

PRAYER.   It is not easy for us to come and stand before you, Father. The many activities of the past week race into our thoughts and we know in our heart of hearts that we are not worthy to be in your presence with all its purity and glory. We have spent our week pursuing the god of commerce, prattling mindless thoughts, moving from moment to moment in maddening haste with no time for reflection and devotion to things higher than the passing moment. We have truly been slaves to relentless schedules, most times in an effort to prove our value to others and to boost our own self-importance. But now we come to silence, accompanied only be the family of faith. The props are gone, talk is hushed, and activity is ceased. We are here, in your presence, most of us ill-prepared to meet you genuinely face to face. For we have played too much in the world with the things of the world and have neglected to be busy about the Father's business and the things of the Spirit.

Forgive us, Father, forgive us. In the light of the truth we see about ourselves we can only cry out for forgiveness for our failures in doing and being what you would have us do and be. Come into our fearful place in this hour and give us victory over our fear. Come into our hurting place and, hearing our deepest sigh, the very groan of our hearts, relieve the pain that has penetrated our lives, minds, and souls. Let us here, this morning, find the medicine that heals and makes whole as the Holy Spirit comes upon us with healing power at the place of our deepest sickness. Come into our lonely lostness and show us the road that leads to life, and that more abundantly, we pray.—Henry Fields

SERMON
Topic: The Tragedy of Having All the Answers, None of the Questions
TEXT: Job 38:1–7

At one stage of my Christian faith I assumed that my right answers were the key to heaven's gates, that correct doctrine was essential to being admitted into God's presence. If that is true, Job was in a lot of trouble.

Job was a good man, as we all know—faithful, obedient, diligent in observing the commandments. Yet tragedy struck. His family, all except his wife, perished, as did his worldly goods. Hearing of Job's disaster, three friends came to comfort him.

The problem they found was that Job refused to believe what he was supposed to believe. The friends agreed, as was commonly known, that suffering was God's punishment for sin. But Job refused to believe it, declaring that he was innocent of such sin as would bring this calamity.

The comforting was fast and furious, with the comforters desiring very much to strangle

Job into submission to the truth. Job refused to acknowledge this as punishment for his sin. Not only that, but Job demanded that God answer him for this unjust suffering. "I have said my last word," declared Job, "now let the Almighty answer me!" (31:35).

Job's actions with God were both intimate and arrogant. He did wrestle mightily with God, trying to understand, wanting to understand in terms of God, seeking God's words. We can admire and emulate Job's persistence and honesty with God. How refreshingly sincere with God he was. How different his words to God were from our formula prayers and platitudes.

But the arrogance of being right is another matter. Job felt he had the answers and God must agree with him. It is a human trait to want and claim certainty; we hunger and thirst for knowledge, and we see ourselves in Job. For all he did know, he did not know what he did not know.

So, Job challenged God. What happened?

I. *God answered him.* God answered from a storm, a metaphor for the storm of Job's turbulent anguish, anger, and searching in the darkness. But God's tone was not fury; no gigantic flyswatter flattened Job. It was as if Job's insistence had prompted God's most intimate answer. "Who is this," God asked, "obscuring my intentions with his ignorant words? Brace yourself, like a fighter!" Indeed this was a rebuke, but an engaging one, a stunning embrace of Almighty and mortal.

II. *God asked the questions.* Job went back to school. It is a moment when all humankind, theologians all of us, go back to school and God becomes the teacher. We see clearly that humanity's very answers, the ossified certainty we love, may absolutely blind us to deeper knowledge of God. This certainty God had to break down to reach Job: "I will question you, and you shall declare to me" (v. 3).

III. *Job could not answer.* From God ensued a barrage of questions and challenges, not of philosophical obscurities but of the simplest matters of everyday life (38:4–41:34). "Excuse me," God seemed to say, "but perhaps I missed something. Where were you when I laid the foundations of the earth? Tell me, since you are so well informed. Where is the home of the light, and where does the darkness reside? Has the rain a father? Who begets the dewdrops? Can you untie Orion's hands? Will lightning flash at your command? Display your greatness, robe yourself in splendor and glory."

IV. *God's questions drew Job closer.* What were these questions but the beckoning finger of God, signaling Job to come closer. "Do you not see my mystery," the little blade of grass asks us? Come closer and see! It is as if Job all this time had stood before the burning bush of God's creation and seen nothing, much less removed his shoes in humility. How tragic to have answers that satisfy and close off the wonder and search for God in all things.

Do you ever sense the longing to wonder again? Do you think maybe of going to the Grand Canyon, hoping you will be awed and feel small? Has our ability to wonder turned into the arrogance of knowledge, into our spiritual poverty? When did we turn in our questions for answers that enslave and dull the mind?

V. *Living the questions.* I don't mean to say that Christianity is without answers. We have profound answers on which we stake our lives. The certainties of our hearts enable us to live with faith, hope, and love. Yet even Paul, whose certainties withstood pressures unknown to most of us, burst into those wonderful words, "O the depth of the riches and wisdom and knowledge of God! How unsearchable are his judgments and how inscrutable his ways!" (Rom. 11:33).

The Jewish rabbi Edwin Friedman somewhere wrote that he prefers to live with life's great questions: the answers are always changing but the great questions remain. Surely that is the spirit God hoped to instill in Job. In fact, Job was humbled and replied to God, "My words have been frivolous: what can I reply? I had better lay my hand over my mouth" (40:4). We know that at that point Job became open to God.

How is it that we stay alive to God? Not by having all the answers but by seeking his face through our questions!—Stuart G. Collier

SUNDAY, AUGUST 13, 2000
Lectionary Message

Topic: The Challenge of Change
TEXT: Eph. 4:25–5:2 (NRSV)
Other Readings: Phil. 3:1–11; James 5: 7–11

Change often means a sort of starting over and usually communicates a freshness that is very invigorating—whether starting a new career, a new educational pursuit, or a new relationship. Yet change can also lead to anxiety and uncertainty—or what we often call "stress." All of life's changes bring a certain amount of stress. In fact, psychologists have identified important "stress factors" that affect our lives and have assigned a "stress value" to each, to help us calculate the amount of overall stress in our lives. Marriage, moving, career change, serious illness, having children, and divorce are each major stress factors.

The idea of change, and the challenge of facing it, is central to our text for today. Earlier, in the book of Ephesians, the apostle Paul made it clear that he is primarily addressing Gentiles who have recently converted to Christianity. He is appealing to them to hold onto the positive changes they've already made, and to make additional ones, in order to experience full Christian maturity (Eph. 2:11–19). In today's text, Paul challenges them to continue on the path of change by using those changes to embrace some very specific instructions intended to bring about growth. Surely the Ephesians faced significant stress in attempting to put these practical changes into practice. After all, they were wrestling against an entrenched and long-held lifestyle.

I. *Speak the truth* (v. 25). Paul begins his challenge to change by first instructing the Ephesians to stop lying and start telling the truth in all things. There is a natural logic in the order of this instruction; before anyone can tell the truth they must first break the old habit of deceit! In the words of the text, he refers to "putting away falsehood," or literally, putting away "the lie" or "the lying" (*to pseudos*). In using this concrete term, Paul makes it clear that he is not referring to some abstract concept but to falsehood in all of its forms. He follows this up with the counsel to "speak the truth" in relating to "neighbors," which harkens back to Zechariah 8:16. It is interesting that Paul speaks of telling the truth as a kind of first step or first sign of an authentic Christian life—and it makes sense that it is. Until a person's basic integrity is established, there is no way he or she can reflect the one who *is* the truth—Jesus Christ!

II. *Express sinless anger* (v. 26). This seems to be a strange piece of advice. For one thing, we tend to think of anger as inherently wrong. Why should Paul be advising these new believers to show any kind of anger at all? Perhaps Paul is recognizing what we sometimes call "righteous indignation"—a healthy, even wholesome, anger that is a response to some terrible injustice and that is not based on selfishness or pride. The NIV translation may actually make Paul's intent a little clearer, as some commentators have noted. It reads, "In your anger, do not sin." What would be an example of this kind of "righteous" anger? Perhaps we can cite Jesus' anger over the fact that merchants were buying and selling in the Temple. In a contemporary context, we might refer to the anger we have when there is a terrorist bombing in which innocent people are horribly wounded or killed.

III. *Do good, honest work* (v. 28). Paul first tells those who might still be thieves at heart, or in actual practice, to stop stealing and to put forth legitimate effort to increase their wealth and prosperity. It is a call to personal responsibility. To take Paul seriously one must seriously apply one's physical skills and intelligence in plying a trade or pursuing a career that will, with honest labor, lead to satisfying one's own needs. But Paul takes this idea a step further. We are to work, not just to squeak by—meeting our own needs—but to have sufficient increase to "have something to share" with those who lack adequate resources (v. 28). Let's be clear that what Paul is actually calling for here is not an "institutional" response to the needy but a personal one! Just as we are challenged to get our "hands" involved in making a living, we are also encouraged to get our hands and hearts involved in sharing the fruits of our labor with others.

IV. *Speak with encouragement and grace* (vv. 29–30). Paul's challenge to change continues with a plea for wholesome, uplifting speech. Paul makes it clear that controlling one's speech is vital to building up God's work. Christians must not only do good but speak it! Paul recognizes that controlling one's speech first requires an inward change, and no doubt this is partly what he is trying to get at. In Matthew 12:34, this issue is clarified by Jesus' statement to the Pharisees, "How can you speak good things, when you are evil? For out of the abundance of the heart the mouth speaks." Paul knew that in calling for pure speech he was actually calling for a deeper change—a change of heart and attitude toward evil.

V. *Be kind and forgiving* (vv. 31–32). Paul's final challenge to change calls us to exercise tenderness and tolerance in all relationships. He asks that all "bitterness and wrath and anger and wrangling and slander" and "malice" be put away in favor of Christlike kindness (v. 31).

Paul closes with the assurance that if the Ephesians accept his challenge to change, and follow these specific instructions, they can, as "imitators of God" (Eph. 5:1–2), experience a dynamic transformation that reveals God's character. We too can claim this assurance if we likewise embrace Paul's challenge to change!—Kenneth B. Stout

ILLUSTRATIONS

THE BUTTERFLY.   It is said that as a caterpillar goes through the vigorous process of freeing itself from its cocoon its body becomes healthier and its wings stronger. The struggle, by nature's design, is absolutely necessary for it to experience successfully its transformation into a beautiful butterfly. An interruption in its struggle would virtually assure its death. And so it is spiritually with us. The very act of our putting forth effort to grow, of struggling against sin, in partnership with God, helps bring about transforming change in our lives.—Kenneth B. Stout

GETTING TOUGH.   A number of years ago, I took a group on a trip to the Holy Land. It was a fairly strenuous journey. We had some late night events and some early morning departures. We had some long days. One lady in the group was a great deal older than the rest and I was worried about her. I was afraid she couldn't keep up the pace. But I noticed that she seemed to keep up the pace better than anybody else. Finally one day I said to her, "You're tough!" She said, "I have had a long time to get tough."—Robert C. Shannon[1]

SERMON SUGGESTIONS

Topic: While You Wait

TEXT: Lam. 3:22–26

(1) You can affirm the Lord's endless mercies (vv. 22–23). (2) You can affirm a special relationship with the Lord that guarantees God's compassionate actions for you (vv. 24–26). (a) You are his and he is yours—"my portion." (b) Therefore, you can wait patiently for him to act.

Topic: Necessary Work

TEXT: Phil. 2:12–13

(1) The Christian life is a serious struggle. (2) It is impossible to succeed in this endeavor without help. (3) God is present in our struggle: (a) in our decision making, (b) in the working out of what we are committed to be and to do.

CONGREGATIONAL MUSIC

1. "Bread of Heaven, on Thee We Feed," Josiah Conder (1824)

    ARFON, Welsh melody; arr. Hugh Davies (1906)

    Although this hymn is usually sung at Lord's Supper services, its first stanza would be a very suitable introduction or response to the Gospel lesson (John 6), which centers on Jesus as the living bread coming out of heaven.
2. "Out of the Depth," Martin Luther (1524); tr. Richard Massie (1854)

    AUS TIEFER NOT, Martin Luther (1524); harm. J. S. Bach

    This classic Lutheran hymn that freely paraphrased Psalm 130 could be sung at the time of the Psalter reading.
3. "Praise the Savior, Ye Who Know Him," Thomas Kelly (1806)

    ACCLAIM, trad. German melody (1873); stanza 4: Bryan J. Leech (1976)

    A fine hymn of general praise, "Praise the Savior," in its fourth stanza by Leech, relates to the Epistle lesson, particularly Ephesians 4:31.
4. "Awake, O Sleeper, Rise from Death," F. Bland Tucker

    MARSH CHAPEL, Max Miller (1984)

    The beginning of this contemporary hymn is based on Ephesians 5:15. However, its later stanzas (especially stanza 4) hark back to Ephesians 5:1–2, in which the apostle Paul exhorts the Ephesian church to "walk in love, as Christ has loved." The unfamiliar tune could be introduced by a choir singing the first two stanzas before the congregation joins in.—Hugh T. McElrath

---

[1] *Christ Above All*

WORSHIP AIDS

CALL TO WORSHIP.   "I wait for the Lord, my soul waits, and in His word I do hope. My soul waits for the Lord, more than those who watch for the morning" (Ps. 130:5–6a NKJV).

INVOCATION.   Every moment we live, O Lord, is or can be a kind of reaching out to you. You have encouraged us with many promises and shining examples, so that even now we await some new experience of your mercies.

OFFERTORY SENTENCE.   "Bless the Lord, O my soul, and forget not all his benefits" (Ps. 103:2).

OFFERTORY PRAYER.   Our gracious and loving Father, you have blessed us with many benefits—forgiveness of sins; escape from many dangers, toils, and snares; bread for our tables and bread to share. Grant unto us a generous portion of your spirit as we contemplate the ways in which our financial resources can further your Kingdom.

PRAYER.   O Lord, whose creative power reaches back behind all beginnings and out beyond all endings, we marvel that you should come to us in our little times.

We wait before you, praying that our times be a time of the grace of our Lord Jesus Christ.

We wait—praising You for the Church, for the churches, and for this church through which your word of grace is a lively word redeeming, healing, making all things new.

Open us to the insight to see that there is a sense in which the church is here, not because of us but in spite of us. There is a grace at work that is of your wisdom and power. There are times when we need to get out of the way, lest we get in the way of that new thing that you are doing in our day. You have brought us from there to here, and you will lead us from here to where you would have us be.

We pray for the human family; we pray for the healing of the nations. How long, O Lord, how long will the violence of war and the violence of neglect continue toward the children of the world? How can we be forgiven our political posturing when today so many are starving, thirsting, on the road with no place to call home?

We pray that our leaders at all levels of government will not succumb to special interests but seek to serve the needs of all.

In the strong name of him who is among us in Resurrection power.—John Thompson

SERMON

Topic: Keeping Faith at Work

TEXT: Luke 16:1–3

Just how relevant is what we're doing here to what you will be thinking about by three o'clock tomorrow afternoon? For most of us, our working hours are the most demanding and significant ones of our week. How much help is our Sunday Christianity by Wednesday or Thursday?

For good reasons and bad, there has long been a divide between the world of Sunday and the world of Monday through Friday. In many ways, in fact, they seem to dwell in mutually exclusive universes.

On Sundays we talk about a world of grace, where everything is given to us, where we are loved unconditionally just for who we are, where life is more about being than doing, where the highest values are love and community. It is a world of abundance.

Then on Mondays most of us enter a world where, to put it mildly, we are saved not by grace but by our works, where the ultimate question is our productivity, where our worth is measured by what we have accomplished and how efficient and effective we are, where the deepest values are ambition, competition, and success. It is often a world of scarcity, in which only the strongest survive; it worships at the altar of profits.

In the strange parable in today's Gospel, Jesus tells the story of a real hustler in the Monday to Friday world, a man caught red-handed cheating his boss who then quickly cuts some deals in order to try to secure his future. On the one hand, Jesus seems to hold him up as a model of scrappy resourcefulness. But on the other, Luke, the author of this Gospel, reports Jesus as saying that these two worlds can't go together: "No slave can serve two masters. . . . You cannot serve God and wealth."

That puts the division as starkly as possible. And yet Christians have always believed that the Lord of the universe is also Lord of the marketplace, and that there should be no wall between our faith and our work. We can't simply live separate, parallel lives. What we do on Sunday is intended to shape and inform what we do all week long at work, and what we do at work should be the expression of our souls, the acting out of the convictions that we express on Sunday morning.

In fact, in the biblical vision, work has always been part of God's vision for our lives. In the creation stories, humans are told to "be fruitful and multiply, and fill the earth and subdue it." We human beings are given a mandate for work and economic life. We are called to be cocreators with God, extending the goodness of creation by participating with God in shaping the world. It is up to us to feed and clothe our fellow human beings; to create a cultural life; to provide shelter, education, health care, and justice for one another. That is our human work. As the medieval mystic Meister Eckhart puts it, "God can do as little without us as we can do without God."

And that means that our daily work is our ministry. What you and I do with our days, whether it is seeing clients or teaching school or programming computers or running a business, we are participating in God's ongoing care for the creation. Not only is work for many of us the primary source of identity, but it is also our principal way of sharing with God in the care of the world.

For far too many centuries of Christianity, going into the ordained ministry was regarded as a higher calling, as if to say, if you are dedicated to God you will certainly become a priest or minister or nun. But in recent decades we have begun to reclaim the essential biblical vision which is that all of us are called to be ministers in our daily life and work. In our baptism we are all ordained to be priests of Christ, and we are all called to live out the priesthood as doctors or accountants or human resources specialists or custodians or nurturers of our children.

So, welcome to the ministry, my fellow priests! It is your vocation to be Christ's head and heart and hands at Fidelity and Fleetbank, in the Boston Public Schools, and at Beth Israel Hospital. We clergy are your support staff. It is our job to gather you here week after week so that we can keep focused on our high calling. Everything we are about here as we start a new year is aimed at equipping you to go out and be Christ all day long, all week long.

But work these days is a complicated business. For one thing, not all work is equally meaningful to us. The distinguished sociologist Peter Berger has said that there are three levels of significance in working: for some of us work is richly rewarding and we find much of our identity in it; for a great many more of us it is not very fulfilling, and we often end up simply enduring it for the sake of our private lives; and for many others work is a direct threat to our integrity, either because of the indignity of the work or the conditions in the workplace. As Studs Terkel puts it in his book *Working,* "Most of us have jobs that are too small for our spirits. Jobs are not big enough for people."

In all this business we are having to face fundamental questions about our values. As a society we say we want a wholesome environment in which to raise children, a good relationship with nature, a life in which work is fair and just. But our economy is based on the bottom line; it runs on the assumption that unlimited growth is necessary, that unbridled competition is a good thing, and that above all owners are entitled to the maximum return on their investments. In work we experience the clash of these two sets of values. What would it take for us to be able more fully to be priests of Christ in the workplace?

I want to close with four simple words of counsel for all of us who are called to be priests and ministers in our workplaces. First, we can do our best. We can perform the tasks we're given at work as effectively as we can. Second, we can build community, using every opportunity at work to build trust, to enhance dignity, to foster a sense of inclusion for everyone around us. Third, we can work for justice. To the extent that we are able, we should see that the work we do is honest and contributes to a fairer, healthier, safer world, and that the people we work with are treated justly. Finally, we can share our convictions. When the time is right, we can be explicit about where our beliefs come from and how they shape what we are doing.—Samuel T. Lloyd III

SUNDAY, AUGUST 20, 2000
Lectionary Message

Topic: Be Careful What You Ask For!
TEXT: 1 Kings 3:3–14 (NRSV)
Other Readings: 1 Kings 4:20–34; Prov. 4:7; 8:13

What would you request if you were asked to identify what you wanted most in the whole world? Particularly if you were asked by someone who actually had the power to make your request come true? Would you ask for a luxurious estate, a winning multimillion-dollar lottery ticket, a model's good looks, or perfect health? For most of us, it would actually be a very, very difficult choice if we were acting from a strictly human and worldly point of view. Especially if it was a single, once-in-a-lifetime choice. Certainly such an opportunity would reveal our real values, priorities, and motivations!

In our text for today, young Solomon, son of David and newly crowned ruler of the nation of Israel, faced just such an incredible decision; he was asked to reveal his heart's ultimate desire. God came to Solomon in a dream and said to him, "Ask what I should give you" (v. 5), or as the NIV puts it, "Ask for whatever you want me to give you." Now this was not a typical dream and Solomon recognized it. This was a unique and supernatural dream in which God confronted Solomon's deep inner consciousness by special, divine intervention.

I. *Solomon's state of mind* (vv. 3–5). Now Solomon was a dedicated young king about to embark on the enormous task of leading the vast nation of Israel. We know that he was spiritually committed because the text says that he "loved the Lord" and walked in the "statutes of his father, David" (v. 3). So Solomon was seeking God—and God responded by appearing to him and giving him a phenomenal opportunity to ask for whatever he wanted. What would he ask for? It seems like his human nature would have had his mind scrolling through numerous "carnal" possibilities, such as fame, fortune, and power—and probably it did. But Solomon carefully zeroed in with single-minded intensity on one thing; the text indicates absolutely no hesitation or uncertainty in his mind. But what if Solomon had not comprehended the import of the moment and asked for something temporary and peripheral? The fate of the nation for years to come hung on how serious this young ruler took God, and on the care and selflessness with which he made his decision.

II. *Solomon's request* (v. 6–9). Solomon first cited God's love and grace, and then he expressed the fact that he felt like a little child, ill-equipped to provide the kind of leadership that his nation needed—a nation that he recognized as belonging to God (vv. 6–8). He answered God's question by submitting his request: "Give your servant therefore an understanding mind to govern your people" and "to discern between good and evil" (v. 9).

What a marvelous moment this was in salvation history! Solomon, thinking only of his people, asked not for a selfish favor but for moral insight and practical wisdom so that he could best administer the nation and serve the people. Amazing! We can truly say that he was never so rich or so wise or so truly great as when he confessed, in childlike humility, "Lord I need your help!" But what if he hadn't? What if he hadn't chosen with such beyond-his-years care? Think of the enormous loss, not only to Israel and the entire ancient world but also to our age. We would not have the three thousand proverbs and over a thousand songs that he left behind (1 Kings 4:32–33), and we would not have the wonderful example that reminds us of how we should make life's choices—always with great care and with God's interests as the primary consideration. If only we and our current political and religious leaders would, today, ask for Godly wisdom and understanding!

III. *God's response* (vv. 10–14). Then, in one of the greatest understatements of human history, the Bible says, "It pleased the Lord that Solomon had asked this" (v. 10). God went on to say, "Because you have asked this, and have not asked for yourself long life or riches, or for the life of your enemies . . . I give you a wise and discerning mind" (vv. 11–12). But God didn't stop there. With incredible generosity God went on to give Solomon what he hadn't asked for—unmatched riches, honor, and long life, conditioned, we should note, on his continued faithfulness in walking in God's "ways" (vv. 13–14).

IV. *Solomon's kingship.* Blessed by the marvelous wisdom and quickness of mind that God had bestowed, the early years of Solomon's reign were golden years for Israel. His administration for many years was characterized by devotion to God, uprightness of principle, and careful obedience to God's commands. It was a time of moral renewal and great material prosperity because he and his government were centered in God's principles. Solomon's influence was so great that "people," including kings, "came from all the nations" to hear and profit from his wisdom (1 Kings 4:34).

From Solomon's experience we learn several important lessons. First, God is eager to meet our needs when our motives are honorable—a point reinforced by Jesus when he said, "Ask me for anything, I will do it" (John 14:14). Second, God is the source of all wisdom—and not just for kings! God proclaims to every one who, like Solomon, faces a new challenge: "If any of you is lacking in wisdom, ask God, who gives to all generously" (James 1:5). Finally, we learn that God enjoys going beyond meeting mere "needs" to satisfying our deepest "desires."

Tragically, in the second half of his reign Solomon forgot the lessons of his early life and had a falling out with God that tore apart his nation (1 Kings 11), until a late-life reconversion, described in Ecclesiastes. This reminds us that humility must be carefully renewed every day and that, as Psalm 111:10 says, "the fear of the Lord is the beginning of wisdom."—Kenneth Stout

ILLUSTRATIONS

TEST OF GREATNESS.   The higher the position a man occupies, the greater the responsibility that he has to bear, the wider will be the influence that he exerts, and the greater his need of dependence on God. Ever should he remember that with the call to work comes the call to walk circumspectly before his fellow men. He is to stand before God in the attitude of a learner. Position does not give holiness of character. It is by honoring God and obeying His commands that a man is made truly great.—E. G. White[2]

PROPER HUMILITY.   Dr. E. D. Jarvis, minister of the famous Wellington Church, Glasgow, relates an experience against himself that underlines the harmonious effect of mutual laughter. He was taking his first session meeting in London, soon after leaving College. The session was composed of an impressive company of men, all older than himself. He knew that they were observing the young minister closely, and he wished to make a good impression. He was nervous and ill-at-ease. Attempting to take the situation in hand, he ventured on a joke. It was not a good joke. No one laughed, except Jarvis himself; and that was due to sheer nervousness. He laughed and leaned back in the chair. The joke had fallen flat, and so did the minister; the chair disintegrated under him. A complete collapse! What a beginning to a first session meeting! The amazing thing was that, before he could pick himself up, he found himself laughing in real earnest, laughing at himself, laughing at the whole ridiculous situation. Moreover, the whole session was laughing, too. And Dr. Jarvis comments, "We were friends and brothers from that moment."—John N. Gladstone[3]

SERMON SUGGESTIONS

Topic: The Potter's Wheel

TEXT: Jer. 18:1–6

(1) Introduction: the poverty and plight of a nation relying mainly on power politics. (2) It is God who makes history. (3) Men sometimes obstruct the will of God for their nation, thus inviting disaster. God is not defeated; he begins to fashion the nation to a new design. (4) Conclusion: our duty is to place ourselves at the disposal of the moral will of God, the primacy of moral responsiveness; our confidence is that the clay of nations is all on the wheel of history, in the skillful hand of God.—Dwight E. Stevenson[4]

---

[2] *Prophets and Kings* (Mountain View, Calif.: Pacific Press, 1943), pp. 30–31.
[3] *A Magnificent Faith*
[4] *Preaching on the Books of the Old Testament*

Topic: Scared to Life

TEXT: John 11:38–44

Some of the most attractive qualities in the lives of those for whom fear has been overcome by faith: (1) to speak out courageously, (2) to claim spontaneity, (3) to accept challenges gladly. Then, when Jesus calls our names, as he called forth Lazarus, we can come running.—Welton Gaddy[5]

CONGREGATIONAL MUSIC

1. "Songs of Praise the Angels Sang," James Montgomery (1819)

   MONKLAND, John Antes (1704)

   This is but one of several hymns emphasizing the importance of song in the grand sweep of Christian history. The last two stanzas constitute a particularly apt response to the apostle's invitation to sing and make music in the heart (Eph. 5:19).

2. "Bread of the World," Reginald Heber (1827)

   RENDEZ A DIEU, Louis Bourgeois (1551)

   This popular communion hymn would be appropriate sung in connection with the Gospel lesson (John 6:51–58).

3. "O Give the Lord Wholehearted Praise," Psalm 111, vers. *Psalter* (1912)

   GERMANY, in *Gardiner's Sacred Melodies* (1815)

   A metrical paraphrase of Psalm 111, this hymn could be alternately sung and read as follows: stanza 1, sung; stanza 2, read; stanza 3, sung; stanza 4, read; stanza 5, sung; stanza 6, read; stanza 7, sung.

4. "O Food to Pilgrims Given," Latin (1661); tr. John A. Riley

   O WELT, ICH MUSS DICH LASSEN, Heinrich Isaac (1539); harm. J. S. Bach (1729)

   This ancient hymn set to a classic tune expands on the theme of the Gospel lesson: receiving Christ's flesh (bread) and blood (wine) is necessary for eternal life.—Hugh T. McElrath

WORSHIP AIDS

CALL TO WORSHIP.   "The fear of the Lord is the beginning of wisdom: a good understanding have all they that do his commandments: his praise endureth forever" (Ps. 111:10).

INVOCATION.   All-wise God, our loving Father, forgive our reckless pride that so often causes pain for ourselves and for others, and give us hearts that seek your wisdom and ways.

OFFERTORY SENTENCE.   "What good is it, my brothers and sisters, if you say you have faith but do not have works? Can faith save you?" (James 2:14 NRSV).

OFFERTORY PRAYER.   We know, O God, that it is one thing to say we have faith and another to do what real faith will lead us to do. Strengthen our faith, that we may naturally and joyfully do what faith will lead us to do.

---

[5] *Tuning the Heart*

PRAYER.   O You who are not only the covenant-making but the covenant-keeping God, we come in intercession in behalf of all those we have named and all others where there is special need of your mercy and grace.

We are able to come in faith, for we know that you are faithful in keeping all your promises. You are here in an everlasting mercy, calling us each by name. In your love you are calling us to fulfillment, whatever our incompleteness.

By your grace in Christ in his life, in his ministry, in his passion, in his Resurrection—heal our brokenness. Where there is not to be health of body, we pray for that miracle of the Spirit that transcends all physical brokenness.

We pray for all those wrestling with decisions that their own ill health or the illness of a mate has forced on them.

Be with any among us broken by loneliness, that we may know the meaning and depth of your companionship—the love that does not let us go.

Grant to those challenged to grow a new self by the changed circumstances of their life the courage to believe.

Fulfill the joy of those privileged to celebrate the fidelity of married love through many years.

For the unique journey of each of us we pray that faith may be excited, that love may persevere, that grace may fulfill.

We pray through him who is your Word of grace to us, to the Church, to the nations, to all humankind.—John Thompson

SERMON

Topic: How Do You Handle a Miracle

TEXT: John 21:1–14

I am asking you to focus your attention today on the fourth verse of the chapter, which reads, "Just as day was breaking, Jesus stood on the beach, yet the disciples did not know that it was Jesus."

Discouraged, depressed, defeated by the awful events of Calvary—the crucifixion of Jesus—they were blinded to some wonderful thing that God was trying to reveal to them. They looked at Jesus. They had been with him for three years. They had heard him preach, they had heard him give the Sermon on the Mount, they had watched him with his healings, they knew him well. Teacher, Rabbi, Master, Lord, Friend. And yet they looked at Jesus on the beach and they knew not that it was Jesus. A miracle was at hand but they couldn't handle it!

How do you handle a miracle? The disciples looked at Jesus on the shore shortly after Easter—the Risen Christ—and they knew not that it was Jesus. How *do* you handle a miracle?

I am going to make three suggestions that could change your life:

1. *Get ready.* Believe that a miracle can happen.
2. *Get set.* Believe it will happen.
3. *Go!* Believe it has happened and do something about it.

To get ready, we look to God and we talk with God. We focus our faith on the face of God, our Heavenly Father, revealed to us by Jesus Christ. We focus on his goodness and his love and his strength. He is God, the Father Almighty. If we keep the Lord ever before us, as the psalm enjoins us, then we will have confidence that great things can happen. We will *believe* that miracles can happen. We will know that God is more eager to give us a miracle than we in our prayers do ask for it. Jesus gave us this picture of God as a Heavenly Father, and that does it all. He said, "Don't you see, if an earthly Father knows how to give good gifts to his children, how much more will the Heavenly Father want to give good gifts to you?" A hundred thousand miracles are around you every day. God is wanting to give good gifts to you because he is our Heavenly Father. *Believe* that a miracle can happen. *Get ready. Get set.* Believe—it will happen. There is nothing more important than the attitude with which you confront the vicissitudes of life. Not the "facts" of your life but your attitude toward them is the important thing. There is no situation that can't be changed if you change your attitude. Believe, expect, hope that a miracle will happen.

A little while ago Norman Vincent Peale was asked to give a message to America and he gave it in six words: "Expect a miracle. Make it happen." Six words for America. And what gets in the way? Our negative thoughts, our worries, our anxieties, our depressions, our fears. These blanket our lives and we can't see anything good. Someone asked a positive thinker, "Don't you ever entertain negative thoughts?" and he said, "I have negative thoughts; they come to me—but I don't entertain them. I don't bid them welcome. I don't hold on to them; I don't nurse them." If instead of nursing your negative thoughts you would reverse them, you would be on the upward way. Negative thoughts can blind us to wonderful possibilities that God is trying to make known to us.

All kinds of things are possible. In our age I don't need to tell you that the impossible has become possible. Things that we see and enjoy and experience today were not possible fifty years ago. With God all things are possible.

Jesus told us that—if you can believe! He said to the father of the epileptic boy—if you can believe—"all things are possible to him that believes." So, *expect* a miracle. *Get set. Go!* Believe that a miracle has happened and *do* something about it.

In the case of the disciples, as they fumbled about, Jesus asked them to *do* something and suddenly the light broke upon them. He asked them to cast their nets. They had been fishing all night and hadn't caught any fish. The one thing they didn't want to do was keep on casting the net. It seemed silly, futile, hopeless. All kinds of negative thoughts were in their minds and a spirit of defeat and depression weighed them down. But Jesus said, "*Do* something: cast your nets!" And when they did, things began to happen. First there was the wonderful catch of fish—153. John tells us how many big fish there were. But of course the real miracle was that they knew it was the Lord. Something of the glory of Easter was beginning to come through to them. What gets in our way? I think we are put off by appearances. We don't know just how to recognize a miracle when it comes.

Some people say, "Well, a miracle—that doesn't belong in my everyday life, in my business life in the office, in my housework at home." Jesus came to the disciples in the everyday. They had given up all their dreams and they had gone back to their old way of life. They were fishermen, so they went back to their work of fishing; and they had gotten out their boats and nets again and they were back in the old routine. It was the *everyday*. And Jesus gave a miracle in the *everyday*. Don't forget that, because he can do it to you, and he will, if you *get ready*, if you *get set*, and then if you *go!*

Sometimes we are put off by the appearance of a miracle because it comes in the form of a problem, but the problem has implicit in it possibilities; and when you have solved the problem, something has been done and you are a finer person. Sometimes we worry about the obstacles to what we want to do, but obstacles give us a real opportunity to grow and strengthen our agility. Why do they have obstacle courses to train police people, for instance? It is because the obstacles present the opportunity to grow, to develop, to be stronger, more agile.

And tragedy? Tragedy weighs us down, tears blind our eyes. Calvary—the disciples were completely dismayed by the happenings of Calvary. They could no longer see the goodness of God at work. Jesus came to them in the everyday and revealed how God can change Calvary into the Easter Glory, and the Risen Christ is their hope.—Lowell M. Atkinson

SUNDAY, AUGUST 27, 2000
Lectionary Message

Topic: Preparing for Battle
TEXT: Eph. 6:10–20 (NRSV)
Other Readings: James 4:7–11; Phil. 3:12–4:1

When preparing for battle, troops in a modern army are concerned about making sure not only that they have sufficient offensive weaponry and ammunitions, but also that they have strong defensive capabilities. Shrapnelproof helmets, bulletproof vests, and camouflaged uniforms are put on, and radios are distributed so that the soldiers can call for backup and get information about the location and strategy of the enemy. Furthermore, tanks and planes are put in position to come to their aid should they need additional cover.

Today's text, likewise, discusses how a Christian soldier prepares for his or her personal defense in battle against evil. An analogy is made between the defensive attire and equipment of the ancient Roman soldier and the equipment needed for the Christian. Paul describes the specific pieces of equipment needed by a typical soldier of his day: a breastplate, a shield, a sword, and so on. Paul was in chains at the time he wrote this letter, and some commentators suggest that he may have used his personal Roman guard as a model for the equipment he describes in the text. Though the specific equipment he mentions may be out of date for effective modern warfare, the analogy still works when applied to contemporary "spiritual" warfare against our age-old enemy, the devil. The fact is that we must be defensively prepared for the devil's spiritual attacks.

I. *Making careful preparation for a fierce battle* (vv. 10–12). Paul first makes it clear to the Ephesians, who are relatively new converts, that as long as they are striving faithfully to practice their new lifestyle and grow in Christ, they will be under constant spiritual attack. The devil will try to reclaim them as his followers. Paul compares their attempt to remain faithful to a battle in which they are engaged as God's soldiers needing effective defensive armaments. In fact, he describes, in detail—and in language that the Ephesians could well understand—the spiritual equipment that can and must be employed to keep them from becoming a "casualty" in the war between Christ and the devil. He discusses six specific pieces of equipment and what they represent: (1) the belt of truth, (2) the breastplate of righteousness, (3) shoes to proclaim the gospel of peace, (4) the shield of faith, (5) the helmet of salvation, and (6) the sword of the spirit. Paul makes it clear that each piece of equipment functions in the hand of faith by God's power. Our part is simply to choose to "strap on" each piece spiritually and trust its effectiveness.

II. *Using the word of God as an offensive weapon* (v. 17). It is interesting to note that the "sword of the Spirit" is the only one of the armaments that was used as both a defensive and an offensive weapon. The meaning seems to be that this one weapon, representing the "Word of God" (v. 17), is sufficient to attack the devil and his forces offensively and put them on the run; no other offensive weapon is needed, provided that it is used effectively. And this fact is supported by Jesus' own victory in the wilderness when, in direct conflict with the devil, he defeated him with the simple "it is written" of Old Testament Scripture (Luke 4:1–13).

III. *Not getting careless and fighting at less than full strength* (vv. 11, 13). Another point to be drawn from Paul's counsel is that no single piece of armor, by itself, is adequate for maximum success. All of the armor (*panoplia*) must be on each of God's soldiers for them to have complete, head-to-toe protection. Paul twice mentions that believers should put on the "whole armor of God" (vv. 11, 13). A helmet would not protect against a chest wound, as a breastplate would not absorb a blow to the head. The spiritual lesson is clear. The "wily" devil (v. 11) is a great student of human weakness and knows just when and where to attack. If on a given day a Christian comes out to battle with a crucial piece of protective armor missing, the devil will be able to exploit that vulnerable area of his or her life.

IV. *Knowing that your enemy is extremely powerful but not invincible* (vv. 11–12). Paul explains why the battle must be taken so seriously and fought so hard—it is against "cosmic powers" (*archoi*), not "blood and flesh" human enemies (v. 12). The battle is against the devil and the powerful spirit beings who were cast out of heaven with him (Rev. 12:9). The believer's individual battle, then, is part of a much larger, ongoing "great controversy" between Christ and the devil. Yes, other human beings, under the devil's influence, will work against believers, but believers must not be fooled into thinking that that is where the real battle is or where their attention should be focused. Believers must understand that the real attack they face comes from the devil, whose "flaming arrows" (v. 16) come in the form of many temptations and distractions. This imagery is drawn from the fact that, anciently, soldiers shot arrows dipped in pitch and set on fire in order to burn the enemy's defenses.

Paul repeatedly pleads with believers to "stand" up against the devil (vv. 11, 13), despite his power, because Paul is confident that the devil can be routed as we fight relying on the Lord's great might. According to Paul, standing up to the devil with confidence is a key to success. First, standing is important because—using the analogy of fighting with heavy ancient armor—once you are knocked to the ground it is difficult to get back up, making you extremely easy to kill. Second, to "stand" (*stele*) against the devil is a key to success because it implies a mental, physical, and spiritual toughness—what we call faith—that allows soldiers to hold their ground against the devil's advance while setting the stage for a strong counterattack.

Paul is convinced that if we therefore stand up against the devil and employ all of the equipment that the Lord makes available to us, trusting in God's divine power, we will be able to defeat the devil and glorify Christ.—Kenneth B. Stout

ILLUSTRATIONS

NO THROWAWAYS.   Throughout history, battles have often been won by generals who simply threw overwhelming numbers of soldiers against the enemy, rather than employing a careful strategy of minimizing the loss of troops. Consequently, such conflicts resulted in massive casualties. The life of a soldier seemed to count little to the political leaders and military commanders sending them into harm's way. A more recent example of this is when Iran and Iraq were at war back in the 1980s. Iran sent tens of thousands of its soldiers to their death, including young men barely in their teens, against the superior armaments and chemical warheads of Iraq. It seemed that their soldiers were mere "throwaways" to achieve their military goals. And Iraq did much the same. This is not the case with our general, Jesus Christ, who wants no one to be lost. Thus the Lord carefully prepares each of his troops and assures each one his supreme spiritual protection and ultimate victory—if we put on the spiritual equipment that he offers and exercise authentic faith in his leadership. In fact, he goes into battle with us to assure our success!—Kenneth B. Stout

FEAR IN BATTLE.   When Marshal Foch found an officer punishing a French corporal for showing fear in battle, the marshal said: "None but a coward dares to boast that he has never known fear."—Charles L. Wallis[6]

SERMON SUGGESTIONS

Topic: The Discouraged
TEXT: 1 Kings 19:11
The words of the text were addressed to a man who wished that he might die. What would we have done with such a man! What did the Lord do? (1) The first thing he did was feed Elijah and tell him to lie down and get a good night's rest. (2) After the sun was up, the Lord reminded the discouraged man that there were many good people in the world. (3) The discouraged man was also brought face-to-face with the Lord. (4) The Lord also gave that discouraged man something to do.—Charles R. Brown[7]

Topic: The Rim of Your World
TEXT: Mark 1:38
(1) The physical horizon is an artificial one for the soul of man. (2) There is the liability of accepting prematurely an artificial horizon for our own character and personality, of losing the horizon of the possible person we might be. (3) We all face the danger of the too-near horizon of personal interest and advantage. In our text we see Jesus facing it and rejecting it.—Halford E. Luccock[8]

CONGREGATIONAL MUSIC
1. "Soldiers of Christ, Arise," Charles Wesley (1742)
    SILVER STREET, Isaac Smith (1780)
    This hymn tune with its trumpetlike call reinforces the mood of this Wesleyan hymn that relates directly to the Epistle lesson (Eph. 6:10–20).
2. "How Lovely Is Thy Dwelling Place," St. 1, 2, Scottish Psalter (1650); St. 3, 4, Carl P. Daw Jr. (1984)

---

[6] *A Treasury of Sermon Illustrations*
[7] *Dreams Come True*
[8] *Marching Off the Map*

This composite metrical version of Psalm 84 would make a good opening hymn for today's worship.

3. "All Glory Be to God on High," Nikolaus Decius (1523); tr. F. Bland Tucker (1983)

ALLEIN GOTT IN DER HOH, Nikolaus Decius (1525)

An English translation of a German paraphrase of the Gloria in Excelsis, this confessional hymn glorifies the "Holy One of God" (John 6:69) and can therefore be used meaningfully in connection with the Gospel reading.

4. "Be Strong in the Lord," Linda Lee Johnson (1979)

STRENGTH, Tom Fettke (1979)

Based on Ephesians 6:10, this modern hymn with its vibrant tune offers a strong response to the Epistle lesson.

5. "How Blessed Is This Place, O Lord," Ernest E. Ryden (1924)

SOLOTHURN, Swiss melody (1826)

In keeping both with the Psalter reading and the Old Testament lesson describing the bringing of the Ark of the Covenant to the Temple and Solomon's prayer of dedication, the singing of this twentieth-century hymn would be appropriate.—Hugh T. McElrath.

WORSHIP AIDS

CALL TO WORSHIP.   "How amiable are thy tabernacles, O Lord of hosts! My soul longeth, yea, even fainteth for the courts of the Lord: my heart and my flesh crieth out for the living God" (Ps. 84:1–2).

INVOCATION.   We need your help, O God, today, tomorrow, and in every circumstance. Bless us now with your presence and your redeeming judgments, so that our lives may be purified for your worship and service.

OFFERTORY SENTENCE.   "By love serve one another. For all the law is fulfilled in one word, even in this; Thou shalt love thy neighbor as thyself" (Gal. 5:13a–14).

OFFERTORY PRAYER.   As our love for you, O Lord, is deepened, so our love for other people will be deepened, our service strengthened, and our joys multiplied. When we are so blessed, these tithes and offerings leave our hands with your blessings upon them.

PRAYER.   O God, you are the prodigal—the prodigality of your love that seeks us out in the far country of our willfulness no matter how far we have wandered from home.

O God, we pray for your love in all relationships—personal, family, national, international. Your love is patient and kind; it does not parade its own importance; it is not easily provoked; it looks for ways of being constructive, creative—even to dying on a cross.

We pray for the strength to love, to love you with your love; to will the good of the other, not his destruction—to will life, not death. We pray for the wisdom to love with the love that returns good for evil; that reconciles, not alienates; that builds bridges, not walls. We pray for the perseverance to love with the love that never gives up. Your love follows us even to the pit of our own digging; your love pursues and perseveres. You are not willing that one should perish.

We pray in the spirit of him who said, Greater love has no man than this, that he lay down his life for his friends, and who went out and laid down his life for his enemies and is vindicated in his Resurrection from the dead and is among us as Risen Lord, teaching us to pray and live.—John Thompson

SERMON
Topic: It Matters How You Get Where You Are Going
Text: 2 Tim.

In the wonderful film *Chariots of Fire*, Eric Liddell, a young Scotsman born in China to missionary parents, is in Scotland with his family for a visit. It is time for the family to return to China, but Eric wants to stay to train and run in the national and Olympic races. His sister opposes him. She says his first duty is to return to China as a missionary. He resists her, saying, "God made me for a purpose. For China. But he also made me fast. When I run, I feel his pleasure. To give it up would be to hold him in contempt."

His father understood and said to him, "Eric, you are the proud possessor of many gifts. And it is your sacred duty to put them to good use. . . . Run in God's name, and let the world stand back in wonder!"

Liddell felt God had set a course before him. He did return to China as a missionary, and died there, but not before he ran for God. His life was not his own, but it was for a purpose, God's purpose, and it was Liddell's joy to live out the course set for him.

Paul is writing to Timothy about the life of faith, and Paul puts it in terms of "getting there." "The course that I was set I have finished," Paul says. "The time of my departure has arrived" (4:6, 7).

This is such a different perspective that Christianity gives to life. Our faith provides life a solemn and awesome importance, completely beyond the usual concerns and standards measuring success.

I. Paul puts his life as a follower of Christ in terms of a battle: "I have fought the good fight." The most difficult battles are not physical but spiritual. We can live with many physical problems if we are spiritually healthy, but if our spirits are sick we cannot live with a healthy body. The questions of being faithful to Christ in our individual lives and faithful to Christ's mission in our church lives are spiritual issues.

II. We should notice that Paul believed the course he had run was set before him by God, and he kept faith in running it as well as he could. Paul, we know, felt the call to work with the Gentiles. The question arises for each of us, "What fight has God given me? What course has been set for me?" No matter how you answer that question for yourself, you will find new meaning and purpose for your life when you see it as bound under the calling of God and devoted to finishing the course on which God has set you.

In one particular race, Liddell fell down in the first turn. As the others continued running, the camera in slow motion focused on the fierce look of determination that came over Liddell's face as he scrambled to his feet and took off again. He ran with his heart and soul, and when the race was done he collapsed on the sidelines, gasping for breath and life.

An old running coach came over to him, cradled his head in his hands, and said, "That's not the prettiest [race] I've ever seen, Mr. Liddell. Certainly, the bravest."

For some of us, we are called to run brave races, not to finish first, with honors, but to finish, with honor.

III. Then Paul said to Timothy, "I have kept the faith." The power of a personal example is greater than all the words in the language. Timothy, struggling in Ephesus, could look at Paul and see how to live life. Paul reminded him of all the difficulties along the way in Antioch, Iconium, and Lystra (3:10, 11), then said, "You know what I have faced, and the Lord has seen me through." Paul's life authenticated his message. When the great missionary doctor and New Testament scholar Albert Schweitzer was criticized for his radical beliefs, he always refused to argue, but responded simply, "My life is my argument."

IV. Beyond the power of your example, you give the power of your belief in someone. Have you ever been in a situation in which no one believed in you? Only the rare person will be able to maintain self-confidence, but when someone believes deeply in you, you can do marvelous things.

Timothy was in the dumps. He was young, inexperienced, lonely, confused, and needed support. Maybe his faith was shaken. He apparently wrote to Paul, telling him all his problems. Paul wrote back exactly what he needed to hear—not criticism but this: "I thank God as I remember you constantly. . . . I often think of that genuine faith of yours. . . . I remind you to stir up that inner fire which God gave you. . . . Be strong in the grace that Christ Jesus gives. . . . Guard the treasure entrusted to you" (1:3–14).

In other words, "Timothy, I believe in you. I am often amazed at the genuine and deep faith you have. Don't be discouraged, but stir up the fires in your spirit, and rely on the strength Christ gives."

IV. Some of the best words Paul could give Timothy were *endure* and *take your part in suffering* (2:3–5; 4:5). Endure your share of hardship as a loyal soldier of Christ, Paul told him. Some dislike images of soldiery in our old church hymns, but they don't bother me, because the soldier image brings the proper implications of hardship and difficulty and loyalty that belongs to God.

In the final scenes of *Chariots of Fire,* Liddell is running the four-hundred-meter Olympic race. The world is watching. In the stands everyone knows that Liddell is running the longer race at the last minute because he will not run the shorter one-hundred-meter race on a Sunday. He has never even practiced the four-hundred-meter distance. An American coach tells his runner not to worry about Liddell because he has already run that day and will be tired. Another American runner knows the depths of Liddell's convictions and says, "Watch out for Liddell. He has something to prove—something that guys like coach wouldn't understand in a million years." Then another American runner, who has already won a gold medal, comes up to Liddell in the starting blocks and places in his hand a piece of paper. Liddell opens it and reads, "It says in the good book, 'He that honors me, him I will honor.'" Liddell crumples the paper in his hand, and runs—and runs and runs, and wins the gold medal. He has put God first, and he runs for God, and he finds in his running, not in his winning but in his running, the glory of God.

If we are faithful, we will be joyful when our time of departure arrives and we can say, "The glorious fight that God gave me I have fought. The course I was set I have finished and I have kept the faith. The future holds for me the crown of righteousness, which God, the true judge, will give to me."—Stuart Collier

SUNDAY, SEPTEMBER 3, 2000

Lectionary Message

Topic: Signs of an Authentic Christian

TEXT: James 1:17–27

Other Readings: Song of Songs 2:8–13; Ps. 45:1–2, 6–9; Mark 7:1–8, 14–15, 21–23

I grew up in a very conservative religious environment. A good Christian was identified by what he or she did not do—drink, smoke, chew tobacco, dance, curse, gamble, or play cards. Though these behaviors are those a Christian could refrain from doing, they do not describe what a Christian is or does. James 1:17–27 lists several signs or marks of an authentic Christian.

I. *Christian faith begins with God* (1:17–18). Every thing good comes from above. Verses 13–16 need to be read as a preface or background to James 1:17–18. Good comes from above and not from below. Every gift that God sends is good. When compared with God's gift, all other gifts lack perfection. A person's relationship with God is not something he or she can create of his or her own accord or will. As Christians we come into existence not as an act of our own; we owe that relationship solely to God's will. James emphasizes that God is unchangeable; all other created things have variability or change. While lights change and vary, God who created them never changes. The word of truth is "the gospel." A kind of first-fruits obligation indicates that we are to give God the very best that we are. In biblical times, first fruits were sacred to God. As the first fruits of the harvest belong to God, so do we as his children.

II. *Practicing self-control* (1:19–21). We are to practice self-control, for the anger of a person does not show the righteousness of God. As Christians we are to submit all of our habits, attitudes, and emotions to God. A Christian's dominant desire is to have the approval of God, and this desire restrains one from angry outbursts, which God cannot approve. If we are to listen to God, our mind cannot be distracted by resentment, ill-temper, hatred, or vengeance. Converted Christians bring into this new life in Christ much that is inconsistent with it. As believers we should be more anxious to listen to God than to try angrily to get God's attention. Anger usually indicates a clash of wills, a conflict of selfish interests, a struggle for power. Our lives are to be lived as God's Word dwells within us—the engrafted word. It is a part of who we are and thus controls and guides our behavior. If we are to influence others either as teachers or parents, we will do it more by encouragement than by harsh anger. The accent must be on love because it has more power than the accent of anger.

III. *Authentic Christianity involves both hearing and doing* (1:21–25). Christianity is essentially a life to be lived. James admonishes his readers to get rid of everything that would keep them from receiving the true Word of God. We can receive the knowledge of the true Word of God from two sources—from the depths of our own being as it comes from the Holy Spirit, the teachings of Jesus, and from the preaching of humankind. What the Christian needs is a teachable spirit. When we have a teachable spirit it means that we are humble enough to learn, that we are able to face the truth without anger even when the truth hurts and condemns, that we can willingly accept the discipline of learning. Many people feel that just going to church is adequate. However, what one hears in church must by lived and done in life. James states that the practical value of going to church is realized when the word heard becomes the word in action. What the authentic Christian hears in church must be lived in the marketplace. Some feel that responding to the Word of God and accepting obedience to God narrows the scope of one's living. The question is, When is a person really free? Freedom is not a restriction of choices, but it gives guidance to what the choices should be. Choosing the law of liberty leads to enrichment of life, being truly free, and happiness, which is the lot of one who does the will of God. The person who fulfills the purpose for which God sent him into the world will be the person God intends and will make the contribution to the world he or she should make. As long as a person obeys his or her own passions, emotions, and desires, that person is a slave. When a person accepts the will of God, then he or she is free to be good and agrees to be what he or she ought to be. A Christian loves God's commandments and is eager to obey them.

IV. *Control of one's tongue—the mark of an authentic Christian* (1:26–27). The outward expression of religion is ritual, liturgy, and ceremony. These externals are unacceptable to God unless accompanied by a genuine desire on the part of the worshiper to render sympathetic and practical service to others. The prophet Micah describes it well in chapter 6, verse 8: "He has told you, O mortal, what is good; and what does the Lord require of you but to do justice, and to love kindness, and to walk with your God." A Christian's relationship to God is not determined by any external activities but by a simple and sincere devotion to God, and by having a compassionate relationship with one's fellow beings. In addition, one is to avoid even the appearance of evil. One is to keep oneself pure by continual remembrance of the demands of a holy God. For James, real, authentic worship lay in the practical service of mankind and in the purity of one's own personal life.—Jerry M. Stubblefield

ILLUSTRATIONS

ATTITUDE TOWARD THE WORD.   Some years ago I was asked to teach Paul's first letter to the Corinthians to a nearby church. There were some who fairly hung upon the word; there were others who did not. At the close of one period a lady sitting near the front came up with a radiant face and said, "Why didn't you go on? I could have listened another hour." As I went out the door, I heard one girl draw a deep sigh and say, "O—oh! I thought he would never quit."—P. I. Lipsey[1]

ANGER EVALUATED.   Too easily we represent what in fact springs from wounded self-esteem and thwarted pride as "righteous indignation." In Paul's writings when anger is named, it stands in company with obviously evil qualities, which a Christian must seek to discard (e.g., Col. 3:8, Eph. 4:31). It is true that in Eph. 4:26 there appears to be a kind of permissive acceptance of anger (though a slightly different word, *parorgismos*, is used): "Be angry but do not sin: do not let the sun go down on your anger." These words, however, should not be understood as an approval of anger, but rather a clear insistence that if anger does occur, it must be clear from all that taint of self which makes almost all anger sin, and moreover, even if it be free from sin, it must not be allowed to continue overnight."—C. Leslie Mitton[2]

---

[1] *Tests of Faith*
[2] *The Epistle of James*

SERMON SUGGESTIONS

Topic: God's Kind of Love

TEXT: Jer. 31:1–6

(1) It is everlasting. (2) It rebuilds what is damaged. (3) It leads to rejoicing. (4) It gives hope for the future. (5) Its culmination is worship.

Topic: The Bottom Line

TEXT: 1 Pet. 3:8–9

(1) The goal: harmony. (2) The means: love. (3) The reward: God's blessing.

CONGREGATIONAL MUSIC

1. "O Brother Man, Fold to Thy Heart Thy Brother," John G. Whittier (1848)

    WELWYN, Alfred Scott-Gatty (1902)

    The great Quaker poet Whittier has given us this expression of what it means truly to worship. The second stanza harks to the teaching of the apostle James (1:27) that pure religion includes ministering to the needs of orphans and widows.

2. "For the Beauty of the Earth," Folliott S. Pierpont (1864)

    DIX, Conrad Kocher (1838)

    The James 1:17 verse confessing that every good and perfect gift comes from the Father finds appropriate response in this hymn that recounts in gratitude the gifts that God has freely bestowed.

3. "As a Chalice Cast of Gold," Thomas H. Troeger (1984)

    INWARD LIGHT, Carol Doran (1984)

    Here is a contemporary hymn based on the teaching of Jesus in the Gospel lesson appointed for this day. Basically it is a prayer to be saved from the accusation of Isaiah, repeated by Jesus, that this people honors the Lord with their lips but in vain worship their hearts are far from him. A choir could introduce the hymn by singing the first two stanzas, after which the congregation should be able to join in.

4. "Come Away to the Skies," Charles Wesley (1755)

    MIDDLEBURY, Ananias Davisson, *Supplement to Kentucky Harmony* (1825)

    This little-known hymn by the eighteenth-century master Charles Wesley was written for an anniversary of the birth of his wife. It is based on the love song found in the Old Testament reading (Song of Songs 2:10–13). The folk-hymn tune is especially suitable for children's voices.—Hugh T. McElrath

WORSHIP AIDS

CALL TO WORSHIP.   "Your throne, O God, will last for ever and ever; a scepter of justice will be the scepter of your kingdom" (Ps. 45:6 NIV).

INVOCATION.   Bless this service of worship, Lord, with new depths of understanding and new heights of insight, that the wisdom of God in Christ might make us faithful in every good work to honor the Lord our maker.—E. Lee Phillips

OFFERTORY SENTENCE.   "In his name, then, let us continually offer up a sacrifice of praise to God, that is the fruit of lips that confess his name . . . and forget not to be kind and liberal; for with that sort of sacrifice God is well pleased" (Heb. 13:15–16 Montgomery).

OFFERTORY PRAYER.   God of grace, grant that we may learn what it is to give sacrificially, for earthly life is but for a while and a gift for the Kingdom of God is filled with eter-
nality.—E. Lee Phillips

PRAYER.   Thou, O God, art pleased with the humble and with the contrite, with such as
are of broken spirit; thou art pleased with the first and most imperfect sigh of repentance and
forsaking of evil and yearning to the truth. Thy smile is enough to bring thee to us with sweet
attraction and instant relief. We ask not that thou shouldst accept an offering today glorious
in its fullness; we come as imperfect creatures in the school of development; all that we bring
is imperfect, and much is most sinful both by omission and commission. We come to thee
knowing that we are spared; that it is mercy which guards our hearts; that it is the long-suf-
fering of God with our indolence, helplessness, pride, and selfishness, that gives us leave to
be and to have comfort in being by drawing near. We come not bringing purified gold and
silver as offerings to thee; but faint, and hungry, and weary, and often discouraged, and conscious deeply of our own demerit and sinfulness.

We come before thee because thou hast revealed thyself a God of tender mercy, a Saviour
of sinners. Lift thou upon us the light of thy countenance, for we are in darkness. Send us
mercies, for we are weak. Love us, not because we are able to repay thee, but because thou
knowest, in the royalty of thy nature, how to love the unworthy and even the unlovely. Grant,
we beseech thee that today we may have developed toward us the Divine nature, in magnanimity, in generosity, in all tender mercy and kindness.—Henry Ward Beecher[3]

SERMON
Topic: Aspects of the Life in Grace
TEXT: Eph. 4:25–5:2

One Lord, one faith, one baptism. These are the ties that bind us together in one body, one
Spirit, and one hope. All of that is the gift of the grace of one God, the Father of us all,
through all things and in all things. As we open our lives to the spirit and power of God in
faith, we become part of the body of Christ; we find ourselves and all of our gifts being
enriched, being changed, being used, being fulfilled, being redeemed. Our prayers for justice
are being put to work through missionaries, through agencies, through other lives that are
sustained by our gifts and the links of support through the Church. Our hopes for the new
Kingdom are visible in all the places where there is an ongoing debate about what the world
ought to look like.

In Jesus Christ we see, hear, and feel the new life that is God's gift and desire for all of us.
By our response, by our faith, by our identification with that life, we bring our gifts and our
energies into the Kingdom of God to be at work for the purpose and will of God, but Paul
says that purpose and will of God will flow back into our lives and we will see our lives
marked by changes. As we put ourselves into the body of Christ, the body of Christ puts itself
into us and we begin to see that we have been changed, are being changed, and desire to be
changed even more.

---

[3] *Prayers from Plymouth Pulpit*

Paul says there are lots of dimensions of life where these changes can be seen. There are certain qualities about life that will begin to become natural characteristics of our lives. We are part of the same body of Christ. Christ becomes part of our bodies, minds, and hearts, and as we become more and more influenced by the Spirit and power of Christ, we find that we stop trying to control and manipulate words and sentences in order to make ourselves look better. Paul says it simply: "We are part of the same body. Stop lying and start telling each other the truth." In the body of Christ we have confessed that we are forgiven sinners; there is no need for us to try to pretend that we are so much better or kinder than we are.

So often these few words, "Speak the truth in love," have been used by some as the justification for all kinds of bluntness and cruelty to others, insults and harshness that are defended as just speaking the truth in love. For Paul, as the Spirit of the body of Christ becomes more and more alive in us, we share Christ's forgiveness so we no longer have to protect ourselves, so we can speak the truth about our responsibility for our mess, and we invite you to take the responsibility for your part in the mess.

So you find it surprising that no sooner does Paul affirm that we are all one body in Christ but he starts off by telling us to stop lying. Does that mean that the first place the Spirit of Christ coming into our lives will have an effect is in the integrity of our speech, or does it mean that the integrity of our speech is the aspect of our lives that needs the greatest improvement? Does the will and personality of Christ come into our lives and affect our ability to speak honestly about ourselves and our lives because it is the easiest reform to accomplish or because it is the most needed?

Certainly the nature and the quality of our speaking, of our language, of our use of language, has dramatically shaped the nature of our community as a people. There are some who are shocked by the cynicism and sarcasm of the public around them. There are those who are wistful for more patriotism, more idealism, more optimism, more devotion to values. Nobody believes what anybody says. Everybody is skeptical of anybody else. We seem to be creating a people who are willing to believe only themselves and they don't believe that they have to keep the promises they have made to anybody else.

When the grace and Spirit of Jesus Christ flows into us as we are united in the one body, by one faith and one baptism, our anger becomes an expression of our opposition to evil in life rather than simply our rage that we did not get what we wanted. Don't become so angry that you sin. Sin is when we separate ourselves from God so that we decide for ourselves what is good and what is evil. Cain became so angry that his sacrifice wasn't received that he decided to eliminate the competition. But God had told Cain that sin was waiting outside his door till the anger gave him a chance to come in. Don't allow your anger to become so great that it separates you from God.

It is a relief to discover in these words the fact that it is not sin to become angry. Paul does not seem to indicate that just because we get angry in life we have sinned. In fact, there is good evidence in the Scriptures that the more we are filled with the spirit and power of God, the more we indeed should become angry at the evil and injustices we discover around us. Illegal deaf Mexicans being used as slaves ought to produce in us some legitimate indignation and anger. But as we are united in the body of Christ by spirit and faith, the anger does not provoke us to play God, to take justice into our own hands, to speak or act in some pompous and judgmental way, to lose our focus on the face of the person before us.

In the body of Christ, under the influence of the works of the Spirit, work becomes different. If you have been a thief, stop. If you have been a taker, stop. The Spirit of Christ begins to bring us to the place where we see work as the source of obtaining what we can give. Work so that you will have something to give. What a radical transformation for us in our culture. We work so that we can acquire. We work so that we can have something to get what we want. We work so that we can buy all the things that we would like to have. Paul says that as we are part of the same body, the body of Christ, we will discover that our perspective, our desires, our reasons for working move from working so that we can get, from that of taking, acquiring, accumulating, to where we work so we will have something to be able to give, to bless others, to help, to contribute.

The more we merge into the body of Christ, by faith, by hope, by love, the more we are changed; the more we struggle to have integrity about our speech, to stop lying, the more we discipline our anger so that it does not give opportunity to sin, and work becomes the means of obtaining something to give rather than just the means for us to have whatever we want.—Rick Brand

SUNDAY, SEPTEMBER 10, 2000
Lectionary Message

Topic: Faith in Action
TEXT: James 2:1–10 (11–13), 14–17
Other Readings: Prov. 22:1–2, 8–9, 22–23; Ps. 125; Mark 7:24–37

I. *Showing proper respect* (2:1). We live in a world where discrimination is considered a normal way of life. In the Christian fellowship there is no room for either humiliation or arrogance. Jesus set the example of how we are to treat others. Jesus treated everyone with proper respect. He was never snobbish or showed prejudiced favoritism. It is human nature to be influenced and thus to show favoritism because of a person's social standing, prestige, position in life, or wealth. God shows fairness, justice, and complete impartiality to all people.

II. *Snobbery within the church* (2:2–4). Showing partiality reveals a divided allegiance, a hypocritical desire to serve God and humankind. Those who differentiate between rich and poor may show themselves to be judges with impure motives. James was afraid that snobbery might invade the early Church. In the ancient world the Church was the only place where social distinctions did not exist. Because there were no distinctions, going to church created some very awkward situations—a master might find himself sitting next to his slave, or a master might find himself in a service in which his slave was the leader of worship. In its beginning the Church was predominantly poor and humble. When people meet in Church there can be no distinctions of rank or prestige; all are equal in the sight of God. In God's presence all people are one; there is an equality of rank, place, and prestige.

III. *The paradox of poverty and riches* (2:5–7). For James the poor of this world have been chosen by God to be rich in faith. They are also rich in the gifts of God's Spirit. Christianity has always had a special message of hope for the poor. The essential message of Christianity was that those who mattered to no one else were significant and important to God. Those who bear the honorable name of Christ must stand with the oppressed. James insists that those who profess to serve Christ must show justice and mercy to all. Part of the gospel appeal to people was that it offered much to the poor and demanded so much from the rich, so that many people were swept into the Church. James emphasizes that there is high value upon those whom the world regards as valueless. In James's world the rich were notorious for abusing and oppressing the poor. The rich were the most violent oppressors of the Christians. They frequently dragged the poor to the law courts. James is not condemning riches but condemning the use of riches without empathy. A Christian takes the name of Christ, is called after Christ.

IV. *The royal law* (2:8–10). James connects the royal law and the previous passage. The law that James feels is the supreme law is "Love your neighbor as yourself." James may mean that this law is of supreme excellence, the highest part of the law. This is the law that governs all other laws concerning human relationships. The law of God is used in the light of all other laws and is used, judged, and applied in that light. Emphasis is placed on the law of God, so that to break any part of God's law is condemned. For James the whole law is the will of God; thus to break any part of it is to infringe on the will of God and to be guilty of sin. A person may be a good person in almost every aspect of life, yet one can spoil it all by one fault. Christians cannot subtract the laws we do not like. One should so live that by doing one thing everything is not spoiled and all goodness goes for naught. The plea is for the Christian's conduct to be consistent. When one loves another one cannot disparage them. The intention of the royal law is the good of humankind. If one violates the law's intention, then one is guilty of violating the underlying principle that governs all the commandments of God.

V. *Faith in action* (2:14–17). James points out the futility of any profession of Christianity that does not express itself in right conduct. He has already condemned showing partiality; now he addresses the issue of faith that does not carry over into life or action. What he is attacking is the idea that a confession of faith guarantees salvation regardless of the way the believer lives. A faith in word only is not worth calling faith; real faith unites a person with Christ so that one's thoughts and actions come under the control of Christ's Spirit. James is disputing the notion that the recital of a creed makes a person acceptable to God in spite of his or her behavior toward other people. There is a belief that is primarily intellectual, in which we accept a fact only with our minds; another way to view belief is that we take that belief into every area of our lives and live by it. It is a guiding principle, one that directs and guides us in our daily living and actions. Salvation is the free gift of God; we cannot secure our salvation by deeds we do. A proof of our salvation is the good works we do because we are saved. Counterfeit faith has no saving power.—Jerry M. Stubblefield

ILLUSTRATIONS

SOMETHING TO DO.   One New Year's day, a minister's phone rang and a voice asked if interviews were ever granted on a holiday. The man came. He was very tense. His mother, to whom he had given himself, had passed away some six months before. He was not in financial distress, but he had no job, no interests, no friends. The ache of loneliness was like a terrific physical pressure. His mind was so distraught that he could not read or sleep. He was at dead center. He was consulting various persons, talking over and over his problems. But talk was not enough to get him off dead center. That man had to put his hand to something. He had to force himself to start doing something, however little, something which would get him out of himself.—Ralph W. Sockman[4]

WORK TO DO.   You remember that terrible scene in Hamlet, where the uneasy prince first learns the cause of his father's death. He sinks to the ground under the weight of it, muttering to himself:

> The time is out of joint; O cursed spite!
> That ever I was born to set it right!

When suddenly he realizes that his friends, Horatio and Marcellus, are standing beside him! He gets to his feet then, and with a brave gesture, linking both arms in theirs, strides off the stage, saying to them, "Come, let us go together!" There's the world, and there's God's will for it! Together we have our work to do!—Paul Scherer[5]

SERMON SUGGESTIONS

Topic: Punishment Deserved—Forgiveness Restored

TEXT: Gen. 50:15–21

(1) Joseph's brothers: a story of jealousy and murderous intent. (2) Joseph himself: a story of incredible forgiveness. (3) The God of Abraham, Isaac, and Jacob: a story of the will and power to bring good out of evil, foreshadowing the cross of Jesus.

Topic: How to Give

TEXT: Various references

Give the self: (1) first (2 Cor. 8:5); (2) voluntarily (2 Cor. 8:3; 9:5); (3) proportionately (2 Cor. 8:12); (4) generously (2 Cor. 8:2; 9:11); (5) sacrificially (Luke 21:1–4); (6) spontaneously (Matt. 6:2–4); (7) systematically (1 Cor. 16:2).—Richard B. Cunningham[6]

HYMN SUGGESTIONS

1. "O for a Thousand Tongues to Sing," Charles Wesley (1740)
    AZMON, Carl G. Gläser (1828); arr. Lowell Mason (1839)
    The healing ministry of Jesus described in two instances in the Gospel lesson (Mark 7:24–37) finds an exuberant response in the stanzas of this Wesleyan hymn. It would be especially appropriate for the beginning of worship.
2. "When the Church of Jesus," Fred Pratt Green (1968)
    KING'S WESTON, Ralph Vaughan Williams (1925)
    This contemporary hymn makes a good response to the Epistle reading (James 2:1–17), which states that faith without works is dead.
3. "All Who, with Heart Confiding," Psalm 125, vers. Psalter (1912)
    KNOWHEAD, Charles H. Gabriel (c. 1930)

---

[4] *The Higher Happiness*
[5] *The Place Where Thou Standest*
[6] In James W. Cox (ed.), *Handbook of Themes for Preaching*

Alternately singing this paraphrase and reading Psalm 122 can effectively bring out the meaning of this "Song of Accents." The plan would be: Ps. 125:1–2, read; stanza 1, sung; Ps. 125:3–4, read; stanza 2, sung; Ps. 125:5, read; stanza 3, sung.

4. "Footsteps of Jesus," Mary B. C. Slade (1871)

FOOTSTEPS, Asa B. Everett (1871)

Because the lesson from Proverbs (22:1–2, 22–23) focuses on ministry to the poor, this gospel song would be appropriate (especially the third stanza) to use in connection with the reading.—Hugh T. McElrath

WORSHIP AIDS

CALL TO WORSHIP.   "They that trust in the Lord shall be as mount Zion, which cannot be removed, but abideth forever" (Ps. 125:1).

INVOCATION.   O, God, give us the faith that refuses to be satisfied with things as they are, a faith that puts us on the front line of action, serving you through love and deeds of mercy.

OFFERTORY SENTENCE.   "Be ye doers of the word, and not hearers only" (James 1:22a).

OFFERTORY PRAYER.   Allow, O Lord, that what is begun here will eventuate in strong faith played out in the broken places of a sinful world where Christ waits.—E. Lee Phillips

PRAYER.   O God, our help in ages past, beyond our knowing you have cradled us in the heart of your providence. You have surrounded and sustained us with grace upon grace. Morning by morning, new mercies we do see, and this Lord's day, we rise and gather to worship you and lift our hearts and praise to you. Great is your faithfulness!

O God, our hope for years to come, beyond our knowing, by your love and goodness, forgiveness and redemption, you are sealing our destiny with your blood and life. Indeed, you are our eternal way, our eternal truth, our eternal home, and we give thanks for the will and privilege to walk each day in your call to discipleship.

Wondrous God of help and hope, may we worship you and serve the good news with glad and generous hearts, even in this Lord's Day hour.

Timeless God, author of our days and seasons, the shorter daylight, the cooler mornings, the different angles of the sunlight, all remind that autumn is near upon us. Though changeless you are, you grant us the beauty and mystery of your changing creation. We give you thanks.

For this extended season of service in this sacred place alongside these gracious folk who embody the Christ, I thank you, O God. It has been a sacred trust, an endeared gift of love and service, and we have been honored to labor together in your name. Through many dangers, toils, and snares, we have come, reminded that grace, indeed, has brought us safe thus far, and grace will lead us home. Thanks be to God for a Savior of grace!

Wondrous, abiding God of this day and this place, of our past and our future, we do give thanks for all that has been. And in the goodness of God, fully revealed in the living Christ, may all that we breathe, say, and do help to live the Christ rather than kill the Christ. May

we embrace all that is to come in the Yes of God, Jesus Christ our Lord, in whom we pray.—
William M. Johnson

SERMON
Topic: The Power of Integrity
Text: Eph. 6:10–13

The entire story of the New Testament can be understood as a power struggle. Had Jesus posed no threat to the authority of either the Jewish establishment or the Roman government, he might have lived to a ripe old age and died of natural causes. But Jesus was viewed as a dangerous presence. Jesus was viewed as a religious threat; he taught a revolutionary new standard of righteousness. He was a political threat; he proclaimed a new Kingdom. He was a social threat; he attracted a significant following rivaling the popularity of John the Baptist. He challenged the accepted understanding of the law and spoke with an uncommon authority. The solution to the Jesus problem was the cross—destroy the man, eliminate the threat. The cross became a symbol of the unique power of the gospel.

The devils believe in God, and tremble. Jesus was executed out of fear. Especially religious leaders were terrified by his existence. The cross was not the product of a popular uprising—some lynch mob aroused by mass hysteria. The cross was an official execution. Jesus was terminated legally and officially by the established authorities. Both the authorities and the disciples saw the cross as a sign of weakness. Jesus was overpowered. But the cross turned out to be only the beginning. Paul even declared a victor: "He disarmed the rulers and authorities and made a public example of them, triumphing over them on it [the cross]" (Col. 2:15). The threatening presence of Jesus did not end with the cross. The gospel of Jesus Christ exploded from Jerusalem to Judea and Samaria and the ends of the Earth. The man became a movement. The challenge to the powers of domination in the world has continued to this day. Regardless of what you or I may believe about the Resurrection of Jesus from the dead, the authorities of his time were terrified by the haunting presence of Jesus in the world. The Kingdom of God proclaimed by Christ could not be stopped.

Alternatives to the cross are symbols of failure. Jesus would not be seduced by the powers of evil. The appetites of the body, the appeal of public acclaim, and the lust for political power were options before Christ in his temptations—alternatives to the cross. The temptations continue to stand before us, with radically diverse results. Jesus was a threat because of his unconventional manner of dealing with the powers of this world. He refused the sword. He did not come to destroy but to save. He also refused to acquiesce to the authorities or to compromise before the beast devouring the children of God. Jesus chose the cross, not as resignation to the power of evil in the world. The cross was the final stand of Christ—a positive strategy for the final destruction of the demonic powers. The cross was then and is now a stand of strength and victory.

We stand in the power of Christian integrity. Our model is Christ, and our symbol is the cross. You can almost hear the breeze blowing in the background as the apostle warns Christians about a weak, passive relationship with the world: "We must no longer be children, tossed to and fro and blown about by every wind of doctrine, by people's trickery, by their craftiness in deceitful scheming. But speaking the truth in love, we must grow up in every way into him who is the head, into Christ" (4:14–15). The alternatives of fight or flight are rejected for the first principle of Christian strength in this world—to stand firm. We shall not be moved! Followers of Christ shall neither compromise with the powers of evil in this world nor imitate the behavior of the enemy. The military figure, "Put on the whole armor of God," is far from an endorsement of militarism. The armor of God prepares for the struggle with principalities and powers—the enemy within. The Christian is here to change the world rather than to imitate the world. Too often the Church has gone out with the words of the Great Commission ringing in our ears only to be converted by the very world we have been sent to save, and no resistance to the Word of God in this world can be more effective than compromised Christians.

Every shrewd dictator has recognized the power of religion and sought ways to use spiritual power to enslave his subjects. Domination must go beyond ownership of property and physical enslavement of people. People are more than bodies; we are souls. People are controlled from the inside out. If you would rule the world, first command the mind and spirit. In spite of his failure to see the ultimate effect of a state church, Luther recognized the power of the cross: "Let goods and kindred go, this mortal life also. The body they may kill: God's truth abideth still."

The power struggle goes on. Battles for power are all around us. The struggle to win, to dominate, or simply to have is basic to human nature, past and present. The popular football team is the winning team, the one demonstrating the power to excel over the competition. The popular politician is the one who convinces the public that he or she is defeating the public enemies. The financial wizard is the person who has learned to translate wealth into power. The respected intellectual is one who has demonstrated that "knowledge is power." We cannot afford to ignore the ultimate mission of Christ, the Kingdom of God. Thus the one who humbled himself, who took the role of servant, who was obedient even to death on the cross is the one whom God has highly exalted "that at the name of Jesus every knee should bend."—Larry Dipboye

SUNDAY, SEPTEMBER 17, 2000
Lectionary Message
Topic: Control Your Tongue, Control Your Life
TEXT: James 3:1–12
Other Readings: Prov. 1:20–33; Ps. 19; Mark 8:27–38

I. *The awesome responsibility of a teacher* (3:1). Earlier James stated that faith without works is dead; now he says that words are works. A teacher's words often leave an indelible impression for good or evil upon receptive and often immature minds. Teachers in the early Church were highly respected and honored. The role of the teacher was significant in the early Church because the converts were entrusted into their care. They were to instruct these converts in the facts of the Christian gospel and for edification in the Christian faith. The awesomeness of the teacher's responsibility was that he would put the stamp of his own faith and knowledge on these new converts who were entering the Church for the first time. James was aware of the heavy moral responsibility he had as a teacher. He was concerned about false teachers; he believed that teaching was a very serious responsibility for any person; he himself was a teacher. Teachers, especially Christian teachers, must be careful that they teach the truth, and not their own opinions, or even their own prejudices. Teachers must use caution that their own life does not contradict what they teach.

II. *The danger of the tongue* (3:2). Speech differentiates humans from the animals. One's character is revealed by one's speech. Speech is important for people because action is preceded by thought, which is prompted by verbal suggestions. The way human beings cooperate with one another depends on verbal communication. Every human sins in some way. Sin can be that which one does, a sin of commission, or that which one neglects to do, a sin of omission. Often sin occurs when we let our guard down, when we least expect to sin. The innocent person is one who has the tongue completely under control. By controlling one's tongue, one possesses the power to bridle the whole body, because sin uses the body as the medium of its self-expression. Every person commits sin, thus one cannot be prideful for the life one lives. James stated that the gravest sin is the sin of the tongue.

III. *The tongue—small but powerful* (3:3–5a). It is interesting how such a small thing as a bit in the mouth of a horse can control such a large animal. If we can control our tongue, we can control our whole body, but if the tongue is out of control, one's whole life is moving in the wrong direction. What is true of horses is also true of people. By using the bit one can guide the horse in the desired direction. A rudder is small in comparison to the size and weight of a ship, but with a little pressure on the rudder one can change the direction of the ship and guide it to safety. Though the tongue is small, it can direct the course of the whole body and the life of a person. Life is safe when the mind controls every word and emotion and when the mind itself is controlled by Christ. A little bit and a small rudder achieve big results. James was not encouraging silence; he was appealing for the control of the tongue. Abstention is never a substitute for control in the use of anything. He was urging the wise use of speech—the tongue.

IV. *The tongue—a destructive fire* (3:5b–6). The fact that it takes only a spark to set on fire a great mass of material illustrates the destructive power of the tongue in individual lives and in human relationships. Damage done by the tongue is like a fire in that it is far-reaching. The tongue can damage at a distance. Because the range the tongue can reach makes it the tongue's greatest peril. Like a fire, the tongue is uncontrollable. No person can control the damage the tongue can do. While one cannot control what one speaks, one will definitely answer for it. The tongue has the possibility of kindling a destructive fire that can destroy all life. Herein lies the danger and terror of the tongue. Fire that is kindled by the Holy Spirit can be used to purify.

V. *The tongue—untamable* (3:7–8). Every animal can be tamed. Tame means to control something and make it useful and good. The tongue is untamable when one has lost control over oneself.

VI. *The tongue—an instrument for blessing and cursing* (3:9–12). The highest use of human speech is the praise of God, who is acknowledged to be Lord and Father. There is the potential in all of us to be both a saint and a sinner. This is seen in the tongue. With the tongue we can bless God and we can curse other people. One of life's hardest tasks is to see that one's tongue does not contradict itself but speaks only words one would wish God to hear.—Jerry M. Stubblefield

ILLUSTRATIONS

WELLSPRING OF WORDS.   In the *Journal* of John Woolman, there is a well-known scene which took place in an Indian village along the upper Susquehanna River in Pennsylvania. John Woolman rose to pray in a religious meeting held among the Indians and an interpreter who stood up to render Woolman's words into the Indian language was asked to sit down and let the prayer go untranslated. After the meeting, the Indian chief, Papunehang, approached Woolman and through an interpreter said of the prayer whose English words he had not understood, "I love to feel where words come from."—Douglas V. Steere[7]

THANK CONSEQUENCES.   Both God and life are complex: the primary dimension of each is infinite mystery. In consequence man might almost be defined as the *anxious* creature. To suggest that good intention has no place in Christian doctrine would be wrong, but to make it the major part of piety is a disaster. The mind is at least as important an instrument of grace as the heart, and understanding the facts contributes as much to the redemption of the world as willing the good. If anything is more blasphemous than the suggestion that the Christian life is easy, it is the promise that it can be kept simple.—William Muehl[8]

SERMON SUGGESTIONS

Topic: Help for the Downhearted
Text: Ps. 42
(1) We are sometimes downhearted from disappointment or disillusionment or anxiety. (2) Hope is the remedy: (a) because we have been assured of God's love, (b) because God's love is strong and God is able to make his love effective (Isa. 40:27–31), (c) because God's love triumphs in his ways—not necessarily in ours—winning over his people's slavery in Egypt, their wandering in the wilderness, and their exile in Babylon (Hos. 2:15).

Topic: A New Family
Text: Gal. 3:28–4:7
(1) Our Father—God. (2) Our Mother—the Church. (3) Our Elder Brother—Jesus Christ. (4) Our Brothers and Sisters—all Christians.

CONGREGATIONAL MUSIC

1. "The Heavens Declare Your Glory," Psalm 19:1–6, 14, vers. Thomas R. Birks (1874)
   FAITHFUL, J. S. Bach (1735)
   This paraphrase of the opening verses of Psalm 19 is effectively set to the charming tune of J. S. Bach. This theme of praise for all creation should be sung by the people in unison to sparse accompaniment.
2. "Nature with Open Volume Stands," Isaac Watts (1707)
   ELTHAM, Nathaniel Gawthorn (1730); harm. S. S. Wesley (1872)

---

[7] *On Listening to Another*
[8] *All the Damned Angels*

Also relating (particularly in its first stanza) to adoration of the God of all nature, this is one of Watt's finest hymns. The angularity of its eighteenth-century tune may make congregational singing difficult. However, after a choir has sung two or three of its opening stanzas, a willing congregation should be able to join the singing with fervor.

3. "Yield Not to Temptation," Horatio R. Palmer (1868)

PALMER, Horatio R. Palmer

This gospel hymn could be sung in connection with the Epistle lesson (James 3:1–12), for it speaks specifically (stanza 2) of shunning bad language, swearing, and the other evils that result from an uncontrolled tongue.

4. "Where He Leads Me," E. W. Blandy (1890)

NORRIS, James S. Norris (1890)

Based on Mark 8:34, this gospel song makes an admirable response to Jesus' summons to deny self, take up one's cross, and follow him.—Hugh T. McElrath

WORSHIP AIDS

CALL TO WORSHIP.   "The worship of the Lord is good; it will continue forever. The judgments of the Lord are just; they are always fair" (Ps. 19:9 TEV).

INVOCATION.   Today, O Lord, let the words of our mouths, and the thoughts of our hearts please you, for so much is at stake for us as individuals and for the triumph of your Kingdom.

OFFERTORY SENTENCE.   "If our faith is strong, we should be patient with the Lord's followers whose faith is weak. We should try to please them instead of ourselves" (Rom. 15:1 CEV).

OFFERTORY PRAYER.   Help us, O Lord, to overcome our reluctance in our stewardship because some of those we have tried to help have not made the best use of our efforts to bless them in your name. Give us patience to match our faith and love.

PRAYER.   O Lord, our God, we pray that thou wilt help us in our various situations of life to bear the burdens that thou dost call us to bear; and though we may ourselves be instrumental in bringing those burdens upon us, thou art employing them as moral instruments, thou wilt by them help us in the end. May those that are weak be helped of God, in those troubles that spring from weakness, whether of mind, conscience, or affection. May all those that are in the midst of sickness, of troubles and pain, find thee a present help in those necessities. May those that are bereaved find that God is an able physician for this trouble; and may those who desire to get rid of their difficulties understand the sweetness and depth of the promise, "My grace shall be sufficient for thee"; and may they more and more find out the sacred lesson of bearing.

May we, O Lord, find strength in enduring things which at first we utterly despised and hated. May we know how to make our lower nature serve faithfully, cheerfully, and gladly our higher; and in all things may we accept the overrulings of our lower experience, of our physical sensations, of our earthly connections, and of our time interests, in behalf of generosity, magnanimity, purity of life, spiritually, and the hope of God and heaven. And we beseech of thee that thus we may be led everyday as in a Sabbath, finding rest every hour, and everywhere a sanctuary, and our heart a perpetual altar, and every affection sweet incense.—Henry Ward Beecher[9]

SERMON
Topic: Lord, Teach Us to Pray
TEXT: John 17 (selected verses)

Whatever number of years we have had experiences with prayer, there is still a need to know more about the prayer times of Jesus. There are more than twenty accounts in the Gospels about Jesus and prayer. When we read that he withdrew from the crowds for long periods of solitude we want to know what he prayed for. In his model prayer Jesus outlined what we need to pray for. We know this prayer in worship as the Lord's Prayer. From reading about his prayer in the Garden of Gethsemane, we know that it was an agonizing experience. Haven't we all had moving, disturbing, and close encounters with God?

It has always been helpful, uplifting, and instructional to sit at the feet of Jesus and let him "teach us to pray." Let us do it again and again and we will have a "Closer Walk with Jesus."

Jesus prayed before the temptation ordeal, before the appointing of the twelve, before delivering the Sermon on the Mount, before instructing the disciples, before serving the multitudes, and before his glory was manifested. In addition, his prayer from the cross reached deep into our own desire to be forgiven.

In the great prayer recorded in John 17, he prayed for himself, for his disciples, and thank God, he prayed for us and those yet to be (John 17:20).

I. *Jesus prays for himself.* Just as Jesus prayed for himself, so we need to pray for what we may become through intimate fellowship with him. The blind beggar prayed for himself by crying out, "Jesus, thou son of David, have mercy upon me." The publican prayed, "God be merciful to me a sinner." This is the personal prayer that has delivered us from death to life eternal. In the letter of James we read, "You do not have because you do not ask. You ask and do not receive, because you ask wrongly, in order to spend what you get on your pleasures" (James 4:3 NRSV). Praying for self will help us to achieve goals Christ has for us.

In my earliest recollections I felt a sense of mystery about prayer. There was prayer at every meal. No one was even to taste the food until we bowed our heads and Father prayed words of gratitude for God's provisions. Why at every meal? Couldn't we have had one big prayer for the food in the morning and let that be enough? Not in a pietistic religious environment. Furthermore, our father led the family, ten in number, in a devotional service after breakfast. There were readings from the Scriptures and another prayer. Then father would go to the parlor, a special room reserved for receiving special guests and for his personal devotions. As a curious child I wanted to know what my father did during his personal devotions. I eavesdropped by the hot air register from the furnace that connected both the parlor and the kitchen. First, there was silence. I assumed he read from the Bible and a devotional leaflet. Then I heard a thump as he knelt and then prayed audibly. He followed the pattern in the

---

[9] *Prayers from Plymouth Pulpit*

great prayer by Jesus. He prayed for himself, his family and church, sometimes for persons who were ill physically or spiritually. Because my father and mother honestly lived their faith, they became my best teachers on behalf of Jesus. Most of what I gleaned about a meaningful prayer experience came from them.

What has kept believers faithful to Christ in regions of the world where it has been or is still not permissible to practice openly their religious faith?

While visiting and preaching in the former Soviet Union, which at that time allowed only government-controlled religious gatherings, lay people and pastors repeatedly stated that "we can always pray in private." There are countless thousands who have survived imprisonment and great suffering by praying for themselves. Thank God that computers cannot register or put on the Internet what we think or pray in private.

II. *Jesus prayed for his disciples* (John 17:6–19). Jesus enumerated all that had been achieved in their lives. The total review of his ministry with the twelve focused on the need for them to be loyal and protected. "I am not asking you to take them out of the world, but I ask you to protect them from the evil one" (v. 15). He prayed, "Sanctify them in the truth; your word is truth. As you have sent me into the world, so I have sent them into the world" (vv. 17, 18). At this point in the prayer we may wish to have been one of the disciples, because Jesus prayed so earnestly for them. But as we read on further, Jesus did include us.

This portion of Jesus' prayer must be for us who are believers now. It is one of the most cherished assurances he gave us. How reassuring to know that we have not been left to ourselves to try to live the Christlike life. No matter where our journey has taken us, we are fortified by the Master, who prayed for us while on Earth and continues to pray for us. Do our fellow believers know this spectacular fact? "And remember, I am with you always, to the end of the age" (Matt. 28:20b NRSV).

Jesus spent much time away from the crowds—to pray. Does that encourage us to engage in longer sessions of prayer? We must meditate on our concerns and allow the Spirit of God to bring to mind persons, situations, opportunities, and problems that take more prayer time. Are sleepless nights God's invitation to "think on these things?" The fast pace of our times calls for disciplined prayer. Does silence before the Lord make us uncomfortable? A psalm that I have recited many times when calling on the sick and elderly states, "For God alone my soul waits in silence; from him comes my salvation. He alone is my rock and my salvation, my fortress: I shall never be shaken" (Ps. 62:1, 2 NRSV). Almost the same words are repeated in verses five to seven. Walking close to God takes time, meditation, and contemplation. This is what Jesus illustrated in his prayer times and expressed so personally in the words of his great prayer.

The fruits of a devout prayer life are illustrated by a man who lived on a farm one mile away from our home. His German name, Gottlieb, literally translated, is GOD LOVE. He came to America in 1889. A pioneer in North Dakota, he homesteaded 160 acres of land that would become fully his after tilling the ground for five years. He was a most genuine example of what a Christian should be. A group of believers met in his house because they had no church building. First it was a house constructed of sod. After a few years he was able to build a house that could accommodate the larger number of people coming to worship. The community needed a cemetery plot, which Gottlieb gave—six acres of his 160. Not long after that they needed land for a church, and again Gottlieb, a man of great dedication, gave the four acres needed right next to the cemetery. Schools were needed in the community, and Gottlieb again gave the six acres that were needed. This added up to the tithe of the homestead plot that America provided for pioneers.

The prayers of Jesus for his followers will continue to bear fruit for the Kingdom of God if we remain faithful.—Gideon K. Zimmerman

SUNDAY, SEPTEMBER 24, 2000
Lectionary Message

Topic: The Source of True Wisdom
TEXT: James 3:13–4:3, 7–8
Other Readings: Prov. 31:10–31; Ps. 1; Mark 9:30–37

I. *Person who should not teach* (3:13–14). His basic question is, "Who among you wants to be a man of real wisdom and a real teacher?" Wisdom is more than knowledge or cleverness or astuteness; it is an understanding of what the good life is or ought to be. If one wants to be a person who has real wisdom and to be a real teacher, one must show to everyone that gentleness is the controlling power and influence in one's life. A person of wisdom and a teacher is always under two temptations. It is hard for a teacher or a preacher to remain humble, yet it is absolutely necessary. Both the teacher and preacher are used to being listened to; they are used to having their words accepted; they are used to telling people rather than listening to people. All of this leads to the temptation to be arrogant. The other temptation is resentment. It is almost impossible to argue without passion. This passage describes four characteristics of poor teaching. One is fanaticism, holding truth more with unbalanced fierceness than with reasoned conviction. Another characteristic is resentfulness, regarding one who opposes as a person to be annihilated rather than as a friend to be persuaded. Another negative quality is to have selfish ambition, being more interested in the victory of one's own opinions than in the victory of truth. The last characteristic is arrogance, taking pride in one's own knowledge, than having humility in what one does not know.

II. *Wisdom that is wrong* (3:15–16). Resentful and arrogant wisdom is quite different than real wisdom. Resentful and arrogant wisdom has three effects. It is earthly. Everything about it is worldly—its standards, its sources, its measure of success, and its aims. It is also characteristic of the natural man. A part of our lower nature is that which we share with the animals. The wrong kind of wisdom is devilish. It issues in disorder; instead of bringing people together, it drives them apart. It produces strife instead of peace. It also produces disruptions in personal relationships rather than producing fellowship. This kind of person who is active in church life causes trouble, drives people apart, foments strife, makes trouble, and disturbs personal relationships.

III. *True wisdom* (3:17–18). True wisdom always comes from above—it is the gift of God, not human attainment. James uses eight words to describe this true wisdom. First, it is pure. True wisdom has become pure enough to see God, because it is cleansed of all ulterior motives, cleansed of self. Second, true wisdom is peaceable. True wisdom produces right relationships—right relationships between one person and another and between one person and God. It is the kind of wisdom that brings people closer to each other and closer to God. Third, true wisdom is considerate. True wisdom gives a person the ability to give to others kindly consideration that we wish to receive ourselves. The possessor of true wisdom knows how to forgive, knows how to make allowances, knows when not to stand on one's rights, knows how to temper justices with mercy, remembers that there are greater things in the world than rules and regulations. Fourth, true wisdom means one is ready to obey or is easy to persuade. A truly wise person is always ready to obey God when he or she hears God's voice. Being easy to persuade means one is not stubborn and is willing to listen to reason. True wisdom is being willing to listen, to be persuaded, being skillful in knowing when to wisely yield. Fifth, true wisdom is full of mercy and good fruits. Christian mercy is for any person who is in trouble. Mercy issues in good fruit, in practical help. Sixth, true wisdom is undivided; it does not waver, hesitate, or vacillate. True wisdom knows its own mind, chooses its own course, and abides by it. It has certain convictions that it will not change. Seventh, true wisdom is without hypocrisy. Christian wisdom is honest; it never claims or pretends to be what it is not. Eighth, true wisdom produces right relationships. This means that people are in uninterrupted friendship and fellowship with one another. Without right relationships between people, righteousness cannot exist. One's religion must show itself in what it does, in its works.

IV. *Seeking our pleasure or God's will* (4:1–3). Desire is at the root of all the evils that ruin life and divide people. A person is drawn between seeking to please oneself or to make the ultimate choice in life, between choosing to please oneself and pleasing God. Basic desires are for the same things—money, power, prestige, worldly possessions, gratification of bodily lusts—all these place people into a competitive arena. The energies and ambitions of people must be radically redirected. The ultimate question is this: Is God or pleasure the dominant concern in one's life? On the contrary, obedience to the will of God draws people together. When one obeys the will of God, it makes a person essentially selfless; to serve the will of pleasure makes one essentially selfish. Craving pleasure shuts the door to prayer. A selfish person seldom can pray properly; we can pray correctly only when self is removed from the center of life and God is placed in the center of one's life.

V. *A demand for moral purity* (4:7–8). God's demand is a moral demand, not a ritual demand. The ethical demand of the Bible is that a persons' words, deeds, emotions, and thoughts should be cleansed inwardly and outwardly, for only the pure in heart will see God.—Jerry M. Stubblefield

ILLUSTRATIONS

A PLACE OF PEACE.   After entering the desert and wrestling with your demons and discovering your angels, you come to "the still point"—a place of peace, a point at which you begin to feel at home with yourself and with life. At the center you discover a fountain of grace that offers you a reconciled relationship with God, with yourself, with others, and with life itself. At the center point, do not expect too much or settle for too little. Accept life, the real life in the world, in God. At the center point you will be infused with courage to become what you were created to be!—Ben Campbell Johnson[10]

HOW A CALL MAY COME.   What happens to the worshiper that turns him into a minister? He may have brought with him certain seeds out of which ministry could flower or he

---

[10] *To Pray God's Will*

may have come without any expectation that he would that day be called into the ministry. What he is and what moves in him is slowly disclosed before the living Listener, who gathers the meeting to himself, and there in that tendering presence an ordering takes place.—Douglas V. Steere[11]

SERMON SUGGESTIONS

Topic: The Suffering Man and the Silent God

TEXT: Ps. 88

(1) The intensity of pain (vv. 8c, 15–17). (2) The isolation from friends (vv. 8, 18). (3) The interrogation of God (vv. 13–15). The interrogation of God does not mean the absence of God. God is present even in and through his silence. God stands "within the shadow, keeping watch above his own."—Charles E. Crain[12]

Topic: On Being a Whole Person

TEXT: 1 Cor. 12:12–14:1

(1) Ideally, the Church functions as a smoothly running organic whole. (a) This is God's intention. (b) This is symbolized in baptism. (c) This is affirmed by the one Spirit. (2) However, problems arise, such as individualism and jealousy. (3) The solution is to be found in the practice of *agape* love: (a) by pursuing love, (b) by striving for the spiritual gifts.

CONGREGATIONAL MUSIC

1. "O Master, Let Me Walk with Thee," Washington Gladden (1779)

    MARYTON, Henry Percy Smith (1879)

    A popular hymn that prays for the kind of selfless service that Jesus was calling for (Mark 9:35), it could be sung either to introduce or to respond to the Gospel lesson assigned for this day.

2. "Before Thy Throne, O God," William Boyd Carpenter (1925)

    ST. PETERSBURG, Dimitri S. Bortiniansky (1822)

    The exhortation of the apostle James (3:14–4:3, 7–8) for wise behavior and righteous living calls for a response in a hymn like this. It is a poignant petition for forgiveness for one's sinfulness and for assurance of God's presence as one strives to rise to a life of purity and true wisdom.

3. "The One Is Blest," Psalm 1, *The Psalter* (1912)

    DUNFERMLINE, *The Scottish Psalter* (1615)

    A venerable paraphrase of Psalm 1, this hymn could well be sung in place of the reading of the psalm. If preferable, the psalm could be read in alternation with the singing as follows: Ps. 1:1, read; stanza 1, sung; Ps. 1:2, read; stanza 2, sung; Ps. 1:3, read; stanza 3, sung; Ps. 1:4, read; stanza 4, sung; Ps. 1:4–5, read; stanza 4, sung; Ps. 1:6, read; stanza 5, sung.

4. "Near to the Heart of God," Cleland B. McAfee (1901)

    MCAFEE, Cleland B. McAfee (1901)

---

[11] *On Listening to Another*
[12] In James W. Cox (ed.), *Best Sermons* (1st ed.)

This informal devotional song would be effective if sung as a response to the Epistle reading, especially if it follows the last verse (James 4:8a) of the reading: "Draw near to God and he will draw near to you."—Hugh T. McElrath

WORSHIP AIDS

CALL TO WORSHIP. "The Eternal cares for the life of the just, but the ungodly life shall perish" (Ps. 1:6 Moffatt).

INVOCATION. Help us, O Lord, to see that every opportunity of worship provides another measure of your care of us. Grant that your wisdom may permeate our decision making and give permanence, even eternal significance, to our lives.

OFFERTORY SENTENCE. "Thanks be unto God for his unspeakable gift" (2 Cor. 9:15).

OFFERTORY PRAYER. We thank you, O God, for the incredible gift of Jesus Christ and for all the good things that come to us because of him and through him. Now grant that good things may flow through us into your Kingdom's work because of all that you have given to us.

PRAYER. You have been our dwelling place in all generations. Before the mountains were brought forth, or ever you had formed the earth and the world, from everlasting to everlasting, you are God.

You are the great God and the great King above all gods, yet you are present to each one of us as though there were no other person in the world to love. You are uniquely loving us even down to the tips of our fingers.

You are God, yet you come among us as one who serves. This indeed is strange. It is so strange that many missed you in your coming, and many of us are still missing you.

You are such a stranger, strange to our ways. You *do* move in mysterious ways your wonders to perform. To you, "One day is as a thousand years, and a thousand years as one day."

We wait for you, O God, as those who wait for the morning, anxiously and impatiently; in our incompleteness, we cry out for wholeness; in our brokenness, we long for healing; in our weakness, we desire the strength of the everlasting arms; in our estrangement, we yearn to be at home with you and with all others; in our loneliness, we weep for a love that does not die and leave us.

For the meaning of church affirmed and celebrated in our life together, we are grateful. We are members one of another and no member suffers without the whole body suffering; and when one rejoices, it is the occasion for all to celebrate. For the comradeship of the way experienced in this time and place, we praise you.

Pour out your Holy Spirit upon us all that we may dream dreams and see visions of what you would have us be and do as your people. We pray for special anointing of those who have the awe-full responsibility of seeking out ministerial leadership for our church—your Church. May we support these with our prayers, love, patience.

Renew us in such a sense of mission to faithfully proclaim and lovingly live out the gospel in all the world and all the worlds of men and women, boys and girls, and young people.

We pray in the spirit of him in whom word and deed are one, who is present among us as Risen Lord teaching us to pray and live.—John Thompson

SERMON
Topic: The Goodness of God
TEXT: Matt. 5:17

You and I claim that in the special revelation of the Scriptures and in the life of Jesus Christ we know something of the nature and personality of the Sovereign God. The whole story of the Scriptures is rooted in the bold and daring claim that God is Father to his people. God does not come looking through the Smokey Mountains of the Garden of Eden for Adam and Eve the way the FBI is looking for Eric Rudolph. God comes looking like a frantic parent who is looking for his lost children. "Where are you?"

This Old Testament story claims that God the Father picked out a people for himself and entered into covenant with them. God the Father revealed himself as the God of goodness who is known in righteousness. The people of the Old Testament were stunned by the very idea that God would bind himself to a promise, to a covenant, to the law.

These were people in a world where the gods acted any way they wanted to. These were random and capricious gods who toyed with human beings for sport or sadistic pleasures. These were the three-hundred-pound gorilla gods who slept anywhere they wanted, and human beings were servile and frightened. What an amazing love, that God would come and enter into a relationship of covenant with human beings he called his own.

Too many variables in life: imagine how many variables there are in God's world. So just imagine how wonderful the people of Israel must have felt when the Sovereign God of all creation offered to enter into an agreement with them. This God is good. He is just. He is kind. He is righteous. The goodness of God to us is seen in the desire of God to enter into covenant. God will no longer surprise us. We will no longer have to wonder what God wants us to do. God will not want sacrifices today and refuse them tomorrow. God is a righteous God who shows his love for us by entering in and keeping his agreement with us. We will know what God wants from us and God will tell us what he will do for us. God has made clear the expectations of this relationship.

Some of you may remember that Dr. Jim Moore, when he was here for the Royster Series, spoke one afternoon about the dangerous and destructive games we play with those we love. The first one he mentioned was the game of secret expectations. One person in the relationship begins to think, *if* she loves me, really loves me, if she loves me and cares about me, she will know that I am getting longings for rocky road ice cream for dessert tonight. If she really loves me, she will surprise me tonight with rocky road ice cream. Now we do not tell the other person we want rocky road for dessert, but we expect the other person to have it for us. When they attempt to surprise us with some homemade brownies, we are disappointed. We are hurt. They are hurt. But we won't explain why we are hurt because that would make us look foolish, so there is a wound in the relationship because of secret expectations.

God the Father has come to us and entered into an open and clear agreement in the Old Testament Covenant. God has no secret expectations of his people. God says, here are the ways you can show your love and gratitude to me. Keep these rules. These are my expectations. And here is what you can expect from me. I will be your God and you will be my people. God the Father shows his goodness to his people by being the God who makes clear the expectations and obligations of the relationship he wants with his people.

Certainly one of the great reasons for so much joy at Christmas is that children make specific lists of what they want, and Santa and his helpers work hard at giving them what is on the list and the children are happy and families are happy. The covenant makes it very clear what the people are supposed to do to worship God and to live faithfully and fully as the people of God.

Jesus comes and takes the goodness of God the Father beyond the goodness of the covenant. The Covenant was a gift of grace and mercy. It is a real step up from reckless and selfish gods who toy with creation and indulge their passions with no regard for creation. But Jesus says, I have come to fulfill that covenant even more. There is a goodness that goes beyond a covenant agreement. There is a justice, love, and mercy of relationship that expands and inspires that relationship. There is more to a living and loving relationship than can be contained in an agreement. Every covenant has a way of becoming a burden, an obligation, not a joy; a covenant can sink into legalism and pettiness.

Jesus says, I have come to fulfill the law and the prophets, to show you a goodness that transcends the goodness of the contract, to live out a faithfulness and joy of relationship that is larger than laws. There is a marriage joy that is more than just the license. There is a love and respect for the game that is greater than any multimillion-dollar contract.

The life, teaching, death, and Resurrection of Jesus so clearly demonstrates that there is a fascinating beauty and attractiveness about goodness. We are still reminded of the winsomeness and power of a life such as Mother Teresa's. Even her enemies could not deny a fascination, a mystery, a curiosity about her. Why did she care for those sick so well? What an amazing spirit of humility! Jesus still attracts and invites disciples by the alluring beauty of his goodness. Herein is love, that you love one another as I have loved you. The goodness of the covenant could so easily become a chilly righteousness, a harsh dogmatic cruelty. Arthur Miller, in *The Crucible,* has a husband say to his good wife, "Elizabeth, your righteousness can freeze beer." In Jesus Christ we see an attractive beauty of God's goodness.

But in the life of Jesus there can also be no doubt about the fact that the beauty of goodness demands a high price. To live and to share that kind of goodness has a way of leading us to high demands and great sacrifices. Jesus says that the goodness of God expects from each of us a cross of suffering. Goodness cannot care about the world without feeling the great desire to be able to help those who need help and to do all that is within one's ability to help.

It is our weekly confession that we are never able to get comfortable with that kind of goodness of God. In the light of the beauty of God's holiness and love, of the high sacrifices and calling, we come each week to confess that we have not been faithful to that goodness, nor lived in accordance with that goodness. The brilliance of the light of that goodness is so great that our eyes never fully adjust to the light. That is what troubles some of us at all these informal worship services. It is not the time or the style or the music, but they seem so comfortable, so familiar, so at home, in the presence of God's awesome goodness.

I was not familiar with the names so they have not stayed with me but an American tour group was in a cathedral where Johann Sebastian Bach was the church organist. One of the crowd was a church organist who slipped onto the bench and played a few measures. He turned and laughed and said, "That almost sounds like" and he named a very famous contemporary organist. The tour guide quietly said, "Not really, when he was here he did not feel worthy to sit on the bench." In the presence of the goodness of God, how can we not feel a little uncomfortable and unworthy to be here.

We have seen the goodness of God in the land of the living and that goodness wore the face of Jesus of Nazareth. It is a goodness that still attracts and still demands and still judges us like nothing else. We believe and trust in the goodness of God.—Rick Brand

SUNDAY, OCTOBER 1, 2000
Lectionary Message

Topic: Depending on God
TEXT: James 5:13–20
Other Readings: Esther 7:1–6, 9–10; 9:20–22; Ps. 124; Mark 9:38–50

Ours is a world that depends on computers, television, and cellular phones. These and other inventions have made life more enjoyable and, at least in some respects, easier. This is true until something goes wrong. Try to reason with a computer! Nothing is more frustrating than trying to have something corrected when there is no person with whom one can communicate. What happens when the power goes off? We feel isolated and at a loss. That on which we depended has proven fallible. James reminds us that our ultimate dependence is on God, not ourselves.

I. *Prayer* (vv. 13–15). Perhaps the most direct way of showing our dependence on God is through prayer. But if we are not careful, prayer can become a superficial act. We say thank you to God and make our requests to him although we may secretly think we are capable of taking care of ourselves. But when the crises of life come, we realize there is nothing that we or any other person can do in our situation and we learn to trust in God and depend on him. The Israelites in the days of Esther were like that. Their destruction had been decreed. Only God could save them. Although he used Esther as his instrument, it was still God who brought about their deliverance. The psalmist understood that had God not interceded, his enemies would have destroyed him. So James reminds us of the need of prayer in the crisis times of life. When suffering comes, pray. When good things happen, give praise to God. When sickness develops, get the best doctors and medicines available and pray. We can do only so much for ourselves. Others can do only so much for us. Our real dependence lies with God in every situation of life.

II. *Confession of sin* (vv. 16–18). In our better moments we acknowledge that we are guilty of sin and that we fail God. Much of the time, however, we may not be aware of personal sin. We look around us and see the failures in the lives of others, and we rejoice that we are not guilty of the terrible things they do. This can be dangerous because it leads us to think that we are all right and our lives are pleasing to God. But when we feel most comfortable about our lives, we are farthest away from God. As we draw nearer to him, and he to us, we are made ever more aware of our sin. When we stand in the very presence of God, we know we are sinners and cannot help ourselves. We can give nothing to God to atone for sin. It is impossible to live good enough to make up for even one of our failures. We can offer no sacrifice, no gift, that will bring us back into relation with God.

Our only hope is to make confession of our sin and receive God's forgiveness. Confession is more than simply the recognition of sin. It is more than regret that we have been caught. Confession is admission of sin and the commitment that, with the help of God, we will refrain from such sin from this time forward. Confession is closely tied to repentance. This means a total change of direction, a change from pleasing self to pleasing God. We desire that God's will be done in our lives. Sin has broken our fellowship with God, and it is a stumbling block to others. Confession is vital, and we have the promise that when we confess, God is ready to forgive and restore us to a proper relationship with him. Prayer is powerful, whether it be a prayer of petition or a prayer of confession

III. *Restoration* (vv. 19–20). James closed his letter with an appeal to his readers to allow themselves to be instruments of God in restoring others to fellowship with God. It is easy for a believer to stray into sin. Sometimes it can happen without the individual even being aware of it. Restoration takes place only in dependence on God. The person involved in sin can no more restore himself or herself than he or she could originally bring about forgiveness of sin. Only God can bring one back. No individual has the power to restore another to God. And we can only serve as agents of God in assisting others. All too often, when we see another believer involved in sin, we may rejoice or even seek to make life worse for the person. It is easy to condemn. But James calls on us to be God's instruments in bringing others back. This requires love and forgiveness on our part. We must realize that we are subject to the same danger. We need to see these people as God sees them, and allow ourselves to be used in assisting them. We can be God's channels of love and forgiveness so that they see their need and seek to return to him. Such a ministry may be just as rewarding as bringing someone to an initial confession of Jesus. God desires to keep those whom he has saved in a loving relationship with himself. When we stumble, he restores us and accepts us as though we had never fallen. He is dependable in every situation of life.—Clayton K. Harrop

ILLUSTRATIONS

DEPENDENCE.   Forty-five years ago I stood before a group of students in a seminary classroom. I had taught classes occasionally when the professor was absent. But for the first time the responsibility for the class was mine. It was a frightening experience. It made me especially aware that I had to depend on God for the wisdom and the strength needed to guide these students, these prospective ministers, to learn what they needed, that they might go out and teach others. I could not do it by myself. I had to depend on God.—Clayton K. Harrop

RESTORATION.   The man was a Sunday School teacher and deeply loved by the men in his class. One day he disappeared. No one seemed to know where he had gone or what he might be doing. Only when he returned some days later did anyone begin to realize that this had been a recurring problem in his life. While he was away, his conduct had been anything but what a Christian's conduct should be. He came back repentant and confessing his failure. He tried to resign as teacher of his class because he felt he was not worthy to teach them God's Word.

The men of the class were marvelous. They forgave him, they insisted that they wanted him to continue as their teacher. They allowed themselves to be used by God to restore one who had strayed into the paths of sin.—Clayton K. Harrop

SERMON SUGGESTIONS

Topic: A Mother's Prayer

TEXT: 1 Sam. 1

(1) Hannah felt a deep despair in her heart. (2) Still, there was real hope for her—she had faith in God. (3) After some days God brought joy to Hannah's heart.

Topic: For Those Who Need Him

TEXT: Mark 2:17

(1) The kind of people Jesus was concerned about: (a) the flagrantly sinful, (b) the respectably sinful, (c) sinning disciples. (2) How Christ calls people today: (a) through the regular ministries of the church; (b) through the special ministries, such as personal work and counseling, evangelism and revival. (3) How you and I fit in: (a) realize that confession of Christ is not a once-for-all act but a continuous testimony; (b) understand that evangelism is every Christian's task; (c) be aware that you and I need him—his forgiveness and his empowerment.

CONGREGATIONAL MUSIC

1. "Praise, My Soul, the King of Heaven," Henry F. Lyte (1834)

    LAUDA ANIMA, John Goss (1869)

    Although this hymn is based primarily on Psalm 103, its general mood and theme fit that of Psalm 124, as well as the spirit of celebration in the Old Testament reading (Esther 9:20–22) praising the God who "rescues us all from our foes" (stanza 3). This would make an admirable opening for this Sunday's worship.

2. "If God the Lord Were Not Our Constant Help," Psalm 124, vers. Calvin Seerveld (1981)

    GENEVAN 124, *Genevan Psalter* (1551)

    This free paraphrase of Psalm 124 could be sung antiphonally between two halves of the congregation or between congregation and choir.

3. "Where Cross the Crowded Ways of Life," Frank M. North (1905)

    GERMANY, W. Gardiner's *Sacred Melodies* (1815)

    A great early-twentieth-century hymn of service, "Where Cross the Crowded Ways of Life" would be effective if sung in connection with the Gospel lesson in Mark (9:38–50). Its third stanza refers specifically to Mark 9:41.

4. "Trusting Jesus," Edgar P. Stites (1876)

    TRUSTING JESUS, Ira D. Sankey (1876)

    Following the exhortation of James, "Is any among you suffering? Let him pray. Is anyone cheerful? Let him sing praises" (James 7:13), the singing of this gospel song would be suitable. Note especially stanza 3.—Hugh T. McElrath

WORSHIP AIDS

CALL TO WORSHIP.   "Our help is in the name of the Lord, who made heaven and earth" (Ps. 124:8).

INVOCATION.   We need your help, O Lord, not as a last resort but in every moment we live. We come to you now, asking for your presence to strengthen us, to embolden us, for the doing of your will and work in this world, your world.

OFFERTORY SENTENCE.   "You will be my witnesses in Jerusalem, in all Judea and Samaria, and to the ends of the earth" (Acts 1:8b NRSV).

OFFERTORY PRAYER.   We thank you, O God, that you have given us of your Spirit to empower us to tell the world of your love revealed and confirmed in Jesus Christ. Now let that love tug at our hearts until our gifts of self and possessions make a real difference in us and in those whom you want us to reach.

PRAYER.   In the stillness of this sacred moment, we eagerly listen for your approach to our hearts, Father. Out of the stillness and silence let your message come to us with clarity, bringing conviction that leads to action on our part. You know the ways we have walked. For those times we have turned away from the paths of righteousness, pray forgive us. As only you can, take the wrong we have done, which cannot be undone, and make it of no effect. If possible, turn it into a means of doing good. Deliver us from the sins that so easily beset us. Open before us the path leading to what is right, and enable us to walk in it.

As we follow our several ways and go about our varied tasks, make us aware, Father, of the nearness of your Holy Spirit. In the hour of confusion may we let Christ's Spirit show us the way to certainty. In the hour of weakness may we be strengthened by the indwelling of your Spirit. In the moments of our ignorance may we be instructed by the presence of your Spirit, that we may find sufficient knowledge to meet life's demands. Indeed, may Christ's presence be our guide as the Holy Spirit makes him known to us in every situation of life.— Henry Fields

SERMON
Topic: Communion Meditation (Worldwide Communion Sunday)
TEXT: Luke 17:5

"Lord, make our faith greater." That was the apostles' request. When the Session of First Presbyterian Church of Henderson put down its goals for 1998, one of them was to strengthen the spiritual life of its members: to make their faith stronger, to increase the spiritual gifts of the members. When young people come through the confirmation classes and we ask them what difference they think being a member of the church will make in their lives, they say they think it will make their faith stronger. This is why they join. They want to increase their faith and to make it greater. Luke says that the apostles said to Jesus, "Make our faith greater."

They want more faith. We want more faith. They want their faith to have a greater impact in their lives. We want our faith to play a larger role in our lives. They want their faith to be greater. We want our faith to be greater. Isn't that what holy and devout people have always wanted? Aren't we supposed to pray, "O dear Lord, three things we pray, to see thee more clearly, follow thee more nearly, love thee more dearly, day by day." We want to be more Christlike. We know that we will have to have more of the Spirit and power of Christ in us. We think that more faith will bring us more power to change.

We keep asking for more and more faith. "Make our faith greater." But it certainly doesn't sound to me like Jesus was very impressed with the disciples' request. Jesus answered their request with what sounds to me like a rather blunt putdown. "If you had faith as big as a mustard seed, you could say to this mulberry tree, 'Pull yourself up by the roots and plant yourself in the sea!' and it would obey you."

The apostles say they want more faith, a greater faith, and Jesus seems to suggest that if they had any faith, if they had faith even the size of the mustard seed, they could do miracles that are beyond their wildest imaginations. If this exchange between Jesus and his disciples does nothing else, it certainly shoves me against the question of how much faith I think I have to have before I am willing to use it.

There is a comic strip in *The News and Observer* called *Curtis*. Curtis has a friend from the Island of Flyspeck. And Curtis will never believe his friend when his friend tells him of the superpowers of fertility of the soil from Flyspeck. So Curtis is always creating monster plants that take over the whole house or the entire pizza parlor by sprinkling too much of the Flyspeck soil on the plant. Jesus tells his apostles that the power of faith is so awesome that even the tiniest little bit of faith can accomplish wonders and changes and deeds that they would never have imagined and would hardly dare to suggest. What would you do with more faith?

The apostles said to the Lord, "Make our faith greater." If we take what they say seriously, if we take what we say seriously, that we want to grow in faith, that we want more faith, then Jesus would ask us, What have you done with the faith you suggest you already have? If you want more, if you want the faith you have to become greater, if you pray that God will strengthen your faith, if you come seeking to have your faith deepened, then you claim to have some faith and Jesus wonders what kind of miracles you have done with the faith you already have. If you want more, then you must have some, and all it takes is a mustard-seed-size amount to accomplish miracles. What have you done with the faith you already have?

One of our most persistent and universal defenses as Christians is that we aren't ready yet. We can't invite others to share fellowship with us because we don't have that fellowship now, so we need to work on our own fellowship first before we go out to invite. We can't talk about prayer with other people because we don't think we pray well, so we have to work on our own prayer life first. We have been coming to Sunday School and worship for thirty years but we don't feel able to talk to others about Jesus, we don't know enough yet, so we need better Sunday schools for adults before we send them out to invite others to follow Jesus. If you had faith the size of a mustard seed in the power of God in Jesus Christ you could move trees and plant them in oceans. With a little mustard seed faith we ought to be able to talk to our friends and neighbors about Jesus.

The apostles say they want more faith, a greater faith, a deeper faith, a richer faith. Jesus says, "More faith, deeper faith, I'm not really sure you even have any, because if you had even a little, there would be miracles and wonders happening that would shock the world: trees being uplifted and plunked down in the seas. More faith, deeper faith, greater faith—the only way that comes is by using what you already have. What would you do with more faith? How would you know when you had enough faith to live on it? What would you do with greater faith that you can't begin to do with the little faith you have now?"

Lord, make our faith greater. Jesus says, "Use the little faith you have now to do great wonders." Come to this table. Look at what a little piece of bread and a small cup can do. Come to the joyful feast of the people of God.—Rick Brand

SUNDAY, OCTOBER 8, 2000
Lectionary Message

Topic: Objects of God's Care

TEXT: Heb. 1:1–4; 2:5–12

Other Readings: Job 1:1; 2:1–10; Ps. 26; Mark 10:2–16

The Hebrew people had a long history of God's care. They could look back to Abraham and think about how God had led the founder of their race. They especially looked back to the wilderness experience, as God led their ancestors out of Egypt, through the forty years in the wilderness, and finally into the Promised Land. They had no doubt about his care.

I. *A new revelation* (1:1–4). The author of the Epistle to the Hebrews accepted the fact of God's care in the past. He wrote about how God had spoken to the people through his prophets. But now someone far better had been sent by God. This was his Son. The description of Jesus in the opening verses of this Epistle is one of the greatest to be found in all of the New Testament. Jesus surpassed even the greatest of the prophets in every way. God's revelation in the past was partial; now it was complete. The prophets were only God's spokesmen. Now God had spoken through his own Son. This Son was the one through whom he had created all things. This Son shared the greatness of the being of God himself. And he did the most important thing of all: he sacrificed himself for human sin. He completed his work and sat down at the position of power, the right hand of God. All of this was a clear demonstration of God's care for his creatures.

In a world where angels played a large role in the minds of people, it was comforting to realize that God's care was not for angels but for human beings. Angels were God's servants. They served people because people were the ones for whom God cared. It is easy to lose sight of this fact. In a day when our understanding of the universe has expanded with constant new revelations of the extent of creation, it sometimes seems difficult to imagine that God can care for what takes place on this earth. In a world of billions of people, it is easy to be lost in the crowd and forget that God cares for the least and the most insignificant. It was hard for the disciples to imagine that Jesus could be interested in the welfare of little children during the busy days of his ministry. They tried to keep parents from bringing their children to Jesus. They did not want him to be bothered. What a shock it must have been for them to discover that these little children were the very ones for whom Jesus cared. They were an object lesson of what it meant for one to receive the Kingdom of God.

II. *The expression of care* (2:5–9). Jesus came into what appeared to be an uncaring world. In Jewish life, a woman was the property of her father or her husband. Children had few if any rights. Aliens were despised. In Greek culture, unwanted children were exposed to die. Divorce was common. Jesus had to teach people who did not care for others that God cared for them. He demonstrated this in his life. He healed the sick, comforted the sorrowful. He welcomed the despised—tax collectors and sinners, women and children. He showed that God cared for those for whom other people did not care. God visited mankind in the person of his Son. He cared so much that he gave his own Son on behalf of sinful human beings. Jesus became for a little while lower than the angels. He came to serve, not to be served. Because of his faithfulness to death, he has been crowned with glory and honor. He experienced death that others might not die. What greater expression of God's care could be imagined?

It is still difficult for many people to understand that God cares for them. In the face of loneliness and the indifference of other people, can it be that God cares? Indeed, he does, and he shows this care in ways that help to meet the needs of all people. The good news is still the message of God's care, not simply for the spiritual needs of people but for their total need. To be sure, sometimes this total need is not supplied as we may desire. Nevertheless, God's concern is still present and is demonstrated in ways large and small. He continues to visit his people, and whenever he visits his people he provides help for them.

III. *Like one of us* (2:10–12). From the earliest days of the church, Jesus has been seen as something more than simply human. We are accustomed to seeing pictures of him with a halo above his head. He is always seen as someone's ideal of the perfect man. Yet he became one like us. The New Testament points out that Jesus was a true human being. He shared his flesh and blood (2:14). He shares the same Father with us. It was necessary that he suffer, even to the extent of death on the cross. He knew what it was to be tempted, yet he never yielded. He experienced everything that we experience, with the exception of the guilt of sin. Jesus was never ashamed to claim that relationship with us. He lived in the midst of the suffering and struggles of everyday human existence. He could stoop so low as to wash the feet of his disciples. He could touch the leper. He could weep at the death of a friend. He was not an angel sent down to earth to pretend to share life. He called us brothers, he called his followers his friends. The care of God for us knows no limit. And we are called to care for others in the same way God cares for them.—Clayton K. Harrop

ILLUSTRATIONS

A VARIETY OF MERCIES.   God's care is shown in small ways and large, in everyday affairs and seeming miracles. During World War II, I served as an instructor for recruits in a "village fighting" training course. Live ammunition was used. On more than one occasion it appeared that the hand of God was present to prevent serious injury. Perhaps the most dramatic case was one day when a soldier jumped into a room through a window. Instead of backing against the wall, he went to the center of the room, turned as the instructor was coming through the window, and fired his rifle. Surely the instructor would be killed. But the rifle did not fire. God does care.—Clayton K. Harrop

A SPECIAL GIFT.   During the time when I was pastoring my first church I had the privilege of becoming acquainted with a fine lady of devout faith. What seemed a tragedy was that she had been crippled for many years and was confined to a bed. Yet God cared for her. He did not give her healing, but he gave her the gift of being a blessing to those with whom she had contact. One could not visit her without coming away with a stronger faith. She never complained. She knew, even in her situation, the deep love of God, and there was a fellowship between her and her God that human conditions could never erase. God's care may not always be expressed in the way we expect or desire, but it is always there if we will open our eyes and our heart to experience it.—Clayton K. Harrop

SERMON SUGGESTIONS

Topic: How Good Is Your Aim?
TEXT: Judges 20:16; Isa. 55:8–9
(1) How we miss the mark: (a) by uncritical conformity, (b) by making shortcuts to happiness.

(2) How we can reach the goal: (a) by seeking God's loving purposes for us, (b) by following what God teaches us.

Topic: On Getting Rid of Our Sins
TEXT: Rom. 5:1, 8
(1) Why God opposes sin: (a) sin hurts us, (b) sin hurts the world we live in, (c) sin hurts God. (2) What God has done about our sins: (a) he has set the moral agenda for our lives, (b) he has put forward Jesus Christ, his Son, as the means of dealing with our sins. (3) What we can do: (a) confess our sins to God, (b) accept the forgiveness of God, (c) forgive ourselves, (d) attempt to right the wrongs we have done.

CONGREGATIONAL MUSIC

1. "God Has Spoken by His Prophets," George W. Briggs (1952)
   ODE TO JOY, Ludwig van Beethoven (1824)
   Based on the opening verses of Hebrews, this fine twentieth-century hymn emphasizes the truth that God spoke by the prophets and through Jesus Christ but continues to speak by his Spirit. It would be ideal for the beginning of worship.
2. "I Love Thy Kingdom, Lord," Timothy Dwight (1801)
   ST. THOMAS, Aaron Williams (1763)
   This, the oldest American hymn in continuous use, is based on Psalm 137, but its first two phrases echo Psalm 26:8 and therefore could be used as a sort of antiphon to be sung in connection with the Psalter reading.
3. "Jesus Loves the Little Children," C. H. Woolston (1913)
   CHILDREN, George F. Root (1864)
   This refrain from a gospel song now forgotten relates beautifully to the Gospel lesson (Mark 10:13–16) in which Jesus blesses the little children. Its singing would naturally follow the Gospel lesson.
4. "In the Cross of Christ I Glory," John Bowring (1825)
   RATHBUN, Ithamar Conkey (1849)
   Job's question, "Shall we indeed accept good from God and not accept adversity?" (Job 2:10b) is answered from a Christian perspective in the last stanza of this great hymn glorying in the cross of Christ.—Hugh T. McElrath

WORSHIP AIDS

CALL TO WORSHIP.   "Lord, I love the house where you dwell, the place where your glory resides" (Ps. 26:8 REB).

INVOCATION.   We are reminded, O God, that so much of what we know of you has come to us in this holy place, where you dwell not only in a house made with human hands and raised toward heaven with many a prayer, but also with grace and love in the hearts of people who love you. Let this be a place and experience in which we are touched again by your glory.

OFFERTORY SENTENCE.   "All the Israelite men and women who were willing brought to the Lord freewill offerings for all the work the Lord, through Moses, had commanded them to do" (Exod. 35:29 NIV).

OFFERTORY PRAYER.   We thank you, O Lord, for the many examples in Scripture and in Christian service today of the loving and generous offerings for the building of your Kingdom. Now make us partners in this succession of faithful stewardship, and bless the offerings that we bring, even as you bless us in the giving of them.

PRAYER.   Day by day, day by day, is more than a song, isn't it, O God? It is how you give us life, movement, our being. Day by day new mercies we see, fresh grace upon grace; day by day new bread you provide, forgiveness lavished upon us, hope embodied, goodness and mercy surrounding us. May we, in all these daily gifts and wonders, learn how to see you more clearly.

Day by day, speaking God, you are teaching us your ways. We give you thanks for your moral foundations that give anchor and direction and substance for our lives. We give thanks for our salvation story, for our heritage as the people of God in this place, for the good news, and for the best gift of all, Jesus Christ, our Lord. May we, in grateful response to all your grace and guidance to us, follow you more nearly. We do long for a closer walk, for a greater sense of your presence in our lives and our daily steps. Be thou our vision and our guide.

Day by day, faithful, revealing God, your love is being made known and present to us. As we gather to worship this Lord's day, your love has joined us in the Spirit. Through the events of the week past, your love has not let us go. In the presence of death, the despair of dying, in the trials and demands of just making it through, your love abides with us, bringing light to our darkness, calm to our storms, hope to our fears, redemption to our sorrow. Gladly we respond to your love, fully revealed in Christ and alive today in this your family, who loves us, too. And we seek to love you more dearly.

Wondrous God of Presence, Word, and Love, we worship you in praise and thanksgiving. May it be said of us as it has been said of our early Church family, that we live and work, worship and serve, with glad and generous hearts. And may it be so, day by day, in the Christ.—William M. Johnson

SERMON
Topic: Use the Servant's Entrance
TEXT: Jer. 28:1–9; Luke 13:22–30

Somebody was bound to ask this sooner or later: "Will those who are saved be few?" It's the obvious question. Look at what he has been asking of them: everything, total commitment.

Jesus answers, "Strive to enter by the narrow door; for many, I tell you, will seek to enter and will not be able." Then he tells a story about a banquet. One of these days the householder will get up from his chair, walk to the door, and close it, and when that happens, that's it. It's all over. And if you happen to find yourself on the outside at that time, pounding on the door, protesting this terrible injustice, the householder will say, "I don't know you. Go away." And if you continue to protest and say, "But we ate and drank with you, and you taught in our streets," it won't do any good either. The door still won't open. These protests won't be heard. It won't do any good.

Then he concludes, "And men will come from the east and west, and from north and south, and sit at table in the Kingdom of God. And behold, some are last who will be first, and some are first who will be last." Talk about hard sayings! I think that is about the hardest because it is so ultimate. No appeal.

"We ate and drank with you. We heard you preach." You know what that sounds like? It sounds like some people thought that just being acquainted with Jesus was enough. Just having met him once some years ago, that's sufficient.

"We ate and drank with you, and we heard your teachings. So let us in. We've earned the right to be here. We sat through all those sermons. Let us in."

"I don't know you."

The lesson is one we all know. You know this, don't you, that being a member of the Church does not guarantee your salvation? Of course, being a Methodist helps, but it doesn't guarantee it. There is no guarantee, because reversal stories (there are so many of them in the Gospel, of which this is one) are about those who thought they were in the Kingdom. So they're just taking their time, doing a little shopping, a little sightseeing on the way to the Kingdom. No problem, because we have reservations. We have guaranteed seating at the banquet.

They arrive. The householder has already closed the door. No problem, just knock on the door. He will let us in, because, after all, we have reservations. We are among the saved. The reversal is that some who thought they were going to be in there aren't in there, and some whom you would never imagine would even be there have the places of honor. There are no certainties.

There is a story about the bishop of Durham who was accosted on the street with this question, "Are you saved?" The bishop replied, "That depends on whether you're talking in the past tense, the present tense, or the future tense. If you mean, did Christ die for me, absolutely yes. If you mean, are my feet set on the highway of salvation, I trust so. But if you mean, am I safe at home in the Kingdom, certainly not."

You see why they asked, "Are those to be saved going to be few?"

So, if we have no guarantees, what about guidelines? Are there any guidelines, any hints, any clues here? I think there is a clue here. This is it: "Strive to enter by the narrow door." What is the narrow door? There has been lots of speculation about it. I was taught when I was growing up that the narrow door meant a disciplined life, *narrow* meaning "disciplined," or "strict."

You know what the narrow door is? It's the servants' entrance. It's the rear door. It's the one he used, you know. Luther loved to point that out. When Jesus entered our world he went down the back stairs, through the servants' entrance, into a stable in Bethlehem. Through the servants' entrance.

Jean and I lived in Boston many years ago in one of those stately brownstones in the back bay of Boston built in the nineteenth century. We lived in the servants' quarters. I was the janitor in exchange for that apartment in the building. The front door of the building was just grand, magnificent, with double-hung doors, carved wood, spacious, and so tall, about ten feet tall. It was designed for receiving important guests graciously.

But around the back, down the stairwell, there was another door. The narrow door. And it was short, too. I had to stoop to go through it. That's the servants' entrance.

Enter the Kingdom of God by the narrow door. Humbly. You can't go storming the Kingdom, demanding entrance, showing them your credentials, boasting all the time. You enter the Kingdom the way God entered this world. What did Paul say in Philippians? How did he put it? He came to us as a servant (Phil. 2:7, 9).

The point of that parable is that those who didn't serve the wretched and pitiful in this world didn't get into the Kingdom. And those who did serve were surprised. "When did we see you?" "When you served them." So there's no certainty. Salvation is a gift of grace. Salvation is not something you can earn.

But if you want some advice, I guess that's what is being offered here in this passage in Luke. Some might call this a warning, but it's offered in the spirit of good advice. It says, I wouldn't try to enter through the main door if I were you, the door for VIP's, even if you are one. I wouldn't do that. That elegant door that is set there for important people is closed now, forever. It has been closed for two thousand years. So if somebody told you that you have a reservation, all I can say is, I'm sorry, but that door is closed.

But there is still a door that is open. You go around the back, down the stairs, through the entrance that says "Servants."—Mark Trotter

SUNDAY, OCTOBER 15, 2000
Lectionary Message

Topic: A Matter of Priorities
TEXT: Mark 10:17–31
Other Readings: Job 23:1–9, 16–17; Ps. 22:1–15; Heb. 4:12–16

Life is filled with choices. Some may be trivial. Others are of greater importance, some even having life or death consequences. Some are even concerned with our eternal destiny. Some choices are almost automatic; we hardly think about them. Others are made only after agonizing struggle. It comes down to the matter of having priorities. What is going to be the major focus in my life?

I. *Possessions or Christ* (vv. 17–22). People often approached Jesus to ask questions. On one occasion a man came with the most important question of all: "What must I do to inherit eternal life?" He had evidently been impressed with what he had seen and heard about Jesus. He knew that the power of God worked in Jesus to bring healing. He knew Jesus' teachings were different. They challenged the old, accepted ways. Jesus did not simply repeat the traditional religious phrases. He confronted people with a fresh message from God. So this man wanted to hear what Jesus had to say about his crucial question. Jesus instructed the man to obey the commandments. From the list of Ten Commandments, he listed six that deal with a person's relations with other people. The man responded that he had been obedient to these commandments since he was a young man. Evidently he took seriously his responsibility to God and other people. Jesus loved him and gave him one further word: he must sell all his possessions, give the proceeds to the poor, and follow Jesus. Tragically the man, who was rich, was not willing to do this, and he went away grieved. Jesus did not give this command to all, but only to this particular man. It was necessary in his case, for he loved things more than he loved God. His priorities were wrong, and it was necessary for him to get them straight. Others might not have had the same problem. Yet we know that the love of possessions can be a real danger for many of us, whether we are rich or not. Although we may not be asked to sell all and give it away, our faith must be so strong that we would be willing to do so if God required it.

II. *First things first* (vv. 23–27). Jesus knew it would be difficult for many people to make the right decisions. Wealth was a great attraction, although most of the people who heard him were not wealthy. Galilee was not an economic paradise. But the temptation to accumulate wealth was always present. To have it made life more comfortable. It gave one assurance about the future. We know its appeal in our day. The great danger with possessions is that we come to depend on them for everything. Not only do they give us security against hunger, but they also make it possible for us to have shelter. With wealth we can have the best health care. We feel we do not have to depend on anyone for the necessities and comforts of life. Jesus knew that one could not depend on wealth and God at the same time. We are faced with a choice: God or possessions. Poor people may have less of a problem at this point. They do not have enough wealth to trust it to care for their needs. They know they need God, a recognition that the rich may not have.

Jesus said it is difficult for those who have riches to enter God's Kingdom. One must abandon dependence on wealth and put complete trust in God. Jesus continued by saying that it is hard for anyone, rich or poor, to enter the Kingdom. To emphasize this, he spoke a hyperbole about it being easier for a camel to go through the eye of a needle, an absolute impossibility, than for a rich man to enter the Kingdom. In the ancient world, riches were looked on as a sign of God's blessing. If the rich could not enter, what hope was there for the rest? It was impossible for any person to enter the Kingdom by trusting in self and things. But when one placed dependence on God, the impossible became reality. God must be first, not things.

III. *Following Jesus* (vv. 28–31). Jesus' comments about the danger of riches reminded Peter that he and the other disciples had left everything to follow Jesus. Peter was probably wondering what rewards they were going to receive for their faithfulness. We live with the law of recompense. Someone does something for us, we do something in return. We do something for someone, that person does something for us in return. We leave all to follow Jesus. What will he give us in return? Put that way, we realize this is a wrong attitude, but it is common. Jesus' response to Peter's question contains two parts. First, there is present reward for following him. What has been left will be returned many times over. This does not mean that we will become rich by following Jesus. That was never promised, and experience has shown that it seldom happens. But it does mean that God will provide what is needed for a life committed to service to him. This has been proved again and again in the lives of Christians through the centuries. Second, there is the promise of eternal life. This is the new quality of life that one receives at the moment of putting trust in Jesus, and a life that continues through all eternity. This is the promise made to the one who is willing to abandon everything and place absolute trust in Christ. It means getting our priorities right. Jesus must come first.—Clayton K. Harrop

ILLUSTRATIONS

AN EYE FOR THINGS.   The man often attended the church where I was pastor. He knew the Bible fairly well, and one of his favorite passages was this story of Jesus telling the rich man to give away all his possessions to the poor. As we talked frequently about this command of Jesus I became aware that the man was not interested in whether the rich got to heaven. His concern was that they give away their wealth so he could have some of it. His priorities were no different from theirs. His eyes were on things, not on God.—Clayton K. Harrop

THE RIGHT PRIORITIES.   More and more seminary students are second-career people. They have worked for many years in the secular field and many have been quite successful. It is not unusual to learn of students who have given up significant careers, successful businesses, high-paying jobs, spacious homes, to come to seminary to be equipped to serve Christ. They have their priorities right. They have given up much to follow Jesus.—Clayton K. Harrop

SERMON SUGGESTIONS

Topic: The Things That Shape Your Life
TEXT: Various
(1) The thoughts you think (Prov. 23:7; Phil. 4:8). (2) The company you keep (Ps. 1:1; 1 Cor. 15:33). (3) The books you read (2 Tim. 4:13).

Topic: Straightening a Wobbly Conscience
TEXT: 1 Cor. 8:1–13; 10:23–33; Rom. 14
(1) The source of conscience. (2) The functions of conscience. (3) The improvement of conscience.

CONGREGATIONAL MUSIC

1. "Alleluia! Sing to Jesus!" William C. Dix (1806)
   HYFRYDOL, Rowland Hugh Prichard (1831)
   This noble hymn of praise relates directly to the passage in Hebrews 4:12–16. Christ has passed through the heavens to be our High Priest and Intercessor. Therefore, in our need for mercy and grace, we can draw near to him in confidence. This hymn would be a good selection for the opening of worship.
2. "O Jesus, I Have Promised," John E. Bode (1866)
   ANGEL'S STORY, Arthur H. Mann (1881)
   Written to encourage young people to remain steadfast in their Christian walk, this hymn can be sung in response to the Gospel lesson that concerns the rich young ruler.
3. "Nobody Knows the Trouble I See," African American Spiritual (early nineteenth century)
   DUBOIS, African American Spiritual
   Both Job's lament (Job 23:1–9, 16–17) and the cry of anguish in the Psalter reading (Ps. 22:1–15) find a sympathetic echo in this plaintive spiritual. It could be sung by a soloist, with all the group joining in the response, "Oh, Yes, Lord" and in the refrain.
4. "In the Presence of Your People," Psalm 22:3; paraph. Brent Charmers (1977)
   CELEBRATION, Brent Chambers (1977)
   This contemporary praise-and-worship song is based in part on the Psalter verse: "Thou art holy, O Thou who art enthroned upon the praises of Israel" (Ps. 22:3). It could be used as an antiphon, sung before, during, and after the Psalter reading.—Hugh T. McElrath

WORSHIP AIDS

CALL TO WORSHIP.   "All the ends of the world shall remember and turn unto the Lord: and all the kindreds of the nations shall worship before thee. For the kingdom is the Lord's: and he is the governor among the nations" (Ps. 22:27–28).

INVOCATION.   Lord God, whom we praise and adore, begin mighty deeds in us this hour, send great hopes, fortify firm resolves, because the world needs the gospel and Jesus Christ bids us share with all in need of the Savior.—E. Lee Phillips

OFFERTORY SENTENCE.   "We do not live to ourselves, and we do not die to ourselves. If we live, we live to the Lord, and if we die, we die to the Lord; so then, whether we live or whether we die, we are the Lord's" (Rom. 14:7–8 NRSV).

OFFERTORY PRAYER.   For all of your blessings, great and small, we thank you, O Lord. We are awed and overwhelmed by your wonderful world, with its gifts to us and its joys. We confess that we are sometimes tempted to think more highly than we should of these good gifts when we need to put you first, so that whatever is good in this world will bless us and not hurt us or others. So guide us as we decide our true priority.—E. Lee Phillips

PRAYER.   O, God, in our new estate as brothers and sisters, our lives are so intimately bound together that no one lives or dies unto himself or herself. Your fatherly love calls us as your children to pray and live for one another. As members of the body of Christ we are being called, as he was, to give our life for the life of the world. This is a high calling! Who is ready for it? In our sense of weakness and inadequacy may we know the strong word of your grace that prepares us for anything. With the ill, the bereaved, the lonely, the estranged, the homeless, may we celebrate your grace mediated through the cross to heal, to make whole, to comfort, to strengthen, to set free, to reconcile.

As we reach out to the other, whoever the other may be, we pray for the healing of the nations that "instead of the thorn the cypress shall spring up; and instead of the brier shall come up the myrtle," through him who is the pioneer and vindicator of our faith and is here praying with us.—John Thompson

SERMON
Topic: Song of Creation
TEXT: Ps. 104

It was Karl Barth who spoke of "the strange new world" of the Bible. He meant that the Bible again and again comes to us with a newness that seems strange, as if we had not heard it before. That fresh word surprises us and reorients us to a new world.

Psalm 104 is one of those passages many of us have heard a thousand times but perhaps never *really* heard. It is lyrical, unsurpassed Hebrew nature poetry; but more than that, it is a profound statement of humanity's proper relationship with all of creation. Psalm 104 is not a celebration of God and humanity, but of God and creation: a celebration of the living relationship between God and the creatures, the lightning, the sun and the sea monsters, the oceans and mountains, wind and clouds, wild goats and rock badgers, springs flowing in the valleys, and countless creatures, large and small, all of which humanity is just a part.

In our national life, indeed in our planetary life, we discuss "the environment" as if it were a matter of how it all relates to us as the central figures. Even the word *environment* stands for that which is around *us*. The self-centeredness that is sin causes us to see the world as related to *us*.

The Bible, however, speaks a very strange word to us! In this psalm, God is the central figure. All that is created—oceans robing the earth, the winds that God rides, the cedars, storks nesting in fir trees, young lions roaring, people going to and fro—all that is created, is related to God, and we simply, happily, are part of a glorious creation that together, as a whole, glorifies God. The psalmist, awed by what he sees and understands, sings this psalm, this song of creation.

Rather than surveying all this for his own possible uses, the psalmist simply delights in it, declaring, "I will sing to the Lord all my life. . . . May he be pleased with my song" (vv. 33, 34).

What may we say of God and creation that will help us understand how to live in God's world?

I. *The earth is the Lord's*. To say this is to invite yawns, even from children. We have heard it all our Christian lives. Perhaps this familiarity makes the truth so toothless. How little we understand that God is not an absentee landlord but the one of Genesis who walks through his creation, intimately relating to everything. If we could but see as the psalmist saw and exclaim, "May the Lord be happy with what he has made" (v. 31).

Israel knew that everything, animate and inanimate, belongs to God. The psalmists often declared it: "The earth is the Lord's and the fullness thereof, the world and those who dwell therein" (Ps. 24:1).

Perhaps we do know this. Perhaps it is the application we have missed. If God notices the sparrow's fall, God also notices what we do with the delicate, intricate world of leaping, buzzing, splashing, flashing, soaring things that God has also made. The commission in Genesis to tend the garden and have dominion over the world around us call us to have this mind in us, not of carelessness or exploitation, but of carefulness and preservation of that which is God's. The Kingdom of God is a place where predation has vanished and former enemies live in harmony.

II. *God delights in creation*. In the New Testament era there was a strain of heretical thought called gnosticism. Gnostics believed that the material world was evil and only the spiritual was good. But in the Hebrew faith, the God of Creation remained intimately involved with the world. The images are truly beautiful: God walked in the garden in the cool of the evening, and knit people together in the womb. God fed the birds and had a whale swallow Jonah. The natural world responded to God's commands for plagues to fall and seas to part, for the sun to stand still and the spider to spin a web.

In it all God delighted, and does yet. God rides "on the wings of the wind," covers himself with garments of light, makes springs gush forth, grass to grow for the cattle, the volcanoes to smoke. He looks at the earth and it trembles, and makes it all miraculously, incredibly, work together for the good of all, whether Leviathan or wild donkey or rushing waters. This almost childlike, playful creative genius seems to give pleasure to the master craftsman: "Lord, you have made so many things! How wisely you have made them all! The earth is filled with your creatures" (v. 24).

III. *All things find their value in God.* The psalmist relates all of creation not to its human inhabitants but to God. It reveals the marvels and gloriousness of God; "May the glory of the Lord last forever" (v. 31). The "countless creatures . . . large and small alike," the trembling earth, the breath and dust of life, the moon marking the seasons, the sun knowing its time to rise and set—all these are inseparable from God.

No doubt this is a troubling concept to a consumer-oriented, profit-oriented society. It can only be an unwelcome prophetic word that judges and reorients us. But the psalm relates all things to God: "All of them depend on you. . . . You give new life to the earth" (vv. 27, 30). To God, an acre in Death Valley or in the middle of the Everglades is not a low-rent district compared to Palm Springs or Manhattan—all is equal because all is God's, and because of God's love for all. A snail darter, a spotted owl, an ancient redwood, a seabird fouled with oil, or an old turtle trapped in a gill net are easy to dismiss when the standard of measure is human, but not so easy when the standard is God's ownership, love, and delight.

From this song of creation we have a vision of human spirituality that is based not on possession and dominance but on a harmonious relationship with all that God has created.— Stewart G. Collier

SUNDAY, OCTOBER 22, 2000
Lectionary Message

Topic: A Throne or a Wash Basin
TEXT: Mark 10:35–45
Other Readings: Job 38:1–7 (34–41); Ps. 104:1–9, 24, 35; Heb. 5:1–10

If you were to ask people who they consider to have been the great people in American history, they would probably list such people as George Washington, Abraham Lincoln, Franklin Roosevelt, and Dwight Eisenhower. They would include those who were prominent in political or military life. Some might include the names of Billy Graham and Martin Luther King Jr., but they would be lower on the lists because most people consider that greatness is expressed in the exercise of power. Jesus taught that God's standard of greatness is based on service, not power.

I. *A selfish request* (vv. 35–37). Jesus' disciples found it difficult to accept new ideas that went against what they had been taught and had seen in the lives of others. Their list of great men would have included David, Solomon, and Moses, men of power and authority. They might have included Elijah and Elisha, prophets who exercised power on the political as well as the religious scene. Jesus understood life differently and tried to instruct his disciples that God's standard was different. On two previous occasions Jesus said that he was going to Jerusalem, that he would be arrested and executed, and that on the third day he would rise from the dead. The disciples did not understand. In the first instance, Peter responded that this could not happen to Jesus. But Jesus told his disciples that they must deny themselves, take up their cross, and follow him. To seek to save life meant to lose it, but to be willing to lose life for his sake meant to gain it (8:34–38). On the second occasion, the disciples were arguing about which of them would be the greatest (9:30–33).

Now, for the third time Jesus told the disciples what was going to happen to him in Jerusalem. Immediately afterward James and John came and requested the chief positions in his Kingdom. They were convinced that greatness is measured by the power one possesses. They wanted the positions of power in the Kingdom. They were much like us. We hear what we want to hear and we discard that which does not conform to the conclusions we have already reached. For this reason, we do not consider some of the things God would teach us because they do not agree with what we have already decided. We want power because the world measures greatness by the exercise of power.

II. *Man's standard* (vv. 38–42). James and John followed man's standard for greatness. They wanted positions of power. Seeking power has its price tag. Jesus asked if they were willing to pay the price. Drinking a cup and being baptized probably refer to his approaching suffering and death. Were they willing to suffer with him in order to achieve their goal? They thought Jesus was to be the king. Trivial suffering involved in gaining the Kingdom could not compare with the honor they would receive when they reached their positions.

Such ambitions brought jealousy. The other ten disciples became angry with James and John when they learned what had happened. They wanted these positions for themselves and were displeased that someone else had asked for the positions first. Man's standard of greatness inevitably brings strife and animosity. People are in competition. Each wants the best for self without regard to the desires and qualifications of others. Man's standards are selfish, and to a large extent they are never satisfied. One gains a position and wants a higher one. One gains power and wants greater power. We want more and more. This leads to conflict and the sacrifice of all that is holy and good. So the human standard is for tyrants. It is not God's standard.

III. *God's standard* (vv. 43–45). God's standard is different from the human standard. He measures greatness in terms of service rendered. Jesus told his followers they must not follow the world's way. They are not to seek power. Rather, whoever wishes to be great must be a servant, a slave to others. Such a word upset perceived values. It meant that people would have to be willing to submit to others. They could not fight back. They could not claim rights for themselves. Service meant to put the other person in the place of prominence. Even in such a small group as the disciples, such a practice would not be easy. How much more difficult it would be in a larger community. Yet Jesus insisted this was God's way. As an example, he pointed to himself and said that he did not come to be served by others. He came to serve.

Jesus demonstrated this standard of service throughout his ministry by the way he lived and the way he reacted to the needs of others. He healed the sick, he cast out demons, he welcomed the outcast, he showed God's love to those whom the world did not love. He refused to condemn those who were humble and realized their need of God's grace. And the supreme example was the fact that he was giving his life as a ransom. Jesus, God's own Son, gave his life on the cross as the payment for our sins, that we might live rather than die. This is God's way. Jesus illustrated it vividly on the occasion of his last meal with his disciples. As they were at the table, Jesus rose, took a basin of water and a towel, and went around and washed the feet of his disciples. He performed the most humiliating service for them, a service they were not willing to perform for one another. And then he commanded us to serve in a similar way. This, and this alone, is God's standard of greatness.—Clayton K. Harrop

ILLUSTRATIONS

SACRIFICE.   Albert Schweitzer was a skilled musician. He could have had a wonderful career in music. He would have been praised, honored, and served by others. But he gave all of this up to go to Africa and serve there for Christ. He did not seek a throne but was willing to do the most humble service out of his faith in and loyalty to Christ.—Clayton K. Harrop

SERVICE.   The church of which I am a member has developed a significant ministry in a state prison. Not only do men and women go in and worship together with inmates, but men go into the cell blocks to talk with the prisoners and share with them the good news of Jesus Christ. It is not a ministry that is widely known. It does not bring much honor to those who go. But it is following God's way of rendering service to others in need.—Clayton K. Harrop

SERMON SUGGESTIONS

Topic: Length and Depth of Life
TEXT: Gen. 5:27
(1) Methuselah and the opportunities a long life may offer. (2) Jesus and the boundless blessings of his short life.

Topic: What Our Lord Desires for Us
TEXT: John 17:13–26
Our Lord prayed: (1) that we might have joy—his joy; (2) that we might have security; (3) that we might be consecrated by the truth; (4) that we might have unity; (5) that we might have love for one another.

CONGREGATIONAL MUSIC

1. "O Worship the King," Robert Grant (1833)
    LYONS, attr. Johann M. Haydn (1815); HANOVER, attr. William Croft (1708)
    An excellent hymn for the opening of corporate worship, "O Worship the King" is a free, rather romantic paraphrase of Psalm 104. Sung to either of its tunes, it could well replace the Psalter reading for this Sunday.
2. "The Lord Ascendeth up on High," Arthur T. Russell (1848)
    ACH HERR, DU ALLERHOCHSTER GOTT, Michael Praetorius (1609)
    Although this hymn was written essentially for Ascension Sunday, in its third stanza it draws attention to the High Priesthood of Christ, which is the theme of the reading from Hebrews (5:1–10). The lilting tune would go best if sung in unison.
3. "The Servant Song," Richard Gillard (1974)
    BEACH SPRING, *The Sacred Harp* (1844)
    This modern hymn stressing service to one another offers an appropriate response when sung after the Gospel lesson (Mark 10:35–45).
4. "Bless the Lord, My Soul and Being," Fred R. Anderson (1986)
    RUSTINGTON, C.H.H. Parry (1897)

Stanzas 1, 2, and 5 of this contemporary paraphrase of Psalm 104 relate to the selected verses in this day's Psalter reading. The vibrant tune reinforces the spirit of high praise for God's abundant care over all God's works.—Hugh T. McElrath

WORSHIP AIDS

CALL TO WORSHIP.   "I will sing to the Lord all my life; I will sing praise to my God as long as I live. May my meditation be pleasing to him, as I rejoice in the Lord" (Ps. 104:33–34 NIV).

INVOCATION.   How wonderful it is, O God, to be privileged to sing to you with your people, as we praise you for your loving care of us and as we join hearts with one another in your spirit. Deepen our devotion as our hearts are raised to you.

OFFERTORY SENTENCE.   "And now faith, hope, and love abide, these three; and the greatest of these is love" (1 Cor. 13:13 NRSV).

OFFERTORY PRAYER.   Lord, we have placed our trust in you and we have received assurance of the good things that await us in this life and the next. You have poured out your love to us in your Son Jesus Christ. Now faith presents to you these offerings that your love has inspired.

PRAYER.   O God, awaken the spontaneity, the joy, the love—of the child in *us*—that we may enter the Kingdom. The sage of old is right: a child *shall* lead them. We pray that our stewardship will be not dutiful but in joyful response to your grace in Christ. As we grow in the grace and knowledge of Christ, we do grow in the grace of giving. To follow him who began with a tithe and ended with a cross is not easy but it is the way that leads to joy— "who for the joy that we set before him endured the cross, despising the shame."

In the experience of your love so genuinely experienced in this fellowship, we realize we are all family. No person lives or dies unto herself or himself; therefore we pray for one another and for all others. We pray for those shaken because of life-threatening news. Grant to them the poise of faith to handle creatively whatever life holds for them. Where the ache of loneliness persists, may you minister the Balm of Gilead—the sense of your presence. May those walking through the valley of the shadow have the faith to pray: "I will not fear, for you are with me." Free those who are ill from fear and anxiety to be trusting and open to receive the health of your healing grace. We pray for the health of the nations.

It is of your grace that there *can* be a new beginning in the affairs of men and of nations. Awaken us as citizens that we may be vigilant. No generation can afford the luxury of business as usual when you are calling us to open our eyes to see the new thing you are doing in our day—the coming of your Kingdom. Grant us wisdom, grant us courage for the living of these days, that we fail not the child among us, nor his or her parents or grandparents, nor the generations to come, nor thee. To whom much is given, of him much is required.

How can we pray except in the name of him who is your Word of grace from the beginning, present here and everywhere, teaching women and men, girls and boys, and youth to pray as your family.—John Thompson

SERMON
Topic: A Majority of One
TEXT: John 17:22–23

One is a majority!

When we ally ourselves with God, even if we stand alone, we represent the majority, for we stand on God's side. God is a majority! Even without you or me, he remains a *majority of one.*

It is this powerful oneness of Father and Son that Jesus spells out in his *high priest prayer.* Jesus does not exclude us but seeks rather to include us in this exclusive unity, this marvelous majority of one. He prays to his Father, "The glory that you have given me I have given them [meaning his followers], so that they may be one, as we are one, I in them and you in me, that they may become completely one, so that the world may know that you have sent me and have loved even as you have loved me."

Here is the challenge for all of us: never yield to anyone less than God himself. As we meet the temptations of time and the treachery of others, it is important that we never shortchange our unity with God in Christ for something less. Even if you stand alone, when you stand by the cross of Christ you stand with the majority of one. It is in him that we are set free. It is in the Messiah Jesus that we know the truth, the truth that must never be discounted and made cheap—for it cost the life blood of God himself, and it sets us eternally free. That truth drew life out of death so that the Resurrection of Christ is the sure sign of the conquest of all the evil forces that seek to battle God but fail.

Friend, stand with God! He is the majority of one!

Stand with him in the cause of morality. Battle the evils that plague our civilization—from abuse of drugs and drink to abuse of children and women; from abuse of the planet to abuse of its wildlife. Stand with him in the concern for the poor. Stand with him in loving the handicapped and the troubled, the persecuted and the wrongly imprisoned. Stand with the Lord of love against all those who seek to perpetuate prejudices, hatred, and animosity, who prefer violence and bloodshed to neighborliness and peaceful adjustments. Stand on the side of God to forgive those who oppose him, by ministering to his opponents with Jesuslike compassion.

All you need is the majority of one—to stand united with God as completely one.

Friend, where do you stand?

Charles Swindoll tells the story of a small boy who hated to practice the piano. He sat at the keyboard thirty minutes a day doing scales and chords and detested every minute of it. His mother thought he might see the results of practicing scales and chords if she took him to a concert of a renowned pianist. The famous Ignace Jan Paderewski was to perform in their town, so she obtained tickets. The Polish pianist, composer, and statesman made his debut 110 years ago and performed until 1941, traveling all over the world giving concerts that are legendary today.

The child sat stiff and uncomfortable in his suit and tie in the gilded concert hall. While his mother busied herself chatting with someone next to her, the lad wandered off and went up on the stage. To the shock of the assembling audience, he began to play *Chopsticks* on the master's concert grand. Paderewski, who was standing in the wings, came out and sat down beside the boy, put his arms around him and kept shouting to him, "Don't stop! Don't stop!" as he accompanied the lad's rendition of *Chopsticks* with an improvisation of his own.

Here is what it's like to be on the side of the majority of one. It is to feel the arms of God enfolding you, shouting for you to keep on, as he himself plays the accompaniment, taking the contribution we make and turning it into beautiful music.[1]—Richard Andersen

SUNDAY, OCTOBER 29, 2000
Lectionary Message

Topic: Sight for Body and Soul

TEXT: Mark 10:46–52

Other Readings: Job 42:1–6, 10–17; Ps. 34:1–8 (19–22); Heb.7:23–28

When Jesus began his ministry in the synagogue at Nazareth, among the things he read and applied to himself was "the recovery of sight to the blind" (Luke 4:18). When John sent from his prison cell to inquire whether Jesus was the coming one, among the events the messengers were to report to John was "the blind receive their sight" (Luke 7:22). The most astonishing account of giving sight to a blind man is found in John 9.

I. *The despair of blindness* (v. 46). Those of us who have good eyes cannot know the despair of the person who cannot see. We see such people with their white canes or their guide dogs. But it is difficult to put ourselves in their places. We are so accustomed to seeing the beauty around us, we cannot imagine what it would be like to be in total darkness. Blindness was a special tragedy in the ancient world. A blind person was reduced to begging. He had to depend on the generosity of other people. Such was the man Bartimaeus. He was sitting beside the road near the city of Jericho. Perhaps this was a good place to beg. Many Jews would pass that way going to Jerusalem for the various religious activities. They might be more generous because religious duties were on their minds. But even so, blindness brought despair. There was no hope of improvement in the situation. The person was blind and would remain so.

Despair is a terrible feeling, whether it comes as a result of a physical condition or a spiritual condition. And the despair of a spiritual condition can be just as devastating as that which grows from a physical condition. In a person's own soul there is no more hope for spiritual despair than for physical despair.

II. *Hope of renewal* (vv. 47–50). Suddenly, blind Bartimaeus had a surge of hope. He heard that Jesus of Nazareth was passing by. Probably Bartimaeus had never met Jesus, but certainly word about him had spread even to Jericho. He had heard that Jesus was able to do amazing things. He had healed the sick, he had cleansed lepers, he had cast out demons, he had raised the dead, and he had even restored sight to some who were blind. Perhaps he would do something for Bartimaeus, so he was determined to appeal to Jesus for help. He cried out, using the strongly nationalistic title "Son of David," perhaps sensing that Jesus was the Messiah. He made no specific request, only that Jesus would extend mercy to him.

---

[1] Donald L. Deffner, *Seasonal Illustrations* (San Jose, Calif.: Resources Publications, 1992), p. 97.

He was not easily discouraged, although many urged him to be quiet. Their efforts simply resulted in louder cries to Jesus. When Jesus heard him, he asked that Bartimaeus be brought to him. What an excitement must have possessed Bartimaeus. Here was his hope, his one hope. He was going to come face to face with one through whom the power of God worked.

Hope can come from many directions when one is in despair. But the greatest hope is the assurance of God's concern and care. Human help is important, but it can never take the place of God's help. People may have given much to the blind man. Only Jesus could give him sight. People may help in our physical and spiritual despair, but only God can bring us into the relation with him that dispels all worry and despair. We must share the determination of Bartimaeus and insist on meeting Jesus and receiving blessing from him.

III. *Receiving beyond asking* (vv. 51–52). When Bartimaeus reached Jesus' side, the Lord asked what he wanted done for him. Bartimaeus' request was simple and direct. He wanted to be able to see again. This was the greatest gift he could receive. His main interest was focused on the physical. So often this is true for us as well. Physical conditions can be so intense that we fail to consider the spiritual situation of our lives. Our one concern is to ease physical suffering, whether that be hunger, thirst, or some disease. Jesus did what Bartimaeus asked. He gave him sight. God hears and answers his people, but he does not always satisfy every need in the way we desire. Not that every disease is cured. But even when our specific request is not granted, we find that God is able to relieve our despair simply because he is present and shows concern for us.

Sometimes God gives more than is asked. This may have been the situation with Bartimaeus. He asked for physical sight and received it. But did he also receive spiritual sight? He began to follow Jesus on the way. Though Jesus was accompanied by a large crowd, only a few were actually following him *on his way.* Even his disciples had difficulty at this point. They could not believe that the Messiah would die. How could they follow him on the way to the cross? But Bartimaeus was following on the way. He may not have known all that was involved, but he was willing to follow Jesus wherever that might lead and whatever might be the consequences. This is what God desires for us. We ask for specific things, and he often gives us more than we ask for. He gives spiritual sight so that we can follow him along the way. Physical sight is wonderful, but spiritual sight is even more wonderful. We need to seek it from the only one who can give it, Jesus himself, so that we can follow him on the way.— Clayton K. Harrop

ILLUSTRATIONS

KEENER VISION.   We are told that when one loses the use of one of the physical senses, the other senses become more acute. Even spiritual perceptions may become more aware. This must have been the case with Fanny Crosby. Although she could not see with her eyes, no one can read or sing her hymns without an awareness that, although God did not give her physical vision, he gave her something even more important: spiritual sight. She had a vision of God that few of us ever attain.—Clayton K. Harrop

A NEW LIFE.   Despair gives opportunity for God to work. A friend from long before had come to visit us. We had witnessed to her on numerous occasions but she had refused all we said because she did not believe the Bible. Now she was obviously in despair. She was addicted to alcohol. For two days she did not get out of bed. Then, on Sunday afternoon she came downstairs and asked how she could get what she had seen in our lives. We shared God's wonderful love in Jesus with her. She opened up her heart to Christ and her despair was taken away in a newfound joy in Christ. God is the source of hope in a dismal world.—Clayton K. Harrop

SERMON SUGGESTIONS

Topic: Thinking Ahead

TEXT: Eccl. 12:1

(1) Every successful life is made up of right choices. (2) Some of these right choices are made on the basis of lessons learned from bad or foolish choices. (3) Vital choices made early prepare one for forced decisions that life imposes later. (4) The key to wise decision making is an early recognition of God.

Topic: What Is Your Opinion of Yourself?

TEXT: Luke 18:9–14

(1) The Pharisee: an example of self-esteem built on wrong reasons. (2) The Publican: an example of a realistic assessment of the human situation. (a) All of us are sinners. (b) None of us has a claim on God. (c) Confession of unworthiness is called for. (d) Faith realizes the nature of God as loving and merciful.

CONGREGATIONAL MUSIC

1. "Hail, Thou (O) Once-Despised Jesus," attr. John Bakewell (1757)

    ARFON, Welsh tune (c. 1784)

    This Easter hymn is also appropriate for use in connection with Hebrews 7:23–28, with its emphasis on the Christ who ever lives to make intercession for us. It is a fine worship hymn, often overlooked.
2. "Fill Thou My Life, O Lord, My God," Horatius Bonar (1863)

    ELLACOMBE, *Gesangbuch,* Wittenberg (1784)

    Bonar's fine hymn centering on praise in every part of one's being is a good one to sing before or after the reading of the Psalter lesson (Ps. 34:1–8, 19–22).
3. "Word of God, Come Down to Earth," James Quinn (1969)

    MT. ST. ALBAN'S NCA, Richard W. Dirksen (1983)

    A hymn rich in theological images of the Word of God, it would be especially suitable to introduce the reading of the Gospel lesson. Its plainsong tune may require a choir to introduce it before the congregation is asked to join in.
4. "God Moves in a Mysterious Way," William Cowper (1773)

    ST. ANNE, attr. William Croft (1708)

    Job was tried sorely and sought persistently to fathom the reasons for the ways God was dealing with him. But in restoring Job's fortunes God finally revealed his mercy and his grace. This classic hymn reflects the truths to be gleaned from the story of Job and thus could be profitably sung in connection with the Old Testament reading (Job 42:1–6, 10–17).—Hugh T. McElrath

WORSHIP AIDS

CALL TO WORSHIP.   "O magnify the Lord with me, and let us exalt his name together" (Ps. 34:3).

INVOCATION.   As we praise your name, O God, give us clearer vision of who you are, what you can do, and what you are causing to happen with us and among us. Let our worship become a new experience of truth, truth as embodied in your Son, our Lord, and illuminated for us by your Holy Spirit.

OFFERTORY SENTENCE.   "You are worthy, O Lord our God, to receive glory and honour and power, because you created all things; by your will they were created and have their being" (Rev. 4:11 REB).

OFFERTORY PRAYER.   We offer to you, O God, what is already yours. But you have entrusted to our hands, hearts, and minds all that we call our own, so that we now bring a portion and dedicate it to the special cause of your Kingdom.

PRAYER.   Ever-present Father, in these moments of silence we build small places of solitude in our souls where we seek to commune with you. Pray, speak to us now in ways that will bring us to see ourselves as we are and gain determination to become more than we can ever be apart from you.

Gazing on your matchless beauty we see our own ugly selves. The more we discover of your goodness, the more we are aware of the evil that dwells within our hearts and expresses itself in our lives. Your forgiveness for our sins and misdeeds ever confronts us with our failure to forgive those who have offended us. This morning, grant that our weakness may be turned to strength, that our failure may be channeled to success and our fears changed into courage.

Give us today the spirit of forgiveness even when it is human to seek revenge. Kindle within us a desire to do what is right in all circumstances and undergird our weakness with your strength, that right may be done in all things. Grant that as your followers we may care about those who do care about the things of God, that we may love those who do not love us and pray for those who despitefully use us. Then we will begin to become more like true children of God.

As your children seeking to serve the world and our fellow human beings in your name, we ask that we be granted the high gifts of compassion for the needy, love for the lost and straying, serving ability for the frail, comfort for the lonely wanderers, and words of guidance for the straying and lost on the road through life.—Henry Fields

SERMON

Topic: Is Reformation Past Tense?
TEXT: 1 Pet. 2:1–10

Today is Reformation Sunday. Now, that statement is not likely to generate a great deal of spontaneous enthusiasm, and little if any interest. Most of us know that the Reformation had something to do with the reforming or the renewal of the Christian Church, and that Luther,

Calvin, and others helped to set this force for change in motion. But that's not enough to grasp our attention on a crisp fall morning. Perhaps we are not all that interested in history. You may even agree with Henry Ford's famous assessment: *history is bunk.* You may remember the church of Flip Wilson and Brother Leroy: *the Church of What's Happening Now!* That's the church we are interested in: be up to date, be contemporary, speak not of the sixteenth century. To put it in an even more direct way, we did not come this morning to hear a history lecture. We came to worship (or find) a living God. You and I have come to receive wisdom and courage for the living of *these* days.

Yet is it not one of the rules of living as well as sport that we must often take a step back before we can move forward? Could it be that the great ideas of the Protestant Reformation feed gnawing, spiritual hunger in the twentieth century? Can such a truth as the *priesthood of all believers* become again more than words for us, as it was for Luther and those who heard him? What a difference it made to men and women to believe that before God all are equal. It is not a faith for the elite—*by grace we are saved.* I am freed from sin and death, but also free to be a priest to my brother and sister, and they to me. Christianity is not a spectator sport!

Bud Wilkinson, the architect of so many winning football teams at the University of Oklahoma, had an oft-quoted definition of football: *It's fifty thousand people who are in desperate need of exercise sitting and watching twenty-two men who are in desperate need of rest!* Doesn't that sound like the church? We become spectators and summon the few to do our praying, proclaiming, and priesting for us. What has become of the *priesthood of all believers*?

I. The first mark of a true Reformation will be an authentic *recovery* of a lost, or misplaced, biblical truth. In this case, I mean a universal priesthood. Malachi describes for us the duties of the priest: to teach, to practice the faith, and to minister to or serve the people. Malachi also mourns the results of an unfaithful priesthood: the people of the land are disillusioned. They stumble and fall.

Jesus confronted a similar situation in his day. The religious leaders were busy measuring the people's responsibility. Their narrow, legalistic code of some 615 laws was a burden to the common man or woman who wanted to obey God. What's more, these leaders would not, Matthew tells us, lift their little fingers to relieve the burdens of their brother and sister who needed to experience forgiveness, acceptance, love. Jesus goes beyond criticism. He gives us a new model of leadership and priesthood. This priest is not only one who stands before God for others, but also the one who leads us into new and abundant life by becoming a servant! If we would lead people out from darkness, despair, anxiety, it would be as humble servants.

II. Now, if that's the truth that needs to be recovered from the Bible, the next step is to *reform* it, recast it into terms that can be understood in our times. Being called to be priests to each other can first have a tremendous effect on the structure of the Church. It will be seen in the way we act toward one another; the marks of status in our fellowship will begin to disappear. Unfortunately, it is a mark of modern Protestantism that we place so much emphasis on the pastor as superstar. When he or she arrives, then our worship, stewardship, and witness will be what it should be. People will be visited and encouraged, and injustice will be corrected. Of course, pastoral leadership is important, but in focusing on that call, do we miss hearing our own call as priests of our God (Rev. 5:10)? You and I are members together of equal rank in that priesthood, and according to the Reformed tradition, *there is no hierarchy among equals.*

As priests we will minister to each other, and serve people in the secular precincts where we lead our lives. Our priesthood begins in servant ministries in the Church. Is the care of members a sensitive ministry, praying and standing by the side of one person or a whole committee? Second, that aspect of the priesthood of all believers that has been most neglected in the modern Church is that our ministry is not limited to what we do here on Sunday mornings or in committee meetings. The real evidence of our ministry is how we are enabled to live in the places away from here. In our gathering, are we refreshed and challenged to live a life of humble service? That is the vocation of the priest. What your office, family, club, school cries out for is not the priest who calls attention to his status or her piety. No, true priesthood will mean at times laying down your own ego needs, the tribute you deserve, the attention you demand, so that another may come to life in a new way.

III. If our churches are to overcome the spiritual power shortage and cease neglecting the opportunity to be priests to one another, we must not only *recover* the biblical message and *re-form* it for our community, but finally we must come to a sense of personal *renewal.* The priesthood of believers cannot wait for someone else to begin. There is a prayer used by Chinese Christians that begins, *Renew your church, O Lord, and let it begin with me.* The church can be transformed if we recover our lost heritage. You remember Jesus' charge against the religious of his day. They did not raise a finger to lift the burden of their brothers and sisters. It is the true priests who know the power of even their fingers to lift others in times when they cannot lift themselves. In these past few weeks I have observed people in this church helping lift others through times of grief and loss. I have watched people here this morning minister to those who felt like strangers in an alien land. The example of some of this congregation has taught others of us what it means to be a steward, giving not of the leftovers but from the top of God's gracious bounty. Yes, priests are lifters of burdens.

When we really begin to exercise our priesthood, we will be pointers as well. Paul Tillich has said that the Church should be like John the Baptist in Grunewald's painting: *there his whole being is in the finger with which he points to the cross.* When we become servants, not self-promoters, we are priests. Even without words, we are pointing to the one servant-leader who leads us away from wanting always to be served and honored. It is still his loving presence that enables us and others to do the impossible: to seek the lesser place, to move beyond self-interest. If in and through Christ, that's what we have to offer, why are we so shy to be his priests?—Gary D. Stratman

SUNDAY, NOVEMBER 5, 2000

Lectionary Message

Topic: Love's Demands
TEXT: Mark 12:28–34
Other Readings: Ruth 1:1–18; Ps. 146; Heb. 9:11–14

There are times when it pays to be cautious. Financial advisors will counsel their clients to "hold something back." As with finances, so also with the early stages in a relationship: one might do well to hear and heed the advice, "Don't overcommit yourself." Certainly there are areas of life in which such admonitions constitute good advice. Such cautionary warnings, however, are seldom appropriate in determining actions having to do with our relationship to God. In that area, the reality is that nothing must be held back. There it is total commitment that is called for. For some a life of satisfying discipleship will never become a reality because of a failure to surrender *all* in total commitment to Christ. Yet in our text for today, Jesus makes clear that it is only in meeting the demands of loving God with the whole of one's being that such satisfying religious experience will come. There, against the background of disputes and attempts to have him misspeak in the presence of his enemies, Jesus is provided the opportunity to declare the essence of God's expectations for those who would follow him. And in our Lord's words we are reminded of the great demands that love places on us.

I. *The asking of an honest question.* The opportunity to declare love's demands comes in response to the asking of a specific question. Unlike the trick questions asked earlier concerning taxes and whose wife a thrice-married widow will be at the resurrection (Mark 12:12–24), a man of sincerity raised a question that had profound implications. Impressed with Jesus' earlier responses and obvious insights, this sincere scribe asked a most significant question: "Of all the commandments, which is the most important?" There are indications that at the time there were some 613 different commandments—some defining what a person must do and others indicating what one must not do. With all of those, the question became, What is basic? What is the most important of all? Where is one to begin? What is to receive priority?

Must not Jesus love this kind of question? The man did not ask it as a participant in a plan to entrap Jesus. He sincerely wanted to know; he desired to learn. Jesus seldom responds to our attempts to manipulate him, or to persuade him to substitute our will for his will in our lives. But he does respond to one properly motivated who comes to him humbly with serious and sincere questions. Jesus invites us to come to him with everything that is on our hearts and everything that is a part of our lives. The invitation to "come unto me . . . and learn from me" (Matt. 11:28–29) is always open.

II. *Christ's honest answer.* Many times God's answers to our questions and the deepest longings of our lives do not come to us in specific words. Often we do find the answers we seek in sacred Scripture. But there are times when we experience the answer in subsequent events or outcomes, in what we describe as "divine impulses," or in a sense of direction that becomes unmistakably clear to us. On this occasion, however, the scribe received his answer in clear and specific words. Jesus declared that the most important of all the commandments was not to be found in some hidden text somewhere but in words so well known to every Jew that perhaps for many the common knowledge of them had caused those words to lose their cutting edge. The most important commandment of all is that one love God with all one's heart, soul, mind, and strength (Mark 12:30). Life is to be centered in God. The demand to love is all-encompassing. This command to love God demands that we hold nothing back, that our commitment be total.

III. *The call for an honest response.* The questioner on this occasion knew that he had received a clear and correct answer. The scribe approved of Jesus' teaching. Jesus responded by noting that the man was "not far from the Kingdom of God" (Mark 12:34). But he was not yet in. For the challenge of the "most important commandment" required more than an affirmation of the truth of Christ's teaching. It demanded the response of a total life commitment.

That is the demand if one is to truly love God. And, the proper response, the only really honest response, will include acting on the "second" most important commandment: "Love your neighbor as yourself" (Mark 12:31). The evidence of our love of God with the totality of who we are will be reflected in the way and manner in which we love others. The command challenges us to shift our affections away from paralyzing self-centeredness to where we hold back nothing from others in their need.

True discipleship occurs when we reflect our love of God in our love of others. Truly satisfying discipleship results when we experience God's love in our lives in a way so real and overwhelming that we hold nothing back in our commitment to Christ. For as we so often sing, "Love so amazing, so divine, demands my soul, my life, my *all.*"—Dwight A. Honeycutt

ILLUSTRATIONS

POSITIVE AND CERTAIN LOVE.   It was St. Augustine of Hippo (354–430) who gave us that wonderfully well-known statement "Our hearts are restless, O God, until they find their rest in Thee." The same Augustine shared his own pilgrimage of faith in that classic spiritual autobiography *Confessions*, and therein wrote of his own love of God: "My love of you, O Lord, is not some vague feeling: it is positive and certain. Your word struck into my heart from that moment I loved you. Besides this, all about me, heaven and earth and all that they contain proclaim that I should love you, and their message never ceases to sound in the ears of all mankind, so that there is no excuse for any not to love you."[1]—Dwight A. Honeycutt

RADICAL OBEDIENCE.   Michael Sattler (who died in 1527) was one of the early leaders among the biblical Anabaptists—a group that composed a significant component of the "radical" reformation of the sixteenth century. He died a martyr's death as he was burned at the stake. Even after the fire was burning his body, his voice could be heard in prayer and praise. When the ropes on his hands burned through, he raised the forefingers of both hands, thereby giving the signal he had agreed on beforehand with his fellow believers. The signal indicated that such a death was bearable and represented his testimony that he had remained firm in his faith. Michael Sattler represented a group that emphasized total commitment and radical obedience as they gave themselves to a life of discipleship. In his teachings Sattler had emphasized three points: (1) Saving faith implies radical obedience to the commands of Christ; the Sermon on the Mount is the manifesto for Christian living. (2) The key to victorious discipleship is in following Jesus; Christ is the Christian's example, but more, he is the head of the church, and we are to follow him as Lord. (3) Christians are to be conformed to the image of Christ; they are to reflect the character and integrity of Jesus; indeed, they are to be like Jesus.—Dwight A. Honeycutt

SERMON SUGGESTIONS

Topic: The Help of God

TEXT: Ps. 33

(1) The Lord has helped us up to this point: (a) when we were not aware anything was happening; (b) when we thought the opposite was happening; (c) when we knew what was happening. (2) Who has the Lord helped? Us: (a) those with whom he has made a covenant, (b)

---

[1] St. Augustine, *Confessions* (London: Penguin Books, 1961), p. 211.

those who reverence him, (c) those who hope in his steadfast love. (3) Some facts to hearten us: (a) The counsel of the Lord stands forever; God is still sovereign. (b) Apparent weakness does not rule out ultimate victory. (c) Rejoicing is in order in all circumstances, in view of God's loving purpose.

Topic: Paul's Prayer for Us

TEXT: Eph. 3:16–19

(1) Prayer for power (vv. 16–17a). (2) Prayer for insight (vv. 17b–19a). (3) Prayer for fullness (v. 19b).—Grant R. Osborne[2]

CONGREGATIONAL MUSIC

1. "I'll Praise My Maker While I've Breath," Isaac Watts (1719)

OLD 113TH, *Strassburger Kichenamt* (1525); attr. Matthias Greiter

Watts's powerful paraphrase of Psalm 146 was one of John Wesley's favorites. It's words were on his lips when he died. It is the appropriate hymn for the beginning of worship on this Sunday.

2. "Where Charity and Love Prevail," Latin; tr. J. Clifford Evers (1961)

CHESHIRE, Este, *The Whole Book of Psalms* (1592)

A hymn especially appropriate for a communion service, this modern translation from the Latin could be sung to introduce the Gospel lesson in Mark (12:28–34) where Jesus answered a scribe's question concerning the greatest commandment. The second stanza is especially appropriate.

3. "Come, Thou Fount of Every Blessing," Robert Robinson (1758)

NETTLETON, Wyeth's *A Repository of Sacred Music, II* (1813)

This familiar hymn also could be used for the opening of worship. It relates particularly to the reading in Hebrews 9:11–14 where the theme is the Christ who has obtained our redemption through the shedding of his own blood.

4. "We Are One in the Bond of Love," Otis Skillings (1971)

SKILLINGS, Otis Skillings (1971)

The bond that Ruth had with her mother-in-law, Naomi (Ruth 1:1–8), can be reflected in the bond of love that ties Christians together. This chorus affirms the oneness of true believers in Christ.—Hugh T. McElrath

WORSHIP AIDS

CALL TO WORSHIP.   "Praise ye the Lord. Praise the Lord, O my Soul. While I live will I praise the Lord: I will sing praises unto God while I have any being" (Ps. 146:1–2).

INVOCATION.   We know, O God, that you do not have to have our praise, but we confess that we need to praise you in song, prayer, and life itself. To that end, O Lord, rekindle within us the fires of true devotion.

OFFERTORY SENTENCE.   "So then every one of us shall give account of himself to God" (Rom. 14:12).

---

[2] *The Hermeneutical Spiral*

OFFERTORY PRAYER.   Day by day, O God, help us to do and to say and to give, so that we render our proper stewardship of what we are by your grace, knowing that truly we are in business with you, to your glory and for our blessing.

PRAYER.   How we thank you, O God, for the Church that has called us out to be and become, for the churches that have nurtured us along the way, for the meaning and experience of church we celebrate in the history and life of this congregation.

Help us together to perceive more insightfully what it means to be the Body of Christ in the world—in the kind of world in which our lives are set. To the opportunities of this place and the possibilities of these times may we bring that sense of destiny of those who have gone this way before us, who through their faithfulness are cheering us on toward the goal of your high calling in Christ Jesus.

Help us discern your word in the exigencies of our present life together. Grant us the long look of faith lest we become frustrated in our instant expectations. May we not mark time in some border country but move forward and possess the land of your promise. As your command to the children of Israel was *go forward,* so your word is for us in our journey through the wilderness.

We rejoice in the signs of your coming—for healings among us, for strength in the face of infirmity, for comfort in our bereavement.

Awaken us at depths not yet fathomed, challenge us to heights not yet climbed, inspire us with visions never before dreamed, that we may live at the growing edge of the coming of your kingdom present and promised in Christ.—John Thompson

SERMON
Topic: Body Language—Christian Style
TEXT: Mark 1:41; 1 Cor. 12:27

I read an interesting paperback by Julius Fast entitled *Body Language.* He suggests in this book that we speak most clearly by the signals we make, often without being aware of them.

I turn to the Gospel records and read Mark's account of one of our Lord's first miracles of healing, the healing of a man with leprosy. The arresting sentence is this: "Moved with pity, Jesus stretched out his hand and touched him." It is fascinating to realize that our Lord Jesus Christ was anticipating a contemporary emphasis, actually employing body language, the language of touch. I turn the pages of the New Testament to Paul's first Corinthian letter and read there the magnificently daring metaphor the apostle uses to describe the function and responsibility of the church: "You are the body of Christ." To be a Christian and a church member is to be the presence of the living Christ in the world today—to be his hands and feet and eyes, a continuation of the Incarnation. Moved with pity, the living Lord Jesus Christ still stretches out his hands—and with them he reaches the world he loves through you and me.

We are touching the lives of others, and being touched by others, all the time. The towering question is, Is it with the touch of Christ?

Sometimes we touch others consciously and deliberately. More often we touch others unconsciously and unintentionally. We are all radiating centers of influence, professing to be Christians, members of the body of Christ. What is our body language, our language of touch, saying and doing? Are we speaking in this way with the accent of Christ?

I. *What were the reasons for the touch of Jesus?* I dare say Jesus could have healed this man with a word or with a thought. When a man with leprosy came out and knelt before Jesus, crying for cleansing, "moved with pity, he stretched out his hand and touched him." What were the reasons for this body language of touch? I find three reasons.

To begin with, it was a touch of *indignation.* He was indignant because of the fact of disease in God's clean world, because there was such an ugly intruder. It had to be fought and destroyed.

Here is a second reason for the touch of Jesus. It was a touch of *imagination.* Jesus saw in a flash what hurt the leprosy sufferer most. It was not so much the physical pain or the bodily disfiguration but the psychological anguish, the alienation, the hell of being shunned like the plague. So Jesus dealt with him delicately, sensitively, imaginatively.

Ezekiel, God's prophet, summarizes his own preparation for a ministry to his people: "I sat where they sat." Anyone who can say that is sure to be what Christ would have them be in serving the needs of contemporary society.

Finally, it was a touch of *identification.* Ignoring the formidable barriers of physical repugnance and ceremonial uncleanness, Jesus made himself one with the stricken man, becoming his friend and brother. He identified himself fully with the man in his disease and desperation and took upon himself the social stigma with which a leper was branded.

So, sometimes literally and always symbolically, we must identify ourselves with those whom we would help and heal.

II. We turn now to our second main question: *What were the results of this touch of Jesus?* "And immediately the leprosy left him, and he was made clean."

The touch of Jesus communicated *the gift of inner peace.* That man had never known a moment's peace from the time he first saw the telltale signs of a dreaded disease on his body.

The touch of Jesus also communicated *the gift of personal dignity.* A person has no sense of dignity, no self-respect when, because of a loathsome disease, society shuns and depersonalizes him. He accepts society's estimate of his value. He lives with an appalling inferiority complex. But Jesus touched this man

It's our privilege and duty, as followers of Christ, to touch others, in his name and by his power, in a way that enriches and ennobles their lives, in a way that restores their sense of worth and dignity.

Then, finally, the touch of Jesus communicated *the gift of new life.* He said to the man, "I will; be clean. And immediately the leprosy left him, and he was made clean." This was more than a physical healing. That in itself would be wonderful—a restored body, the right to return to society and take his place again among men and women. But Jesus was more than the Great Physician; he was the Divine Saviour. He came to do more for us than meet our physical needs: he came to bring us new life, life of a new quality, life lived in communion with God, life with the tang of eternity about it.

There is a Christian-style body language. Jesus used it, and his touch still has its ancient power, through people like you and me. For we are "the body of Christ, and individually members of it."—John N. Gladstone[3]

---

[3] *Living in Style*

SUNDAY, NOVEMBER 12, 2000

Lectionary Message

Topic: A Study in Contrasts

TEXT: Mark 12:38–44

Other Readings: Ruth 3:1–5; Ps. 127; Heb. 9:24–28

What makes life meaningful? For many with a secular mentality it has to do with things such as prestige, prominence, and power. It is to receive the accolades of peers and to be judged by the world's standards as a "success." For others, the perspective is altogether different. What makes life meaningful is to be guided in Christ's way, the way of faith, love, sacrifice. In today's Gospel text we see both perspectives graphically illustrated. We see religious leaders who functioned with a secular mentality preoccupied with their own prestige, prominence, and power. Jesus declared that they, in the end, would receive punishment rather than praise. On the other side is the contrast of those religious leaders with the poor widow who in giving out of her poverty reflected a life of sincere faith and sacrifice. Jesus praised her actions.

Twenty centuries later we "religious people" still struggle with the issue of what makes life meaningful. From the text it would appear that our choice is still between these two contrasting possibilities.

I. *There is the way of scandalous religion.* In recent years scandals have been too much a part of the religious landscape. One need only recall those associated with the so-called tele-evangelists. Most of us do not struggle with temptation in the direction of such grandiose scandalous behavior. Yet the temptation is still there for us, but in more subtle forms. It is the temptation to adopt and apply the ways and standards of the world and the secular culture to our religious practices. It is the temptation to use religion to gain prestige, prominence, and power for ourselves, and thus to measure up to the standards of success employed by the secular world.

In his day Jesus warned against this very thing. Note that he warned his disciples to see the fallacy of the lifestyle of the teachers of the Law: they were concerned about their clothing, that it reflect a position of significant status; they wanted only the best seats at religious occasions; they desired positions of honor at social events; they wanted to be esteemed for their ability to offer lengthy prayers (12:38–40). And scathingly Jesus pointed out that for their own financial gain they took advantage of the less fortunate, even to the point that they "devoured widows' houses" (12:40). This is scandalous behavior for anyone. But for religious leaders, how much more scandalous could it be? Their concerns were self-centered and undergirded with greed. What gave meaning to their lives was the achievement of status and the acclaim of the world. Mark indicates that Jesus warned his disciples about these kinds of leaders and the temptation to succumb to those kinds of values. In this world of ours, filled with the same kinds of temptations, we need to hear that warning as well.

II. *There is the way of sacrificial religion.* There could be no greater contrast to the greed and self-centeredness of the status-seeking religionists who chose the way of the world than that of the "poor widow" whom Jesus observed placing her offering in the Temple treasury. Could she possibly have been one of the poor widows whose houses had been devoured? Obviously she was a woman who knew a life of sacrifice, some of which would have been the result of outside forces imposed on her. But one gets the impression from reading Mark's account (12:41–44) that her sacrificial spirit in large part was the result of her own true devotion to God. Rather than being driven by the desire for prestige, prominence, or power, she was guided by a life of faith and trust in God. Thus her offering "out of her poverty" was a true sacrifice "wholly acceptable to God."

Earlier Jesus had declared as the most important commandment, "Love the Lord your God with all your heart and with all your soul and with all your mind and with all your strength" (12:30). Here in the action of the widow as she "put in everything—all she had" is a vivid and classic illustration of one who must have approximated the ideal of that greatest commandment of all. Many others had come that day and made their offerings; "many rich people [who] threw in large amounts" (12:41). But it is the poor widow to whom Jesus calls the attention of his disciples. It is she who becomes the object lesson to enhance their understanding. For it is she, he says, who "put more into the treasury than all the others" (12:43). While the ways of the religious leaders earlier had received his condemnation, the faith, love, and sacrifice of this woman now received his commendation.

The text provides startling and vivid contrasts between two ways. To follow Jesus through the pages of the New Testament is to be confronted again and again by such contrasts. They challenge us. They judge us. In Matthew's account of the Sermon on the Mount, Jesus speaks in vivid word pictures about what gives meaning to life. If it is simply to impress others and to receive their praise, than that in and of itself is very possible to achieve. But that will be *all* the reward that one will receive, he says; that is to say, only those lofty but ultimately empty words of praise. Yet Jesus teaches us that it is possible to move beyond a life of superficiality and hypocrisy, and in faith to choose to do the will of God. In that we are promised meaning for life. And Jesus said, "Your Father . . . will reward you" (Matt. 6:1–4).—Dwight A. Honeycutt

ILLUSTRATIONS

SELF-PROMOTION.   In *Selling Out the Church*, the authors call attention to Adam Smith's famous "invisible hand" theory of economics. "That theory suggested that the most efficient way of meeting needs is for every person to look after his or her own interests. Thus if people engage in voluntary exchanges with an eye to their own interests, the general welfare of all people will be promoted, even though unintentionally." Christian faith looks to the interest of others, and thus is an inversion of the Adam Smith theory. Otherwise, one is motivated only by self-interest or egotism. Maximus the Confessor, writing in the seventh century, is cited as having noted that "Egotism is the source of the passions. From egoism spring gluttony, avarice, conceit. . . . From conceit springs pride. All the other vices, without exception, are merely consequences of egotism. . . . At the beginning of all the passion there is egotism, just as at the end there is pride."—Dwight A. Honeycutt[4]

RICH IN FAITH.   When Mr. Goldfinger comes to the assembly, he is given special treatment, flattery, perks such as special valet parking, and a special couch to sit on. This is the way one may expect to be treated at an expensive boutique, but not in a church. The reason

---

[4] Philip D. Kennson and James L. Street, *Selling Out the Church: The Dangers of Marketing* (Nashville, Tenn.: Abingdon Press, 1997), p. 57.

people fawn over the rich and honorable is not because they love them but because they want to win their favor. The poor, on the other hand, are treated with contempt because people ask themselves, "What can they ever contribute to us?" Jesus looked at things from God's vantage point. The gleaming reputations of the pious and wealthy were stained by a mean-spirited oppression of the helpless and poor. The widow, however, was rich in faith, the only thing that counts with God. She had the only honor worth striving for.—David E. Garland[5]

SERMON SUGGESTIONS

Topic: How God Honors His Name

TEXT: Ps. 25:11–13

(1) By forgiving our sin (v. 11). (2) By guiding our ways (v. 12). (3) By blessing our obedience (v. 13).

Topic: His Victory and Ours

TEXT: 1 Cor. 15:57–58

(1) Our victory in Christ (v. 57). (2) Our consequent resolve and service (v. 58a). (3) Our ultimate reassurance (v. 57b).

CONGREGATIONAL MUSIC

1. "Unless the Lord the House Shall Build," Psalm 127, *The Psalter* (1912)

BOURBON, attr. Freeman Lewis (1825)

An alternation of reading Psalm 127 and singing the stanzas of this metrical version would be meaningful. The plan could be as follows: Ps. 127:1, read; stanza 1, sung; Ps. 127:2, read; stanza 2, sung; Ps. 127:3–4, read; stanza 3, sung; Ps. 127:5, read; stanza 4, sung.

2. "Hark! The Voice of Jesus Calling," Daniel March (1868)

ELLSDIE, Levitt's "The Christian Lyre" (1831); arr. H. P. Main

This rousing gospel hymn would be an effective response to the Gospel reading about the widow's mite (Mark 12:41–43), further challenging the singers to faithful Christian stewardship.

3. "Praise Him! Praise Him!" Fanny J. Crosby (1869)

JOYFUL SONG, Chester G. Allen (1869)

A praise song that exalts the one who is not only Redeemer but also Rock, Prophet, Priest, and King, it is appropriate for singing in connection with the reading in Hebrews (9:24–28) where the high priestly and judging functions of Christ are set forth. This song would be suitable for the beginning of worship as a call to praise.

4. "I Have Decided to Follow Jesus," Garo Christians (1950)

ASSAM, Indian Folk Song; arr. W. J. Reynolds (1959)

Ruth followed the instructions of Naomi and as a result became the mother of Obed, father of Jesse, father of David, and thus in the lineage of Jesus (Ruth 3:1–22). By the same token, Christians decide to follow Jesus and his will for their lives. This Christian folk song affirms that commitment.—Hugh T. McElrath

---

[5] David E. Garland, *Mark, The NIV Application Commentary* (Grand Rapids, Mich.: Zondervan, 1996), p. 486.

WORSHIP AIDS

CALL TO WORSHIP.   "Except the Lord build the house, they labour in vain that build it: except the Lord keep the city, the watchman watcheth but in vain" (Ps. 127:1).

INVOCATION.   Lord, as we are busy planning our services of worship and our programs of outreach, grant us the wisdom and the will to do things your way. To that end, teach us again that our first duty is to you and that our best work is for you and with you. So we pray for the leadership of your Spirit and the joy of the Lord as we prepare to do your bidding.

OFFERTORY SENTENCE.   "I have told you this so that my joy may be in you and that your joy may be complete. My commandment is this: love one another just as I love you. The greatest love a person can have for his friends is to give his life for them. And you are my friends if you do what I command you" (John 15:11–14 TEV).

OFFERTORY PRAYER.   Because you have loved us and because we love one another we bring our offerings today. Deepen our love, that we may give more and more in the spirit of our Savior, who gave his all for us.

PRAYER.   Stewardship Sunday. Who can stand in Your presence, O God, except that your abounding grace invites him. Yours is a grace mighty to save—to save to the uttermost.

The law came through Moses, but grace and truth came through Jesus, the Messiah. The truth that we discover in Christ about ourselves would be overwhelming except that the greatest truth is your word of grace. Where sin abounds, grace does much more abound. Thanks be to you, O God, for victory in Christ.

What grace! To be cocreators with you in the building of your Kingdom. Grant us such a sense of destiny to believe that we have been born to the Kingdom for such a time as this—that we fail not others, or you, or ourself.

Not only for this season but for all seasons we pray that our stewardship will be not dutiful but in joyful response to your ludicrous grace in Christ. You are such a spendthrift! You who spared not your own Son but gave him up for us all. To grow in the grace and knowledge of Christ is to grow in the grace of giving. In this day of unprecedented opportunity, may we as a church move from victory to victory.

In the family of faith we are sisters and brothers. And we are very conscious of the many needs among us. Where there is any brokenness in illness, in sorrow, in love, in disappointment, in failure, we pray for the healing of your grace that alone can make whole.

We believe that grace is your Word not only for our health but also for the healing of the nations. When we say of an enemy, "All they understand is power," maybe this is all that we have shown them. We are haunted by that Word of grace spoken by him who is the full measure of your abounding grace: "Pray for your enemies! Do good to those who spite you."

O Father of all, grant us courage to so believe and live, grant us the wisdom, too, that it is not in deprivation but in giving, in sharing, in helping that we get rid of our enemies—they become friends. As leaders and citizens, help us to realize that wealth and power are a stewardship from you, that all people may enjoy their inalienable right to freedom and the blessed bounty of the good Earth.

O Christ of God, help us to leave this place less of what we have been and more of what you would have us be as you teach us to pray and live.—John Thompson

SERMON

Topic: Exalted Happiness

TEXT: Pss. 89:15; 84:4; 32:2; 1:1–2; 41:1–2; 128:1

Realistically, as one person has said, "Happiness is not a state to arrive at but a manner of traveling." This desired objective is more a by-product of how we live than an end in itself. Happiness turns out to be the afterglow of other endeavors. It becomes a matter of realizing that we have been blessed and enriched because of certain actions or involvements.

Jesus knew this full well. He spoke directly to the pursuit of happiness when he said things like, "Blessed are those who hunger and thirst for righteousness, for they will be filled."

Though we probably are familiar with the Beatitudes Jesus taught, we may be much less familiar with significant Beatitudes found in the Psalms. I highlight the message of each Beatitude, beginning with the one which says, "Blessed [or happy] are the people who know the joyful sound, who walk, O Lord, in the light of your countenance."

What is "the joyful sound" which in this verse evokes happiness? The reference is to a vibrant trumpet call and to singing that took place during the religious festivals of the people of Israel.

Entering into worship with companions in faith, we make our own joyful sound, achieving satisfaction for our spirits and true pleasure for the living of our days. Our worship bestows these gifts.

The next Beatitude from the Psalms says a similar thing: "Blessed are those who dwell in thy house, ever singing thy praise." It is the house of worship that is being described; those who dwell in that house are the Temple priests of Israel. Theirs was a happy vocation, as this verse testifies.

Another word of the psalmist said, "I was glad when they said to me, 'Let us go to the house of the Lord.'" A Beatitude, remember, equals a statement of exalted happiness. Such was the experience of the biblical poets. Such can be our experience as well when we regularly engage in the worship of God.

A third Beatitude from the Book of Psalms is entirely different. We read, "Blessed is the person to whom the Lord charges no guilt and in whose spirit there is no deceit." As if to amplify that message and make it even clearer, a fourth Beatitude tells us, "Blessed is the person who walks not in the counsel of the wicked, nor stands in the way of sinners, nor sits in the seat of scoffers, but his delight is in the law of the Lord, and on this law he meditates day and night."

From these verses we learn that the good life consists in being forgiven, and then in being faithful. Oh, the happiness of putting behind us past failures and faults and all those things that separate us from God.

Once we have been forgiven, our calling is to be found faithful. Such a requirement is imparted by the very first psalm of the Bible, Psalm 1, when it explains, "Blessed [or happy] is the person who does not follow the advice of the wicked or take the path that sinners tread, or sit in the seat of the scornful." Immediately the psalmist shifts to a positive mood by writing that such a person's delight is found in meditating and studying the law of the Lord, and in doing that constantly, "day and night."

Transferring this text to our time, we can say that the law of the Lord embraces everything that declares the mind and heart of God, including preeminently the witness of Jesus.

Yet another Beatitude addresses us from the Psalms. Its words are these: "Blessed is the person who is considerate of the weak! The Lord delivers him in the day of trouble, the Lord protects him and keeps him alive. He is called happy in the land." What an array of promises for those individuals who care for the weak! But then, we should not be surprised. Our entire Bible advocates concern for the least of Earth's peoples: for the poor, the sick, the rejected, the disadvantaged.

World attention has been drawn to the life and death of Mother Teresa of Calcutta, India. There is a strong movement within the Catholic Church to name Mother Teresa a saint, not simply because she founded a worldwide religious order to serve the poor, but because she herself personified what it means to care for society's forgotten people. She sometimes was criticized for not boldly challenging those social structures that produce poverty and wretchedness. But for her there always was the immediate need of a hurting person, and meeting that need consumed all her energies.

In summary of these scriptural directives, these several Beatitudes of the Old Testament, we can resonate with the words of a final one: "How happy is everyone who reveres the Lord, who walks in all his ways!" Love of God and the pursuit of God's ways thus stand unchallenged as the prescription for life abundant, life happily consummated, life joyous and fulfilled.—John H. Townsend

SUNDAY, NOVEMBER 19, 2000
Lectionary Message
Topic: God Helps Those Who Cannot Help Themselves
TEXT: Heb. 10:11–14 (15–18), 19–25
Other Readings: 1 Sam. 1:4–20; Ps. 16; Mark 13:1–8

Many of us grew up in a culture and society that stresses initiative and self-reliance. Perhaps you were reminded more than once of the popular saying, "God helps those who help themselves." The truth is, however, that there are times in life when no matter how much initiative we exert, or how much self-reliance we muster, things just don't go very well. We find that we are inadequate and helpless in the face of many situations and circumstances. We feel we're doing our part, so why doesn't God help us? Well, the truth of the matter is that according to the gospel (the good news), God helps those who cannot help themselves. The writer of the New Testament book of Hebrews seems to make just that emphasis. God does, and has done, for us what we cannot do for ourselves. As we look at today's text, we see that clearly. We also see that when we accept the reality of that particular dimension of the gospel God energizes us with his power to live life victoriously.

I. In Christ's sacrifice, he has done for us what we could not do for ourselves. The author of Hebrews is writing to encourage believers as they face the enormous challenge of living faithfully in a hostile environment. In the first part of our text (vv. 11–14), he emphasizes the fact that repeated sacrifices by any priest, or any atoning action that we ourselves might attempt on our own behalf, will not result in the forgiveness of our sins. But because on the cross he did for us what we could not do for ourselves, we know the reality of forgiveness. Likewise, we are given the assurance a few sentences later (v. 17) that our "sins and lawless acts [he] will remember no more." Thus the redemptive act of his Crucifixion signals the completion of that sacrifice on his part, and we are reminded that Christ now sits at the right hand of God (v. 13). No matter what we do, it is only what Jesus has done that atones for our sins. Here indeed is good news!

II. The impact of his sacrifice sets us apart for his service. As recipients of God's grace through the sacrifice of Christ we enter the process of being shaped into the people of God, a process by which we are "being made holy" (v. 14). These words are reminiscent of those of Peter as he too wrote to early Christians words of encouragement: "You are a chosen people, a royal priesthood, a holy nation, a people belonging to God, that you may declare the praises of him who called you out of darkness into his wonderful light" (1 Pet. 2:9). In the midst of all the trials and challenges faced by the early church, they came to be imbued with hope and energized with purpose. Here indeed is more good news for us! For we too, living in a sometimes hostile world, because of what Christ has done for us, can live our lives dominated by hope. We can accept the challenge of God's call to be his holy people today, and in radical obedience prove ourselves faithful.

III. We are challenged to a "life together" in which we find strength for the journey of faith. In some circles of the Christian movement, individual faith experience is so emphasized as to be guilty of denigrating the corporate dimension of life in the community of faith. Not so in today's text. Against the backdrop of the glorious declaration of what God has done for us, which we could not do for ourselves, the author of the letter to the Hebrews challenges those who have experienced forgiveness of sin to join with others and to "spur one another on toward love and good deeds" (v. 24). They are challenged to continue meeting together in order to "encourage one another" (v. 25). In this passage is to be found an answer for those in our day who say that Christianity is too abstract or esoteric, that it is void of anything practical. Is there anything more practical than what is found here? The joining together of lives where individuals who together constitute that "holy nation," that "people belonging to God," might draw strength and encouragement from one another. That, indeed, is practical! Thus the call to Christ is a call to others also. We are called to watch over one another with a view to steadfastness in our faith and fruitfulness in our lives. The call to be involved in Christ's work in the world is no less a call to be involved with the whole family of God.

The issues addressed by our text are larger than any single facet of the Gospel story. They have to do with the reality and significance of the Incarnation itself. Christ came to us to be with us, to make clear the way to victorious living. In our strength that victory always seems to be characterized by elusiveness, and always seems to exceed our grasp. But here we are challenged to remember that Christ walked this way before us, and now he walks this way with us. In our weakness he promises to come to us with his strength, and he promises to bring into our lives and our experience others who will share with us the journey of faith. In those experiences of walking with him and our brothers and sisters in Christ, we discover again and again that God really does help those of us who cannot help ourselves.—Dwight A. Honeycutt

ILLUSTRATIONS

JESUS DOING WHAT ONLY GOD COULD DO.   Jesus does for men what only God could do. Here I am thinking particularly of the experience of being forgiven. Consider it like this. Suppose I do something which I know to be wrong. Suppose that thereupon I "rationalize" my action, finding palliating circumstances, and justifying myself to my own satisfaction. Is that the end of the matter? In my heart of hearts I know that something else is needed to deal with what has happened and to right the wrong. For what my act has done is to throw me out of gear, not only with my better nature, or with a moral ideal, but with the universe. The barrier is . . . between me and God. And that is the real barrier that must be dealt with. In other words, it is God who must forgive—else there is no true forgiveness possible. It is God who must put me right, or else the wrong remains unannulled. "Thou must save, and Thou alone."—James S. Stewart[6]

LIFE TOGETHER.   Dietrich Bonhoeffer (who died in 1945), the German pastor-theologian-martyr who was imprisoned and killed at the hands of the Nazi Gestapo, wrote a small volume on the significance of the church out of his experiences in an underground fellowship. The book was *Life Together*. In it, Bonhoeffer stressed the need for Christian community, that Christians are called in Christ to one another. Addressing the issue of the Church's ministry and the involvement of all within the community of faith, he wrote: "Strong and weak, wise and foolish, gifted or ungifted, pious or impious, the diverse individuals in the community, are no longer incentives for talking and judging and condemning, and thus excuses for self-justification. They are rather cause for rejoicing in one another and serving one another. Each member of the community is given his particular place, but this is no longer the place in which he can most successfully assert himself, but the place where he can best perform his service."[7]—Dwight A. Honeycutt

SERMON SUGGESTIONS

Topic: Whom Can We Trust?
TEXT: Jer. 17:5–10
(1) *Mere mortals*? (a) In most circumstances it is realistic and necessary. (b) Often it is perilous when we and they are out of sync with the Lord. (2) *The Lord*? (a) In all circumstances, when we "let God be God." (b) Experience will confirm the rightness of our trust.

Topic: Temptation
TEXT: James 1:12–18 REB
(1) Scripture counters the notion that temptation is necessarily evil. (2) Scripture emphatically denies that God is the source of temptation. (3) Yet God gives us the freedom to choose in the hour of trial. (a) Our own desires can lead us astray and culminate in our destruction. (b) Yet God brings his grace to bear in the lives of those who welcome his "good and generous action" to bring obedient choice to a fruitful, happy outcome.

---

[6] James S. Stewart, *The Strong Name* (Grand Rapids, Mich.: Baker Book House, 1972), p. 85.
[7] Dietrich Bonhoeffer, *Life Together* (New York: HarperCollins, 1954), pp. 93–94.

CONGREGATIONAL MUSIC

1. "I Come with Joy," Brian Wren (1968)

   DOVE OF PEACE, trad. American melody; arr. A. C. Lovelace

   This contemporary hymn written for communion captures the spirit of Psalm 16:11—by coming into God's presence we experience "fullness of joy." It is not inappropriate for the beginning of a worship service.

2. "Lord Christ, When First You Came to Earth," Walter Russell Bowie (1928)

   MIT FREUDEN ZART, Bohemian Brethren *Kirchengesänge* (1566)

   This is a good twentieth-century hymn on Christian responsibility to accompany the Gospel lesson (Mark 13:1–8) in which Jesus predicts the destruction of the Temple. Parts of stanza 1 are based on Mark 13:2.

3. "I Am Thine, O Lord," Fanny J. Crosby (1875)

   I AM THINE, William H. Doane (1875)

   The refrain of this familiar gospel song echoes Hebrews 10:22, in which we are encouraged to draw near to God with a sincere heart in full assurance of faith. It would make a meaningful introduction or response to the reading in Hebrews.

4. "When All Your Mercies, O My God," Joseph Addison (1712)

   WINCHESTER OLD Este's *Psalms* (1592); attr. George Kirbye

   The spirit of Psalm 16 is admirably reflected in the stanzas of this venerable hymn by one of the giants of English literature. After the reading of the psalm, the singing of this hymn in response would be meaningful.—Hugh T. McElrath

WORSHIP AIDS

CALL TO WORSHIP.   "You have made known to me the path of life; you will fill me with joy in your presence, with eternal pleasures at your right hand" (Ps. 16:11 NIV).

INVOCATION.   Lord, who loved us first and loves us always, draw us close as we draw close in worship. Speak to our deepest needs. Forgive our sins. Give us new visions for service and accept our fresh commitment for Jesus' sake.—E. Lee Phillips

OFFERTORY SENTENCE.   "If you try to save your life, you will lose it. But if you give it up for me, you will surely find it" (Matt. 10:39 CEV).

OFFERTORY PRAYER.   O God, our Father, you have given your people much work to do, works of love and mercy, as well as routine tasks important to your Church. We bring to you our offerings for all that you will do because of us and through us, thankful for our partnership with you and praying for your guidance and blessing as we serve.—E. Lee Phillips

PRAYER.   We are pilgrims in a dry and thirsty land, Father. With parched souls and hungry hearts we come today to the fountain of life for sustaining refreshment. The cares, burdens, and responsibilities of the day have sapped our strength and left us weary and worn. The struggles have taxed our resolve and sins have clogged our vision of you. Refresh us this morning, we pray, as we wait before you.

Refresh our hope today, we pray. Events of past days and known happenings coming to us in the near future dim the light of hope within our lives. Rekindle the fires that have long smoldered on the altar hearth of our hearts. Remind us anew that Christ, the giver of all hope, has not been defeated by past events, nor will he be stymied by a fearful future. In the light of his truth refresh our hopes today, we pray.

Refresh our love this morning, we pray. It is easy to allow the fringes of hate to intrude into our emotions and stain the purity of real love. We have all been crippled by hate's claim upon us, making us less than we are meant to be. In this sacred moment of time, break every barrier down, cleanse every stain from our hearts and let all hate, jealously, malice, and envy be swallowed up in a love that seeks the highest good for other persons no matter how we feel about them, no matter what they have done to us, and no matter the cost of meeting their need. Call us to you and refresh our love from the fountain of your redeeming heart, we plead.

Refresh our faith as we worship this morning. Let it truly remind us of the foundations of sacrifice, truth, love, and redemption that sustain every believer and follower of the Lord. Impress on our hearts and minds the strength of the Lord's living presence, that we may go from this hour to meet the world with a renewed and fortified faith in him who is light and life eternal.—Henry Fields

SERMON
Topic: Servants Together
Text: Luke 22:17–27

I. *Who is the greatest?* "I am among you as one who serves." These words were spoken by Jesus to his twelve disciples. Jesus clearly was the leader of those men, yet he said, "I am the one who is servant among you." The situation was a most interesting one when that statement was made. It was the occasion when Jesus took bread and wine at the supper table and interpreted these things as his body and blood—as his very life, which would be sacrificed for the sake of his friends.

No sooner had Jesus spoken in such a startling way than a dispute arose among the twelve. Because Jesus had said that one of them would betray him, they debated about who could possibly do such a thing. A turn in the discussion suddenly found them on another subject, specifically, who should be considered the most important. How quickly the initial message was forgotten—Jesus' dramatic statement about offering his life. Concerns about their own lives became enormously important instead. Patiently Jesus dealt with this new issue. Before he was through he reassured the disciples of their individual importance in the sight of God; they would not be forgotten. But there was something they first needed to understand. "Your greatest man must become like a junior and your leader must be a servant." Then he asked them, "Who is greater, the one who sits down to dinner or the one who serves it? Obviously, the one who sits down to dinner—yet *I* am the one who is the servant among you."

Another thing happened at the Last Supper Jesus shared with his disciples. As Luke's Gospel has it, he talked to them about servanthood, redirecting their thinking about personal status and importance, and he named himself as a servant in their midst. Lest there be any mistake about this, Jesus then turned from speaking to acting. The Gospel of John records that action. We read that Jesus rose from the table, removed his outer garment, and wrapped a towel around his waist. Pouring water into a basin, he proceeded to wash his disciples' feet, drying them with the towel he was wearing.

His gesture was unprecedented. That is to say, Jesus as their leader appropriately might have been waited on in this way but never would be the one to do it. In the Palestine of that time, foot washing was commonplace as people concluded their walking journeys. Dusty roads and open sandals made such activity a welcome amenity. Apparently no one had rendered this bit of hospitality when Jesus and the twelve had gathered for their Passover meal. So it was that he did it—the one whom they called teacher and Lord assumed the menial duty. Jesus stooped to wash the feet of his friends.

The force of this drama was not lost on the disciples. Their earlier squabble about who was the most important paled to insignificance. A tense moment occurred when Peter staunchly refused to let Jesus wash *his* feet. This behavior violated Peter's sense of what was socially proper and acceptable. By resisting, Peter thought he was setting things right again. But it was not to be. Jesus responded simply, "If I don't wash you, you don't really belong to me." Thereupon Peter, with typical extravagance, answered, "Lord, don't wash just my feet. Wash my hands and my head." That was not necessary, said Jesus; what mattered was this, as Jesus explained: "You call me your teacher and Lord, and you should, because that is who I am. And if your Lord and teacher has washed your feet, you should do the same for each other. I have set the example, and you should do for each other what I have done for you." Servanthood is honorable, Jesus was saying, and the distinctions people tend to make among themselves are totally irrelevant.

II. *The indispensable ingredient.* Servanthood: it was the example given by Jesus and the pattern of living expected of his followers. Apart from being told about Peter, we are not told how the disciples reacted as Jesus made his point. What we know of their subsequent behavior indicates that some of them, at least, took to heart this fundamental instruction. It is a message that cries to be repeated, declaring that the servant nature is the Jesuslike nature.

It is also correct to say that we are servants together—all of us who seek to follow Jesus and witness to his way. In church life as we know it there are varieties of gifts represented among us and different responsibilities, but we all bear the same title: servant. We are in our world as those who serve. This is an unpretentious identification, but one possessed with an exalted meaning. Because of the one whose example we follow, we are involved in holy and sacred acts whenever we live to serve.—John H. Townsend

SUNDAY, NOVEMBER 26, 2000
Lectionary Message

Topic: Christ Our King!
Text: John 18:33–37
Other Readings: 2 Sam. 23:1–7; Ps. 132:1–12 (13–18); Rev. 1:4–8

In the Western world today, where kings and queens wield little power and assume positions more as figureheads or national symbols, many people are still enamored with royalty. Multitudes gather outside palaces hoping to catch a quick glimpse of some royal figure. Great curiosity attends kings, queens, princes, and princesses. It seems that such curiosity is capable of supporting a whole publishing industry that keeps those who are interested informed of royalty's every move. Even people in countries where there is not royal family will show great interest in someone else's king or queen. In the text from John's Gospel, we see one who long ago was viewed as a king. It is Jesus. And in that particular setting, Pilate, in asking if Jesus is the king of the Jews, causes the honest reader to ask himself, Whose king is he? Is he someone else's king? Or is he *our* king?

I. *A strange kind of king.* Pilate asked, "Are you the king of the Jews?" Pilate certainly knew a king when he saw one, and Jesus did not look at all like a king. Even a few days earlier, on Palm Sunday, when Jesus entered Jerusalem some had sung his praises and acclaimed him as a king. But what a strange kind of king he seemed to be. There was nothing about him that appeared "kingly." In response to Pilate, Jesus did not cite any earthly territory for which he claimed sovereignty as an earthly king. Indeed, the response of Jesus must have sounded exceptionally strange to Pilate: "My kingdom is not of this world." But a king he was, because in a further response he said to Pilate, "You are right in saying I am a king. In fact, for this reason I was born."

II. *Kingship redefined.* When we recognize Christ as King, it is obvious that his kingship is in many ways radically different from what those in Pilate's day would have understood. Kings prided themselves on their status. All of society's response was geared to exalt them. Kings used their authority, power, and might to exact loyalty and obedience. They did not hesitate to inflict punishment in order to get their way. But what about this King Jesus? His way appears totally antithetical to that kind of kingship. Here in Jesus was a king who showed compassion to his people, and wept in the face of their suffering and need. Here in Jesus was a king who sought not to extract something from people but to give them forgiveness, salvation, and hope. Here in Jesus was a king who through grace transformed servitude into friendship. Here in Jesus was a king exalted not on an earthly throne with a gold crown, but on a cross, and who in humility bowed his thorn-crowned head. Here in Jesus was a king who did not set out to punish his enemies but to forgive them and to die for the whole world. Yes, the Jesus standing before Pilate so long ago was a king. His kingship defied understanding then, and subsequent generations have continued to grapple with understanding kingship in the mode cast by Jesus.

III. *Christ, our King!* Pilate initially asked, "Are you the king of the Jews?" Whose king is he? Is he the king of a particular people? Do we see him in our day as a king of ancient curiosity? Someone interesting to read about, like the Royals of England? Is he someone else's king? He is a king. He said so himself. But whose king is he?

His life, his teachings, his death, his Resurrection—everything about the Christ event—challenge us to face that question: Whose king is he? It ultimately comes down to that. It is a question much more applicable to our lives than to Pilate's. For to confront Jesus is to confront ourselves. The real question is, Is he our king? Is he our king, the one whom we, in our attitudes and actions, seek to honor and exalt? Pilate questioned Jesus. But today it is Christ who confronts us with the questions. Will we permit Jesus the Christ to rule in our lives as *our* King?

There he is, Jesus *our* King! And take notice that our King does not ask us to keep our distance but rather invites us to come close into his circle of friends. In conversation with his disciples, Jesus, this most unlikely of kings, once said: "Greater love has no one than this, that he lay down his life for his friends" (John 14:13). Of course it is true that in all our lives there will be those moments and seasons when we will not be able to understand, when we will be hurt, and when we will be met with silence. But even in those moments, even in the darkness, will be found the presence of *our* King—*our* friend. And the good news is that we need never cower before him in fear, but simply respond to him in faith, with assurance and hope.—Dwight A. Honeycutt

ILLUSTRATIONS

A SAD CLAIM TO FAME.   Henry Sloan Coffin, in a masterfully written small volume on the cross, gives a characterization of several individuals whom he calls "crucifiers" of Jesus. One of the persons he treats is Pilate. Coffin offers this sad description: "To the last Pilate was uncomfortable about the case. He did his best to shift responsibility—on Herod, on the crowd, on the priests. But the priests knew their man and played skillfully upon his loyalties and his fears. The fourth evangelist makes them say: 'If thou release this man, thou are not Caesar's friend.' Fidelity to Caesar was both a Roman's patriotism and his religion. They were appealing to Pilate's principles, and they won their point. Pilate washed his hands, but throughout the centuries his name has been coupled with this event as responsible for it on the lips of thousands who repeat 'crucified under Pontius Pilate.'"[8]—Dwight A. Honeycutt

THE KINGDOM NOT OF THIS WORLD.   If Jesus' kingdom were "of this world," he would certainly have been rescued by his disciples. If the gospel needed to be vindicated by a show of power, his trial and execution would have been the moment to provide it. The fact that nobody came to Jesus' rescue, even though he could have called upon legions of angels to defend him, is a good indication of the nature of this kingdom. It means that the kingdom is present without our being rescued from our difficulties and the consequences of our sinfulness. God is present in our lives and deaths just as they are. Whatever happens, the divine presence and action—not as we would like it to function, but as it actually functions—is secretly changing, not the painful circumstances of our lives, but our attitude toward them. In this kingdom we experience our brokenness and our trust in God rather than our virtue and our trust in ourselves.—Thomas Keating[9]

SERMON SUGGESTIONS

Topic: Prayer from the Depths of Need

TEXT: Ps. 51

(1) For mercy and forgiveness (vv. 1–2). (2) For wisdom (v. 6). (3) For purity of heart (v. 10). (4) For protection (v. 14). (5) For freedom to praise God.

Topic: Special Reasons for Praising God

TEXT: Eph. 1:4–14.

(1) We should praise God because he has elected us in Christ (vv. 4–6). (2) We should praise God because he has dealt with us according to the riches of his grace (vv. 7–12). (3) We should praise God because he has sealed us with the Holy Spirit until we acquire full possession of our inheritance (vv. 13–14).—Haddon W. Robinson

---

[8] Henry Sloan Coffin, *The Meaning of the Cross* (New York: Scribner, 1959), p. 19.
[9] Thomas Keating, *The Kingdom of God Is Like. . . .* (New York: Crossroad, 1997), p. 87.

CONGREGATIONAL MUSIC

1. "Lo! He Comes with Clouds Descending," Charles Wesley (1758)

    HELMSLEY, Augustine Arne (1761); harm. R. V. Williams (1906)

    Based on Revelation 1:7, this Wesleyan hymn is eminently appropriate for the emphasis of this particular Sunday preceding the beginning of Advent.

2. "God of Jacob, Please Remember," Psalm 132, vers. Calvin Seerveld (1983)

    BLAENWERN, William P. Rowlands (1915)

    The last three stanzas of this free paraphrase of Psalm 132 equate with the assigned reading in the Psalter. God's promise to bless the progeny of David from which ultimately Christ would come is in keeping with the celebration of Christ the King.

3. "My Song Is Love Unknown," Samuel Crossman (1664)

    LOVE UNKNOWN, John Ireland (1818)

    This ancient hymn is a profoundly effective reflection on the entire passion of our Lord, of which the Gospel lesson (John 18:33–37) is an excerpt. The third stanza recalls the triumphant entry into Jerusalem in which Christ was adored as King—a thought central to this Sunday's focus.

4. "Our World Belongs to God," Marie J. Post (1987)

    RHOSYMEDRE, John D. Edwards (c. 1840)

    David's last words (2 Sam. 23:107) affirmed God's everlasting covenant with his people, thus ensuring the divine plan of salvation. This very modern hymn in stanza 2 speaks of God's great covenant love that many have ignored as it celebrates God's sovereignty and providence. Its tune is quite accessible for congregational singing.—Hugh T. McElrath

WORSHIP AIDS

CALL TO WORSHIP.   "Then the seventh angel blew his trumpet, and there were loud voices in heaven, saying, 'The power to rule over the world belongs now to our Lord and his Messiah, and he will rule forever and ever!'" (Rev. 11:15 TEV).

INVOCATION.   Spare us not from the reality of thy presence, Holy God. Let us lay aside every encumbrance, so that in worship we may find God and be found of the God who brought us in love to this hour.—E. Lee Phillips.

OFFERTORY SENTENCE.   "Offer unto God thanksgiving; and pay thy vows unto the most High" (Ps. 50:14).

OFFERTORY PRAYER.   None of us, our Father, has failed to promise thee better than we do, or at least to yearn to do better. Now may we begin to pay off our promises in earnest and bring our good intentions to definite expression. Receive our tithes and offerings today as our sacrifices of thanksgiving and as payment of our vows.

PRAYER.   O Lord, our Maker, Uncreated Light, in whom we live and move and have our being, all glory and honor to your name. Know our hearts and accept our worship this day.

We confess, O Lord, to saying what we do not mean, acting before praying, being smug instead of concerned. Forgive all detachment in us that runs from the need clearly in our path. Show us the Christ who took time for the needy, turning interruptions into Epiphanies of new faith.

Not just at this season, Lord God, but all through the year, we are grateful for gifts of sustenance and friends. But at this time of harvest, ripe with pumpkin and gourd, bright with scarlet leaves and berries of orange, doused with glad sunshine and refreshing rain, we are especially grateful. Here is epitomized freedom and liberty paid for at no small price; let us not forget. We enjoy the highest rate of living in the world; may we ever be grateful. And "to whom much is given much is required." Therefore let us ever be generous stewards in Christ's name.

And no matter how much we give, how many programs we begin, how many buildings we build, or how many people we serve, never let pride usurp compassion nor wealth negate sacrifice, lest we lose sight of the Christ of Calvary, whom to serve is joy and to avow in the need of others is true purpose for living.

We pray for those who do not pray—they don't know how or they disbelieve. We remember those who have barely enough to get by, in refugee camps across the globe and in our own backyard. We pray for those whose pain is greater than they can share. Aid those who are embedded in ways of life that are ruinous and want out. Some have too much and others never have enough and thus have turned to darkness and shadows that are always counterfeit. Some here are in the throes of grief while others barely hang on, the victims of belittlement for whom the battle of self-esteem and sanity never seems to end. Lord, comfort those who hurt, lift the fallen, hide powerful Scriptures in broken hearts. Lead each of us to speak the Word of faith from a God of love, then put foot to our prayers in the blessed name of Jesus. As a tree at harvest is known by its fruit, let our fruit be a harvest in which God is well pleased.

Now, Father, God, as we journey from Thanksgiving to Advent, cause us to recall again the miraculous inbreak of our Savior in human form in the most inauspicious of surroundings. Let gratitude merge with incarnational hope to make this people in this community of faith reflectors of holy light that never flickers, never vanishes, can never be extinguished because it is the light of God proclaiming news of "great joy" that "is come for all people," even Christ the Lord, in whose name we pray.—E. Lee Phillips

SERMON
Topic: Every Knee Shall Bow
TEXT: Rev. 1:4–8

It is one of the great questions of life: Why are we here? Where did we come from? What are we supposed to be doing? And where does it all lead? What happens after death?

What happens when you die? If nothing else happens, we at least ought to get a chance to get answers to all our questions. Where is Jimmy Hoffa and who killed him? Why did Algie Toomer get paid $100,000? Did the au pair girl kill that baby? Why did we always make the same mistake over and over with the ones we loved? Was the hole in the ozone layer really getting larger or not? Heaven ought at least to be a place where all mysteries are solved and all questions answered. And at the end of that discussion somebody else asks, "Do you think we will even care in Heaven?"

How does life end? How does history end? Where do we end up at the end? For one, a place where all questions are answered; for another, a place of such different quality of life that the old questions won't even be important. Ian and Sylvia, a Canadian folk singing group in the late sixties, had a song about the painful pilgrimage to paradise, and they observed: "Some people speak of pastures where the milk and honey flow, but I have no such illusions of the place I want to go." Isaiah talked about the place where the lion and the lamb would lie down together.

There has always been the tendency among Christians to say more than they know. We get caught up in trying to give answers to questions for which we really have no answers. Somehow we think the existence of God depends on being able to give answers to impossible questions. Faith may be the playing of God's silences over and over again in our lives. Faith may be the sharing of our hopes about such questions, our visions in response to questions.

For after all, if we are to be bearers of good news, if as Christian people we have a story to tell that is to bring joy, comfort, and hope to people, the story will have to suggest an ending that is fitting for the good news. What kind of good-news story would it be if our story were about all these people who are all good looking, all famous and rich, about all the children who were above average and had wonderful, helpful, caring lives and died a tortuous death with bubonic plague? John on the island of Patmos wondered about the end of the story and had a revelation.

He had been sent to the island of Patmos as his punishment. Other Christians of the early church were suffering from persecution, taunting, and discrimination from the Jewish communities out of which most of them had come, and from the Roman officials, because as Christians they refused to acknowledge the crazy Caesar as God. John shared his vision in which he saw that in the end the grace, mercy, and peace of Jesus Christ will be recognized, worshiped, and celebrated by all people.

"Oh, brothers and sisters," John suggested, "it is obvious that we are not being treated well now, but the story ends with our Lord being recognized as Lord of all, our statement that Jesus is Lord and not Caesar being said by all, and our vision that Jesus was God at work for our redemption being celebrated by all people. Don't give up. Don't capitulate. Do not forsake your faith, for the story ends well. Our story as Christian disciples ends just as Jesus' story of the Crucifixion ends, in resurrection, not death; in recognition, not oblivion; in celebration, not tears."

It was a gift of the Holy Spirit to John to create a vision of the end that they could hold onto and by which they would be inspired in faithful living. By the gift of God's Spirit John evoked a vision of the new reality, the new kingdom, the consummation of history—a vision that brought the story to a fitting end. John gave them a vision of a new reality.

John created the vision of a new way of living, a new way for history to come out, that brings the good news of the story of the Christian faith to a fitting and hopeful ending. With that new alternative, that new vision, the early Christians could live, holding onto the vision of how the story ends.

Where do we go when we die? What happens to us? What can we say of this vision of how the story ends? The astrologers, astronomers, and rocket scientists tell us they do not see this place called heaven within the spaces above us. The theological bean counters attempt to imagine the spaces necessary to sustain all the lives and animals and creatures that have existed from the first time. Where could such a huge number of people be? How would we ever find our own family members when we get there?

John's vision was that all will end as it began, in the love and providence of God. The end will be in the beginning, Alpha and Omega. Creation began because God called it into being and creation will end when God calls it home to himself. The end will be the fulfillment of the beginning. God created because God desired fellowship with creation. Creation will end in complete fellowship with God. At the end of creation God celebrated that great Sabbath Rest, God's great smile and satisfaction with all that he had made, and creation will end in the establishment of the eternal rest of the final coming of God, God's great smile of satisfaction that all is as God intended it to be.

The Omega is the Alpha. The end is the beginning. The love of God that began us is the love of God that has redeemed us and the love of God to which we will come home in the end.

This week we are all getting our great wish. Why doesn't the media tell us good news, happy things, nice stories? Lots of the news this week has been about the amazing accomplishment and intimidating prospect of what in the world do you do with seven babies? But those seven babies are now discovering what the rest of us discovered, that the first six months of your life do not properly prepare you for the rest of it. All human beings begin in darkness. For six months those seven babies lived like fish, in water; they breathed through a tube in their stomachs and they received their nourishment by an internal IV system. What kind of credence do you think they would have given to anyone who told them about living in dry air? If you had told them that there was such a thing as sunlight or simply light? Told them they would have to breathe through their noses and chew their own food? That they would have to stand and walk? Very little of what we experience for the first nine months of life prepares us for the rest of it, and yet it all is critical development for the rest of it.

Whatever our vision may be of the coming home to God, of God coming to gather us into his home, of God coming to be recognized by all as Lord and Sovereign over all history, whatever there is next for human reality, it too is God's gift. It too is God's purpose, it too grows out of God's love for us and for all creation. Maybe it is a place of milk and honey. That would be nice if hunger no longer troubled a single stomach, if there were enough for all, except that would not be new because there already is enough for all to eat in this life and we just haven't discovered how to share. It may be streets of gold and pearly gates, and the Dow Jones over 10,000 and everybody fully vested in social security—if life were only economic. It may be a new spiritual reality that abides right here in this creation but that our current physical realities cannot and will not see.

But John's vision saw the end of the story where it had begun, in God's love. John described a new possibility for how the story would end that continued the good news of the gospel to those in times of persecution. John's poetry still is our faith claim: life began in God and will end in God. And when it comes to an end, all will recognize, affirm, confess, and celebrate that love.—Rick Brand

SUNDAY, DECEMBER 3, 2000
Lectionary Message
Topic: Get Ready—Here Comes Jesus

TEXT: Luke 21:25–36

Other Readings: Jer. 33:14–16; Ps. 25:1–10; 1 Thess. 3:9–13

The purpose of the Advent season is to get us ready for the coming of Christ. That is why Advent services bump up against Christmas every year as we celebrate the birth of Jesus. But our text is about events that happened immediately before Jesus' death, not his birth. Why choose this text for the first Sunday of Advent? Hold that question until we explore some other questions that may help us discover the answer.

I. *Three questions that surround the text* (Luke 21:25–36).

(a) Question 1: Who was responsible for destroying the Temple and capturing Jerusalem? Answer: Titus, the Roman Emperor in 70 A.D., with his legions; God in his providence, fulfilling a number of Old Testament prophecies; and the Jewish leaders, when they refused to receive their King as he came into their city a few hours before they crucified him.

(b) Question 2: How did Jesus initiate his Kingdom? He made two entries into Jerusalem as the promised King.

(1) He entered Jerusalem riding on a donkey, knowing he would be rejected. He came to the Temple as Israel's promised King amid shouts of hosannas and with palm branches strewn in his path, received in triumph on the day we call Palm Sunday. But the leaders rejected him and by the following Friday they had crucified him.

(2) He entered the city again in relative secrecy to keep the Passover in an upper room with his disciples. "I have eagerly desired to eat this Passover with you before I suffer," he said. "For I tell you, I will not eat it again until it finds fulfillment in the Kingdom of God" (Luke 22:15).

(c) Question 3: Why did Jesus talk about the destruction of Jerusalem and the Temple in the same breath as the end of the world? Probably because the catastrophic events of the fall of Jerusalem foreshadowed the even greater catastrophic events to come at the end of the world. Jerusalem had rejected her King, and God would bring utter destruction on the Holy City and the Temple. They would have a few more years to repent after the death, burial, and Resurrection of Christ and the founding of his Church, but in 70 A.D. the power of Rome demolished Jerusalem. Jesus warned them to flee from the city; he lamented women with child and mothers with young children, he warned that many would die by the sword or be taken prisoner, and he stated that Jerusalem would be trampled on by the Gentiles until their time is fulfilled.

II. *Two questions that address the Scripture text* (Luke 21:25–36).

(a) How can we know when he will return to earth in triumph as he promised?

(1) The answer is not simple because Jesus himself said, "You do not know the day nor the hour when the Son of Man comes." The truth is that only God knows when.

(2) The answer is not simple because many false prophets will come into the world in Christ's name claiming "I am he" and "the time is near." "Do not follow them," Jesus warned (Luke 21:8).

(3) The answer is not simple because Jesus prophesied his return with certainty: "There will be signs in the sun, moon, and stars. On the earth, nations will be in anguish and per-

plexity at the roaring and tossing of the sea. Men will faint from terror, apprehensive of what is coming on the world, for the heavenly bodies will be shaken. At that time they will see the Son of Man coming in a cloud with power and great glory" (Luke 21:25–27).

(4) The bottom line is this: we may not know the day nor the hour when he will return, but he is certain to return and we need to be ready. "Heaven and earth may pass away," he said, "but my word will never pass away" (Luke 21:32).

(c) What can we as Christians expect when he comes again (or when through death we go to be with him)? He tells us to stand up and lift up our heads because our redemption is drawing near. He assures us that the Kingdom of God is near. He tells us not to be weighed down by sin and anxiety. He urges us always to watch and pray in order to escape all that is about to happen and to be able to stand before the Son of Man. And Christ modeled that for us. In just a few hours he would be betrayed and crucified, and he was already talking about his victorious return.

III. Now we return to our opening question: Why choose this text to usher in Advent? Because it helps us to see the big picture. His birth is to be seen in the light of his life, his ministry, and his second coming. Advent is not just about a baby and a stable but about the cross and the empty grave and about Christ's ascension and second advent, and about God's great scheme of redemption for the human race. Ours is to be a life of service in light of his coming and his coming again. Get ready, here comes Jesus.—Wayne Shaw

ILLUSTRATIONS

THE END OF HISTORY.   Our generation is able to listen with fresh attentiveness to those passages in the New Testament which speak about the end of history. We can understand their urgency for we also carry on our activities with a haunting sense that time may be running out. And we can understand their sharp clarity; for most of the desires and ambitions which seem to be important when an indefinite number of years stretch ahead turn out to be petty and worthless when seen in the white light of eternity.—David E. Roberts[1]

COME, LORD JESUS!   "Batter my heart, three person'd God!" And you can say, if not that, at least something like it. "Lord, here am I. I really want to let you in. But I have so little faith. I have forgotten how to pray. I am such an ordinary, unspiritual creature. I have tried to open the door but, Lord, there is the rust, the accumulated rust of years upon the bolts. You must do it for me. Break through! Smash that rusty lock. Batter my heart, three-personed God! And even so—yes, even so—come, Lord Jesus!"—James Stewart[2]

SERMON SUGGESTIONS

Topic: Human Greatness and Divine Greatness

TEXT: Isa. 57:15

(1) That in which the greatness of God consists. (2) That in which human greatness consists.—F. W. Robertson[3]

---

[1] *The Grandeur and Misery of Man*
[2] *King for Ever*
[3] Adapted from *Sermons*

Topic: A World Gone Sane
TEXT: Phil. 2:5
(1) A world gone sane would put human life and welfare at the center. (2) In a world gone sane, people would seek the things that bring lasting satisfaction. (3) A world gone sane would see that adjustment to the moral and spiritual order is the indispensable condition of human survival and welfare.—Halford E. Luccock[4]

CONGREGATIONAL MUSIC

1. "Jesus Came, Adored by Angels," Godfrey Thring (1866)
   LOWRY, Gerald Near (c. 1984)
   This contemporary hymn with its comprehensive sweep of thought concerning the comings of Jesus could be meaningful used as a response to the Gospel lesson (Luke 2:25–36) where Jesus teaches about his second coming.
2. "O Heavenly Word, Eternal Light," Latin
   O HEILAND, REISS, *Rheinfelsische Deutsches Catholisches Gesangbuch* (1666)
   The apostle Paul's prayerful wish for the Thessalonians (1 Thess. 3:11–14) finds a musical parallel in this ancient hymn. The prayer that love may increase so that we may be established in holiness, looking to that day when all hearts will be judged, is voiced here. It is set to a simple though doubtless unfamiliar tune that can be easily learned when led by a good organ and choir.
3. "O Come, O Come, Emmanuel," Latin (ninth century)
   VENI, VENI, EMMANUEL, plainsong (fifteenth century)
   No advent season should pass without the use of this plaintive hymn calling for the coming of Emmanuel—God with Us. It relates particularly well to the Old Testament reading from the prophecy of Jeremiah (33:14–16), with its reference to the Branch of David ("Branch of Jesse's Stem").
4. "Lord, to You My Soul Is Lifted," Stanley Wiersma (1980)
   GENEVAN 25, Louis Bourgeois (1551)
   This contemporary metrical setting of Psalm 25 could be sung antiphonally by choir and congregation in place of the Psalter reading.—Hugh T. McElrath

WORSHIP AIDS

CALL TO WORSHIP.   "Lift up your heads, O ye gates; even lift them up, ye everlasting doors; and the King of glory shall come in. Who is this King of glory? The Lord of hosts, he is the King of glory" (Ps. 24:9–10).

INVOCATION.   You come to us, O Lord. Into our poverty comes your wealth. Into our emptiness comes your wealth. Into our emptiness comes your fullness. Into our ugliness comes your beauty. Make us ready to open ourselves to you. Break down the walls behind which we hide ourselves. Quench the fear that burns in us, and our shame before you. You come, and make us rich and great and lovely. Come, Lord, come soon.—Jürgen Moltmann[5]

---

[4] Adapted from *Unfinished Business*
[5] *The Power of the Powerless*

OFFERTORY SENTENCE.   "Forget not to be kind and liberal; for with that sort of sacrifice God is well pleased" (Heb. 13:16 Montgomery).

OFFERTORY PRAYER.   Our Father, we confess that often we have sought everything but thy kingdom and thy righteousness. Guide us and strengthen us as we attempt to establish our true priorities, assured that if we attend to what is most important, the less important things will fall into place.

PRAYER.   We come to you, O Lord, with the glint of heavenly radiance in our eyes. Your star has shone before us and we have followed its light. Our pathway has been made plain by the illumination of the meaning of life through Jesus Christ, our Lord. We have seen the light and we have chosen to follow.

The pathway in this season of Christmas sparkles with the hopes and fears of all the years. Memories take us back to loved ones now gone who have taken up residence in their eternal home. Their celebration of Christmas this year is a celebration of the manger experience they have never before known. The light they follow has the aura of eternal brightness. Gone is all fear as the security of being welcomed fully into the family of God is secured.

The hope we all feel is in the fact that once again we are reassured by angel voices, the trumpet calls of the messengers of love, telling us of the coming of the Prince of Peace. We are grateful that in all things, O Lord, you are working for the good of your whole creation, restoring us to our truest home. And so we gather, sisters and brothers in the faith, in adoration of the miracle of Christmas, to celebrate the birth of God's Son into the manger of our hearts.

With all the expectant faithful on earth and in heaven we cry out, "Come, Lord Jesus," in whose name we pray.—Robert F. Langwig

SERMON
Topic: The Urgency of the Hour
TEXT: Matt. 4:17

It was with a sense of finality that Jesus burst upon the scene in ancient Galilee to deliver God's ultimatum to Israel. His first public act was to identify with the conviction of John the Baptist that "the Kingdom of God is at hand" (Matt. 3:2; 4:17). No insistence was more characteristic of everything he said and did.

A close look at all of his parables suggests that the urgency of Jesus was rooted in three dominant convictions.

I. *The house of crisis will be sudden.* First, Jesus was convinced that the crises of life are sudden. His stories were full of examples of unexpected developments that changed everything at a moment's notice. By reminding his hearers of these everyday occurrences, Jesus was asserting that we cannot control our crises, that they often come when we least expect them, and therefore the time to get ready for them is now!

Almost every day I deal with someone floundering through an ordeal simply because it erupted with such suddenness. The best way to be free of fear is not to forget deathbed realities but to remember that we are all vulnerable and so get ready before the unpredictable strikes. The Boy Scout motto effectively summarizes this concern of Jesus: "Be Prepared!"

II. *The hour of crisis will be surprising.* A second conviction of Jesus was that the crises of life are not only sudden but also surprising. The basic reason for this lay in his assumption that our standing in heaven is fundamentally different from our standing on earth, that human status in the sight of man has no bearing on eternal status in the sight of God. The Lukan Beatitudes tersely describe a great reversal: those who are poor now shall receive the Kingdom then, those who hunger now shall be satisfied then, those who weep now shall laugh then, those who are hated now shall rejoice then (Luke 6:20–23).

This dramatic turnabout was vividly depicted in the parables of Jesus. He told of a rich man clothed in purple and fine linen who feasted sumptuously every day while at his gate lay a beggar who ate scraps from his table as the dogs licked his sores. When they both died, however, the rich man was consigned to the fiery torment of Hades while the poor man was transported to the bosom of Abraham (Luke 16:19–31). He told of a Pharisee who prayed like a virtuoso in contrast to a lowly publican who dared not pray at all except to cry for mercy. The shocking verdict on their efforts, however, was that the sinful publican rather than the pious Pharisee was justified in the sight of God (Luke 18:9–14).

Perhaps the most vivid illustration of this truth by Jesus was his depiction of the last judgment, which we may call the Parable of Great Surprises. The shocker was not that a process of sifting would occur, but that both groups would be startled by the results. Sheep and goats alike incredulously confessed that they were oblivious to those opportunities that had determined their destinies. Imagine, those certain that they would be favored found themselves excluded, while those with no hope of inclusion found themselves accepted (Matt. 25:31–46).

In defining eternity as one big surprise, Jesus was not shattering all religious assurance or destroying all hope for the future. Rather, he was insisting that our confidence must rest not in anything earthly but only in God. Hence the urgency of his plea: if you would be ready for the great reversal, and not be dumbfounded by its decrees, then deal decisively with God himself on his own terms and do it *now!*

III. *The hour of crisis will be soon.* A third conviction of Jesus is also disturbing in its import, that the crises of life are not only sudden and surprising but they are sure to come very soon. We are tempted to complain that if one cannot evade either the swiftness of crisis or its startling demands, then at least God should stay his hand until we can get ready for such an ordeal. But Jesus would not have it so. For him, a showdown was already looming on the horizon. Events were rushing to their intended consummation. A new day was dawning. The Kingdom of God was at hand (Matt. 4:17).

Everything in the proclamation of Jesus breathed this note of imminence.

At first glance it might seem impossible to sustain that incredible intensity for two thousand years, but experience teaches otherwise. Perhaps our most frequent failing in spiritual affairs is to misjudge the amount of available time. The southern church thought it could put off dealing with the slavery issue only to find itself in the bloodbath of a national conflagration. For too long Christian leaders dodged the evolution controversy, hoping that those nasty theories of Darwin would simply fade away, only to discover that once-sympathetic universities had left them to embrace the new scientific secularism. History has a rude way of rushing on past those who suppose that God will let the clock stand still.

To recover the urgency of Jesus is not to attack the virtues of prudence and patience. We may grant that long slow years are needed to fashion a solid character. But to those who contend that "Rome was not built in a day," we would respond that it was begun in a day and that, precisely because it may take so long to complete the job, there is no better time to get started than now!—William E. Hull

SUNDAY, DECEMBER 10, 2000
Lectionary Message
Topic: The Proclamation of a Tongue-Tied Priest
TEXT: Luke 1:68–79
Other Readings: Mal. 3:1–4; Phil. 1:3–11; Luke 3:1–6

I. *A tongue-tied priest.* Zechariah was disciplined by God for his unbelief. He had been faithful all his life, faithful enough to be chosen as a priest for special duty in the Temple at Jerusalem. His wife Elizabeth had stood by his side and shared his faith, though it had not always been easy. There remained one great disappointment in their lives. They had asked God for years to give them a child to bless their home and to erase the shame of their being childless, but their prayers had gone unanswered, and as the years aged them they gave up on ever becoming parents. Then suddenly, dramatically, Gabriel, the angel of the Lord, appeared to Zechariah and told him he was to be a father of a son named John who would lead many back to the Lord and who would prepare the way for the Messiah. But the news was so stupendous that he didn't believe it. He believed that the angel was a messenger sent by God, but he didn't believe the message he brought. And because he didn't believe the messenger of God, he was struck dumb. He completed his Temple service as usual, but he couldn't utter a word. The Bible makes it clear that it was because of his unbelief. After all those years of faithful service, he lost his speech in a moment of unpremeditated disbelief.

Does this scenario sound familiar? It hardly seems fair. A person you know well has attempted to live for Christ all across the years. He or she is a faithful worker in the church. Then, in a sudden moment of crisis, faith caves in and all those years of trusting God evaporate like the morning dew. God seems far away and a deep sense of failure sweeps across the soul. Aren't we ever allowed to slip into unbelief? Don't we do it all too often? And if a veteran priest has lapses in his faith, what chance do we have?

Is God too demanding? Well, at least he knows how to get our attention. We have our religious routine down pat and it works for us—perhaps for years. And then something happens to shake our faith to the core. It may be some unexpected tragedy that runs through our soul like a white hot knife, or it may be an unexpected blessing that takes us by surprise—a sudden new challenge or answer to prayer that causes us to shrink from it in bewilderment and disbelief that this could be happening to us. When this happens, at the very least God expects us to stay at our Christian duties and keep worshiping him like Zechariah, who, unable to talk, kept on serving God while he processed what was happening to him.

When the neighbors asked Elizabeth the baby's name, they were astonished at her answer. Contrary to custom, she chose not to name him after Zechariah or one of their family members. The relatives and neighbors couldn't understand it and harassed her about her choice. Then they turned to Zechariah as he came out of the Temple, still unable to speak, and tried to persuade him to give their son an appropriate name, but he wrote on a tablet that his name would be John, the name God had chosen. Zechariah's tongue was untied and he came from being mute to uttering a magnificent prophecy. His faith had been restored, his trust in God was stronger, his commitment was back on track, and he surrendered to God more deeply than ever before. Furthermore, the neighbors were filled with awe, and the news spread like wildfire.

II. *The proclamation.* Beyond God's gift of a son to a tongue-tied priest and his barren wife that filled their family and friends with awe, what is the good news for us in Zechariah's proclamation? Filled with the Holy Spirit, he began to praise God because "he has come and has redeemed his people" (1:68). Although the saving work of God had just begun (remember, Zechariah was standing by his son lying in a cradle, and Jesus had been conceived of the Holy Spirit but had not yet been born), Zechariah prophesied about God's redemption as if it were already accomplished because he believed that God would finish what he had started.

Zechariah's song reminded his listeners of how God was keeping faith with three of the most important events in Israel's history: (1) He linked God's redemption from sin with the Exodus, when God freed Israel from slavery in Egypt. (2) He linked God's raising up a "horn of salvation" through the house of David with the Messiah, who was to be of the royal lineage of King David but destined to be a far greater king. The horn of salvation was Jesus. (3) He linked God's covenant promise to Abraham with the salvation of his people from their enemies so that we can "serve him without fear in holiness and righteousness" all our days (1:75).

Only when he was two-thirds of the way through his prophecy did he mention his son John and his ministry. Something more important than the birth of a prophet was happening; the Messiah was coming. John was only the Messiah's forerunner, and he was already outshone by the rising sun. God had intervened, his Son had come to earth, the long night of Israel's waiting was over, and the dark shadow of death was defeated forever.

All this was happening because of the compassion and tender mercy of God. Jesus brought with him the offer of salvation and the opportunity to serve him as long as we live (1:77–79). This is the greatest of all good news. That message is still worth having at any cost. It is worth untying our tongues to proclaim it. It is worth unstopping our ears to hear it.—Wayne Shaw

ILLUSTRATIONS

OUR TASK.   It is our God-appointed office to lead men and women who are weary or wayward, exultant or depressed, eager or indifferent, into "the secret place of the Most High." We are to help the sinful to the fountain of cleansing, the bond slaves to the wonderful songs of deliverance. We are to help the halt and the lame to recover their lost nimbleness. We are to help the broken-winged into the healing light of "the heavenly places in Christ Jesus." We are to help the sad into the sunshine of grace. We are to help the buoyant to clothe themselves with "the garment of praise." We are to help redeem the strong from the atheism of pride and the weak from the atheism of despair. We are to help little children see the glorious attractiveness of God, and we are to help the aged realize the encompassing care of the Father and the assurance of the eternal home.—J. H. Jowett[6]

---

[6] *The Preacher: His Life and Work*

HOW THE SONG COMES.   The song springs from a man's heart, and breaks through the barrier of his lips, when he stands with God against some darkness or some void, and watches the light come: when he is having a go where he is at shaping, by God's grace, whatever he can of what God wills, as a potter shapes a vase.—Paul Scherer[7]

SERMON SUGGESTIONS

Topic: We Break New Seas!

TEXT: Ps. 139:1–18

(1) Why do we respond so readily to stories of adventure and exploration? (2) Life being what it is, we are all explorers and we need a faith adequate for that fact. (3) Living in an era of revolutions, for the most part unfinished, we have to find a firm path through the perils of the future. (4) The church we belong to has never stood still.—Harold A. Bosley[8]

Topic: Why I Am a Christian

TEXT: 1 Pet. 3:15b

(1) Because my parents were. (2) Because it meets certain of my needs. (3) Because I choose to be.

CONGREGATIONAL MUSIC

1. "Blest Be the God of Israel," James Quinn (1969)
   KINGSFOLD, English folk song; arr. R. V. Williams (1906)
   This contemporary setting of the Song of Zechariah (Luke 1:68–70) would be useful as an opening hymn during worship on this Advent Sunday.
2. "More Love to Thee, O Christ," Elizabeth P. Prentiss (1856)
   MORE LOVE TO THEE, William H. Doane (1870)
   As a response to the Epistle lesson in which the apostle Paul not only expresses his great love for the Philippian church but also calls on the members to abound more and more in love, this simple devotional hymn would be effective.
3. "On Jordan's Bank the Baptist's Cry," Charles Coffin (1763)
   WINCHESTER NEW, *Musicalisches Handbuch* (1690)
   Relating to the message of John the Baptist (Luke 3:1–6), this venerable Advent hymn is a natural selection for use in connection with the Gospel reading.
4. "Comfort, Comfort, Ye My People," Johann G. Olearius (1671)
   PSALM 42, *Genevan Psalter* (1551); tr. Catherine Winkworth
   This traditional Advent hymn relates both to the prophecy of Malachi (3:1) and the Gospel account of John the Baptist. It therefore could be sung in connection with either reading.—Hugh T. McElrath

WORSHIP AIDS

CALL TO WORSHIP.   "The dayspring from on high hath visited us, to give light to them that sit in darkness and in the shadow of death, to guide our feet into the way of peace" (Luke 1:78b–79).

---

[7] *The Word God Sent*
[8] Adapted from *Sermons on the Psalms*

INVOCATION.   As the light of your love dawns upon us, O God, let us reflect that brightness in our faith, hope, and love, so that all may know of your grace in the coming of our Lord Jesus Christ.

OFFERTORY SENTENCE.   "God can bless you with everything you need, and you will always have more than enough to do all kinds of good things for others" (2 Cor. 9:8 CEV).

OFFERTORY PRAYER.   Take these coins and bills, Father, and turn them into bread for the hungry, clothes for the naked, medicine for the ill, shelter for the homeless, and good news for the lost. In faith we give these offerings and send them through your guidance to the world, in Jesus' Name.—Henry Fields

PRAYER.   Almighty God, you who are the great God and the great King above all gods, how foolish are our ways when we think that we can contain you in our neat creeds. How unsearchable are your judgments and how inscrutable your ways! Why should we think it so strange that beyond our wildest imagination there is the freedom of your grace to save the uttermost?

God of grace, God of glory, help us to realize that the mystery of your coming is the elusiveness of your grace—the meaning of your coming is the glory of your grace always present with us but not to be manipulated by our cleverness, nor to be comprehended by the finite mind, never to be apprehended but only to be received as a gift freely given.

That we should be recipients of your grace in Christ when there are so many others as deserving, or even more deserving, who have never heard of you, brings us to our knees "lost in wonder, love and praise."

That we should be channels of your grace is indeed a high calling, but may we not turn from the challenge but pray for faithfulness that through our brokenness your grace may be mediated to others in their need. To be the "wounded healer" *is* our calling. By his stripes we are healed; through his brokenness we are made whole. O miracle of miracles—the grace of our Lord Jesus Christ.

This is the day that you have made, O God, unlike any other we have ever lived. By life's dailiness may we not become so callous as to be blind to its newness or insensitive to its freshness. With both hands may we grasp its opportunities, for today *is* the day of salvation— there is no other.

Cleanse us and we shall be clean; heal us and we shall be whole; save us and we shall be new, through him who is the Alpha and the Omega, the beginning and end of all things, present in the eternal now of our time, teaching us to pray: Our Father. . . .—John Thompson

SERMON
Topic: What Kind of a Place?
TEXT: John 13:33–35; Gal. 5:22–25

I found my text—or maybe my text found me—in this encounter that Jesus had with his disciples that Edna has already read this morning. He was getting ready to leave, and leave-taking communications are most impressive. When we come to that part of the Gospel we need to listen closely. What would he say to his disciples there as he prepared to leave? What was most important? He said: "I give you a new commandment, that you love one another. Just as I have loved you, you also should love one another. By this everyone will know that you are my disciples, if you have love for one another."

I. *The first thing he says is that the nature of his fellowship was always to be a relational place.* The acid test of a church and a family is how we relate to one another. If we flunk this test, we flunk church and family. What we discover from the Lord Jesus is that his love is unconditional. And this is what we are trying to help families with. This is what we are trying to model as church. This is not an easy thing to do. It's what we said that first week when we talked about long-range planning here in this sanctuary. It really is the struggle to make love a living possibility for us all. In our time, we need all the help we can get, don't we?

We're learning a lot of things in the long-range planning committee from all of these surveys that you are tired of filling out, I am sure. But one of the things we have learned is that this church has never in all of its history handled conflict very well. It's a perennial theme that keeps cropping up everywhere. If you think you need to feel not OK about that, I would remind you that I don't know very many churches anywhere that handle conflict very well. But I do know that we have a lot of work to do in presenting unconditional love to people.

II. *I hope this is a values place.* Hopefully it will be a place where we deal with the values of our lives. In the book of Galatians, Paul says that the fruit that comes from the tree flows from the kind of tree it is. He talks about the "fruits of the Spirit." Some Wednesday nights, maybe in the spring, I want to talk about these wonderful concepts that he says are fruits on the tree. They are rich and they are part of our standards: *love, joy, peace, patience, kindness, generosity, faithfulness, gentleness, self-control* (Gal. 5:22–23). These are the fruits of the Spirit.

Somebody said that the best thing about marriage is that you have somebody to blame for everything that goes wrong for the rest of your life. Well, that's the lowest common denominator. That's not what we are here to teach. For you see, we really do affirm that hate never, ever is a family value. So we are trying here in this place to live up to the name of this church—*Covenant*—which is a promise that we will love and care for and strive to give out love and peace and joy and patience and kindness and generosity and faithfulness and gentleness and self-control. We are to model this among one another and we are to let our little children see that as they see us. That's the best Christian education we ever give. If we fail here, we have failed in the value part of what we are to be.

III. *The third thing I want to say to all of us is that this is to be a serving place.* We have all driven up to the service station to get our oil checked and to get the tire that's kind of low checked. So you put your card in the wrong way and finally figure out how to put it in the right way. Then you get the gas pump handle and punch what you think is the right button, and then you discover you've got premium instead of regular because they always put the premium where the regular ought to be so you will buy the expensive gas. So you put that back and get the right one and turn it back on. You ask the attendant standing there smoking a cigarette if he could help you and he says, "I can't do that." You get the squeegee and get your windshield clean. You try to get the top up and figure out how to check if the oil is all right and hope the tire is going to make it to your next destination. Then you get through and get your bill, which is $17.82, and put it in your pocket. The attendant who is standing there and has done nothing is still smoking a cigarette, and as you drive away you look up at the sign that says "Service Station" and you wonder what happened. Something has gone wrong.

When we come here people are looking for a place called church where their needs are met, where their lives are touched, where they are served. When Jesus called us stewards, he wasn't just talking about money. He was talking about being trustees of everything we have. You see, when you enter the ER unit, they don't say, What are you going to do for us? No! They take you and they wheel you down and they do all that stuff to you and it scares you to death. But they serve you.

And our task here is to strengthen one another, to help one another along. And we are not forever to be asking, of course, Are my needs being met? People who ask that the most are the most miserable people I know. Jesus reversed the order and said if you really want to be happy, you reach out and help somebody else and quit worrying about yourself. To build up the people around us. To help those who need.

But you know, I have learned the hard way that you really do save your life when you lose your life in the life of a child or a mate or a parent or an aunt or an uncle or somebody.

And the challenge to all of us is a great one: that we hold out unconditional love to everybody. That we help families work on values that are straight and healthy and whole in a crooked world. That we turn outward and help somebody in need.—Roger Lovette

SUNDAY, DECEMBER 17, 2000
Lectionary Message

Topic: A Defining Event

TEXT: Luke 3:1–20

Other Readings: Zeph. 3:14–20; Isa. 12:2–6; Phil. 4:4–7

When a U.S. president or legislator enters office amid promises of constructive change, we tend to listen with a skeptical ear. And with good reason, because we have heard it all before. But when God promises change, you can count on it.

In this account, Luke records one of the most powerful defining events in human history. William Barclay calls it "one of the hinges on which history turned." The Son of God is about to begin his earthly ministry, and God has appointed his special messenger to announce it. "The Word of God came to John, the son of Zechariah, in the desert" (3:2).

Across the centuries God had called other prophets to announce other messages. What makes this event so defining? Our text shows us four ways that John's message is more important than any prophetic message in the past.

I. *It comes at a defining moment* (3:1–2). Luke pinpoints the date in six different ways. Careful historian that he is, he wants us to know exactly when John the Baptist began his ministry. But there is more than a date on the calendar at stake here. The message of John set the ministry of Jesus against the backdrop of the powerful Roman Empire and the Jewish religious system. The announcement of the Messiah's ministry changed the human situation forever by confronting it with the Word of God.

II. *It contains a defining metaphor* (3:3–6). John began preaching a message of forgiveness based on repentance and baptism. Luke declares that his words fulfill the prophecy of Isaiah 40:3–5. At the heart of Isaiah's prophecy is a defining metaphor.

The picture is this: when a person of royalty was about to visit a city, a courier would be sent ahead to announce his coming and to command the people to prepare the road into the city. Isaiah prophesied that one day Israel would be called on to prepare a highway for God (40:3, 9–10). John declared that the time was now. Jesus is the fulfillment of Isaiah's prophecy, and John is his courier. He proclaimed that to see the glory of the Lord and his salvation, they must build a highway for him in their hearts.

III. *It proclaims a defining message: a baptism of repentance for the forgiveness of sins (3:3).*

(a) His hearers understood what he meant by baptism because they were familiar with proselyte baptism. They had seen Gentile converts initiated into the Jewish faith by being immersed in water for purification and for covenant fellowship. Now John extends baptism to the people of Israel at the beginning of Jesus' ministry. Later, on the birthday of the Church at Pentecost, the apostles extended baptism to everyone who would turn to Christ in faith and repentance (Acts 2:36–38).

(b) Repentance was the way for Israel to prepare a highway for God. John did not mince words. He warned them of the wrath to come, he urged them not to rely on their Jewish ancestry for salvation, and he challenged them to produce fruits that demonstrated that their repentance was real (3:7–14).

Genuine repentance is not only being sorry for our sins; it requires us to make Christ's purposes central in our lives. It leads us to share what we have with others, to be honest and fair in our business dealings, and not to defame or take advantage of others (3:10–14).

(c) The most therapeutic thing in the world is to have our sins forgiven, and it is still our greatest need. God wants his salvation offered to all men and women (3:6) just as it was offered to us. Jesus came to announce that the Kingdom of God is open to all who believe and obey him.

IV. *It points to a defining Master* (3:15–18). John was having spectacular success preaching to large crowds and baptizing great numbers of them in the Jordan River. So great was his impact that people began to wonder if he was the promised Messiah. John made it clear that he was not the Son of God but only his messenger: "But one more powerful than I will come, the thongs of whose sandals I am unworthy to untie" (3:16).

John draws the contrast further. He baptized with water, but Jesus would baptize with the Holy Spirit and with fire. That happened the day the Church was born (Acts 2). The event started with the Holy Spirit coming on the apostles accompanied by a violent wind and tongues of fire, and it ended with the apostle Peter admonishing the crowd to repent and be baptized for the forgiveness of sins to receive the gift of the Holy Spirit (Acts 2:38). Like John, we can baptize with water, but only God can give us his Spirit.

And only God can exercise final judgment. The church must stand courageously for the truth and declare it with conviction, but we can only go so far. "His winnowing fork is in his hand to clear his threshing floor and to gather the wheat in his barn, but he will burn up the chaff with unquenchable fire" (3:17). John could preach repentance, but God dispenses his wrath against ungodliness.

Many have claimed that John's message is all judgment and no gospel. True, he rebuked Herod for his sordid marriage and "all other evil things he had done" (3:20), and Herod responded by locking John up in prison. But the text also says, "And with many other words John exhorted the people and preached the good news to them" (3:18). It is bad news to learn we are sinners and need to repent of our sins, but it is good news that Christ offers to cleanse us from our sins and to give us his Spirit. "And now what are you waiting for? Get up, be baptized and wash your sins away, calling on his name" (Acts 22:16).—Wayne Shaw

ILLUSTRATIONS

WORLDLY LANGUAGE.   "The Word became flesh and dwelt among us, full of grace and truth," the prologue to the Gospel of John says. A dream as old as time of the God descending hesitates on the threshold of coming true in a way to make all other truths seem dreamlike. If it is true, it is the chief of all truths. If it is not true, it is of all truths the one perhaps that people would most have be true if they could make it so. Maybe it is that longing to have it be true that is at the bottom even of the whole vast Christmas industry—the tons of cards and presents and fancy food, the plastic figures kneeling on the floodlit lawns of poorly attended churches. The world speaks of holy things in the only language it knows, which is a worldly language.—Frederick Buechner[9]

POWER FROM ABOVE.   I think of a parish in western New England which once had a minister who was too good for the church. He was a man of culture who wished to develop a dignified service of worship. The people preferred a slipshod, emotionally effervescent form of churchmanship. And the minister found it rough going. An opportunity came for him to go to a more congenial parish. He was tempted to take it. But he remained in the hard place. Then things began to happen. Disagreements were softened. Hearts were opened and a fruitful ministry followed.

By staying in the hard place, the city of Jerusalem, the disciples filled one prescription for receiving the "power from on high."—Ralph W. Sockman[10]

SERMON SUGGESTIONS

Topic: When God Arrives

Text: Isa. 12:2–6

(1) He brings salvation. (2) He causes thanksgiving. (3) He transmits his grace through us to all the world.

Topic: God's Inescapable Nearness

Text: Phil. 4:4–7, esp. v. 5b

Because "the Lord is at hand": (1) We will rejoice (v. 4). (2) We will be thoughtful of others (v. 5a). (3) We will trust God in all circumstances (v. 6). (4) We will experience the peace of God (v. 7).—Eduard Schweizer[11]

CONGREGATIONAL MUSIC

1. "Rejoice, Ye Pure in Heart," Edward H. Plumptre (1865)

   MARION, Arthur H. Messiter (1889)

   The apostle Paul's invitation to rejoice in the Lord (Phil. 4:4) finds its echo in this grand processional hymn and would be a natural choice for the opening of worship.

2. "Surely It Is God Who Saves Us," Isaiah 12, vers. Carl P. Daw (1982)

   LORD, REVIVE US, early American tune; harm. Dale Grotenhuis (1985)

---

[9] *A Room Called Remember*
[10] In G. Paul Butler (ed.), *Best Sermons*, Vol. 10
[11] *God's Inescapable Nearness* (James W. Cox, trans.)

The singing of this modern metrical paraphrase of the Isaiah reading appointed for this day could be alternated with the reading as follows: Isa. 12:1–2, read; stanza 1, 1st half, sung; Isa. 12:3, read; stanza 1, 2nd half, sung; Isa. 12:4, read; stanza 2, 1st half, sung; Isa. 12:5–6, read; stanza 2, 2nd half, sung.

3. "O for a Thousand Tongues to Sing," Charles Wesley (1739)

AZMON, Carl G. Gläser; arr. Lowell Mason (1839)

Those preferring to focus on the spirit of Isaiah 12 (4–5) by singing a great well-known hymn rather than following the alternation suggested above can use this exuberant proclaiming of the deeds of a gracious God penned by Wesley near the anniversary of his conversion.

4. "Hark! A Thrilling Voice Is Sounding," Latin (c. sixth century); tr. *HAM* (1861)

MERTON, William H. Monk (1850)

The startling message of John the Baptist (Luke 3:7–18) is incorporated in this ancient Advent hymn. Though possibly unfamiliar, the tune is very simple and quite suitable for enthusiastic congregational singing.—Hugh T. McElrath

WORSHIP AIDS

CALL TO WORSHIP.   "Surely God is my salvation; I will trust, and will not be afraid, for the Lord God is my strength and my might; He has become my salvation" (Isa. 12:2 NRSV).

INVOCATION.   This is the day you made, O God! Let us live life on tiptoe lest we miss the new thing you are doing in our time. Quicken our minds with your Spirit, enlarge our hearts to receive the fullness of your love in Christ, empower our wills by your grace that we may follow the highest when we see it. For your goodness to us and to all peoples, praise be to you—Father, Son, and Holy Spirit.—John Thompson

OFFERTORY SENTENCE.   "Like good stewards of the manifold grace of God, serve one another with whatever gift each of you has received" (1 Pet. 4:10 NRSV).

OFFERTORY PRAYER.   O Giver of all, may our giving be gracious—not out of any sense of compulsion but in joyous response to the fullness of your grace in Christ, in whose name we give and live.—John Thompson

PRAYER.   Your ways, Father, are higher than our ways and your thoughts higher than ours. When we stop in our busy lives and ponder you, we are entranced by wonder, subdued by awe, and induced to worship you truly.

We can't comprehend you, Lord. We cannot understand how you can be the mighty creator of heaven and earth and yet condescend to bless a little village maid with the wonder of a heavenly child. And how can it be that the light of heaven shines in a crude, smelly animal stable? How can it be that ignorant shepherds, field hands of their times, are thrilled with the symphony of angels' songs while kings are troubled by their dreams and fears?

Father, this morning open our eyes and warm our hearts and touch our lips, that like the shepherds of old we may glorify you for the things we have seen and felt. Grant us an appreciation for Christmas by a rebirth of Christ in our hearts. Then enable us to translate the joy of the Christmastide into a spirit of goodwill and of peace, active in the world.

Permit us, Father, to become agents of light and love and the life of Christ, bringing them to bear wherever we are and in whatever we do, so that a new day may be born in our world and people may live together in peace and harmony. Let this desire rise in the hearts of all people, that it may overcome our ill will toward one another, our hatreds that eat us alive, our greed that leaves want in the pathway of its satisfaction, and our sin that destroys our very soul. Grant to us this morning the miracle of grace experienced so that Christ may come into our hearts and homes and be carried to the waiting world as we venture forth in his Name.—Henry Fields

SERMON
Topic: The Coming of Christ Means Judgment
TEXT: Mal. 3:5; 2 Cor. 5:10

This sermon is about judgment, and judgment simply means that we are accountable for our wrongdoing. We have presumed to remove God, so to speak, from his judgment seat and put him in an easy armchair from which he watches his foolish children with an indulgent eye.

The Bible never makes any attempt to get around the idea of judgment. You might almost say that it never gets over it, for you find it on page after page. Almost the very last words of the Old Testament are these, "Then will I draw near unto you for judgment, saith the Lord." And St. Paul spoke for all of the New Testament writers when he said, "For we must all stand before the judgment seat of Christ."

Neither does the Prayer Book make any attempt to get around this idea of judgment. Again you find it on almost every page.

The collect for Christmas Day says this, "Grant that as we joyfully receive him for our Redeemer, so we may with sure confidence behold him when he shall come to be our Judge."

Such a matter as this is therefore not to be taken lightly. If it is true that we are held accountable for what we do, we ought to know it and behave accordingly and, what is more, we ought to know to whom we are held accountable.

I. Jesus told a story at the end of the Sermon on the Mount that will help us and start us on our way to appreciate what the idea of judgment means. It was a very short story with almost no details, a story about two men who built houses. As far as we know, both were good houses and both men lived in their houses perfectly happily and safely. And then the storm came—a severe storm. The man who had built his house on a rock foundation found that his house stood the test of the storm, but the man who had built his house on sand soon discovered that his house could not withstand the storm and it fell. Why did it fall? There is a requirement in the natural law of things that if you wish to build a house that will withstand the strains of the weather, you must build it on a solid foundation. If you do not, it will fall. And the implication in the story of Jesus is simply this: One man was foolish and did not fulfill the requirements of the natural order and he suffered the consequences thereof.

Jesus made this very clear about judgment, and I think this will be an advance for some of us if we can grasp it firmly in our minds: *Judgment is not punishment inflicted arbitrar-*

ily from above, but consequences incurred from within because of a failure to fulfill the requirements.

One thing that we can say right at the beginning about Jesus and this notion of judgment is that he took the penal idea out of it. Jesus does not show us a picture of an angry God taking almost peevish delight in punishing us when we have made mistakes. Heaven forbid! He shows us rather a moral God who stands by his laws and lets his children suffer the consequences of their foolish ways no matter how severe that suffering may be. In other words, we are accountable in the long run for what we do. Only the foolish ones will ever forget that.

II. Jesus also makes it clear in this same short story that these consequences do not always occur immediately. I picture the men who built the two houses living in them happily for quite a long time. The man who built his house on sand may have thought to himself, How smart I am; my house cost a lot less than the other man's house because I built it on a sand foundation, and look at me, I'm doing all right; my house is just as good as his house and everything is going well. It was not until the rains descended and the floods came and the winds beat on the house that the weakness involved was revealed, and in that moment of judgment the house fell, and the man suffered the consequences of it.

Rome was not built in a day, nor did it fall in a day. Two or three centuries before the actual fall of Rome, Roman citizens were gaily wasting their substance in riotous living. They were playing with their resources, they were using their extraordinary power and position in the world for ends that were not according to the requirements of God, and we can imagine some of them rather smugly and complacently saying to themselves, See, we are defying all the laws of the prophets and we are getting away with it; we are having a wonderful time, and Rome was never brighter, happier, merrier than it is at this moment. Then the barbarian hordes came down from the north like an avalanche, and the civilization that had been rotting for centuries revealed those cracks and crannies in its foundation and could not stand the strain of the storm and it fell under the judgment thereof.

That is why, I suppose, in Christian imagery we are likely to talk about the *last* judgment, when history comes to an end, because in one sense there cannot be a final judgment until all the facts are in. In one sense, our judgment is always in the future.

III. There is one further consideration and that is what the requirements are. If I am to be held accountable for what I do and if I must fulfill the requirements, what in the world are they? Jesus in that same little story about the two men who built houses makes that indubitably clear also, for he said that the wise man who built his house on rock was like the person who heard what Jesus said and did it, whereas the foolish man who built his house on sand was like a man who heard what Jesus said and ignored it. In other words, Jesus had what we might call the sublime audacity to make himself the requirement and himself the judge.

So, it is not that we do not know what the requirements are, is it? There is no use in deceiving ourselves about that. We know all too well what they are. Love God with all your heart and mind and soul. Love your neighbors, the people around you, as much as you love yourself. Love your enemies, do good to them that hurt you and persecute you. Trust God the way a child trusts his father. Be humble, not proud. Be gentle, never violent.

But never forget this. The judge is one of us. He has faced the same temptation that every one of us faces. He knows whereof we are made and he is willing to make every possible allowance for our weakness. He woos us, as it were; he pleads with us, gives us chance after chance after chance to try again and do better. He loves us even when he lets us suffer the consequences of our mistakes and our follies, just as a father who must be true to himself and to what he believes sometimes must let his child suffer the consequences of his foolishness; but in letting him do that he still loves him and the child knows that he loves him, and in that love is the child's salvation.

And Jesus, the judge, asks only one thing of us ultimately, and that is that we cling to him, and in some mysterious way that Christians have intuitively felt even though they are not able to express, the fact that we are associated with him is the fact that saves us from that ultimate despair that would inevitably be ours if we faced the single fact that we are held to the requirements of his word.—Theodore P. Ferris

SUNDAY, DECEMBER 24, 2000
Lectionary Message

Topic: The Virgin's Heart
TEXT: Luke 1:46–55
Other Readings: Mic. 5:2–5z; Heb. 10:5–10; Luke 1:39–45

It is an understatement to call Mary's pregnancy unusual. Not because mother and baby were not healthy—Dr. Luke would surely have noted any physical problems. It was a normal pregnancy. But the circumstances surrounding her pregnancy were absolutely astounding. The gossips sent the rumors flying that she was pregnant out of wedlock. Joseph, the man to whom she was betrothed, believed it. The evidence would soon be there for all to see, and he planned to dissolve the betrothal quickly and privately so as not to embarrass her any more than necessary, but he could not live with what he believed was her unfaithfulness to their betrothal. Let's not be too critical of Joseph. After all, would you have believed it? In fact, a virgin birth happened only this one time in human history. No wonder Mary pondered all these things in her heart. A young Jewish maiden who never had known a man, pregnant for the first time, probably in her teens, had been given more than enough to ponder. And while the baby was growing in her womb, awareness of God was growing in her heart.

I. *The faith in her heart.* When Mary pondered all that God was doing in her life, she realized that God had been confirming her faith, and she came to trust him with a heart full of faith.

(a) Her faith was confirmed through the Old Testament prophecies she had heard read in the synagogue. The Old Testament was full of predictions that the Messiah would come, and all Israel had looked for him for hundreds of years. The Gospel of Matthew, for example, points specifically to Isaiah 7:14 to declare that "a virgin will conceive and bear a child, and you shall call his name Jesus for he shall save his people from their sins." She believed that the prophecy was being fulfilled through her.

(b) Her faith was also confirmed through the appearance of the angel who assured her that the child she was carrying was of the Holy Spirit. Joseph, who had been shaken to the core by her unexpected pregnancy because he knew he couldn't be the father, had had God confirm in a dream that he didn't need to be afraid to take Mary as his wife. And because he believed God, he called off his plan to divorce her. Through it all Mary kept her faith centered in God. She trusted that God was confirming his plan through her in spite of the ugly rumors circulating about her.

II. *The song in her heart.* Praise always follows genuine faith, and Mary's song that God had put in her heart is one of the most beautiful hymns of praise ever sung.

(a) Mary's song is beautiful because of its style. When we read these exalted words of beauty, we find it hard to believe that they could come from the lips of an uneducated peasant girl. But remember, the only exalted language she had heard repeatedly was from the Old Testament in public worship. The Psalms, for example, had evidently saturated her soul, and when the Holy Spirit gave her her song, the style of the Psalms was the one she knew best in which to praise the Lord. Few songs ever written can compare with hers.

(b) Mary's song is beautiful because of its content.

(1) She begins by praising God for who he is (1:46) and expressing her overwhelming joy at what is happening to her. She contrasts her present humble circumstances with the honor that will be hers. "All generations will call me blessed," she sings, but she does not add, "because I am to be the mother of God's Son." Instead she sings, "because the mighty one has done great things for me." She puts the emphasis not on herself but on God, and she does not claim that she is divine; rather, she praises God for his holiness (1:49).

(2) She praises God for all that he does: for his acts of mercy (1:50), for his choosing the humble and not the proud (1:51–53), and for keeping his promise to Abraham and his descendants across the centuries (1:54, 55). God's promise to Abraham had called them into being and shaped them as a nation. It had given them their identity for centuries among the nations of the world. When Abraham had been too old to be a father and his wife Sarah was barren, God promised them a miracle birth. They would have a son, they would call his name Isaac, and through Abraham, Isaac, and their descendants God would bless all nations. The time had arrived on God's timetable, and in another miracle birth the Son of God was coming to Earth incognito in the womb of a virgin. God gave her a son, he gave her a song, and he gave us a savior. No wonder she praised God with this magnificent song.

"Mary pondered all these things in her heart." That led her to a faith deep enough to sustain her through all the pressures of her pregnancy and to put a song of joy, praise, and salvation in her heart. Her way is ours: first faith comes by pondering in our hearts what God is doing through the testimony of his Word and his activity in our own lives, and then praise comes to our lips from our hearts in grateful worship.—Wayne Shaw

ILLUSTRATIONS

THE GOSPEL ACCORDING TO MARY.   The gospel according to Mary speaks not only of the tremendous mercy of God but also of his rejection of every human pretension, his condemnation of our arrogance, our acquisitiveness, and our pride. Through this song we already hear the words of Jesus. He spoke about the man who boasted that he was "not as other men are, and prided himself on his religious virtues." "He hath scattered the proud in the imagination of their hearts," says Mary. Jesus stood helpless before Pilate, who boasted of his power to have Jesus crucified, and said, "Thou couldest have no power at all against me, except it were given thee from above." "He hath put down the mighty from their seats," said Mary. (And what a putdown!) He told the story of the man who concentrated on the accumulation of material and planned to retire and enjoy it. "But God said, Thou fool, this night thy soul shall be required of thee; then whose shall these things be, which thou hast provided?" "The rich he hath sent empty away," said Mary.

The gospel of Mary is the gospel of her child, which means that it is the good news of God's grace for all whom come to him in the rags of the Prodigal Son.—David H. Read[12]

ACTIVE WAITING.   You must give ear to a God who is speaking to you now, and act on what He says. For here is today's manger, the way Christ comes to you in helplessness. No longer a baby, but just as important.

This fresh kind of Advent—active awaiting, ears tuned to the Spirit, eyes awake to Christ in a thousand Gethsemanes—this will cost you: "a sword shall pierce you too." Discipleship, like grace, does not come cheap. But for your comfort and strength, be aware that you wait, like Mary, with your Lord already within you. Don't envy our Lady to excess; for, as Jesus told you, if you love him and keep his word, his Father loves you and they come to you and make their home with you (cf. Jn 14:23). Christ deep in you and Christ all around you—your whole life can be a ceaseless Advent, a splendid prelude to his final coming. All you have to do is murmur with Mary "Whatever you say, Lord," and then do whatever he says. That's all. . . . That's all?—Walter J. Burghardt[13]

SERMON SUGGESTIONS

Topic: It Sounds Like Jesus!
Text: Mic. 5:2–5a
(1) In his humble earthly origin. (2) In his divine significance. (3) In his universal mission of peace and wholeness.

Topic: An Important Vitamin for Spiritual Growth
Text: Acts 20:35
(1) Why some people do not give: (a) Some say, "Charity begins at home." (b) Some say, "I don't like the way my money will be spent." (c) Others say, "I don't have enough for myself." (d) The real reason may be a deep sense of insecurity and an unwillingness to trust God. (2) Various motives for giving: (a) bargain, (b) duty, (c) gratitude, (d) love. (3) Methods of giving: (a) regularly, (b) systematically, (c) impulsively, (d) as God has prospered.

CONGREGATIONAL MUSIC
1. "O Little Town of Bethlehem," Phillips Brooks (1868)
   ST. LOUIS, Lewis H. Redner (1868)
   To introduce the Old Testament reading from the prophecy of Micah, which is concerned with the future fame of Bethlehem, this familiar American Christmas hymn could be appropriately sung.
2. "Tell Out, My Soul," Timothy Dudley-Smith (1961)
   WOODLANDS, Walter Greatorex (1916)

---

[12] In James W. Cox (ed.), *Best Sermons*, Vol. 1
[13] *Still Proclaiming Your Wonders*

This excellent contemporary version of the Song of Mary could be sung in connection with the reading of the Magnificat (Luke 1:47–55) or could actually replace that reading.

3. "That Boy-Child of Mary," Tom Colvin (1969)

BLANTYRE, trad. Malawi melody; adapt. Tom Colvin (1969)

Using the call-and-response method, this Malawi Christmas carol could be sung with the congregation doing the refrain and a soloist or soloists singing the various stanzas. It focuses on the important place of Bethlehem in the Christmas narrative.

4. Because this is Christmas Eve, any of many Christmas carols, familiar and unfamiliar, would be suitable for worship on this day. Listed here are a few that might be sung: "Hark! The Herald Angels Sing"; "The First Noel"; "Once in Royal David's City"; "Go, Tell It on the Mountain"; "Angels, We Have Heard on High"; "O Come, All Ye Faithful"; "Sing We Now of Christmas"; "Good Christian Friends, Rejoice"; "Infant Holy, Infant Lowly"; "He Is Born, the Holy Child," and so on.—Hugh T. McElrath

WORSHIP AIDS

CALL TO WORSHIP.   "Listen! I am standing at the door, knocking; if you hear my voice and open the door, I will come in to you and eat with you, and you with me" (Rev. 3:20).

INVOCATION.   We are keenly aware, gracious Lord, that you await our welcome, as individuals and as a people gathered for worship. Enter, we pray, that you may have your rightful place in our hearts and in all our relationships in life.

OFFERTORY SENTENCE.   "But you will receive power when the Holy Spirit has come upon you; and you will be my witnesses in Jerusalem, in all Judea and Samaria, and to the ends of the earth" (Acts 1:8 NRSV).

OFFERTORY PRAYER.   We pray, Lord Christ, that in our giving we may be truly instruments of your Spirit, that your name and love may be made known in our community and to the ends of the Earth.

PRAYER.   The feeling of the love of Christmas is in the air, dear God, and the celebration of the birth of your loving Son is in full swing. We hear carols being sung, the melodies of angelic choruses filling the winter air. We see a star shining brightly on the pathway we are to follow. The colors of the rainbow are upon the trees of Christmas. The warmth of heart and home acknowledges the Christ Child's birth. We come to say thanks, our parent God, to congratulate you on your new birth, and to tell you how happy we are that all this has come to pass. With the heavenly angels we sing of your glories and bring our hopes for peace on Earth and goodwill to all parts of this universe.

Help us, O God, to celebrate the advent of your love, the fullness of your presence in our everyday experiences of life. May the glow of Christmas past become the light of the world in the Christmas present. Enable us to be a part of your light so we may shine so brightly that others will know we are a part of your family and sisters and brothers of Christ. Let our love so glow in this darkened world that others will find their way to the manger to discover once again the Prince of Peace, come to Earth as a loving child.

Help us, O Lord, to fill the years ahead with the full celebration of life that Jesus has begun through his birth. In his Name we pray.—Robert F. Langwig

SERMON
Topic: What Shall I Give Him?
TEXT: Matt. 2:7–14

O. Henry, master of the short story, gave us "The Gift of the Magi," which has become an American literary Christmas classic to rival Dickens's "A Christmas Carol." It is about new-lyweds Jim and Della. It is about personal sacrifice. It is about the element of surprise, which sometimes turns into irony. Della sold her hair to buy a chain for Jim's watch. Jim sold his watch to buy combs for Della's hair. With a slight touch of sarcasm, O. Henry connected his story to the birth of Christ and suggested the origin of exchanging presents at Christmas: "The magi, as you know, were wise men—wonderfully wise men—who brought gifts to the babe in the manger. They invented the art of giving Christmas presents. Being wise, their gifts were no doubt wise ones, possibly bearing the privilege of exchange in case of duplication."

There you have it. Blame the Wise Men for the mobs at the mall, the traffic jams, the confusion of Christmas bells with the ring of the cash register, the measure of love by the size of the gift, the bulge of advertising in the December newspapers—shall I go on? If the mystery guests at the manger are responsible for the tradition of exchanging gifts, maybe we need to look again. To pattern our giving from the point of origin, our whole attitude toward Christmas gifts will need to be adjusted. We can begin with the clarification of the identity of the characters here.

I. *Who are the givers?* The three gifts that are presented to the child of Bethlehem have long been the basis for assuming three Wise Men instead of two, four, or ten. Matthew offers no count. The gifts speak for themselves. They say more about the child in the manger than they do about the number or the character of the Magi. Before gifts are presented, the Magi kneel before the child and pay him homage. Martin Luther, along with other early Christian writers, speculated about the symbolism: gold for a king, incense for a god, and myrrh to anoint the dead. The only clear evidence from the Old Testament is that gold and incense are appropriate gifts for a king, supporting Matthew's theme that Jesus is born King of the Jews. The Magi are the only visitors to the birth of Christ in Matthew. Luke's visitors are shepherds who have been called from the fields by an angelic host, and they apparently came without gifts. Because the Magi are foreign guests, the gifts have international significance. Protocol has not changed. State visitors and foreign guests usually bring gifts when they cross cultural lines. Such gifts identify the giver while stating the importance of the recipient.

II. *Who is the recipient?* If Christmas giving is to be consistent with the message of the Magi, our gifts should center on the Christ. Their giving was unconditional and without re-ciprocation. They did not draw names and exchange presents. The gift of God can never be treated on a reciprocal basis. The gift of God is Immanuel, God with us. The person of Christ is incomparable.

Hugh Haynie has long been the political cartoonist for the Louisville *Courier Journal.* Each year at this time he runs the same cartoon, a shopping list that forms an image of the head of Christ. The character making the list asks, "Who have I left out?" You have probably heard enough sermons by now on leaving Christ out of Christmas. The cultural celebration of Christmas departed from the Christian center long ago. I cannot find fault with the family traditions or the children's fantasies, which have grown like kudzu on a Tennessee hillside. Giving to one another and loving one another are certainly compatible with the gospel. Jesus is the one who set the children in our midst as models of the Kingdom. But there is more. The center is not home and family. It is not even marriage and children. Advent centers on the Christ.

The practice of giving to foreign missions at Christmas is more than a good fundraising trick that exploits the generosity of the season. To set our attention on the world of missions is to look beyond ourselves. We are following the universal love of God that is represented by the foreign visitors at the manger. As we shift the center from ourselves to the needs of the world, we begin to recover the center.

III. *Who are you?* Giving is an act of worship. Long before the birth of Jesus, his people had learned to worship through sacrifice. If God is God, our offerings do not enrich the divine coffers. The very nature of the God we worship denies any dependency on creatures or the gifts of creation. Worshiping God and giving are synonymous for the wise of every age. Our sacrifices do not enhance divine authority. God is Lord regardless of our behavior. So what is the point of giving to God? We gather to celebrate the incomparable gift of God in Christ. We give in response to the giving love of God, and every authentic Christmas gift will identify not only the importance of the Christ but also the character of the giver. The paradox of giving is in the effect of the giver. Character is formed by acts of generosity. When you are gathering the abundance of gifts for your family at Christmas, ask, "How will this gift help us to grow?" Will your child learn higher respect for other people by the wealth invested in his or her presents? Will you be a more moral person because you have what you want? The worst problems with Christian stewardship have tended to come more from affluence than from poverty. Why? Poverty helps us to adjust our wants to our needs. Poverty opens our hearts of compassion to a starving world.

Della and Jim tell us about sacrificial giving—the meaning of love. O. Henry has painted a beautiful portrait of human love at its best, but consider the gift of the Magi. They gave more than precious objects. They presented themselves before the Christ. James reminds us, "Every generous act of giving, with every perfect gift, is from above, coming down from the Father of lights, with whom there is no variation or shadow due to change" (James 1:17).— Larry Dipboye

SUNDAY, DECEMBER 31, 2000
Lectionary Message

Topic: The Temple Prodigy
TEXT: Luke 2:41–52
Other Readings: 1 Sam. 2:18–20, 26; Ps. 148; Col. 3:12–17

This story is the only account of Jesus' childhood in all the Bible. Luke opened and closed it with two verses that tell us nearly the same thing: that Jesus grew strong and wise, in favor with God and men, and God's grace was upon him during those years (Luke 2:40 and 2:52). Something very important happened in this incident that we need to hear.

I. *The story.*

(a) Mary and Joseph made their annual trip from Nazareth to Jerusalem during Passover week. That year was a rite of passage for Jesus because he had turned twelve, and therefore became of age under Jewish law. This was his first Passover as a young man. After the feast was over, his family joined the others to begin their four-day journey back to Nazareth. The men usually traveled at one end of the caravan and the women at the other with the children in the middle, so it was not until they stopped to make camp for the first night that they discovered that Jesus was missing.

(b) In a panic they retraced their steps, and for three long days and nights they searched frantically for him. They finally found him in the Temple quizzing and being quizzed by the Temple teachers in a fairly deep theological dialogue. This twelve-year-old lad was confounding and amazing the learned theologians. Mary and Joseph were overjoyed, and upset at him for causing them so much anguish. "Why have you treated us like this?" his mother demanded.

One of my students told about going camping with his family. While his wife and he were putting up the tent, their five-year-old son wandered off with his three-year-old sister. "We searched in the worst places first, including the lake," he said, "and when we found them safe, I swatted our son on his bottom out of joy and relief."

II. *The omission.* There is so much that Luke does not tell us. Why did they leave without Jesus? Why did he not leave with them and why did he not tell them that he was staying? At the very least, the family had a communication problem. Where did he sleep? What did he eat and who fed him? Because he grew up without sin, we know there has to be a logical explanation, but Luke doesn't give it. All we know is that it took them three days to find him in the Temple holding his own in a theological dialogue. And we have Jesus' reply to his mother. It quieted her heart but she didn't understand its meaning. Though he addressed it to Mary, it must have sent shock waves through the Temple crowd. "Why were you searching for me?" he asked; "Didn't you know I had to be in my Father's house?" Neither Moses nor any of the Old Testament prophets ever dared make that statement. It would have been blasphemy. But Jesus as a twelve-year-old lad proclaimed it.

III. *The proclamation.*

(a) Jesus declared his deity to Mary and Joseph in no uncertain terms. He knew he was where he belonged—in his Father's house. They needed to be reminded that they were parenting the Son of God, but this did not mean that Jesus was a rebellious young man. He went back to Nazareth and was obedient to them, but they would never forget that trip. Mary pondered these things in her heart. She seemed to be always pondering something about Jesus in her heart.

(b) Here was the temple prodigy astonishing both his earthly parents and the doctors of the law with his claim. As Israel's promised prince, soon to become the King of the Jews, he had come home to his Father's house. Twenty-one years later he would return to his Father's house and they would turn him out, take him outside the city, and crucify him.

IV. *The application.*

(a) What is the bad news in this text? The Son of God was revealing himself in their midst, but Mary and Joseph didn't get it, and neither did the temple leaders. Mary and Joseph finally caught on, but the leaders never did and they crucified him.

(b) The good news is that he did all of these things for us. We can be saved from our sins if we submit to him, and he will take us home to his Father's house. "Trust in God; trust also in me," Jesus said. "In my Father's house are many rooms; if it were not so, I would have told you. And if I go and prepare a place for you, I will come back and take you to be with me, that you also may be where I am" (John 14:1–3).

(c) The question for us today is "Do we get it?" It is his Father's house, and you and I have an engraved invitation to follow him there. Until then, may we grow as he did, in wisdom and stature, in favor with God and men, and with the grace of God upon us.—Wayne Shaw

ILLUSTRATIONS

THE REAL JESUS.   The only New Testament story about Jesus' youth is not the story of a juvenile. It says nothing about his development, the roots of his ministry in his early experience, the beginnings of his later gifts (v. 47 at most). On the contrary, Jesus knows from the very beginning who his Father is. The real Jesus is therefore not "our" Jesus, the Jesus whom we can explain and understand. At most his appearance as a student in Jerusalem might characterize him as an early achiever, but its real meaning becomes apparent only in his words. Remarkably enough he demonstrates this in a way of life in which he integrates himself in the household of his parents, but also in the history of Israel and its Temple—in no way apart from others. That this will go beyond all power of human imagination will be shown by the Passion.—Eduard Schweizer[14]

THE PERFECT SON.   "Your *father* and I," said Mary, "have been searching for you." "Did you not realize," said Jesus, "that you would find me in my *Father's* house"? See how very gently, very definitely Jesus takes the name *Father* from Joseph and gives it to God. At some time Jesus must have discovered his own unique relationship to God. He cannot have known it when he was a child in the manger and a baby at his mother's breast or he would be a monstrosity and an abnormality. As the years went on he must have thought; and then at this first Passover, with manhood dawning on him, there came in a sudden blaze of realization the consciousness that he was not as other men are, that in a unique and special sense he was the Son of God. Here we have the story of the day when Jesus discovered who he was. And mark one thing—the discovery did not make him proud. It did not make him look down on his humble parents, the gentle Mary and the hard-working Joseph. He went home and *he was obedient to them.* The very fact that he was God's Son made him the perfect son of his human parents.—William Barclay[15]

SERMON SUGGESTIONS

Topic: We Have a Ministry, Too!
TEXT: Exod. 19:5–6a
(1) A challenging prospect (v. 5). (2) A status with obligation (v. 6a) (see also, 1 Pet. 2:9–10).

Topic: Our Christian Identity
TEXT: Col. 3:12–17
(1) We are special in God's sight (v. 12a). (2) We are spiritually obligated (vv. 12b–14). (3) We have a many-splendored calling (vv. 15–17).

---

[14] *The Good News According to Luke*
[15] *The Gospel of Luke*

CONGREGATIONAL MUSIC

1. "Praise the Lord, Ye Heavens, Adore Him," anon.; *Foundling Hospital Collection* (1797)

AUSTRIAN HYMN, Franz, J. Haydn (1797); HYFRYDOL, Rowland H. Pritchard (c. 1830)

A good hymn to open worship, "Praise the Lord" is an anonymous paraphrase of Psalm 148. To either of the tunes, it could be sung antiphonally phrase by phrase between choir and congregation.

2. "Christian Hearts, in Love United," Nicolaus L. von Zinzendorf (1725)

CASSELL, trad. German melody (1735)

The apostle Paul's most emphasized exhortation to the Colossian church, to "put on love, which is the perfect bond of unity" (Col. 3:14), is reflected in this great Moravian hymn. Its singing could appropriately follow the Epistle lesson.

3. "Christ, the Worker, Born in Bethlehem," Ghanian work song; tr. Tom Colvin (1968)

AFRICAN WORK SONG, adapt. Tom Colvin (1969)

The first two stanzas of this folk song pertain specifically to Jesus as a youth who "increased in wisdom, stature, and in favor with God and man" (Luke 2:52). This simple work song may be sung as a round by having a second group of singers begin the tune after the first group has sung the first measure.

4. "Angels, from the Realms of Glory," James Montgomery (1816)

REGENT SQUARE, Henry T. Smart (1867)

On this Sunday during Christmastide and before Epiphany, this hymn of adoration could be used to recall each group that worships the Christ Child: angels, shepherds, the Wise Men, and yes, even the singers present (stanzas 4–5).

5. Many other Christmas hymns, spirituals, and carols are available for singing during the worship services of this season. Moreover, because this is also New Year's Eve, it would be appropriate to sing hymns such as the following: "O God of Bethel, by Whose Hand," Philip Doddridge; "O God Our Help in Ages Past," Isaac Watts; "Another Year Is Dawning," Frances R. Havergal; "God of Our Life, Through All the Circling Years."—Hugh T. Kerr

WORSHIP AIDS

CALL TO WORSHIP.   "Let the message about Christ completely fill our lives, while you use all your wisdom to teach and instruct each other. With thankful hearts, sing psalms, hymns, and spiritual songs to God" (Col. 3:16 CEV).

INVOCATION.   We come to you, O Lord, because we have heard the good news of Christ and because we yearn to let that message truly change us. We thank you for all your blessings and believe that there are more to come. Help us to share freely with one another from what we have already received.

OFFERTORY SENTENCE.   "God chose what is weak in the world to shame the strong" (1 Cor. 1:27b).

OFFERTORY PRAYER.   Lord, we believe that you can take the widow's tiny gift and multiply it a thousandfold. We pray that you will receive what we have, gifts both large and small, offerings faithfully given, and use them for your glory and for the blessing of many.

PRAYER.   O, Lord Jesus, what wondrous condescension! O, what is there in us, that thou shouldst take such pains to love us; that thou shouldst be willing to punish us; that thou shouldst be willing to take the part of father or mother and watch over our outgoings and incomings, reproving us and teaching us the right way; and that with many experiences thou shouldst enforce thy rules, still following after us to deliver us from our troubles! How sacred is this care of God over us who deserve nothing; who have no claim; who are less than the last before the mightiness of God; yet how dost thou make thyself humble like us to dwell with the heartbroken.

O Lord! thou are revealed in the majesty of thy greatness, but more in the fruits of thy humiliation than any thing else to our thought; that thou shouldst weep with us in our distresses; that thou shouldst bind up our broken hearts; that thou shouldst cheer us in the midst of fragmentary hopes; that thou shouldst make the disasters of this world reflect from so many faces of diamond stones, each face a vision of heaven; that thou shouldst make us to see in our darkness ten thousand suns shining afar off in the heavens; that thou shouldst continue thy way and never be weary, not forgetting more than the mother her child; that this should be God eternal, and everywhere, spreading abroad, filling heaven and overflowing the earth; our God, in whom we have a right, and whom we call Father; who lays sacred hands upon us day by day; who numbers our sleeping hours and watches our waking hours, who is before us and behind us, and all round about us with thoughts of grace and mercy! O what wealth, what undeserved riches, what grace beyond all conception, is thine to us!—Henry Ward Beecher[16]

SERMON
Topic: Follow the Light
TEXT: Isa. 60:1–5

We took down the tree and put away the creche for another year. The miniature characters in the nativity fit very well on a shelf above our front door. Modern orthodoxy places the shepherds on the right while the eastern visitors bearing gifts of gold, frankincense, and myrrh stand on the left. The star is centered over the stable. There the infant Jesus lies in an animal feeding trough surrounded by Mary, Joseph, and the animals. The picture is so fixed in our heads that any improvisation of the scene seems like blasphemy. Yet early Christians followed the Gospels to a different mental picture of the coming of the Christ.

Luke remembers the census, the crowded city, laying the newborn in a manger, and the visitation of shepherds—Christmas. Matthew locates the infant in a house and centers attention on the threat of Herod and the visitation of the Wise Men. By the fourth century, Eastern Christians began to celebrate Matthew's story as a distinct event. Eventually the birth of Jesus on Christmas Day was followed twelve days later by the celebration of Epiphany, or the "manifestation." Luke was about Christmas. Matthew's story was the epiphany of God that seemed to stand as a distinct, later event. The light that led the Eastern Gentiles to the infant Jesus recalled Isaiah's vision of the restoration of Israel. The glory, the light of God, will appear, and Gentile pagans, who live in total darkness, will be drawn to the light

---

[16] *Prayers from Plymouth Pulpit*

of God. The prophet's vision sounds like nationalistic arrogance in view of today's international situation, but we must remember that Second Isaiah spoke to the defeated people who had suffered not only the loss of property but also the loss of pride. They desperately needed a vision of strength and hope. Besides, the nations were not attracted to the superior government of Israel. They were attracted to the light of God.

I. *The big picture is revealed in Christ.* Whatever else we might be celebrating here today, Isaiah and Matthew saw an act of God. The glory of God in Christ that draws all people to the center of God's grace appeared in Christ. As the light of God has broken through our darkness in Christ, the light of God is breaking though the darkness of the world through the Church that follows the light. We are compelled by the commission of Christ to share the light of the gospel. One of our families recalled a Christmas Eve candlelight tradition in another church in which the people carried the candles out into the night as a symbol of the church's mission to a dark world. This is the vision of Epiphany. If we pay attention to the whole gospel, we cannot set up camp at any point along the way. We cannot be satisfied with being C & E (Christmas and Easter) Christians. Just as Peter, James, and John wanted to set up camp at the Transfiguration, we are prone to set up camp at the manger. But the gospel of Christ calls us down the mountain and into the world of darkness. Epiphany brings us to our feet and takes us into the world. The tradition of bringing an offering for world missions is an appropriate expression of Epiphany, even if the connection is only coincidental.

We need to bring our precious gifts to the altar as an expression of our worship, but we need to take care of some other business while we are here. God's people have been struggling with myopia throughout the ages, and every generation seems to find its own expression of exclusive religion. The racism of Israel was little different from the racist view of the world that has distorted the Christian world vision. Jesus taught us to leave something at the altar before our gifts. Worship begins with repentance. Before we come to God asking for forgiveness, we must be forgiving. Before we come to God celebrating God's love for the world, we need to enlarge our vision and give up our narrow view of other people. We received two messages at Christmas from CBF missionaries working with the Parsees. The Magi are Parsee priests often identified with the Wise Men from the East. For political reasons, the missionaries could not reveal either a name or a place, but they appealed for our prayers. The call to prayer was also a call to respect and love for this warm and loving people.

The light of God appears in the strangest places. We do not look for God among the poor and the weak, but that is where God looks for us. Second Isaiah called Israel to observe a different kind of fast, to break every yoke of oppression, to share your bread with the hungry, to bring the homeless poor into your house, to provide clothing for the naked. "Then your light shall break forth like the dawn . . . the glory of the Lord shall be your rear guard" (Isa. 58).

II. *What is your vision?* A few years ago the Louisville newspaper contained a humorous article about all the misplaced churches in the city. Ninth and O was located on Taylor Boulevard, Walnut Street was on Third Avenue, Green Street was on Gray Street, etc. All of the churches named were Baptist churches. We have a strong tendency to name our churches for a location, and when the location changes, we just carry the old name with us. Even the St. Matthews Baptist Church in Louisville and the St. Johns Baptist Church in Charlotte are named for communities rather than for saints. I have never quite been certain of whether being First Baptist makes us Number One or just the first one in town. The Church of the Epiphany is a common name among Catholic churches. It fits the vision of the gospel well.

The church ought to be a place where the light of God is revealed to all people. Maybe the name would not fit too well for a Baptist church, but that is my vision for our church.

I read recently that 99 percent of our light comes ultimately from the sun. We do not create the light. We find creative ways to make the stored energy visible. That is the responsibility we have for the gospel. We do not initiate or create the light. We find ways to make God's light visible to a dark world. We allow God's light to shine through his people. God acts; we react. God initiates; we respond. Then the world sees.—Larry Dipboye

SECTION III

MESSAGES FOR COMMUNION SERVICES

SERMON SUGGESTIONS

Topic: You Are Welcome
TEXT: Luke 15:1–2

The school cafeteria comes fairly close to the social structure of the Gospels. The school "who's who" is played out every day at lunch as "birds of a feather flock together." Everyone wants to sit at the same table with the handsome, the popular, and the star of last week's game. Clusters of friends gather daily with varying degrees of exclusivity. A stranger may be allowed at some tables, but some kids are not welcome anywhere. Geeks and nerds are abandoned to each other's company, and the uncool eat alone.

I. The table is more than a place to eat. Put Jesus in the school cafeteria, and you will always find him with the wrong people. Sometimes he will invite himself to the table of the outcast, like the day he invited himself to the home of Zacchaeus, the tax collector. Height was not the only problem that put Zacchaeus up a tree. He was not welcome anywhere. He was scum. He stole social security checks from the handicapped and the elderly as a vocation, and he did it all legally with the full support and cooperation of the Roman authorities. The Romans were not stupid. They preferred to get a local to do their dirty work. The collectors were neighbors who had sold out to the enemy. Like a cat in the company of dogs, Zacchaeus preferred to watch the show from the branch of a tree. Jesus looked right past the clusters and cliques to the little guy in the tree and invited himself to the table of the most hated man in town. Obviously Jesus did not know about the protocol of the school cafeteria. Then again, maybe he knew but didn't care.

Even when Jesus chose to eat with the right folks, he seemed to be a genius at closing the door to any future invitation—like the day he was the guest of honor at the table of Simon the Pharisee. According to Luke 7:36, "He went into the Pharisee's house and took his place at the table." A woman of the city walked into the dining court off the street with a container of very expensive perfume. She probably intended to anoint his head as a sign of honor, but she was overcome with emotion. She began to shed tears of gratitude as she knelt at his feet. Then she wiped the tears from his feet with her hair, kissing his feet and anointing them with the perfume. Then came the judgment. According to Simon the host, no real prophet would allow a woman of her reputation actually to touch him! Evidently this was a woman of some reputation, even though John identifies her as Mary, the sister of Lazarus. The story has striking similarities to the account in Matthew and Mark of the woman who anointed Jesus' head, only the disciples played the role of the self-righteous.

In Luke, this is the long version of the prying, critical inquiry of the Pharisees about the table manners of Jesus, about why he associated with sinners. It is a living parable illustrating the common accusation found at the beginning: "Look, a glutton and a drunkard, a friend of tax collectors and sinners!" Evidently the social life of Jesus was quite an item among the

Pharisees. The criticism emerges again in Luke 15 as the key issue in the three parables—the lost coin, the lost sheep, and the lost son. These are not stand-alone parables, and they cannot be separated from the accusation leveled at Jesus: "This fellow welcomes sinners and eats with them." As a shepherd celebrates the recovery of a lost sheep, a woman celebrates finding a lost coin, and a loving father celebrates the return of a lost son, Jesus opens his arms in welcome to the kids who eat alone in the back corner of the lunchroom.

II. The real difficulty is in knowing who you are. The line of distinction is not drawn between saints and sinners, as we usually assume. Through the window of the gospel, the line stands between the ignorant and the informed. Jesus did not endorse prostitution any more than he endorsed murder and robbery. The notorious sinners seemed to know who they were. Folks who were in real danger were the self-righteous, like Simon, who thought they were good. Jesus never challenged the high moral tone of the Scribes and Pharisees. The Kingdom standards of righteousness are higher. We can read this as either trying to out-Pharisee the Pharisees in a nit-picking religion of behavioral perfectionism, or as a humble acknowledgment, "All have sinned and fall short of the glory of God." The Pharisee and the Publican (tax collector) who went up to the Temple to pray stood on the same ground. One was conscious of his sin before God while the other thought of himself as beyond the need of divine grace. The elder brother's faithfulness to his father certainly deserved commendation, but he failed to see himself in his younger brother's failure. He had cut all family ties from the wanderer, but brothers are always brothers regardless of where they roam or how bad they behave. Cain is always his brother's keeper. The practice of self-righteousness is more dangerous than the worst of sinful behaviors simply because we lose sight of our identity with one another.

III. You are welcome. Barbara Brown Taylor sees Jesus at the local Huddle House eating with "an abortion doctor, a child molester, an arms dealer, a garbage collector, a young man with AIDS, a Laotian chicken plucker, a teenage crack addict, and an unmarried woman on welfare with five children by three different fathers." Then enters the local ministerial association, who sit across the room, join hands and pray, and stare at the odd bunch and click their tongues at the other table. Jesus should know better than to hang out with the wrong crowd.

The scene repeats itself in churches all of the time. We are prone to forget who we are. Then someone walks into our Wednesday dinner gathering poorly dressed, of questionable personal hygiene, and uncertain moral history; and finally someone says, "Come and sit at my table." And I can almost hear the word of Christ, "I was hungry and you gave me food, a stranger and you welcomed me."

The table stands before us in worship as a symbol of our acceptance of God demonstrated in our acceptance of one another. It is the table of the Lord. You are welcome!—Larry Dipboye

Topic: Communion in God—Life Together
Text: John 15:1–17

One of the great images that Jesus provided to his followers was that of the vine and the branches. To those followers he said, "I am the vine, you are the branches." Moreover, it is God who is the vine grower. God prunes the branches of the vine so that they are productive and strong. God then is glorified as each branch grows and becomes fruitful.

Jesus was talking about what it means to follow him. He said that anyone who would be his disciple will live his or her life in Jesus, and Jesus' words will also live in each disciple's heart. This sharing of Jesus' divine life with our human lives yields a positive result. To paraphrase the Scripture, it is the person who shares Jesus' life and whose life Jesus shares who proves fruitful. The plain fact is that apart from Jesus, a person "can do nothing at all," as the Gospel of John explains. That separation is like a branch broken off from the vine, no longer pulsing with meaningful energy. It is fit only to be cast aside or perhaps used for firewood. Attachment to Jesus, on the other hand, signifies continuing growth, with every possibility of truly productive living.

We experience both communion in God and life together. We abide in our Lord, and beyond that we are connected to one another as well.

The warning of Scripture immediately applies: if we fail to sustain this attachment to the Master, our effective power for living is gone. We cannot bear fruit alone. A withered branch is next to useless. Furthermore, a community of disciples detached from Jesus becomes merely a random collection of individuals. Not much can be expected of them. Without communion in God, there is very little experience of life together.

The image of the vine and branches describes the union between Jesus and his followers. This union then bears its full fruit as those followers live and serve together.

We need constantly to abide in Jesus and to allow him to abide in us. As that happens, our ties to one another become firm and lasting and what we call the Church develops as God intends. Always we must look to the source of spiritual life: to Jesus, who is the vine, and to God, who is the vine dresser. Faithfulness there translates into faithfulness here, in our congregational life and service. None of us would want to be part of a church that had forfeited its understanding of the vine and the branches. We would not want to be cut off from the Lord of the Church, from Jesus himself. So it is that individually and collectively we cultivate the kind of relationship, as Jesus said, that will lead to his joy being in us and to our joy being complete.

The joy about which Jesus spoke relates to bearing fruit, to imparting good things as his representatives in the world. *Love* is one of those good things. "As the Father has loved me," said Jesus, "so I have loved you; abide in my love." He went on to say, "I appointed you to go and bear fruit, fruit that will last. . . . I am giving you these commands so that you may love one another." Love is the chief fruit or product of the branches that draw their nourishment from the vine. Love identified the Christian community. "Behold how they love one another," it was said of Christians in New Testament times. The same is said of Christians today insofar as their life together centers on communion in God. The closer we get to our Master, the closer we get to one another. Love is the name of that relationship.

It is not only within this particular congregation that we demonstrate the fruitfulness of love. It is also with all Christian fellowships wherever they are found.

Someone has written, "Unmistakably, love is the true essence which the vine distributes to the branches, so that the greatest fruit of the kingdom is this fruit of love which we, the branches, are expected to bear."

As the branches remain connected to the vine and in relationship with one another, the power of God finds outlet in the world.

A very practical explanation of how we need one another comes from the ancient wisdom literature of Israel. In the Old Testament book of Ecclesiastes, a section of material makes the contrast between solitary living versus mutual cooperation. The writer has no kind words for people who envy and vainly compete against their neighbors. His positive feelings are toward those who encourage life together. "Two are better than one," he writes, "because they have a good reward for their toil. For if they fall, one will lift up the other; but woe to one who is alone and falls and does not have another to help. Again, if two lie together, they keep warm; but how can one keep warm alone? And though one might prevail against another, two will withstand one. A threefold cord is not quickly broken." These thoughts sharpen the meaning of life together and even anticipate Jesus' teaching that no one can bear fruit alone.

Someone has dared to say that communion in God—life together—makes all things possible. Could this have been Jesus' meaning when he taught, "If you abide in me, and my words abide in you, ask whatever you will, and it shall be done for you"? That dramatic promise has been claimed by heroes of Christian faith through the ages. It is a promise you and I also can claim if indeed our spirits are in harmony with Jesus' spirit and our vine and branch relationship is secure. Seemingly impossible issues yield to the power of our Lord as he works through us and the fellowship we share. Enormous potential is ours as we experience communion in God—life together.

The path before us is plain. Day by day we serve well and live at our best as we draw nourishment from the vine. Acting in concert with other Christians, we bear the fruit of love to an often loveless world. Dedicated to communion in God and life together, we find ourselves blessed with the joy of the Lord and are able to spread that joy. All of these things are realized by prayer and faithfulness on the part of each of us.—John H. Townsend

Topic: Come to the Table
TEXT: Luke 13:22–30

As a way of renewing our lives and being in touch with the realities of Christian faith, observance of the Lord's Supper may seem an odd practice indeed. Among the accusations brought against early Christian believers by their enemies was that of cannibalism. These people, it was charged, eat the body and drink the blood of their leader. Even when it was explained as a symbolic act, outside observers had trouble understanding this fundamental practice of the early church. Still today it is not always understood.

Recognizing the simplicity of communion is a helpful place to begin. By simplicity I mean the association of our Lord's life with one of the most regular and elemental experiences of our own lives: that of eating and drinking. Jesus said that every time we break bread, every time we drink from the cup, we have an occasion for remembering him—remembering specifically his broken body and shed blood at the time of crucifixion. Recalling his sacrifice points us to the outcome of it, namely, to the forgiveness and reconciling love of God. By his death Jesus revealed the lengths to which God, manifest in Jesus, was willing to go to draw all people to himself. Though this awesome blessing can be described theologically, though it can be read about in the pages of the Bible, though it can be a subject for study and discussion, above all it can be known personally through the two simple acts of eating and drinking. Remembrance of God's redeeming love expressed in Jesus Christ can be experienced anew as we again come to the table; it is as uncomplicated as that. Here we eat and drink basic food elements in remembrance of our Lord.

In the teachings of Jesus, coming to the table had another meaning as well. The table fellowship represented a sign of God's kingdom—which is to say, it signified the gathering of all of God's people, all who have lived by faith and have sought to be true servants of God. At the conclusion of one of his parables Jesus said, "People will come from east and west, from north and south, and will eat in the kingdom of God." A mighty gathering will occur—and it will be at a feast, at a banquet. God, as the psalmist said, will prepare a table before us; our cups will overflow. These are images readily grasped because they relate to those primary experiences we know so well, the experiences of eating and drinking.

It was at a dinner attended by Jesus, during which he told a parable about the welcoming hospitality of God, that one of the guests exclaimed, "Blessed is anyone who will eat bread in the Kingdom of God!" That remark prompted yet another parable about a banquet. Jesus in his next story contrasted indifference with willing acceptance, relating to a certain host's invitation. The comfortable and well-fed who constituted the first guest list all made excuses and failed to show up at meal time. Their host felt compelled as a result to search out the poor, the maimed, the blind, the lame. These people, the often rejected ones of society, willingly responded and enjoyed the feast. Jesus' point was that individuals gathered around God's table are those keenly aware of their needs. They are not the self-centered, who place other priorities ahead of the divine invitation. Implied by Jesus as he told his parable were some questions, specifically, Will you be there? Will you be at the table of the Lord? or Will you make an excuse and stay away?

Recorded in the New Testament is another statement of Jesus that continues this line of thought. "Listen!" he said, "I am standing at the door, knocking; if you hear my voice and open the door, I will come into you and eat with you, and you with me." Here is a picture of intimacy predicated on the willingness of each of us to allow Christ into our lives. Most interesting is the image of that resulting fellowship found in Jesus' words, "I will eat with you, and you with me." Once more, the routine act of coming to the table becomes a way of accessing spiritual truth.

It is not by happenstance that eating together is a chief characteristic of Christian congregations. Whether it is the time-honored potluck supper or a formal, served meal, breaking bread with one another is an important part of church life. We may not always be aware of it, but by this kind of fellowship we are anticipating the mystery Jesus described. At that Last Supper Jesus had with his disciples, when he established the practice we follow at communion he said, "I tell you I will never again drink of this fruit of the vine until that day when I drink it new with you in my Father's Kingdom." These words direct us beyond present understanding, to the mystery of eternal fellowship and the coming together at the table of the hosts of God's people. We can say that our commonplace meals foreshadow a greater and heavenly banquet, in company with Christ himself. Sharing meals together thus becomes one of the very important things we do.

It is important not only because eating together anticipates that further and future relationship with Christ; it is important also because you and I and all of us together thereby form a community, a company, a fellowship. That we are not Christians alone is one way to look at it. Our assembling at a meal strengthens the ties that bind; we are drawn closer to each other through such occasions, with our faith encouraged and enhanced.

It is by gathering together in so ordinary an event as eating a meal that Christians nourish both body and soul—for themselves and potentially for many others beyond themselves. From the ordinary and commonplace, the sacred is born.—John H. Townsend

Topic: Remembering the Grace

TEXT: Isa. 55:1–9; Eph. 1:3–10; 2 Cor. 8:9

If I had but one sermon to preach—that is a sobering thought—what would it be? The subject would be the theme of our biblical text this morning: "Remember the grace of our Lord Jesus Christ who was rich, yet for our sakes became poor, that we through his poverty might be rich."

In this single verse is the Advent/Christmas story according to the apostle Paul. Here the mind-boggling fact of the Incarnation is stated as poignantly as anywhere in the New Testament. In their original context, these words were written to the Christians at Corinth, challenging them to a generous offering for their needy brothers and sisters in the Church in Jerusalem. There is no higher motive for Christian giving—for Christian living—than the grace of our Lord Jesus Christ.

I. The grace of God as we come to know it fully in Jesus of Nazareth is an amazing grace. That Almighty God, the Creator of the heavens and the Earth, the Lord of the universe, the Eternal Spirit, should come in person, in the flesh and blood of one of us, to Earth of all the planets that he has created and set in motion—what grace, what an amazing grace.

God, the infinite God, the Everlasting One, the God above all gods, comes to save you—to save me. He does not send an emissary, some ambassador, not even an angel; he does not phone long distance; he does not wire a fax—he comes in person. Can you think of anything more amazing than that? "He was rich, yet for our sakes became poor." "He emptied himself of being God to become a person to identify with us in our every need."

The amazing grace of God in Christ that prompts so much celebration in this season has nowhere been more aptly expressed than by John Newton in his popular hymn "Amazing Grace." The lyrics of this song are so moving, for they are autobiographical.

For much of his life John Newton was a lost soul. He was the captain of a ship that brought slaves from Africa to be sold on the auction block in London. He seemed to have no conscience concerning the evil of his trade and the deplorable conditions that the slaves survived on his ship. But then on one trip off the coast of Africa, en route to England with his cargo, the ship ran into a storm in which he nearly lost everything, including his own life. Out of this experience there came a strange turning in his life that no psychologist could ever have charted. Out of this crisis he heard the call of God, gave up the slave trade, educated himself, and was ordained to the Christian ministry.

The story of his conversion has become one of the most beloved hymns ever written, with an almost universal appeal.

> Amazing grace, how sweet the sound,
> That saved a wretch like me!
> I once was lost, but now am found,
> Was blind, but now I see.

The amazing paradoxical nature of grace—the grace that judges but also saves—is the theme of the second verse:

'Twas grace that taught my heart to fear,
And grace my fears relieved.

II. Remember the grace of our Lord Jesus Christ—as amazing grace and abounding grace. As the apostle Paul writes in our lesson, "In him we have redemption through his blood, forgiveness of our sins, according to the riches of his grace that he lavished on us." Where sin abounds, grace does much more abound, the apostle assures. God is such a spendthrift; his grace is never stintingly given; but he lavishes it upon us; his abounding grace covers all our sins—addresses our every need.

"In Christ I am ready for anything," the apostle Paul declares. How could he say that? Because he knew the abounding grace of God in the Beloved. Is not the apostle's Creed speaking of the depths to which God's abounding grace will go when it declares of Christ, "He descended into hell"? What blessed assurance that Jesus is with us in all the hells that we encounter—the fiery furnaces of our trials.

III. Remember the grace of our Lord Jesus Christ—an amazing grace, an abounding grace, and a free grace. When the Bible scholars of an earlier generation spoke of "free" grace, they did not mean that grace does not cost anything. It is costly—it cost God his only Son. When we say that grace is "free" we mean that it cannot be earned; it is not for sale, even at Saks Fifth Avenue. It is the gift of God freely given. As the apostle writes in our lesson, "God destined us for adoption as his children through Jesus Christ, to the praise of his glorious grace that he freely bestowed upon us in the Beloved." This characterization of grace as free— "without money and without price"—is the theme of our Old Testament lesson.

Listen, everyone who thirsts
come to the waters;
and you that have no money,
come, buy wine and milk
without money and without price.

What an invitation to God's feast of grace!

Grace is free in that it is the gift of God, and it is free in that it is out of our control. We cannot manipulate it. We cannot apprehend it, even comprehend it. Grace is free in that it is serendipitous, unpredictable, full of surprises. God does move in mysterious ways, his wonders to perform.

We discover God's grace in the most unlikely of places—in the most unpromising of persons. Perhaps the serendipitous nature of grace is nowhere more strikingly illustrated than in the Church's doctrine of the virgin birth. We often affirm our faith by repeating the Apostle's Creed: "I believe in God the Father Almighty, Maker of heaven and Earth; and in Jesus Christ his only Son, our Lord, who was conceived by the Holy Ghost, born of the Virgin Mary. . . ." The Church through much of its history has been so literal and biological in interpreting this doctrine that it has missed its profound theological meaning.

Whatever else it may be, the doctrine of the virgin birth is the Gospel writer's attempt to declare in the most radical terms possible that salvation is of God. God takes the initiative.

Our salvation is from on high. God's coming is free; he can come to this planet in any way he chooses and not as we in our little minds and diminutive hearts scheme that he should.

> They were all looking for a king
> To slay their foes and lift them high;
> Thou cam'st a little baby thing
> That made a woman cry.

Remember the grace of our Lord Jesus Christ. To remember the grace of God in Jesus of Nazareth is to remember the waters of our baptism. The whole of the gospel is dramatized in this sacrament. When in his struggle with the Roman Pope and the German princes Martin Luther was hard-pressed, he would renew his faith by affirming to himself, "I have been baptized." To make this affirmation is to say, "I am a child of the covenant. I am saved—and I am saved by the grace of God. I need not fear what man can do unto me." In baptism we remember the grace of God at work for our salvation and the salvation of humankind.

Our partaking of the bread and the cup must be a participation in the life and spirit of Jesus, through faith, as real as though we were eating of his body and drinking of his blood.

The mystery and meaning of the sacrament are the mystery and meaning of the Incarnation—the Word becoming flesh. "This is of the Lord's doing and it is marvelous in our eyes!"—John Thompson

ILLUSTRATIONS

THE SECRET OF GENERAL BOOTH.   Read Richard Collier's tremendous book *The General Next to God*, the story of the rise and progress of the Salvation Army, and of General Booth in particular. It is magnificent. What was the secret of this giant of a man who led his motley army to such monumental achievements, sweeping aside physical violence and fanatical opposition, ignoring social obloquy? "If there is any secret," the General himself modestly said, "it is this: Jesus Christ has had the whole of me." He offered himself, keeping nothing back. This is the least we can do, and the best.—John N. Gladstone[1]

COMPANIONS IN SHARING.   Theologian Robert McAfee Brown has said, "I believe that we are placed here to be companions—a wonderful word that comes from *cum panis* ("with bread"). We are here to share bread with one another so that everyone has enough." Out of such sharing, as Dr. Brown indicated, sensitivity to human need is achieved. As we become companions among ourselves, awareness grows that such companionship deserves to be extended. Our bread—our faith—increasingly is shared. Another writer, a woman named Abbie Graham, explained it like this: "God lives not, I think, in bread and wine, but in the breaking of bread, in the sharing of wine. Bread unbroken does not fortify the heart, but bread divided among all who hunger will sustain the spirit."—John H. Townsend

WHERE JESUS WALKED.   In visiting the Holy Land, the amazing grace in God's Incarnation becomes real, perhaps as in no other way. This happened for me at Capernaum on the

---

[1] *All Saints and All Sorts*

shore of the Sea of Galilee, where Jesus began his public ministry. There are ruins of two synagogues there, only a short distance apart, and we cannot be sure in which one Jesus spoke his inaugural sermon.

"But," our Jewish guide said to our traveling party, "this is not the important thing, to be able to determine which synagogue Jesus attended. The important thing for you Christians is that he was here—that he actually walked these dusty roads, that he was a person, that he was as anyone of you, that he was for real. This is the strategic thing for your faith—that the Incarnation really happened."

In talking with one of our members before she left with the group traveling to the Holy Land, she simply said to me: "I want to go to as many places where Jesus was as I can." In those words I hear her saying, "I want to celebrate the fact of the Incarnation for myself—God becoming a person and dwelling among us."—John Thompson

SINNERS BREAKING BREAD.   A German pastor, thrown into a concentration camp, had lived for three years in solitary confinement. One night, a uniformed S.S. man came into his cell. He said: "Pastor, I have been condemned to death. Will you hear the confession of my sins, and give me the Lord's Supper?" So he confessed, and his sins were many and grievous. Then the pastor took the stool which had been his seat for three years and placed on it a piece of bread left over from his dinner. Beside it, he put a mug of water. Then the two men knelt on either side of the stool, each a sinner in the sight of a gracious God. They broke bread together. They received the assurance of pardon and peace. And they were filled with joy.—John N. Gladstone[2]

THE SOURCE OF COURAGE.   One of you shared with me your story of experiencing an abounding grace. You had major back surgery at Sarasota Memorial. When I called on you a day or two later, you shared with me that you had a most difficult night. "If I have ever been through a dark night of the soul, this has been it," you confessed. You shared that in enduring your most excruciating pain you had discovered faith and courage as you recalled the grace of our Lord Jesus Christ. You saw him on the cross in his suffering, and you knew you were not alone. You heard his assuring words: "Take courage! I have overcome the world." And you found yourself repeating, "In the cross of Christ I glory, towering o'er the wrecks of time."—John Thompson

---

[2] ibid.

SECTION IV

MESSAGES FOR FUNERAL AND BEREAVEMENT

SERMON SUGGESTIONS

Topic: Not Made with Hands
TEXT: 2 Cor. 5:1–5

I'm glad that we share a belief that one of the ways God speaks to us is through the Holy Scriptures, and furthermore, that part of what God says to us in the Bible is there for our comfort. Our passage from the apostle Paul is a practical and theological reflection in which many people do find comfort.

Paul was not always in the mood for comfort, but he managed here in spite of himself. He told the Corinthians, at some other place, that he was better at building up than he was at tearing down. This brief passage is part of that reality.

Paul had a keen eye for what mattered, and much about which we worry day by day really doesn't matter. He could look beyond the limitations of our earthly existence and set the value of life here and now in the context of eternity.

One fact about which he was certain is that there is more to human life than the body in which we live during our years on earth. This body is important and essential in the way God has created us. We won't overlook that, and we don't want to. Paul was quick to remind us that when this body fails—and it will—it's not the end of us by any means. "For we know that if the earthly tent we live in is destroyed, we have a building from God, a house not made with hands, eternal in the heavens" (v. 1).

The "tent," when set up properly and well cared for, can last and give those who use it protection and enjoyment, but there are no delusions about its durability. A tent is something humanmade, not permanent; we could not live there long. Paul contrasts a tent with a *house that God builds*—a heavenly, eternal home. This eternal home with God is promised to all who are children of God. We want it, and we need it. "Here indeed we groan, and long to put on our heavenly dwelling" (v. 2).

Life lived in relationship with God is so rich and full. When we begin to understand just how wonderful it is, we don't want to lose out on such life—ever, and we don't have to. God's children don't lose out on it. Instead, what happens is that, in God's vast plan, mortality is "swallowed up by life" (v. 4). The essence of who one is, is transformed into fullness in the heavenly realms—no more weaknesses or limitations.

It's hard to believe, isn't it? "[The one] who has prepared us for this very thing is God, who has given us the Spirit as a guarantee" (v. 5). Through the Holy Spirit of God there are constant renewals in our lives and in the lives of many people we know, and these take place in an imperfect world. If this goes on here in this life and we can know a sense of renewal and resurrection in this life, how much greater will be the transformation God has waiting for his children in heaven! The best of life in the present is only a foretaste of all that God has for God's own.

Dear friends, your loved one and our friend has moved out of his tent and into a most elegant heavenly home, a heavenly body in which he can celebrate his wholeness even as he joins the celestial choirs singing praise to God. He has begun to receive the gifts of eternity; he is in a new home, not a home made with hands but a home made by God. Though separated from you for a time, he is well cared for. After all, to be away from the body as we know it is, for God's children, to be "at home with the Lord" (v. 8). And so he is. Amen.—David Albert Farmer[1]

Topic: Our Very Present Help

TEXT: Ps. 46

We join you today in this painful event as friends who share in your grief and disbelief. We share your sense of deep loss and the profound wish that there might have been some other way. We have no answers or explanations; we, like you, are inclined to search for ways to understand, but we have all already discovered that such a search is in vain. And still, without answers, explanations, or ways to grasp what has happened, we stand alongside each of you with the hope and confidence in Jesus Christ that the last word has not been spoken. Even in this situation of what feels to us like finality in the extreme, the God of life will not let it be. The God who gives life—physically and spiritually—has already taken the one you love into his divine arms and welcomed her into her heavenly home.

We understand all too well that those of you nearest her remain in a state of confusion, heavyhearted and bereaved, lonely and confused. Of course; how could it be any other way? What I have to offer today is a simple reminder that the God who loves and has provided for her eternally also loves you and is ready to help you bear the heavy load. This is the abiding message of the Christian faith and the only basis through which we can face life's grim realities with a sense of hopefulness intact. God loves you, abides with you, and will not forsake you in these moments and in the days of readjustment and reorientation that are ahead of you.

This surely is the message of the psalm 46. Where could we find stronger words of comfort? These are words especially for you today.

Not only are the psalmist's words beautifully rendered and reflective of profound insight, but also the very logic provides a pastoral word of comfort and inspiration. The writer begins with the full force of theological reality, a statement of religious confession and assurance that gives order and hope to his life and to the whole human family. This is the beginning point. This is the lens through which we view world events and the more immediate circumstances affecting our lives. Any other point of departure, any other frame of reference, will distort not only how we see but also how we hope. The psalmist began with God, and so must we.

Not just any god, mind you, but with the one true God, the creating, redeeming, and loving God. The God on whom his people may depend; and with only a little bit of experience in our uncertain and many times cruel world, we see that this is the God on whom we *must* depend. "God is our refuge and strength, a very present help in trouble" (Ps. 46:1). Therefore,

---

[1] *Basic Bible Sermons on Hope*

let us come to grips with our grief, anger, fear, and loneliness, which result from this untimely death, by looking first to and through such a God as this, the God to whom Jesus also pointed. Because of his own reliance on God and because God was so much in him, Jesus could say, "Come to me, all who labor and are heavy laden, and I will give you rest . . . rest for your souls" (Matt. 11:28, 20).

The psalmist's assessment of God does stir us to reach out to God because God is reaching out to us in a living presence that helps us fend off enemies from without and enemies from within. God is our refuge; in relationship with God we may take shelter from outward attack, such as a tragedy over which we have absolutely no control. Oh, there will come a time to step out of the shelter and take on the enemy; but even then God will be with us, because God, too, is our strength. The psalmist's summary of theological affirmation is that God is a present help in trouble; come what may, God's presence is what we need to cope and keep on searching for the divine meaning in life. Again, this is where we begin, not with the trouble.

The trouble is real, and God never asks us to ignore it; that would be disastrous. However, in spite of trouble, the psalmist still draws our attention Godward. As an example of trouble, the psalmist recalls a personal experience—perhaps the most horrifying experience he could have imagined: an earthquake. Even in that time when he feared for his own life amid death and destruction all around, he could still affirm that God was his refuge and strength.

What you have been living through for the last several days is like a personal and emotional earthquake—with much of your joy and stability threatened and even dying. Finding peace and courage to rebuild will not be easy. You can find some courage and encouragement that you're not up against it all alone. In both the material and emotional rebuilding and healing, the Lord of hosts is with you; the God of Jacob is your refuge.—David Albert Farmer[2]

Topic: Christians Will Rise Again
TEXT: John 11:1–44

Death often shakes our faith in God. The reason is not that we stop believing in God. No. Our problem is that we know God could have healed our loved one if he had chosen to do so.

Today is no different. We mark the passing of a loved one, a loved one who knew and loved Jesus. The Lord of life could have spared her for now, but chose to take her while we still need her. How does God help us in these times? What promises does he make? This text tells us that God responds to our concerns, asks us to have faith in him, and pledges eternal life for all who believe in him. Let us take comfort in these truths.

I. *God responds to our honest concerns* (11:21, 32). Many of us were raised by people who told us not to question God. These good folks (and they were good folks) thought that God does not like or respond to questions asked in pain. But Jesus did not blast Martha and Mary for wondering why he did not come when he was told of Lazarus' death. He did not rebuke them when they said he could have kept their brother from dying. Rather, he spoke kindly to them. He dealt with their honest questions.

---

[2] *Basic Bible Sermons on Hope*

Faith in Christ does not solve every earthly problem. We still know that God could heal but allows death. We trust the Lord, yet still the death of a loved one hurts.

Take your questions to the Lord. He loves you and made you smart enough to raise important issues. Take heart. As long as you ask in faith, trusting that God wants to answer, you will find God a loving, responsive father.

II. *God builds our faith* (11:23–32). When Martha and Mary were honest with Jesus about Lazarus' death, he built their faith. He asked them to affirm that those who live and believe in him never die. He meant that death cannot hold a Christian. We pass from this life into life everlasting. This truth can only be accepted by faith, for none of us has experienced death yet. Martha and Mary believed, and they were comforted. Do we believe?

Ultimately Jesus asked the sister to believe *in him*. Our faith must be in what Jesus teaches, of course, but we believe what he teaches because we believe in him. The two cannot be separated. When we trust Christ we trust the one who made us (John 1:1–14). We trust the one who saves (John 3:16), heals (John 5:1–15), forgives (John 8:1–11), and gives abundant life (John 10:10). When we trust him we are secure (John 10:28–29).

So let the person and promise of our Lord fill your hurting hearts and your questioning heads. Know that at these times he is worth trusting and that trusting him makes us strong.

III. *God gives eternal life* (11:25, 33–34). Of course you know that Jesus raised Lazarus from the dead. Martha and Mary's brother came stumbling out of his tomb, wrapped tightly in his grave clothes. Jesus raises the dead, just as God raised Jesus from the dead. Lazarus died again, but death had no power over him, for Christ rules death.

Now, our friend will not come back to life today. Nor did everyone Jesus loved come back to life when he was on Earth. But everyone who trusts Jesus will be raised on the last day, the day when God will banish death (1 Cor. 15:51–58) and take us to a new heaven and a new Earth (Rev. 21:1–8). Truly those who live and believe in Christ never die; we can and do believe this truth, and we are comforted by it.

In 1963 C. S. Lewis met with some friends for what he thought would be the last time. As they parted, he shouted across a busy Oxford street, "Christians never have to say goodbye!" He was right. We are now separated from our friend, but we have not said goodbye. She lived and believed in Christ, and he will raise her just as surely as he raised Lazarus, just as surely as he will raise us. If you believe this, then depart in hope to serve the living God, who responds to our concerns, who teaches us to believe in him, who guarantees us eternal life.—Paul R. House

Topic: The Lord of Our Days

TEXT: Eccl. 3:1–8

We come together today on a sad occasion, the death of Frances Moore.[3] But times like these give us cause to think, and they offer us the possibility of growing stronger. We still grow stronger as we trust in God, depending on him to meet our needs. For it is God who is Lord of our days, our work, our play, our hopes and dreams, and especially of our pain. God ordered Frances's days, and we would do well to consider how he orders ours as we consider this text.

---

[3] Frances Moore was a member of our community whom I did not know. I developed this sermon for use in this situation, and preached it on several other, similar occasions.

I. *A time to be born* (3:2). God is the Lord of creation. He made Frances, and he made us, for God created the universe. Genesis 1 teaches that God made all things good. James 1:17 adds that all good gifts come from God, who never changes, never fails to be just and loving. Everything good that Frances did was God's work through her.

Further, God made us for a specific purpose. Men and women are created in God's image and have the capacity to know and love him. The main reason we were born is to love and serve God, who died for us so that we might have eternal life. The book of Ecclesiastes claims that it is not always easy to relate to God, yet urges us to do so. As we walk with the Lord we find that the God who created us orders our days.

II. *A time to live* (3:3–8). The Lord of our days fills our days with important work to do. Frances was a homemaker, one who made a living easier for others. You may be a farmer, a computer expert, a secretary, or a teacher, or you may do some other type of worthy work that makes you gather, sew, or plant. All honorable work is given by the Lord of our days to benefit others and to meet our family's needs. In our work we find meaning, and this meaning takes us back to God.

God also gives family, as Frances's gathered loved ones demonstrate. In families we learn to laugh and to weep, to mourn and to dance, and to love and hate. Whatever your family's current level of love and trust, I ask you at this crucial time to draw together. A death reminds us that petty squabbles and old hurts only separate us from those we need most. A death also reminds us that family closeness is a wonderful gift.

Most of all, God gives himself. Work and family enrich our lives, but even these blessings do not match the grace and love of God. Just as you need family now, so you need the love of your heavenly Father. Reach out to him as the Lord of your days who gives good work and good people during the living of your life.

III. *A time to die* (3:2). A funeral reminds us that life on Earth ends. We all die. And under normal conditions none of us really longs for death. Yet death is a reality, and we must prepare for it.

Frankly, many of us fear death. Paul speaks of his fear when he mentions that sin is the sting of death (1 Cor. 15:54–55). Why does sin make death sting? Because it separates us from God unless we have believed in Christ. If we commit our lives to the Lord of our days, though, there is no sting in death, for our sins are forgiven (1 Cor. 15:56–57).

Through Christ we need not fear death. He has defeated death on our behalf (1 Cor. 15:54–58). He has promised life after death (John 3:16). He has promised a place where death, separation, and pain—such as we feel today—will no longer exist (Rev. 21:1–8). All who prepare for death by trusting in Christ can claim these promises as their own.

The Lord of our days desires to give us endless days with him. The one who made us, who gave us work and family, desires to spend eternity with us. As we take comfort in these truths, may we learn to walk with the Lord of our days.—Paul R. House

From Everlasting to Everlasting, Thou Art God

A sermon by James W. Crawford
The Old South Church in Boston

On November 24, 1995, I received a telephone call from my brother-in-law Walter B. Smith in Arlington, Virginia. My sister Polly, after a long, painful, and frightening struggle with ovarian cancer had died in hospice during the night. She left not only her husband, whom we call Uncle Waldo, but also three sons, Charles, Jimmy, and Walt Jr., ranging in ages from sixteen to ten years old. Polly was forty-four.

On May 27, 1997, I received a telephone call from my brother-in-law John Francis in Toledo, Ohio. My sister Jane, after a long, painful, and frightening struggle with ovarian cancer died in her home during the night. She left her husband, whom we call Uncle John—U. J. for short. Jane was forty-nine.

Ovarian cancer is one of those diseases still afflicting womankind that kills, so to speak, on contact. Just to discover it means you're too late. A variety of highly sophisticated procedures enables those stricken to live longer, to be relieved of significant pain, and to remain lucid and alert almost to the end. I have no doubt that the antidote to these killer cells will someday be discovered, but to this day the invasion of ovarian cancer cells means that the body's defense systems will ultimately be subverted and overwhelmed. The invasion renders premature death virtually inevitable.

That our family has been profoundly grateful to the immediate care of skilled and compassionate physicians, nurses, and health care workers is an understatement. Lewis Thomas wrote a compelling history of twentieth-century medicine entitled *The Youngest Science,* a book reminding us time and again that medicine is no less an art than a science, that a judgment based on facts, experience, and intuition forms the core of a physician's true authority, and that medicine can be called, in the true sense of the expression, a *practice.*

I claim no uniqueness for our family amid this four-year vigil. Heaven knows—I know—men, women, and children in this congregation who themselves fought the battle against cancer in their own bodies and won a reprieve. All of us know others who bore with it in their spouses, partners, and children and best friends. Health professionals worship with us this morning who battle this illness every day. Let me say simply that we wrestled with many of the anxieties and angers, the frequent sense of helplessness and powerlessness that you *did* and *do* through your vigils. We clung desperately to every sliver of news suggesting an oncological breakthrough at Bethesda's National Institute of Health, in Stockholm, or in London. We stood baffled by the disease striking two sisters within a year of one another. We speculated on diet, stress, the location of our childhood home, genetic predisposition, sympathetic response, the asbestos surrounding our high school swimming pool. We oscillated between seeing the illness as just another piece of nature going on about its business, or viewing it as a weapon of the devil to be cursed and sought and then finally in exhaustion and despair surrendered to. Because conversation consisted of the World Series, "Celtic pride," the weather, miserable golf scores, hanky-panky in Washington, our joint plans for our summer place, the fortunes of Dartmouth basketball, euphemisms became the order of the day; we denied the inevitability of their succumbing to this damned thing; we danced around death.

And yes, while this went on, so did the miraculous support of family and friends. What a fantastic network of human beings took shape amid our anxious pilgrimage. Thank God for the congregations with their prayer calendars, their carefully designed visiting schedules, their tape-recorded services. God bless those with "chipper" entrances into hospice and sick room, their wacky and sentimental presents, off-the-wall joke books, and sublime flower arrangements, their potluck suppers and boxes of candy, their weird and riotous get-well cards. As the author of Hebrews says, a veritable "cloud of witnesses" formed around these women and their families, offering humor, compassion, chit-chat, and from time to time the silence of solidarity in recognition of being jointly involved for a time in the marvel and mystery of mortality.

So there, you catch a glimpse of our story. My brothers-in-law would highlight different things. Our mother, who possesses an enormous capacity to embrace and share human suffering with serenity and courage and who provided inspiration to all of us would surely bring another perspective. Many of you this morning can tell stories containing similar components. On this occasion let me say I know a few of these stores, shared a piece of them with some of you, and am grateful to serve as a witness to, and receiver of, your constant faith and abiding hope as you and your loved ones over the years make your way through the "valley of the shadow." The witness of this congregation to me as you deal with the frailty and glory of the human condition grounded in the faith and hope of the gospel continues to inspire, encourage, and sustain my own faith. To you, my deepest thanks.

I. Now, friends, the true test of any religious tradition lies in its capacity to handle the grandeur and misery of human existence, the dimensions of human suffering, the threat and reality of death. Faith and hope begin and end on life's boundaries. In our family's encounter with these two deaths our faith has been threatened and deepened, and in the time remaining I want to point to a couple of markers we discovered out there on the boundary.

The first comes from a lesson we read a few moments ago: Psalm 90. Psalm 90 formed the base of Isaac Watts's hymn we sang to open our service this morning, "Our God, Our Help in Ages Past." By general consent that hymn stands as the greatest hymn ever written. How could it help but be so? Psalm 90, read at almost every memorial service, uses a variety of images for human life. The psalmist describes life as short as a three-hour watch in the night. He draws it as fresh grass growing in the morning, scorching in the midday sun, withering and dying by evening. He pictures life as a sleep we forget when we wake. But he sets this transience in God's eternity. Our life appears brief, transitory, partial because its measure lies not so much in our counting of the days, months, and years, but as one translator puts it, "with the God in whom we dwell in age after age, before the mountains were born or the earth and land labored in pains of birth." From the perspective of eternity we measure our temporality. To be sure, this marvelous psalm bears a melancholy note. The poet grasps the limitations of life, its vulnerability, its suffering, its final demise. In portions of the psalm we omitted this morning, the poet understands our life as incomplete and separated from the divine intentions designed for it. He understands us to be in danger of self-injury, if not self-destruction. Yet, though the poet expresses melancholy, we find him neither cynical nor in despair. No, he rejoices in our finding our true home within the embrace of one whose eternity sustains us, one who bears us through and across all of life's boundary situations, enabling us to live with security and courage in the face of life's contingencies. The psalmist lives with one who offers "a dwelling place in all generations," a God "who from everlasting to everlasting" is home to us.

II. A second marker set at the boundaries of life, indeed at the boundary of death itself, resides in the affirmation of what Paul calls the "resurrection of the body." The other day I passed a Hare Krishna house on Commonwealth Avenue and saw on their bulletin board a reference to the body's being an embarrassment to the soul. That's one way to look at life. But the biblical faith follows another way. We deal with the resurrection of the body because we believe that human personality includes all of our created being. Our bodies are not irrelevant husks incarcerating some pristine soul waiting to escape this prison house. Hardly! Our bodies help to define who we are; our bodies play a role in creating, expressing, and representing our personhood. Let me illustrate with a little piece I wrote for my sister for her memorial service a week or so ago in Ohio. After a short introduction indicated a fierce inner determination and phenomenal physical coordination, a paragraph or two centered on Jane's capabilities as an athlete and competitor. It went like this: "She could ski faster and more gracefully than the rest of us; she could swim with both suppleness and power; and Jane with her sister Polly dazzled us as a water-ballet duet. She became a superior tennis player, an excellent golfer, an intimidating bowler, a wicked ping-pong aficionado. We all thrived on her eagerness to excel. But did you know she could water ski in a fashion worthy of Cypress Gardens as a teenager? And did you know that she and Uncle John preempted the affections and attentions of all their nephews and niece during vacation? Why, you ask? Because between the hours of 6 and 9 P.M. on a glorious New Hampshire lake when the father of this nefarious brood headed for some barren fishing hole, Aunt Jane, in collusion with U.J., pointed to some obviously ridiculous and sterile eddy or shoal—and found fish. I suppose some of the fun hinged on her colorful expletives, heard and sympathized with by many of us when the bass spit out the hook, the putt rimmed the cup, or the ping-pong ball dribbled into the net."

Do you see? Her arms and legs, her muscles and brain, her feet and fingers played a vital role in the unity of her person. When Paul affirms God's power as raising our bodies, he's talking about God's hanging onto the whole of us, loving and treasuring, not some evanescent, gutless soul, but all of who we really are. "Resurrection of the body" serves as a metaphor for the complete, whole, full *you*. God loves all of you, and beyond the boundaries of life, God receives all of each of you home.

III. And briefly, just a word about the Communion of Saints, heaven, the so-called afterlife. In faith we confess that God receives us unto a loving, embracing self and we affirm our joining with others in this divine condition we call eternity. We dare not exclude anyone from God's boundless acceptance, nor deny anyone the capacity to change. I believe that the compassion and hope God holds for each of us continues to sustain and invites us to perfection through eternity. Nor dare we speculate on what Reinhold Niebuhr called "the temperature and furniture of heaven." But how about a wild, unverified conjecture? In the case of my sisters, I've wondered if Jane has recruited a golf foursome including Cleopatra, Joan of Arc, and Eleanor Roosevelt, and since it's heaven, tied them all—on earth she'd have whipped them—and is right now (since in heaven they need no churches) enjoying a cool lemonade and potato chips at St. Peter's nineteenth-hole cafe. As for Polly and her artistic gifts, she's no doubt looked up your spouse, or mother, or father, or son, or daughter—someone you love and miss—and made them a funny little doodad to pin on their wings or dangle from their halo. Regardless of what they're doing, we know where they are, where those whom you love and miss are, and where, by the promise of the everlasting God, we may be headed. We know what promise we finally live and die by. Paul lays out that promise for us by asking a brilliant rhetorical question. You know it as well as I. Remember? "Who shall separate us from the love of God? Shall tribulation or distress, or nakedness, or peril or famine or sword?" Then he answers the question, confessing, like our psalmist, the sovereignty of God over all of life and death. "No," he says, "in all these things we are more than conquerors through him who loves us. For I am persuaded that neither life nor death nor angels nor principalities, nor things present nor things to come, nor height nor depth nor anything else in all creation can separate us from the love of God in Christ Jesus, our Lord."

ILLUSTRATIONS

A GOOD GIFT.   A famous minister of a generation ago was James McIntyre. In an address illustrating the love of God he told of this incident.

James was the last boy to go into the room, because he was the youngest—then a lad of fifteen. In his own words, this is how he tells of that scene:

"I entered the room in which my father was dying. His face was as white as the pillow on which he lay. A deep sense of my unworthiness came over me. I remembered the times I hadn't done the chores, and other occasions when I had been unruly. As I tiptoed to his bedside it seemed as though there couldn't be a greater sinner in the world.

"But my father had only one word for me. Taking my hand, he said, 'Jim, you've been a good boy; always.'"

So the old farmer passing saw only the good and beautiful in his boy.

Which reminds us of what Jesus said: "If ye then, being evil, know how to give good gifts unto your children, how much more shall your Father which is in heaven give good things to them that ask Him?"—Archer Wallace[4]

ENRICHMENT AND GROWTH.   After a rather lengthy and extensive apologetic for the resurrection of the dead and the final triumph of God in Christ, the apostle Paul writes, "If only for this life we have hope in Christ, we are to be pitied more than all men" (1 Cor. 15:19 NIV). We are confronted by the affirmation that the Christian life is one lived out under the presence of death, but not under its power. This life, as we live it and know it and breathe it is to be valued as the place of our enrichment and personal growth. Yet this life has been transcended, extended if you will; it has been given a new horizon, the borders have been pushed to the limits, which are no longer limits at all.—Albert J. D. Walsh[5]

NOW AND FOREVER.   Diligent discipleship does not eliminate a future *eschaton*; the full arrival of what we have experienced in Jesus as a foretaste. There is an optimism in this regard that in theological terms is known as *realized eschatology*—that the Kingdom is being fully realized now. And surely there are present benefits of life in Christ (Rom. 6:4; Eph. 2:6); and the Gospel according to John tells us that we have passed from death into life (already) (John 5:24), and whoever has the Son has eternal life (John 3:36), and life eternal is to know God and to believe in the one whom God has sent (John 17:3).

Either view that denies the other breaks apart the Kingdom formula: already but not yet, in our midst and still to come, has come and will come. We can be "laborers in fields white unto harvest," but we cannot rush the Kingdom. We can calendarize human endeavors, but the when and where of God's Kingdom in its fullness are tucked away in the Father's wisdom. But above saying all in this parable of the sower, hopefully we have heard our Lord's

[4] *In Grateful Remembrance*
[5] *Reflections on Death and Grief*

voice saying, "Fear not, little flock, for it is your Father's good pleasure to give you the Kingdom" (Luke 12:32).—John Huffman

A VISION.   The stream of life through millions of years, the stream of human lives through countless centuries. Evil, death and dearth, sacrifice and love—what does "I" mean in such a perspective? Reason tells me that I am bound to seek my own good, seek to gratify my desires, win power for myself and admiration from others. And yet I "know"—know without knowing—that, in such a perspective, nothing could be less important. A vision in God *is.*—Dag Hammarskjöld[6]

COMPLETED.   In a harbor two ships sailed: one setting forth on a voyage, the other coming home to port. Everyone cheered the ship going out, but the ship sailing in was scarcely noticed. And a wise man said: "Do not rejoice over the ship that is setting out to sea, for you cannot know what storms it will encounter, what fearful dangers it may have to endure. But rejoice rather over the ship that has safely reached port, and brings home all its passengers in peace."

And this is the way of the world: when a child is born, all rejoice; when a man or woman dies, all weep. We should do the opposite. No one can tell what trials and travails await a child; but when a mortal dies in peace, we should rejoice, for he has completed his long journey and is leaving this world with the imperishable crown of a good name.—Adapted from the *Talmud*

WORTH.   This is the point of most temptations; we are tempted to create our own solutions rather than coping with anxiety by trusting in the wisdom and goodness of God.

If we are to learn of our worth from the accepting love of God, if we are to maintain the plausibility of God's purpose for our lives, and if we are to be able to yield to the gracious provision of our Lord, then we must be careful to keep the ring of his voice in our ears. "Hast thou not seen how thy desires e'er have been granted in what He ordaineth?"—John Huffman

---

[6] *Markings*

SECTION V

LENTEN AND EASTER PREACHING

SERMON SUGGESTIONS

Topic: What Sacrifices?

TEXT: Phil. 3:4–14

I. Paul had been good at the game. "Mirror, mirror on the wall, who's most righteous of them all?" Paul's name was at the top of the list. But it wasn't a game, and it isn't a game for us either. Most of us are troubled by the haunting questions about life. What is the purpose of life? What am I living for? What are we supposed to be doing with our lives? How do you measure the success and failure of living? Santa Claus may know whether we have been bad or good, but most of the time it is so hard to know. Have we done the right thing for the wrong reason, as T. S. Eliot ponders? Have we sought to do evil and God meant it for good, as Joseph told his brothers? How do we "earn our keep"? What are the things of importance in life and how much of the rest of the stuff would we be willing to give up to get that which is good?

So often those questions boil down to the question of what must I do to be saved? What is expected of me to receive the "well done, good and faithful servant" from God? And according to the real-life version of the game Paul was playing, he was way ahead. He was born a Jew, circumcised on the eighth day according to the Law. Not only was he born into the covenant people, but his ancestors also come from the tribe of Benjamin, one of the old first families, and they still spoke Hebrew at home. And it wasn't all just a matter of being born into the right family. He had gone to the finest schools and been educated as a Pharisee. His zeal for the Kingdom of God had taken him into the leadership of the persecution of all who opposed the Jewish faith. He knew the Law. He kept the Law. Straight A in righteousness. Blameless before the Law of Moses. Mirror, mirror on the wall, who's most righteous of them all? Well, Saul of Tarsus holds the number one spot.

II. Yet here is Paul, saying that all of the things he had counted on to make him acceptable to God, to earn him a spot in God's Hall of Fame, he counts now as worthless. Everything that he looked at to give him standing and value as a human being before God he now says is nothing but trash to be thrown out in order that he might receive and enjoy the grace of God given in Jesus Christ. All the stuff he counted on to establish his own righteousness he now rejects in order to have a righteousness whose source is God and whose basis is faith. He has turned his back on all of the proud achievements and privileges of his past and yet he seems to be laughing and rejoicing in his newfound relationship with God.

It is not easy to know what kind of torment and pain this conversion may have caused Paul. We do not know of the penalties and insults from the Jewish community. We do not know if his family disowned him, whether his property was confiscated; perhaps he was taken out of the will; he certainly became a traitor to all his friends. But Paul writes about it with great force and freedom. The power and peace of the righteousness with God that comes in the gift of God to us in Jesus is worth every sacrifice it may involve. We hear those words of Paul in church and we have heard that kind of language so often that it may not get our attention, but on *Prime Time,* Diane Sawyer had a story about a group called the Brethren. This is a group of thin-bearded young men who hang out in beautiful college communities, and they talk to young, bright, attractive, well-educated, serious, athletic, devout, religious young people and invite them to become members of their group. It is the desire of the young people to be good and religious people that takes them into this group. Inside this group they live off of the garbage from fast-food places. They are encouraged not to contact their parents. They spend their time reading the Scriptures and copying the words of Scripture in a prescribed writing style. One of them told Diane Sawyer that she was all dolled up, painted up like a hussy.

These young people have forfeited everything we think makes them wonderful; they have left their great schools, they have sold their stereo systems, they now move on bikes and public transportation, they wear nondesigner clothing. They now have made the same kind of sacrifices that St. Paul made. They have forsaken everything for a different relationship with God.

The parents of these children do not think it is wonderful. They engage in twenty-year searches to try to find their children and to "rescue" them. Diane Sawyer kept talking about how these young people have been kidnaped, brainwashed, and are now poor misguided people, under the authority and control of a religious fanatic. In the eye of the TV camera the kind of renunciation these young people make is not something to be applauded; rather, it is a pity, some kind of tragedy that parents need to warn their children to avoid. It is not a kind of lifestyle that any right-thinking American would want to choose.

Paul talks about forfeiting everything of importance to his previous lifestyle and we hear that with approval, but when twenty or thirty college-age young people in America make that kind of sacrifice for their religious convictions, they are considered sick.

III. So just what kind of sacrifices would be appropriate in order to receive the gift of righteousness of God given to us in Jesus Christ?

For Paul, the supreme joy and good of the knowledge of Christ is worth the sacrifice of everything else he counted as important in his life. The great relief and peace that comes in receiving the righteousness of God rather than the constant pressure and worry of trying to earn our own righteousness is worth every sacrifice. When we try to make our own kind of music, when we try to make the good life, when we try to earn our own salvation, there is never any rest. All of our past accomplishments suddenly seem so small and we feel like there is so much more we ought to have done. When we are working to be blameless there are so many dangers we have constantly to be on guard against. It is just so hard. Life is so complicated and confusing and there is no rest. Then there is the offer of a righteousness that God gives us. We don't have to make our own, we don't have to kill our own children for our own righteousness' sake, Abraham; God has provided the lamb. There is a gift of righteousness that you can have.

But make no mistake about it. There comes the giving up of all that we have counted on to make our own righteousness. We are to understand that for God to be revealed as the source of our righteousness involves the dislodging of a person from his estimation of his own freedom. For us to be seen in the righteousness of God means that we have to stop trying to be seen in our own accomplishments. To receive the freedom, that relief, that liberation from the burden of trying to make ourselves look good, to receive the freedom of being a child of God, means we have to sacrifice our freedom to decide what we think our righteousness should look like.

Paul has already discovered that to receive that great freedom of his acceptance as a child of God by the gift from God means that he has to throw out everything he used to elevate himself in his own eyes before God. To look like a real child of God by grace means that we have to throw away all that we took pride in that made us look good.

IV. All the advantages of birth and upbringing Paul had formerly set down in the assets column; now he had transferred them to the column of liabilities. That is not always easy for us. Look at how shocked we are when some of our brightest and best college students forfeit it all to become Brethren. Clearly as long as we keep wanting to think about things from our own personal advantage, to hold onto something, inherited or acquired, to maintain control over some little area of our lives because we think it might be our ace in the hole with God, those are obstacles to our joy.

There have been very few couples who have come for premarital counseling whom I have refused to marry, but there was one. They were very nice. He was a most accommodating young man. Whatever she wanted, he was willing. But when asked where they thought there might be a problem in their relationship, they knew immediately. He would give her anything she wanted. He would do anything she told him, except that on the first week of deer hunting season, he was going hunting. He did not care what else was happening. Birth of their first son—didn't matter. Deer hunting. During that week she could do what she wanted to. Go shopping, spend a million dollars. He didn't care. He was going deer hunting, and it made her furious. You could see the blood boiling even as they discussed it. It was that he was going deer hunting, it was that there was this little piece of him that he was refusing to sacrifice to the relationship. If he would just put the relationship ahead of deer hunting and say that he was going deer hunting most years but that there might be something with her that was more important than deer, she would not have a problem with it. He said she could have him as he was or not at all, but he was not changing.

"All to Jesus I surrender, all to thee I freely give." That is what we sing in the hymn. In that Paul has found his great joy. In the sacrifice of all that he had once trusted to make him somebody he found the freedom to accept the gift of righteousness that God makes possible for us in Jesus Christ. The knowledge of Christ, the knowledge that God has a lover's relationship with creation, that God has a welcome for the lost, brings the good news of Jesus who says "come unto me all ye who are weary and overburdened, exhausted by trying to make yourself worthy, and I will give you rest." The knowledge of Christ is the knowledge that all that is expected by God is for us to be willing to receive his gift rather than to continue to try to advance our own standing.

If there is any sadness in those who sacrifice to become Brethren, it is that they sacrifice one way of trying to earn their righteousness for another way to make their own holiness. As they say in Final Four language, they have taken their game up a notch but they are still playing to win. They have not yet accepted the fact that the win has already been given by God.

V. When we come to the place where we discover that great relief, that great joy of being freed from the curse of the Law, freed from the constant message that if you don't behave, don't measure up, don't achieve, don't keep your nose clean, don't mow your grass, don't tithe, if you don't love everybody, you are going to hell. When we accept the knowledge of Christ that we are welcomed into the family of God by the gift of God, that whosoever will may come, life becomes marked by a deep, abiding and ever-flowing peace and contentment. It is an abiding sense of hope and joy. Beneath all of the pain and suffering of daily life, there is for Paul and there is for those who live in the knowledge of Christ an abiding smile. One of the Brethren was asked if he ever smiled, and he said he tried not to. Why not? The gift of God's grace in Christ ought to bring a profound sense of hope.

For the joy of accepting the gift of God's righteousness, we have to open our hands and drop all to which we have been clinging to make us righteous; and yet when we receive that gift of God's acceptance, we discover that we have so much that all we thought we had before looks a lot like the trash we threw out yesterday.—Rick Brand

Topic: A Living Parable
TEXT: Mark 11:1–11

My first real experience with farm life was as a student pastor of a rural congregation east of Dallas. One of our deacons had a small farm with a few head of cattle surrounded by his neighbor's cotton fields. I was always fascinated by the careful attention given to the care and feeding of animals destined for the slaughterhouse. When the pastor was invited to Sunday dinner, it was never the traditional fried chicken. We feasted on T-bone steaks like I had never tasted before. I enjoyed every gram of fat marbled in those beautiful cuts of meat—until I learned the route from the hoof to the plate. The process was tainted with an element of dishonesty, which I was wise enough to keep to myself. The calf was penned and fed nothing but mother's milk and grain. There was no foraging for grass, no munching on dry hay. The chosen ones were treated like royalty—all that they could eat every day of the week. They were given the impression that they were a cut above the rest of the herd. Little did they know that *cut* was the significant word. The whole time the calf was being dined on a daily feast of the very best grain, the farmer was really feeding himself. The final disposition of the calf was not royal green pastures where "seldom is heard a discouraging word, and the skies are not cloudy all day." Something more sinister was in mind, like feeding the preacher on Sunday.

I. Things are never quite what they seem to be. Surface reality is always somewhat superficial. Truth always lies somewhere beneath the surface in the depths that are exposed by the passing of time. The arrival of Jesus in Jerusalem on the last Sunday of his earthly life and ministry stands in stark contrast to the events of Thursday night and Friday. He entered the Holy City as a conquering hero, treated as royalty. By Friday he was the lamb being led to the slaughter. How do we get from Palm Sunday to Good Friday? Is this a lesson in human nature? Do people normally crucify their kings? Inaugurations are never real pictures of the presidency. The pomp and circumstance of protocol and formal courtesy can become a smoke screen to hide subterranean public hostility and the struggle that is to follow. The calf is en route to the slaughter. In the ministry we talk about the beginning days in a pastorate as the "honeymoon." Sometimes the honeymoon lasts for months or years; but we all know that a marriage is not measured by the honeymoon. I recall the early speech of Gerald Ford in which he expressed a preference for a good marriage to a beautiful honeymoon.

The entry of Jesus into Jerusalem is a moment in messianic politics, and public opinion is like the weather—sunny and bright on Sunday, dark and stormy on Friday. Yet the mission of Jesus was never politics as usual. The polls meant nothing to Jesus. Had he not refused the invitation to leap from the Temple to dazzle the crowds? Public relations was neither the forte of the Christ nor even his concern. He was driven by the purpose of God in history rather than by either the "hosanna" of Sunday or the "crucify him!" of Friday. Whether the same people who lined the road singing Psalm 118 were the ones who were gathered at Pilate's court demanding crucifixion is unclear. Even in messianic politics, the leader seldom has the total support of all of the people. Given the right time and place, a handful of angry, manipulated people can seem to be the whole population. Given the right time and place, the very people who sing messianic hymns of praise on Sunday can easily be swayed by the spirit of mob violence into a swarm of bloodthirsty piranha. Nothing about this week is really beyond the reach of human nature as we know and live it.

II. God comes in Christ. All of us do it. We struggle to get a message across to the parents or friends. Words are not adequate to carry some messages, so we act out our message. Wise parents and spouses learn to be attentive to the message behind the act as well as to the spoken or written word. Like the prophets of old, Jesus often acted out his message. Many of his miracles were messages, "signs" of a word more profound than the Sermon on the Mount. The very person of Christ is pictured by John as the Word become flesh. Thus Jesus was deliberate in his decision to head toward Jerusalem. The disciples were disturbed by the prospect of heading toward the Holy City, a citadel of growing hostility; but Jesus was driven: "See, we are going up to Jerusalem, and the Son of Man will be handed over to the chief priests and the scribes" (10:33). Jesus was deliberate about the entrance into the city. Luke records a reflective moment of compassion as Jesus approached the city. It was almost a vision of the events of 70 A.D., when Rome would turn to the final solution to the Jewish problem by utterly destroying the Temple and everyone in sight. (The Jews have never been strangers to holocausts.)

The plans were meticulous. Just the right beast of burden had to be selected. Matthew is so literal in remembering the messianic message of Zechariah that he has Jesus riding on two animals at once. Perhaps this is meant only to be an event that ties the whole mission of Jesus to the covenant of God with the Chosen People of the Old Testament. But the people want a military messiah. They are seeking a crusader on a white stallion. The horse is the animal of champions, not the donkey. The events of the day are almost comic in ridicule of the king who comes to claim his throne. As you read, you keep looking for the crossed fingers or the wink that betrays the hypocrisy of the moment; but this is not a pretentious event. This is the way of salvation. "Hosanna!" salvation rides into town on a donkey. On the surface, it appears that our God does dumb things, like send the Son into a peasant's home and to a criminal's death. We are reminded of the reflection of Paul: "God's foolishness is wiser than human wisdom, and God's weakness is stronger than human strength" (1 Cor. 1:25).

As Jesus enters the city, he enters our lives. He comes on a donkey with nothing more compelling than his compassion to move us to worship. As Jesus enters the city, his people enter the world. We are sent out as sheep among wolves. Like Christ, the Church comes to the world in the humility of service. We are called not only to praise but also to discipleship, to take up our cross and follow.—Larry Dipboye

Topic: "In the Praetorium with Jesus
TEXT: John 18:33–37

When was the last time you stood in the praetorium with Jesus? I know you have. All of us have stood there. When was the last time you were in a place where you felt strange and unusual, alone perhaps, and alien?

There in Pilate's palace, the center of worldly authority, stood Jesus of Nazareth, the creator of the universe on trial before the people he created. The one whose laws existed long before the laws of Rome, whose decrees would still be giving life and hope long after the last of the Caesars was gone, here he was asked to justify himself, in the praetorium. What should he do? What do you do?

The praetorium is not just the center of political power. It is where all the powers and pressures that try to control our lives are centered. It is where our religious convictions stand face to face with all those other powers that have authority over us. If you're a high school student and you've ever been to a party where your friends started drinking or couples retreated alone to rooms behind closed doors, if you've ever been in a situation where your loyalty to Jesus put you in conflict with your loyalty to your friends, you've stood in the praetorium with Jesus. If you work in an office where it's hard to be a Christian, where the culture of the workplace is totally focused on the bottom line and the relationships with people are determined by what they can do to help you get ahead, then you've stood in the praetorium with Jesus. We've all been there when the authority of Christ confronted the authority of the world.

One way we can react when confronted with the demands of the world around us is withdraw. There is a long and distinguished tradition of withdrawal in the Christian Church. The first monks in the early years of the Church withdrew to the desert to form holy communities when they became convinced that the world was too corrupt a place for them to live as faithful followers of Christ. They prayed for the world, and many of them wrote of their faith.

Even if we don't live in a monastery we all need to withdraw from time to time. It's something that God's people do time and again throughout the Bible. Ezra commanded God's people to have nothing to do with foreigners, to the extent of divorcing their foreign wives and husbands. Whenever we gather here on Sunday morning, we're reaffirming our identity as people who are different from others. When we tithe our income, we're making a statement that there's something about Christians that causes us to use our resources differently than others use theirs. When we control what our kids watch on television, when we don't let our fourteen-year-olds watch R-rated movies, we're making a statement that there are things about the world around us that we don't want our children to participate in. We stand in the praetorium with Jesus, and we don't compromise on who we are.[1]

But withdrawing isn't the only thing to do when we find our faith confronted with worldly powers. Sometimes the places we live and work and play are the very places where God is hardest at work. After all, John's Gospel opens by telling us that all things were made through Christ. Without him was not one thing made. There is no place where God is not present, no

---

[1] H. Richard Niebuhr, *Christ and Culture* (New York: HarperCollins, 1951), pp. 45–82.

situation where he cannot work his will. In the Old Testament, God used the Assyrians and the Babylonians to punish Israel, and God used Cyrus, King of Persia, to restore them to their land. Those were all pagan emperors who worshiped idols and probably did all kinds of things God's people wouldn't do. They didn't know God was using them. Yet God had made them and God worked though them.

Jesus appeals to the best in us. Even among those who don't accept him as their Lord and Savior there are many who admire him and work alongside his followers. The praetorium isn't a totally bad place. After all, Pilate was a lot more sympathetic to Jesus than the religious leaders who refused to go into the governor's headquarters out of fear that they would contaminate themselves and not be pure enough to perform their rituals.[2]

Sometimes we need to see the world around us as our friend, a place where God is still active just as God was when the world was made. But then we have to make sure we realize that something isn't good just because it exists. We've seen too many times, from the Crusades to the Balkan wars, that the name of Jesus has been added like a veneer over unspeakable deeds that have nothing to do with his gospel.

Sometimes we need to withdraw from the world around us. Sometimes we need to embrace it as our friend. For most of us most of the time, we do what Jesus did when he was in the praetorium. We enter into the places where others hold power, where Jesus is hardly noticed, let alone worshiped. And by being present in the world yet distinct from it, we transform the world, as Jesus, in the very heart of Roman power, procured our eternal salvation by dying at the hands of Pontius Pilate.

That's what Jesus does with each one of us. He comes to us where we are, accepts us as we are, and changes us into something better.

Isn't that what he does with our families? Jesus blessed the family by growing up in one. He stayed with his mother until he was thirty. His first miracle was performed at a wedding, where a new family was being formed. He responded to the heartfelt cries of parents whose children were ill. Jesus affirms our families, yet he fundamentally transforms them by telling us that we have to be willing to leave them to follow him.

Jesus affirmed the government by telling his followers that they had to pay taxes to Caesar. The book of Romans in the Bible says that God established governments to maintain order and restrain evil. It was a government census that got Mary and Joseph to Bethlehem where Jesus was born. Yet Jesus transformed our relationship to governments by standing before Pilate and refusing to answer his questions, because the government had no authority over him. He was from a different realm.

Jesus had no quarrel with business or labor. Many of his parables are about relationships between workers and managers, about business practices and investments. He advocated no economic revolution or overthrow of the existing structures. Yet he transformed our relationship to work and money by telling us to be like birds of the air and lilies of the field and to live by grace not by work.[3]

When Jesus stood in the praetorium, he could have overthrown Pilate. He could have summoned legions of angels to fight for him and get rid of his enemies. Or Jesus could have fled. The one who walked on the sea and slipped away from the hometown crowds who wanted

---

[2] ibid., pp. 83–115.
[3] ibid., p. 3.

to throw him over a cliff surely could have escaped from Pilate and fled to the hills to live for another day. But Jesus stayed there in the heart of worldly power, and by his love for the world he made, he transformed the human race.

The next time you stand in the praetorium, the next time you're face to face with a power that has control over your life and you feel helpless before it, remember who stands there with you: Christ the King.—Stephens G. Lytch

Topic: The Transforming Encounter
TEXT: 1 Cor. 15:5–8

The Resurrection of Jesus is not a human symbol of hope, like springtime lilies and bunny rabbits and Easter eggs and beautiful sunrises. Rather, it is a divine event not captive to any day of the week or any season of the year. Easter is not even about our yearning for immortality; it is about the availability of a deathless presence that can live with us here and now. Easter is not a remembered symbol but an experienced power! It is nothing less than a transforming encounter with the Lord of the universe.

This is clear from the earliest and most basic passage in the New Testament about the Resurrection of Christ (1 Cor. 15:3–10a). There Paul used passive verbs to say that God, not earthlings, engineered Easter. Christ "was raised" and "was seen"—we had nothing to do with it. In reporting the appearances of the Risen Lord, Paul lays to the rest the idea that they involved only believers who were trying to conjure them up as an escape from despair. Notice how this is proved by the three individuals singled out for mention: Cephas, James, and Paul (1 Cor. 15:5, 7, 8). We know enough about each of them to demonstrate that they were the most likely candidates for Easter. In fact, they were the last people on earth who would ever make up a story like that as an exercise in wishful thinking. Let us look more closely to see what Easter really meant to them and can mean to us today.

I. *Cephas: Easter and our despair.* How incredibly life can change in a single week. Peter entered Jerusalem amid hosannas as the leader of the Twelve, ready to be chief viceroy in a glorious kingdom about to be established. Casual bystanders in the courtyard shattered Peter's defenses and three times he denied his Lord (Luke 22:54–60), only to have Jesus "look at him" as he passed by (v. 61). There was nothing left for this beaten, broken man to do but go out and weep bitterly (v. 62). Peter was nailed to his own wretched cross of defeat.

But Easter meant that Jesus had other plans for this miserable failure now wallowing in despair. His first message, left with angels guarding the tomb, was, "Go, tell his disciples *and Peter* that he is going before you to Galilee; there you will see him" (Mark 16:7). And it happened, even before that, in Jerusalem: "The Lord has risen indeed and has appeared *to Simon*" (Luke 24:34). What does this mean but that Jesus singled out the one who needed him most and came to him first with forgiveness and restoration (see John 21:15–17). It forever changed a broken, disconsolate disciple into a courageous, confident apostle!

Easter finds many of us in the predicament of Peter. We have made bold resolves and firm promises but have failed to carry them out. We have boasted of faithfulness but then denied Christ over and over again. We "blew" it when Christ was counting on us to be faithful and true.

The transformation in Peter's life was hardly self-induced. Left to himself he would have destroyed his future in an orgy of self-inflicted recrimination.

Easter offers the only savior who can forgive so deeply and love so strongly that he can stand us on our feet and help us to begin to live again.

The whole point of Easter is that no one ever overcame defeat like Jesus. True, the failure was not his fault, but tragedy nevertheless buried him in a tomb and sealed it shut. His Resurrection meant that God's power was sufficient to overcome even that ultimate failure of the cross. His appearing to defeated disciples is an offer to us to overcome our lesser failures in his strength.

II. *James: Easter and our disbelief.* The second individual named in our text is James, the brother of Jesus (v. 7). This is not the James who was a brother of John, one of the "sons of thunder"; nor was it the James who was a son of Alpheus. This James was not even a member of the Twelve, because during Jesus' earthly life this James did not believe in Jesus' mission. In Mark 3:21, Jesus' family came to take him home to Nazareth thinking that he was "beside himself," meaning "out of his mind."

This family tension became explicit as Jesus faced his last supreme challenge in Jerusalem. Like Peter and the Twelve, his brothers were all too willing for him to journey to the capital and "show himself to the world" (John 7:4). This self-seeking strategy of playing to the crowds, which Jesus could not accept, was based on the fact that "even his brothers did not believe him" (v. 5). Presumably James went to Jerusalem, as Jesus suggested (John 7:8), for their mother was there to the bitter end (John 19:25) and would have traveled with her sons for protection and care. There is not a hint that James ever changed his attitude toward Jesus during their earthly sojourn. Just why he could not see anything different in Jesus remains a mystery. Perhaps it was the "familiarity that breeds contempt" (see Mark 6:2–3), living too close to his humanity to see his divinity.

But suddenly that was a change. No sooner was Jesus risen and ascended than the disciples gathered for prayer in an upper room "together with Mary the mother of Jesus *and with his brothers*" (Acts 1:14). What could have happened except that the Risen Christ appeared to the disbelieving James, and this encounter wrought a transforming change that Jesus' earthly ministry could not effect. Like Peter, James was totally unsuited as a candidate for Easter. He had proposed a worldly strategy for Jesus, only to have his more famous older brother do just the opposite and suffer bitter rejection as a result. At the other extreme from Peter's despair, James could have wallowed in self-justification: "I was right. He needed a broader power base. If only he had listened to me."

Despite this natural sense of pride and superiority, the Easter encounter convinced James that Jesus had been right after all. So totally did James change that, when Peter gave up his leadership of the Jerusalem church, he identified James as his logical successor (Acts 12:17), a role to which James immediately succeeded despite not having been one of the Twelve. Not only did he lead the church amid great pressures (Acts 21:18–25), but like Peter he finally gave up his life in martyrdom (62 A.D.).

Far from creating an Easter fiction, James was transformed by the Easter fact. Suddenly the habits of a lifetime were changed with the realization that everything for which Jesus stood had been vindicated by God.

Think how hopelessly we view those "gospel-hardened" adults whose muscles of resistance have grown rigid from rebuffing the claims of Christ.

Frankly, could we blame Jesus if he left James to his self-centered ways?

Instead, he singled out James for special attention, which is just what he continues to do with unbelievers today. They may be "hopeless cases" to faithful church folk, but to Jesus they are potential leaders needing only a change of heart to make a fresh start.

What is the missing piece of evidence? Not more arguments or explanations, nor even more examples of good Christian living. No, what is needed is for the Risen Christ to be seen, living and powerful, triumphant over sin and death. Even more, what is needed is a realization that he is concerned to claim the most reluctant disbeliever in our midst! Jesus does not shun skeptics or avoid atheists or reject doubters. Instead, it is to them that he offers the ultimate evidence of his resurrected life.

III. *Paul: Easter and our dogmatism.* Paul had personally interviewed both Peter and James (Gal. 1:18–19) and thus knew from firsthand reports of their Easter experiences. Now he dared to add his own name to the list of personal appearances (1 Cor. 15:8), which means that he had verified for himself what he had reported about the others. Paul's problem was not that of Peter's. Instead of backsliding, he had advanced beyond his contemporaries, outstripping them in religious zeal (Gal. 1:14). Far from being weak and undependable, he was strong and determined. Further, Paul's problem was not that of James. He was deeply religious, very concerned for spiritual matters, hardly a crowd pleaser who wanted to impress the world.

Of the three, Paul's dogmatism may have been the hardest to change, even more so than the despair of Peter or the disbelief of James. The true zealot is so sure of his position, so confirmed in his fanaticism, that he will not listen to others because he is certain that God is on his side.

As Paul set out on the Damascus Road, he was not trying to create a lovely springtime celebration. Instead he was "breathing threats and murder" against everything Christ stood for (Acts 9:1). The heavenly light that blinded him was neither sought nor understood (Acts 9:3–5a) but came as a total surprise.

Yet that encounter was powerful enough to turn his life in a totally new direction, so much so that his former supporters were now ready to kill him (Acts 9:23), even while his former enemies were still afraid of him (Acts 9:26). Everything changed: all of those things about which he once boasted, he now counted as loss (Phil. 3:4–7). And it lasted for a lifetime!

So do we have Easter today because a handful of wishful thinkers in the first century wanted it badly enough? No, we have Easter because even those moving as fast as they could in the opposite direction were overtaken by its reality. If anything, Easter prevailed in their lives despite the fact that they were not the least bit ready when it arrived! And what a multitude of problems the Resurrection of Jesus overcame. Look at our trio of stars in the cast of the first Easter drama. Peter was beaten and broken, James was callous and indifferent, Paul was proud and unyielding. Yet the same Lord changed them all: totally, permanently, against their wills, despite their resistance. That, my friends, is sheer miracle!

If you want nothing to do with Easter, then you are just like those for whom Easter was intended originally. If Jesus would appear to Peter, James, and Paul, why would he not appear to you as well? Add your name to eternity's list with the confession, "He appeared also to *me!*"—William E. Hull

ILLUSTRATIONS

TRIUMPH.   The tragedy of Calvary is not a promise of triumph at Easter. The cross itself a triumph. In Christ's death there is life. Lifted up in crucifixion, he draws men and women into his life. That is why the Church puts palms and thorns together. The King is triumphant not simply when he rises from the rock; he is triumphant when he is raised on the cross. Today I rejoice; on Good Friday I rejoice; for in Jesus' dying the world comes alive.—Walter J. Burghardt, S. J.[4]

A DIFFERENT PERSPECTIVE.   Today, upon Palm Sunday, Jesus comes riding into Jerusalem in the midst of palm branches and hosannas. Next Thursday, He is prostrate in Gethsemane. Next Friday, He is hanging on the Cross. Next Sunday, He is rising from the tomb. The great experiences come quick on one another. Joy crowds on sorrow, sorrow presses on the steps of joy. To each comes the quick end. Each is but born before it dies. But one thing never dies—the service of His Father, the salvation of the world, the sum and substance of His life! Set upon that, with His soul full of that, joy comes and pain comes, and both are welcomed and dismissed with thankfulness because their coming and their going bring the end for which He lives more near.

Such be our lives! As Jesus was, so may we be, seeking an end so great, so constant, so eternal that every change may come to us and be our minister and not our conqueror; that even our cross may come as His came, and men may gather round it and say, "Alas, then this is all! Alas, that finally it should all come to this!" While we who hang upon the cross cry, "It is finished," with a shout of triumph, counting the finishing but a new beginning, and looking out beyond the cross to richer growth in character, and braver and more fruitful service of our Lord!—Phillips Brooks[5]

THE RECONCILING CROSS.   Bishop Lesslie Newbigin writes in *A South Indian Diary* of Sundaram, the pastor of a village church in his diocese. A colorful figure, this pastor sported a military mustache, wore huge army boots, a faded battledress, a toupee, and always carried a long stainless steel baton. Sundaram had been in Burma when war broke out, and was unable to escape to India. He stayed on in Burma doing evangelistic work. He was arrested as a spy, taken to a Japanese guardhouse, and bound to a post. All his belongings, including his Bible, were confiscated. A Japanese officer came in and began idly turning over Sundaram's scanty possessions. He came to the Bible and looked across enquiringly. He could not speak Tamil and Sundaram could not speak Japanese. He made the sign of the Cross in the palm of his hand. Sundaram nodded. Then the officer crossed the room, stood in front of Sundaram, and stretched out his arms in the figure of the Cross. Cutting the prisoner's bonds, he signaled him to go free. Before Sundaram went, he handed him, apparently as a souvenir, the stainless steel baton which was his officer's staff. Across the gulf of warfare and unintelligibility there stretched the healing, reconciling Cross of Christ. Two men were at peace with one another through faith in Him who made peace by the blood of His Cross. "Beloved," says John the Apostle, "if God so loved us, we also ought to love one another."—John N. Gladstone[6]

---

[4] *Grace on Crutches*
[5] *The Light of the World*
[6] *A Magnificent Faith*

TRUE KINSHIP.   Do you know the name of Rabbi Blouch? He was a Jewish padre in the French Army in the first World War. Men of the Jewish faith in the French Army are naturally not numerous and the padre's chance of finding one whenever he went out into no-man's land was light. For the larger number of dying men were Roman Catholics. The Rabbi, therefore, always carried a crucifix with him to comfort any sinking Christian he might find. It was, indeed, as he was holding the crucifix before the eyes of a dying soldier that the fatal bullet came and drilled the Rabbi through.

What an argument some doctrinaires would make of that! "But he wasn't a Christian himself! What could a crucifix mean to him? What would other Jews think?"

Let them argue! It was love, compassion, magnanimity. . . . It was all understood by our ascended Lord. Our true sacrifices reflect His own.

Our humanity is in heaven.

One nature holds us kin.—W. E. Sangster[7]

PARTAKERS.   It is all important that each one of us consider himself included, a partaker of God's mercy in the life of our Lord as revealed in his resurrection from the dead on Easter morning. It is all important that we believe humbly yet courageously that we are those born again in him to a living hope: *You will live also.*

I am at the end. We are privileged now to approach the Lord's table. The Lord's Supper is quite simply the sign of what we have said: Jesus Christ is in our midst, he, the man in whom God himself has poured out his life for our sake and in whom our life is lifted up to God. Holy Communion is the sign that Jesus Christ is our beginning and we may rise up and walk into the future where we shall live. The Lord himself gives us strength, food and drink for our journey, from *one* bread and from *one* cup, because he is One, he the One for us all.—Karl Barth[8]

---

[7] *Westminster Sermons*
[8] *Deliverance to the Captives*

SECTION VI

MESSAGES FOR ADVENT AND CHRISTMAS

SERMON SUGGESTIONS

Topic: Christmas Is Coming

TEXT: Isa. 13:32–37

Years ago the great prophet Isaiah put his hands to his lips and cried to the children of Israel who were in captivity. "Prepare, prepare a way for the coming of the Lord who is going to set you free." Centuries later Jesus would say to his disciples, "Watch, because you do not know when the son of man will come." Though he was talking here about his second coming, the words are still true for us today concerning his first coming. Watch.

Mary did not know when God's Messiah would come the first time. It is really astounding how God prepared the world for that particular moment when Christ would be born. He took centuries in the preparation. The God who could wait for the right moment for the coming of his son took his time in preparing for this moment. Decades and centuries before, God had called Abraham to come searching and following after him to go to a place that was unknown to Abraham. God began with a small tribe. That small people slowly began to grow. Later, after they were formed into a nation, they were carried captive into Egypt. God raised up Moses, who liberated the people from Egypt. While they wandered in the wilderness looking for the Promised Land, God gave them his commandments and helped forge them into a particular people. Later, after they became a nation and settled in a particular land, the Babylonians arose against them and took them into captivity in Babylon. Later the Persians came along and conquered them. All of this took place more than six hundred years before the coming of Christ.

While they were in captivity, they began to hear the words "prepare the way" because the deliverer was coming. Then God sent a deliverer called Alexander the Great who moved his armies across the stage of history. This prince had been a student of Aristotle, the Greek philosopher, and everywhere he went he wanted to give the people the Greek philosophy. Soon this philosophy began to spread across the land, and the language of Greece was spoken from the Himalayas to Britain. Then Rome conquered the armies of Alexander the Great. When Rome settled their peace over that part of the known world, they built roads from one end of their empire to the other so that their soldiers could travel back and forth to reinforce and keep the peace. The Jews were dispersed during all of these times. They would be resettled in one part of the country and then another, but every place they went they would establish a synagogue. There was a universal language. There were roads across the land.

Now what is the point of this lesson in history in understanding Christianity? God picked the particular moment when Rome was in power to send his Son. If he had sent his Son forty years later, there would have been no Temple. If he had come twenty years earlier, there would have been no peace. But he came when roads stretched across the world so travelers could journey on them and carry the gospel message to others. The Jews were dispersed around the world and their synagogues were often used as a base from which the message of Christ was shared. Greek was a universal language, and the New Testament was written in the universal language of the people of that day. God prepared the time through centuries, and then his Son came. Watch. Prepare. But even in his first coming, many missed it.

Some of us will miss celebrating the real meaning of Christmas again. We will get involved in the festivities, the gift giving and merriment. But somehow or other we will still miss the essential meaning of Christmas. Part of the reason some of us will miss it, just like some missed it then, is because when God comes he often comes in unexpected ways. As we get older Christmas becomes very routine for many of us. It seems so routine that we lose our sense of excitement about it. Can you recall when you were a child, or as you watch your own children as Christmas approaches can you the sense of excitement they have about it? Their eyes get big with wonder as the day gets closer; they can hardly contain themselves; they count the days and jump with anticipation. As we get older, many adults find that sense of excitement fading. It becomes routine, ordinary, and too familiar for us.

Elizabeth and Zechariah, the parents of John the Baptist, were ordinary people. Zechariah would be considered a country preacher today, but God chose him as the father of the forerunner of Christ. Mary, a simple maid, became the mother of Christ. These were ordinary people who seemed to live routine lives. We sometimes miss Christmas because we do not expect God to speak to us through the ordinary and routine places or people of life. Even in the ordinary celebration of Christmas, we may again miss it because we are not prepared for it.

Christmas is coming soon. Prepare for it. Watch! Be alert! Some of us will expect too much. Some of us will not expect enough. Some of us won't expect anything. Watch, lest you miss the real meaning of Christmas. Watch, so you, like the shepherds, may come and kneel down before the Christ. Watch so that like the Wise Men you can bring your gifts to the Christ. Watch so you will see the star glowing once again and follow it to the Christ who has come to bring salvation. Watch so that you will hear the angelic song once again. Make preparation for Christmas. Prepare your heart so that God can speak tenderly to you and so you may experience his great love that he has revealed through his Son, Jesus Christ. Watch. Remain alert. Be prepared. Christmas is coming.—William Powell Tuck

Topic: New World Coming
TEXT: Isa. 2:1–5

In the Broadway place *Fanny,* Marius, a young man hungry for adventure, challenges his father, Cesar. "You think Marseilles is the center of the earth!" And old Cesar quickly replies, "It is. That is north, this is south, that east, this west, I am here, the center!" Marius protests, "But there are others!" to which Cesar firmly declares, "They are off-center." From the point of view of a compass, the center is where you happen to be standing. To suggest that the compass defines the universe is a bit naive, but we all do it. We never completely outgrow the egocentricity of childhood. The geographical form is provincialism locating the center of the universe in one's own place under the sun.

I. The vision of peace in Isaiah is at once majestic and childish. Certainly nothing is wrong with the dream of peace, beating swords into plowshares and spears into pruning hooks, but why Jerusalem? Why not Washington or Athens, Rome or Moscow—or even Oak Ridge? In spite of the vision, Mount Zion is hardly "the highest of the mountains," and Israel has never quite qualified as a world power, much less as the arbiter of international peace. When you think about it, the Jews have always been a bit like Old Cesar, thinking that the world revolves around their little piece of earth—even to the point of believing that God maintains an exclusive dwelling in the little house that they constructed on Mount Zion. Even today the Wailing Wall, the remaining piece of the ancient Temple, has become such a sacred shrine that it borders on idolatry. You recall the controversy that was stirred in both Jewish and Christian circles when the United Nations debated the declaration, "Zionism is racism." Of course it was all politics, but it was world politics. The Arabic world wanted to identify the provincial, place-centered religion of Judaism with the ugly racial hatred that constantly tears at our nation. The vision of Isaiah is a scandal on the world political front. To even suggest that Jerusalem is the center to which all nations will turn for counsel and from which the authority of God will be enthroned is offensive to non-Jews, especially the neighbors of modern Israel.

I recall a missionary to Lebanon in the early 1960s telling about the sensitivity of Christian missions where all of the borders are under dispute. He noted that the Lebanese mission did not sing, "On Jordan's stormy banks I stand and cast a wistful eye/To Canaan's fair and happy land where my possessions lie." Walter Brueggemann in *The Land* claimed, "Land is a central, if not *the central theme* of biblical faith." Not just the Old Testament but the entire Bible is about a place called Zion, about the land given by promise of God to the ancestors, but finally about the greater promise of God to all of the peoples of the earth. For the most part, Christians have "displaced" Jerusalem as a geographical city. Jerusalem is that ideal vision, "The Holy City," which has ceased to be just a place. Jerusalem has become the center of the new world, the Kingdom that God is bringing from dream to reality.

II. Think big. In spite of the scandalous particularity of time, place, and person that we celebrate in the coming of Christ, the boundaries of the vision are beyond imagination. "How odd of God to choose the Jews" does not qualify as great poetry, but it is a valid question to take to the Bible. After a friend had been ill for several weeks I spotted him one day at church and said, "I did not know that you were here," to which he replied, "Everyone has to be somewhere." That makes more sense than we could imagine. The redemptive revelation of God had to start somewhere. Why not the Jews?

We begin where we are. Everyone comes from some "where." Every creation myth has provincial roots. Every culture tends to think of itself as the cradle of civilization. Why not? Even God had to start somewhere. The Jews thought in terms of Jerusalem much as we think in terms of Washington—although few these days would locate God's dwelling in the District of Columbia. The Mormon claim to have found a lost tribe of Israel in prehistoric America is little different from other misguided beliefs that God has chosen America over all the nations of the earth. Non-Christians are understandably amused by the claim of universal importance in the coming of Christ. It has not been too long since *The Atlantic Monthly* captured the vision of Christmas from outside our little world: a Japanese department store displayed Santa carrying baby Jesus in his sleigh pulled by the seven dwarfs.

A wonderful irony is embedded here. Neither Jerusalem nor the Christ of God belongs to some cultural claim for superiority. With J. B. Phillips we need to denounce publicly all local visions of God that are culturally too small for the God of creation. Just as the vision of Isaiah looks beyond Israel to the Kingdom of God, Matthew looks beyond the moment in time and the babe in Bethlehem to the great salvation of God.

III. Advent leans forward. We know that the answers are not in the past. We have been there. There is no peace in history. Even the message of Advent as history is a cry of pain for a world at war with itself. The suffering innocents of Bethlehem are not so far away from the child who was tortured to death by her mother or the Tennessee children abandoned to die in a hot car.

I was asked to answer questions about Christianity in a high school sociology class my second year out of seminary. The community had a significant Jewish population. The Vietnam war was at is worst. A Jewish girl framed an accusation in the form of a question, "How can Christians say that Messiah has come when the world is still at war?" The question was right on target.

We sing, *"Gloria in excelsis Deo!* And on earth peace. . . ." We cannot duck the question. Christ has come, and we still wait for peace. My response was less than an answer. I mumbled something about the unfinished business of God, that Christians also live with hope for the day of peace.

The Advent of Christ is the beginning of peace, not the end, and we live by the promise, not the possession, of God. While we wait for God to finish the new creation, God waits for the world to receive the promise.—Larry Dipboye

Topic: Messianic Politics
TEXT: Isa. 11:1–10

Historian John Bach McMaster tells of a visit to the White House when he was a very small boy. The guests were lined up to walk past the president; but because of the war, no one was allowed close enough to shake hands. Disappointed at the security, one guest stopped before Mr. Lincoln and shouted across the distance, "Mr. President, I'm from up in York State where we believe that God Almighty and Abraham Lincoln are going to save this country!" The president waved back and replied jovially, "My friend, you are half right."

I. God or Government? The question is, which half? Does the fate of the world rest on the politicians at the throttles of power or on Almighty God, whom we worship as Creator and Lord? Isaiah is a blend of both God and politics. So is the birth of Christ. Can you imagine a sweet little girl like Mary singing a song of revolution? "He has scattered the proud in the thoughts of their hearts, he has brought down the powerful from their thrones, and lifted up the lowly, he has filled the hungry with good things, and sent the rich away empty."

The prophet writes about a tiny, primitive world from a Jewish point of view. No real distinction between God and politics, no separation of church and state, is necessary in a perfect world. The stump or root of Jesse is a clear reference to the political dynasty of David. To restore the rule of David is to recover the divine purpose that Israel had lost in political history. Nostalgia about the past is an indulgence that seems always to accompany a sense of futility about the present. The Jews longed for David's dynasty to be restored to power for political salvation; thus universal peace and justice always wait for the rule of David. Only Isaiah would think of little Israel as the source of ultimate peace and the location of universal government. Even at the time, the very idea of establishing political control of the world through Israel was laughable. Yet Isaiah envisioned political realities. The appetite for peace and justice is stimulated by the horrors of tyranny and war. Thus the hope was political—and more than just politics. Nothing in the past would indicate that peace and justice should come merely through the restoration of David's throne, so the Spirit of the Lord will rest on a descendant of David and inspire wisdom, understanding, counsel, might, knowledge, and reverence. He will create a society in which justice will depend not merely on the human ability to receive and process information, where justice will be anchored in righteousness and faithfulness. God will rule. All wickedness will be destroyed. All hostility will cease. Political and natural predators will cease to threaten. That is the messianic hope.

In the absence of evil, "a child shall lead them." Why not? In a world without evil, who needs government, much less an iron-fisted dictator? In Isaiah, the demise of government is in direct proportion to the increase of righteousness. There resides the problem. Government is supposed to be the wedge between predators and prey. Paul observed (Rom. 13), "rules are not a terror to good conduct, but to bad." Government will fade only in a perfect world.

II. The hope of the world rests on the ridiculous. Isaiah's vision does not seem so far-fetched in light of the claim of the Christian gospel. Luke writes of political realities, the time when Quirnius was governor of Syria, the time of Caesar Augustus, by modern calculation, about 6 B.C. A child born in Bethlehem to peasant Jews would determine the destiny of the universe. That makes about as much sense in the real world as the suggestion that a child of black immigrants from Jamaica to Harlem might become president. In case you have not heard, politics and theology never conform to pure reason. Both politics and theology rest on the possibility of the ridiculous.

The message of Advent—the child of Mary is Emmanuel, "God with us"—proclaims the mind of God. God is found with the innocence and hope of the child. Children are always the first to suffer in war and in economic depression. The message is carried forward into the New Testament. Only when the child becomes the focus of society will the door open for the rule of God. Jesus identified the Kingdom with the child (Mark 10:15) and repeatedly used the model of the parent-child relationship in describing the bond between God and humanity. He taught us to pray as children, "Our Father." The tragedy of suffering innocence in the birth of Jesus is a shocking dose of reality. Herod represents a political attitude that views the child as threat, where children can be sacrificed on the altar of political expediency.

The deliberate execution of babies is unthinkable, but I participate in a world that practices execution by neglect. Children die slowly and painfully by starvation, they are exploited for labor and prostitution and abandoned to violence. What will be our political inheritance? The destiny of the world rests on the child born in Watts, Harlem, Calcutta, and Sarajevo. Children born of violence, fed on anger, and bathed in deprivation are growing up to run the world, being raised to be political messiahs to murder and plunder. Isaiah's hope and the message of Advent is that, through the power of God, the dynamics that bring the world to the brink of destruction will literally save the creation. Children are God's unfinished business in the world, still capable of being shaped.

Advent has always been about politics, but not about politics as usual. Advent concerns the political reality of the care and feeding of children. The natural law of cause and effect, of sowing and reaping, applies to the movements of history. We sow the wind and reap the whirlwind. As we shape the children we shape the world that is to come. Isaiah was right. A child leads and the world follows either to salvation or destruction.—Larry Dipboye

Topic: God with Us
TEXT: Isa. 7:10–16

We are dealing with budget issues for a city association of Baptist churches. The needs of a large city always seem to overwhelm the resources, and one can hardly expect folks who live at a safe suburban distance to understand, or to care for that matter. Budgets usually mean making hard choices about how much and where, and no one should have been surprised that the poverty of city missions held less interest than some glitzy church-growth projects. After the suburban majority won the day and budget priorities had been set, I happened to be standing in the line of fire when one of the layman began to express his disapproval. His righteous indignation was significant in light of the fact that he was one of "us" not "them." Why should he care what happened to the city? He should have been pleased to know that the bulk of the budget was in "our" expansion needs rather than in "their" survival needs, but he was not happy. He raised a rhetorical question: "If Jesus came to this city, where would he go—to the slick programs and promotions of bigger and better churches or to the broken people living on the margin?"

I. *God is with us.* In my personal hierarchy of need I am more likely to ask, "Where do I stand" than "Where would Jesus go?" The question is central to Advent, the coming of God. It is an uncomfortable question of personal values that goes to the issue of priorities, power, and politics. In light of the obscenity of selfish indulgence that dominates this season of shopping, we ought to question where Jesus might be found in the celebration of his birth. Would Jesus go to our shopping malls or bless our Christmas trees? We would do well to ponder the question before we leap to conclusions. Immanuel is a sign of God's loving presence with his people, not an endorsement of our values.

Isaiah spoke to the immediate time and place of Judah, 740 years before Christ. Yet the oracle is more quoted from Matthew than from Isaiah, more closely connected to the birth of Christ than to Jewish history. King Ahaz was terrified by news that Aram and Israel were forming an alliance against him, but he was more afraid of God. He would not put Jahweh to the test. Impatient with the ineffective regent, Isaiah prophesied a sign of protection from God. A child born to a young woman would be the sign Immanuel, the comforting presence of God. The identity of the child may well have been known to Isaiah—perhaps even Hezekiah, son of Ahaz. A conservative, literal interpretation of the Hebrew is "young woman," but Matthew quoted in Greek and used the word "virgin." Roman Catholic scholar Raymond Brown made the honest observation that nothing in Jewish understanding would have naturally connected the Isaiah prophecy to the future hope of a messiah or to the virgin conception of Jesus. Matthew made the connection. Unfortunately controversy has obscured the message as debate has revolved around the virginity of the mother to the neglect of the sign Immanuel, "God with us." Actually, the sign Immanuel is central to both Isaiah and Matthew. No controversy or contradiction is necessary. The sign given to calm the fears of a weak king who lived more than seven hundred years before Christ took on new meaning for a beaten and oppressed people at the birth of Jesus. In Christ, God is with us. Paul may have said it best: "God was in Christ reconciling the world to himself."

II. *Do not be afraid.* Immanuel meets us in our fear. God spoke to the fear of Moses in the call to begin the Exodus: "I will be with you" (Exod. 3:12). The Isaiah of the exile would comfort the captives (41:10): "Do not fear, for I am with you; do not be afraid, for I am your God." Every visitation of angels in the birth narratives of Matthew and Luke addresses the fear of the people. When Gabriel revealed to Zechariah the conception of John and to Mary the conception of Jesus, the world of comfort, "Do not be afraid," is preface to the revelation. Joseph is advised not to fear taking Mary as his wife. The proclamation of the angel of God to the shepherds was, "Do not be afraid; for see, I am bringing you good news of great joy for all the people."

The wisdom of Solomon declared, "The fear of the Lord is the beginning of knowledge" (Prov. 1:7), and Malachi warned, "for he is like a refiner's fire and like fuller's soap. . . . He will purify the descendants of Levi and refine them like gold and silver" (Mal. 3:2). Fear of the holy presence of God is the normal response of a pious Jew. Addressing fear suggests that these are people who are serious about God, but what kind of God approaches us in the help-lessness of infancy? Why is the sign Immanuel about an infant born of a young woman? Remember Elijah. The Word of God came not in the earthquake, fire, or storm, but in the veiled silence. The child shall lead us, lead us to know the God who has come to us not in raw power but in pure grace. Jesus continued to calm fears. He quieted a storm on the sea for his disciples. He quieted their fear when he walked on the sea. At the Transfiguration, Jesus lifted the disciples to their feet when they fell to the ground in fear. At the Resurrection, "Do not be afraid" was the greeting to the first witnesses on Easter morning, and the promise of peace met the fear of separation.

What scares you? Death is supposed to be the ultimate threat, but I suspect that many of us are more frightened of life. This is the season to be jolly for those who turn a deaf ear and a blind eye to the sin of the world. This is a season of terror for folks who are struggling with real threats. Christ does not meet us in superficial joy or saccharin sweetness. The message of Advent is for the frightened of this world. God has not abandoned the sick, the poor, the weak, and the lonely. Immanuel dwells at the center of the greatest fear and the deepest need. God is found with young Jewish peasants struggling with the hard economic political issues of the day. He is revealed to Gentiles from the East who have absolutely no reason to look for salvation from the Jews. God meets rough shepherds in fields, an elderly priest in the Temple in his last days, and a prophetess called Anna. Like Isaiah's prophecy, this child is a threat to kings. Let all of the powers of this world tremble, and let the hearts of God's people take courage. God has come to us. Immanuel, God is with us, and his promise stands forever: "I am with you always, to the end of the age."—Larry Dipboye

Topic: Walking in the Light of Christmas
TEXT: Isa. 9:2–7; Luke 2:1–20

It was on this night that God reached down from his unreachable height, from a distance so far that human beings could never scale it, and opened for us a tunnel into God's distant light.

Coming into that manger, God pierced a tunnel through the darkness of our human condition and focused the pure bright light of heaven on us. That light shines in the darkest expanses of the Earth, in the most shadowy corners of our lives. And not only does it come down to change this world where we live, but it is also a beacon drawing us upward out of our darkness toward God's holy light.

For those of us who are dependent on our eyes for making sense of our world, light can completely change the way we understand what's going on around us. There's a wonderful children's book that I used to read to my children called *Bedtime for Frances*. It's about a little girl who has a hard time falling asleep. As Frances lies in the dark shadows of her room, she sees a tiger in the corner getting ready to pounce on her. She tries all kinds of things to relieve her fears. She sings songs and recites the alphabet backwards. Finally she can take it no longer, and she runs to her father crying that a tiger is going to eat her up. Her father goes with her to her room, turns on the light, and shows her that all she saw was the shadow of her bathrobe crumpled in the corner—her bathrobe that she should have hung in her closet, by the way.

This heavenly light whom God sent at Christmas, our Savior Jesus Christ, casts light on all the things we fear and exposes them for what they really are. He shines in the darkness of our loneliness to let us know that we are never alone, for he has promised that his spirit is always with us. He casts his eternal light on our greatest fear, the fear of death. By his light he shows us that we have nothing to fear from death. As awesome and terrifying as it looks to us, Jesus shows by his own death that dying is not the end of life.

Light also shows us the true character of things. There is a restaurant in Columbia, South Carolina, where I ate lunch from time to time. At noon it was an ordinary downtown restaurant whose decor was nothing special. But one time I ate supper there after dark. The lights were low and candles gleamed on each table. It looked like a completely different place in the dark.

Jesus casts light on those things that look so attractive in the dark so we can see them for what they really are. In the darkness of this world, evil can look so appealing. In Bosnia and Rwanda, in Northern Ireland and the Middle East, there are those who coddle hatreds that are generations old and that make their life's goal revenge on those who have wronged them. We too with a darkened sense of righteousness nurture grudges and find pleasure in evening scores. Jesus our light shows how stupid and futile it is to nurse our grudges. In the darkness of this world, financial security, at whatever cost to our health or our family's welfare, can look like the ultimate good. The light of Jesus shows us the futility of committing our lives to shallow things. The light of Jesus can show us that some of the things we hold most important are really pretty insignificant when we see them in that heavenly light.

And that light from heaven not only exposes evil for what it is and uncovers shallow purposes for what they are, it also reveals the good things that we might never notice in the shadows. Like groping for your slippers in the predawn darkness of your bedroom, only to discover that they're right beside you, sometimes the things we want and need most are right by us, but we can't see them unless they're illuminated by the light of Christ. In a world that puts a premium on looking out for number one, who would ever expect to find true happiness in serving others? In a culture where it pays to have connections with the right people, who would ever expect to get anything out of helping the homeless and the dispossessed? In a world that values wealth and power, who would ever look for the Son of God in a manger?

That tunnel of light that God opened at Christmas changes the way we see everything around us. But Jesus does more than cast light on our lives. He also leads us to that greater light that is far more glorious than anything we can ever conceive, more brilliant and awe-inspiring than even the light the shepherds saw when the angels surrounded them in the fields outside Bethlehem.

Through the light God sent at Christmas, through the child Jesus, we have a tunnel onto a distant light. That light shines into the world, overcoming all our darkness. And it points us to the father of all lights, the beginning and the end of all creation. That light is God's gift to us on this holiest of all nights. May it shine in the depth of your heart this night and for eternity.—Stephens G. Lytch

ILLUSTRATIONS

IMPORTANCE.   The year was 1809 and the place was Hardin County, Kentucky. A traveler met a local farmer who lived in that county at the crossroads and they were engaged in conversation. The farmer asked the traveler, "What's new in the world?" "Well they are talking about establishing a National Bank," he said, "and we may be having some more trouble with Great Britain. What's new here in Hardin County, Kentucky?" "Ah, shucks, mister," the farmer responded, "nothing ever happens here. Nancy Hanks and Tom Lincoln had a little baby boy last night. But nothing important ever happens here." It is really amazing how some of the most important things that ever happen in the world come in the form of babies, and we do not even know of their importance. A lot of us will find Christmas coming upon us and soon past us and we will not know what the real meaning of Christmas was because we will have missed it entirely.—William Powell Tuck

CHRISTMAS FRUSTRATION.   Christmas is very frustrating for many because Christmas is supposed to be a time of great joy. But how do you find it when you don't have it? I think it's sad that so many celebrate the Christmas season by getting drunk, trying to cover up their emptiness. One woman who became an alcoholic traced the beginning of her plight to a Christmas party where, with her Christmas whiskey in her hand, she staggered to the bar and sang in discordant tones, "Silent Night, Holy Night." Such superficial joy dies. It does not last. Suicide rises to great heights during the Christmas season. Depression overwhelms many during Christmas because they come face to face with the fact that they are not happy; they have not found joy.

The reason is simple. They have sought to find it outside things and have not understood that joy begins from a relationship with God who made us all. Joy is found when he becomes part of our lives, and we remember that we are in his hands, and nothing can take him away from us. God has not left us. He has brought joy to the world.—Hugh Litchfield[1]

A MODEST ENTRANCE.   I used to drive past Appomattox, Virginia, almost every week when I was in college. I never stopped. My hometown was just a few miles from Appomattox, which was one of the most historical places in the Civil War, but I never bothered to stop there until many years later. I took a friend one day to visit Appomattox, the place where the Civil War ended. It was too familiar, a common place to me. Some of us will miss the meaning of Christmas because it comes routinely and we will not be ready for it. Some of us will miss it because we do not expect God to come in such an ordinary way. If you and I had been in charge of the universe, we certainly would not have made our entrance into the world in an obscure village in Bethlehem. We would have had a brass band. We might have chosen a

---

[1] *Preaching the Christmas Story*

palace or something more spectacular. We would not likely have chosen the quiet, modest way that God did to make his entrance into the world.—William Powell Tuck

SMALL BUT SIGNIFICANT.   "I should go so far as to say that, spiritually speaking, everything which is gigantic is spiritually suspect." Gabriel Marcel, a truly fine French philosopher, uttered these words. And Lancelot Andrewes, the sixteenth-century son of English piety and ordered loveliness, in a Christmas sermon, sums up the immortal message of the manger: "The great lesson is to be little, seeing this day infinite greatness become so little. Eternity a child, the rays of glory wrapped in rags, Heaven crowded into the corner of a stable, and He that is everywhere wants a room."—Johnstone G. Patrick[2]

SEARCH FOR THE CHRIST CHILD.   There is an old legend about a woman named Befana who is the gift giver in Italy like Father Christmas is in England or Santa Claus in America. The legend says that when the Wise Men came by her home, they invited her to go with them to find the place where the birth of Christ was to be, but she was too busy with her chores to go with them. We are told that today she spends all of her time looking for the birthplace of the Christ Child because she had been too busy when he first came. We can be so busy with all the preparations that are very important and somehow miss the very meaning of Christmas itself. Watch. Prepare yourself.—William Powell Tuck

ANSWERING PRAYERS.   A church gathered together to pray for a needy family. This family needed food for Christmas, and members of the church gathered together to pray for them. A young boy came and knocked on the door where the church group was praying and said, "My father said he can't come tonight because he is busy unloading his prayers at the Jones's home. He said he had taken a side of beef, a sack of potatoes, a bushel of apples, some jars of jam. He said he couldn't be here tonight to pray, but he has taken his prayers and unloaded them at their home."—William Powell Tuck

---

[2] In G. Paul Butler (ed.), *Best Sermons* (1959–1960 Protestant Edition)

EVANGELISM AND WORLD MISSIONS

SERMON SUGGESTIONS

Topic: The Glory of the Gospel
TEXT: Rom. 1:16

I. *"I am not ashamed of the gospel."* That opening retort, "I am not ashamed," was not a proud boast but a costly confession. Simply for preaching the gospel, Paul had been imprisoned in Philippi (Acts 16:19–24), smuggled out of Thessalonica (Acts 17:5–10), hounded out of Beroea (Acts 17:13–14), laughed out of Athens (Acts 17:32), and driven out of Ephesus (Acts 19:28–20:1). If he was not ashamed of his cause, then he was certainly one of the few!

The realization that his gospel was a scandal came early for Paul, and he faced the crisis squarely in the opening chapters of 1 Corinthians (1:18–2:5). Because the essential content of that message concerned a crucified Messiah, it would always be "folly" to the wise and clever (1:18–19). Both to Jews demanding signs and to Greeks seeking wisdom, the preaching of Christ seemed to be foolishness and weakness (1:22–25).

It was this conviction, that divine power is most clearly seen in human weakness, that enabled Paul to resist the strong temptation to become ashamed even when his enterprise seemed on the verge of collapse (2 Tim. 1:8).

All too often pulpit and pew engage in a conspiracy of silence to keep the radical claims of the gospel from surfacing. But the issue must be faced, for we will never grasp the full glory of the gospel until we prove in our own experience that we can endure its deepest offense without becoming ashamed!

II. *"It is the power of God unto salvation."* How could Paul maintain such an unwavering confidence in the gospel despite its ridicule and scorn? Supremely, by realizing that his message was not what it appeared to be. Instead of a foolish story of human weakness, it was in reality "the power of God unto salvation" (Rom. 1:16b). A few verses earlier, Paul had identified the content of his gospel as Jesus Christ, who became "Son of God in power . . . by his resurrection from the dead" (1:4). A few verses later he will explain that his gospel is a divine revelation "from heaven" (1:17–18). The context, therefore, guides us to understand that all of the supernatural power vested in the Risen Lord of glory flows through that scandalous message that proclaims his earthly shame!

Note well: Paul did not say that the gospel is a proclamation *about* the power of God; rather, he said that the gospel *is* that very power at work for human redemption (1 Cor. 1:18). The gospel does not merely bear witness to salvation but has within itself the strength to save. The preacher of the gospel literally recreates the Christ event every time he tells the sacred story. When his message is faithfully uttered, Christ actually *happens* again in human affairs.

The gospel does not merely *announce* or even *anticipate* the outcome. Rather, it *inaugurates* the pilgrimage of salvation and *actualizes* the experience of its reality here and now, in advance of the end.[1] We may pay our respects to military might, to the rule of law, to education, and to culture, but still ask of them the ultimate question: Do you have the power to save? Paul had actually seen lives changed, hopes awakened, purposes redirected, churches established. He knew what his gospel could do. His own transformation was living proof that it was, indeed, "the power of God *unto salvation.*"

Such power will come not from our size or our structures but from the consistency and integrity with which we embody the gospel of Jesus Christ in word and in deed.

Paul put it so well: "that our faith might not rest in the wisdom of men but in the power of God" (1 Cor. 2:5).

III. *"To everyone who believes."* Complete reliance on the sufficiency of God is demanded not only by the divine aspect of the gospel as "the power of God unto salvation" but also by the human aspect of the gospel as available "to everyone who believes" (Rom. 1:16c). In its biblical definition, faith is not some human action that would base our salvation on works; rather, it is a reaction to the divine action declared in the gospel (Eph. 2:8–9). It is that absence of self-assertion that makes room for the divine initiative.

But because everything is given in the gospel, the scandal of faith as the opposite of religious works is fully vindicated. Through simple trust we discover that our emptiness is his filling, our weakness is his strength, our abdication is his coronation, our humiliation is his exaltation.

The glory of a gospel received by faith alone is that salvation thereby becomes available "to everyone" (Rom. 1:16c). We cannot all share the same citizenship, for national boundaries divide us, or the same culture, for social classes divide us, or the same prosperity, for economic differences divide us. But thank God we can all share the same salvation, for the possibility of believing unites us. When the gospel defines faith as man's "nothing" in the face of God's "everything," it offers each person a second chance, regardless of the first chance provided by heredity, environment, or attainment.—William E. Hull

Topic: When God Knocks at the Back Door
TEXT: 2 Cor. 12:1–10

Once when I was ill, a couple from our church family sent me a most interesting Charlie Brown get-well card. Charlie is philosophizing about life, as he so often does, and is saying, "Wouldn't it be nice if our lives were like VCRs . . . and we could fast forward through the crummy times?"

It is our thesis this morning that what we often think of as "crummy times" can be some of the most *constructive* in our lives.

The more I struggle with my life and share the struggles of others, I see that crises are the backdoor through which God often gains entrance into our lives. It may be the only way that he can ever gain access, because the front door is closed, bolted, and locked. It is as though life is always calling us to higher ground through experiencing it at deeper levels.

The Lord of life has not trusted us with his precious gift to only half live it. But for so much of our life it seems that we are given to coasting rather than to climbing. We are not

---

[1] C. K. Barrett, *The Epistle to the Romans*

growing. We are not experiencing the fulfillment that life promises. We are paddling around in the shallows when life challenges us to launch out into the deep. We are complacent. We have given up the struggle of being and becoming. Our top priorities are comfort and ease.

And we resent our comfortable lifestyles being threatened and sometimes altered by changing circumstances: ill health, failure in business, rejection in love, the death of a loved one or friend; but it may be that only through these adversities God gets our attention, and we are willing to listen to him.

Robert Browning, the English poet, has unforgettably expressed this insight in his lines:

> Just when we are safest, there's a sunset touch,
> A fancy from a flower-bell, someone's death,
> A chorus-ending from Euripides.

Although God does not inflict the crises, many of them we choose for ourselves at depths of which we are only beginning to understand; but God *can* use the crises to prod us, nudge us, provoke us to the road that leads to life. Many of us do not know where we are going, but we are in an awful hurry to get there. We may be hell-bent rather than heaven-bound and a crisis affords an opportunity for us not only to catch our breath but also to get our life turned around, to get our priorities in order. Often it is *only* through some adversity that we ever take time out to reflect about what is *really* going on.

Our New Testament lesson from the apostle Paul is all about the knock at the door that came to him as "a thorn in the flesh," as he characterizes it. Evidently it was a very prickly thing—irritating, frustrating—something for which there was no cure, no escape; it was a fact of his life. Even though he prayed many times for its removal, it did not go away.

Although God said no to the apostle's prayers, he did answer Paul, the person. The answer: "My grace is sufficient for you; my strength is made perfect in your weakness."

Paul bowed to a wisdom that was greater than his. He saw that because of the great visions that had so dramatically come to him in his conversion, he might be inclined to be egotistical, and this thorn, whatever it was, would remind him that all is of grace.

Is not a mark of true maturity when we get beyond asking *why* the thorn and ask *how* can this impediment become a means of grace? How can God's grace get into this situation so that we may see the rose blooming alongside the thorn?

There *is* a knock at the door through an accident, the diagnosis of a life-threatening disease, a failure in relationships or in business. We can run for cover, trying to protect ourselves—to escape back into the womb—or we can be open, grip whatever happens with both hands until it yields up its amazing treasure of grace.

Someone has said that the best commentary on the Bible is the Bible. James, the Lord's brother, makes a very striking statement concerning our theme in the initial chapter of his little epistle. As translated by J. B. Phillips, James writes: "When all kinds of difficulties come into your life, don't resent them as intruders, but welcome them as friends" (James 1:2, 3).

When there *is* the knock at the door with the visitation of some adversity, open the door to the possibility that this contingency can become a friend. Is this not the insight in our contemporary text, as Shakespeare so poignantly pens:

Such are the uses of adversity,
Which like the toad, ugly and venomous,
Wears yet a precious jewel in his head?

There *are* "treasures in darkness." Don't miss them!

Don't miss the day, or the night, of your visitation, when God is so near. God is never so present as when he seems most absent. When some calamity strikes, how often we cry out in resentment, if not in rebellion, "Where is God?"

As the Good Shepherd, he is with you, leading you through every valley of the shadow. He is with us as the Divine Host, preparing a table for us in the presence of our enemies. His gracious hospitality is symbolized in that he hands to us a cup that is not only full but running over. When we have experienced the fullness of his grace to heal, to bind up the brokenhearted, to anoint with the balm of Gilead, who does not find himself, herself, rising from the Lord's table refreshed for the journey and confidently singing with the psalmist: "Surely, goodness and mercy shall follow me all the days of my life."—John Thompson

Topic: Faith: The Saving Response
TEXT: Eph. 2:8–9

While it is grace that saves us, we can speak of faith as the saving response.

God does not overwhelm us; we make a free response. We are passive, not like a cup into which God pours his grace. We sing of God's being the potter and our being the clay, of his molding us and shaping us after his will. Though the imagery tells an important truth, being very concrete and vivid, it is quite inadequate. We are not like inert clay in the hands of God. We have the power to respond to God or reject the shaping power of his grace.

I. *The importance of faith.* If faith is what I have said it is—reliance on the goodness of God, trusting his steadfast love, and responding to his saving grace in Christ, then faith is important. That is what the New Testament says about it.

Jesus, on coming down from the Mount of Transfiguration, found his disciples at the base with an epileptic boy whom they could not heal. After rebuking them, Jesus said: "For truly, I say to you, if you have faith as a grain of mustard seed, you will say to this mountain, 'Move from here to there,' and it will move; and nothing will be impossible to you" (Matt. 17:20–21).

The father of this epileptic boy came to Jesus half doubting and half believing, imploring him: "If you can do anything, have pity on us and help us." And Jesus said to him: "If you can! All things are possible to him who believes" (Mark 9:22b–23).

Jesus was always disappointed by little faith and always exulted in great faith. (See Matt. 8:10, 26; Luke 24:25.)

When the author of Hebrews looked back over the history of his nation, the real heroes were men and women of faith. In the eleventh chapter of his book he gives a roll call of the faithful. They had done impossible things because of their faith, and they had suffered much because of it. The world was not worthy of them. He spoke of how Moses "endured as seeing him who is invisible" (v. 27a). But that was true of all of them. They trusted unseen reality and lived as if the things hoped for were real. These stalwart men and women of faith inspired one of the most unique definitions of faith in the New Testament: "Now faith is the assurance of things hoped for, the conviction of things not seen" (v. 1).

John, writing possibly near the end of the first Christian century, marveled at how far the Christians had come and the victories they had won. What was the secret of it all? "This is the victory that overcomes the world, our faith" (1 John 5:2).

II. *Faith in an inhospitable climate.* As you study your Bible you will discover that faith often flourishes in an inhospitable climate. It is not a fair-weather faith; it often walks in shadows and darkness. It is a faith that originates not in quiet and sequestered harbors but on the high seas, where the winds are high and the storms are fierce. Often life seems to argue against justice, goodness, and God. Yet men and women, while sometimes doubting, go on believing. It is a tenacious faith. It keeps on holding on.

The God of biblical faith does not accommodate himself to our little categories, does not satisfy our childish and immature ways. He does not come at every beck and call. He refuses to be a cosmic valet carrying our luggage for us. The psalmists would argue with God: Why are you so far away? Why are you silent? Why don't you speak?

You remember the Babylonian captivity. The Israelites were captives in a strange land. Back home their land was despoiled, their sacred places desecrated, and their Temple, where they had made their sacrifices and where God was present as nowhere else, lay in shambles. You feel their anguish in one of their psalms (Ps. 137: 4–6).

Yet here emerges one of the most significant things about Israel's history: it was in that strange land that they came to their best understanding of God. In that inhospitable climate, their finest flower of faith grew.

One of the things that helped biblical people to go on believing when the situation was not conducive to faith was the feeling that God was present, although hidden, in the tragedy of life; that while he himself was not evil, he was often in the midst of evil bringing forth good out of it.

Israel had been a nomad people of the desert, where they learned the ways of eagles. One of the seemingly most ruthless things was to see an eagle claw away the nest from beneath her eaglets. God is likened to an eagle stirring up its nest: "Like an eagle that stirs up its nest, that flutters over its young, spreading out its wings, catching them, bearing them on its pinions" (Deut. 32:11).

The imagery is vivid and meaningful. High up on some craggy rock an eagle has built her nest. The time comes when the eaglets must learn to fly. There will be danger and risk in this adventure. Then one day the nest is ruthlessly torn from beneath the eaglets, and what is so completely mystifying is that it is not an enemy but the mother that destroys the nest.

The eaglets find themselves falling to the rocky earth beneath. They spread their wings and flutter, but still they continue to fall. And just before they hit the earth, the mother swoops down, spreading her great pinions beneath them, on which they are gently and strongly borne upward. Then they understand that there was love in the ruthlessness, that it was a caring act. So God is often like an eagle that stirs up her nest.

A young Jewish girl in the Warsaw ghetto managed to escape over the wall and hide in a cave. She died there shortly before the allied army came, but before her death she had scratched on the wall three things: first, "I believe in the sun, even though it is not shining"; second, "I believe in love, even when feeling it not"; and third, "I believe in God, even when he is silent."

We should give attention to faith. There is no joy, vitality, or hope without it. It opens up life to God, in whom are the springs of life. And while it does not save us, it is the saving response.—Chevis H. Horne[2]

Topic: Men Need Religion, Too!
TEXT: John 6:66–69

I have never forgotten the man's words. He said very forcefully, "I don't go to church. Religion, you see, is for women and children. Strong men don't need it." That man echoes the sentiments of more people than we can begin to realize. They believe that religion for a lot of folks is just a prop that holds them up. Religion is for the weak or the insecure, those who are not able to face the difficulties and struggles of life within their own resources. "Religion," he said, "is for women and children."

I. First, men think they can be moral, ethical, and good without religion and without the Church. They can rely on their own resources and their own strength. They have self-confidence, but unfortunately their self-confidence often becomes conceit and begins to cripple them.

They have become their own standard for morality. They measure all things by what they think is right, without anyone challenging it or coming to them with higher principles or higher ideals. They think they can be good without religion. Yet they never thought they could become attorneys, doctors, dentists, pharmacists, or anything else without discipline, guidance, and direction.

Second, I think there are some, especially many men, who have turned primarily to the pursuit of happiness.

Third, I think, there are some men who are not in church today because their primary pursuit in life is for money, power, and fame.

Fourth, there are many men who go through life with their jobs taking first place. If God has a place, they do not have much time to let God interrupt their business.

Fifth, there are others who turn away from church and religion primarily because they are influenced too much by the negative things they see, hear, or think about religion.

Sixth, there are others who are simply indecisive. They cannot make a religious decision with all of the other demands on their lives. There are a lot of people who go through life in their relationship to God "just browsing, just looking." They never can make a decision.

There are others who do not turn to Christ because of cynicism and agnosticism. They have become cynical about religion because they have seen its weaknesses, its disgraces, and its problems. They also have all kinds of questions about God, life, the Church, and Christ. Nobody has ever answered all of their questions.

If you wait until you get to the point that you have all the answers, then you will never decide.

I believe, however, that all persons, all men and women—but we are talking primarily today to men—have gods in their life. Oh, you have some kind of god. It may not be God the Father of Jesus Christ, but it is a god, nonetheless. Whether it is power, wealth, our job, financial

---

[2] *Preaching the Great Themes of the Bible*

security, or our own self-confidence, we all have some type of god. Too often we kneel at that shrine and let that force and power dominate us, instead of the power of God.

Often we think we are so strong and self-confident that we do not need God or religion. Then we suddenly discover, to our surprise, that we are crushed down at our strongest point. We discover that we cannot handle a crisis, grief, an accident, the loss of a job, or some other situation. Hundreds of things come into our lives and we are crushed to our knees and do not know where to turn.

II. Let's respond now to that man who said that religion is for women and children. Let me begin by saying, "Yes it is!"

The apostle Paul wrote that "in Christ there is neither male nor female." In Jesus Christ we are all one.

Yes, religion is for women, but it is also for men. Where did we get this notion of Jesus meek and mild? There is a little song, "Jesus meek and mild, look upon a little child." Oh yes, Jesus is meek and mild in a sense. There is a tenderness in Christ. As the Good Shepherd, he cares for us in our times of hurt and in our times of need. We are aware that we can turn to the one who says, "Take my yoke upon you." He is the one who is concerned with our grief and our burdens. He helps us bear our sorrow and burdens. We know we can turn to him.

Look at this Jesus Christ who walked into the Temple in Jerusalem, the chief religious place of its day, and kicked over the tables of the moneychangers who were there robbing the people. He declared, "You have made my Father's house a den of thieves." That would not have made him very popular with the Jewish leaders. Can you imagine the courage it took to do that? Jesus often challenged the religious leaders and their understanding of Moses as the greatest lawgiver of all. Jesus said, "Well, now, Moses has said unto you, but now I say unto you—" Oh, my goodness!

If a person, especially a man, will not turn to Christ because he thinks he is weak, he does not know Jesus Christ. Jesus was a man of great courage. He walked through a crowd in his home town that was getting ready to stone him. The crowd was ready to stone him when he opened the Scripture and then declared, "This Scripture is fulfilled today." They knew that Jesus was talking about himself. They were going to stone him, but he did not run. He just walked through the midst of the crowd. Remember, Jesus died on a cross, bearing not only his own awful, physical suffering and death, but he also bore the sins of humanity. In no way is Jesus seen as weak. The Son of God came into the world that we might know fully what God is like.

If there is any problem with religion today it is that those of us in the churches, preachers and laypersons, have made the Christian faith too easy. Jesus Christ never said his way would be easy. My question is, Are you man enough, are you woman enough, to follow Jesus Christ?

Christianity is for the weak? Who are you kidding? Look at the apostle Paul. When he started telling other people about Jesus Christ he was imprisoned by the Romans, the Greeks, and the Jews. He was beaten forty times, he said, on five different occasions. He was beaten by rods; he was stoned and left for dead. Do you want to call the apostle Paul a weak man? Look at the courage of that man as he went about sharing the good news of the Gospel of Christ. Every single disciple of Jesus, except maybe John, and we are not sure about John, died as a martyr as they shared the good news of Jesus Christ.

Look at society today, and those persons who have dared to follow Jesus Christ. They have lifted up their lives to walk in his way. It takes great courage and great strength to follow Jesus Christ as Lord. Are we men enough? What the Church needs today are men who will lift up their heads, boldly, and look to Jesus Christ, who challenges the best and highest in us.

I believe that Jesus Christ draws a line in the sand today. He asks us, Are you man enough to walk across that line and live your life for me? Will you stand for my way of justice and righteousness and receive eternal life? Are you man enough, are you woman enough to do it? Christianity is not for weaklings; it is for individuals who have courage, fortitude, and commitment. Will you say, I want to surrender my life to Jesus Christ and serve Him?—William Powell Tuck

ILLUSTRATIONS

GOOD NEWS.   Christopher Morley, one day while observing the telephone, began to think of the people who were waiting somewhere to hear some good news. There were the parents waiting anxiously for a call from a boy or a girl far from home. There was the lonely young man in the city wishing that someone would call him and talk to him. There was the girl who was waiting for the young man to announce he was coming to take her to dinner. And he says that suddenly he wished he could call them all and give some good news to each. Well, this is what I have been commissioned to do. To every man, to every woman, to every young person who is dissatisfied, my word is that God wants you to possess a better life than you have ever known, and best of all, he will help you possess it.—Gerald Kennedy[3]

MADE TO FLY.   Do you remember the story of the ugly duckling? He didn't walk like a duck, he didn't quack like a duck, and he didn't look like a duck, but he lived among the ducks in the barnyard. Then one fine day he heard a call from above. He had never heard it before, but in him was an instinct that answered that call. In the sky he saw a speck. The speck became a long trail. The call became louder and more insistent. The ugly duckling began to flap his wings. He found that he could fly. Up above the barnyard, higher and higher he flew, to answer that call and to join that company. He disappeared from the barnyard. The ducks never saw him again. They said that he died, but we know better. "They that wait upon the Lord shall renew their strength. They shall mount up with wings as eagles."—Robert C. Shannon[4]

WEAKNESS?   Was Martin Luther a weak man when he nailed his ninety-five theses onto the church door and challenged the corruption of the Church of his day? Was he weak when he stood before the synod and said, "Unless I can be convicted by the evidence of God's word, I will not recant"? Was David Livingston a weak man when he went to Africa? Was Albert Schweitzer a weak man when he gave up his position as a professor and great musician to become a medical doctor and go as a medical missionary to Lambarene to serve Christ in that godforsaken jungle? Was Bill Wallace a weak man when he went to China to serve Christ? Was Walter Rauschenbusch a weak man when he worked in one of the worst parts

---

[3] *Fresh Every Morning*
[4] *Christ Above All*

of New York City, Hell's Kitchen? Was Martin Luther King Jr. a weak man when he stood up and cried for justice and righteousness for all races?—William Powell Tuck

PROPER DEFENSE.   If you have ever been to the fascinating city of Edinburgh, Scotland, you know that on one end of a street is the Edinburgh Castle. It sits high up on a mountain, with one side a sheer cliff. There was only one time during war that the Edinburgh Castle was captured by its enemy. Do you know when that was? It happened when they did not fortify what they thought was the strongest side. They were being attacked by their enemies and they assumed that nobody could possibly climb up the cliffs and get in that way. So they defended the city at all of its weakest points. But the enemy came up the side of the cliff, at its strongest point. It fell at the point that they thought was impregnable. It was captured not at its weakest point but at the strongest.—William Powell Tuck

BIBLE STUDIES

BY EDUARD SCHWEIZER

Bible Study I: God Makes Free
TEXT: Exod. 6:2–9; Gal. 5:1–15

Most of us are living in a free nation. Most of us are not slaves of a foreign power, as the Israelites were slaves of the Egyptians in the time of Moses. We are, perhaps, even living in a country that has recently been liberated. Are we not free, at least most of us?

I have seen students captivated in a traditional university system against which they could only rebel in bloody battles. Are we not free, independent nations? And yet we are not able to be freed from our own free institutions and their old and fixed structures. Are we not all boasting of our independence? And yet, we are so totally lost in problems that nobody seems able to solve. Even if we, as individuals, oppose the politics of our government courageously, thinking that we would know some way out of the disaster, how should we succeed against powers that are beyond any possible influence from private individuals? But are our problems not rooted even more deeply than that? While sitting in a lecture hall of a Paris University, I read an inscription carved with a knife in the table before me: "Poem of the student of the twentieth century: I am fed up with everything, I am fed up with everything, I am fed up with everything—and you?" Beneath that, someone else had engraved: "I too." Are we not free, oppressed by nobody? But our young people are overcome by a hopeless nausea. I have good friends in the USA and in Europe who are no longer able to speak to their own children. The parents are living in their world of values, of aims, of ethics, and their children are living in another world of quite different values, of quite different aims, of quite different ethics. They may even esteem each other, but they no longer have any common language that would enable them to communicate, because each one is totally fixed in his own way of understanding life. Are we not free and independent? Yet each one of us is fastened as with chains to his views, his traditions, his dreams. In the Fiji islands I have seen young people trained in modern agricultural methods come home to their tribes and nobody was willing to change anything of the traditional way of cultivating the fields. Fathers and sons were living in silent opposition. They did not speak of it, but they were separated from each other, as if high walls had been built between them. Are we not free to go on our own self-chosen paths? Yet we are unable to do so, because each one of us is stamped by his origin and family and education. Where is freedom, real freedom?

I. *"And God said to Moses, 'I am the Lord. I appeared to Abraham, to Isaac, and to Jacob, as God Almighty'"* (vv. 2–3). God? Could God be of any help? For generations, people have spoken of him, but to what effect? To be sure, it is a favorite custom during the hoisting of the flag to sing of "the Almighty, the Ancient of days." It is a widely accepted adornment of a patriotic speech to refer to the protection of the Almighty—even Herr Hitler did so. But the God of the tradition, the God of the forefathers does not help. There are so many things of our grandfathers still hanging in our huts or houses—old bows and arrows, old pictures or diplomas, charms or books, revered and liked, but no longer of any use. Is God just one among these old-fashioned, outmoded relics? Revered and liked, but not contributing anything to a new, modern, changing world?

II. *"But by my name the Lord I did not make myself known to them"* (v. 3b). What an extraordinary thing! God himself wants to become a new God, a modern God for his people. The world has become another world, and God becomes not another but a new God. He changes his name; he will no longer remain the revered God of our grandparents; he wants to become our God, no longer simply the Almighty of whom the choir speaks when singing hymns of the last century, of whom grandfather spoke, and also Herr Hitler, but now our Lord. But have we not all experienced this? When we were small children, who was God for us? A giant, somewhere up in heaven, perhaps like our father or grandfather or a mighty chief, sometimes good to know about, sometimes to be feared. And then we grew up and we realized that it was not as simple as that. He did not always fulfill our wishes, he did not merely protect us from all suffering; on the contrary, he expected us to go on difficult roads and do things that we did not like to do. Sometimes he spoke to us, and sometimes he seemed to be silent. So God became a new God in our life, quite different from the picture we had as children. This was not always easy. Sometimes we doubted and rebelled against him; sometimes we did not know what to think and believe. Of course, we understood later on that it was one and the same God who spoke to us in a new way, showed himself from a new side; but how many difficult hours of doubt and trouble did this create for us, until we had understood it! Why should we wonder when some of these doubts and troubles shake the world today? We may live in a time when God wants to get out of his old traditional place in which we have locked him so that he can be revered but cannot become effective or disturb us in our ways. Might not the worldwide problems and uproars be signs of the fact that God is on his way to becoming a new God, to becoming Lord anew?

III. *"I also established my covenant with them . . . and I will take you for my people, and I will be your God"* (vv 4a–7a). Indeed, God is not satisfied with being merely revered as a relic of old times and getting a favorite place in our home like the yellowed photograph of our great grandfather hanging over the settee. He wants to enter into a covenant with us, to become *our* God, not only the one of our grandparents. He wants really to enter into our life, to disturb us, to rouse us, to send us to new tasks, to enter into our present state of the world.

IV. *"Moses spoke thus to the people of Israel; but they did not listen to Moses, because of their broken spirit and their hard work"* (v. 9). Very often God is indeed on his way to becoming a new God, to becoming in reality our Lord. But the Israelites do not listen to Moses "because of their hard work." They have no time for him; there is so much to do. Modern life is breaking into our homes everywhere; there are too many changes, there is too much to learn, so many problems to think about. Business is so demanding that even after closing hour it continues to operate in our minds and hearts; it jumps out of the newspaper into our thinking, it occupies our hearts while with our mouths we talk to our wives and our children, and we listen as little to God as we listen to our family, or even less. No, God has no chance to get out of the gilt frame of his old-fashioned picture. Of course, we have time for him—ten minutes in the morning, ten minutes in the evening at least; but in these ten minutes our thoughts are unable to reach him, because they are spinning around and around, always around our problems and hopes and wishes. One of my colleagues at the faculty of medicine of our university pronounced that *the* malady, *the* neurosis, of the twentieth century was the loss of our soul, the idiotic idea that man could be understood on a rational basis as a mere physical being without, as he expressed it, the eternal or divine dimension. It might well be that Asian and African Christians could teach us a better understanding of man.

And the Israelites did not listen to Moses because of their "broken spirit." Again we understand. We know what a broken spirit means when we are so hopeless, when we think that we are unable to change anything. The world runs its course, disasters come, men are killed, and we are simply powerless. Hatred grows, other races, parties, or beliefs are persecuted, and we disagree in our hearts, but this does not alter the facts. In a modern novel, author Bulgakow lets Jesus say that the worst sin is just this broken spirit, this lack of courage, which never leads to action and kills every new enterprise. We are so anxious, so full of fear, that perhaps we should be disillusioned if we dared to tackle something new. Some have grown so skeptical that God himself is no longer protected against their skepticism. This is the broken spirit of his people that kills everything from its beginning and renders it impossible for God to start something new in and through his Church.

Yet there was one for whom God had become too strong, stronger than all the hard work and the business waiting for him, and stronger than all the cowardice in the person who shrinks back from every new road. Moses had a dream, but he did not remain a dreamer. He had a dream that no desire for calm can kill. He saw an aim that God had put to his people. He heard God's voice: "I am the Lord, and I will bring you out from under the burdens of the Egyptians, and I will deliver you from their bondage, and I will redeem you with an outstretched arm and with great acts of judgment" (v. 6). Now we prefer a Buddha-like god with entwined arms who would leave us alone. Outstretched arms are always a bit dangerous; they might bless or give, but they might also hit or threaten or send us on new ways. Who knows? And the great acts of judgment might hit not only our enemies, but first of all ourselves. This is, at least, what we read in 1 Peter: "The time has come for judgment to begin with the household of God." God's redemptive work always begins with his judgment over us, and a revolution that is not, first of all, insight into our own deficiencies is probably due not to God's revolutionary acts but to our own ideas. With Moses, it starts with God's unrest coming over him so that he can no longer resign himself to the situation as it is. He has a vision of what God plans for his people, and this vision looks quite different from what the present realities are.

Moses has heard God: "And I will take you for my people and I will be your God; and you shall know that I am the Lord your God who has brought you out from under the burdens of the Egyptians" (v. 7). This is what God has promised. But how does this look in reality? When Moses dared to start on a new road with his God, he met merely unbelief and rejection from his own people and a total refusal from the Egyptian king. And when he had overcome all this and led God's people out of Egypt, the real difficulties began: the Egyptian army behind, the Red Sea in front, and death for all seemingly unavoidable. And even the miracle of God, saving them through the Red Sea—Where did it lead? Simply into desert, famine, thirst. Rations grew meager and hope diminished. And then the nights came in which they dreamed of the pots of meat they'd had in Egypt.

Whoever sets out with God is not protected against nostalgia about his earlier life that was undisturbed by God and his plans. There will always be times in which he will long for a traditional God, for the God of dead formulas and fixed liturgies who will not disturb him with new tasks. Even more must be said. Neither Moses nor any of the Israelites who started with him, trusting in their God, saw the promised land. They saw only desert and danger, doubt and death. Moses was allowed to see the land, but just from very far away before dying. Their daring adventure with God was to create possibilities for the generation after them, but not for their own. Not their feet but those of their children and grandchildren would tread on the promised soil that Moses had seen in his vision.

Moses died cheerfully. This is what faith means. For forty years he had seen nothing but desert. Even those who were with him as his companions on his way with God were full of mostly nostalgia for the earlier, godless times that they had spent in slavery in Egypt, not even ready for the freedom of God to which Moses tried to lead them. They even rebelled against him and made his work as difficult as possible. Up to his death he had not seen the land of promise except from very far away. He could easily have asked: Where is God? Where is his promise? He could easily have declared God dead. Yet he goes on and on, trusting, hoping, cheerful. He dies without seeing, yet also without doubts. He knows that God will reach what he, Moses, cannot reach. Just because he expects everything from God and not from his own courage and skill and force, he wins the fortitude to lead his people every morning anew on the day's march. It is his faith that gets his entire people through to their final destiny, to the Promised Land. Sometimes one man believes for a whole people, believes his whole people through to their goal. He can do so because, on the one hand, he considers himself not more important than he really is; he, Moses, will not change the world and its politics of force; nobody but God can do this. He can do so because, on the other hand, he considers himself not less important than he is; it is through him that God wants to free his people, and everything depends on his readiness to be inspired by his God and to stick stubbornly and patiently to his task, even if he cannot see beyond the next two or three days' march. And then God, determined in his saving will and unyielding in his grace, does the work and reaches his goal with his people.

One man was faithful to the end for the sake of his whole people. More than a thousand years later, one man was faithful to the end for the sake of our whole world. He was God's Son himself. The end was not a cheerful death with a glimpse of the promised land, at least from some distance. It was a death, in which all the experiences of desert, famine, and thirst, and more than that, all the despair about that incomprehensible God were concentrated. It was a death exploding in a cry: "My God, my God, why hast thou forsaken me?" But even so, Jesus has stuck to his God, and cried: "My God, my God." This is the miracle of a faith, in which man's heart was one, totally one, with God's heart. This is the faith that won, that got us through forever. "For freedom God has set us free," writes the apostle Paul (Gal. 5:1). There are times when we have to fight for social, political, and economic freedom, for quite concrete freedom, as was the case in the time of Moses, when he freed his people from slavery. But there are lords other than national powers. Moses' people were freed from their slavery, but they were not free. Passions and doubts and rebellion mastered them so that they grew more and more nostalgic about their former slavery. We spoke at the beginning of all the so-called free nations today where there is not real freedom. "Stand fast therefore, and do not submit again to a yoke of slavery" (v. 1b), writes the apostle Paul. There are old, traditional ideas, maxims, views that are holding us under their yoke. An older generation can no longer understand the younger, nor the younger the older. A father may have very old-fashioned ideas that his son should be raised exactly as he was raised thirty years ago and force him into an outmoded frame that prevents him from finding his identity. Or he may have very modern ideas and know exactly what ideal goal must be reached by his son and may force him into a very modern frame, nonetheless inflexible and dreadful. Whole nations may be ruined by very old-fashioned colonialism or by very modern subjugation; the difference is minimal. There is but one real freedom, because there is but one totally free man: Jesus Christ. And those who are given the gift of living in Christ, as Paul expresses it, share something of his real freedom. For they have understood that God has, in Jesus, said yes, once for all, to all people. If one understands this, he is no longer forced to make more of himself than he is, to bully and to burden all who have to live with him. Because God has accepted all the others as he has accepted one person, that person becomes free to live together with the others without forcing them into his own frame. And if one understands this, he is no longer forced either to make less of himself than he is, to be a drudge, discouraged and full of inferiority complexes, and to drive all others to despair. Because God has accepted him, why should he not accept himself? In brief, God has finally and definitely freed us from all our horrible fears; and what else is at the root of all inhumanity and oppression but fear?

When I was a boy, there was an old lady in our neighborhood, who was a bit queer. We really feared her because we thought she was one of the witches of the fairy tales. And just because of this we had to show her that we did not fear her, by shouting, from the security of our garden behind the tree, all sorts of insults at her. Now she began to fear us in turn and she had to use her powers, too. When she saw our mother next time, she complained, of course. Thus the whole story ended in a good spanking. This was not tragic; but exactly the same happens on the level of whole nations or races, and it ends tragically. It is nothing but naked fear that leads to the ruthless battles in commerce, to the police terrorism against those whose power we dread, to fixed viewpoints and a propaganda that paints the other in the dirtiest colors. And God has, in Jesus, definitely and totally taken away our fear. "For you did not receive the spirit of slavery to fall back into fear, but you have received the spirit of sonship" (Rom. 8:15). People who know about this are freed to fight for the real freedom, for which we have to strive in the political, social, and national arenas. These are the people who have to spread something of this fearless freedom into the political and social problems created by fear. They are those who know the right direction. Therefore they get moving, even if they see not more than the first day's march. They are not discouraged if they earn only ingratitude and aggression. They are not in despair if things go backward rather than forward sometimes. They are certainly not protected from going astray, but they come back from the wrong way humbly and courageously and ready to search out the right way again. They are not protected against the nostalgia for the fleshpots of a traditional church or bourgeoisie, but they can never quite lose the dream that God has given them, the dream of a world of justice in which the nations are living together and not against one another. They do not give up, even if they realize that they themselves will not reach the goal. They know from the beginning that it will be God who will reach it, not they with their own strength, and this is why they are never discouraged but are marching on, trusting their God.

From the faith of people who have understood that God has said yes to them in Jesus Christ and will use them therefore for his plans, an atmosphere of courage and modesty, of hope and soberness, of unyielding firmness and all-understanding love spreads into our world and becomes infectious. This is how God will free us and will get, through us, into even the offices where worldwide business is managed, into the rooms of diplomats where worldwide policies are made, even into the conscience of those who determine the social conditions. God is on his way; he wants to become a new God, a God who will be able to shake us and get us moving.

Bible Study II: The Strong and the Weak
TEXT: Rom. 15:1–13; Judg. 19–20

"We who are strong ought to bear with the failings of the weak" (v. 1a). No doubt there are strong people and there are weak people. In the Church of Rome there was a real struggle between them. There were weak Christians, still haunted by old superstitions, not daring to eat meat, which might have been offered to idols, still fearing some witchcraft or spell. And there were strong Christians, fearing nothing but God, knowing that idols are powerless and that eating meat could do no harm. Paul considers himself one of these strong Christians.

There will always be strong ones: strong fathers, righteous and successful; strong husbands, determining everything; strong politicians, smashing all oppositions; strong chiefs, keeping their tribes in total dependence; strong theologians, terrifying the simple believers. There will also be strong nations, oppressing others; strong parties, dominating all political life; strong races, wearing down people of other colors. It is a most astonishing fact that Paul does not ask too much whether the strong ones are right or wrong. He asks but one question: Do the weak ones suffer from the conduct of the strong ones? If so, then something is basically wrong. Whether or not the strong ones are right in their thoughts or programs is not so important; as long as the weak ones have to suffer from them, the strong ones fight against God's will. More and more the weak ones become fanaticized; they stress their views, they pity themselves; they want to show how strong they are and they easily overdo it. We know exactly how it works with teenagers rebelling in opposition to strong and righteous fathers, with wives escaping from husbands who want to show who the boss is, with political parties changing into underground movements and then suddenly and unexpectedly flaring up, with church groups organizing themselves in opposition to an official church that oppresses them. We know exactly how it works with nations deprived of all freedom, with parties prohibited by a ruling majority, with races cut off from the privileges of others. We know exactly how it works. And this is exactly what could have happened in the Church of Rome or even in the worldwide Church, consisting of Jews and Gentiles, in the time of Paul. It did not happen. Why not?

"We ought not to please ourselves; let each of us please his neighbor for his good, to edify him" (v. 2). This is what Paul proposes: for the good of the other person and his party or nation or race. His edification should become our aim. This is said, first of all, to those in strong positions, but of course it would be equally applicable to the weak. This would mean that it would no longer be important to be successful, to overcome the other, to reach the first rank. Life would receive a new meaning. We would find a task worth living for: namely, the good, the edification of our fellow persons of a different color, belief, party, or nation.

However, is this not a mere illusion? Life is more difficult. It is not to be mastered with sentiment. There are hard facts, and they are not removed by a few kind hearts full of good-will. Are we not forced to fight—to fight against all injustice and all repression?

"Christ did not please himself; but as it is written, 'The reproaches of those who reproached thee fell on me'" (v. 3). There were, in Christ's time, people fighting against injustice and repression. There were the zealots hiding weapons in their huts, writing pamphlets against the Roman occupation army, making propaganda for their cause and recruiting fighters for justice. After a short period of success, they led their whole nation into a deadly disaster. There was Jesus, fighting too, but fighting in a different way. Fighting in such a way that the reproaches of all fell on him. It was a totally unsuccessful life. At the beginning he filled some people with enthusiasm. A few fishermen even followed him, leaving their homes to wander with him. But very soon the enthusiasm died. When he came to Jerusalem, some of it flared up while he entered the city. But again the masses were very quickly disappointed. Nothing happened except that he drove out some merchants from the Temple. The end was a miserable death on the cross and, worse than that, he died in total loneliness, deserted by all who had for some time gone with him. When he died he had no followers, no one to carry on. It was the total, seemingly hopeless end of a man who had failed all along the line. This is the way of God's fighting: it is a heart that refuses absolutely to be incited against others; it is a heart living for the good and the edification of others, even when it seems to be completely hopeless. This is the way God fights. This is God's "godness," that he is able to humiliate himself absolutely. God's full godness is not to be found in his majesty. People also come along in majesty. God's full godness is to be found in the life of Jesus, where the reproaches of all fall on him without so much as a word of insult on his part. Perhaps people are sometimes living this way because any protest would deteriorate their situation; however, when they so choke down all their hatred, it may explode any day. Jesus went his way without retaliating, without barking back, without choking down the insults. This is God's way of fighting. Forty years after that seemingly senseless and hopeless way, the successful fighters for freedom, who had stirred up the whole nation to war, had succeeded in bringing their people into total and hopeless slavery. At the same time, some thousands of Jews and many more Gentiles were living together in the small communities that they called after the name of Jesus, inside and outside of Palestine. This is God's way of fighting.

It began with small groups like that Christian community in Rome, insignificant in the context of the city and without any hope of influencing the life of the capital. It began with the admonition of the apostle: "May the God of steadfastness and encouragement grant you to live in such harmony with one another, in accord with Christ Jesus" (v. 5). There God's miracle started. There a few hundred men learned to live in "accordance with Christ Jesus," which means, the whole life and death of Jesus became a power that entered more and more into their lives and deaths. What they knew of Jesus became so important that they could no longer escape from it, it grew more and more powerful and began to determine all their actions, words, and feelings. This power of Jesus Christ became so infectious that the strong ones in Rome could no longer despise the weak ones by eating their meat in front of them in order to show how sophisticated they were. Neither could the weak ones rebel against the strong ones by founding a party of religious vegetable eaters.

They had learned what Paul wrote to them: "Welcome one another, therefore, as Christ has welcomed you, for the glory of God" (v. 7). Here we are at the heart of our problem.

Christ has welcomed us; that means that in Jesus God himself has accepted us into the crowd of his children. Now, you see, this is so utterly astonishing: we are his children! But are we not the queerest sort of children of God one could imagine? Doubting and rebelling and fighting against him and against one another, forgetting our Father time and again until we need his help, going astray in all directions, some of us being very clever and therefore even more proud, some of us being very simple and not much more modest because of it, some of us rather pious but seldom ready to do something for God, some of us very active but seldom grateful to the one who gives us strength day by day. What odd sort of children we are! And he has welcomed us, in Jesus Christ, and has welcomed us just as we are. What an incredible sense of humor God must have to cope with his children day by day and century by century. Would such a sense of humor not infect us so that we might learn to look at our fellow people with the eyes of God? We shall certainly never learn to do it as perfectly as God does it with the eyes of Jesus Christ. But should we not at least start to do so? Nobody asks us simply to close our eyes. The weak ones in Rome, or wherever they might live, are sometimes rather ridiculous in their scruples. Paul clearly says so in the preceding chapter. And the strong ones in Rome, or wherever they might live, are sometimes rather conceited and not at all concerned with the needs of others. This is why Paul admonishes them here. Yet if we think just a little bit about what it must cost God to welcome us anew every morning and to bear us and all our oddities, how small are all these grievances under which we suffer in our common life with other people. This is what they have learned in Rome.

It was an insignificant, small group of people within a giant city. To be sure, life was, even in that group, not always harmonious; there were also struggles and envy and gossip. Nonetheless, maybe there was some unity of thought and some harmony; it may perhaps be quite nice to know of some small circles in which some harmony can be found. But how would this help the big problems of the city or even of the world? Paul goes on writing: "For I tell you that Christ became a servant to the circumcised to show God's truthfulness, in order to confirm the promises given to the patriarchs, and in order that the Gentiles might glorify God for his mercy" (v. 8–9a). Within this insignificant group, the Church at Rome, something much more significant has taken place. Two nations, two races, two creeds, Jews and Gentiles, have been brought together. And because this became true in these small, relatively insignificant groups of Christians, it set foot in our world and nobody can destroy it. Just as was the case with Jesus himself, when he had been brought to death, not exercising, as one thought he would, any influence on the course of the world, so it happens again with his small, insignificant, poor Church. What happened with Jesus—that he had taken God more seriously than anyone had ever expected—became a power in our world that nobody could remove from then on. What happened with his disciples—that they had learned to take God so seriously that they could no longer take all their differences and frictions more seriously than him—became a power in our world that may be laughed at, that may be fought against, but that nobody can make disappear. Because there were Jewish Christians together with many non-Jewish Christians in the churches of Germany under Hitler, he never succeeded in convincing real Christians that the Jews should be extinguished or at least be separated from Germans. There have been many who have gone to prison and even died because this togetherness of Jews and non-Jews that started, for instance, in the small church at Rome almost two thousand years ago, was still a power, mightier than their fear.

And yet, is this all that is to be said? Does not just this example show how much our situation has changed? First, the weak ones in Rome who feared the spirits of idols that could hurt them when they would eat meat did not bring suffering to others. When Herr Hitler, out of a mad fear of the Jews, began to kill them, he was no longer simply the weak brother, no more than whites killing blacks in their fear or captains of industry suppressing all movement within the body of their workers out of fear. Second, in the time of Paul, the Church was a very small minority without any possible influence on the course of the world; is this not quite different today? I am not so sure about this. The real Church, as God sees it, is probably still a small majority, whether smaller or bigger than it was in Paul's time, who knows? The disaster of the Church in preceding centuries has often been that we have believed in Christian nations, even in a Christian world. Too much has been identified with the Church and has been carried out in the name of Christ: cruel crusades against so-called unbelievers, bloody wars against so-called heretics, inhuman colonization against so-called primitive nations, antisocial rule over so-called low classes. And always, for centuries, the name of Christ has been misused in horrible ways. We have even read about a slave ship with the name "The Good Ship Jesus." Atrocities like this have happened, and we have shamefully to confess it. It is not that men who have never been Christians have misused Christ's name, but that the Church has not been spiritually awake to draw the borderline between the disciples of Jesus and those who have simply abused his name. Consequently, many real believers, full of goodwill and devotion, have taken part in such terrible enterprises without being able to "prove what is the will of God" (Rom. 12:2). Let us beware, lest we identify again too quickly our own cause with the cause of Jesus Christ.

And yet something has changed. Most of us are citizens of nations in which we share the responsibility for the political, social, and economic life. There is no Caesar as in the Rome of the time of Paul—the only one responsible for the welfare of his empire. Most of us have to vote for and are allowed to criticize our governments; therefore, our responsibility has grown. In some way we are therefore closer to the situation of Israel in the Old Testament, particularly if we are living in a nation that still calls itself Christian. Hence it is perhaps not unwise to read one of the unknown and rather strange stories of the Old Testament in Judges 19 and 20. It tells us of a man in Gibeah, himself a foreigner, who invited a traveler and his concubine to be his guests for a night. But "the men of the city, base fellows, beset the house round about, beating on the door; and they said to the old man, the master of the house, Bring out the man who came into your house, that we may know him" (v. 22). Finally, after long debate, they seized his concubine and put her out to them; and they knew her and abused her all night until the morning. And as the dawn began to break, they let her go. And as morning appeared the woman came and fell down at the door of the man's house where her master was, till it was light" (vv. 25–26). In the morning the traveler found her dead in front of the house of his host. The news about this deed got around the whole land of Israel "and the people of Israel said, 'Tell us, how was this wickedness brought to pass?'" (20:3) Then the whole nation took counsel and decided that the inhabitants of Gibeah had "committed abomination and wantonness in Israel" and prepared for war (12:13). "And the tribes of Israel sent men through all the tribe of Benjamin, saying, "What wickedness is this that has taken place among you? Now therefore give up the men, the base fellows in Gibeah, that we may put them to death, and put away evil from Israel." When the Benjaminites did not listen to this ultimatum, they fought against them "and smote them with the edge of the sword, men and beasts and all that they found. And all the towns which they found they set on fire" (v. 48).

There was one concubine who had been raped and one man who had lost his companion. Yet a whole nation rose and went to war against the guilty city. Why? First of all, it was not their own advantage that they sought. It was the harm done to a totally powerless woman and to a foreign guest. Second, it was an "abomination and wantonness of Israel" that should have been put away from Israel; that is to say, they fought against themselves, against the evil in the midst of themselves. This means that the Church is called to fight, most of all, wherever and whenever weak, powerless people suffer from the strong ones, and first of all, wherever and whenever this oppression arises from their midst and is exercised under the name of Christ. In this case no peace is possible. In this case the true Church has to resist the false church. Certainly, Israel had to defend herself many times against foreign aggressors; but she always knew that the main foe was her own wickedness.

Our Bible study guide asks, "Under what conditions should the church make an open and public attack?" There is no law with clearly fixed rules that would take the decision off our shoulders. We are to prove anew in every situation what is the will of God. Yet our two texts have given us some guidance. Paul has made us wary against all too quick identification of Christ's cause with our own causes. Paul has called us to a life "in Christ," to a life shaped and determined by Jesus' way, which ended in victory on a cross. Paul has helped us to understand that faith that knows that supporting one another, even welcoming one another in accordance with Christ Jesus, will in the long run win many more victories than flaring up and fighting. And the Old Testament has summoned us to see, first of all, the misdeeds in our midst, the so-called Christian atrocities, the "abomination in Israel." The place to fight is primarily in our own church, our own nation, our own circle. Moreover, in the Old Testament story it is a real fight, in which many had to die; it was not a cheap resolution uttered from outside the danger zone. It meant real action in the center of this danger zone. Thus, if it is our own wickedness, and if it is not we but some powerless, weak people who must suffer by it, then there is no peace, then we must rise and fight.

Twice in this section on the strong and the weak Paul writes about the aim of this struggle for unity. This unity is to be strived after, he writes, in order "that together you may with one voice glorify the God and Father of our Lord Jesus Christ" (v. 6), or a little later, "and in order that the Gentiles might glorify God for his mercy" (v. 9a).

This indeed is the answer to our question. I know well, how often this has been abused, how often abominable deeds have been done for the glory of God. Yet there are no other criteria. If we ask ourselves quite seriously whether God himself is really our goal, then we know whether our way of bearing others or of combating others is right or wrong. To be sure, we cannot expect all our fellow people to agree with this criterion. For many of them, God means nothing. Nonetheless, we may cooperate, we may be very grateful for their greater knowledge, courage, or strength; we may feel quite humble and follow along after them. We may be sure that in the last judgment many who have not been able to believe will be high above us, because they have really done God's will with more courage and commitment than we ourselves; yet there will always be the point at which we have to say no because by going along with them all the way we can no longer "glorify God." The prophets of the Old Testament knew that God had given Israel its kings; but when the king stole the vineyard of Naboth (1 Kings 21), Elijah arose and fought against him. Jesus knew that God had given

Israel its worship service and he participated in it; but when he interpreted the Scriptures to them, they tried to lynch him, because he let the Bible speak against them and not against those outside. Furthermore, when he entered the Temple, he drove out those who used it for their own advantage and no longer for the glory of God. Elijah was nearly killed and Jesus was really killed because of their courage to say no to those with whom they had gone quite a long way. Whether it is the way of bearing others in silence or of fighting against others, as long as we go our way in order truly to "glorify the God and Father of our Lord Jesus Christ," our way will always resemble the way of Jesus himself.

SECTION IX

PREACHING ON HOPE

BY BRUCE E. SHIELDS

I must admit that I was surprised. My survey was anything but exhaustive, yet I do have a pretty good collection of sermons in my library, including two multivolume sets: *Twenty Centuries of Great Preaching* and *The World's Great Sermons.* I looked through their indexes and also through a dozen or more books of sermons and found only six sermons with *hope* in the title! Of course many sermons in those collections deal with hope in some way or another, and there are sermons with words like *heaven, immortality,* and life *everlasting* in their titles. But all in all I was surprised not to find more sermons dealing primarily with hope.

My surprise only increased when I surveyed the Bible for passages dealing with hope. There is no doubt that hope is a major theme of biblical texts, so the contrast with my sermon survey was great. Therefore I would suggest that if you intend to preach on hope, you would be well advised to begin not with books of sermons but with the Bible itself.

I offer the following six steps to preparing to preach on hope, not as a law to be obeyed in sequence but as a listing of various things the preacher can do to prepare for preaching on this important topic.

I. *Survey the Bible.* You might already have in mind a specific text or even a series of passages. Even if you do, it would be a good idea to read pertinent Bible passages. And if you are starting from scratch, do a survey of texts that deal with your subject. In this case, the words *hope* and *promise* are especially helpful.

(a) *Hope.* I find it most helpful to make use of a topical concordance. To prepare this section I did two different computer searches on the topic of hope in the Logos computer Bible study system. One of those searches turned up passages under twenty-seven different subtitles, referring me to seventy-two different texts of the Bible. The other search produced a straight listing of texts, this time sixty-one different texts, many with multiple verses. This would surely be enough biblical material to keep a preacher busy for a week, but other topics and terms might produce helpful material also.

(b) *Promise.* The term *promise* and other future-oriented words will produce similar lists for reading in the Bible. The preacher who is developing a series of sermons on hope will want to do more extensive searches than will the preacher working on just one sermon. The line must be drawn somewhere, but we don't want to overlook texts that might prove helpful.

II. *Do collateral reading.* Read challenging and stimulating material. There are many books, articles, and sermons on hope that could stimulate the preacher's thinking on the subject. I deal here with just a few that I have found especially helpful.

• Jürgen Moltmann, *Theology of Hope,* trans. by James W. Leitch (New York: Harper-Collins, 1967). Moltmann deals extensively with the biblical concept of promise. On page 30 he points out that God's "name is a wayfaring name, a name of promise that discloses a new future, a name whose truth is experienced in history inasmuch as his promise discloses its future possibilities." He follows this up on page 42 with the insight that Old Testament theology shows that "God reveals himself in the form of promise and in the history that is marked by promise." Moltmann characterizes the theology of the Reformers in this way: "Faith is called to life by promise and is therefore essentially hope, confidence, trust in the God who will not lie but will remain faithful to his promise." Later, as he connects hope in God with the Resurrection of Jesus, he points out that "through the raising of Jesus from the dead the God of the promises of Israel becomes the God of all men" (p. 142).

These statements are indicative of how reading a book like this can help the preacher clarify his or her thinking and relate the many biblical texts listed with the help of concordances and other reference works. This kind of reading also often offers insights into preaching in general. A good example is Moltmann's statement, "What unites our present age with past ages in history is, to the extent that we have here a 'historic' relationship, not a common core of similarity nor a general historic character attaching to human existence as such, but the problem of the future" (p. 189).

• *The Living Pulpit*, Jan.-Mar. 1992. This journal is filled with brief articles and even briefer quotations on broad topics for preaching. This inaugural issue dealt with hope. It is composed of articles by outstanding theologians and preachers on various facets of hope. In an article titled "Preaching from Within Our Own Hope," Don Wardlaw writes, "We preach hope effectively to the extent that we recollect the experiential ground of our own hope."[1]

• *Sermons by other preachers.* As I said earlier, you will be hard pressed to find many sermons that deal directly and primarily with hope, although the few I did find are very helpful. As James Cox says in the opening minute of his sermon "Hope Unashamed," "Hope, as an essential ingredient of the Christian faith, has never completely dropped out of our vocabulary, though it has been sometimes ignored."[2] Cox's sermon, along with other contemporary sermons, such as those by Karl Barth and Frederick Buechner,[3] can help the preacher to be open to new ways of saying things.

III. *Delve into Christian experience.* One's own experience is too often overlooked as a source of understanding for the development of sermons. In his article quoted from earlier, Wardlaw writes, "Our people need to know that we, too, experience what it is like to be lost in the woods, to be immobilized by our rage over injustice, our fears for our health, and our depression over sagging self-esteem. Above all, our congregations need to sense that we have glimpsed the way out and have even scouted some paths up the mountain of hope" (p. 44) In hopes of sharing my own experience of the way up that mountain, I recently began a sermon with the following paragraphs:

> This sermon was prepared in circumstances that could appear hopeless. Our youngest child, who is now a thirty-three-year-old man with a wife and daughter, spends twelve hours a week on a kidney dialysis machine. He is waiting for a new kidney from his older sister, who was

---

[1] p. 44.

[2] James Cox, *Surprised by God* (Nashville: Broadman Press, 1979), p. 87.

[3] Karl Barth, "My Hope Is in Thee," *Deliverance to the Captives* (New York: HarperCollins, 1961); Frederick Buechner, "A Sprig of Hope," *The Hungering Dark* (New York: Seabury Press, 1981), pp. 34–44.

ready to give him one two years ago when the donor tests determined that she was pregnant. Following the birth of her baby (a second beautiful granddaughter for us) and the obligatory wait until her body chemistry was back in order, further tests revealed some complicated blood connections on both her kidneys. One transplant team then ruled her out as a donor, but we found a more experienced team that was willing to do it provided she lose some weight. She is nearing her goal, but it has been a long wait.

At the same time, our other child, a thirty-six-year-old man with Down Syndrome, had developed a staph infection that settled in his spine and left him paraplegic. For two years now he has been in and out of physical therapy following spinal surgery and a sixty-eight-day stay in the hospital.

Then my wife's mother collapsed with heart trouble and apparently had a slight stroke, from which she has since recovered. During the same period my mother was diagnosed with bladder cancer at age eighty-six. Surgery and radiation have gotten rid of the cancer, but they have left her with reduced capabilities in managing her house. So we have moved her from Pennsylvania to Tennessee—first with us, then into a local Christian retirement center.

Now, at our age my wife and I are supposed to be slowing down and enjoying life, looking forward to retirement. But our so-called sandwich generation finds itself pulled between the needs of our parents and those of our adult children. Does this sound familiar to some of you? I am telling you all of this not to elicit your sympathy—we don't need that. I tell you because it recently dawned on me that people were amazed that we were not depressed or at least in despair. But hopelessness is not an option for us.

Hopelessness or despair makes sense only within this world's way of looking at life—a way in which hope means incremental progress based on human effort and optimism. We say we have hope that if all goes well the stock market will improve next week. Or we hope that if nothing unexpected happens we will take that long-planned vacation next month. That is the way the world we live in speaks of hope.

But the texts I have chosen for today do not fit this pattern of the world. They show hope not as a condition arising from positive experiences of human life but as an experience of God arising in spite of life's circumstances. Let's hear the texts: Isaiah 40:1–5 and Colossians 1:24–29.

Biographies of other people can also offer us strong examples of living in hope. The life of Saint Francis of Assisi offers many examples of a person who can live through negative circumstances because of a vision of another, more powerful dimension of existence than that offered in the here and now. Dietrich Bonhoeffer is a more recent example of the victory of hope over suffering. As much as his writings emphasized total commitment to service in the here and now, he was impelled forward by a vision of the future envisioned by Jesus.

IV. *Exegete.* It is hardly necessary here to describe in detail the process of exegeting a biblical text in preparation for preaching. However, I cannot overemphasize the importance of careful study of the text or texts one intends to refer to in a sermon. Such study should include a careful look at the history of the text itself (see my upcoming sermon synopsis on Rom. 8:28); attention to the literary, historical, and cultural context; analysis of the syntax and word meanings; and consideration of the theological issues dealt with in the passages.

Exegesis of the audience is also vitally important to ensure that one's preaching touches human life. Even if the preacher is quite familiar with the hearers in general, when we preach on hope we should think again about the circumstances in which these individuals and families live their lives and about the meaning for them of certain future-oriented phrases. This is more than the proverbial "Bible in one hand and newspaper in the other." This is a look at the joys and sorrows of the people who will hear the sermon.

V. *Meditate.* Let those bundles of information (facts, events, ideas) interact until a message or series of messages begins to form. European works on preaching deal extensively with meditation in sermon preparation, but American homiletics has neglected this step. Fred Craddock comes close when he describes the preacher's playing with the text. He indicates that in this step one should relax the analytical mind and let the imagination take over.[4] However, meditation can include even more than free association; it can also be praying a text, following minor themes of a text, and reading a text aloud or hearing a recording of it, so as to receive it through the ears, as will the congregation, instead of through the eyes alone.

However one meditates on a text, the objective is to deal with it at deeper levels of the person than the analytical mind. In this process the text becomes a dialogue partner with the preacher, whereas in analysis the text is an object under the control of the preacher. Here is where the tables are turned and the text makes demands on the preacher instead of the other way around.

VI. *Formulate the sermon.* Determine the text or texts or issues and topics around which your ideas are clustering. Study these with your hearers in mind until a sermon approach, form, or both arises. Then fill it out!

Preaching on hope can take many forms. The following are samples. They lack the illustrations and insider talk that are so important between preacher and congregation, but they show how one can use five different sermon forms in preaching on hope.

(a) *Narrative.* Abraham is the choice of the apostle Paul as an example of faith and hope for all people. I would use Genesis 17:1–8, 15–22, and 21:1–7, and Romans 4:13–25 as texts for this sermon. Reading Frederick Buechner's retelling of the story of Abraham and Sarah could help the preacher who is not naturally creative to translate the ancient story into contemporary thought forms.[5]

Title: Hope Against Hope

The plot, of course, would emphasize the human impossibility of having a baby when over ninety years old. This could be done with descriptions of the "old and worn" couple as well as with dialogue between the two of them and between them and God.

This emphasis is further underscored by reference to the all-too-human attempt to make dreams come true when Sarah gives to Abraham Hagar, her servant, as a surrogate mother. But of course that is not what God had in mind.

As with other stories in Scripture, God waits until all human hope is gone before working his will. The story of Jesus and the death of Lazarus (John 11) is similar in this regard and could be brought in at this point to show that Abraham's experience was not totally unique.

---

[4] See Fred Craddock, *Preaching* (Nashville: Abingdon Press, 1985), pp. 105ff.
[5] Frederick Buechner, *Telling the Truth* (San Francisco: HarperCollins, 1977), pp. 49–53.

Romans 4:13–25 can then be used as a conclusion, either paraphrased or read in its entirety to bring together the Creator God, the God who keeps promises, and the God who raised Jesus, his Son, from the dead.

(b) *Expository.* In this style the preacher needs to explain somehow the meaning of the text and help the people to actualize its meaning in their lives. This can be done either indicatively, inviting the hearer along on the journey toward understanding, or deductively, in a more pedantic mode. I usually find myself combining these approaches, as in the following example.

Title: Working for Good

TEXT: Rom. 8:28

Several modern translations read, "God works for good in all things for those who love him," but my research into the textual variants leads me to doubt that in the original text God was the explicit subject. I must admit that such a translation fits my personal theology nicely.

However, I am left with a text that says, "We know that all things work together for good for those who love God, who are called according to his purpose" (NRSV). On the other hand, this sentence appears between a paragraph dealing with how God's Spirit interprets our deep groaning as prayers in the presence of God, and the rest of the chapter, which assures us that God is in charge and that nothing can "separate us from the love of God in Christ Jesus our Lord."

Thus the context leaves no doubt about who is the primary actor in this drama we call life. It is not that "things" work out but that under God's direction we who love God will eventually experience good things. *Eventually* is, of course, an operative word here. We human beings tend to want God to operate on our schedules. Illustrations of this tendency are easy to find in our own experience.

Furthermore, we human beings tend to define *good* in our own ways. Each of us has a picture of how we think our lives should look—what kind of car is parked in our garage, what house and what neighborhood we live in, how many children and of what sort we have, how our bosses treat us, how we relate to our spouses, and so on.

In other words, we human beings would in some measure like to be God. We want to control the timetable of life. We want to decide what is best for us. But our text is also close to verse 18, which refers to "the sufferings of this present time." That doesn't sound like either the schedule or the good that we desire. No, such things are pretty much out of our hands.

Perhaps we should rejoice in that fact. The history of human dealings is not very encouraging. (Earth-shaking as well as individual examples of human decisions and actions can easily be found and used as illustrations.) Hopelessness is the normal result of humans trying to control their own lives.

Hope happens when we get out of the way and let God take charge. (The Bible and the history of God's people are full of illustrative stories of how good happens when God controls.) "All things"—circumstances that appear to harbor no hope, objects that seem to have no power, persons who usually have difficulty controlling anything, even themselves—"all things work together for good" in and for the persons "who love God and are called according to his purpose."

In other words, the person working with God finds that the most surprising situations bring God's good into his or her life. The person working with God discovers the patience to wait for God's timing. The person working with God learns to recognize God's good gifts when they come. As those experiences multiply, the person working with God builds hope. In fact, hope can become a primary characteristic of life for the person who works with God, because that person grows to expect "all things" to "work together for good" in his or her life as well as in the lives of all those "who love God and are called according to his purpose."

(c) *Compare and contrast.* Isaiah 40 and Colossians 1 contrast the difficulties of life with hope in God. Sangster's sermon, "When Hope Is Dead—Hope On!"[6] contrasts optimism with Christian hope. The following sermon synopsis contrasts the sufferings of life with the eternal hope found in God's faithfulness.

Title: The Hope of Glory
I begin this sermon with the personal information given in the earlier section on delving into personal experience. My experience teaches me that a preacher must indicate some acquaintance with suffering in order to preach convincingly about hope.

Hope against hope. Isaiah's message of promise was preached to a nation of people in deep trouble. They were being used as pawns in a high-stakes game of international politics. The "big boys" of the Middle East were fighting one another to see who would rule, and most of the fighting seemed to endanger little Judah. Isaiah preached in Judah during the time of the destruction of the Northern Kingdom, Israel, and then during the invasion of Judah by the Assyrian king, Sennacherib. But Isaiah continued to remind people in no uncertain terms that the greatest danger was that they were taking God for granted. They were going through the motions of service to God, but they seemed to have forgotten that such service was more than ritual. They were neglecting the needs of their kinfolk and neighbors, and God was displeased with such neglect.

So in the midst of prophetic proclamation against the sins of God's people, Isaiah also delivered the message of comfort, and the comfort came in the form of a promise: "Then the glory of the Lord shall be revealed, and all people shall see it together, for the mouth of the Lord has spoken" (v. 5).

Likewise, the apostle Paul writes to the Christians in Colossae, "I am now rejoicing in my sufferings" (v. 24). A bit later he explains to them that his sufferings are not only the physical and mental concerns of his person; even more important, they are his concern about them. He is concerned that they are being tempted to adopt some practices of worship that will lead them and their children away from the heart of the gospel of Christ, which focuses on the promise of the grace of God. But in verse 27 he practically shouts out, "Christ in you, the hope of glory."

In a time of stress and anxiety Isaiah had shouted out, "The glory of the Lord shall be revealed." And eight hundred years later, in a time of stress and anxiety, Paul proclaimed, "Christ, in you the hope of glory."

---

[6] *Twenty Centuries of Great Preaching,* Vol. 11 (Waco, Tex.: Word, Inc., 1971), pp. 363–368.

These are just two examples of what the Bible is full of—what Paul describes in Romans 4:18 as Abraham's example of "hoping against hope."

There was no earthly reason for Abraham and Sarah to think that at their advanced age they would finally have a son—no earthly reason, but they expected God to do something, just because he had promised.

There was no earthly reason for Isaiah to think at that late stage in Judah's rebellion against God that there was any hope for the nation—no earthly reason, but he expected God to do something, just because he had promised.

There was no earthly reason for Paul to think at that late stage in the Colossian's heresy that there was any hope for that church—no earthly reason, but he expected God to do something, just because he had promised.

Against human hope they hoped in God, just because he had promised. Hope is expecting God to do what he promised. As Hebrews 10:23 puts it, "Let us hold fast to the confession of our hope without wavering, for he who has promised is faithful."

The God of hope (Rom. 15:13). And there is no earthly reason for me or you at this point in our complicated and often painful lives to do anything but despair—no earthly reason but that we believe in a God who has inundated us with promises of salvation, presence, help, comfort, strength, rest, and ultimately blissful eternal life. We believe in that God, so we expect him to do something, just because he promised.

Our God is the God who kept his promise to Noah to never again destroy the earth with a flood.

Our God is the God who kept his promise to the Hebrews enslaved in Egypt that he would lead them safely to their homeland—the Promised Land.

Our God is the God who kept his promise to restore his sinful people to Jerusalem from their captivity in Babylon.

Our God is the God who kept his promise to send a Messiah to suffer and save people from their sins.

Our God is the God who kept his promise that the gates of Hades would not prevail against his Church.

I dare say that every believer here could add to this list because our God is the God who has kept his promises to all of his people in all circumstances of life.

As important for our faith as what God has done in the past is—as vital for our lives as what God is doing in the present is—our God is truly Lord of the future. It is hard to find in the Bible a pivotal event or doctrine that has no connection with the future. The early Church recognized even Genesis 3:15 as a promise of the gospel fulfilled in Christ.

Even our celebration of the Lord's Supper is described by the apostle Paul with an eye to the future, when he writes, "As often as you eat this bread and drink this cup, you proclaim the Lord's death until he comes" (1 Cor. 11:26). Yes, even the communion service is a promise that offers us hope for the future.

Christians have long recognized that the gospel consists of facts to be believed, commands to be obeyed, warnings to be heeded, and promises to be enjoyed. I fear that the promises are the part of the gospel most in danger of our neglect. Let's shout it from the housetops, let's show it in our lives: Our God is the God who keeps his promises.

Standing on the promises. Let's recall some of those promises, recognizing that this is only a sampling:

Acts 2:38–29	You can stand on that promise!
Matthew 11:28–29	You can rest on that promise!
Matthew 18:19–20	You can depend on that promise!
Matthew 28:19–20	You can win the world on that promise!
1 Corinthians 10:13	You can live on that promise!
John 14:1–3	You can die on that promise!

Perhaps you have a favorite Scripture promise. Will you quote it for us? (Give time for people to quote their favorites.)

I guess my favorite is Romans 8:38–39: "For I am convinced that neither death, nor life, nor angels, nor rulers, nor things present, nor things to come, nor powers, nor height, nor depth, nor anything else in all creation will be able to separate us from the love of God in Christ Jesus our Lord." You can find security on that promise!

These are promises that a person can stand on, promises that we can build lives on, promises that we can found families on, promises that we can grow churches on, promises that we can die on. They are promises founded on the God who does what he promises. They are promises that depend on no earthly power or reason. They depend on the power of the Creator of the universe. They are sealed by the sacrifice and Resurrection of God's Son, Jesus Christ. They are promises of "Christ in us, the hope of glory."

Just where do you stand? Are you standing on the promises of God, or are you dependent on the support of the world? Believe me, this world can throw enough negative stuff your way that it will lead you to hopelessness—to despair. The appeal of your Creator and Redeemer is, "Hope in God." Take your stand on God's promises, and nothing this world dishes up can drive you from true hope.

(d) *Problem–solution.* See John 11, in which Jesus is with Mary and Martha at the death of Lazarus. The first sixteen verses of this chapter make clear that Jesus established the problem at the center of the report. The specific problem here is the ultimate problem of human life—the problem presented by death. At the tomb of Lazarus we see Christ, the Lord of life, in the presence of the primary symbol of the destroyer of life. He is deeply moved by the conflict, but his power is victorious.

Title: A Matter of Death and Life

A. Death is the problem.

Death is a problem for followers of the Lord of life. A look at the variety of funeral practices familiar among Christians shows how confused we are about death. We mix pagan philosophies of immortality and dualism with the Christian proclamation of the Resurrection. It is no wonder that many people claim not to be able to believe in God because of the presence of pain, illness, evil, and death in the world.

Death is a problem for survivors of the deceased. The pain of grief is real, no matter how deep the believer's faith is. The world looks totally different to the grieving person than to others. Deep questions about life demand to be dealt with when we have lost somebody near and dear to us.

Death is a problem for the deceased. It is natural to fear the uncertainty of death. Faith in God does not eradicate the fear of the unknown. On the life side of death we can imagine neither the fear nor the joyful anticipation of the person going through the gateway called death.

B. Jesus deals with problems.

His timing is right. One of our problems with death is timing. In some instances people seem ready to die, yet they live on. In many other instances people are struck down in childhood or in the prime of life. We say that they are taken prematurely, which indicates that we can't understand the timing. Mary and Martha were upset that Jesus came so late, but he did what he went to do. His timing was and is just right, in spite of our lack of understanding.

His manner is right. Jesus was and is an understanding helper in all situations. He says what needs to be heard, but his presence at a graveside is more important and more powerful than his words. We can be assured that when we feel the pain of grief, our God feels it with us.

His method is right. The Lord can do what nobody else can. He alone has the power of life and death. He alone has won the victory over pain and death. He alone can guide us through death into life and at the same time comfort those who are left to grieve.

C. Jesus is the solution to the problem of death.

In Jesus the Creator is present. Believers throughout history have recognized in Jesus the Creator of life. Following Jesus is being in the presence of the only one who can overcome death and turn it into new life for us.

In Jesus the Creator is active. We cannot fully understand the mystery of God's work in our lives through Christ, but as we rest in our faith in Jesus, we find that we can face and overcome everything life throws at us. The only satisfactory explanation is that God is at work in us through Jesus Christ, our Lord.

In Jesus' Resurrection the Creator declares victory over death. The human war with death is all but over. The decisive battle was won when God raised the crucified Jesus from the grave. Jesus gave his followers a preview of this victory when he called Lazarus forth from his grave. We still face the fact and the experience of what we call death, but as Paul indicated in 1 Corinthians 15:55, death has lost its sting.

The Christian hope does not spring from our circumstances or abilities, nor is it endangered by the circumstances of life or death. It springs from the power and faithfulness of God and it destroys death through the Resurrection of Christ.

(e) *Topical or doctrinal.* This type of sermon lends itself naturally to a logical form. Following is an outline of five logical moves that should lead hearers from a superficial understanding of hope as our world sees it to a more helpful understanding as our faith teaches it.

Title: The Christian Hope
The world's concept of hope depends on human ability and circumstances.

   A. Our hope is based on God's ultimate promise in Christ.
   B. God's promise is sealed by Christ's Resurrection and Ascension.
   C. Christ's lordship includes his control of the future.
   D. The eternal future of Christians rests in the hands of Christ.
   E. We can live and die in the Christian hope.

Let us hold fast to our hope and encourage one another in it.

CONCLUSION

Perhaps the most important aspect of the sermon for the preacher to consider is the sermon's aim or objective. This appears to me to be doubly important with sermons on hope. We always run the risk of giving the wrong signals when speaking of future glory. We can cause people to conclude that work for the betterment of human beings or the rest of the universe in the present is unimportant. We can lead people to be dangerously satisfied with the way things are in their lives, because God will make it better in the future. We can even cause people to withdraw from others into a self-centered meditative state to prepare for the end.

What we should be aiming for is to lead people to the kind of hope in the living and active God that will strengthen them and us for the ministry of reconciliation that awaits us every day we live. Such an aim is formulated well in the prayer that Frederick Buechner uses to close his sermon on hope titled "The Hungering Dark":"Give us back the great hope again that the future is yours, that not even the world can hide you from us forever, that at the end the One who came will come back in power to work joy in us stronger even than death."[7]

Amen.

---

[7] Frederick Buechner, *The Hungering Dark* (New York: Seabury Press, 1981), p. 125.

SECTION X

CHILDREN'S SERMONS

January 2: Choosing the Right Road

TEXT: Ps. 25:4–5 [*Print scripture on a card and give to each child.*]

Object: Road map

Boys and girls, I hold in my hand an item that most travelers would not be without. Who can tell me what it is? [*Unfold road map. Display in front of the children.*] Yes, this is called a road map. By knowing how to "read" a map and follow directions, we end up at our destination.

Let's say we begin at point A [*point to a city*] and drive to point B [*follow a path to another city*]. To use a map effectively, we need to know directions, such as north, south, east, and west. We should also know the scale of the map, or how many miles equal one inch.

Of course some routes have obstacles. Detours may lead away from the main road. High mountains create barriers. Rivers require a bridge to cross. If we venture off the main road, we may take the wrong route. In fact, sometimes drivers get lost.

Following the route is important in reading a map. And following Jesus is important when we love him. Can any of you tell me how boys and girls take the wrong road in life? [*Pause.*] What do children do that makes God sad? [*Pause for responses.*] What about disobeying your parents? Cheating on a test? Repeating gossip? Staying away from the Lord's house? Yes, these and other things keep us from taking the right road to the Christian life.

In your hand you have a Scripture that tells you the way to go. Read with me: "Show me your ways, O Lord; teach me your paths; guide me in your truth and teach me, for you are God my Savior, and my hope is in you all day long" (Ps. 25:4–5 NIV).

[*Ask the pianist to play while a soloist sings "All the Way My Savior Leads Me" as the children return to their seats.*]—Carolyn Ross Tomlin

January 9: Don't Give God Leftovers

TEXT: Exod. 23:19a

Object: Two snack food packages, one open and stale

Listen to this story about two boys, Billy and Johnny. Johnny was at Billy's house one day after school and Billy said he was starving. Billy, the host, got out two snack cakes. Billy kept one wrapped in cellophane and handed to Johnny a cake that was wrapped in a torn napkin that had scribbling on it.

Johnny took the ragged napkin off the snack as Billy tore the cellophane off his cake and began to devour it hungrily. Johnny noticed that his little cake was stale and hard. He was a little confused and asked Billy why the snack was wrapped in the napkin.

Billy was still munching his snack and brushing the crumbs off his face when he answered Johnny. He said, "I started to eat that snack a few days ago and decided I wasn't hungry, so I wrapped that napkin around it to save it for later."

Johnny had always been taught "company first" when serving guests. The stale snack cake made him lose his appetite, so he left it on the kitchen counter. Billy didn't notice that his buddy was all mixed up because of what Billy had done to him.

Later that evening Johnny talked with his mom about what had happened. His mother explained that most folks tend to put themselves first and have to learn to be more kind. She told Johnny that people treat God the same way. Instead of putting God first in their thanksgiving, offerings, and efforts, people just give God their leftover time and resources.

Johnny's mom said that the Bible teaches believers to put God in a place of honor. Listen to this verse. [*Read text.*]

When God is first in our lives, we worship him by our best actions and service. God deserves more than leftovers. He expects our very best. When the Lord is in the place of honor in our lives, the puzzle pieces of our lives fall nicely into place.—Ken Cox

January 16: Let Your Light Shine
TEXT: Matt. 5:16
Song: Sunlight in My Soul Today
Object: Flashlight and a paper bag

Boys and girls, I have something in this bag that many of you have at home. In fact, you may have one for your own personal use. Let me give you some clues. First, this object needs batteries to work. Second, there is an off-and-on switch. Then, it works best in a dark place. People depend on it when they are lost. And last, it shows you the way to go. Does anyone know what I'm holding in this bag? [*Pause for response.*]

That's right, the object in this paper bag is a flashlight. Flashlights comes in all shapes and sizes. Some are yellow, blue, or even black. Some flashlights float if you drop them in water. I would say that a flashlight is an amazing discovery. Have any of you ever had an unusual experience using this object? [*Pause.*] But there's something about this that makes it work. [*Turn the light off and on several times.*] I wonder what would happen if I removed the batteries? Does anyone know? [*Take the batteries out and turn the switch off and on.*] What happens? Nothing—absolutely nothing. Without the batteries this light will not work. It will not do what a flashlight is supposed to do. It has become a useless piece of plastic and metal. But what happens when I place the batteries back into the case? [*Replace batteries.*] Now I have a light that shines brightly.

You know, our lives are a little like this flashlight. When we have Jesus inside our hearts, our entire lives light up. We are joyful. We sing. We help others because we love Jesus.

Listen as I read from God's Word: "In the same way, let your light shine before men, that they may see your good deeds and praise your Father in heaven" (Matt. 5:16).

[*Have the pianist play softly "Sunlight in My Soul Today" as the children return to their seats.*]—Carolyn Ross Tomlin

January 23: Don't Be a Stumbling Block
TEXT: Rom. 14:13b
Object: Building blocks

These are building blocks. By carefully stacking them we can construct some impressive structures.

The Bible describes another kind of block. It is a stumbling block. A stumbling block is like a rock or rope that people trip over then hurt themselves. We become a stumbling block if we set a bad example that someone follows. We would be a stumbling block if we ran across the street without looking. A friend following us might run across the street without looking both ways and be hit by a car. Of course we know that the proper way to cross a street is to look both ways and walk across, preferably with a parent. To be a good example, we must consider how our lives affect other people, for either good or bad. Listen to this verse. [*Read text.*]

We must try to be sure that our lives are building blocks for people. That means we will build other people's lives up by our good examples. If our lives are stumbling blocks, our bad examples will cause others to get into trouble. Most of life is spent copying what others do. We talk like others, dress like others, and act like others. What kind of life will people live if they copy your life? The Bible tells us to spend our lives building people up, not putting blocks in front of them to make them trip and fall.

We can build people up by encouraging them. Encouragement is important because some people go for days without hearing a compliment. It is sad that some are kidded about the clothes they wear or the way they talk. We become an encourager whenever we spot the good in people and praise them for it. When we encourage someone, we build them up.—Ken Cox

January 30: Where Is Our Primary Place of Worship?
TEXT: Josh. 24:15
Object: A church directory

God has shown a special way for us to learn about him. This directory has a picture of our church on the cover. We might point at the cover of this directory and say, "The church is the best place to learn about God." We would say this because we pray, sing praises to God, and learn from the Bible at church. However, according to God's plan, the family is the best place to learn about Jesus. On the pages of the directory, we see all of the families of our church. These families are what God intends to use to teach others about him.

A man named Joshua was a great leader of Israel. After coming into the promised land, the people were at a point of decision. They had to make up their minds about the one they would worship. Joshua knew exactly what he was going to do. Listen to this verse. [*Read text.*]

Joshua told the people of his community that his family would be devoted to God. He understood that his family came first in religious training. He didn't look to others to teach his children about right and wrong. Joshua knew that faith starts in the family.

Another Bible passage tells parents to teach their children. Families are to use every opportunity at home or when walking or resting to impress upon their children the truth of the Bible (Deut. 6:7). When we hear the truth about God over and over, it becomes a part of the way we think and act.

This church directory contains the answer to the question, "Where is the best place to learn about God?" The answer is not on the cover, it is on the inside; the pictures of the family of the church. When at home, be sure to ask your parents questions about Jesus. Also, whenever you pray at the table before meals or hear one of your parents read from the Bible, pay close attention. Your home is the best place to learn about God.—Ken Cox

February 6: Helping Someone Who Feels Embarrassed
Text: Luke 15:17–20

Have you ever done something bad and been embarrassed by it? One day when I was a little boy I was in a store with my friends and we didn't have any money. We were hungry so we decided to steal some candy bars. One of us went to talk to the man at the counter to make sure he couldn't see the rest of us. We took the candy bars and put them under our shirts and walked out of the store really slow and acting cool. When our friend who was at the counter caught up with us on the other side of the street, we ate the candy bars.

Just as I was finishing my candy bar, who should walk by but my mother. As she walked toward us, all my friends ran away. My mom asked, "Where did you get the money for the candy bar?" My mother could always tell when I was lying, so I told her the truth. My mom made me tell the man at the counter what we had done and how we had done it, and she made me promise to pay for the candy bar! I was so embarrassed! I couldn't believe that I had done something so stupid and so dishonest, and I was afraid of what the man at the counter thought of me. But when I went to pay for the candy bar, the man said, "I know you realize that you made a mistake and that you will never do it again. You are a good kid." Then he patted me on the head. He was so kind to me! It made me feel better. I was no longer embarrassed to be around that man or to be in his store.

When someone forgives you for the bad things you have done, it does make you feel better. That is what God does for us; he forgives us and we feel better. God wants us to forgive others when they do something bad to us and make them feel better, too. They are embarrassed because they did something bad. Let's help them feel better by forgiving them, just like God does for us.—Michael Lanway

February 13: Our Special Bodies
Text: Ps. 8:5 NIV
Object: Band-Aid

Our bodies are fascinating, wouldn't you say? Nerves transmit reflexes and help our limbs move. The heart pumps blood through the veins and sends it throughout the body, our lungs make breathing possible, and our skin serves to protect our bones and muscles. In fact, I would say that our body is a marvelous machine.

Think of your body as a gift from God. Each part of your body allows you to do certain things. What can hands do? [*Clap, fold in prayer.*] Fingers? [*Hold a pencil, draw, pick up objects.*] What about feet and legs? [*Run, skip, hop, climb, march, and so on.*] Yes, each part of our body serves a specific function. God made our bodies to perform special purposes.

Because God loves us, he wants us to take good care of our bodies. Can you think of some ways we can keep our bodies safe? [*Pause for answers.*] Yes, those are important. Did we mention eating the right kinds of food? Getting enough sleep and rest? What about exercise? These are only some of the things that keep us healthy.

But there's another gift from God. This is the ability of our bodies to heal themselves. Have you ever skinned your knee or cut your finger? Did the cut heal? We don't know exactly why but usually healthy bodies are able to heal themselves. [*Hold up a Band-Aid. Place one on a child's finger.*] Perhaps Mom or Dad has placed a Band-Aid over a cut or scratch.

Yes, God has given us a wonderful gift. No amount of money can replace your body. He wants us to take care of this special creation and use it to serve him! [*Hand out a bright-colored Band-Aid to each child.*]—Carolyn Ross Tomlin

February 20: God Called Moses
TEXT: Exod. 3:10
Object: A bush

A calling is a special job God gives us. Every believer has a calling to serve Jesus Christ in God's Kingdom.

A man named Moses had a calling from God. Moses was born in Egypt long ago. His people, the Israelites, were in slavery. There were millions of Israelites serving a cruel pharaoh. When Moses was a young man, he tried to help a few of his people. That small group didn't like Moses meddling in their affairs and they told him to mind his own business. Feeling like a failure, Moses ran away from home.

Moses ended up living in a desert and being a shepherd. Many years passed and Moses became an old man. His strong feelings of helpfulness toward his people had died like a long forgotten dream. One day while Moses was with his sheep in the desert, he noticed a bush, like this, burning in the distance. He couldn't take his eyes off that fiery shrub and he went to investigate.

When Moses got close to the strange sight, God spoke to him out of the bush. This was God's way of explaining to Moses the special task Moses was to accomplish. Listen to this verse. [*Read text.*]

Moses went back to Egypt and, demonstrating the power of God, led his people to freedom. Later the Israelites arrived in the Promised Land. The Israelites' freedom was possible because Moses was true to his calling.

God has a calling for each of us. When we are trying to accomplish what God has given us to do, we discover that God is working through us. God may not give you a calling out of a burning bush, but he will surely speak to your heart.—Ken Cox

February 27: Putting on Our Clothes
TEXT: Eph. 6:14–17

Can you get dressed all by yourself? I still need some help myself. My wife still picks out some of the things she wants me to wear. But I can get dressed by myself if I have to.

Knowing what type of clothing to wear is important. Imagine wearing just your bathing suit when there is snow on the ground and it is freezing outside. We would get sick! So it is important to know what type of clothes to wear and how to put them on the right way.

Let's see how much you know about getting dressed. [*Have available child-sized underwear, socks, shoes, pants, T-shirt, shirt, tie, and coat.*] What would you put on first? Second? Why wouldn't you put on the tie first? Or the coat?

There are other things that can protect us besides clothes. The Bible tells us that if we tell the truth, God will protect us. If we have faith, know the Bible, and love Jesus, God will protect us. And it tells us to pretend that our faith, and our trust in Jesus, and all the other things are like clothes. Why? So that we will pray to God every morning right after we get dressed and tell him that we know he will protect us and be with us because we love Jesus. Let's pray to God right now and tell him those things, and pray to God every morning after we get dressed. [*Avoid using the clothes when you talk about the spiritual themes; the symbolism will not be communicated.*]—Michael Lanway

March 5: Coming to Church

TEXT: Ps. 122:1
Song: "Tell Me the Stories of Jesus"
Objects: Small bag or suitcase, Bible, Sunday school book, hymnal, offering envelope, paper plate with a happy face drawn on one side

How many of you boys and girls have packed a suitcase or overnight bag and stayed away from home? Perhaps you and your family went on a vacation. Perhaps you spent the night with a friend. Wherever you went, you packed things you would need. Let's think a minute about what boys and girls might put in a bag like this. Can you help me? [*Pause for response.*] Would you pack your pajamas? What about a toothbrush, extra clothes, some type of game or toy, a book? Yes, these are things one might need.

Do you think I have these things in my bag? Would you like to see? But first, think about where I am today. [*Pause.*] I am in church. So, if I'm coming from my house to church this morning, what would I need? Let's open the bag and see what I packed.

[*Hold up each item as it is mentioned.*] Here is a Bible. It's the most important thing I brought because in it God gives us rules to live by. In these pages are the stories of Jesus. Then I have my Sunday school book. I want to be prepared as my teacher discusses the lesson. Look, I even have a hymnal. No, I didn't bring it from home. But singing is such a big part of worship and I want to participate in praising God's name. Here is my offering envelope. I want to give back to God a portion of what he has given me. And last, this is something each of you can give others. It is a happy face. When you wear a smile at church, you show others you are happy to be in God's house.

The psalmist realized how important it is to worship God. "I rejoiced with those who said to me, 'Let us go to the house of the Lord'" (Ps. 122:1 NIV). [*Lead the children in one stanza of "Tell Me the Stories of Jesus." Invite the congregation to sing along.*]—Carolyn Ross Tomlin

March 12: God Makes Worthless Things Special

TEXT: 2 Cor. 4:7
Object: Any art work made from trash

This is a colorful scene from a farm. If you look closely you will see that the cows, sheep, and fields of corn have been painted on the back of an old saw blade. After many hours of cutting wood, the teeth on the saw became dull and wouldn't quickly and neatly cut lumber. This blade was worthless and bound for the junk pile. But luckily for us, some creative soul spotted the scrap piece of steel and dreamed that it could be used for a beautiful painting.

That's what God does with us. The Bible describes every human as a sinner. Sinners break God's commandments and are not willing to cooperate with his plans. Sinners are worthless to God in his perfect plans for our world. Thankfully God still sees potential in every sinner. He sent Jesus to save us through the forgiveness of our sins. Also, the Lord puts his presence into our lives. God's Spirit in our lives brings joy and love into our cold hearts.

When we realize the wonder of God's power in our lives, we begin to feel like the saw blade might feel if it were a living thing. We begin to realize that our lives are worthwhile only because God has loved us and sent Jesus to help us. We feel like a paper cup that has been filled with a very expensive wine. Listen to this verse. [*Read text.*]

Instead of trashing us, God enables our lives to become beautiful treasures. We should thank God today for making our lives beautiful by his love and grace.—Ken Cox

March 19: Keeping Our Lives in Place

TEXT: Prov. 3:3

Objects: Buttons, zippers, and strings

Boys and girls, I'm holding in my hand something that manufacturers use to hold clothing together. These are buttons. Here's a zipper. And this is a string. [*Show each object as you speak.*] Look at your own clothing. Do buttons fasten your clothes? If so, count them. What about a zipper? Any strings or cords? [*Pause for response.*]

Buttons, zippers, and strings have several purposes. They keep our clothes in place. On a cold, windy day, they help keep our bodies warm. A zipper may secure a pocket or keep money or other possessions from becoming lost. Have you ever lost a button? Have you ever had a zipper that broke? [*Pause for response.*]

Yes, we need buttons, zippers, and strings to keep our clothes in place. But more important, we need Jesus to keep our lives in place. Will you share some ways that Jesus helps boys and girls? [*Allow time for children to respond.*] Yes, those are good ways. What about helping us make the right choice? Sharing toys with friends? Respecting our parents? Coming to church? Talking to God? When we allow God's love to enter our life, he helps us to keep our lives in the right place. Listen as I read this verse: "Let love and faithfulness never leave you; bind them around your neck, write them on the tablet of your heart" (Prov. 3:3 NIV).

Please bow your heads as we pray. Dear God, please help each boy and girl present to include you in his or her daily life. Even little decisions are easy when we pray for your guidance. Amen. [*Ask the pianist to play "Blest Be the Tie That Binds" as the children return to their seats.*]—Carolyn Ross Tomlin

March 26: Jesus Takes Away Our Sin

TEXT: Rom. 11:27

Object: One clean white cloth, one dirty cloth

[*Ask a pianist to play softly "Whiter Than Snow" as the children gather. Read two verses from the song or ask someone to sing.*] Children, I am holding two cloths in my hands. What can you tell me about these two pieces of cloth? [*Pause for response.*] Are they alike or different? Yes, the one in my right hand is clean. You might say it's "as white as snow." [*Hold cloth up to a light.*] But look at the one I'm holding in my left hand. See those dark places? I believe that someone has used this cloth to wipe mud off their shoes. Or to remove grease from a car. And I believe that this spot is mustard. Even ketchup's on here! It's really a mess. [*Hold up to light.*] In fact, after handling this cloth I need to wash my hands.

After seeing these two cloths, which one would you choose?

There's another reason why I'm using these two cloths today? Does anyone know? [*Pause for response.*] The dirty cloth represents a life filled with sin. The clean cloth represents our life when we allow Jesus to take away our sins. After we become a Christian, he washes away our sins. He forgives our wrongdoings.

At this time we are like a newborn baby. We experience a fresh beginning. When others see our lives, they see Jesus living in us.

Let me ask you this: Which cloth represents your life? If you are not a Christian, would you ask Jesus to come into your heart? Ask him to forgive your wrongdoings and cleanse your life.

The Bible speaks to us many times about sin. Listen as I read this verse: "And this is my covenant with them when I take away their sins" (Rom. 11:27 NIV). Keeping our lives clean is a way to live as a Christian.

[*Ask boys and girls to bow their heads.*] Dear Father, please help these precious children to keep their lives clean. Guide them to always choose what is right and just in their hearts. Let them know the love of Christ working in our church teachers and leaders. Amen.—Carolyn Ross Tomlin

April 2: Moses Lost His Temper
TEXT: James 1:20
Object: A golf club

I once saw a man get red-faced and angry on the golf course. He was trying to hit the ball near the hole but it went splashing into a pond instead. He took his club, like this one, and bashed it against a tree. The golf club bent around the trunk of the tree. The club was ruined because of a the man's fit of temper.

A sad story about anger is in the Old Testament. A man named Moses was on a special mission for God. Moses was trying to help God's people by guiding them through the desert. The people constantly grumbled and complained. One day the people were grouchy because they were thirsty, and Moses lost his temper.

God provided a source of drinking water for the thirsty people. He instructed Moses to strike a special rock with his staff and the refreshing water would flow out of the rock like a stream. Instead of obediently doing what God had told him to do, Moses angrily struck the rock twice. This rash action made God unhappy. Because of his tantrum, Moses was not permitted to enter the Promised Land. Moses' anger was a regretful thing.

Every time we lose our temper we feel sad about it later and wish we could take back what we said and did. The Bible warns us that anger does not accomplish what God desires. Listen to this verse. [*Read text.*]

Nothing good comes out of a fit of temper. Whenever anger boils up inside us, we need to stop and slowly count to ten. Stopping, thinking, and praying for a moment enables us to control our anger. Things always turn out better with patience than with anger. Patience is the way God can do good things through us.—Ken Cox

April 9: Seeds Determine the Plant
TEXT: Luke 8:8 NIV
Song: "Fairest Lord Jesus"
Object: Handful of Seeds

What do I hold in my hand? [*Pause, show a mixture of seeds.*] Yes, they are seeds. But can you tell what they are? There's no package or picture to show what kinds of seeds I'm holding.

Look at this one. [*Hold up a kernel of corn.*] It's a kernel of corn. What happens when I plant this seed? Yes, a corn plant grows. And this one? [*Hold up a bean.*] This one will grow into a bean plant. Can we say that what we plant determines what we grow?

Our life is a lot like these seeds. When we follow God's rules and love him, we become what he expects of us. When we disobey his commandments, we disappoint God. And we will never reach our full potential if we live outside the will of God.

Boys and girls, think with me a minute. What do people your age do that displeases God? [*Allow time for response.*] Are some of these the same things that adults do also? And even people during biblical days had the same sins.

Luke 8:8 says, "Still other seeds fell on good soil. It came up and yielded a crop, a hundred times more than was sown." Just like the seeds, if we love God, He will bless our lives.

[*Ask a boy or girl to read the stanzas of "Fairest Lord Jesus." As they return to their seats, the pianist may continue to play.*]—Carolyn Ross Tomlin

April 16: How to Do God's Will
TEXT: Mark 14:36
Object: Hofmann's painting of Gethsemane

This painting portrays a crucial time in the life of Jesus. He is kneeling and praying in an olive garden named Gethsemane. Where Jesus prayed is not important. How he prayed is what matters.

When Jesus knelt by this rock, he was facing a big decision. He knew that if he was true to his mission, the cross awaited him. Jesus could avoid the cross, but he would have to be untrue to God. So Jesus prayed for strength to do what God wanted him to do. Listen to this verse. [*Read text.*]

We have to make a decision just like Jesus did. The Lord has a special purpose for our lives, but we must ask him to help us discover it. God's plan for our lives will bring us joy and happiness. He doesn't want to hurt us or make us unhappy; he wants to give us abundant life.

By living for the Lord, we not only please God but we also please ourselves. If Jesus hadn't followed God's will, none of us would have salvation and the promise of eternal life. The Bible describes Jesus as a triumphant savior. He won over the force of evil and rejoiced. If we don't seek God's will for our lives, others will never hear about God's love in Jesus. Furthermore, we will never share in the victory of Jesus.

Jesus prayed that God's plan would be completed in his life. We need to ask God to help us know the special reason that we are here. When we ask to know God's plan for our life, he will show it to us.—Ken Cox

April 23: Christ Is Risen!
TEXT: 1 Cor. 15:19–26
Object: A picture of the empty tomb

Good morning! Who can tell me what we are celebrating today? [*Let them answer.*] That's right! Today is Easter, and who can tell me what happened on Easter that makes us happy today? [*Let them answer.*]

On the first Easter morning nearly two thousand years ago, Jesus rose from the dead. He had died on the cross and been laid in a tomb like the one in this picture. [*Show the picture.*] What do you see in this picture? Can you describe what you see? [*Let them answer.*]

The most important thing we see in this picture is that the tomb where Jesus was laid after he died is empty! He is no longer there! He has risen from the dead! Now why do you think that fact is so important to us? Why are we all so happy on Easter Day? [*Let them answer.*]

The thing we are most happy about is that because Christ was raised from the dead, we who believe in him will also be raised from the dead. We don't have to be afraid of death because we have God's promise that he will raise us from our tombs, just like he did Jesus. Isn't that something to be happy about? [*Let them answer.*]

Dearest Father in Heaven, we praise you for raising Jesus from the dead and promising to raise all of us so that we can be with you in heaven forever. Amen.—Robert R. Roberts[1]

April 30: God Sends the Rain
TEXT: Acts 14:17
Song: "For the Beauty of the Earth"
Object: Glass of water

Boys and girls, I am holding in this glass something that is vital to life. What do we call this clear liquid? [*Pause.*] Most of you agreed that this glass contains water.

Water is necessary for life. Let us name some ways we use water. [*Pause for response.*] Yes, it is necessary to drink water daily. This keeps our body working. We depend on water for keeping our bodies clean, for washing clothes, and for cooking. We may water our vegetable garden and flowers. What about swimming? Boating? Fishing? Water is a necessity, but it is also often used in family recreation.

Industry depends on water for power. Since man discovered how to use water power, machines have made work easier for people.

Without water, our Earth would dry up and wither away. In some parts of the world, famines occur when rains do not come at the appropriate time. When this happens, crops do not grow. Other times, too much rain falls and the land is flooded. Too much and too little rain cause problems. The amount of rain affects all living things made by God. People, animals, and plants depend on moisture to survive.

Often we take something, like rain, for granted. Perhaps you live in a section of the country that has just the right amount of annual rainfall.

[1] *CSS PLUS*

Often boys and girls don't like rainy days. Has this ever happened to you? [*Pause.*] Rain may keep you inside when you would rather be playing outdoors. But the next time that happens, think about what we've talked about today. Instead of complaining, thank God for sending the rain. Think of an activity your family can enjoy together when you must play inside.

The Bible has several verses that speak of rain. "He has shown kindness by giving you rain from heaven and crops in their seasons; he provides you with plenty of food and fills your hearts with joy" (Acts 14:17 NIV).

[*Ask someone to sing a verse of "For the Beauty of the Earth" as the children return to their seats.*]—Carolyn Ross Tomlin

May 7: Hearing Your Father When He Calls You
TEXT: John 8:47

When you are outside playing away from your house (such as in a neighbor's yard) and your mother or father wants you to come home, how does she or he call you?

When my parents wanted me to come home, my mother would yell for me, "Michael, come home." Sometimes I would hear her; most of the time I wouldn't. After hearing that excuse several times, my mother decided that my father would call for us by whistling. My dad is the loudest whistler you will ever hear. He whistles so loud that it can make your ears hurt if you are close by while he is whistling. [*Demonstrate a shrill, loud whistle.*] So there is no way I could ever say I didn't hear my dad call for me. Whenever I heard that whistle, I stopped whatever I was doing and got home fast, just as my dad expected me to do. And to this day I still do.

I noticed something else about my dad's whistle. Whenever we heard it, we would come running, but everyone else who heard it just ignored it. Do you know why? Because they were not his children. We were his children, so we came as fast as we could.

God says the same thing is true about his children. He says that if we are his children we will listen to what he has to say in the Bible, and we will do what he says for us to do. Let's show the world that we are God's children by doing what he says for us to do and love others.—Michael Lanway

May 14: Sarah Becomes a Mom
TEXT: Gen. 21:2, 5–6 (Mother's Day)
Object: A picture of grandparents

God does things that amaze us and even make us laugh. This is a picture of some grandparents. These grandparents are about seventy years old. Once God allowed a husband and wife who were ninety years old, much older than this couple, to become parents. Not grandparents—parents!

The Lord made a promise to a man named Abraham that he would be the father of many nations. God said that Abraham and Sarah, his wife, would have children, grandchildren, and great grandchildren that numbered as many as the stars that shine at night. Abraham and Sarah looked forward to this promise coming true. However, the years went by and Abraham and Sarah didn't have any children. Not one.

Abraham and Sarah became as old as grandparents and still they had no children. Finally God kept his promise and Sarah learned that she was going to have a son. She was more than ninety years old. When Sarah found out that she was going to have a child, she laughed. She named her son Isaac, which means laughter. Listen to these verses. [*Read text.*]

The Lord waited to keep his promise so that his act would be an amazing thing. God completes his promises in such a way that humans will know that the Lord is responsible for what has happened. Otherwise humans would take the credit. The Lord is so amazing, he even makes us laugh, like Sarah. Sarah had a great Mother's Day. She knew that the present she had received was from God.

The Lord Jesus wants to do amazing things with your life, too. If you will ask him and allow him to work in your life, God will do amazing things.—Ken Cox

May 21: God Is Like a Mighty Tree
TEXT: Mark 4:6
Object: Small branch from a tree

While walking the other day I noticed a very tall tree. This tree seemed to be balanced on top of the ground. But we know that isn't true, don't we? Something was holding this tree in place. Who can tell me what holds a tree in the ground? [*Pause.*] The underground roots serve as a support system. Reaching out like fingers they hold the tree in an upright position. The roots also supply the plant with water and nutrients. If something happens to the roots, the plant will not grow.

This branch that I'm holding in my hand was once part of a tree. The tree had a root system, a trunk, and branches. The roots held the tree steadfast in the ground.

Listen to what the writer of Mark 4:6 says: "But when the sun came up, the plants were scorched, and they withered because they had no roots" (NIV). When we remove a plant from the soil, it soon dries up and dies. It has no means of support.

God is to us what a root system is to a tree. He anchors our life. He supplies all our needs. He gives us life today, and eternal life in heaven. We can't see God, but his presence surrounds us in everything we do.—Carolyn Ross Tomlin

May 28: Pretending to Give
TEXT: Acts 5:1–11

When I was a little boy, every Sunday morning my daddy would give me three quarters. He would tell me to put two quarters in my Sunday school offering and use the other quarter to buy a doughnut after Sunday school. So every Sunday morning I would put two quarters in the offering basket and use the other quarter to buy the doughnut after Sunday school.

One Sunday, I put only one quarter in the offering. Do you know why? Because I had decided that I wanted to buy two donuts after Sunday school. I thought, "No one will ever know the difference. So what if I keep an extra quarter for myself?" After Sunday school I went to buy my doughnuts. The first donut I ate really fast. Then I bought the other one. I had taken just one bite of it when I felt a hand on my shoulder. It was a hand that I had felt before. It was my dad.

My dad asked, "Is that your first doughnut?" I lied to my dad and said, "Yes." My dad said, "Son, I watched you eat the other doughnut." I knew I was in big trouble. My dad made me spit out the bite of donut in my mouth and throw the rest of the doughnut away. Then he explained to me that I had not only lied to and stolen from my dad, but I had lied to and stolen from God, too. My dad told me that God knows the difference when I do not give him what I should, that it was wrong and that what I did hurt my dad's feelings and God's feelings, too. I felt very bad and decided never to pretend to give to God and keep the extra for myself. I don't do that any more.

I hope that you never try to pretend to give to God and keep the extra for yourselves. God knows it when we do that, and it hurts him. All God wants is for us to be honest with him and give what we can. Let's promise God that we will do that.—Michael Lanway

June 4: Going to Church
TEXT: Heb. 10:24, 25

Every Sunday you and I do the same thing. What is it? We get dressed in a nice outfit and go to church. I always get excited about going to church. Do you? What do you like best?

There are so many things I like best. I like my Sunday school class. My teacher is real nice and does a good job of helping me learn more about the Bible and about God. I have friends in my class who I get to see. We talk to each other about the things that have happened during the week. I like that. Oh! I almost forgot the doughnuts. I really like the doughnuts.

I like the church service, too. The music is nice and I like to sing. I like to hear other people sing and to hear the pianist and organist play. I like to shake hands with everyone.

Do you know what one of my favorite things is about the service? Each one of you is one of my most favorite parts of going to church. I really like talking with you during the children's sermon. I get excited thinking about what I am going to say and thinking about what you may say. It makes me so happy to see your faces and to hear your laughter.

I am so glad that God has made this church and has brought each one of us here so we can be together and bring joy to God and to one another. I never want to miss a Sunday of seeing you.—Michael Lanway

June 11: The Best Way to Evangelize
TEXT: Acts 8:34–35
Objects: Some tracts and a computer Bible

One way to tell others about Jesus is by distributing tracts. This is a tract. There is information about God, Jesus, and salvation printed in this tract. If someone were to read this tract, they would have enough truth to accept Christ as their savior. I read of a missionary who drives around in a country in Africa and throws tracts out of his jeep. He has learned that people have accepted Jesus as savior based on a tract they found lying on the side of the road.

Another way to tell others about Jesus is through computer resources. This little disk has the entire Bible on it. Also, on the Internet are Web sites that contain information about Jesus. Persons browsing the Internet can discover truth about Jesus.

The best way to tell people about Jesus has not changed over the years. A specially printed tract or a high-powered computer is not required for this method of evangelism. Friendly encounters and casual discussions are still the best way to share knowledge of Jesus Christ. Listen to these verses. [*Read text.*]

We can tell our friends about Jesus. We don't have to be able to quote a bunch of Bible verses or preach a sermon. All we need to do is tell what we know to be true about Jesus and what he means to us.

People have a way of knowing when they are hearing the truth. Our sincerity and concern for someone else are the primary ingredients for a witnessing recipe. Be sure to tell your close friends about Jesus. Your personal testimony to them is better than a fancy tract or a powerful computer.—Ken Cox

June 18: Fathers Make Us Feel Safe

TEXT: 1 John 4:18 (Father's Day)
Object: A sack containing safety devices

This sack contains things that are supposed to make our lives safer. Here's a toy pistol. Some folks feel better when they are carrying a gun. Here's a cell phone. With a cell phone, 911 can be dialed at anytime. Here's some pepper spray. There are all sorts of devices that are intended to make us feel safe.

This is Father's Day. Dads make us feel safe. Dads are great to have around when we are scared.

A fellow told a story of going to a late afternoon horror show with his friends. He was only seven years old when it happened. Afterwards, when it was dark, the boys began nervously walking home. One by one the frightened friends dropped off as they came to their houses. Finally, the little boy was all by himself. He was trembling with fear as he headed down the last dark, tree-covered street. Up ahead he saw something lurking in the shadows of some twisted oak trees. The little guy thought it was a werewolf, just like in the movie. He was scared and his heart was beating loud enough for the werewolf to hear. Just before he turned to run for his life, the werewolf called his name! The panicked boy realized he knew the voice. As he looked again, the huge figure stepped out from the shadows and the boy saw his dad. He ran and leaped into the arms of his father, who had been waiting for him to come home. As he hugged his father, the boy was not afraid of anything, not even a werewolf.

Why do fathers make us feel so safe? The Bible has the answer. Listen to this verse. [*Read text.*]

Dads make us feel secure because they love us. Also, they are bigger than we are, and we know that they are trying to take care of us. Today, thank your Dad for loving you and taking care of you. God, our heavenly father, loves us and will protect us. As we pray, let us give thanks to our earthly and heavenly fathers for holding us in their arms.—Ken Cox

June 25: Your Church Needs You

TEXT: Luke 4:16 NIV
Song: "Dear Lord, Lead Me Day by Day"
Object: A brick

Boys and girls, I am holding something in my hand that you've seen many times. This object is called a brick. Can anyone tell me how we use bricks? [*Pause for response.*] I hear you say that we use bricks to build churches, houses, walkways, to edge flower beds and numerous other things. Yes, a brick is useful for many things.

Now this brick wasn't always in this block shape. The materials in this object come from nature and God provides all the necessary ingredients. A long time ago people realized that they could mix sand and clay, mold it, then bake it in an oven. This produced a hard block form that could be used in construction. In this design they can be stacked one on top of another to make a wall.

But there's something else about a brick. One brick by itself isn't very useful—unless it's used as a doorstop. It takes a lot of bricks to build a church, or a garden wall. While walking one day I noticed a wall that had one brick missing. This didn't make the wall fall, but everyone who passed noticed that one brick was absent. They didn't see all the other bricks still in place and doing their job.

When you are away from church, you are like that missing brick. Yes, we will have our worship service. Yes, we will have Sunday school. But without you, something is lacking. You are important. Your church needs you. Will you make the commitment to try your best to be in church every Sunday?

The writer of Luke 4:16 tells us about Jesus as a young boy and how he loved to go to church. "He went to Nazareth, where he had been brought up, and on the Sabbath day he went into the synagogue, as was his custom. And he stood up to read."

[*The pianist plays a stanza of "Dear Lord, Lead Me Day by Day" as the children return to their seats.*]—Carolyn Ross Tomlin

July 2: Jesus Says

TEXT: 1 Thess. 3:8 NIV
Song: "Stand Up, Stand Up for Jesus"

How many of you boys and girls like to play games? Good, that's everyone. Yes, games are fun. When I was a child my friends and I often played games like Red Rover, Red Rover; Kick the Can; Swinging Statue; and Simon Says. I suppose Simon Says was my favorite. In this game the leader calls out a direction. But you have to wait until the leader says the words "Simon Says" before you follow the directions. If not, you are out. Let me demonstrate. Do you think you can follow? Hold up your left hand. Did I say "Simon Says?" Did I catch someone? Now, Simon says touch your nose. What good listeners you are. Simon says stand up. Very good.

As I saw you rise I was reminded of another time when we should stand up and follow God's directions, that is, when we need to stand up for what we believe. Jesus wants his children always to do what is right. Can you help me think of other things that boys and girls who love Jesus can do? [*Pause for response.*] What about telling the truth? Minding our parents? Helping our friends? Doing our homework? Saying no to drugs. Yes, these are all ways we can show others that we are boys and girls who love Jesus. We are not ashamed to stand up for him.

Jesus loves each one of you so much. It makes him sad when we don't take care of our bodies or when we fail to obey our parents or do our best work in school.

So, what can we do when we are tempted to do wrong? Just remember this little game of Simon Says and you'll think of Jesus Says. That way, we will always stand up for what is right.

Let me share a Bible verse with you (1 Thess. 3:8): "For now we really live, since we are standing firm in the Lord."

[*The pianist plays softly "Stand Up, Stand Up for Jesus" as the children return to their seats.*]—Carolyn Ross Tomlin

July 9: We Must Tell the Story
TEXT: Acts 5:20
Object: Quietness

I am so glad that you are here this morning. I have the best news to tell you. This news is crucial for your life. [*Long pause.*]

I am happy that you are ready to listen. The message that I have for you will make a difference in eternity for you. [*Another long pause.*]

That's irritating, isn't it? It's disappointing to have someone inform you that they have great news and then give you the silent treatment. If someone has some critical news for us, we need to hear it, and the sooner the better.

Quietness may be the result of fear. If we are afraid, we will not talk. We like to be comfortable and confident before we start sharing information. Whatever our reasons, we must never be quiet and fail to tell others about Jesus. Listen to this verse. [*Read text.*]

Salvation has always spread by one witness telling another. If we fail to tell others about Jesus, the growth of the Kingdom of God will come to a screeching halt.

There are times to be quiet, like when we are in the library or in church. But we must never be quiet about Jesus. We must tell everyone that God loves them.—Ken Cox

July 16: God's Purpose for Your Life
TEXT: Rom. 8:28
Object: Toy duck in a paper bag

Children, I have something in this paper bag. At this time you don't know what the sack contains. Listen and I'll give you some clues. Then you can guess.

This object has webbed feet. It is a good swimmer. Soon after the young are born, they like to get into the water. Now, can someone guess what I'm talking about? [*Remove the object from the bag.*] Yes, I'm talking about a duck. A duck is a very good swimmer. Its webbed feet make it easy to paddle in water. Its feathers are made so the water runs off instead of soaking in. What happens to your hair when you get in water? Yes, it gets very wet. But a duck is made so that the water runs off the feathers.

The duck has a purpose in life. God planned for the duck to swim in water. He planned for the feet to serve as paddles.

What is your purpose in life? Do you think that God in all his greatness made you special? I think he wants boys and girls to tell others about his love. What are some ways we can show others that we love Jesus? [*Pause for response.*] I hear you saying that we can pray, sing with our congregation, invite others to church, read our Bibles, and ask our parents to read the Bible. Yes, there are so many ways to find God's purpose for our life.

The Bible speaks to us many times about finding God's purpose for our lives. The writers of the Scriptures use many examples of people who found God. Listen as I read this verse:

"And we know that in all things God works for the good of those who love him, who have been called according to his purpose" (Rom. 8:28 NIV). Finding his purpose is the way to love Jesus.

[*Ask the pianist to play "Jesus Loves the Little Children" as the boys and girls return to their seats.*]—Carolyn Ross Tomlin

July 23: Mother, May I?
TEXT: Matt. 6:10

Does anybody here know how to play Mother, May I? Explain the game to me. [*Allow them to explain.*] OK, let's play the game. I will play Mother. [*Give an instruction, after which they must ask "Mother, May I?"*]

That was a fun game! Playing it reminds me how important it is for us to ask for permission from others before we do something. If we are at home and we want to do something special or different, who should we ask for permission before we do it? [*Moms and dads, older sister, and so on.*] What if we are in class at school or church? [*Teacher.*] It is important to ask for permission, to make sure that what we want to do is okay with our parents and teachers.

Do you think we should ever ask God for permission? The Bible says we should pray and ask God's permission and for his will before we do something. That is really important, too, because we need to know that what we are doing is okay with God.

Let's remember that asking for permission is not only a fun game but also a very important thing to do. Let's be sure that we ask for permission from our parents, teachers, and especially God.—Michael Lanway

July 30: Hold Me
TEXT: Phil. 3:12

Have you ever asked your daddy to hold you? My kids have. Whenever we had been walking for a long time, perhaps at the shopping mall, my children would stop and hold their arms up to me, like this. [*Demonstrate.*] What do you think they wanted? They wanted me to pick them up and hold them. They were tired and didn't want to walk anymore.

What do you think I did? Do you think I just looked at them and walked away? No, of course not. I am a good daddy. I would bend over and pick them up and hold them. I would carry them as far as I could. Then I would give them to their mother.

Now my children are too big for me to carry them. They still ask for me to hold them, but in a different way. Now when they ask me to hold them, they want a hug. I really like to do that, because a hug is a way for us to show how much we love each other. I know your mommy and daddy feel the same way.

When our daddies and mommies hold us and hug us, they are showing us not only how much they love us but also how much God loves us. That is one reason that God has given us mommies and daddies, and brothers and sisters, and aunts and uncles, and grandmothers and grandfathers, and everyone around us. Every time we get and give hugs, that is God saying, "I love you, too!"

Everyone, no matter how old they are or how big they are, still needs someone to hold them at times, to be reminded that somebody loves them, that God loves them. Let's give somebody a hug today, and let them know that we love them and that God loves them, too. [*Hug the children as they leave, and tell them God loves them.*]—Michael Lanway

August 6: Wear a Smile
TEXT: Ps. 144:15
Object: Distribute happy-face stickers as the children gather, or draw a smiling face on an index card for each child.

Boys and girls, you are special. There are many unique things about you. And there is one thing you can give that belongs only to you. It's called a smile.

What happens when your face shows a smile? [*Pause for response.*] Yes, people return it. They smile back. This brightens their day. As a baby, your parents waited for your first smile. This facial expression was a first sign of recognition, and it made your mom and dad love you even more.

Think of a smile as a gift from God. Let's talk about places where we can use this special gift. At home we can have a helpful attitude. We can be pleasant when parents ask us to do chores. At school we can help friends. And remember those with handicaps, or new students. Could your teacher use a smile to lighten her day? At church we can welcome visitors, assist senior adults, hand out bulletins, and open doors for people. In fact, we can allow a smile to become part of everything we do.

Yes, a smile is important. It shows others how we feel about being a child of God. The Bible says, "Blessed are the people of whom this is true; blessed are the people whose God is the Lord" (Ps. 144:15 NIV).

Let's ask God to help us use this special gift throughout each day.

[*Ask the children to sing "Jesus Loves Me" or have the pianist play the song.*]—Carolyn Ross Tomlin

August 13: We Help Jesus by Helping Others
TEXT: Matt. 25:40
Object: A glass of water

Years ago Mr. Jones lived with his family on the second floor of his general store building. One night he had a dream that Jesus was coming to his store.

The next morning Mr. Jones was excited as he opened the store. As he was hurrying about, the little bell over the front door rang. It was Bobby from the Smith family that lived across the tracks. Mr. Jones helped Bobby find shoes to put on his bare, cold feet. He told Bobby not to worry about lacking a few dollars of the price.

Before long the little bell rang again. It was old Herman. Mr. Jones listened as Herman talked about the unhappy things in his life. After about an hour, Herman bought two apples and went on his way.

When the bell on the door jingled again, it was Mrs. Moore and her three children. They asked for some groceries on credit. Mr. Moore had lost his job and they already owed for three weeks of groceries. Mr. Jones scratched his head with worry, but he looked at the children and told Mrs. Moore it would be okay. He sacked up her milk and bread and stashed some candy in the bag for the kids.

It had been a long day by the time Mr. Jones trudged up the stairs to his family. When he dropped off to sleep he had another dream. He saw Jesus walking down a street and went running after him. Mr. Jones asked Jesus why he hadn't come to his store as promised.

Jesus answered that he had come to Mr. Jones's store. Jesus said that he was in Bobby needing shoes, in old Herman needing a friend, and in the Moore family needing help. Jesus said that each time he had come, Mr. Jones made him feel welcome.

Mr. Jones was glad he had been patient on that special day when Jesus came. He learned that by doing even the smallest kind acts, like giving a glass of water, like this, we are being kind to Jesus. Listen to this verse. [*Read text.*]—Ken Cox

August 20: Don't Worry About Tomorrow
TEXT: Matt. 6:25–26

I remember when I was going to school for the first time. I worried about what would happen. I remember when my mommy was late coming to pick me up at school and I was worried that something had happened to her. I remember riding my school bus for the first time. I was scared and was worried about who would sit next to me. Have you ever had a day when you were worried? [*Let them respond.*]

When we are worried, it doesn't feel good. Our tummy gets nervous and it feels like a bunch of butterflies are trying to fly through it. Sometimes even our head hurts, and we feel scared.

God knows that there are times when we will be nervous and scared and worried. That is why God uses the Bible to remind us that he will always take care of us. The Bible says that God takes care of the birds and he certainly will take care of us.

So when we are worried, we can pray, "God, I remember that you have promised to take care of me and everyone I love. So please help me and take away that awful feeling in my tummy. Please take away my headache. Help me not to worry right now. Thank you God."—Michael Lanway

August 27: Signals We Give Others
TEXT: Jude 21
Object: A Bible

[*Ask a pianist to play softly "All the Way My Savior Leads Me" as the children gather.*] When your grandparents learned to drive, they had to know and use hand signals. Automobiles did not have turn signals. Let me demonstrate. Of course the window had to be down. If you wanted to turn right, you would bend your left arm at the elbow with the hand upright. For a left turn, the arm and hand were extended out straight. And if you slowed down, you dropped the hand into an eight o'clock position. Would you like to try? [*Stand with your back to the children and allow them to go through each turn signal.*]

Today cars have turn signals that show others where we plan to go. It's much easier, don't you think?

We also use another type of signal. These signals tell others about our life. When we love Jesus, we want others to see him in our actions. The words we speak are a type of signal. As you grow older, the choices you make in friends send a message. So are your choice of clothing and doing your best in school. And the places you choose for leisure time are important. Can you think of others? [*Pause for response. List the choices the boys and girls make.*]

All of you made the choice to be in church today. That's a good signal. What does this tell others about our lives? Does it show our love for Jesus?

The Bible speaks to us many times about love. Listen as I read this verse: "Keep yourselves in God's love. . . ." (Jude 21:2 NIV). Sending the right kind of signal shows our love for God and others.—Carolyn Ross Tomlin

September 3: Is God Your Rock?
TEXT: Ps. 18:2
Object: A rock

This is a rock. In the Bible, God is compared to a rock. Listen to this verse. [*Read text.*]

God is compared to a rock because rocks are strong and steadfast. This is a small rock, but some rock formations are as large as a three-story building. Huge stone structures are impressive and radiate a sense of strength. God is like that. He is strong and steadfast.

I like to think that each time David the shepherd walked by a boulder marking the boundaries of his homeland, he thought of the steadfastness of God. The stone was the same regardless of turnovers in governments or shifts in the economy. The rock was a constant fixture in a world of change. David believed that the same qualities applied to God. The Lord was always there, unchanging and faithful.

Also, God is likened to a rock because he offers a place of safety. In large stone formations there are caves or holes. The Bible describes people scurrying to hide in the caves in the mountains when their enemies attacked them. The caverns were a place to conceal themselves until the enemy left their country. God is a rock because he offers a place of refuge for us with our problems.

Most important, the Psalm calls God "my rock." The Lord was personally known to be a steadfast, faithful place of refuge. God is our personal Savior and Lord. Jesus is alive and real in heaven now. We can know him just like we know and talk to each other. We know him by our belief and trust in him. God is not just a rock; he is "my rock."—Ken Cox

September 10: Doing What My Parents Do
TEXT: John 5:19, 20

My daddy is smart. So is my mommy. They have taught me a lot of things. They have taught me everything: how to get dressed, comb my hair, brush my teeth, ride my bike, and a whole lot more. Do you know how they taught those things? They showed me how to do it. They would do it first, then tell me to try, and then correct me to keep me doing it right.

Do you know how to tie your shoes? I remember learning to tie my shoes. At first I thought I would never be able to do it! It looked like a lot of twisting and all I could do was get my shoelaces in a great big knot and my shoes were still too loose and would fall off. But my daddy stuck with it and told me I could do it. One day I did it! I tied my shoelaces perfectly. I was so happy about it that I kept on practicing tying my shoes just to see how fast I could get them done. Pretty soon I challenged the rest of the kids on my block to a race. Guess who won? Me!

I am glad that God gave me a mommy and daddy who were willing to show me how things work and teach me to do them. That is how God taught Jesus, too. God would show Jesus what to do and then Jesus would do it. Aren't we lucky to have God, who loves us so much that he gives us parents who will teach their children just like God taught his Son Jesus? Let's thank God and let's thank our parents for the things they show us how to do.—Michael Lanway

September 17: God Doesn't Bench People
TEXT: Matt. 25:21
Object: Photo of an athletic bench

This is a picture of basketball players sitting on a bench. Only five players per team can be on the court at one time. The best players get to be in the game and the others have to watch from the sidelines. It is pretty hard to be benched. All of these players watching the game would rather be out on the court scoring points.

I saw a television report of a high school basketball star who received a scholarship to play at college. When he started playing at the big university, his coach thought that most of his teammates were better than the basketball star was. He spent the majority of his college basketball career on the bench. He rarely got into the game. The otherwise exciting games were frustrating for him and his family. That's one of the sad things about sports—not everybody gets to play.

In the Lord's Kingdom, everybody gets involved in God's game plan. God doesn't have a bench where people have to sit and watch others score all the points. The Lord wants everybody on the court.

God gives all believers a gift to use in his Kingdom. This special ability has been given to us by the Lord to bring about his perfect will on the Earth. The Lord expects all of us to use our talents for him. If we don't use our abilities for him, those qualities go to waste.

Talents in God's Kingdom include being a missionary, Sunday school teacher, preacher, organist, pianist, singer, or youth director. There is no end to the list of abilities that God has given to his children. Anywhere there is work to be done, whether it is witnessing or working in the kitchen, the Lord wants to see all believers involved in his Kingdom.

When we consistently use the ability God has given us, he is very pleased with us. Listen to this verse. [*Read text.*]

If you aren't exactly sure what your special ability is, ask the Lord Jesus to make it clear to you. As the years go by, the more you use your gift, the more valuable that ability will become to you and others.

Christianity is not a spectator sport. God never puts his children on the bench; he always puts them in the game.—Ken Cox

September 24: Little Things
TEXT: Mark 9:41
Object: A glass of water

Tell me some of the people who are heroes to you. [*Let them answer. Some may name great athletes, musicians, or television or movie stars.*] You have told me about people who have done great things. [*Here retell, or ask the children to retell, how a person's great accomplishments have made his or her name a famous name.*]

When we think of great people, we think of them as being great because of all the big and important things they have done. My hero is . . . [*Here share your hero or heroine's story.*]

Now, how many of you have heard about a person who became famous because he or she offered a glass of water to someone? [*Let them answer.*] I don't know of anyone. We don't think that offering a thirsty person a glass of water is anything very important. But it is important to God!

One day Jesus' disciples came to him telling about another man who was doing some great things for God. They might have been jealous of the man who was doing such great things for God. They even tried to stop the man from doing these things. But Jesus said not to stop anyone from doing anything that helps God's cause. Even little things like offering a drink of water are important to God.

If offering a thirsty person a glass of water to drink is important to God, what other kinds of things might also be important? [*Let them answer.*] I am glad that everything we do to help others is important to God. There are no little things, are there?

Dearest Jesus: Help us to keep in mind that we are always serving you. Amen.—Dennis Fakes[2]

October 1: Fruit Trees
TEXT: Matt. 17–18; Gal. 5:22–23
Object: An apple and a banana

What type of fruits are these? Apples and bananas. Where do we get apples and bananas? We get them at the grocery store in the produce aisle, where there are lots of bananas and bags of apples.

Do apples and bananas grow in the grocery store? Of course not. Apples and bananas grow on trees. A lot of different types of fruit grow on trees: apples, bananas, peaches, pears, plums. How can we tell which trees are peach trees and which are apple trees? We can tell by the fruit that is on the tree. Only apples can grow on apple trees and only peaches can grow on peach trees. Apples cannot grow on peach trees and peaches cannot grow on apple trees. That is how we can tell trees apart.

God says that is how we can tell the people who really love Jesus and others apart from those who do not really love Jesus and others. Those who love are always helping other people to feel special and good. They try to do good things and say good things that bring joy to somebody else's life. Those who don't love are always doing things and saying things that make others sad. How will others know you love them and Jesus? By making them feel special and loved in the things you say and do.—Michael Lanway

October 8: The Lord of the Harvest
TEXT: Matt. 9:37–38
Object: An apple

This apple grew on a tree. It began as a blossom, turned into a little hard piece of fruit, and then ripened into this beautiful red color. This apple is crisp and sweet. It was picked at just the right time.

---

[2] ibid.

Apples grow on a group of trees called an orchard. If you can imagine it, this apple was one of many tasty apples that became ripe and ready for harvest at the same time. Harvest time in an apple orchard is an extremely busy time. There are thousands of apples that must be picked and put in boxes for shipping in a very short time. If the apples aren't picked when they become ripe, they will fall from the tree and rot on the ground. Such a loss of delicious fruit would be a tragic waste.

God has compared the world to a field that is ready for harvest. Instead of being concerned for pieces of fruit, the Lord is concerned about people. According to the Bible, there are many people ready to hear the story of Jesus. When these hundreds of people are told about Jesus, they will believe in him and have eternal life. If the people are not told about Jesus, they will be lost. Like beautiful ripe, red apples ready to fall from a tree, many persons must be told about Jesus before the time of spiritual harvest is lost. Listen to these verses. [Read text.]

Jesus was concerned that enough harvesters would be working in the field of the world. Today most apples are picked by machines. In Jesus' field the harvest is still brought in by hand. Each person is lovingly sought, told the good news, and brought to salvation, one at a time.

The Lord wants all of us to be involved in his harvest. When we commit ourselves to him, the production from his fields will be great. Let's get busy so the harvest is not lost.—Ken Cox

October 22: Let the Lord Get in Front of You

TEXT: Deut. 31:8

Object: Picture of a shepherd and some sheep

In school we have to wait in line. I remember every now and then letting someone get in front of me in line. That person had to be very special. By letting them get in front of me, they didn't have to wait a long time to get a drink of water or food in the cafeteria. We should let Jesus get in front of us. When Jesus is allowed to be in front of us, we begin to follow him.

This is a picture of a shepherd and his sheep. In the land of Palestine, the shepherds lead their sheep. In city streets shepherds whistle and call to their sheep. The sheep know their shepherd's voice and trust in him, even if it means walking close to honking horns and screeching tires. The sheep follow wherever their owner goes. The sheep have learned to trust the shepherd, because he cares for and feeds them every day.

Once a man named Joshua was frightened about becoming a leader of his people. Moses, an older man whom Joshua trusted very much, reminded Joshua not to worry. Moses told Joshua that God would always be in front of him, leading the way, just like a shepherd. Listen to this verse. [Read text.]

For our lives to follow the right pathway we must be certain that we are following Jesus. Jesus calls himself the good shepherd. The good shepherd loves all of his sheep and leads them to pastures that are safe and full of nutritious grasses. Unlike sheep, we choose whom we will follow. Let's make certain that we let the Lord get in front of us. When the Lord is leading our line, we will always end up in the right place.—Ken Cox

October 29: I Can't Help It

TEXT: 2 Pet. 1:4–7

When mommies and daddies take their newborn babies home from the hospital, one of the things they think about is getting their babies to sleep. That is because some babies cry for a long time and have a hard time sleeping by themselves in their crib.

When we brought Whitney home from the hospital, we wondered how long it would take her to fall asleep. Can you guess how long it took? To our surprise, about ten minutes. Why? Because she would suck on her two middle fingers, which made her feel good and settled her down. It usually took her about ten minutes to find her middle fingers on her right hand and put them in her mouth. We were very glad that she sucked those fingers and went to sleep so easily.

As Whitney got older, we noticed that she sucked her fingers during the day, too. By the time she was five years old, it seemed that she had her fingers in her mouth all day long. Do you know what happened? Her middle fingers became thicker than the others and her teeth started growing the wrong way. So we knew she had to stop sucking her fingers, but every time we reminded her to stop doing that, she'd say, "I can't help it!" She really thought she couldn't stop, because she'd been doing it all her life.

Today Whitney is twelve years old. Do you think she still sucks her fingers? No. She stopped before she started kindergarten. You know how? One day, she decided she wasn't going to do that anymore. She had learned that big girls and boys don't suck their fingers and she wanted to be a big girl. It was real hard for her to stop, but she did it. She asked God to help her stop sucking her fingers, and he did. He promises to do that (2 Pet. 1). If you have a bad habit that you want to stop, ask God to help you and he will. That is his promise.—Michael Lanway

November 5: A Life with Jesus

TEXT: John 3:16

Object: Basketball enclosed in a box or sack

Boys and girls, I have an object in this container. At this time you could only guess what it is. It could be anything that would fit into this space. After I give you some clues, most of you will know the answer. Please wait until I finish to make your guess.

First, this object is used in a game. Usually a team plays. The team with the highest score wins. The object is round. You can bounce, kick, throw, spin, and roll this object. Now, raise your hand if you know the answer. That's right, it is a basketball. [*Remove the ball from the box or bag and show to the children.*]

Notice another thing about this basketball: it is filled with air. [*Bounce the ball once or twice.*] For a basketball to do what a ball should do, it must have air. A ball without air is useless. Have you ever tried to play with a flat basketball?

Let's compare the lives of boys and girls to a basketball. For you to live happy, meaningful lives, you must have Jesus. A life without Jesus is missing what he wants us to enjoy.

Listen as I read from God's book: "For God so loved the world that he gave his only begotten son, that whosoever believeth shall not perish but have everlasting life" (John 3:16 NIV).

God cares so much for you that he sent his Son to be born. Jesus lived and taught others about being a Christian. Then he died for our sins on a cross. That is how much God loves you and me.

Just like a basketball player needs a team, we need other Christians. The Church is a team of people who love God. Aren't you glad we can do this in our church?

Boys and girls, bow you heads as we thank God for loving us.—Carolyn Ross Tomlin

November 12: Esther Risked Her Life to Save Others

TEXT: Esther 4:14

Object: A hero certificate (or medal or trophy)

About 2,500 years ago a beautiful young lady named Esther lived in the magnificent palace of King Xerxes. King Xerxes had total control over his whole kingdom. Everybody instantly did whatever the king said to do. One day an evil man named Haman deceived King Xerxes into being angry at God's people, the Jews. King Xerxes ordered that every Jew be put to death.

King Xerxes didn't know that Esther was a Jew because she had not made a big deal about her national identity. Because of her beauty and winning ways, King Xerxes liked Esther very much. Esther didn't know what to do. If she went forward and tried to protect the Jews, she might put herself in danger. However, if she remained quiet and hid behind her secret palace identity, she might save her life, even though the rest of her people would be killed.

Esther's uncle, Mordecai, sent her a message. Mordecai instructed Esther to be brave and act to save her people. Mordecai told Esther that she was wrong to be quiet when her people were in danger. Listen to this verse. [*Read text.*]

Even though Esther was frightened, she took a risk for her people. Because of Esther's bravery, her people were not killed and they reclaimed their status as a mighty nation. The story has a happy ending only because Esther was willing to be brave.

As followers of Jesus Christ, we are commanded to tell others the truth about salvation. It is easier to be quiet than to speak up. We are afraid that people will make fun of us or abandon us if we witness for Jesus.

Like Esther, we must take a risk and be witnesses for Jesus. People's lives can have a happy ending in eternity only if we are willing to be brave and tell them of their need for forgiveness through Jesus. When we are willing to take a risk for the gospel, people will be grateful because of God's gift of salvation. We cannot become heroes unless we are willing to risk something for others.—Ken Cox

November 19: God's Word Should Be Inside Us

TEXT: Ps. 119:11

Object: A Bible with a beautiful cover

This special Bible came from the city of Bethlehem in Israel. There is a shop there that sells Bibles with covers made from olive wood. In the land where Jesus was born there are many olive trees. Olives grow on trees that live to be hundreds of years old. The wood from these trees can be used to make beautiful frames and statues.

However, the most important thing about the Bible is not its beautiful cover. The Bible is important for what is between the covers. The Bible is God's Word. God has revealed himself to us in truth because he loves us. The Bible is a book all about Jesus.

God's word is to be planted in our lives like a seed. When we memorize or learn the meaning of verses, we are planting or hiding the word of God in our hearts. Listen to this verse. [*Read text.*]

When I hide something from you, I don't want you to find it, at least until our game is over. But when we hide God's Word in our hearts, we want everyone to know where it is. When God's Word is hidden in our hearts, his truth becomes a part of our thoughts and actions. His Word is blended in with everything else we know.

The cover of a Bible is not that important. What is significant is inside the Bible. Furthermore, it is even more important that we hide God's Word in our hearts. The cover holds the Bible together, and our lives contain the truth of God.—Ken Cox

November 26: Knowing the Bible
TEXT: Acts 18:24–26
Objects: A bible and a dictionary

What is this book I am holding in my hands? It is the Bible. What is this book I am holding? It is a dictionary. These books are important for us to read and to learn from.

A dictionary helps us to learn new words, to learn what words mean, and to spell words correctly. How many of you have a dictionary at home? Good. Which words from the dictionary do you know? Good.

God has given us the Bible so we can learn all about him and all about Jesus. From the Bible we learn all about how we can be with God forever in heaven when we die, and how to live good lives. Which stories from the Bible do you know? Good. How many of you have a Bible at home? Good.

It is important to read the Bible so we can learn from it and so we can help others to learn from it. That is one reason we come to church—so we can learn more about God and Jesus. Let's be sure that we read the Bible at home, too. Ask your mommy or daddy to read a Bible story to you. Try your hardest to remember those stories. Then tell the story to others so they can learn about God and Jesus, too.—Michael Lanway

December 3: God Is Our Friend
TEXT: Prov. 17:17
Object: A Bible

[*Ask the pianist to play softly a couple of verses of "What a Friend We Have in Jesus."*] Boys and girls, today we are going to talk about friends. How many of you have a friend? Why did you choose this person? [*Pause for response. If time permits, make a list of activities that boys and girls can participate in with friends.*] A friend is someone who plays with you. Perhaps you share toys with your special friend. A friend is a person you like, who you spend time with, and who you can trust. When you have a friend, you have someone to talk to. And a friend listens. God wants us to choose good friends. Listen as I read what the Bible says about this topic.

Proverbs 17:17 says, "A friend loves at all times." When you're sick or when you can't come out and play, a true friend still loves you. This person may be your age, someone older, or a senior adult. Yes, friends are very important. If we want friends, how do we have them? [*Pause for response.*] Now think about how you can be a friend. Isn't it the same? You must become a person who can be trusted. Get to know boys and girls in your neighborhood, school, and church. Find ways to help older adults your family knows. Friendships take time. To spend time with others, you may have to give up some of your favorite activities.

Has a friend ever disappointed you? Of course. Regardless of how much you love your friend, sometimes this happens. But there is one who will never forget you. He will always be ready to listen when you pray. His name is Jesus. Jesus is always our friend. [*Hold up Bible.*] The Bible is God's book. It tells us how to be friends by loving one another.

Let us bow our heads as I ask God to help us be good friends.—Carolyn Ross Tomlin

December 10: Jesus Is Our Light

TEXT: John 1:4; 1 John 4:18
Object: A flashlight

A dark bedroom can be scary. When I was growing up I would take a flashlight to bed with me. When I heard an unusual noise, I would shine the light into the darkness and see for sure that nothing dangerous was there. Knowing that I had the light nearby always made me more comfortable. When I was really scared, I would crawl into bed with my folks.

I wish that all fears left when a person becomes an adult. They don't. Grown-ups may not take a flashlight to bed with them, but there are things to be afraid of. There is the fear of getting sick, losing loved ones, and losing jobs. These few things are not a complete list of fears. All sorts of things can make us frightened. Light and love are the solution for all fears. The light doesn't come from a flashlight, it comes from Jesus. God is love and cares for us. Listen to these verses. [*Read text.*]

The light and love of Jesus keeps fear from draining all of our energy away. When we believe that Jesus is with us, the light of his truth makes us confident. By living for him we know we are on the right pathway for our lives. We don't have to be afraid of being lost. Furthermore, the love of Jesus' presence gives us courage, and we can see and enjoy all the blessings the Lord sends our way.—Ken Cox

December 17: God Makes Us Wait

TEXT: Exod. 32:1
Object: A picture of a traffic light

This is a picture of a traffic light. When the light is green, we are happy to hurry up and go. If the light is yellow, we have to be cautious and get ready to stop. When a traffic light is red, we are made to do something that is very difficult for humans. We have to stop and wait.

Long ago God called Moses up on Mount Sinai to receive the Ten Commandments. Moses told the people to wait for him to come back down the mountain. After nearly forty days had passed, the people were feisty and impatient. They were tired of waiting for Moses. Listen to this verse. [*Read text.*]

The people made a golden calf to take the place of God. The idol was easier to worship than the God who had revealed himself through Moses. The people could make their own rules with idols. Humans like idols because they can be manipulated, and idols don't make us wait. However, there is a problem with idols. All idols are worthless, whether they are ancient golden calves or modern careers, possessions, or dreams.

Even though at times we have to wait on the Lord, God is worth whatever time we have to invest in his Kingdom. When we ask God for help, it may take more than a few hours for him to work out a perfect answer to our prayers. We may feel like yelling, "Hurry up!" at heaven. All the while God is fitting our request into his perfect plan for our lives and his world.

When humans get anxious, mistakes are made. An old saying is "haste makes waste." The Lord will not do anything that will cause problems now or in the future. So the Lord is worth waiting for. We may get upset when we don't control the schedule of God's answers, but the Lord is worthy of our trust and time.—Ken Cox

December 24: Gabriel, God's Messenger
TEXT: Luke 1:26–38
Object: A Christmas tree angel or nativity set angel

Good morning! I brought an angel with me this morning to tell a wonderful story about God. God doesn't work the way we work. We often see people based on their importance. We think some people are very important and we treat them special. Can you tell me about some people we consider very important? [*Give the children an opportunity to tell about important people.*] We treat kings and presidents in special ways in which we don't treat others.

Sometimes when a person is very poor or doesn't have a really good job, people are tempted to treat him as if he is not as important as other people. That's the way many people are. It was true a long time ago as well.

Many years ago in a little town—which itself was not important—there lived a young woman. Many would say that she was not important at all. She was poor and she had no important job. She did not have a high position, such as being a princess or queen. Many people probably thought that this poor woman was not at all important. Does anybody know this woman's name? [*Let them answer.*] Her name was Mary and she lived in Nazareth.

Others didn't think much of Mary from the unimportant town of Nazareth, but God thought she was very important. God sent a messenger to this woman. The messenger's name was Gabriel. Gabriel was one of these—an angel. Does anyone know what God wanted Gabriel to say to Mary? [*Let them answer.*]

God told Mary that she was to have the baby Jesus. That was important. That was the most important thing anyone could ever do.

One thing I think this story tells us is that every person is precious to God. God could have chosen anyone to have Jesus, but God chose a person everyone else thought was not important. Now we consider Mary very important, but she was important to God long before anyone else thought she was important.

Do you know what? *You* too are important to God.

Dearest God: Thank you for making us important people. Amen.—Dennis Fakes[3]

December 31: Running on Empty

TEXT: 1 Pet. 5:7 NIV

Song: "Jesus Loves the Little Children"

Object: Toy car

Boys and girls, I'm holding an object behind my back that represents something your family may own. In fact, you may have come to church in it today. Can you guess what I'm holding? [*Pause for response and show children the car.*]

Cars of today do not look much like those your grandparents or great grandparents drove. But in some ways they are the same. Both have four tires, a steering wheel, brakes, lights, and a place for the driver and passenger. And something else, cars of yesterday and today require gas to run.

Fuel or gas is necessary to make the motor operate. This drives the engine. Have you ever been with your parents and the car ran out of gas? What happened? What choices did you have? [*Pause for response.*] You might have called a service station to bring you gas. You might have called a family member or friend. Perhaps you had to walk to a telephone.

Did you know that sometimes boys and girls are like a car without gas? Sometimes we are running on empty. How can this happen? If we fail to eat healthy food, our bodies may not grow. If we do not see a doctor when we are sick, we may not feel well. If we fail to get enough sleep, our bodies tire easily. And if we do not pray, read our Bibles, and attend church regularly, we may not learn of God's love. Just like a car without gas, our bodies cannot be what God intended them to become.

The writer of 1 Peter 5:7 reminds us of God's love. "Cast all your anxiety on him because he cares for you." Let us repeat this verse together. Ask God to help your body and mind grow strong.

[*As the pianist plays "Jesus Loves the Little Children," the boys and girls return to their seats.*]—Carolyn Ross Tomlin

---

[3] ibid.

SECTION XI

A LITTLE TREASURY
OF SERMON ILLUSTRATIONS

NEED TO FORGIVE.   A man once came to his minister in great distress of mind. He said that his prayers no longer appeared to bring him any comfort. He seemed, so he confessed, to have lost all contact with God. He uttered the same words as he had done for many years, but he remained without any assurance of being heard, or of any touch of God's Spirit such as he had known. Why was this, he pleaded? The two talked for some time, and then, quite by accident it seemed, he mentioned that he was at that time suing his own brother in court for payment of a twenty-year-old loan. He did not want the money, that is to say, he did not need it; but, as he said, he wasn't going to let his brother get away with it, and so laugh at him. No, not he! He would fight him till he got every penny of it back!

It was only when he was asked how much he thought he had been forgiven; it was only when he was reminded of the irredeemable debt he owed to God; it was only when he was invited to say the Lord's Prayer, and deliberately stopped at the place where he would have blandly repeated "as we forgive those who trespass against us" that he suddenly realized why it was that his prayers had been so unavailing and so ineffective.—John Trevor Davis, *Lord of All*

LOVE AND UNDERSTANDING.   Understanding, then, can lead to love. But the reverse is also true. Love brings understanding; the two are reciprocal. So we must listen to understand, but we must also listen to put into play the compassion that the wisdom traditions all enjoin, for it is impossible to love another without hearing that other. If we are to be true to these religions, we must attend to others as deeply and as alertly as we hope that they will attend to us; Thomas Merton made this point by saying that God speaks to us in three places: in scripture, in our deepest selves, and in the voice of a stranger. We must have the graciousness to receive as well as to give, for there is no greater way to depersonalize another than to speak without also listening.

Said Jesus, blessed be his name, "Do unto others as you would they should do unto you." Said Buddha, blessed be his name as well, "He who would, may reach the utmost height— but he must be eager to learn." If we do not quote the other religions on these points, it is because their words would be redundant.—Houston Smith, *The World's Religions*

THE IMPORTANT THING.   Sir Christopher Wren was a prince in many realms of science as well as in architecture, and in 1659 he pioneered a medical advance and discovered blood transfusion, which has saved many lives today; but he considered St. Paul's Cathedral his greatest work, and in his later years loved to go in and sit in its lofty precincts. The Church has an incomparable mission, because the saving of character is more momentous than the saving of life. Whatever turns men to the worship of God is more decisive for human progress and happiness than scientific discoveries and material improvements, and that is why those who love the Church attest to the living presence of god in their heart.—Arthur A. Cowan, *Crisis on the Frontier*

THE GOODNESS OF GOD.   Once I decided that I could not believe in the goodness of God in the presence of the world's evil, and then I discovered that I had run headlong into another and even more difficult problem: What to do about all the world's goodness on the basis of no God? Sunsets and symphonies, mothers, music, and the laughter of children at play, great books, great art, great science, great personalities, victories of goodness over evil, the long hard-won ascent from the Stone Age up, and all the friendly spirits that are to other souls a "cup of strength in some great agony"—how can we, thinking of these on the basis of no God, explain them as the casual, accidental by-products of physical forces, going it blind? I think it cannot be done. The mystery of evil is very great upon the basis of a good God but the mystery of goodness is impossible upon the basis of no God.—Henry Emerson Fosdick, *Living Under Tension*

THE JOY OF LOVE.   There is an ad for a bubble bath for children that suggests that it can be almost as much fun to get clean as it is to get dirty. That strikes me as a good ad for a church, for while it recognizes a certain fun in wrongdoing, it also acknowledges that it is a joy to scrub one's mind and soul—and the world—of dirt. It really is a joy—a bubbly joy—to be with irrepressible people who are so precisely because they know and love the Lord. It is a joy to be loved. It is a joy to love others.—William Sloan Coffin, *The Courage to Love*

WORDS THAT DEFINE.   Carlyle Marney used to say that one of the great challenges of our human venture is "getting the adjectives and nouns of life in their proper places." An adjective, according to Marney, points to some important characteristic about a human being but never tells the whole story. For example, the words *tall* and *short* are adjectives. Each says something very significant about the shape of a human body, but neither of these words says everything there is to be said about the mystery of a person. *Human being* or *child of God* are the definitive nouns; all other words simply point to one facet of a given human being.—John Claypool, *Glad Reunion*

LOVE'S DIMENSIONS.   The story that Christianity tells, of course, claims to give more than just a clue, in fact to give no less than the very meaning of life itself and not just of some lives but of all our lives. And it goes a good deal further than that in claiming to give the meaning of God's life among men, this extraordinary tale it tells of the love between God and man, love conquered and love conquering, of long-lost love and love that sometimes looks like hate. And so, although in one sense the story Christianity tells is one that can be so simply told that we can get the whole thing really on a very small Christmas card or into the two crossed pieces of wood that form its symbol, in another sense it is so vast and complex that the whole Bible can only hint at it.—Frederick Buechner, *The Magnificent Defeat*

UNCERTAINTY.   Don't elevate your every whim into a conviction. Having an opinion is one thing, delivering the Ten Commandments is something else. Intellectual honesty demands that unless you're a bona fide expert in the field, a hint of tentativeness should accompany all your views and decisions. Indeed, a hint of uncertainty is appropriate even if you *are* an authority. Here's a simple device to ensure that you have the proper humility when offering your opinion: When you speak, imagine that an expert is sitting right across from you. Now offer that opinion.—Joshua Halberstam, *Everyday Ethics*

CALLED TO ACCOUNT.   "In Him we live and move and have our being." Whoever lives with the feeling of emptiness and tedium has ceased to realize this truth. If he is courageous enough to reflect, he will of course become aware that it is precisely in the sense of void which oppresses him that God is speaking to him and asking him questions: questioning him about himself and calling him to account as to what he has made of his life.—Rudolf Bultmann, *This World and the Beyond*

LOVING GOD AND CARRYING CHRIST.   The cross is a constant in our lives; death in some form haunts us each day. But you are less than Catholic if you fail to see that "cut it off" is not mutilation but liberation: It frees you to love God with every fiber of your being. You are missing the depth and the thrill and the joy in Catholic living if you carry Christ only *into* church, if you fail to carry him from Communion to the concrete and glass outside, to the condo and the slum, to your desk and your bed—in a word, to the men and women who people your days.

    Love God above all else and you won't have to calculate just how you carry Christ to your turf; it will be second nature, as easy as breathing. All you will need is to be yourself; for that self will be Christ. It may not be all fun—Christ himself did not laugh on Calvary. But I can promise you a delight in human living that will only grow richer as you grow grayer, a fascination with your creation that will rival the breathless day when God looked on what He had shaped "and behold, it was very good" (Gen. 1:31).—Walter J. Burghardt, S. J., *Lovely in Eyes Not His*

THE COMMANDING CROSS.   What of the road Jesus walked? He consented to a messy little gallows set up on the city dump. He asked nothing for himself, except to love God and men. He courted oblivion. He should have been lost in the ruck of history. But he keeps coming back: lovers and liars, kings and commoners, the Mafia and the misfit saints all date their letters from his birthday. The centuries have knelt before him daringly: the *Bach Mass in B Minor* is only one instance. The Cross is empty now, yet never empty. It has stolen the skyline of every city. All prayer begins in that adoration.—George A. Buttrick, *The Power of Prayer Today*

A SURE AND CERTAIN SOUND.   A bugle is blown from Castle Rock in Edinburgh at sundown. Once we heard the bugle through heavy fog. We could not see the rock, still less the sunset. But we knew then that there is a rock and a sun's light. How else to describe Jesus? His life is a bugle blown "from the hid battlements of Eternity."—George A. Buttrick, *So We Believe, So We Pray*

TRICKY FEELINGS.   One woman, being asked how she felt, said, "I feel good today. But I always feel the worst when I feel the best because I know how bad I am going to feel when I get to feeling bad again."—Clovis G. Chappell, *Sermons on Biblical Characters*

MEANING.   Looking to the crucified and living Christ, even in the world of today, man is able not only to act but also to suffer, not only to live but also to die. And even when pure reason breaks down, even in pointless misery and sin, he perceives a meaning, because he knows that here too in both positive and negative experience he is sustained by God. Thus faith in Jesus the Christ gives peace with God and with oneself, but does not play down the problems of the world. It makes man truly human, because truly one with other men: open to the very end for the other person, the one who needs him here and now, his "neighbor."—Hans Küng, *On Being a Christian*

WHEN GOD HIDES.   The Spiritual Presence can never end. But the Spirit of God hides God from our sight. No resistance against the Spirit, no indifference, no doubt can drive the Spirit away. But the Spirit that always remains present to us can hide itself, and this means that it can hide God. Then the Spirit shows us nothing except the absent God, and the empty space within us which is His space. The Spirit has shown to our time and to innumerable people in our time the absent God and the empty space that cries in us to be filled by Him. And then the absent one may return and take the space that belongs to Him, and the Spiritual Presence may break again into our consciousness, awakening us to recognize what we are, shaking and transforming us.—Paul Tillich, *The Eternal Now*

THE SPIRIT AT WORK.   There may be death in your house. It may be filled with poisonous gases, but if you will throw it open, if you will lift the windows and swing wide the doors, the sweet, pure air will rush in, laden with life and health. You need not be an expert in science and understand all about the laws of ventilation to understand that. Just trust the wind, remove the barriers, let it come in, and all the foul exhalations will make way for it, and your house will be sweetened and purified.

So, you see, when the Lord teaches us that God is spirit, and then uses the air as a symbol to bring the thought down to the level of our comprehension, he teaches us something most practical and beautiful. What royal bounty, what boundless provision, what fullness, and freeness it suggests for all the wants of our nature. As spirit he touches every life, he presses upon every heart, he waits for us to make room for him that he may enter in to cleanse and bless.—Robert F. Coyle, *The Christianity of Christ*

PRIORITY.   When a boy grows up in a bad environment, where nobody loves him, he has to try to find a substitute for mother-love. A puppy or a teddy bear may then take the place of the mother. After a while, he cannot live without it. When this boy comes into a new atmosphere where he is loved and can feel at home, he will not automatically throw away his puppy or his teddy bear. Rather, they resume their proper place; they no longer supplant the mother and her love; they move a bit closer to the periphery of his life. That is exactly what happens where "the name of our Lord Jesus Christ" and "the Spirit of our God" are active in our life. Even then, of course, we love and cling to a host of things. But no longer do they possess us; no longer are they idols, for they stay in their proper place.—Eduard Schweizer, *God's Inescapable Nearness*

UNDERSTANDING PEOPLE.   There was a little girl who got rather mixed up when she tried to write an essay on "People." She said: "People are composed of girls and boys, also men and women. Boys are no good at all until they grow up and get married. Men who do not get married are no good either. Boys are an awful bother. My mother is a woman and my father is a man. A woman is a grown-up girl with children. My father is such a nice man that I think he must have been a girl when he was a boy." We all get confused when we try to understand people. And how very difficult it becomes when we try to live in harmony and happiness with people!—John N. Gladstone, *A Magnificent Faith*

CHRISTIAN LOVE.   "Blest Be the Tie That Binds" was born of a bond between a pastor and a church. John Fawcett was a young pastor of a small congregation in Yorkshire. In 1772, he was called to a large city church in London to succeed the famous Dr. Gill. The young pastor's head was turned by the prestige and affluence of London. He resigned his charge, preached his final sermon, and prepared for the big move. The wagons were loaded, and the Fawcetts were ready to go. As they looked into the faces of the people they were leaving, they sank down onto one of the crates with an overwhelming sense of grief. They unloaded the wagons and returned to finish out their ministry with the modest congregation at Yorkshire. Out of this event, so expressive of the "ties which bind," came the hymn. From the hymn has come a new understanding of the new commandment which was given by Christ—to love one another as he has loved us.—Larry Dipboye

THE LURE OF THE WORLD.   If you go to Las Vegas as I do, and I hasten to add I go there to preach, you will find two blocks downtown which are even brighter than Times Square. Out on the Strip spectacular electric displays stand in front of the casinos with breath-taking beauty. But when you remember that all this is to lure people into gambling halls, it makes it all look cheap and disappointing. Watch the gamblers in the morning haggard, sad, and despondent, and the glamor becomes ashes.—Gerald Kennedy, *Fresh Every Morning*

A HEALING VISIT.   Florence Nightingale was a lovely visitor. Do you recall that exquisite bit of poetry in conduct on the field of Crimea? A soldier was to go through a painful operation. An anesthetic could not be administered and the doctor said the patient could not endure the operation. "Yes, I can," said the patient, "under one condition: if you will get the 'Angel of the Crimea' to hold my hand." And she came out to the little hospital at the front and held his hand. Glorious visit. No wonder the man went through the operation without a tremor.—Clovis G. Chappell, *Sermons on Biblical Characters*

WAITING FOR THE CHRIST.   I remember a Jewish boy I had in a New Testament class for a while who said one day in a burst of real impatience and anger, "Don't you get sick and tired, you Christians, of waiting for someone to come back who never comes back?" And I found myself asking him if to wait for a Christ who never comes back is all that much harder than to wait for a Christ who never comes at all, and in that moment we became brothers as we'd never been before, both of us Jews in the sorrow of our waiting, of our seeing, yes, sometimes a little something, somewhere, but never enough, of seeing but not seeing.—Frederick Buechner, *A Room Called Remember*

JOHN 3:16.   A humorous tradition in the Talmud reports how the great and gentle Hillel was once asked to explain the whole Law of Judaism while he stood on one leg, and that Hillel succeeded in doing so by quoting the Golden Rule. In an age of digests such as ours, it is not unlikely that we too might be asked to do something similar for our faith, to give in a nutshell the meaning of the gospel committed to us. Should that ever happen, I suggest that we could do no better than quote the verse from the Gospel of John that I have chosen as a text. It seems to me to summarize the essential content of the Christian faith. It is the *gospel* within the *Gospels.*—W. D. Davies, *The New Creation*

GOD'S FACE.   I think back to my days of working in Dorothy Day's Catholic Worker soup kitchen. One afternoon, after several of us had struggled with a "wino," a "Bowery bum," an angry, cursing, truculent man of fifty or so, with long gray hair, a full, scraggly beard, a huge scar on his right cheek, a mouth with virtually no teeth, and bloodshot eyes, one of which had a terrible tic, she told us, "For all we know he might be God Himself come here to test us, so let us treat him as an honored guest and look at his face as if it is the most beautiful one we can imagine." At the time I had a great deal of trouble seeing God in that face, even as the faces of God some children have presented to me seem improbable candidates for such an honor—"and yet," as Dorothy Day would sometimes say, never finishing her sentence, thereby leaving open any number of possibilities. God's face is *His* to reveal—so she and any number of children seem to have known.—Robert Coles, *The Spiritual Life of Children*

A MOTHER'S TOTAL MOTHERING.   My "earliest love story" is "strangely intermingled with a story of severing, of gently pushing away, of farewell." That final, triumphant thrust that launched me into an unsuspecting world, that severed umbilical cord, these were only the beginnings, the symbols, of a love bent on liberating, bent on gradually freeing me from bondage to her, so as to live my own life, to be open to others, open to loving and sharing. Even when I left home for good, at the ripe age of sixteen and a half, I can remember only her sweet, encouraging smile; I was not allowed to see the tears.—Walter J. Burghardt, S. J., *Sir, We Would Like to See Jesus*

YOUR IMPORTANT GIFT.   Did you never read of Rossini, who had to write an opera for a company whose contralto had only one good note to her voice—middle B flat? How easy to complain! How easy to give up! Instead he wrote one of his loveliest pieces, making her sing a recitative on that one note, meanwhile surrounding it with great orchestral music.—D. W. Cleverly Ford, *An Expository Preacher's Notebook*

TRUSTED WITH SORROW.   J. Wallace Hamilton tells the story of a letter he received from his sister in Africa, the wife of a missionary. They had lost their nine-year-old son by tragic death. Just one line in the letter told a great story about two great souls. Here is the line: "God has trusted us with a great sorrow." Think of all the patience, all the trust, all the confidence, all the love that these parents must have had to write that one sentence! "God has trusted us with a great sorrow."—Gaston Foote, *How God Helps*

STEWARDSHIP.   Through stewardship it is possible for a man to be an unknown presence and power in some distant place. Someone has written these sentences: "When a medical missionary enters a community he is accompanied by a thousand men—among whom are Pasteur with his knowledge of bacteriology, Fleming with his discovery of penicillin, Jefferson with his understanding of the democratic way of life, Jerome and Tyndale with their translations of the Bible, and St. Paul with his interpretation of Christianity."—Jack Finegan, *Clear of the Brooding Cloud*

WHEN GOD SPEAKS.   Because the word that God speaks to us is always an incarnate word—a word spelled out to us not alphabetically, in syllables, but enigmatically, in events, even in the books we read and the movies we see—the chances are we will never get it just right. We are so used to hearing what we want to hear and remaining deaf to what it would be well for us to hear that it is hard to break the habit. But if we keep our hearts and minds open as well as our ears, if we listen with patience and hope, if we remember at all deeply and honestly, then I think we come to recognize, beyond all doubt, that, however faintly we may hear him, he is indeed speaking to us, and that, however little we may understand of it, his word to each of us is both recoverable and precious beyond telling.—Frederick Buechner, *Now and Then*

FREEDOM AND RESPONSIBILITY.   When I make it possible to my daughter to attend college, and when I send her off, I help to increase her freedom intellectually, socially, and in terms of all the maturity which I have coveted for her. If I did her assignments and wrote her term papers—if I did the things which she ought to do for herself—then indeed I would be a bad father. But when I make it possible for her to increase her freedom and her responsibility, her maturity, then my deeds and even my presence, if I go to visit her, are a help and not hindrance. God never violates human personality in the giving of himself or in the giving of his gifts. God always increases our freedom and increases our responsibility, when we approach him in prayer.—Nels F. S. Ferré, *The Extreme Center*

This has potential

SUCCESSFUL PREACHING.   Recently a friend of mine was telling me of a certain sermon preached by his pastor. He said the preacher made a terrible flop. Possibly he was speaking solemn truth. Possibly, also, this minister had nobody to blame but himself. He may have failed to make proper preparation both of himself and of his sermon. But there may have been other causes. Last summer I went fishing and caught a trout. No sooner had I landed him than he began to make a decided flop. But I did not blame him. My criticism was hushed when I realized that his ridiculous flop was due to the fact that he was trying to breathe in an atmosphere that was so dry that it was smothering him to death. Sometimes this may be the case with your minister. Certainly this is true: The success of a service depends quite as much upon the audiences as upon the minister.—Clovis G. Chappell, *Values That Last*

A COMPELLING MISSION.   Viktor Frankl, an Austrian psychologist who survived the death camps of Nazi Germany, made a significant discovery. As he found within himself the capacity to rise above his humiliating circumstances, he became an observer as well as a participant in the experience. He watched others who shared in the ordeal. He was intrigued with the question of what made it possible for some people to survive when most died.

He looked at several factors—health, vitality, family structure, intelligence, survival skills. Finally, he concluded that none of these factors was primarily responsible. The single most significant factor, he realized, was a sense of future vision—the impelling conviction of those who were to survive that they had a mission to perform, some important work left to do.—Stephen R. Covey, *First Things First*

THIS WORLD AND THE NEXT.   This world and the next world are not, to the pure in heart, two houses, but two rooms, a Gallery to pass through, and a Lodging to rest in, in the same House, which are both under one roof, Christ Jesus; the Militant and the Triumphant are not two Churches, but this the Porch, and that the Chancel of the same Church, which are under one Head, Christ Jesus; so the Joy, and the sense of Salvation, which the pure in heart have here, is not a joy severed from the Joy of Heaven, but a Joy that begins in us here, and continues, and accompanies us thither, and there flowers on, and dilates it self to an infinite expansion . . . though the fullness of the glory thereof be reserved to that which is expressed in the last branch, *Videbunt Deum, They Shall See God.*—John Donne

CONVERSION.   In the Trinity Term of 1929, I gave in, and admitted that God was God, and knelt and prayed; perhaps, that night, the most dejected and reluctant convert in all England. I did not then see what is now the most shining and obvious thing; the Divine humility which will accept a convert even on such terms. The Prodigal Son at least walked home on his own feet. But who can duly adore that Love which will open the high gates to a prodigal who is brought in, kicking, struggling, resentful, and darting his eyes in every direction for a chance to escape? . . . The hardness of God is kinder than the softness of men and His compulsion is our liberation.—C. S. Lewis, *Surprised by Joy*

TRUTH.   Sometime in 1938, it is recorded, a Nazi schoolmaster asked his class of boys, "What is the supreme virtue?" Back came the answer, "Obedience!" from all save one. He said, "Truth, sir." He was a British boy in the school.

That story paints to its own moral, and stands as a sober warning as to what can all too easily happen if we sell our birthright for a mess of pottage.—John Trevor Davis, *Lord of All*

THE FATAL WEAKNESS.   Remember the Chinese Wall? It was two thousand miles long, built as a barricade on the western border of China to keep out the invader. For centuries, the Wall successfully defended their land. But one day an enemy bribed a dishonest gatekeeper; the invaders filed through the door at midnight and conquered China. The ultimate defense of any nation lies, not in its walls or armaments, but in the morality, integrity, and character of its people.—Wayne Dehoney, *Challenges to the Cross*

SCIENCE AND CHRISTIANITY.   There is nothing more inspiring just now to the religious mind than the expansion of the intellectual area of Christianity. Christianity seemed for a time to have ceased to adapt itself to the widening range of secular knowledge, and the thinking world had almost left its side. But the expansion of Christianity can never be altogether contemporaneous with the growth of knowledge. For new truth must be solidified by time before it can be built into the eternal truth of the Christian system. Yet, sooner or later, the conquest comes; sooner or later, whether it be art or music, history or philosophy, Christianity utilizes the best that the world finds, and gives it a niche in the temple of God.—*Henry Drummond: An Anthology,* edited by James W. Kennedy

CHRIST, OUR RIGHTEOUSNESS.   One day, as I was passing in the field, and that too with some dashes on my conscience, fearing lest yet all was not right, suddenly this sentence fell upon my soul, Thy righteousness is in heaven; and methought withal, I saw, with the eyes of my soul, Jesus Christ at God's right hand; there, I say, is my righteousness; so that wherever I was, or whatever I was a-doing, God could not say of me, He lacks my righteousness, for that was just before Him. I also saw, moreover, that it was not my good frame of heart that made my righteousness better, nor yet my bad frame that made my righteousness worse; for my righteousness was Jesus Christ Himself, the same yesterday, and to-day, and for ever (Heb. 13:8).—John Bunyan, *Grace Abounding to the Chief of Sinners*

HONESTY WITH GOD.   The God who sent his Son to die for us is not oblivious to our suffering. He is not defensive even when we lash out in anger at him for allowing us such pain. God has taken our sorrows and suffering and guilt upon himself. He will walk through the darkest valleys with us. Therefore we need to let go of our fear that our true thoughts and feelings will not be acceptable to him and that he will respond in anger at our foolishness and blasphemy. Many who need to lament but are afraid to do so find great comfort when they discover those parts of the Bible that allow them to say out loud what has been lying secretly within their hearts.—Daniel J. Simundson, *Faith Under Fire*

THE POWERFUL PAST.   It is a psychological platitude that a trivial incident can affect the whole course of a man's life. It is said of one of the recent prime ministers of Britain that his whole career as a statesman was colored, and even vitiated, by the circumstances of his early years. It is not for nothing that we speak of the formative years of childhood and adolescence. John Buchan entitled his autobiography *Memory Holds the Door;* but memory holds the door not only to the past but oddly enough into the future, because the past lives in the present and future. That is why we sometimes have to deal severely with our memories. The memory of blessings ennobles, but the memory of injury and disappointment, and especially of our own sin, can blight and curse.—W. D. Davies, *The New Creation*

FOREVER ADVENT.   To be a Christian means to be one who waits for God's future. Hence for the Christian perhaps all seasons are essentially an Advent season. For Advent is characterized above all by this note of expectation. Yes, so it is, and yet it seems good to distinguish the season of Advent in the round of the Church's year as the special time of expectation. It is intended to remind us sharply of what we so easily and so often forget, namely that, as Christians, we are expectant. But also it should make us more certain of the fulfillment of the promise, for it leads us on to that feast which is the very symbol of fulfillment, the Feast of the Holy Nativity.—Rudolph Bultmann, *This World and the Beyond*

GOD'S CARE.   When the events in your life do not make sense, when suffering seems to be way out of proportion to anything that you deserve, when none of the popular explanations for the presence of evil in the world seem to work, then it sometimes helps to contemplate the beauty and order of God's creation. How can you be anxious when you know that God is even keeping track of the gestation period of the mountain goat? How can you be anxious when you know that God cares even for the individual sparrow?—Daniel J. Simundson, *Faith Under Fire*

BEGGARS AND SINNERS ALL.   Not one young idealistic person I have worked with has ever claimed immunity from lusts of various kinds; has ever denied rivalry, ambition. The sin of pride (narcissism, we call it) is a commonplace in these talented and kindly people. As Dorothy Day, who lived one of the most altruistic lives of this century, said when asked about her own motives and purposes: "We reach out to help others as a statement of our own need for help. We are all beggars and sinners. We are all in more jeopardy than we dare acknowledge. When I offer bread to the hungry, I am feeding my soul's hunger—its 'long loneliness' I once called it! When I offer clothes to those who lack them, I am making myself feel more protected from the nakedness of so many moments—when we feel that nothing is between us and the devil! When I offer someone a place to stay, I am reminding myself how homeless we all are—unsure on many mornings or evenings, of where we belong in God's eyes!"— Robert Coles, *The Moral Life of Children*

WHY WE DO THINGS.   A very able surgeon put it to me like this: "What is happening," he said, "is that nobody works for the sake of getting the thing done. The result of the work is a by-product; the aim of the work is to make money to do something else. Doctors practice medicine not primarily to relieve suffering, but to make a living—the cure of the patient is something that happens on the way. Lawyers accept briefs not because they have a passion for justice, but because the law is the profession that enables them to live."

"The reason," he added, "why men often find themselves happy and satisfied in the army is that for the first time in their lives they find themselves doing something not for the sake of the pay, which is miserable, but for the sake of getting the thing done."—Dorothy L. Sayers, *The Whimsical Christian*

FIERY TRIALS.   A great athlete must train rigorously for many years to develop the heart, the lungs, the muscles, and the coordination which enable him to become a champion. The discipline required to develop a godly character is even longer and more exacting; therefore testing is both necessary and constructive. So the Christian is not to consider the "fiery trial" which overtakes him as something strange. It has a beneficent purpose. Furthermore Jesus went through all kinds of testing in order to help us through: "For in that he himself hath suffered being tempted, he is able to succour them that are tempted."—William Douglas Chamberlain, *The Manner of Prayer*

LEARNING TO PRAY.   The first step in learning to pray is just to pray. You can read every book ever written about prayer, and you can attend innumerable discussions on prayer, but still the only way to learn to pray is to pray.

As a young man I took lessons in public speaking. Some time later I met one of the greatest orators of that period and asked him, "How does one become proficient as a public speaker?"

"By speaking," he replied. "Learn the art by practice. Speak every time you get a chance. Keep doing it. Keep practicing constantly, seeking to improve yourself."

That advice applies to all efficiency. It is important to study the rules and techniques of anything you want to master, but in the last analysis you learn by doing.—Norman Vincent Peale, *A Guide to Confident Living*

SUFFERING.   When I wrote *Turn Over Any Stone*, I wrote as a victim experiencing not her first taste of suffering, but her first big taste of suffering. I was running away from my first overwhelming sense of the futility, the immensity, the helplessness of human suffering. The book was myself swinging around to confront the elements I did not wish to see, and in the process of writing the book I discovered more elements inside and outside me that I did not wish to see. But I discovered much more, and by the grace of God and the pondering that I recognize to be the work of the Holy Spirit, I am continually discovering more. Indeed, at times I almost cry out, "Will you leave me alone!"—but immediately postscript, "Please, please don't!"—Edna Hong, *Turn Over Any Stone*

SECURING FAITH.   Ecumenical Christians, for example, generally provide leadership in interfaith dialogues, yet they sometimes tend to be uneasy about stating the claims of their own faith. Evangelicals, on the other hand, give high priority to world evangelization, but many appear reluctant to participate in serious interfaith dialogues with Jews, Muslims, Buddhists, and Hindus.

Frankly, I am convinced that both groups are missing an important opportunity. Evangelicals, for instance, in shying away from open dialogue with those of other faiths, are denying themselves an important chance to grow in understanding of other religious traditions. In addition, they are missing a valuable opportunity to share the faith they hold so dear.—Tom Sine, *Wild Hope*

SPIRITUAL GROWTH.   Watching a redwood seed germinate and begin its growth into a magnificent, towering tree strikes me with awe. That tiny seed has the potential for incredible development and growth. A human soul has potential for even greater growth in this life and unending growth in the life to come. There are many elements which cooperate to bring about unfolding of the potential within the seed. The process of transformation of the life hidden in the husk of a seed into a tree offers a picture of the growth process which is possible in a human soul.—Morton T. Kelsey, *Adventures Inward*

A PLACE FOR JESUS CHRIST.   Arthur Balfour, philosopher and one-time premier of Great Britain, was lecturing after the First World War, it is said, on pathways to a new world. The meeting, if reading memory is right, was held in the hall of Edinburgh University. He pleaded for knowledge in world affairs, for training in stagecraft, and for what he vaguely called "morality." Just as he finished, a Chinese student rose to ask in a voice that all could hear, "But, sir, what about Jesus Christ?"—George A. Buttrick, *So We Believe, So We Pray*

ZEAL AND TOLERANCE.   A monument to Bishop Herber in St. Paul's Cathedral describes him as one who "combined intense zeal and wide toleration." These two qualities are not incompatible. Tolerance is not weakness or vagueness; it is respect for the convictions, ideas, habits, and tastes of others without necessarily accepting them or liking them. Firm convictions and passionate loyalties can exist alongside a warm charity and generous tolerance. Harshness and bigotry are sworn enemies of the peace—and so dreadfully unlike Christ.—John N. Gladstone, *A Magnificent Faith*

A FADING GOSPEL.   Too much of our knowledge of the gospel is like fruit long since plucked and labeled and put away upon the shelf. The rich flavor, the delicious taste, the juiciness it once had, are gone.—Robert F. Coyle, *The Christianity of Christ*

CONTRIBUTORS AND ACKNOWLEDGMENTS

CONTRIBUTORS

Andersen, Richard. Pastor, Evangelical Lutheran Church in America, former pastor of International Church of Copenhagen

Atkinson, Lowell M. Retired Methodist minister, Holiday, Florida

Beavers, David. Chairman, Pastoral Department, San Jose Christian College, San Jose, California

Brand, Rick. Pastor, First Presbyterian Church, Henderson, North Carolina

Collier, Stuart. Baptist minister, Birmingham, Alabama

Cox, Ken. Pastor, First Baptist Church, New Barton, Texas

Crawford, James W. Pastor, Old South Church, Boston, Massachusetts

Dipboye, Larry. Pastor, First Baptist Church, Oak Ridge, Tennessee

Durst, Rodrick. Dean of the faculty, Golden Gate Baptist Theological Seminary, Mill Valley, California

Fakes, Dennis R. Pastor of Messiah Lutheran Church, Lindsborg, Kansas

Farmer, David Albert. Pastor, University Baptist Church, Baltimore, Maryland

Ferris, Theodore Parker. Former rector, Trinity Church, Boston, Massachusetts

Fields, Henry. Pastor, First Baptist Church, Toccoa, Georgia

Gladstone, John N. Pastor Emeritus, Yorkminster Park Baptist Church, Toronto, Ontario, Canada

Hammer, Randy. Columnist, Franklin, Tennessee

Harrop, Clayton, K. Former dean and professor of new testament, Golden Gate Baptist Theological Seminary, Mill Valley, California

413

Honeycutt, Dwight A. Professor of church history, Golden Gate Baptist Theological Seminary, Mill Valley, California

Horne, Chevis H. Pastor for thirty-one years of First Baptist Church, Martinsville, Virginia, and visiting professor of preaching, Southeastern Baptist Theological Seminary, Wake Forest, North Carolina

House, Paul R. Professor of old testament, Southern Baptist Theological Seminary, Louisville, Kentucky

Huffman, John C. Retired Baptist pastor and educator, Louisville, Kentucky

Hull, William E. Provost, Samford University, Birmingham, Alabama

Langwig, Robert. Retired Presbyterian minister, Louisville, Kentucky

Lanway, Michael. Baptist minister, Bardstown, Kentucky

Litchfield, L. Hugh. Professor of homiletics, North American Baptist Seminary, Sioux Falls, South Dakota

Lloyd, Samuel T., III. Rector, Trinity Church, Boston, Massachusetts

Lovette, Roger. Pastor, Covenant Baptist Church, Birmingham, Alabama

Lytch, Stephen. Pastor, Second Presbyterian Church, Louisville, Kentucky

McElrath, Hugh T. Senior professor of church music, Southern Baptist Theological Seminary, Louisville, Kentucky

Phillips, E. Lee. Freelance author and Baptist minister, Atlanta, Georgia

Pinson, William Jr. Executive director, Baptist General Convention of Texas, Dallas

Randolph, David J. Pastor, United Methodist Church, Babylon, New York

Rice, Charles. Professor of preaching, The Theological School, Drew University, Madison, New Jersey

Roberts, Robert R. Retired Missouri Synod Lutheran pastor, Paradise, California

Schweizer, Eduard. Former professor of new testament and *rektor* (president), University of Zurich, Switzerland

Shaw, Wayne E. Dean and professor of preaching, Lincoln Christian Seminary, Lincoln, Illinois

Shields, Bruce E. Director, Doctor of Ministry Program, Emmanuel School of Religion, Johnson City, Tennessee

Stout, Kenneth. Professor of preaching and Christian ministry, Andrews University, Berrien Springs, Michigan

Stubblefield, Jerry M. Professor of Christian education, Golden Gate Baptist Theological Seminary, Mill Valley, California

Thompson, John. Minister of pastoral care, Venice Presbyterian Church, Venice, Florida

Tomlin, Carolyn. Writer for a variety of publications, specializing in church curriculum materials, Jackson, Tennessee

Tomlin, Matt. Pastor, Ward's Grove Baptist Church, Jackson, Tennessee

Townsend, John H. Pastor Emeritus, First Baptist Church, Los Angeles, California

Trotter, Mark. Pastor, First United Methodist Church, San Diego, California

Tuck, William Powell. Pastor, First Baptist Church, Lumberton, North Carolina

Vinson, Richard B. Dean, Averett College, Danville, Virginia

Williams, Joe Priest. Baptist minister, Louisville, Kentucky

Zimmer, Mary. Pastor, Church of the Savior, Cedar Park, Texas

Zimmerman, Gideon K. Former executive secretary of the North American Baptist Conference, Louisville, Kentucky

ACKNOWLEDGMENTS

Acknowledgment and gratitude are hereby expressed for kind permission to reprint material from the following publications:

Excerpts from David Albert Farmer, *Basic Bible Sermons on Hope,* pp. 43–48, © 1991, Broadman Press.
Excerpts from Chevis H. Horne, *Preaching the Great Themes of the Bible,* pp. 157–165, © 1986, Broadman Press.
Excerpts from William M. Pinson Jr., in *Proclaim,* Apr.–June 1991, pp. 8–9, © 1991, published by LifeWay Christian Resources of the Southern Baptist Convention, Nashville, Tennessee.

INDEX OF CONTRIBUTORS

SERMON TITLE INDEX

Children's stories and sermons are identified as (cs); sermon suggestions as (ss).

419

SCRIPTURAL INDEX

INDEX OF PRAYERS

INDEX OF MATERIALS
USEFUL AS CHILDREN'S STORIES
AND SERMONS NOT INCLUDED IN SECTION X

INDEX OF MATERIALS USEFUL
FOR SMALL GROUPS

TOPICAL INDEX